SOUTHEAST ASIA

Also of Interest

Southeast Asia Divided: The ASEAN-Indochina Crisis, edited by Donald E. Weatherbee

The Two Viet-Nams: A Political and Military Analysis, Bernard B. Fall

Laos, Arthur J. Dommen

The Emerging Pacific Community: A Regional Perspective, edited by Robert L. Downen and Bruce J. Dickson

The Rise and Demise of Democratic Kampuchea, Craig Etcheson

Malaysia: Economic Expansion and National Unity, John Gullick

Agricultural and Rural Development in Indonesia, edited by Gary E. Hansen

The Agrarian Structure of Bangladesh: An Impediment to Development, F. Tomasson Jannuzi and James T. Peach

Burma: A Socialist Nation of Southeast Asia, David I. Steinberg

†*The Philippines: A Singular and A Plural Place,* David Joel Steinberg

War of Ideas: The U.S. Propaganda Campaign in Vietnam, Robert W. Chandler

†Available in hardcover and paperback.

About the Book and Editor

Southeast Asia: Realm of Contrasts

THIRD REVISED EDITION

edited by Ashok K. Dutt

From reviews of the second edition:

> "A need for a relatively short geography text on Southeast Asia is met by this book. . . . [It] has the great advantage of leading students on to learn more. It does not stifle their interest."
>
> —The Professional Geographer

Southeast Asia: Realm of Contrasts, an introduction to the geography of the region, is intended for use as both a text and a reference. This third revised edition has an extensive introduction cataloging important recent events, as well as topical chapters and country case studies.

Ashok K. Dutt is professor of geography at the University of Akron. Dr. Dutt is the author of numerous books and articles, including *Public Planning in the Netherlands* (forthcoming).

THIRD REVISED EDITION

SOUTHEAST ASIA

Realm of Contrasts

---

edited by Ashok K. Dutt

Westview Press / Boulder and London

Published in 1985 in the United States of America by Westview Press, Inc.,
5500 Central Avenue, Boulder, Colorado 80301; Frederick A. Praeger, Publisher

Library of Congress Catalog Card Number: 84-52334
ISBN: 0-86531-561-2
ISBN: 0-86531-562-0 (pbk.)

Composition for this book was provided by the editor
Printed and bound in the United States of America

10 9 8 7 6 5 4 3

Contents

PART II
Case Studies

Foreword

The term "Southeast Asia" came into use only during the Second World War, and it has taken some thirty years for it to take on any precise meaning in the vocabularies of most observers, whether Americans or Europeans. Prior to that time, the area frequently was described either in terms of its relation to South Asia as "Farther India," or from the standpoint of the Sinitic world as the "Southern Seas." The concept of a vast subcontinental region, comparable in population to Africa south of the Sahara, possessed of a character of its own though lying between India and China, seemed very difficult for many Europeans and most Americans to grasp. Only with the increasing involvement of the United States in the so-called Vietnam War did the idea of the region begin to penetrate the mental fog which clouds the geographical perception that most Americans have of the world in which they live. Even that breakthrough, however, had its limits, since to most observers Vietnam came to be considered as tantamount to Southeast Asia, rather than the relatively minor part of the region that it really is.

Now, even that constraint happily is beginning to change, and it cannot but be removed more quickly by this important volume, the product of eleven scholars who have pooled their knowledge and wisdom to prepare a cogent, informed, and readable introduction to the geography of Southeast Asia. This is the first general work in the field to appear in the past twenty years, and it is full of remarkable insights as well as a wealth of information and percepts which can only serve to help its readers become more fully informed about one of the pivotal realms of the world.

The organization of the book both reflects and transcends the perennial contradiction between systematic and regional geography. The first half deals with the general and topical, the second, entitled "Case Studies," with individual countries. Part I includes, in addition to the conventional if basic problems of the physical environment and economic geography, illuminating chapters on the political organization of the area and its evolution from colonialism to independence, on cultural history without which the complexity of human ecology in the region cannot be appreciated, on urbanization and the interrelations between city and country which mark the patterns of the future, and on development and planning, an understanding of which is necessary if one is to forecast trends and prospects. Part II is enriched by two major chapters on Indochina, which bring that vast area into proper focus in terms of the historical and contemporary patterns of political and economic forces operating within the region and upon it from extraregional sources.

Despite the number of contributors, there is comparatively little overlap among the chapters, and both style and content suggest more a dialogue among the authors than a congeries of little-related essays. Each chapter is accompanied by numerous footnotes which at the same time provide an extensive bibliography that cannot help but encourage extensive further reading, and the entries are remarkably up to date.

One of the contributions of this volume will be to help bring into focus the idea of the region as it can be applied to Southeast Asia. Having been for so long submerged as part of the vast continent known as Asia, Southeast Asia is beginning to be accepted as one of the great world realms in its own right. The people of Southeast Asia are particularly sensitive about their identification as societies independent of those in South and East Asia. They are equally concerned that they be regarded not simply as part of an area that is negatively defined in that it is neither Indic nor Sinitic in cultural characteristics, but as having major cultures in their own right, with futures that they themselves can and will determine. At the same time, they recognize that their destinies are inextricably intertwined with those of the great neighboring states such as India and China and with those of the other world powers—in Western Europe, the United States, and Japan, from whose dominance they have only recently become emancipated and whose interests and influences continue to be large in the area. Aware of their own weaknesses and problems, they have come to recognize that in unity there is strength, and to that end they have begun to act in concert on a number of important issues that affect them. The Association for Southeast Asian Nations (ASEAN) is one organizational reflection of that view. The fact that several of the countries have been acting as a regional bloc within the Asian Development Bank is yet another. We are privileged to observe incipient regionalism act as a powerful force for regional international cooperation in Southeast Asia, and it is giving additional meaning to the concept of Southeast Asia as a distinctive part of the world order. This book provides an invaluable point of departure for understanding the problems of development and modernization in the area and for glimpsing the directions and trends which will determine its future.

Santa Barbara | Norton Ginsburg

Preface to the First Edition

This book is an introduction to Southeast Asia as a realm. Anyone, as a beginner, wanting to learn about this realm will have little difficulty in understanding it. It is, nonetheless, true that many aspects in different chapters of the book are the result of indepth research conducted by the contributing authors. Many new facts have been pooled together; much of the interpretations and analyses reflects the novelty and originality of the contributing authors.

The contributing authors have written chapters specially for this book. In other words, they have not been published earlier. The authors who have written different chapters specialize in the fields on which they have chosen to write. Hence, in spite of the coverage of varied topics and countries this book has something special to present in terms of scholarly contribution. Though all but one of the contributing authors are either United States citizens or residents, they have a first-hand experience of the realm, which makes them feel at home in writing about this "foreign" land.

The factor that ties the chapters together is the fact that the book has a running theme: diversity, change and development. Chapters portray the theme in historical, economic, social and political perspectives, never losing the spatial dimension and interaction. In spite of the above effort tieing up is far from perfect. I, as the editor, take full responsibility for this imperfection.

Ashok K. Dutt

Preface to the Third Revised Edition

Southeast Asia: Realm of Contrasts has been extensively revised because many events and developments have taken place in Southeast Asia since the publication of the second revised edition in 1976. North and South Vietnam were unified under Communist control in 1976; the Communists took over Cambodia and Laos in 1975 and renamed Cambodia as Kampuchea and Saigon as Ho Chi Minh City; the Filipino capital was shifted from Quezon City to Manila; a bloody civil war began in Cambodia in 1978-79, and thousands of refugees have fled; the Vietnam-backed Communists ousted the China-supported Cambodian regime in 1979; China invaded the northern borders of Vietnam in 1979 to teach the Vietnamese a "lesson" because of their "undesirable" involvement in the Cambodian Civil War; several thousand Vietnamese refugees, known as "boat people," left Vietnam, crossing turbulent seas in boats not meant for sea voyage; Indonesia occupied the Portuguese portion of Timor Island in 1975, thus ending the last vestige of direct colonial rule in Southeast Asia; and Brunei became fully independent of British protection in 1984.

The new revised volume includes many of these developments, along with recent changes in the economy of several countries. Also, a new introduction has been added; each chapter, as well as the tabular information for each country in Southeast Asia, has been updated; the chapters on Thailand and Singapore have been rewritten; and three chapters, including one on Brunei, have been added. Old materials were retained not only because they are still largely valid, but also because they provide a useful historical comparison.

A.K.D.

Acknowledgements to the Third Revised Edition

Thanks are offered to David Liversedge, Ramesh Vakamudi and Margaret Geib for editorial and proof-reading assistance. Linda Rogers, Theresa Barnett, Teri Jares-Blount, Jill Schuler, Abigail Gantenbein and Deborah Phillips-King are particularly thanked for typesetting and putting together the final format of the book. Mrs. Hilda Kendron's help in typing and retyping the manuscripts is gratefully acknowledged. All the new maps and diagrams for this edition have been prepared by Miss Margaret Geib. The editor is indebted to the Department of Geography, the University of Akron, particularly its Head (Dr. Allen G. Noble), and its Cartography Laboratory for continuous help in finalizing this Third Edition of the book.

A.K.D.

Part I

General and Topical

Southeast Asia: An Introduction

Ashok K. Dutt

Southeast Asia is one of the five realms of the Asian continent, the others being South Asia, the Middle-East (Southwest Asia), Siberia (Asian U.S.S.R.) and the Far East. Southeast Asia is separated from the Australian continent by the Timor and Arafura seas. Philippine Sea and the Pacific Ocean lie to the west. The Bay of Bengal, Andaman Sea and the Indian Ocean are situated toward the west and southwest.

The two countries, China and India, each with a 5,000 year old historical heritage, bound the realm on the north and northwest. Southeast Asia has had deep historical and cultural bonds with both India and China because they were not only geographically nearest, but as they traded with each other at least for 2500 years, the Southeast Asian realm enjoyed an intermediate locational vantage. The ancient ships carrying traders and goods made Southeast Asia their midway halt. It is in this way that Southeast Asia started to gain religious ideas, literary treasures and agricultural practices from China and India, though for a short while south Indian kingdoms extended their territories in Burma, and China made North Vietnam a part of its empire for over a thousand years. Vietnam inherited Confusian Buddhism from China, whereas, the other mainland countries (Burma, Thailand, Kampuchea (Cambodia) and Laos) except Malaya were indoctrinated into Theravada Buddhism, originating from India and Sri Lanka.

Australia did not contribute anything significant in the historical development of Southeast Asian civilization, because the latter had a superior level compared to the former. Nonetheless, the accessiblity of Southeast Asia by sea and its situation between two great oceans: Indian and Pacific have attracted other sea-faring peoples from beyond India and China. First the merchants from the Arabian peninsula and then the European traders (starting from 1511 A.D.) came by sea and established themselves in Southeast Asia. The Arabian connection in conjunction with West Indian Moslem traders turned Malaysia and Indonesia into Islam by the 13th and 14th centuries. Spaniards were able to convert the Filippinos to Catholicism *en masse*. The Europeans, by the end of the 19th century, also subjugated all the countries of Southeast Asia, except Thailand, and made them colonies. To the European imperialist countries—Britain, France, The Netherlands, Portugal and Spain—the Southeast Asian countries were the suppliers of specialized raw materials (cotton, rubber, oil, tin, timber, etc.) and the manufactured goods from Europe found a captive market in the colonies. Thus, a true classical form of colonial exploitation emerged.

The United States, however, was a late entrant in the colonial race. When the United States became a super power and was able to compete with the European nations at the end of the 19th century, the world was already divided into colonies owned by the European powers. But, as a result of the Spanish-American War and with the eventual defeat of Spain, the United States entered into colonial ownership by obtaining possession in 1898 of the Spanish colony in Southeast Asia, Philippines. To the United States the Philippines represented a strategic point at the other end of the Pacific and thereby providing the prestige of owning a colony. These were the basic motivations rather than the economic pressure which motivated the European powers to compete with each other for colonial ownership.

When Japan entered the second World War one of the objectives was to extend its colonial empire like its European counterparts. Thus, the Japanese subjugated all of Southeast Asia for four years (1941-45). The Allied strategy to free

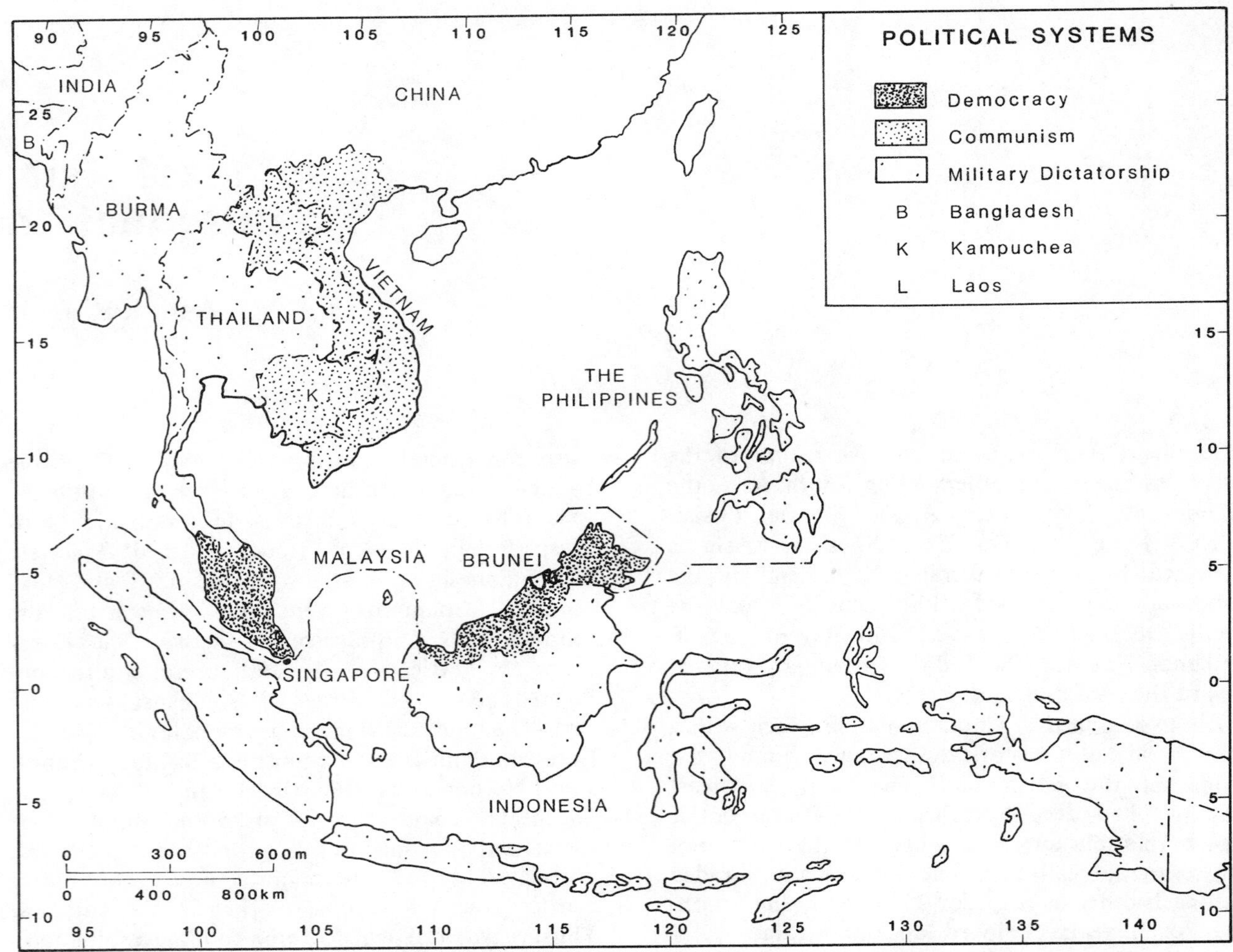

the realm from the Japanese started from the south (West Irian, New Guinia and Papua). Led by General McArthur American and other Allied troops recaptured the Philippines and eventually culminated in the defeat of Japan in 1945. During this War the Southeast Asia was recognized as a strategic realm and since then, its individuality was well acknowledged.

Despite historical influences imparted by countries from all over the world, Southeast Asia has maintained its own identity (languages, distinct cultural bases and a heritage of over 2,000 years) which makes it unique. Ideas came in different forms in Southeast Asia from the north, west, and east and the outside invaders also came to this area from those directions, but like a true accommodative civilization, the Southeast Asian peoples absorbed all of them and maintained individual national identities within the broader framework of the realm. As a result, all of Southeast Asia was infused with a new nationalism after the World War II, which eventually resulted in the attainment of national independence of different countries: the Philippines from the United States in 1946; Indonesia from the Netherlands in 1949, Kampuchea (Cambodia), Laos and North/South Vietnam from France in 1953, 1953 and 1954 respectively; Burma, Malaysia, Singapore, and Brunei from Britain in 1948, 1957, 1963, and 1984 respectively; Timor from Portugal in 1975.

THE SYSTEMS OF GOVERNMENTS

The systems of governments in southeast Asia (including absolute monarchy), in the early eighties, may be classified into three distinct types: democratic, military dictatorship, and communist. The democratic governments of Malaysia and Singapore occupy the core of the realm, whereas, the military dictatorships of Philippines, Burnei and Indonesia have an insular location. Among the mainland countries two (Burma and Thailand) are military dictatorships

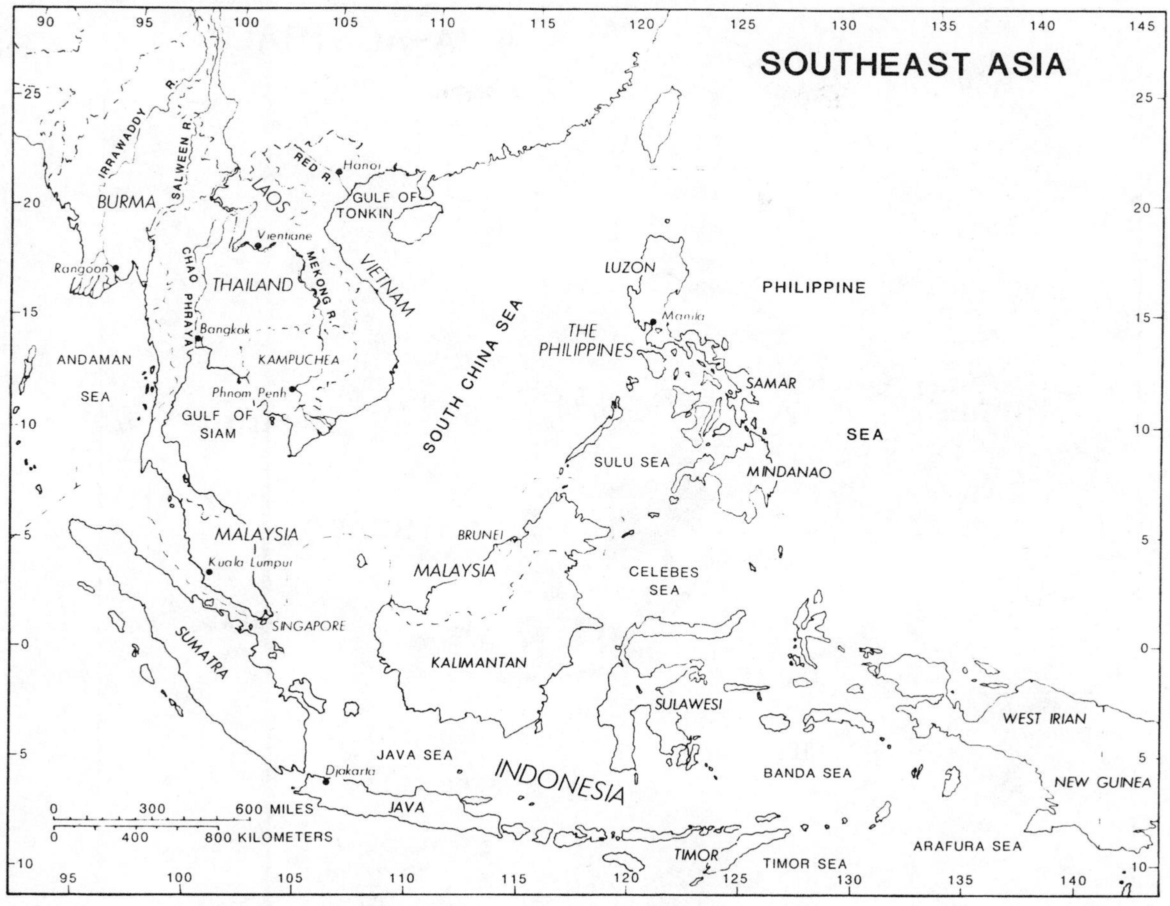

and three (Kampuchea, Laos, and Vietnam) are communist states.

The democracies in Malaysia and Singapore do not guarantee full freedom of speech and rights of organization like that of India and western democratic systems, but nonetheless the governments there are elected by popular vote and are subject to change as a result of regular elections. Both Malaysia and Singapore have inherited the British style of parliamentary democracy and are the only surviving representatives of relatively free systems in the realm, whereas, all the other countries, except Vietnam, had some kind of democratic interlude after World War II for a period of time. North Vietnam turned communist immediately after it ceased to be a French colony and South Vietnam retained a military dictatorship before being united with the North.

The five countries that have military dictatorships resort to national elections with a view to camouflage the systems with democracy. Such elections are often fake and are arranged in such a way that the dictator, who has complete support or control of the military, gets 'elected' as the head of the government. In the case of Thailand the military takes control of the government whenever it feels that its absolute power is in danger. In Burma, Indonesia, and the Philippines, the dictators have organized their own political wings and they stay in power suppressing any viable signs of opposition. In Brunei the Sultan is not only the monarch, but he rules the country with absolute power, backed by a strong military.

The communist systems of Kampuchea, Laos, and Vietnam are based on the Marxist idea of the 'dictatorship of the proletariat' where only a single political party, the Communist Party, is allowed to function. All other political opposition is suppressed as they are considered bourgeois. The Communist Party, thus becomes the main political force and the only organized apparatus for providing directions to the government. Elections are organized in such a way that the representatives are elected from among the Party members and their sypathizers. The Party is led by a central committee, which is guided by a small group of members: the Polit Bureau. In

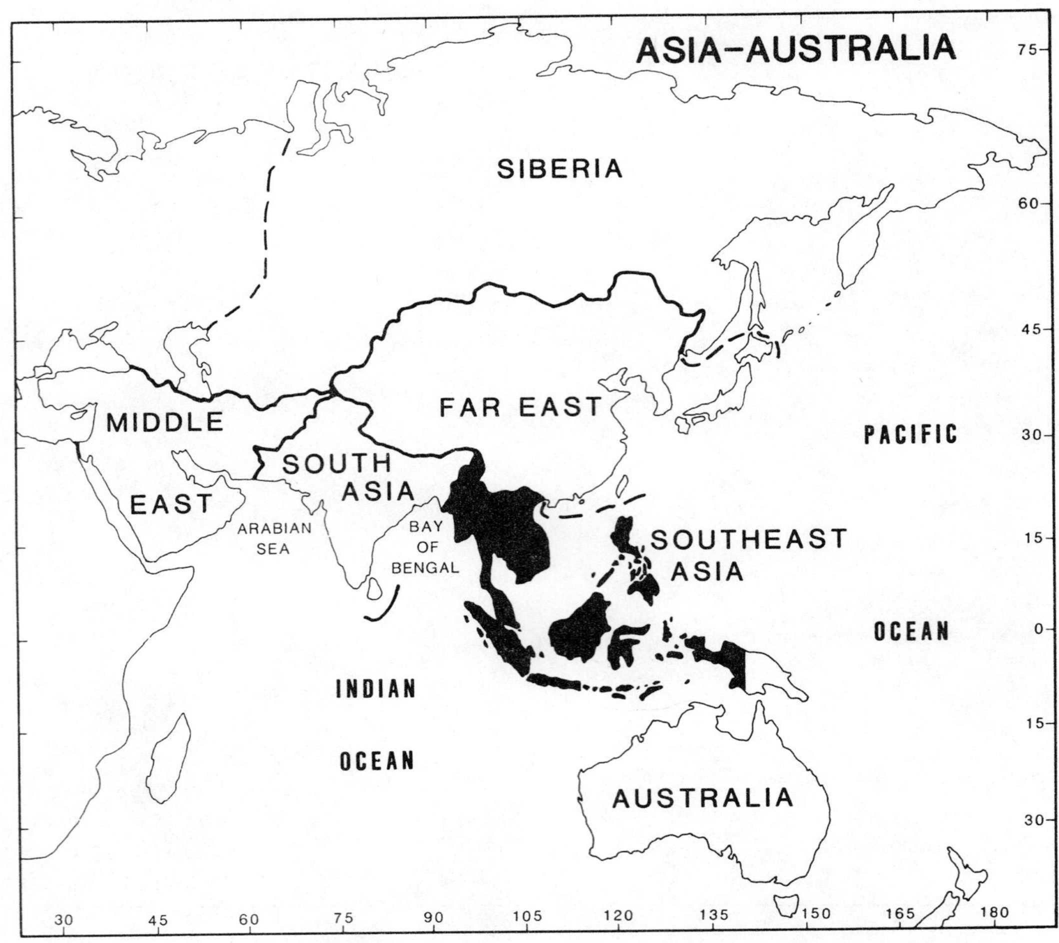

practice it is the Polit Bureau that not only dominates the decision-making process but also rules the country. The main reasons for the establishment of communist governments in Vietnam, Kampuchea, and Laos, were their contiguous land connection with each other and their common borders with the communist Peoples Republic of China, from where came continuous flow of arms for guerrilla war. Moreover, the French rule was crudely imperialistic, which indirectly encouraged the growth of extreme left in the Vietnam politics by suppressing the middle level liberals.

Inspite of the fact that the three systems of government have ideological differences they do co-exist. They influence each others' peoples in generating both positive and negative opinions in their respective countries. There is always a possibility for one system to change into another, but once a communist system takes over a country, it hardly switches hands. Thailand and Burma have common borders with communist countries and are, therefore, most vulnerable to turn communist in the near future.

INDONESIA

The principal goal of the post World War II Indonesian revolution—complete independence from Dutch colonialism—was realized in December 1949, when sovereignty was transferred to the Indonesian Republic. An inherited parliament, continued to have several Dutch appointed members, provided the basis for the parliamentary system, but the army which had attained much strength during five years of revolutionary struggle prior to independence, never stopped playing a significant role in politics. President Sukarno, initially a ceremonial head according to the constitution, was not only extremely popular, but he also used his popularity in collaboration with the army to curb democracy. The first such collaboration was displayed in 1952, when regional coups were engineered in support of Sukarno's call to undermine the parliamentary system.

Though a national election considered to be fair, was held in 1955, no political party attained

Indonesia at a Glance

Name: Republic of Indonesia
Borders with: Malaysia in the island of Kalimatan, and Papua in New Guinea Island
Area: 735,432 mi^2(1,904,769 km^2)
Population: 144,300,000 (1980 est.)
Capital: Jakarta (Pop: 5,000,000)
Other Cities: Surabaya (Pop: 2,000,000), Bandung (Pop: 2,000,000), Medan (Pop: 1,000,000)
Monetary Unit: Rupiah (U.S. $1 = 625 Rupiahs, 1981)
Chief Products
  Agriculture: Rice, rubber, cassava
  Industries: Textiles, light manufacturing, cement
Per capita GNP: U.S. $360 (1978)
Religion: Islam (major), Christianity, Hinduism
Language: Bahasa Indonesia (official) Various Malayo—Polynesian languages, English
Railway: 5,520 mi (8,832 kms)
Roadways: 12,600 mi (20,160 kms)

a majority. The Communists emerged as an influential force with about 20% of vote. As internal unrest accentuated in 1957, martial law was declared and finally in 1959, President Sukarno was assigned dictatorial powers by the parliament. A new dummy parliament was appointed by the president, who became dictator. His policies, by then had swung more to the left and his principal collaborators included the army and the Communists. He ran a centralized authoritarian administration and adhered to unrealistic policies, which caused economic disaster to the country.

The Dutch retained control of the western part of New Guinea until 1963, when its sovereignty was transferred to Indonesia, who incorporated it into the republic and renamed it Irian Jaya in 1973. Another colonial remnant, Eastern Timor, was annexed in 1975 and the following year it became the 27th province of Indonesia.

Though Sukarno proclaimed non-alignment, he was closer to the communist nations. In 1965, an abortive coup attempt, led by the Communists with the tacit support of Sukarno, paved the way for General Suharto's ascendency. Sukarno lost much of his power and two years later in 1967, Suharto became the president.

The unsuccessful coup of 1965 resulted in a massive anti-communist campaign with an estimated 250,000 people killed. This led to the virtual extermination of the Communist Party in Indonesia. Nonetheless, Suharto's regime meant military control because most top government level and lucrative ambassadorial positions were filled with military personnel and one-fifth of the parliamentary seats were guaranteed to the military.

General Suharto was elected president by the parliament in 1968 and civil liberty resrtictions were partly eased. The country went to general elections in 1971, sixteen years after the first one held in 1955. Out of a total of 460 members of the House of Representatives, 360 were elected and 100 were appointed by the president from among the military, who were not allowed to contest. Sixty-five percent of the elected members were from the governing party, Sekber Golkar. Suharto got the necessary majority in the House even without military support. The Communist Party, which was proscribed, was barred from contesting the election. General Suharto was reelected president in 1973 to serve another 5 year term. The second national election during Suharto's regime took place in 1977 and the results were similar to the first. Suharto's Golkar Party received 62% of the vote. The parliament reelected Suharto as president for the third successive term in 1978, when civil liberties were curtailed as a result of mounting opposition activities. The Suharto government responded with further curtailment in civil liberties in 1980s, including freedom of the press.

When Sukarno lost his power in the government in 1965, the Indonesian Republic swung to the right and towards the west seeking foreign investments and aligning itself more closely with the United States.

BURMA

Eight months before Burma attained its independence in January 1948, a constituent assembly was elected to prepare a constitution for the new nation. The constitution opted for a British-type parliamentary democracy, which placed executive powers in a prime minister and cabinet, and made the president a nominal head of state. However, even before the arrival of independence, a political rival murdered six cabinet members including Aung San, who was not only the most popular among Burmans, but was the leader of the ruling Anti-Fascist Peoples Freedom League and an interim prime minister. It was an irreparable loss to Burman political leadership.

Burman democracy was shortlived as by 1958, executive powers for the government were handed over to the chief of the army, Ne Win. After the resumption of civilian rule as a result of the 1960 national election, Ne Win staged a coup in 1962, abrogated the 1947 constitution, and did away with democracy once and for all. A 17 member revolutionary council was formed to rule the country and Ne Win became its chairman. In 1973, the Ne Win regime, with a view to be labelled a 'democratic' drafted a new constitution, modeled on a one-party system in which Ne Win's Burma Socialist Program Party (BSPP) was recognized as the only political organization in the country. The referendum for the constitution managed to receive an 'endorsement' by 90% of those who voted.

The first Burman election was held in 1974 after a lapse of 14 years. Ne Win became the president and a 451 member Peoples Assembly (representing only BSPP) was elected. In accordance with the new constitution, another election was held in 1978; a 464 member assembly was constituted; BSPP remained the only party and Ne Win was retained to serve another 4-year term as president. Thus, Burma staged elections every four years to 'elect' its national government.

Though Burma returned to a 'limited democracy' starting from 1974, the Communist-led insurgency in the north and the west which had lasted since Burma's independence in 1948 continued to cripple the administration. Other insurgent groups were also quite active in the Shan plateau. In 1980, it was estimated that one-third of Burma's budget was spent on combating insurgent forces. Burma maintains a policy of a relative non-alignment in the international policies and stays in isolation.

Burma at a Glance

Name: Socialist Republic of The Union of Burma
Borders with: India, Bangladesh, China, Thailand, and Laos
Area: 261,789 mi^2(678,030 km^2)
Population: 34,400,000 (1980 est.)
Capital: Rangoon (Pop: 2,100,000)
Other Cities: Mandalay (Pop: 417,000), Moulmein (Pop: 202,000)
Monetary Unit: Kyat (U.S. $1 = 6.50 Kyats, 1981)
Chief Products:
  Agriculture: Rice, jute, sesame, ground nut
  Industries: Food processing, textiles, wood products, petroleum refining
Per capita GNP: U.S. $150 (1978)
Religion: Buddhism (Theravada base)
Language: Burmese
Railways: 2,600 mi (4,160 kms)
Roadways: 11,000 mi (17,700 kms)

PHILIPPINES

July 4th is an important date in the Philippines because it was on this day in 1945 that General Douglas MacArthur announced its complete liberation from Japan and on this day in 1946, the United States President Harry Truman proclaimed its independence. Less than three months before the day of independence, national elections were held based on a constitution adopted in 1935 and amended in 1940 and 1948. The constitution was designed to follow an American presidential form. Elections until 1969, generally considered fair, took place every four years signifying the existence of a broad democratic support in the country. During this period, the Communist-led rebels (Hukbalahap) were brought under control, but were not eliminated.

Ferdinand E. Marcos was elected president in 1965 and his Nationalist Party gained a majority in the senate in 1967. Marcos in 1969 became the first Filipino president to be elected to a second 4-year term. A constitutional convention, consisting of 320 members elected democratically, was held in 1971 and decided that the constitution be written in English, with translations in other locally spoken languages, and that the voting age be lowered to 18 from 21 years. A new charter also adopted to change the form of government from presidential to parliamentary and to assign emergency powers to the president.

As a result of the last provision in the charter the democratic processes in force for two and a half decades came to an end in 1972 when President Marcos declared martial law in the name of upholding "law and order" and became the dictator. Since 1973 several mock referenda have been held and Marcos was given a 'popular approval' to continue on with his martial law. In 1976, the name of the capital, Quezon City, a suburb in the Manila metropolitan area, was changed to Manila. The election of 1978, the first one since the imposition of martial law, was full of fraudulence and as expected, Marcos' 'New Society Movement' party members won all the places in the national assembly. With limited opportunities given to the opposition in the midst of an unlimited political repression unleased by the Marcos government, his party won most local elections (governors, mayors, and local councils).

Two insurgencies, one by the Communists in central Luzon with 5,000 armed men, and the other by the Moslems with 10,000 strong armed people in central Mindanao and Sulu, have plagued Marcos martial law regime all through its existence. Internal unrest against martial law has also erupted on several occasions demonstrating a feeling of popular disapproval of a dictatorial regime.

Philippines has stayed a constant U.S. ally and has offered bases to U.S. military.

Philippines at a Glance

Name: Republic of Philippines
Area: 115,830 mi^2(300,000 km^2)
Population: 47,914,017 (1980 est.)
Capital: Manila (Pop: 1,165,990)
Other Cities: Cebu (Pop: 489,208)
Monetary Unit: Peso (U.S. $1 = 7.65 Pesos, 1981)
Chief Products
  Agriculture: Rice, corn, sugar, copra
  Industries: Food processing, tobacco, cement, textiles
Per capita GNP: U.S. $620 (1979)
Religion: Christianity, Islam
Languages: Pilipino (official), English, Spanish. Some 77 native languages are spoken of which nine are of major importance and they belong to Malayo—Polynesian family.
Railways: 715 mi (1143 kms)
Roadways: 84,556 mi (135,291 kms)

Thailand at a Glance

Name: Kingdom of Thailand
Borders With: Burma, Laos, Kampuchea (Cambodia), and Malaysia
Area: 198,250 mi^2 (514,000 km^2)
Population: 47,300,000 (1980 est.)
Capital: Bangkok (Pop: 4,870,509)
Other Cities: Chiang Mai (Pop: 105,230) Nakhon Ratchasima (Pop: 87,371) Khon Kaen (Pop: 80,286) Udon Thani (Pop: 76,173), Pitsanulok (Pop: 73,175), Hatyai (Pop: 67,117)
Monetary Unit: Baht (U.S. $1 = 20.50 Baht, 1980)
Chief Products
  Agriculture: Rice, rubber, tapioca, corn
  Industries: Food processing, textiles, wood, cement
Per capita GNP: U.S. $490 (1978)
Religion: Buddhism (Theravada base)
Language: Thai
Railways: 2,380 mi (3,830 km)
Roadways: 9,180 mi (14,773 km)

THAILAND

After Thailand became a constitutional government in 1932, the monarch's power was restricted considerably and the real power, according to the constitution, rested with the prime minister, his cabinet and the National Assembly. Though a civilian government was formed in 1945–47, repeated military coups occurred, the first one in 1947 followed by another in 1957. After a brief return of civilian rule in 1968, martial law was proclaimed again in 1971. However, a civilian government was proclaimed again in 1973 and national elections were held in January 1975. This election is considered to have been democratically conducted. Over 40 parties contested the election and no party received a majority in the parliament, which had 269 seats. As a result, the first coalition government fell in 2 months and second one, formed in March 1975, collapsed in January 1976. This led to another national election in 1976, contested by about the same number of parties as in 1975, and formation of another coalition government, which was toppled by a bloody military coup in less than six months. In 1977, another bloodless coup occurred and a new constitution was adopted at the end of 1978, based on which a new national election was held creating a 301-member House of Representatives. Parliamentary democracy was partially restored continuing through the early 1980s, but the military has had an overriding control over the government as has been mostly true since the World War II.

The Thai government has generally adhered to anti-communist and pro-western (mostly U.S.) policies. During the Vietnam War (1965–75), it was an ally of the United States and had provided bases for American military operations. Vietnam-supported Kampuchea (Cambodia) government has had border troubles and skirmishes with Thailand starting in 1979. Thai leaders are afraid of the modernized Vietnamese armed forces, which are three times as large as those of Thailand and therefore, they backed anti-Vietnamese Cambodian guerrilla rebels (rival communists) led by Pol Pot. The Thais allowed 50,000 of Pol Pot troops in 1979, to escape to Thailand and let them re-enter Cambodia to avoid encirclement by the Vietnamese. The internal struggle in Cambodia had also caused tens of thousands of refugees to pour into Thailand; many chose to remain in Thailand as of early 1980s.

BRUNEI

Brunei, a maritime country separated into two parts by the Malaysian state of Sarawak, has not only the highest per capita income in Southeast Asia but many developed countries, including the USA, do not reach its level of per capita income. It has the least number of people among the countries of the realm. The British established a protectorate over it in 1888 and used it as a base for trade with China. In 1929, oil was first discovered near Seria, giving this territory a base of prosperity not experienced by its neighbors. The four-year Japanese occupation (1941–45) ended with a British military government lasting until 1946, when the Sultan regained jurisdiction over Moslem and native law. The final word on all other legal matters remained with the British resident.

Brunei became an independent sultanate under British protection from 1959 through 1983. The Sultan adopted a constitution in 1959 setting up privy, executive and legislative councils. Britain was represented by a High Commissioner. In the first election of 1962, the Ra'ayat party swept the elected seats in the legislative council. This legislature was suspended by the Sultan as a result of a revolt led by the leaders of the Ra'ayat party. Later elections have been held, but the Sultan maintains a tight, virtually monarchical control over the administration of this newly independent nation (January 1, 1984). Brunei became the sixth memeber of the ASEAN organization in 1984.

Brunei at a Glance

Name: Brunei
Borders with: Malaysia
Area: 2,226 mi^2 (5,765 km^2)
Population: 193,000 (1981 Census)
Capital: Bandar Seria Begawan (pop. 1982 est. 51,6000)
Other cities: Seri , Kualu Belait
Monetary Unit: Brunei dollar (Aug. 1983 US $1=B$2.12)
Chief Products
  Agriculture: Rubber, Rice
  Mining: Oil, Gas
Per capita GNP: $25,600 (1983)
Religion: Islam, Confusian Buddhism
Languages: Malay, Chinese
Railways: None
Roadways: 916 mi (1466 kms)

MALAYSIA

Malaya, a part of the Malay peninsula of the Southeast Asian mainland, won independence from Britain in 1957 and was then called the Federation of Malaya. The British transferred the power to local nationalists after they had secured the country from communist insurgency. In 1963, the name of the country was changed to Federation of Malaysia because Singapore and northern Borneo (i.e., Sarawak and Sabah of Kalimantan), erstwhile colonies of Britain, joined the new Federation. As Indonesia vehemently objected to the British move of federating northern Borneo with Malaysia and not with Indonesia, the latter's relationship with Malaysia was strained considerably. This also affected Singapore's port based trading. Singapore, which was also experiencing a mounting tension between its two dominant ethnic groups—Chinese and Malays—withdrew from the Malaysian Federation and became an independent state in 1965.

At the national level, the Malaysian constitution was designed on the British model: ceremonial monarch, Senate and House of Representatives. The House election takes place at least once in 5 years and the Senate once in six years. However, unlike Britain the country has a second tier of government—states—which have their own legislature and executive branch.

The national election of 1969 reduced the popularity of the Alliance party which had governed the country and whose leader, Abdul Rahaman, a Malay Moslem, had held the office of prime minister ever since its independence. Ethnic riots emerged following the elections and an emergency was proclaimed with curfews, censorship and suspension of democratic institutions. Rahaman came under heavy criticism. He resigned in 1970 and his deputy, Tun Abdul Razak, also belonging to the ruling Alliance Party became the prime minister. By 1971, emergency prohibitions were lifted and the parliament was summoned after a two-year suspension. To prevent communal outbreaks and to stabilize Malay dominance over the other ethnic minorities—Chinese and Indians—the Constitution was amended, proscribing the following items from public and parliamentary discussion: a) non-Malay citizenship rights, b) special constitutional privileges given to Malays, c) the question of having Malay as the official language and d) the 'sovereign' status of Moslem sultans of Malay. Several politicians were prosecuted for violating the new constitutional provision, which for all practical purposes legitimized the advantage of the ethnic Malays. Thus, Malaysia paved the way for a society where Malays were given special economic privileges despite important Chinese and Indian ethnic minorities.

The national election of 1974, returned the successor of the former ruling Alliance Party: United Malays National Organization (UMNO), to power with 87% of the parliamentary seats, though with only 59% of the votes. On Razak's death in 1975, his deputy Datuk Hussain bin Onn, took the office of prime minister. Hussain continued to be the prime minister even after the 1978 election when his UMNO captured 85% of the seats in the parliament. Malays, who are economically more depressed than the ethnic Chinese and Indians, are progressing at an increasing rate compared to non-Malays. Many Malays feel that not enough is done for them while the Chinese and the Indians feel that the Malay progress is registered at their cost.

Malaysia has an anti-communist government, but it is not totally allied to the United States like Philippines, though it has good relations with the latter.

SINGAPORE

After seceding from the Malaysian Federation in 1965, Singapore became an independent republic based on parliamentary democracy. Since 1965 the Peoples Action Party, which represents multi-ethnic and multi-religious groups, has dominated the political scene and has controlled the parliament as its leader (Lee Kuan Yew) has always acted as majority leader in the parliament and prime minister. In the 1968 election, the ruling Action Party captured all seats of the parliament. A leftist organization, the Peoples Front which was organized in 1971, did not make any significant dent in the popularity of the Action Party, which also captured all the 69 parliamentary seats in 1972, 1976, and 1980 elections. The opposition parties secured about one-fourth of the votes. Singapore has been nourishing a one-party system.

Ever since independence, the Action Party has steered the government by proscribing the Communist Party, initiating an innovative economic policy (Fabian Socialism type), and encouraging private and foreign investments. Stiff penalties were meted out against those who tried to stir communal and racial disharmony. Lee Yew's government adheres to a non-aligned policy internationally.

Malaysia at a Glance

Name: Malaysia
Borders with: Thailand, Singapore, Brunie and Indonesian Kalimatan
Area: 127,315 mi^2(239,746 km^2)
Population: 14,000,000 (1980 est.)
Capital: Kula Lumpur (Pop: 500,000)
Other Cities: George Town (Pop: 280,000), Ipoh (Pop: 255,000)
Monetary Unit: Ringgit (Malaysian $: U.S. $1 = 2.14 Ringgit, 1980
Chief Products
  Agriculture: Rubber, palm oil, pepper, rice
  Industries: Steel, tin, automobiles, electronic
Per capita GNP: U.S. $ 1,090 (1978)
Religion: Islam (major), Buddhism, Taoism, Hinduism
Languages: Malay (major), English, Chinese dialects, Tamil
Railways: 1,138 mi (1,832 km)
Roadways: 18,813 mi (201,008 kms)

Singapore at a Glance

Name: Republic of Singapore
Borders with: Malaysia
Area: 224 mi^2(580 km^2)
Population: 2,390,800 (1980 est.)
Capital: Singapore (Pop: 1,327,500)
Monetary Unit: Singapore Dollar (U.S. $1 = $2.08, 1980)
Chief Products
  Agriculture: Tobacco, vegetables, rubber, coconut
  Industries: Petroleum refining, rubber processing
Per capita GNP: U.S. $6,515 (1980)
Religion: Buddhism (Chinese Confusian base), Islam, Hinduism
Languages: Malay, Chinese, Tamil, English
Railways: 16 mi (25.8 kms)
Roadways: 143 mi (228 kms)

VIETNAM

In 1954, after the French left Vietnam, it was divided along the 17th parallel into two independent countries—North and South—in accordance with the Geneva Agreements, which stipulated a general election in 1956. The South Vietnam president Ngo Dinh Diem refused to abide by The Geneva Agreements and the stipulated election never took place. South and North remained two separate states though the Geneva Agreements conceived of a united Vietnam. The North led by its popular communist leader, Ho Chi Minh, never accepted the separation and named itself the Democratic Republic of Vietnam with capitol in Hanoi. The Republic of South Vietnam had its capital in Saigon.

North Vietnam

North Vietnam had a Communist-led government from the inception with Ho Chi Minh as its founder president. The constitution was apparently democractic, but as in Russia and China, led the way to one-party (Communist Party) dictatorship. At the helm of the executive branch was the president and his cabinet ministers. There was an 'elected' legislative assembly. The Communist Party stayed in full control of executive, legislative and judicial branches.

The National Assembly election was held in 1964, but the scheduled 1968 election was postponed because of severe United States bombing. However, People's Council elections were held in 1967 at different levels. Ho Chi Minh's death in 1969 eventually led to a smooth transition in which the former vice-president Duc Thuong assumed the presidency, but the national assembly endorsed a collective leadership. After seven years, in 1971, elections for a 420 seat national assembly took place. True to the principle of one-party dictatorship, 522 out of 527 candidates contesting the election were approved by the Vietnam Fatherland Front, a broad based popular wing of the Communist Party. Duc Thoung was reelected president and Pham Vam Dong became the prime-minister.

A power struggle hindered the effective leadership and Le Duan, the party secretary became more influential. The election for National Assembly in 1975 chose 425 members and the major cabinet ministers' responsibilities remained unchanged. North Vietnam was officially unified with the South on July 2, 1976 and was given a new name, the Socialist Republic of Vietnam.

Vietnam at a Glance

Name: Socialist Republic of Vietnam
Borders with: Kampuchea (Cambodia), Laos, China
Area: 127,246 mi^2(329,566 km^2)
Population: 53,300,000 (1980 est.)
Capital: Hanoi (Pop: 1,443,500)
Other Cities: Ho Chi Minh City or Saigon (Pop: 3,460,500) Haiphong (Pop: 1,191,000), DaNang (Pop: 500,000)
Monetary Unit: Dong (U.S. $1 = 2.18 Dongs, 1981)
Chief Products
  Agriculture: Rice, sugarcane, tea, cotton
  Industries: Phosphate fertilizer, cement, food processing
Per capita GNP: U.S $170 (1978)
Religion: Buddhism (Chinese Confusian base), Taoism, Christianity
Language: Vietnamese (official), Cantonese
Railways: 1,272 mi (2,047 kms)
Roadways: 3,690 mi (5,980 kms)

South Vietnam

Independent South Vietnam was a monarchy in 1954. Bao Dai was the sovereign and Diem was the premier. A referendum in 1955 abolished the monarchy and led to the formation of a republic, with Diem as the president. Diem's regime lasted up to 1963 when a military coup was staged leading to his murder. Thereafter, nine coups took place in less than two years and finally in July 1965 Vice Marshal Ky established a firm military control. In 1966 an election was held to elect a constituent assembly, which adopted a new constitution the following year. The constitution, patterned on the U.S. model, provided for a two house legislature, an independent judiciary and a presidential form of government. In accordance with the new constitution an election was held in 1967, which was boycotted by the Communists, who had been engaged in anti-Saigon regime guerrilla warfare in the countryside ever since 1954. Though there were eleven presidential candidates, the only non-civilian, General Nguyen Van Thieu, was elected with the largest share (35%) of votes. The fairness of the election was questionable and Thieu became a president with a minority of popular approval. The elected legislature also contained a large number of members who were opposed to Thieu.

While the Thieu government continued to exist with a great deal of political manipulation, repression and encouragement to corrupt practices, the communist insurgents were gathering increasing momentum, culminating in the formation of a parallel "Provisional Revolutionary Government" in 1969. Thieu was re-elected president in 1971 in an uncontested election to serve a second 4-year term, by preventing two of his rivals from entering the contest. This election, by no standard fair, was also the South Vietnam Republic's last. The South Vietnam government fell to the Communists in April 1975 and Thieu left for the Philippines. Thousands of Vietnamese also left the country and were received in the United States as refugees. The problem of the "boat people" refugees fleeing South Vietnam continued through 1980s. The South was joined with the North forming a single state structure in 1976.

Vietnam War

The Antecedents of the War (1930–54). The Vietnamese opposed French repression during colonial times through an indigeneous Communist Party led by Ho Chi Minh, who founded it in 1930. French colonial policy did not encourage the growth of a sizeable middle level intelligentsia and prevented the existence of an influential middle class or liberal party. The Communists in Vietnam came to be regarded as the principal leaders of national liberation.

During the Second World War, the Communists led a struggle against the Japanese occupation and designated the broad-based movement as "Viet Minh." After the war in 1945, they had become quite strong and when the French reoccupied Vietnam, the Communists organized a very powerful guerrilla struggle against colonial reoccupation. The United States not only supported the French, but became the principal financier of French military efforts in Vietnam.

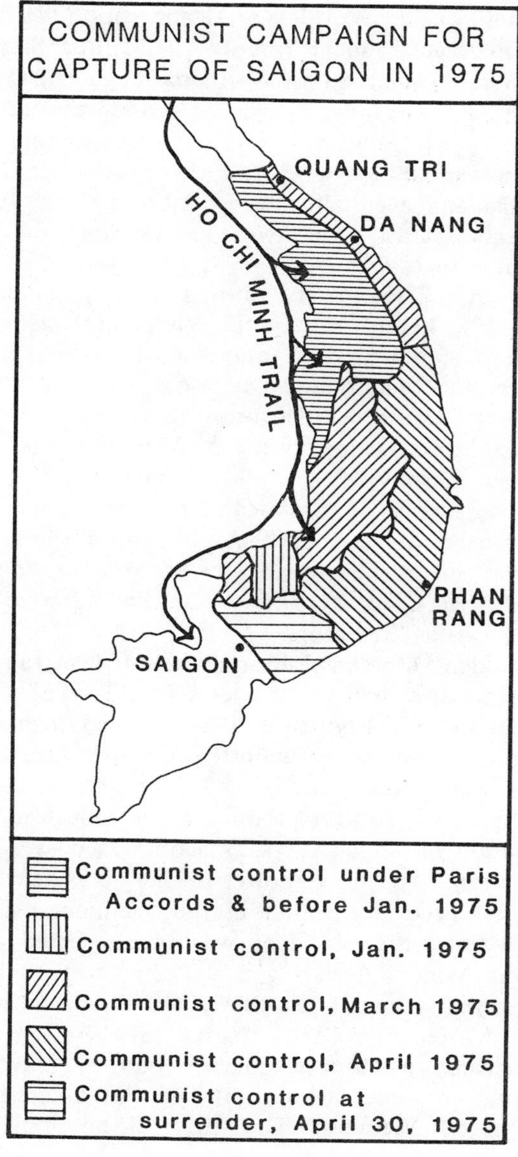

However, the French steadily lost territory, culminating in the spring of 1954 with their defeat at the Battle of Dien Bien Phu in North Vietnam. This led to a negotiated settlement of the conflict in the Geneva Conference (1954); the French left Vietnam which was divided into North and South; the North was ruled by the Communists and was supported by U.S.S.R. and China; the South initially by monarch Bao Dai and later by Diem, both supported by the United States.

War During the Early Days of Independence (1954–64). The United States practically became the successor of French colonial forces after 1954. There were widespread areas of insurgency in South Vietnam mainly manned by local communist groups with arms left over by the Japanese during World War II and captured from the Diem government forces. The United States, however, saw in South Vietnamese guerrilla activities an 'outside aggression' and postulated that if the South Vietnamese anti-communist government should ever fall then the entire Indochina and eventually all of Southeast Asia will turn communist. This was an example of the "domino theory".

Dwight Eisenhower, during his presidency (1952-59), helped the South Vietnamese government to stabilize by sending aid, including arms and military and political advisors. In 1960 when Kennedy assumed the presidency, over 2,000 United States' troops were in Vietnam, and the number increased to over 15,000 in 1963. A massive supply of American arms and ammunition further stepped up the war against the communist insurgents, who were contemptuously called Viet Cong by Diem, but they referred to themselves as 'liberators'.

President Lyndon Johnson was further trapped by aggressive military advice. The Tonkin Gulf Resolution of August 7, 1964 marked a major turnning point. It is doubtful whether American ships were ever attacked by North Vietnamese vessels in the Gulf of Tonkin, but that was the allegation on which the U.S. Congress passed the resolution, which empowered the president to take all necessary action in the Vietnamese conflict. Thus, the president was given virtual war powers without declaring a war. For seven subsequent years the United States was involved in a war which included drafts of the young Americans, a massive military budget, and the sending of increasing numbers of American troops to Vietnam. The first air-bombing of North Vietnam followed immediately upon the passing of the Gulf of Tonkin Resolution.

War Escalation (1965–73). American participation increased like a geometrical progression in 1965 with over 180,000 U.S. troops in Vietnam, and peaking to about 550,000 in 1968. As a result of the Nixon-Kissinger decision to wipe out illusive Viet Cong hide-out headquarters, the U.S. troops entered Cambodia on April 30, 1970. This step, a further escalation of the war, intensified the already powerful American peace movement against the Vietnam War. As an aftermath of this entrance the Kent State University episode of May 4, 1970 took place, which resulted in the killing of four students by Ohio National Guardsmen during a massive campus protest.

At the end of the 1960s and the beginning of the 1970s, though the United States decided to commit a lesser number of troops in Vietnam, it escalated the air-war both in South and North Vietnam and 'Vietnamized' the war by training more South Vietnamese troops and supplying them with a greater amount of American arms. The Thieu government was losing the war gradually because of brutality, nepotism and a lack of an effective land policy in rural areas. In the meantime the strength of communist insurgency increased rapidly physically supported by North Vietnam and with arms supplies from the U.S.S.R. and China.

The Fall of Thieu's Saigon Regime (1973–75). The U.S. wanted badly a way out of the war and finally the Paris Accords were reached in 1973. Vietnamese groups involved in the conflict and the United States agreed that a) all American troops would be withdrawn from Vietnam, b) Communist held rebel pockets in South Vietnam would be maintained, and c) a gradual change over to a 'national reconciliation' government would take place. The Paris Accords gave the United States an opportunity to withdraw peacefully. In two years time the Communists supported by North Vietnam mounted massive attacks first about 125 miles north of Saigon in January, 1975 and then, closing in from the north. In less than four months the shaky Thieu government of Saigon without the American troops to back them, was toppled. On April 30, 1975 the Saigon area was surrendered, completing the occupation of South Vietnam by the Communists.

The Consequences of the War. The war caused widespread physical damage and misery in Indochina, and the United States was also affected by it deeply. On the Vietnamese side war effects were staggering:

a) 1.7 million Vietnamese killed,
b) 5 million tons of bombs and 18 million gallons of poisonous chemicals dropped over the fields, forests, settlements and military targets in Indochina,
c) 12 million Vietnamese forced out of their homes and turned into refugees, and
d) a complete dislocation of both rural and urban economies, especially in South Vietnam.

In the United States the cost of the war totaled $150 billion and 49,933 Americans were killed. Many Americans sustained permanent physical and mental injuries. Chemical warfare (such as, use of Agent Orange) affected a large number of Americans later in their life. The war's long term effects on the American economy were dismal—spiralling inflation and the slowing down of economic growth. Moreover, no other foreign war had ever created such a polarized public response in America with the bitter feelings of 'doves' and 'hawks' lasting for a long time to come. The American involvement in the war was considered by many throughout the world to be unnecessary aggression against the poor Third World peoples, and thus the war damaged the American image of the 'liberator of Europe' and a 'champion of democracy.' In the final analysis, the war ended in a defeat for the United States, the first major debacle in its history.

Vietnam Unified

Over two months before the official unification of north and south Vietnam, for which a protracted and bloody war was fought for 22 years, both parts held elections for a 497 member National Assembly. Though both north and south shared almost equally the number of Assembly members the main core of the unified government and party leadership came from the north. The name of the Workers Party, which ruled the country, was changed to Communist Party in 1976. To conform with the new administrative necessities in a unified setup, the country was divided into 32 provinces, in addition to special provincial status given to three cities: Hanoi, Ho Chi Minh City (Saigon) and Haiphong.

The north and south dichotomy persisted, as the former tried to dilute the long established capitalist-feudal influence of the south. The north supposedly had gotten rid of such an influence because of its two decade old communist rule. The new government planned to relocate 10 million northerners in the south and about 10 million southerners to the "New Economic Zones." In 1976 alone, 700,000 residents of Ho Chi Minh City were relocated to these zones.

By 1978, an estimated 800,000 southerners, mostly former supporters of the Thieu Government, merchants and middle class employees were sent to concentration camp-like "re-education centers" for indoctrination and brainwashing. Not much is known about them.

China invaded Vietnam in 1978, but the war which lasted for only 17 days, was intended to "teach a lesson" to Vietnam for their support to the ouster of China-backed Pol Pot government in Kampuchea. China was also unhappy with the Vietnamese internal ethnic policy because after the local Chinese owned buisnesses in Cholon (a twin city with Ho Chi Minh City) were nationalized, a large number of Vietnamese Chinese (estimated 250,000 in 1979) fled to China. However, the Chinese invasion did not work as expected because the Vietnamese offered strong resistance. Thousands were killed on both sides, but Vietnamese losses were much more extensive. The Chinese eventually withdrew on their own.

In 1980, a new constitution was adopted for Vietnam which established a collective presidency and a council of state headed by a Chairman. Though there was an extensive reshuffling of top guards in 1980, the highest officials: Pham Van Dong, Truong Chinh and Le Duan retained positions as premier, chairman of the National Assembly's Standing Committee and secretary of the Communist Party, respectively. By the early 1980s, a rule by one-party dictatorship seemed to have become quite entrenched, both in the north and the south. Vietnam, allied to the Soviet Union, shared their brand of communism and did not see eye-to-eye with the Chinese Communists.

LAOS

Laos became independent of French occupation in 1953 and was a monarchy. The Pathet Lao communist group created a large insurgent area in the northeastern part of the country and was supported by China and North Vietnam. By the early 1960s, the country was divided into three groups: Communists, neutralists and pro-westerners and they fought with each other for power. In 1962, the neutralist Prince Souvanna Phouma headed the government, but the rightist military men staged a coup two years after. However, Sauvanna Phouma was returned to power as a result of international pressure. Souvanna Phouma continued to stay in power as a result of the 1967 election, which was boycotted by Pathet Lao Communists. Souvanna Phouma's United Front bagged 32 out of 59 Assembly seats. The Communists had control of about one-third of the country's territory in 1967 and three years later they, in collaboration with the North Vietnamese controlled over two-third of the country. The American bombing of the Ho Chi Minh Trail in Laos could hardly prevent North Vietnamese from moving massive arms to the south.

As the Paris Accords were reached for Vietnam, a cease-fire was also agreed upon for Laos in 1973, which left about four-fifths of the country occupied by the Pathet Lao forces. A coalition government of pro-western Souvanna Phouma and the Communists was installed, though earlier coalitions attempts in 1957 and 1962 had failed to produce any long-term results.

As the Communists mustered enough strength by December 1975, the coalition was abolished, monarchy was abandoned and Laos became a communist country. With Kaysone Phoumvihan, a communist leader, as prime minister and Prince Souphanouvong, another long time communist leader and a half brother of Prince Souvanna Phouma as president of the newly formed republic. The real power rested with pro-Hanoi Phoumvihan, who is considered half Vietnamese.

The Laotian communist regime, not as harsh as the neighboring Khmer Rouge, continued to suppress political opponents by sending thousands to "re-education camps". An estimated 170,000 Laotians have fled to Thailand as refugees since 1975.

Though the Laotian Communists are allied to Hanoi, they are not as vociferously antagonistic to China as desired by Vietnam.

Laos at a Glance

Name: Lao People's Democratic Republic
Borders with: China, Vietnam, Kampuchea (Cambodia), Thailand and Burma
Area: 91,429 mi^2 (236,800 km^2)
Population: 3,700,000 (1980 est.)
Capital: Vientiane (Pop: 90,000)
Other cities: Savannakhet (Pop: 50,690), Luang Prabang (Pop: 44,244), Pakse (Pop: 44, 860)
Monetary Unit: **Kip (US $1 = 10 K)**
Chief Products
  Agriculture: Rice, corn, coffee, cotton
  Industries: Tin, lumber
Per capita GNP: US $90 (1978)
Religion: Buddhism (Theravada base)
Languages: Lao, Pali
Railways: nil
Roadways: 2,130 mi (3,412 kms) paved all weather
2,500 mi (4,000 kms) non—all weather

KAMPUCHEA (CAMBODIA)

After attaining its independence from the French in 1953, Kampuchea's King Norodom Sihanouk led the country for about two decades. He abdicated his throne in 1955. In 1960, the National Assembly installed him as the Head of State, controlling major governmental functions. Sihanouk also organized a powerful political party, the Popular Socialist Community. The National Assembly was based on direct elections held every four years.

From the mid-1960s, the Sihanouk government was distressed by internal communist activities and the Vietnamese Communists' use of Cambodia as sanctuaries and supply routes from North Vietnam along the Ho Chi Minh Trail. Sihanouk's policies were shifting more towards the right, when in March 1970 he was overthrown by his general, Lon Nol, in a bloodless coup while Sihanouk was in Moscow.

Lon Nol's pro-U.S. regime which lasted until 1974 paved the way for an extreme internal polarization and military intervention from the United States and South Vietnam. The United States troops entered eastern Cambodia on April 30, 1970 and stayed there for two months to comb Viet Cong hideouts. The American backed South Vietnamese forces continued to stay in Cambodia months after the American pullout. In the meantime, the ousted Sihanouk, regarded by the Cambodian people as a sort of god-king, formed a government in exile supported by the Khmer Rouge (local Communists) and by Peking and Hanoi. The Khmer Rouge by the end of 1970 controlled half of the country and it was only in the southern half that Lon Nol had effective control. The Lon Nol regime dissolved the parliament in 1971 and an emergency was declared. The government was beleagued by inefficiency and corruption. Before the Paris Accords in 1973, American planes bombed Khmer Rouge strongholds routinely. By the beginning of 1975, the Khmer Rouge occupied 90% of Cambodian territory. Lon Nol's control was restricted around Phnom Penh which was over-run by the Communists on April 16, 1975. Lon Nol fled to the United States. The war resulted in total disorganization and the destruction of rice paddies and turned the country from a rice exporter to an importer. Moreover, during the five years of war, half of the country's population became refugees, and 13% were either killed or wounded.

Kampuchea (Cambodia) at a Glance

Name: Democratic Kampuchea
Borders With: Laos, Thailand, and Vietnam
Area: 69,898 mi^2 (181,035 km^2)
Population: 6,000,000 (1980 est.)
Capital: Phnom Penh (Pop: 200,000)
Monetary Unit: Riel
Chief Products
Agricultural: Rice, rubber, sugarcane
Industries: Textiles, cement
Per capita GNP: U.S. $80 (1972)
Religion: Buddhism (Theravada base)
Language: Khmer (official)
Railways: 380 mi (612 kms)
Roadways: 1,628 mi (2,620 kms)

The Khmer Rouge immediately established a government with Sihanouk as the nominal head, and its dominant leader was Khieu Samphan. Phnom Penh was considered to be filled with unproductive "urban parasites" and therefore, over one million from this city were forcibly moved to the villages to augment rice production.

In 1976, a 250-member Peoples Representative Assembly was elected, but Sihanouk resigned being dissatisfied with communist practices. Pro-Peking Pol Pot became the powerful Communist Party secretary and the premier. His regime was ruthless not only in suppressing political opponents, but forcing the people to work in the fields. It is estimated that between 1975-78, one million people died as a result.

As the Pol Pot regime of Cambodia was allied to Peking, the Soviet-backed Vietnam, engineered a counter force led by Hing Samrin, who was installed as Vietnamese puppet in 1979 to govern Cambodia as a result of an invasion in which 200,000 Vietnamese forces participated. Pol Pot's army was pushed to the western side of the country, where it operated insurgent areas. In the early 1980s the Vietnamese forces continued to stay in Cambodia to back their puppet government, while insurgency continued on in the west and in the Cardamom mountains. Cambodia was in disarray, fields were not cultivated and a large number of people faced starvation.

SOUTHEAST ASIAN INDIVIDUALITY

After World War II, when Southeast Asia was rightly rcognized as a realm, its civilization was still considered to be an extension of India, China or the Western nations. The terms used were Indianization, Sinicization and Westernization of Southeast Asia. Though there had been an extensive Moslem influence in Southeast Asia for about 800 years, the Western, and Western-educated, Asian historians, who were mainly trained in Indian and Chinese studies, found it difficult to understand the impact of Islam and therefore, reference to Islamization of Southeast Asia was made only infrequently.

Starting from the 1960s and 1970s, a new generation of historians—both Southeast Asian natives and Western, who were no longer restricted by colonial constraints, started to uncover the ancient civilization of Thailand, Kalimantan and many other areas, and are asserting that in comparison to Indian and Chinese civilizations, they were not inferior. Southeast Asian civilizations are not considered to be copies of either neighbors, India or China. These civilizations stood at a high level and were only influenced by Indianization, Sinicization, Islamization and Westernization processes without losing their inherent individuality. Like all civilizations when established and continued Southeast Asia also received influences from foreign sources. Some civilizations refuse to accept those influences and others such as Southeast Asia accept them in varying degrees. In the case of Southeast Asia such influences had been profound, as the recipient not only accepted them, but enriched their civilization by such acceptance in varying degrees. There is, however, a great deal of spatial variation of such acceptance in Southeast Asia, which reflects divergent forms of civilization by countries, but within a broader unity of the realm .

References

The Americana Annual—Year Book of the Encyclopedia Americana 1968–1981 (Grolier Incorporated), for sections dealing in Burma, Indonesia, Kampuchea, Laos, Malaysia, Philippines, Singapore, Thailand and Vietnam.

D.T. Bayard, "The Roots of Indochinese Civilization: Recent Developments in the Prehistory of Southeast Asia," *Pacific Affairs*, Vol. 53, (1980), pp. 89–114.

Richard Butwell, "Vietnam," in *Encyclopedia Americana*, Vol. 26 (Danbury, Con.: Americana Corporation, 1979), pp. 108–112.

John F. Cady, "Thailand," in *Encyclopedia Americana*, Vol. 26 (Danbury, Con.: Americana Corporation, 1979), pp. 591–594.

Leonard Casper, "Republic of the Philippines," in *Encyclopedia Americana*, Vol. 21 (Danbury, Con.: Americana Corporation, 1979), pp. 759g–759n.

David G. Dickason, "Burma," in *Academic American Encyclopedia*, Vol. 3 (Princeton, N.J.: Arete Publishing Co., 1980), p. 575.

Ashok K. Dutt, "Kampuchea," in *Academic American Encyclopedia*, Vol. 12 (Princeton, N.J.: Arete Publishing Co., 1980), pp. 12–13.

Ashok K. Dutt, "Thailand," in *Academic American Encyclopedia*, Vol. 19 (Princeton, N.J.: Arete Publishing Co., 1980), pp. 140–141.

Donald K. Emerson, "Issues in Southeast Asian History: Room for Interpretation - A Review Article," *Journal of Asian Studies*, Vol. XL:1 (1980), pp. 43–68.

Felix V. Gagliano, "Malaysia," in *Encyclopedia Americana*, Vol. 18 (Danbury, Con.: Americana Corporation, 1979), pp. 163c–163d.

Marvin E. Gettleman, "Vietnam War," in *Academic American Encyclopedia*, Vol. 19 (Princeton, N.J.: Arete Publishing Co., 1980), pp. 584–590.

I.C. Glover, "Ban Don Ta Phet and its Relevance to Problems in the Pre- and Prehistory of Thailand," *Bulletin of the Indo-Pacific Prehistory Association*, Vol. 2, (1980), pp. 16–30.

Karl L. Hutterer, "Early Southeast Asia: Old Wine in New Skins?—A Review Article," *The Journal of Asian Studies*, Vol. XLI:3 (1982), pp. 559–570.

B.R. O'G. Anderson and John R.W. Smail, "Indonesia," in *Encyclopedia Americana*, Vol. 15 (Danbury, Con.: Americana Corporation, 1968), pp. 70c–70j.

Thomas R. Leinbach, "Indonesia," in *Academic American Encyclopedia*, Vol. 11 (Princeton, N.J.: Arete Publishing Co., 1980), pp. 149–150.

Thomas R. Leinbach, "Malaysia," in *Academic American Encyclopedia*, Vol. 13 (Princeton, N.J.: Arete Publishing Co., 1980), pp. 85–86.

Von Leur, "Southeast Asian History and the Social Sciences," in C.D. Cowan and O.W. Wolters, eds., *Southeast Asian History and Historiography*: Essays Presented to D.G.E. Hall (Ithaca, N.Y.: Cornell University Press, 1976), pp. 396–402.

Leonard C. Overton, "Cambodia," in *Encyclopedia Americana*, Vol. 5 (Danbury, Con.: Americana Corporation, 1979), pp. 250–251.

John Paxton, ed., *The Statesman's Year Book 1981–82*, (New York, St. Martin's Press, 1981).

Hugh Tinker, "Burma," in *Encyclopedia Americana*, Vol. 5 (Danbury, Con.: Americana Corporation, 1979), pp. 8–12.

Richard Ulack, "Philippines." in *Academic American Encyclopedia*, Vol. 15 (Princeton, N.J.: Arete Publishing Co., 1980), p. 238.

Richard Ulack, "Vietnam," in *Academic American Encyclopedia*, Vol. 19 (Princeton, N.J.: Arete Publishing Co., 1980), pp. 582–584.

World Development Report 1980 (New York: Oxford University Press, 1980), published for the World Bank.

Chapter 1

The Geopolitical Base

Pradyumna P. Karan
Wilford A. Bladen

Between the two great demographic and cultural foci of India on the west and China on the north, lies Southeast Asia. It occupies a strategic position in the world's circulatory system, where sea routes linking the Pacific and Indian Oceans converge, and where major air routes from Australia to Western Europe and from the western coast of the United States to South Asia meet. Extending over an area of one and a half million square miles (less than half that of the United States) Southeast Asia, in 1983, comprised of nine independent states—Burma, Thailand, Laos, Vietnam, Cambodia (Kampuchea), Malaysia, Singapore, Indonesia and the Philippines. It also includes the British protected state of Brunei, due to become independent on January 1, 1984. The forest-covered mountains and the numerous small separate areas which were easily dominated by foreign powers. All the newly independent states of Southeast Asia are products of western decolonization which began with the independence of the Philippines in 1946, followed by Burma in 1948, Indonesia in 1949, Cambodia, Laos, North and South Vietnam in 1954, Malaya in 1957, and culminating in the establishment of the Republic of Singapore in 1965. The unity of Southeast Asia as a world region is derived from this process of decolonization and the region's transitional character between India and China. Its historic disorganization and political weakness is its principal characteristic as a subsystem of a world political system in the twentieth century.

Southeast Asia may be divided into mainland (or continental) and maritime (or insular) areas.[1] The continental territories of Burma, Thailand and Indochina (North and South Vietnam, Laos and Cambodia) have a predominantly Buddhist population. Some three quarters of the population of continental Southeast Asia live in the deltas if the Irrawaddy, Chao Phraya, Mekong, Song Koi (Red River) and the Salween. Insular Southeast Asia is comprised of Indonesia, the Philippines, Malaysia and Singapore, and is inhabited mainly by Islamic and Christian population. While the great deltas of continental Southeast Asia developed commerical rice production, Insular Southeast Asia specialized in producing raw materials and plantation crops for export to the European market. Lying almost entirely in the humid tropics, its rich endowment of raw materials such as rubber, tin, spices, rice and plantation crops are located in areas with a high degree of accessibility by water.

One of the distinctive features of Southeast Asia is the extent to which it has been subjected to external influences. Even before the advent of the Europeans, the movement of various cultures—Indian, Chinese and Islamic—had a profound impact on the cultural and political geography of the region. During the Dark Ages, when Europe was divided into small, struggling feudal principalities, large areas of Southeast Asia were culturally and commercially developed under the Indian trading empires of Sri Vijaya (7th to 13th centuries) and Majapahit (13th to 14th centuries). The European expanison of Southeast Asia, beginning in the 16th century, following the discovery of a sea route to the Orient impelled by the European desire to participate in the lucrative spice trade, as marked by nearly four centuries of conquest, trade, exploitation and colonization.[2]

THE IMPRESS OF COLONIAL RULE

Great Britain and France carved out valuable colonial dependencies of Burma and Indochina, and in 1896, decided to preserve Siam (Thailand) as a buffer state between their respective spheres of activity. The French interest in Indochina was prompted by the possiblity that the river valleys might provide a back-door route to China. The principal British interest in Burma was to protect the eastern frontier of the Indian empire. During the 17th century the Dutch expelled the Portuguese from their dispersed and percarious footholds in the Indonesian archipelago, with the exception of easter Timor (a Portuguese colony until 1975). The Dutch treated their East Indies colony as a *bedriff* (a business concern) and exploited the territory commerically by concentrating on the cultivation of a wide range of tropical products in Java and a few favorable areas on other islands. In 1898, owing to the war with Spain, the Philippines, an outpost of Spanish power in Asia dating back to the era of lucrative spice trade, passed under the control of the United States.

The major influence shaping the contemporary areal political organization of Southeast Asian lands can be traced to the period of Western Colonial domination which began in the 16th century and ended in the early 1960's. The duration and intensity of colonial domination varied greatly among the Southeast Asian countries. Although Britain treated Burma as an adjunct to its Indian Empire, Britain pursued a policy of developing the country's resources and improving the nation's economy. On the other hand, the French doctrinaire policy of assimilation of Indochina into France, left most of Indochina largely undeveloped. The Dutch colonial policy of commerical exploitation left Indonesia mostly undeveloped and unprepared, economically and politically, for self-government. In keeping with its traditional anticolonial attitudes, the American policy in the Philippines was directed towards the development of self-government in the islands. In 1935 with the adoption of the Commonwealth Constitution, the Philippines began making major advances toward independence.

During the period of colonial rule changes were stimulated in all Southeast Asian lands. Colonial rule, in general, retarded the economic and social development in most countries resulting in a marginal quality of life for a majority of the peoples. With few exceptions, the development that took place was largely related to the needs of the colonial powers rather than to the requirements of the Southeast Aisan countries. Regional disparities in the economic development of various countries was greatly accentuated as a result of unplanned development concentrated in a few favored areas. Under the impact of colonial rule, the spread of sanitation and hygiene, massive immigration of labor for plantations and mines, the incentive to large families prompted by the Dutch Culture System (*cultuur stelsel*), which required farmers to set aside a portion of their land to the cultivation of certain crops whose harvest were handed over to the administration, resulted in a rapid population growth in selected areas of Southeast Asia. In British Malaya, the Dutch East Indies, and French Indochina, while successful plantation developments were taking place, the economic and political needs of the local population were generally neglected. The European powers interfered with the human ecology of Southeast Asia, bringing disharmony which influenced the political geography of the region.[3]

Politically, the European Colonial domination in Southeast Asia produced a pattern of territorial units which have little relevence to the ethnic and historical conditions of the various countries. The territorial form of the Southeast Asian states were derived from European political considerations; the need for coexistence with other European imperial powers, and administrative conveniences. The concept of a viable, spatial, political organization characterized by factors of common tradition, history or identity was not a serious consideration for the Europeans. As a consequence, the boundaries of the Southeast Asian countries drawn by the colonial powers motivated with imperial considerations, included a variety of different physical and cultural identities. In particular, the boundaries defining the political–territorial space of various countries did not coincide with the pattern of settlement of ethnic groups. Often these boundaries bisect homelands or peoples such as the Shans in Burma, or *Montagnards*, of Indochina, or the tribes living along Borneo's interior boundary lines (Indonesian–Malaysian border).

The process of European Colonial expansion, starting with an initial intervention and aquisition of territory, followed by a forward movement under the perceived necessity of protecting and securing the initially occupied territory, did not contributed to the establishment of political units based on unifying factors of common tradition or cultural identity. Each colonial political unit contained diverse cultural identities such as a variety of hill tribes, ethnic groups, and distinct religious communities. Under the weight and authority of colonial powers, the deeply rooted territorially-based rivalries, conflicting interests, and ideological antagonisms were restrained from clashing and the diverse elements coexisted in each colony. In certain cases the colonial powers, impelled by political motives, promoted deep rooted antagonism in their colonies by discriminately soliciting the cooperation of minority peoples such as the Karen in Burma, the Ambonese in Indonesia, and adherents of the Catholic Church in Indochina. No serious attempts were made by the colonial powers to encourage the integration of territorially-based ethnic identities into the spatial political organizations of the colonial territorial units. In addition, the Chinese and Indian migrants who were originally brought to work in plantations and mines, remain as distinct, largely unassimilated groups in various countries.[4] Although most of these Chinese and Indian migrants, having since moved to urban areas, have been evicted from various Southeast Asian countries in recent years, their impressive commerical skills and economic power generate resentment among the indigenous population. Almost every Southeast Asian government regards them as a major obstacle and would like to reduce their economic influence and to integrate them more fully with the local societies.

In the aftermath of decolonization, as the new states assumed responsibility for the maintenance of national boundaries, spatially-oriented local rivalries and conflicting interests emerged in Southeast Asian countries. The removal of colonial rule was not succeeded by a cohesive well-rooted nationalist viewpoint as a common unifying force to integrate the spatial dimension of the political system. Regionally-based ethnic identities created too vast a gulf for even the strong anticolonial sentiment, the most important common ideological denominator in Southeast Asia, to overcome. The new governments, taking over from colonial administrations which had temporarily subsumed ethnic differences and papered over religious cleavages, have not, yet, been able to establish common values and identity to achieve spatial political integration and assumed functioning of the state in the face of a variety of centrifugal forces. Ethnically-based regional feelings are a source of latent disunity in Indonesia where minorities on outer islands contend among themselves as well as with the dominant Javanese of the island-pivot of the Republic.[5] Neglect of the regional needs and aspirations of ethnic minority areas such as the Moslems of Sulu and Mindanao (Philippines), the Hill tribes of northeast Thailand, and the Malay of the southernmost provinces of Thailand have contributed to a sense of separate, territorial-based, ethnic identity in each country. The tradition of ethnic conflict in Burma has made effective territorial control of political space and national integration elusive.

POLITICAL GEOGRAPHIC EVOLUTION AND PROBLEMS OF TERRITORIAL INTEGRATION

The Continental Subrealm

In continental Southeast Asia, a series of overland migrations of Burmans, Thais and Vietnamese was followed by the establishment, by each of them, of kingdoms in the relatively large core areas provided by the great river basins. In all the mainland states, through the process of accretion around core areas in the river basins, the lowland peoples gradually extended their rule over the peripheral hill and plateau country surrounding the core. The spatial organization of large and effective political units around core areas in the early centuries was made possible by maritime Indian contact and the Indianized Kingdoms of Funan.

Champa and Langkasuka, located along the sear route between India and China, played a cruicual part in the formation of early Southeast Asian states. Langkasuka, with its center at Pattani occupied eastern coast of Malay peninsula.[6]

The heart of the Burmese kingdom comprised the great valley and central plains of the Irrawaddy. All the former capitals of the country—Ava, Amrapura, Pagan, Prome and Mandalay—are located along the middle Irrawaddy.[7] The Thai heartland located in the immense rice plain of the Chao Phraya, which extends down to Bangkok, formed the nucleus of the political unit which evolved into the modern state of Thailand.[8]

The great Khmer empire, the predecessor of modern Cambodia, has its core area in the inland basin of Tonle Sap. The empire sprang from one of the early maritime states of Indian civilization, originally founded in the Mekong delta, on key points along the sea route to China.[9]

Although Tonkin is considered the original nuclear base of the Vietnamese people, the Vietnamese inhabit a country without any geographical, and moreover, without any significant political unity. A nation-wide spatial political organization also failed to emerge in Vietnam during the French rule.[10] Between 1954–75, Vietnam developed into a cohesive state based on deep-rooted nationalism. After South Vietnam came completely under communist rule in 1975, it united into a Socialist Republic of Vietnam with a strong Marxist ideological orientation.

The original Lao state, based in the fertile valleys which break up the Laos plateau and Annamite Cordillera, disintegrated in the early 18th century into three segments: A central section focused at Vientiane, a northern section centered at Luang Prabang, and a southern part with its center at Champassak. France established its protectorate over the entire area in the 1890's. Since 1975 Laos has been occupied by communist-led Kaysone Phoumvihan.[11]

The Maritime Subrealm

In maritime Southeast Asian nations there are no core areas analogous to the river basins in the mainland countries. The present territorial extent of Indonesia, the Philippines and Malaysia is the legacy of the Western Colonial rule, far more than that of many of the mainland states whose heartlands were reasonably well-established at the time of the imposition of French and British colonial rule. Indonesia, the most populous of the Southeast Asian states, is characterized by a bipolarity in its spatial political organization which dates back to the two former trading empires of Sri Vijaya, centered on Sumatra, and Majapahit, centered on Java.[12] The small, densely populated, and agriculturally productive island of Java has been a major focus of power in Indonesia throughout historical times. The powerful Hindu Kingdom of Majapahit, centered on Java, reached its supremacy in the 14th and 15 centuries. The lowlands of eastern Sumatra comprise the second major focus of power in Indonesia. They sustained the medieval Indianized Buddhist sea-state of Sri Vijaya between the 7th and 13th centuries. In the 14th century Sri Vijaya was defeated by the Hindu kingdom of Majapahit and for a brief period Majapahit exercise overlordship over nearly all of the archipelago.

In 1518 Majapahit collapsed. Islam, which began to disseminate throughout the Archipelago, beginning in Sumatra, in the late 13th century, made Sumatra the principal focus of orthodox Islam. The strength of the earlier Hindu tradition modified Islam in east Java, thereby accentuating the traditional difference between Java and Sumatra. The two foci of power were united into a single spatial political organization under Dutch colonial rule, which exploited the country to the greatest extent by concentrating development of commercial production for export in a few well-selected areas (such as Java and northeast Sumatra), ignoring the rest of the archipelago. The clash in interests and the differences in outlook between Java and Sumatra, and additionally the outer islands, still presents major ramifications for the spatial organization of Indonesia's political system. In the 1960's, people of the outer islands resented the political dominance of Java; in the 1970's the disproportionately large influence of Sumatra in the national government is resented by the Javanese. The prospect of developing a stable state system in Indonesia rests largely upon the forging of a harmonious relationship between Java, the metropolitan island, and Sumatra and other outer islands.

External cultural and colonial influences, acting upon a dominantly Malay population have given the Philippines a distinctive political-geographic personality.[13] Unlike the historic kingdoms, the Philippines has no native culture of its own. It was not organized politically until the advent of Spanish power in the 16th century. Under Spanish rule, Manila, located in close proximity to the productive lowlands, became the administrative focus of the archipelago. In 1898 Spain ceded the Philippines to the United States. A feature of American colonial rule was the establishment of English as the *lingua franca* of well-educated Filipinos throughout the country. Linguistic diversity, religious distinctiveness, and the segmentary character of an archipelago state impede smooth progress towards an integrated spatial political system.

The multiracial Malaysian Federation, composed of three main ethnic-cultural-linguistic groups (Malay, Chinese and Indians), occupies a central position of great commercial and strategic importance in Southeast Asia.[14] The arrival of the Portuguese in Malacca, in 1509, marked the beginning of European expansion in the area, and the powers of the sultanates progressively declined. The Dutch ousted the Portuguese from Malacca in 1641 and, in 1795, were replaced by the British, who had occupied Penang in 1786. In 1826, the settlements of Malacca and Penang were combined with Singapore to form the Colony of the Straits Settlements. As a result of treaties concluded with Malay states, Britain established its protectorate on the peninsula. The Federated Malay States came into being in 1895, with the union of Perak, Selonger, Negri Sembilan and Pahang sultanates. The western seaboard of the

Federated Malay States developed into a major area of tin and rubber production with the importation of Indian and Chinese workers. In contrast, commerce dominated the economy of the Straits Settlements. After the Second World War the Communists launched a long and bitter guerrilla war which was suppressed. In 1957 Malaya became independent. The British colonies of Singapore,[15] Sarawak,[16] and Sabah[17] (North Borneo) joined the Malayan Federation to form Malaysia in 1963. In 1965 Singapore withdrew from Malaysia.

Despite the lack of effective integration, the territorial pattern of the Southeast Asian states created as a consequence of decolonization has been remarkably stable. While separation and fragmentation have real impact and exist in a defacto sense in Laos and have actually taken place in the case of Malaysia and Singapore, the formal spatial political pattern has been, so-far, remarkably enduring. Each state has retained the formal responsibility for its political space, which enjoys recognized international status. International status, however, does not necessarily correspond to the extent of effective internal control over political territory. In many cases the governments have still to consolidate territorial control. In the majority of the new states, social and ethnic cleavage, economic grievances, and insurrection thwart attempts to establish an integrated political spatial organization.

POLITICAL GEOGRAPHY OF INSURGENCY

The spatial aspects of insurgency in Southeast Asia are of interest and significance to political geography. The locational characteristics of areas of insurgent activities are significant in both the successful operation of guerrilla warfare and in formulating actions to counter the insurgency which undermines the territorial integrity of many Southeast Asian countries. Through attrition of government control over specific portions of the country, insurgency is a means to bring about political change in a state. The establishment of a territorially-based insurgent state, committed to replace the leadership of the state and change the form of government, may be regarded as the first step in a national revolution involving both the national population and national territory. The insurgent areas in Burma,Thailand and Kampuchea represent territorial units possessing all attributes of legitimate states—*raison d'etre*, control of territory and population, a core area, and political and administrative organization. The existence of an insurgent state is evidence of weakness and of the ineffectiveness of the government to control and protect its national terrritory. At the same time, through its complete control over the human and material resources of a territory, the insurgent state has the base needed for its continued development and expansion.[18]

The Burmese Insurgency

In Burma, the guerrilla base area or core area of the insurgent movement against the government is located in Kachin, the rugged mountain region in the north along the Chinese frontier (Fig. 1-1). In this region, which covers an eighth of Burma's territory, with the exception of main towns, the insurgents control an ideal locational position to harass transportation routes (such as the railway from Myitkyina to Mandalay) and expand their movement south toward the "Golden Triangle" border area with Thailand and Laos.[19]

Although some Communist elements have joined the insurgents in border areas, most of the ten to twenty thousand insurgents are ethnic minorities such as the Kachins, Shans and Karens, who are dedicated to winning autonomy or independence from Burma. Despite the increased agressiveness of the insurgent groups, they are not a serious threat to the stability of the central government in Rangoon. However, the insurgency in Kachin state could become far more dangerous if China were to increase the supply of weapons more advanced than the rifles, sten guns and submachine guns which the insurgents now use. The Kachins, who worked with American guerrilas fighting against the Japanese during World War II, are considered good fighters. The Kachin army is reported to be four to five thousand strong. Except for a small left-wing faction, the Kachins are anti-Communist.

In early 1980s, an estimated 700 Shan State Army (SSA) guerrillas held sway over the sparsely populated eastern Burma, seldom penetrated by government forces. The SSA was born out of the Shan revolt against the central government in 1958, and consists of four brigades (1st, 2nd, 4th and 7th) of three battalions each. The 4th brigade, the most distant unit, operates north of Mandalay-Lashio line and draws largely on the Wa population as a recruitment base. The 2nd, on the Thai border, covers areas east of the Salween,

Figure 1-1. Areas of Insurgency in Burma.

but also patrols as far north as the government-held town of Nam Sang. The 7th brigade operates in the east. Soldiers are constantly on the move to escape encirlement by Burmese troops. Nearly ninety percent of the arms at the SSA's disposal are Chinese-made, made available free from the Burmese Communist Party (BCP), which allows the party to exert a good deal of leverage over the SSA. In addition to the control of territory the SSA, the Shan United Army (SUA), Shan State Army Eastern (SSAE), and the Shan United Revolutionary Army (SURA) are also involved in the opium trade. Hill tribes in Burma grow the opium. Insurgents in the Shan State transport it, and ethnic Chinese buy and export it. All insurgents in Burma (except some Karens) profit to some degree from the drug traffic. The Burmese Communist Party also collect tax from opium caravans travelling through areas under its control. About sixty percent of the Burmese segment of the "Golden Triangle" is under the effective sway of the BCP and the rebel SSA.

Guerrilla Bases of Kampuchea in Early 1980s

In Kampuchea the Pol Pot rebel groups have been successful in establishing and operating guerrilla bases around the Cambodian basin. The insurgents control a large territory and have access to key targets, which they continue to harass. In Kampuchea the insurgents, who are indigenous natives dedicated to overthrowing the Heng Samrin government, have the advantage of hiding among the general population in the countryside without fear of detection.

Insurgency Areas of Thailand

In the remote border areas of northeastern and southern Thailand a number of insurgencies are presently under way. The most active insurgent territorial base is in Thailand's northern mountains and they have raided lowland, ethnic Thai village areas to expand their political influence in the country. The primary objective of the insurgents in southern Thailand is to consolidate their base area until the situation is favorable for resumption of full-scale operations. Joint Thai-Malayasian police operations have been organized against them. Communist insurgents in the southern peninsula of Thailand along the Malay border represent a local problem because of the distance separating them from key economic areas in central Thailand. Weak control by the central Thai government, the mountainous terrain, dense vegetation, and the location of insurgent areas along the international borders with inherent problems of suppression, provide an ideal cover for insurgent operations in Thailand. The insurgent areas in north and northeast Thailand represent locations with economic self-sufficency and access to either a Communist state or Communist-controlled areas for external support and supply of arms.

Vietcong Insurgency in South Vietnam, 1954–74

Insurgency in South Vietnam under control of the Vietcong was part of the enduring landscape of the countryside during 1954–1974. Political and military organization, ideology and nationalistic motives all combined made the Vietcong a viable force which extended its territiorial control over large stretches of South Vietnam. In terms of the continuity of government and political organization, the areas controlled by the Vietcong were relatively stable, and able to resist attempts by the South Vietnamese government to extend control within Vietcong insurgent zones.

The success of the Vietcong insurgency, accomplished against opponents with a very great superiority in weapons of modern war, had been derived largely from the voluntary support of the rank-and-file peasantry. The Vietcong offensive could not have been carried out unless secure bases existed to support and supply the insurgent armies. The staying power of insurgent territorial bases had been consistently underestimated by the government of South Vietnam and the U.S. officials. From a series of viable strongholds in 1954, the Vietcong insurgent state covered much of the territory, including key villages (Fig. 1-2). The 1973 cease-fire agreement left a pattern of the military situation in Laos and Cambodia which was favorable for the Vietcong insurgent state in South Vietnam since the Communist control of most of Laos and Cambodia guaranteed supply routes into the Vietcong insurgent state. The Vietcong insurgent state, recognized de facto by the 1973 Paris Accord, set up its capital in the devastated town of Dong Ha in Quang Tri province.[21] Dong Ha was one of the eight district capitals under control of the Vietcong Insurgent State. Its selection as a capital for the Vietcong state gave the Communists unimpeded communications with North Vietnam, and from these insurgent-held pockets the entire country was occupied by 1975.

The "Huks" of the Philippines

The tiny "Huk" (Hukbong Mapagpalaya Nang Bayan, or People's Liberation Army in Tagalog, the predominent language of Luzon) guerrilla army, which has established a following among masses in Pampanga province and in parts of Tarlac, Bucacan and Nueva Ecija provinces north of Manila represents another example of an incipient revolutionary territorial base (Fig. 1-3). The Huks today represent a strange conglomeration of ideal reformers, Communists and farmers. In contrast to situations in both Burma and Thailand, the Huks are apparently not trying to overthrow the government so much as they are attempting to make themselves the most important segment of the society. In Pampanga they have become the effective force protecting the farmers from the landlords and the theft of water buffaloes. The Huks have succeeded in

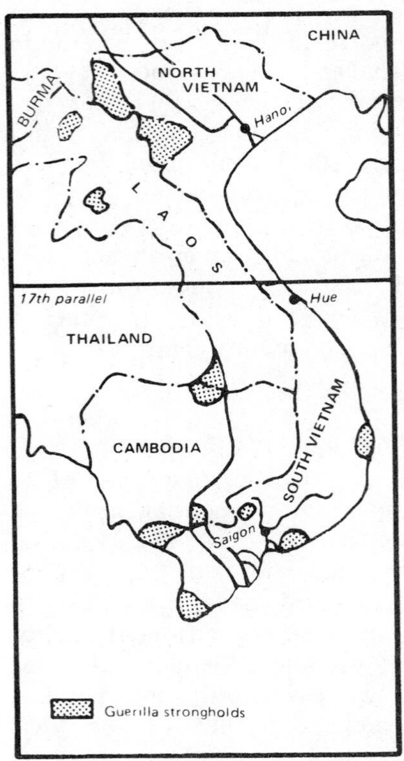

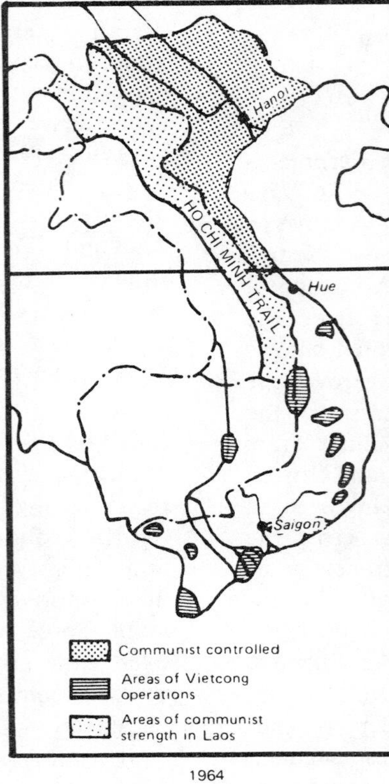

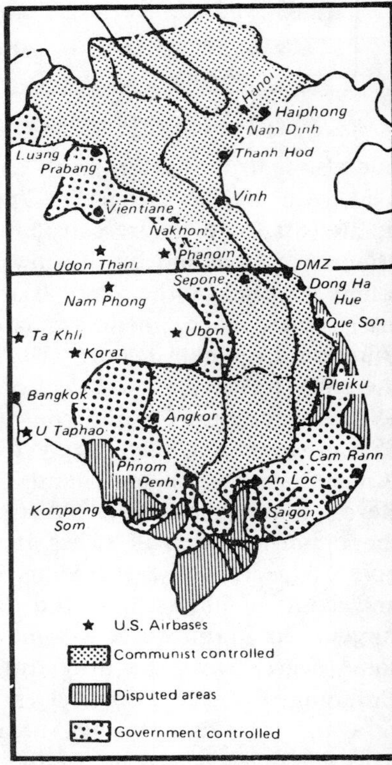

Figure 1-2. Expansion of Insurgency in Indochina (1954–72).

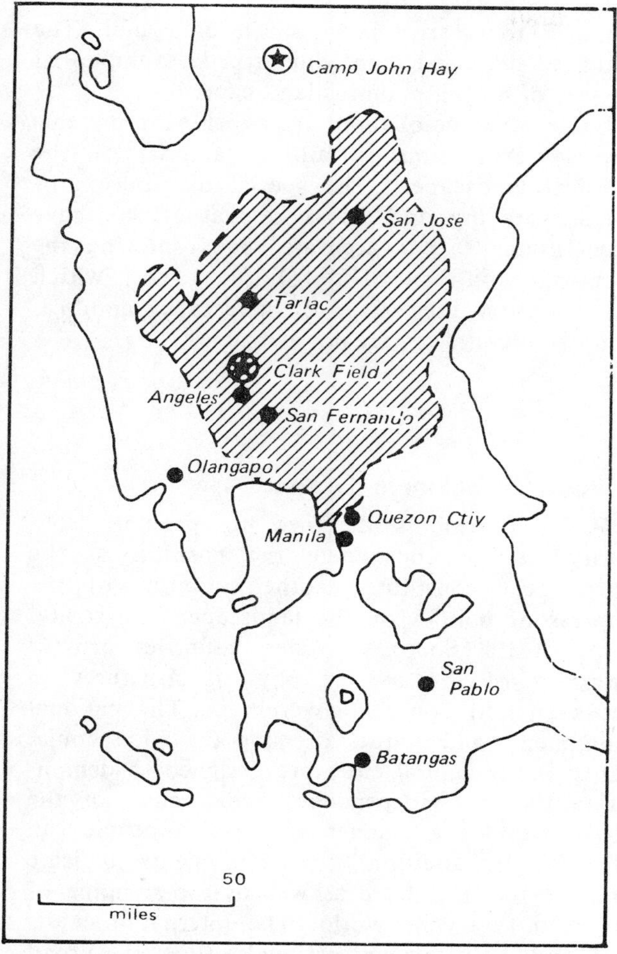

Figure 1-3. Areas in Central Luzon (Philippines) where Huk Guerrillas operate.

establishing a firm financial base ($400–$500 thousand) to pay their new recruits about $5 more a month than a private in the Philippine Army earns.[22] A major source of revenue for the Huks is Angeles, a town on the outskirts of the U.S. Clark Air Force Base. The Huks receive protection money from the owners of the many bars and restaurants in Angeles frequented by the Americans. Automatic rifles, smuggled off the base, have been sold to the Huks. The establishment of the Huk-dominated area, in the rich fertile area of Central Luzon within the Philippine state, gives them a political significance exceeding that which the "liberated" areas suggest in terms of the political geographic structure of the country.

Insurgency in Laos, 1954–1975

By 1970 the insurgent state of Pathet Laos occupied more than half the territory of Laos (Fig. 1-2). All of eastern Laos, and much of the northern and southern regions of the country were controlled by the Pathet Lao. The Pathet Lao insurgent state had considerable strategic significance for the Vietcong insurgent state in South Vietnam because of its logistical reliance upon the Ho Chi Minh Trail (supply route), which ran through eastern Laos. The Pathet Laos, dominated by the ideology of international Communism was closely related to the Communism of North Vietnam. The insurgency movement began in 1954 and gained adherents over the years. With increasing assistance from Communist neighbors, it steadily expanded its territorial occupation and improved its political strength and military organization. The Pathet Lao insurgent state in Laos demonstrated efficiency and effectiveness in its successful operation. Laos, a communist state since 1975, is dominated by Vietnam.[23]

IMPRESS OF POLITICAL ACTIVITIES ON THE LANDSCAPE

Political geographers have long recognized the major impress which political activities leave on the landscape of an area.[24] A variety of political processes such as activities related to the need for security, special features such as military garrisons, and the development of capital cities, are examples by which political activities manifest in the landscape. Southeast Asia provides a unique and dramatic example of a major transformation of landscape and economy under the impetus of the Vietnam War. Activities connected with counter-insurgency such as pacification and relocation, secured areas, strategic hamlet policy and enclave theory have expressions in the landscape and suggest the wide scope of political impress on the environment. In this section two aspects of political impact upon the landscape will be discussed: (1) the dramatic impress of the Indochina war on the environment; and (2) the political symbolism of national capital in the landscape of Southeast Asia which express a country's aspirations and perceived values in the monuments, public buildings and architecture and serve to demonstrate its sovereignty from foreign powers.

Impress of the War on the Indochina Landscape

The contemporary landscape of Indochina provides numerous examples of the ways in which civil war and related activities leave their impress upon the land. In South Vietnam, the strategic hamlet policy of the 1960's has left a major imprint of security in the landscape.[25] In the 1960's thousands of Vietnamese farmers were moved to strategic settlements protected from the Communist guerrillas by mud walls, moats, barbed wire and also bamboo ledges. An elaborate complex of defenses—miles of walls commanding an encircling ditch and dozens of watch towers protected by barbed wire and bamboo stakes are apparent in the landscape as an impress of governmental activity in pursuit of security—one of the most valued elements of sovereignty over an area. This deliberate policy of moving the villagers from their home villages to the strategic villages displaced millions of Vietnamese during the 1960s and early 1970s.

Thousands of Americans, sent to serve as advisers and to provide logistic support to the Vietnamese in their war against Communist guerrillas, have left a significant impress on the country in a variety of ways. The impact of American troops was apparent on the economy of Saigon and other towns. More dramatic landscape, modifications can be seen in the scores of villages which have been blown away as a result of bombing, leaving deep bomb craters. Harvested crops burned to ash, orchards destroyed, and thousands of acres of once-productive rice-farming land in the delta, lying abandoned and choked with weeds, are landscape expressions of the tragedy of the Vietnam War. The dikes and canals that were built by the French in the Mekong Delta, to keep the salt water out, were allowed to fall into disrepair, threatening millions of productive areas by crop-killing salt water intrusion. It had been estimated that nearly 740,000 acres of rice land had been abandoned because of the war.[26]

In the Red River delta of North Vietnam, a network of dikes to protect rice fields from floods has been built by the peasants.[27] This river dike system is highly vulnerable to bombing attacks. In 1971 floodwaters smashed through a 30-mile section of the delta's dikes, wiping out large parts of the autumn rice crop, which forced North Vietnam to import food from the Soviet Union and China. When systematic bombing of the delta began in 1965, a civilian army of men and women was formed by North Vietnam to patrol the branches of the Red River for any ruptures in the dikes. Without the dikes, the Tonkin plain would be a desolate land of marsh and flood. In June 1972 bombs destroyed the dikes protecting Nam Dinh, a town sixty miles south of Hanoi. The damaged dike and dams did provide examples of impress of hostilities on the landscape.[28]

Large scale defoliation in Indochina represents another expression of military activity on the physical landscape.[29] The spatial distribution of forest spraying and its ecological effects have been studied,[30] but accurate maps showing the locational pattern of defoliated areas, which would reflect the extent of landscape modification by military acts, are not available.

Political Symbolism in the Landscape

Political symbols designed to promote solidarity and to consolidate the position of the government constitute another example of the impress of politics on the landscape. The capital cities of the Southeast Asian countries provide examples of the use of physical structures to focus attention on the government. The national monuments and statues dressing the wide boulevards of the capital cities are designed to demonstrate the post-independence achievement of the government in a manner with which people can identify. In addition, the monuments indicate promise for the future as well as the standing of the country in the world. The international airport and the associated national airline, the broad paved streets lined with physical symbols of technological and educational achievements, modern hotels, government offices, stadiums and other structures, comprise symbols of grandeur and modernization stamped on the landscape of the capital city.

Although most of these physical structures are functional, they have the added purpose of engendering a sense of national pride among the citizens. In Southeast Asia, monuments varying from the Soviet-style architecture in Jakarta to the neotraditional buildings in Phnom Penh have been erected to evoke a sense of pride in national achievement. National status symbols, both visual and nonvisual, are relevant for the evocation of appropriate political attitudes to promote solidarity, but the ephemeral trimmings and symbols must be backed by the government's ability to develop a strong economic structure to meet the needs of the people, which is necessary to support a viable political system. Symbols will not build an enduring system if the material necessities are not satisfied. Among the Southeast Asian countries, Singapore provides the most striking visible evidence with a landscape of substantial economic advance in features such as low-cost housing developments and industrial enterprise.[31] Examples of political symbols on the landscape can be multiplied indefinitely. The selected examples mentioned above identify a group of landscape features which have significance in the study of political geography of a region.

VIABILITY OF AREAL POLITICAL ORGANIZATIONS (1974)

Viability of areal political units is a product of a complex set of physical, economic and cultural attributes, which include the ideas, spirit and attitudes possessed by people of a given state. In evaluating viability, political geographers cannot rely on the use of a few features of the country. Viability must be delineated on the basis of the multiple characteristics of sovereign states. An attempt has been made here to delineate, with some precision, the variations in levels of viability among the Southeast Asian states using twenty-five selected variables (economic, demographic, man-land relationships, political stability and social, educational and general development) which measure the internal structure and spatial organization of political areas.[32]

Results of the Application of Factor Analysis

Using a factor analysis procedure, it was found that more than 73% of the variance in viability of political units (with twenty-five variables employed to measure viability) could be accounted for by five dimensions or factors. Factor analysis reduces the large number of explanatory variables into a small number of "factors" or dimensions which help explain most of the variance.[33] Factor loadings indicate which factors are most important in the explanation of variations such as levels of viability of sovereign states. The factors in which a state had the highest loadings are most important in explaining its levels of viability according to their own location in factor space based on scores for five factors derived from twenty-five selected variables for states of Southeast Asia.

The five factors which differentiate viability among the Southeast Aisan states are; (1) relative level of economic development; (2) composite size elements; (3) social welfare and location; (4) level of rural development; and (5) political awareness. Using a grouping procedure that selected states which are most alike in their internal organization and spatial structure, three levels of viability among the Southeast Asian states were delineated. The viability levels take on distinct locational patterns, with member states tending to be clustered in distinct areas within Southeast Asia (Fig. 1–4). States with the lowest level of viability are in continental Southeast Asia; located astride this group in mainland and insular Southeast Asia are states with a moderate level of viability; the state (Singapore) with the highest level of viability lies in the center of Southeast Asia.

The most viable state in Southeast Asia today is Singapore, which is also one of the smallest in both area and population. Singapore exhibits a higher standard of living and a more stable government than any of its neighbors. A high degree of political integration has been reached despite the ethnic variety within its boundaries.[34]

High Level of Viability. Singapore, characterized by a higher level of economic development, cultural and social integration and political stability ranks at the top in level of viability in Southeast Asia. The important strategic location of Singapore has given this microcity state a great advantage in import-export trade, banking, insurance and related activities. Profits from the various industries combined with the political stability have given Singapore one of the highest standards of living in Southeast Asia.

Moderate Level of Viability. The second group of states—Indonesia, Malaysia, Vietnam, the

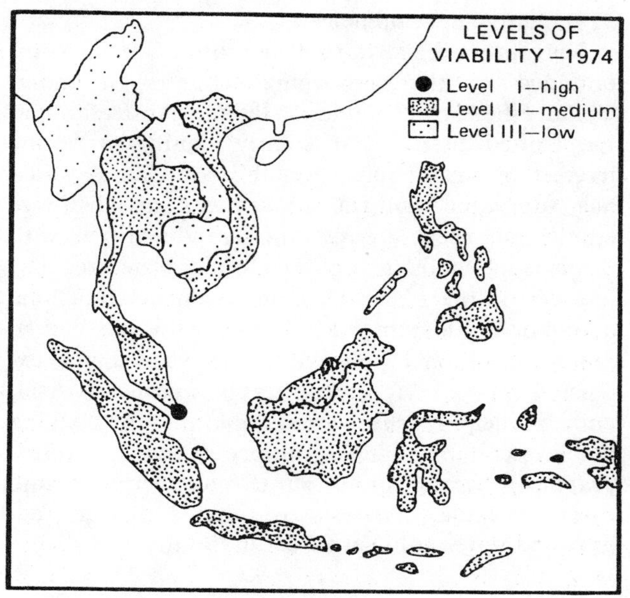

Philippines and Thailand—are characterized by a moderate level of viability. Southeast Asian states at the second viability level are not highly developed but are at about the world average in terms of life expectancy, standard of living, educational levels and stability of government.

Low Level of Viability. Burma, Kampuchea and Laos rank lowest among the Southeast Asian states in viability. Burma represents, in heightened form, the complex of economic, social and environmental problems which have to be overcome on the road to political-territorial integration. The problem of integration in Kampuchea is handicapped by the insurgent control of areas along the Thai border.

THE SOUTHEAST ASIAN GEOPOLITICAL SCENE

The events of the last two decades indicate that none of the newly independent Southeast Asian states is sufficiently strong to fill the vacuum resulting from withdrawal of Colonial powers, and that they are unable to cooperate in establishing a truly united insular and continental Southeast Asia which would be a major force in the world equation of power. The failure of the colonial powers to solve problems of underdevelopment in their former dependencies magnified the political stresses, as each nation tried to assert its individuality and achieve an economic breakthrough by shifting from Western-style free enterprise towards a planned socialist-type model of economic development.

The geopolitical problems have been compounded by the converging interests of India, China, the Soviet Union, Japan, Australia and the United States. Particularly significant is the interest of the People's Republic of China, which has supported political movements of all those ethnic and rebel groups who are dissatified with the existing political and economic structure. The interest of the Communist governments in China and North Vietnam had clashed with the United States' traditional policy of counteracting the extension of Communist power in Southeast Asia, and of helping the various nations in building viable economic and political structures. Geographical juxtapostion of the converging, and often clashing, interests of major powers aggravate the geopolitical forces in Southeast Asia.

Traditional and Contemporary Indian and Chinese Perception of Southeast Asia

The geopolitical role of India and China can best be understood by an examination of the traditional Indian and Chinese perception of Southeast Asia. The traditional Indian view of Southeast Asia was guided by the Hindu *codes of Manu*, by the political thought in the *Mahabharat* and the famous Indian manual on politics called *Arthasastra*, the classic work of Kautilya. These Hindu writings perceived a world of unequal concentric states in constant flux, comprising a "Mandala" or "Circle."[35] Each state in the concentric "circle of states" sought to extend or preserve its security and power by a combination of diplomacy and force among a series of powers which surrounded it. Thus, according to the traditional Indian view, the geographic position and resources of a state determined its foreign policy and world view. Kautilya's *Arthasastra* provides detailed strategems and practices for varying kinds of relationships in the concentric circle of states. The ancient role of India in Southeast Asia is not guided by the traditional Hindu perception of world order. As the largest democracy in the world, surviving the present perils in its own way, India is an example of a working democracy to the nations of Southeast Asia. It has maintained good relations with Burma, despite the existence of some unresolved problems—such as the status of Indians in Burma who, together with the Chinese, have played a major role in the economy of the country. In 1967 India and Burma reached an agreement on the delineation and demarcation of their common border. India's relations with Malaysia, Thailand, Indonesia, the Philippines and Singapore are cordial. India has announced its determination to defend the Indian Ocean and has attempted to promote security in Southeast Asia by strengthening, individually and collectively, the economic and political stability of the nations concerned. In India's view, the security of Southeast Asia is the responsibility of the nations in the area. It has opposed the formation of any military alliance, which lead to a counter-military alliance and, hence to instability. Many internal difficulties inhibit the policies and the capabilties of India to play an active role in Southeast Asia as an effective counterweight to China. Between 1954 and 1971, as chairman of the International Supervisory Commissions in Vietnam, Laos and Cambodia, India tried unsuccessfully to make a contribution towards peace and stability in the region.

In constrast to India's traditional perception of world order, which is no longer the operative principle of her foreign policy, the traditional Chinese perception of world order,[36] comprising inferior "tributary" and "vassal" states surrounding "the Middle Kingdom" continues as an element in China's contemporary policy in Southeast Asia. China's geopolitical role combines a traditional perception of overlordship over the region with Chinese brand of Marxist ideology.

The establishment of Chinese-supported insurgent areas and careful organization of Chinese-oriented Communist parties in various nations are strategies which China has used to gain dominance in the region. The insurgents appeal to young people in rural areas with popular sentiments of nationalism and social justice. The emergence of a network of these Chinese-supported insurgent territorial bases along China's southern flank in Burma, and Thailand, have been noted in the earlier section. Local cells which can become a nucleus for insurgency with fixed territorial bases, exist in the Philippines, Indonesia, Borneo (Kalimantan), Singapore and Malaysia. However, nationalistic tendencies in Southeast Asian Communism, intense ethnic antagonism against the Chinese, and China's disinclination to use its military power for conquest and control in adjoining countries due to fear of massive retaliation, constitute major limitations on the pursuit of China's geopolitical objectives in Southeast Asia.

The Role of the Soviet Union

The geopolitical role of the Soviet Union in Southeast Asia is not as distinct as that of China. However, the Sino-Soviet conflict has made it clear that the Soviet Union has a different ideology and practice for modelling Socialist states in Southeast Asia than do the Chinese.[37] The Soviet-Chinese differences in Communist ideology and practice have turned into a bitter competition between the two countries for the allegiances of Communist parties in all nations of Southeast Asia, particularly in Kampuchea. One of the principal goals of the Soviet Union is to prevent the spread of China's influence in Southeast Asia by developing active relationships with Vietnam, Kampuchea, and Laos and with internal Communist parties in other Southeast Asian countries.

The Soviets are out to consolidate their ties to the new group of Indochinese communist states—Vietnam, Laos, and Kampuchea—to weaken American and Chinese influence among the ASEAN countries, and to prevent ASEAN from joining an anti-Soviet Pacific coalition. The Soviets are intent upon increasing their naval and maritime power in the key areas of Southeast Asia. They have been steadily increasing the size of their Pacific Fleet for many years and now that their fleet has regular access to Vietnamese ports, the Soviet Union's ability to project its naval power throughout Asian waters will be greatly enhanced. The Soviets not only have strong incentives for expanding their power in Southeast Asia, but regional conflicts often provide opportunities for the Soviet Union to insert itself into a position of influence. By supporting Vietnam against China, the Soviets expanded their influence in Southeast Asia.

Japan's Economic Objectives

Japan's contemporary geopolitical role in Southeast Asia has been characterized by an almost exclusive concern for economic and trade objectives,[38] although the potential of Japan's political role in the region is very great. Japan is the nearest industrial market for Southeast Asia's export of primary products. The investment of Japanese capital in Southeast Asia has provided much-needed institutions for the transfer of modern technological skill and management. The Southeast Asian countries can take maximum advantage of Japan's economic capability because of proximity and competitiveness. Japan's political role in the area may develop if she becomes increasingly involved in regional, and national, political problems. With no military intentions and considerable wealth, Japan has confined her role in the region towards broadening the base of economic relationships that flow in increasing quantities between Japan and Southeast Asia.

Australian Motives

Australia is alive to its strategic importance and location in relation to Southeast Asia. It has emphasized her role in the economic development of the region and has shown sympathy with the Nationalist movements. Australia was a prime mover in the Colombo Plan of 1950 designed to give economic and technical aid to non-Communist Asian countries. She sent armed forces in 1955 to Malaya to quell insurgents, and Australian troops were employed in South Vietnam to aid the Americans. Australia has tried to fill the vacuum created by the British decision to withdraw armed forces from Singapore. Two related factors will continue to dominate

Australia's geopolitical role in Southeast Asia in Australia's current and future security and defense; and trade prospects in Southeast Asian nations.

The United States Strategy

The strategic value of Southeast Asia to the United States has undergone changes during the past two decades. After the successful Communist revolution in China in 1949, the United States sensitive to a possible shift of Communist aggression to Southeast Asia, began to develop the concept of a single comprehensive security system for East and Southeast Asia in order to protect the American perimeter of influence running from South Korea and Japan through Taiwan and South Vietnam to Thailand. Convinced that the defense of Southeast Asia was indivisible, the United States sought united action, which led to the formation of the Southeast Asia Treaty Organization (SEATO) in 1955. The "domino theory" assumed that Communist capture of any one of the Southeast Asian countries would endanger all others.[39] The loss of one country or "domino" would necessarily be followed by the fall of a whole series of neighboring "dominoes." This concept of Southeast Asia led the United States to take all possible measures to deter Communist aggression in the region.

The United States attempted to sustain the independence, survival and growth of Southeast Asian states through a program of economic and military aid. In 1964 the United States Congress, in a Joint Resolution, declared that "The United States regards as vital to its national interest and to world peace the maintenance of international peace and security in Southeast Asia."[40] The Resolution authorized the President to use armed forces to defend any Southeast Asian nation threatened by military conquest. To counter aggression in Vietnam and Laos, the United States began using its own military forces in 1965. The United States extricated itself from the Indochina War with the signing of the Paris agreement in January, 1973, but the warring sides in Vietnam did not abandon the causes for which they fought, and deep distrust remained. The 1973 agreement allowed North Vietnam to keep troops in South Vietnam to defend the Vietcong insurgent enclaves.

With disengagement in Vietnam, the United States' policy shifted from the "domino theory," involving containment of Communism in Southeast Asia, to the contemporary policy of coexistence with Communism, based on a balance of forces with the area itself and among the world powers. If successful, this equilibrium could lead to a new stability in Southeast Asia which even the two decades of war could not guarantee. However, in 1974, the sought-for stability seemed extremely precarious. The United States worn out by the internal and external convulsions of the long and seemingly inconclusive war in Vietnam seized the opportunity to make an abrupt turnabout in its relations with China. Accommodation with the United States seemed the only route open to China, in view of its pervasive fear of Russian attack. Further, China's leaders regard the solution of their basic food problems, industrialization, and raising the national income as steps as necessary to China's defense, and it is only the United States—the major non-Communist power—that can offer the technology and capital to accomplish these objectives. The American rapprochement with China frightened and menaced the smaller countries of Southeast Asia. The problem is compounded by the continued presence of guerrilla and other radical movements, owing ideological allegiance to China, which seek to usurp the *status quo* in various nations. The answers to principal geopolitical questions remain open to speculation. To what extent is the United States accommodation with China a stable quantity in Southeast Asian geopolitical equation? Will The United States attempt to build stability in Southeast Asia through an equipoise of power among the countries in the area, including China and the Soviet Union, succeed in the future? Or, was the 1973 Peace Agreement a prelude to continued instability and the possibility of increasing disequilibrium and war and intervention by the great powers, as Soviet-Chinese-supported insurgents attempted to overwhelm various governments in Indochina? In 1975, it was evident in retrospect that the 1973 Peace Agreement was only a stepping stone to achieve full power for the insurgents in Vietnam, Laos and Kampuchea.

MARITIME BOUNDARY PROBLEMS

In 1980 Indonesia declared an exclusive 200-mile economic zone, an area of limited jurisdiction, for the exploitation and exploration of waters, sea-bed and other resources surrounding the territorial sea. Several other nations in the region have declared similar economic zones, and they must negotiate median boundaries with neighboring countries. Theoretically, there is also an area of potential conflict with China, which claims islands in the South China Sea. While overlapping boundaries declared by Indonesia, Papua New Guinea and the Philippines pose no major problems at present, those between Indonesia, Vietnam, Australia, and Malaysia present serious problems (Fig. 1-5).

The most dangerous conflict zone is not accepted by Indonesia and encompasses economic zone waters which Indonesia has already contracted out for oil exploration. The problem lies in the method of determining the 12-mile boundary within which a nation can claim full sovereign jurisdiction. Indonesia uses the archipelagic principle which, for island nations such as Indonesia, defines territorial waters by drawing an imaginary straight line between the outermost points of the country's outermost islands. Territorial waters and economic zones are measured from this base line. On this basis, Indonesia claims a large area jutting out into the South China Sea between peninsular Malaysia and Sarawak. Indonesia's Natuna island is 400 miles south of the Vietnam coast. Vietnam uses the deepest navigable portion of its coastal waters to designate the line from which territorial seas are determined. This line is further from the shore than the normal base-line, and the 200-mile zone calculated by this method includes areas already contracted out to foreign oil companies by Indonesia.

The problem between Indonesia and Australia is more technically complicated. The dispute emanates from two distinct legal frameworks—one, of the sea-boundary based on continental shelf, and the other on overlapping fishing zone of 200 miles. The conflict is centered on fishing rights south of Timor. With Malaysia, Indonesia's potential problem concerns two islands (Pulau Sepadan and Pulau Ligitan) which appear on Malaysian maps as part of Malaysia, and on Indonesian maps as Indonesian. The dispute between the two neighbors has surfaced frequently, with protests over alleged claims of sovereignty flying back and forth.

SOUTHEAST ASIA IN THE 1980s

In the 1980s Southeast Asia is distinguished from many other developing regions of the world by a relatively stable, pro-Western balance of power. Most of the region, with the exception of Vietnam, Laos, and Kampuchea, is tied into a Western alliance system in one way or another. The Philippines provided the United States with key air and naval bases; Thailand is tied to the United States by the Manila Pact; Malaysia and Singapore are both members of Five-Power Pact which includes Great Britain, New Zealand, and Australia. All the ASEAN countries, including Indonesia, rely on the United States or other Western countries for their arms supplies.

An important factor in the stability of Southeast Asia is the ASEAN, the first successful regional organization in the history of Southeast Asia. Formed in 1967 the Association of Southeast Asian Nations (ASEAN) is designed to promote economic progress and political stability in Southeast Asia. The five ASEAN countries—Indonesia, Philippines, Singapore, Malaysia, and Thailand—have adopted a common front against the Vietnamese invasion of Kampuchea; they have developed joint strategies to deal with the industrial countries; and they have taken some cooperative steps to defuse territorial disputes and to discourage the growth of sectionist movements within their borders.

In the 1980s the most serious and bitter confrontations in Southeast Asia are those between contiguous communist states, China against Vietnam, and Vietnam against communist insurgents supported by China in Kampuchea.

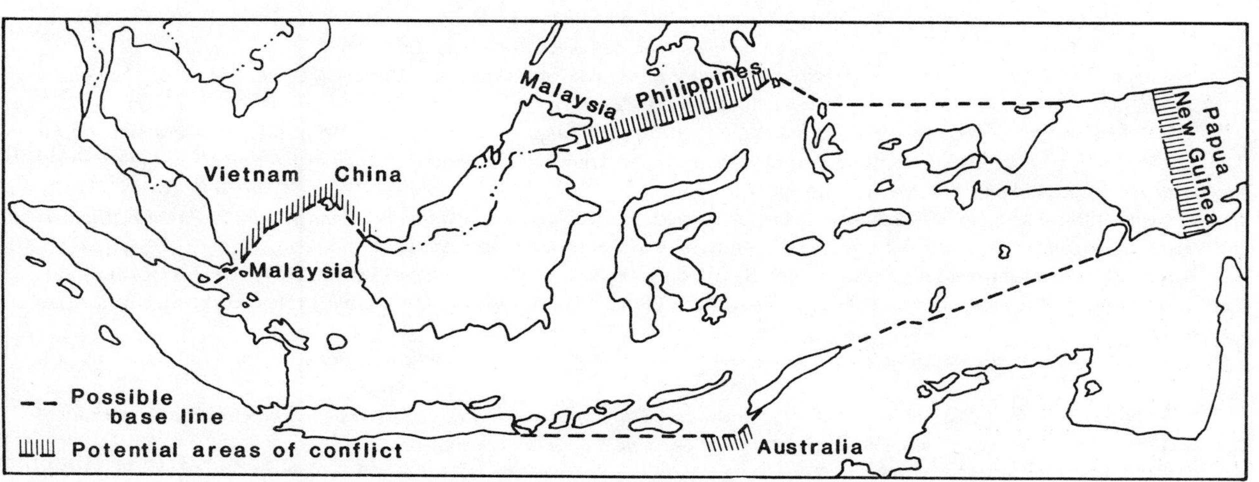

Figure 1-5. Disputed Boundaries of Indonesia.

Southeast Asian communist states are finding that their most active and dangerous adversaries are not far-away Western powers, but neighboring communist states with whom they share disputed and heavily armed borders and an historical record of conflict going back several centuries. These conflicts are not mere transient elements. They are likely to last throughout the 1980s. They have deep historical roots, in which historical power rivalries that were temporarily diminished by the common struggle against colonialism are being revived. The end of Western colonialism, and the retreat of American power from Vietnam in 1975 have led to the return of historial geopolitical rivalry. And both Vietnam and China, Vietnam and Kampuchea, have resumed ethnic and geopolitical rivalries that go back to several centuries before the arrival of the West.

Footnote References

[1]For good recent bibliographic surveys of Southeast Asia including regional and country maps which provide excellent geographic profiles of various countries see *Peninsular Southeast Asia: A Bibliographic Survey of Literature*, D.A. Pam. 550–14 (Washington D.C.: Government Printing Office, 1972); and *Insular Southeast Asia: A Bibliographic Survey*. D.A. Pam. 550–12 (Washington D.C.: Government Printing Office, 1972). C.A. Fisher provides an excellent review of geographical literature on Southeast Asia in *Geographers Abroad: Essays on the Problems and Prospects of Research in Foreign Areas*. University of Chicago, Department of Geography, Research Paper No. 152, 1973, pp. 185–228.

[2]For details see K.M. Panikkar, *Asia and Western Dominance* (London, 1953).

[3]For a discussion of the effects of European interference with human ecology and its influence on political geography see E.H.G. Dooby, "Some Aspects of the Human Ecology of Southeast Asia," *Geographical Journal*, Vol. 108, Nos. 1–3 (July–September, 1946). pp. 40–54; see also Robert Solomon, "Boundary Concepts and Practices in Southeast Asia," *World Politics* (October, 1970), pp. 1–23.

[4]See L. Unger, "The Chinese in Southeast Asia," *Geographical Review*, Vol. 34 (1944), pp. 196–217; K.S. Sandhu, "Chinese Colonization of Malacca," *Journal of Tropical Geography*, Vol. 15 (1961), pp. 1–26; Victor Purcell, *The Chinese in Southeast Asia*, 2nd edition (Oxford, 1965); C. Kondapi, *Indians Overseas 1838–1949* (New Delhi: 1951); K.S. Sandhu, *Indians in Malaya—Immigration and Settlement 1786–1857* (London: 1969); C.P. Fitzgerald, *The Third Chna: The Chinese Communities in Southeast Asia* (Melbourne, Cheshire; 1965).

[5]C.A. Fisher, "Indonesia: A Giant Astir," *Geographical Journal*, Vol. 138 (1972), pp. 154–165.

[6]For a good history see John F. Cady, *Southeast Asia: Its Historical Development* (New York: McGraw-Hill Book Company, 1964); see also G. Coedes, *The Indianized States of Southeast Asia*, 3rd edition (Honolulu: East-West Center Press, 1968).

[7]W. Kirk, "Some Factors in the Historical Geography of Burma," *Journal of Manchester Geographical Society*, Vol. 54 (1947–49), pp. 16–26; see also Frank Trager, *Burma—From Kingdom to Republic* (New York: Praeger Publishers, Inc., 1966).

[8]For details see Robert L. Pendleton *et al., Thailand: Aspects of Landscape and Life* (New York: 1962).

[9]Robert Garry, "La geopolitique du Cambodge et la deuxieme guere d'Indochine," *Etudes de geographie tropicale offertes a Pierre Gourou* (Paris and The Hague: Mouton, 1972), pp. 165–182.

[10]For details see D.J. Duncanson, *Government and Revolution in Vietnam* (New York: Oxford for Royal Insitute of International Affairs); B. Fall, *The Two Vietnams*, 2nd edition (New York: Praeger Publishers, Inc., 1967).

[11]For details see Hugh Toye, *Laos: Buffer State or Battle ground?* (Oxford: 1968); A.J. Dommen, *Conflict in Laos: The Politics of Neutralization*, Rev. edition (New York: Praeger Publishers, Inc., 1971).

[12]For a detailed introduction to Indonesia see Ruth T. McVey (ed.) *Indonesia* (New York: 1963); Missen, *Viewpoints on Indonesia: A Geographical Study* (1972); for recent developments see Arnold C. Blackman, *Indonesia: Suharto's Road* (New York: American Asian Educational Exchange, 1973).

[13]An authoritative geographical treatment is F.L. Wernstedt and J.E. Spencer, *Philippine Island World: A Physical, Cultural and Regional Geography* (Berkeley and Los Angeles: University of California Press, 1967).

[14]An excellent overview of Malaya is by Norton S. Ginsburg and C.F. Roberts, *Malaya* (Seattle, 1958); see also Ooi Jin—Bee, *Land, People and Economy of Malaya* (London: 1963); Rene Peritz, *Malaysia in Search of Stability* (New York: American-Asian Educational Exchange, 1974).

[15]A sound basic survey is Iain Buchanan, *Singapore in Southeast Asia: An Economic and Political Appraisal* (London: Bell, 1972).

[16]Two excellent recent works are J.C. Jackson, *Sarawak: A Geographical Survey of a Developing State* (London: University of London Press, 1968); and Yong-Leng Lee, *Population and Settlement in Sarawak* (Singapore: 1970).

[17]An excellent introduction is provied by Yong-Leng Lee, *North Borneo (Sabah), A Study in Settlement Geography* (Singapore: 1965).

[18]For further details on the "insurgent state" see Robert W. McColl, "The Insurgent State: Territorial Bases of Revolution," *Annals of the Association of American Geographers*, Vol. 59 (December, 1969), pp. 613-631.

[19]"Chinese-supported Rebels Gain in Burma," *The New York Times* (January 21, 1973).

[20]See "Thailand: The Northeast," *Asia*, The Asia Society, No. 6 (Autumn, 1966), pp. 1-27.

[21]*The New York Times* (January 24, 1973), p. 17.

[22]"Huks regaining Luzon Strength," *The New York Times* (April 16, 1967); see also "The Philippines: Problems and Prospects," *Asia*, The Asia Society, New York, No. 23 (Autumn, 1971), pp. 9-10.

[23]Robert Shaplen, "Our Involvement in Laos," *Foreign Affairs* (April 1970), pp. 478-493; R.A. Paul, "Laos: Anatomy of an American Involvement," *Foreign Affairs* (April, 1971), pp. 533-547.

[24]J.R.V. Prescott, *Political Geography* (London: Methuen, 1972), pp. 14-26.

[25]Homer Bigart, "Vietnam Sets up Fortified towns," *The New York Times* (April 1, 1962).

[26]Barry Kramer, "Vietnamese Must Undo Long Economic Neglect as Well as Fix Damage," *The Wall Street Journal* (February 15, 1973), pp. 1 and 14.

[27]Seymour M. Hersh, "Dikes in Hanoi Area Represent 2,000-Year Effort to Tame Rivers," *The New York Times* (July 14, 1972).

[28]Professor Yves Lacoste, a geographer at the Sorbonne who is a specialist on the delta plain, has reportedly mapped the damage to dikes in North Vietnam. For a complete documentation of damage to dikes see *American Bombing of Dikes and Dams in North Vietnam* (Montreal: Association of Vietnamese Patriots, 1972).

[29]J.B. Neilands, "Vietnam: Progress of the Chemical War," *Asian Survey*, Vol. 10, No. 3 (1970), p. 221.

[30]Arthur H. Westing, "Ecological Effects of Military Defoliation on the Forests of South Vietnam," *Bioscience*, Vol. 21, No. 17 (September 1, 1971), pp. 893-898.

[31]Willard A. Hanna, "Singapore Success Syndrome Retested" Part II, *Field Reports*, American Universities Field Staff, Vol. 21, No. 5 (January, 1973), pp. 1-16.

[32]The data was taken from the United Nations Statistical Reports.

[33]For a detailed treatment of this technique see H.H. Harman, *modern Factor Analysis* (Chicago: University of Chicago Press, 1967); and L.J. King, *Statistical Analysis in Geography* (Englewood Cliffs: Prentice-Hall, Inc., 1969).

[34]Warick Neville, "Singapore: Ethnic Diversity and its Implications," *Annals of the Association of American Geographers*, Vol. 56, No. 2 (1966), p. 238; Yong Leng Lee, "Race, Language and National Cohesion in Southeast Asia," *Journal of Southeast Asian Studies (Singapore)*, Vol. 11 (March 1980), pp. 122-138.

[35]George Modeelski, "Kautilya: Foreign Policy and International System in the Ancient Hindu World," *The American Political Science Review*, Vol. 48 (September 1964), pp. 549-560.

[36]Norton Ginsburg, "On the Chinese Perception of a World Order," *China in Crisis, Vol. 11, China's Policies in Asia and America's Alternatives*, Tang Tsou, Editor (Chicago: The University of Chicago Press, 1968), pp. 73-91; J.K. Fairbank, "China's Foreign Policy n Historical Perspective," *Foreign Affairs* (April, 1969), pp. 449-463.

[37]Robert C. North, "Two Revolutionary Models: Russian and Chinese," *Communist Strategies in Asia*, edited by A. Doak Barnett (1963), pp. 34-60; see also Stephen P. Gilbert and Wynfred Joshua, *Guns and Rubles: Soviet and Diplomacy in Neutral Asia* (New York: American-Asian Educational Exchange, 1970).

[38]For details see Josefa M. Saniel, "Japan's Thrust in Southeast Asia in the Sixties," in Bernard Grossmann, *Southeast Asia in the Modern World* (Wiesbaden: Otto Harrassowitz, 1972), pp. 377-422; J.M. Allison, "Japan's Relations with Southeast Asia," *Asia* (Winter, 1969-70), pp. 34-59.

[39]Dwight D. Eisenhower, *The White House Years: Mandate for Change 1953-56* (Garden City, N.Y.: Doubleday, & Company, Inc., 1963), p. 33; see also Russel H. Fifield, *Americans in Southeast Asia: The Roots of Commitment* (New York: Thomas Y. Crowell, 1973), p. 191.

[40]U.S. Congress. Senate Committee on Foreign Relations Background Information Relating to Southeast Asia and Vietnam 89.1 (Washington: Government Printing Office, 1965), p. 128.

Chapter 2

The Physical Environment

Allen G. Noble

American ignorance of Southeast Asia is colossal despite the almost daily coverage by television and newspapers of the United States involvement in Vietnam and other parts of former Indochina during 1965–1975. Several reasons account for this situation among which can be cited; inadequate public school training in geography, the lack of attention in the entire American educational system to foreign areas (except western Europe and the Caribbean), and the remote location and fundamentally unfamiliar culture of Southeast Asia.

Perhaps as important as any other reason for American ignorance of Southeast Asia is the diversity of the area itself. In the words of Norton Ginsburg, "A more highly fragmented part of the globe could scarcely be imagined."[1] The first impression given by a glance at the map of Southeast Asia is one of complicated interpenetration of peninsulas and islands with straits, bays and gulfs. These landforms and water bodies are arranged in such a fashion as to make certain parts of Southeast Asia remote and thus less attractive, while others attain strategic value by virtue of their accessibility.

The physical geography of Southeast Asia may be approached as a series of basic dichotomies, although such simplicity tends to mask the reality of diversity. Each of these contrasts illustrates the fundamental relationships of the physical geography of the area, without the complicating details which tend to obscure the basic associations.[2]

CONTRAST ONE: MARINE AND CONTINENTAL ENVIRONMENTS

Most basic of the simple physiographic contrasts is that between land and water, or more specifically between marine and continental environments (i.e., coastal and interior locations) (Fig. 2–1). Considered from an encompassing viewpoint, water areas exceed land areas as much as four to one.[3] Thus, the sea, dominating vast parts of Southeast Asia, profoundly affects the life and activities of the region. Within continental Southeast Asia the focus has been upon interior development with political units organized about internal lines of communication. Each major lowland carries its own tradition of past glory; the names of Pagan, Angkor Wat, Luang Prabang and Ayutthaya come quickly to mind as representatives of earlier great civilizations. Indigenous development was for the most part introversive, so much so, that European infringement and subsequent domination was comparatively effortless.

Marine Southeast Asia suffered the same onslaught of European colonialism, if anything, more severely and earlier. The essential difference was that in all marine Southeast Asia only Indonesia had produced an elaborated civilization, built partially upon the support of fertile volcanic soils. The complicated arrangement of elongated islands and peninsulas, together with unfavorable physical conditions (i.e., mangrove swamps, tidal marshes, dense tropical rain forests, deeply dissected hills and low mountains) impelled movement in marine Southeast Asia along the narrow, well-defined ocean straits. Thus, in the 19th and early 20th centuries Singapore assumed its function as primary port of the region.

CONTRAST TWO: AREAS OF STABLE OR UNSTABLE GEOLOGY

The complexities of geological structure also may be reduced to a simple contrast; the stable, massive continental blocks and the highly unstable, actively shifting portions of the earth's crust (Fig. 2–2). The latter are expressed geographically as a series of island arcs extending from New Guinea and the Philippines through Indonesia and the Nicobar and the Andaman Island groups. These island arc structures are connected to the Himalayan mountain zone on the Asian continental land mass via the folded

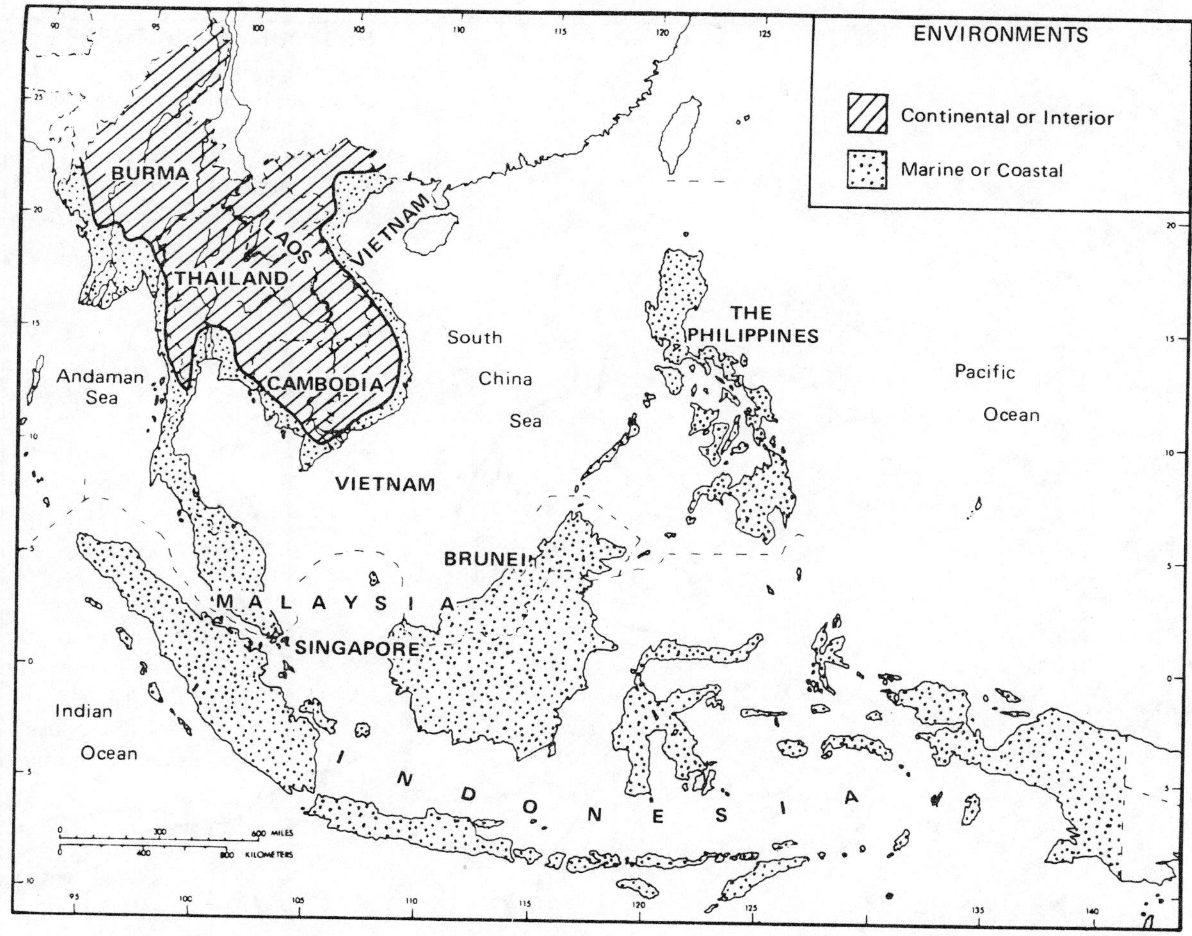

Figure 2-1. Marine and Continental Environments of Southeast Asia.

chain of the Arakan Yoma and its northward extensions. As this area is still in the process of active mountain formation, crustal instability is characteristic throughout this zone.

Earthquakes are commonplace with severe shocks apt to occur at any time and in any area of the island arc zone. As a result of frequent earth movement along fault planes, the short rivers of Indonesia (except Kalimantan) and the Philippine Islands are often remarkably straight for short distances with characteristic right angle bends. Another consequence of active crustal movement is the large number of lakes within insular Southeast Asia. Lake Tempe on the island of Sulawesi has achieved especial economic importance as the supplier of more than three-quarters of Indonesia's fresh water fish requirements.

Earthquakes result from volcanic activity as well as movement along planes of the earth's crust. Certain portions of the zone are among the most active volcanic regions in the world. In the central Philippines there are twelve active or recently active volcanoes. The figure jumps to eighteen for Sulawesi and the Molucca Islands, and to twenty-five in the Lesser Sunda Islands. Java and Sumatra are also highly active volcanic areas with no less than seventeen volcanoes in the former island and twelve in the latter.

One of the most conspicuous and famous of volcanic eruptions was that of Krakatoa in 1883. In a series of awesome explosions, reportedly heard over 3,000 miles away in Australia, the entire top of the volcano, more than six miles in diameter at the base, was blown to bits and dust was hurled high into the atmosphere. So much material was thrown out, and to such elevations, that the coloring of sunsets and sunrises all over the earth was altered considerably for a period lasting eighteen months. The immediate fallout of ash and volcanic dust was recorded on the decks of ocean freighters 1,600 miles from the eruption scene and was sufficiently dense to obscure the sun, requiring all day burning of lamps for several days in Batavia (Djakarta) over 100 miles away. Storm waves created by the volcanic explosions were

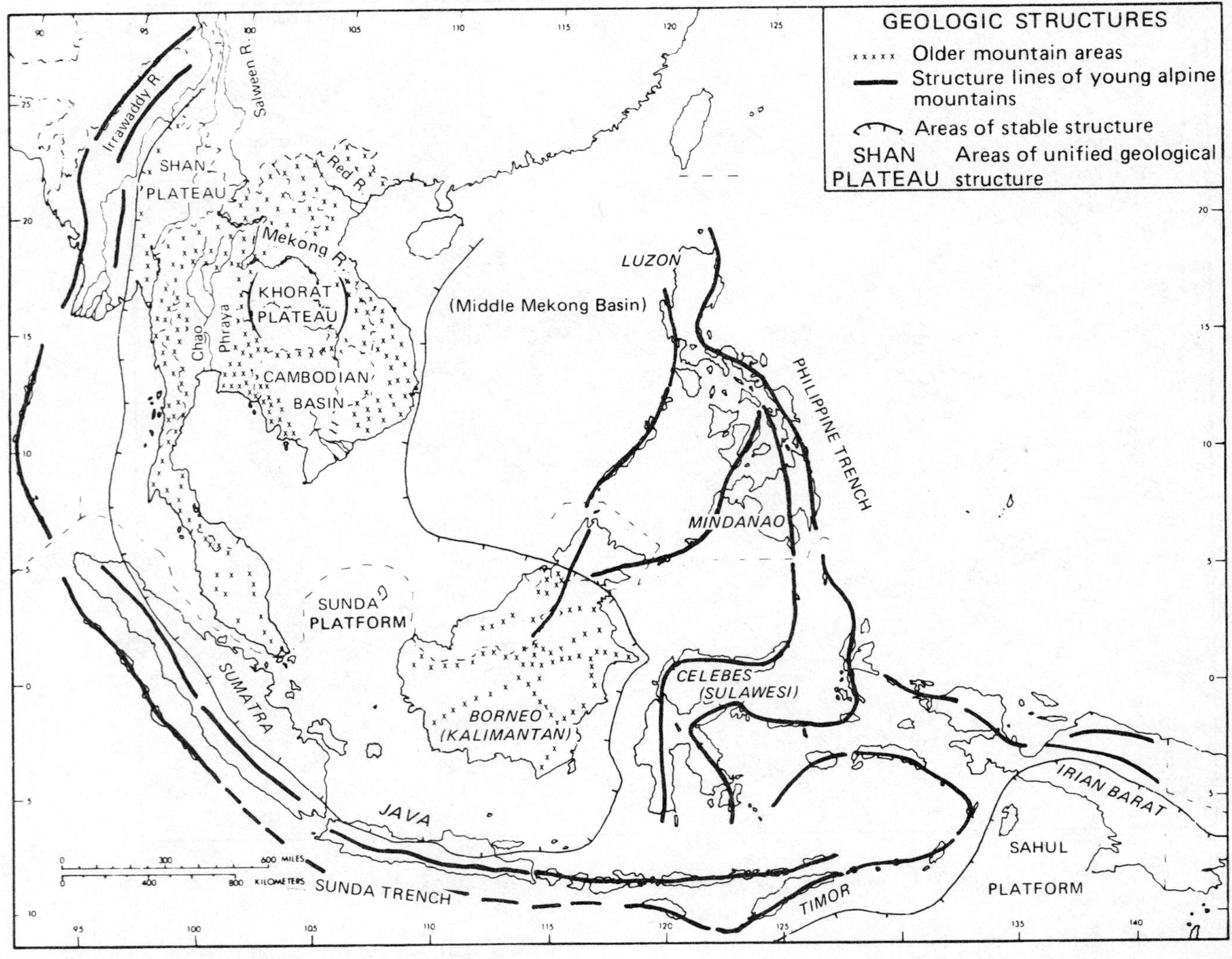

Figure 2-2. Geologic Structures in Southeast Asia.

of such terrifying magnitude that on the coast of Sumatra a Dutch warship was torn from her moorings and driven, anchor dragging, two miles inland. Almost 36,000 persons living along the coasts of the adjacent islands of Sumatra and Java, died in the subsequent floods.[4]

Nor has the Krakatoa explosion been an isolated phenomenon. An eruption of great magnitude occurred in 1815 from the volcano of Tombora on the Lesser Sunda island of Sumbawa. Because of its earlier date and more remote location fewer details are available. Yet it is known that within 300 miles of the volcano the sun was totally obscure for three days by the outpouring of ash and other ejecta. Of twelve thousand persons on Sumbawa Island only twenty-six survived the holocaust.

Even earlier and more obscure were major eruptions in Java in 1772 and 1699. In 1772, the catastrophic eruption of Papandayung resulted in the death of about three thousand persons and the total destruction of forty villages in an area fifteen miles wide and six miles long. The height of the cone was reduced from over 9,000 feet to just 5,000 feet. Details of the severe 1699 eruption of Mt. Salek which caused earth tremors in Batavia, six days journey distant, are scanty. Similarly forceful eruptions may be expected in the future in the island arc zone.

Throughout the unstable area of Southeast Asia, highland topography predominates over plains. Often the mountains rise precipitously from the sea in steep escarpments so recently formed in geologic time as to be only moderately dissected in spite of exposure to heavy tropical rains. The abrupt changes in altitude encountered along the sea coasts of most islands are only modest indicators of the actual differences in height since in most cases deep trenches parallel the shore lines. The deepest and most clearly defined of these *foredeeps*, which are intimate aspects or components of current mountain building activity, are the Sunda Trench south of Java and the Philippine Trench east of Mindanao. In the latter, the depth of the waters reaches almost seven miles.

Quite in contrast are the conditions encountered upon the Sunda and Sahul Platforms. The contrast is demonstrated quite clearly in Sumatra, where the western portions lie in the unstable crustal zone and the eastern part belongs to the stable continental block (Fig. 2-2). In the unstable zone several characteristic features occur. Perhaps most conspicuous are the volcanic peaks which, thrusting up above surrounding lands, give the island its largest topographic differences. Steep slopes are encountered everywhere and offshore to the west is a submarine trench which marks a continuation of the Sunda Trench off Java. Within this trench, rise up a series of islands of folded sedimentary rocks. The overall impression which this zone gives is one of instability and topographic variety.

On the other hand, the eastern portions of Sumatra, although subject to earthquakes due to close proximity to the zone of instability, and broken here and there by isolated volcanic intrusions, are characterized by moderate slopes. Massive limestone and sandstone layers, often in relatively undisturbed condition, account for broad lowlands. Shallow fringing seas, with the land grading almost imperceptively into the sea, produce extensive areas of coastal swamp.

CONTRAST THREE: COMPLEX ERODED MOUNTAINS AND SIMPLE HORIZONTAL STRUCTURES

Even within the Sunda Platform a basic dichotomy exists between the areas of complex eroded and folded upland, and the simpler blocks of unified and more or less horizontal sedimentary rocks. Eroded upland topography characterizes much of Borneo (Kalimantan), the Cardamom-Elephant mountain area of southeastern Thailand and southwestern Cambodia (Kampuchea), Vietnam (except for the two deltas and the eastern coastal plain), Laos, Malaysia, and various portions of Thailand (Fig. 2-2). Within these areas population is either sparse or virtually nonexistent, for the areas are distinctly unproductive except for the extraction of a limited number of minerals, the most significant of which has been tin.

The three principal structures within the Sunda Platform which are not complex mountains are arranged in a steplike fashion on the mainland of Southeast Asia. The highest "step" is the Shan Plateau of eastern Burma, a deeply dissected area of sedimentary rocks some of which have been longitudinally folded and some of which lie in uncontorted massive beds. General elevation is often above 4,000 feet. Much of the surface has been modified by rapid erosion producing a distinctly rough landscape.

Southeast of the Shan Plateau is the intermediate step of the Khorat Plateau of eastern Thailand, lying at a general elevation of just under 1,000 feet. In great contrast to the Shan Plateau, the lower lying surface of the Khorat Plateau consists of gently folded beds of red sandstone, slightly dipping toward the Mekong River, but sharply upturned along the edges. The escarpments thus formed serve to set off the Khorat Plateau sharply from surrounding landforms. Although the escarpments are neither especially high (1,500–2,000 feet normally) nor particularly deeply dissected, "thanks to their continuity and the denseness of their forests they have served fairly effectively to isolate Khorat from the rest of Thailand."[5]

Finally, at the lowest elevation, between 100 feet and 300 feet above sea level, lies the Cambodian Basin. The underlying rocks, which out-crop at various locations, are limestone, but considerable thicknesses of alluvial soil commonly obscure the underlying bedrock. The entire basin structure may be conceived of as a gigantic saucer with characteristically gentle slopes and with a large lake, the Tonle Sap, occupying the central and lowest portion.

The unique aspect of the Cambodian Basin is its relationship to the Mekong River which lies adjacent to it on the east. The Mekong, one of the longest and most actively eroding rivers of Asia, has constructed an enormous delta which begins at about Phnom Penh and extends approximately 175 miles to the sea. Because of the fertility of the alluvial soils on the Mekong Delta, southern Vietnamese settlement has tended to coalesce around this area, which eventually developed as the southern Vietnam heartland. As deposition from the Mekong gradually continues, the accumulating sediments are chocking the channels of the river and causing the speed of water flow to be reduced. Normally, as on other deltas, this process would result in extensive seasonal flooding across the deltaic region. That this does not happen, may be attributed directly to the presence of the adjacent Cambodian Basin. As the Mekong floodwaters rise, a flow westward into the Tonle Sap takes place across an extensive sill of mud held in place by dense swamp vegetation. The Tonle Sap lake increases over six times in average depth.[6] Tonle Sap and the Cambodian Basin thus take up the excess Mekong waters during the monsoon and slowly release them after the height of the rains. As a result, the Mekong delta is largely flood free and possesses little evidence of the extensive diking which is required for safe agricultural development in northern Vietnam on the Red river delta between Hanoi and Haiphong.

CONTRAST FOUR: UPLANDS AND LOWLANDS

Geologic structure and morphologic processes are only two aspects of the physical environment of Southeast Asia. Of equal, or even greater, importance is the surface topography since it often strongly affects man's activity (Fig. 2-3). Although directly related to structure, major landform differences have an additional dimension—suitability for human settlement and economic activity of paramount significance for man. Thus, the complex, older eroded highlands of continental Southeast Asia function as barriers and repellent areas just as do the young folded and volcanic highlands of the island arcs. Each is closer in function to the other than to adjacent lowlands.

Much of Southeast Asia consists of rugged uplands within which population is sparse and economic activity rudimentary. On the mainland, these uplands have tended to keep the cultures of the lowlands distinct from one another, so that a series of quite separate societies evolved, each centered upon its own lowland. Despite the overall ruggedness of the

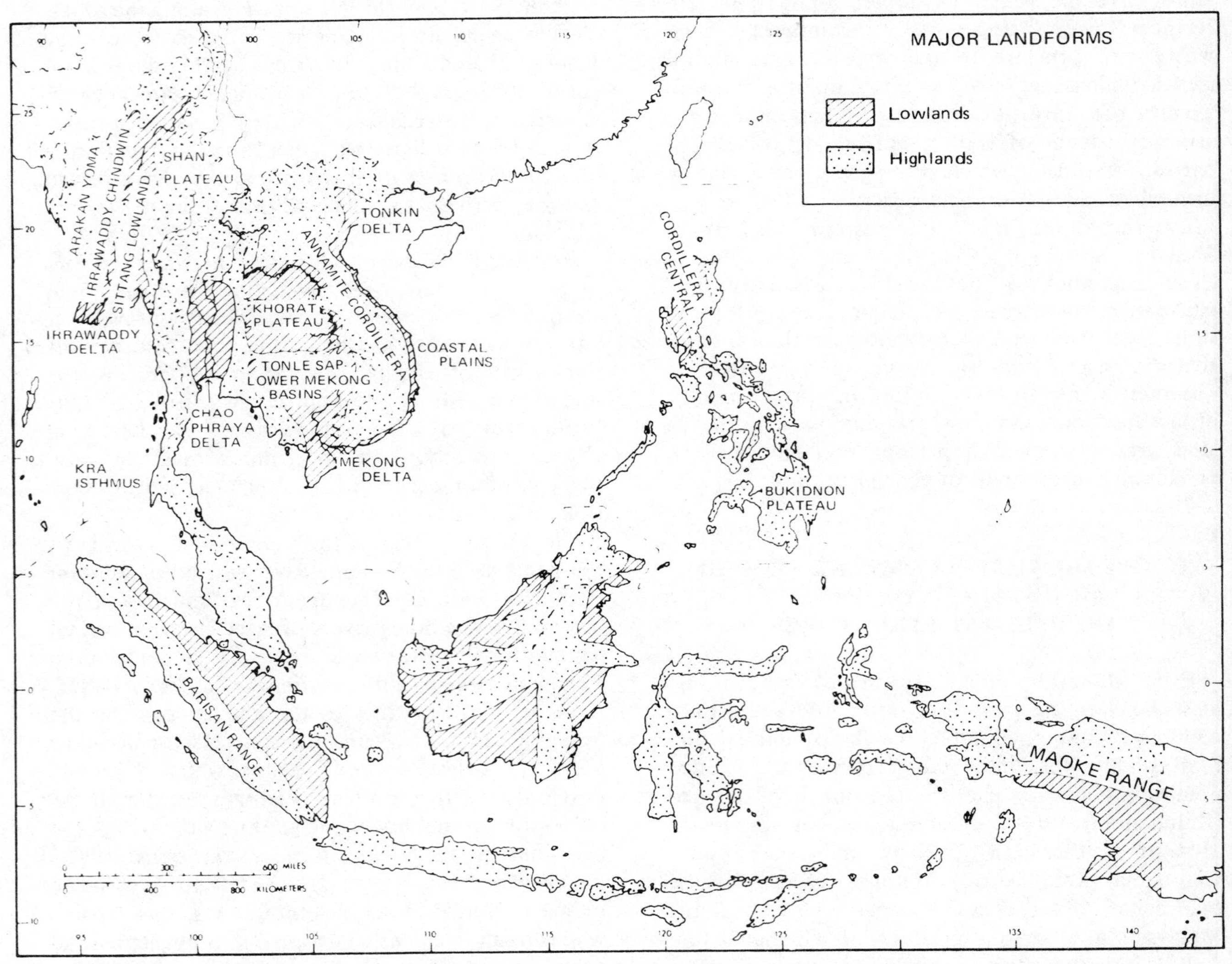

Figure 2-3. Major Landforms in Southeast Asia.

terrain, altitudes of the upland areas are not especially high. Elevations above 6,000 feet are encountered over extensive areas only in northern Laos, on the Indonesia island of Sulawesi, and in the northern portions of West Irian (New Guinea). Elsewhere in the highlands, altitudes above 6,000 feet exist only in isolated volcanic peaks (especially well-illustrated in Java or Mindanao) or in fault-sharpened narrow ridges. The best example of the latter is the Arakan Yoma which forms the western bulwark of Burma.

Within the lowlands themselves several contrasts may be noted. First, is the material of which each is covered or the method of formation of the lowland. The Khorat Plateau, as discussed above, is clearly a structural feature enclosed by surrounding heights. The surface is rolling and composed of soil materials weathered in place. Other lowlands are primarily the product of folding and faulting so that elongated valleys have been produced such as those of Luzon Island in the Philippines, the Chao Phraya lowland in Thailand and the several major plains of Burma. In all these areas, differences between the lowland and the bordering uplands are emphasized by strong contrasts which occur at the junction of the two landforms. Not only does topography change abruptly, and vegetation and soils shift from one adjustment to another, but even the human condition is significantly affected.

Robbins Burling in *Hill Farms and Padi Fields* draws this differentiation clearly.[7] He cites language unity, hydraulic cultivation of rice, high population densities, ease of transportation, and political unity as characteristic of the lowlands, and language diversity, subsistence grain and root cultivation, sparse population, inaccessibility and political fragmentation as characteristic of the uplands.

In contrast, other portions of both the Irrawaddy and the Chao Phraya lowlands are deltaic. The Irrawaddy Delta resembles the nearby and somewhat larger Ganges-Brahmaputra Delta. The Irrawaddy Delta is rapidly being extended seaward in a series of fingers each separated by one of the delta's distributory channels. An actively advancing seaward margin is anchored by dense mangrove and nipa palm vegetation which in its turn is gradually being encroached upon by paddy cultivators eager for new land. Pressure of population is not as great as on the Ganges-Brahmaputra Delta and hence destruction of the forest is much less pronounced.

The Chao Phraya Delta is quite unlike that of the Irrawaddy. Although it is actively building seaward, it lacks the developing fan shape of many deltas since it still is confined within the syncline which marks the limits of its valley and the northward extension of the Gulf of Siam. As a result of its enclosed location, together with the effect of off-shore longitudinal currents, a shoreline of sandy ridges and lagoonal mud flats has been produced rather than the "fingers" of the Irrawaddy Delta.

In structure, the Mekong Delta resembles the Irrawaddy more than the Chao Phraya, whereas the Red River Delta of northern Vietnam tends to be enclosed by surrounding landforms, much as is the Chao Phraya.

The extensive coastal plains of Sumatra and West Irian and the numerous lowlands of Kalimantan are products of alluvial deposition combined with some degradational effect. In general, these vast lowlands are not densely settled and in contrast to the other plains are not yet productively utilized. Construction of expensive dikes and large scale drainage operations will be required before cultivation and settlement of these lowlands can be effective.

CONTRAST FIVE: TEMPERATURE FLUCTUATIONS

By virtue of its situation astride the equator, as well as its exposure to moderating sea influences, maritime Southeast Asia has a remarkably uniform temperature regime. As shown by Table 2–1, temperatures are high throughout the islands and peninsulas of equatorial Southeast Asia. High temperatures are coupled with high relative humidity produced in large part from the surrounding expanses of continually warm ocean waters. This combination, as well as the monotony of both high temperature and high humidity, contributes to make weather conditions difficult for human endeavor. As one book on Indonesia states, with constant high humidity a mean temperature in the eighties "can be mean indeed."[8]

Fortunately, increasing altitude reduces temperature. Even centuries ago, colonial governments recognized the desirability of establishing mountain retreats where temperature aspects of their homelands could be recaptured for short periods. The best known of these hill stations, which persist today as tourist and holiday centers, are Baguio in the Philippines and Bandung in Indonesia. A comparison of average mean monthly temperatures for Manila, which lies close to sea level, and Baguio, at an elevation of approximately 5,000 feet, illustrates well the role played by altitude in reducing temperature. The moderation of temperature is always at least 12° Fahrenheit. Most fortunately the greatest relief occurs at the season of highest temperatures, when Baguio averages 15° cooler than Manila.

TABLE 2-1
Monthly Average Temperatures (in Degrees Fahrenheit) Equatorial Southeast Asia

	J	F	M	A	M	J	J	A	S	O	N	D	Seasonal Variation
Djakarta, Indonesia	79	79	80	81	81	80	80	80	81	80	80	79	2°
Manokwari, Indonesia	79	79	79	79	80	79	79	80	80	80	80	80	1°
Menado, Indonesia	77	77	78	78	79	79	79	80	80	79	79	78	2°
Padang, Indonesia	79	80	79	80	80	79	79	79	79	79	79	79	1°
Penang, Malaysia	81	82	83	83	82	82	82	81	81	81	80	81	3°
Pontianak, Indonesia	78	79	79	79	80	80	80	79	79	79	78	78	2°
Singapore	79	80	81	81	81	81	81	81	81	80	80	80	2°
Zamboanga, Philippines	80	80	81	81	81	81	80	81	81	81	81	81	1°

	J	F	M	A	M	J	J	A	S	O	N	D
Manila	77	78	81	83	84	83	81	81	81	81	79	78
Baguio	64	64	67	68	68	68	68	66	65	66	66	66

In other parts of Southeast Asia, because of the combination of greater land mass and location farther from the equator, a much wider seasonal fluctuation of temperature prevails, although nowhere are true winter conditions experienced (Table 2–2). The seasonal contrast is most noticeable in central Burma and on the delta of northern Vietnam.

Everywhere in mainland Southeast Asia, except for the eastern Vietnam coast, rainfall and cloudiness from the southwest monsoon serve to reduce high-sun temperatures so that the warmest weather is experienced in April, May or June, before the onset on the rains. The highest temperatures of any part of Southeast Asia are recorded here at this season. Throughout Burma, Thailand, Cambodia, Laos and portions of Vietnam, maximum temperatures over 100° F. have been reached.[9] Of the stations shown on Table 2–2 only Hue on the Vietnam coast, subject to the northeast monsoon rather than the southwest monsoon, varies from the pattern.

CONTRAST SIX: ANNUAL PRECIPITATION

Given similar tropical temperature conditions, an annual precipitation of sixty inches may be taken arbitrarily as the dividing line between those areas of copious rainfall adequate for agriculture and those areas where moisture is deficient. The effectiveness of annual rainfall also can be gauged from natural vegetation. Lands with over 60 inches of rain are covered with dense tropical rainforest (selva) or with a more open semideciduous monsoon forest where distribution of precipitation is highly seasonal. Areas receiving less than 60 inches are characterized by savannah grasslands or dry scrub forest. Vegetational conditions are discussed in greater detail below.

In general, the lower latitude and more insular portions of Southeast Asia receive the greatest rainfall (Fig. 2–4). However, even within these areas some stations, because of local topographic conditions or because of other immediate influences, have precipitation totals which are below the arbitrarily defined limit of 60 inches. Zamboanga, on Mindanao Island in the Philippines, for example, has an annual total of only 42 inches (Table 2–3).

Parts of the southeastern Indonesian islands have annual precipitation totals below 60 inches. In general, reduced rainfall here is related to proximity to the desert expanses of Australia out of which the monsoon-strengthened, dry, southeast trade winds blow from March through September. But again, within this area, some anomalies exist. For example, certain mountain slopes, especially at altitudes between 3,000 and 5,000 feet, which are in the path of prevailing winds, show higher totals than those for surrounding lowlands.

Other areas of low rainfall occur in the synclinal valleys and basins of mainland Southeast Asia (Fig. 2–4). Within these areas, low annual precipitation is primarily a function of interior location and the "rainshadow" effect caused by surrounding uplands.

TABLE 2-2
Monthly Average Temperatures (in Degrees Fahrenheit)
Continental Southeast Asia

	J	F	M	A	M	J	J	A	S	O	N	D	Seasonal Variation
Bangkok, Thailand	78	81	84	86	85	83	83	83	82	81	79	77	9°
Chiangmai, Thailand	72	74	77	82	83	81	80	81	81	79	75	71	12°
Hanoi, N. Vietnam	62	63	68	75	82	85	84	84	82	78	71	65	23°
Hue, S. Vietnam	69	67	74	80	83	85	84	85	81	78	73	70	16°
Lashio, Burma	60	63	71	75	77	77	76	76	76	73	66	61	17°
Luang Prabang, Laos	69	73	78	82	84	83	82	82	82	79	74	70	15°
Mandalay, Burma	68	73	81	89	88	85	85	84	83	81	75	68	21°
Vientiane, Laos	70	74	79	83	81	82	81	81	81	78	75	71	13°

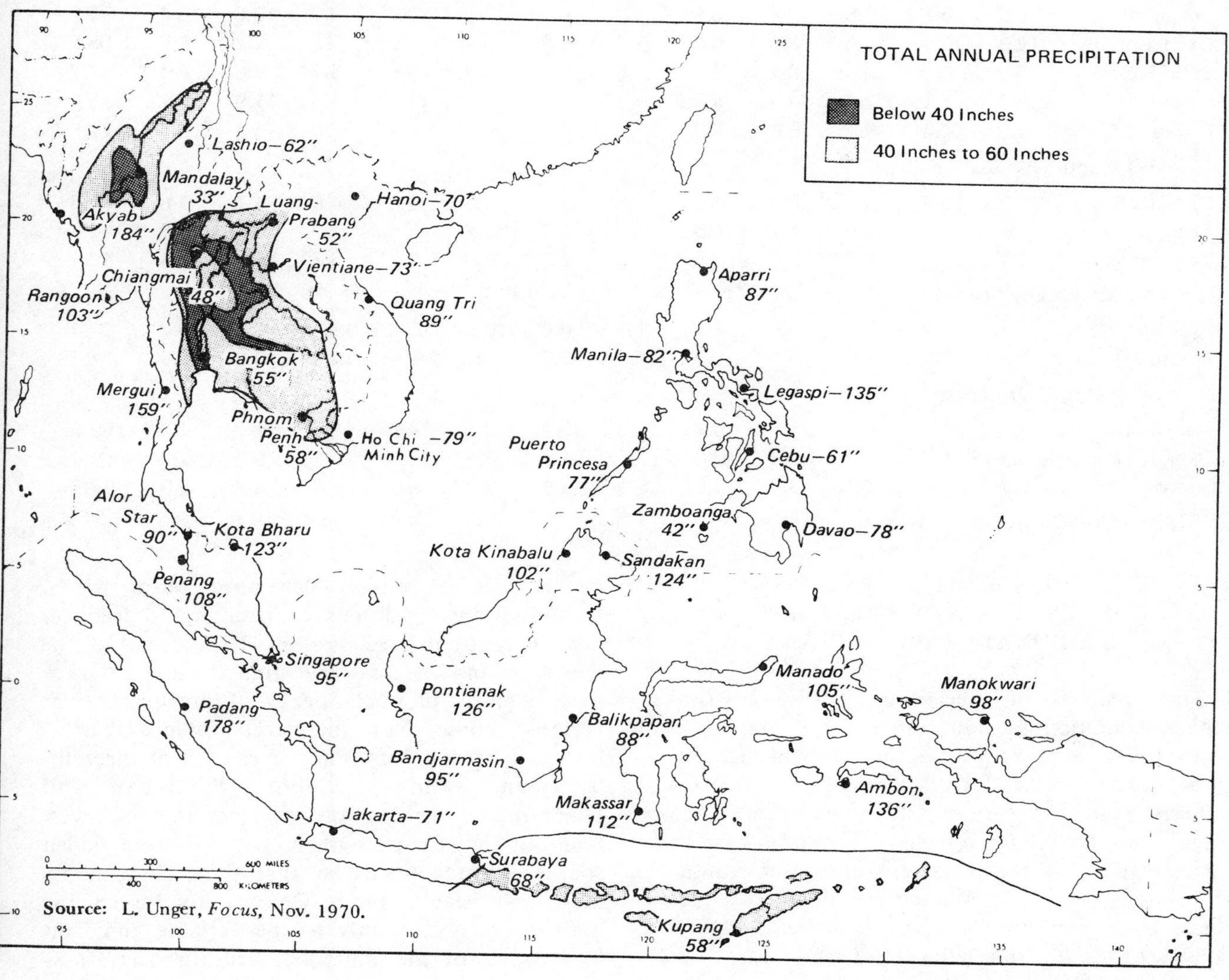

Figure 2-4. Total Annual Precipitation of Southeast Asia.

TABLE 2-3
Monthly Average Precipitation, in Inches, Southeast Asia,
Stations Continually Wet or with Short Dry Season

Station	J	F	M	A	M	J	J	A	S	O	N	D	Yearly Total
No Dry Season													
Padang	13.5	9.9	11.9	14.0	12.6	13.0	11.8	13.7	16.1	20.0	20.7	19.4	176.6
Ambon	5.0	4.7	5.3	11.0	20.3	25.1	23.7	15.8	9.5	6.1	4.5	5.2	136.2
Legaspi	13.9	10.3	7.3	7.2	9.5	5.5	8.9	9.9	9.4	11.9	18.2	22.9	134.9
Pontianak	10.8	7.9	9.8	10.8	10.7	8.7	6.3	8.9	8.4	14.8	15.7	13.2	126.0
Sandakan	19.0	10.9	8.6	4.5	6.2	7.4	6.7	7.9	9.3	10.2	14.5	18.5	123.7
Kota Bharu	10.2	5.5	7.0	4.6	6.4	6.1	5.5	6.6	8.7	12.0	24.0	26.3	122.9
Penang	3.7	3.1	5.6	7.4	10.7	7.7	7.5	11.6	15.8	16.9	11.9	5.8	107.7
Manado	18.3	14.1	12.0	7.8	6.3	6.4	4.7	3.8	3.4	4.8	8.6	14.6	104.8
Kota Kinabalu	5.5	3.1	3.0	5.2	9.7	11.6	7.9	9.9	12.6	12.9	11.3	9.5	102.2
Manokwari	11.3	9.8	13.3	10.9	8.0	7.6	5.7	5.5	4.9	4.3	6.4	10.6	98.3
Singapore	9.9	6.8	7.6	7.4	6.8	6.8	6.7	7.2	7.7	8.2	10.0	10.1	95.2
Bandjarmasin	12.8	12.9	11.6	8.8	6.1	5.7	3.8	3.4	3.9	5.3	8.7	12.5	95.5
Balik Papan	7.9	6.9	9.1	8.2	9.1	7.6	7.1	6.4	5.5	5.2	6.6	8.1	87.7
Aparri	5.3	3.3	2.3	2.4	4.5	6.3	6.6	9.2	11.4	14.8	11.9	8.7	86.7
Davao	4.8	4.4	5.2	5.8	9.3	9.1	6.5	6.5	6.7	7.9	5.3	6.1	77.6
One Month Dry Season													
Djakarta	11.7	13.5	8.4	5.6	4.3	3.6	2.6	1.5	2.8	4.5	5.7	7.6	71.8
Cebu	4.2	2.9	2.0	1.7	4.5	6.4	7.2	5.7	6.9	7.7	6.4	5.0	60.6
Zamboanga	2.1	2.2	1.5	2.0	3.5	4.2	4.9	4.0	4.7	5.7	4.2	3.4	42.4
Two Month Dry Season													
Alor Star	1.7	1.2	5.3	10.5	8.6	7.5	6.6	10.6	10.2	13.7	8.3	6.2	90.4
Puerto Princesa	2.4	1.5	1.6	2.1	6.6	7.8	8.7	7.1	8.4	10.3	10.8	10.0	77.3
Three Month Dry Season													
Mergui	1.1	1.9	2.3	5.5	15.2	30.0	32.7	29.1	24.0	11.6	4.3	1.3	159.0
Quang Tri	6.0	1.2	1.5	1.3	2.8	2.6	4.8	3.9	15.7	26.4	16.0	7.2	89.4
Phnom Penh	.1	.6	1.9	3.8	5.0	6.0	5.9	6.4	9.0	9.6	6.8	2.0	57.1

CONTRAST SEVEN: CONSTANTLY WET AREAS AND SEASONALLY DRY AREAS

Total amount of precipitation is an environmental condition of importance for human utilization of an area; so also is the seasonal distribution of that rainfall. In Malaysia, most of Indonesia, and the eastern Philippine islands, no month has less than 2 inches of rainfall—which may be taken as the limit separating dry months from wet (Fig. 2-5). Within these largely equatorial lands any "dry season" is "dry" only by comparison with the balance of the year. The generally abundant rainfall results in continually moist soils and a luxuriant forest vegetation.

Convectional instability from overheating, the passage of local tropical disturbances, and the convergence of weakly developed warm winds, are important conditions contributing to frequent but intermittant precipitation. The advent of the monsoon and the seasonal strengthening of trade wind systems produces peaks of precipitation at various stations. Note the effect (Table 2-3) as illustrated by concentrations of rainfall at three Indonesian stations, Ambon, Sandakan and Djakarta. At Ambon, the effect of the southwest monsoon is to strengthen the moisture laden southeast trade winds so that they blow across the small island. From October to March the island is subjected only to the variable and light local winds of the equatorial belt. In contrast to Ambon, the reverse situation is demonstrated by data for Sandakan, which lies north of the equator and on a north facing coast. At Sandakan the northeast trades affect the station from late

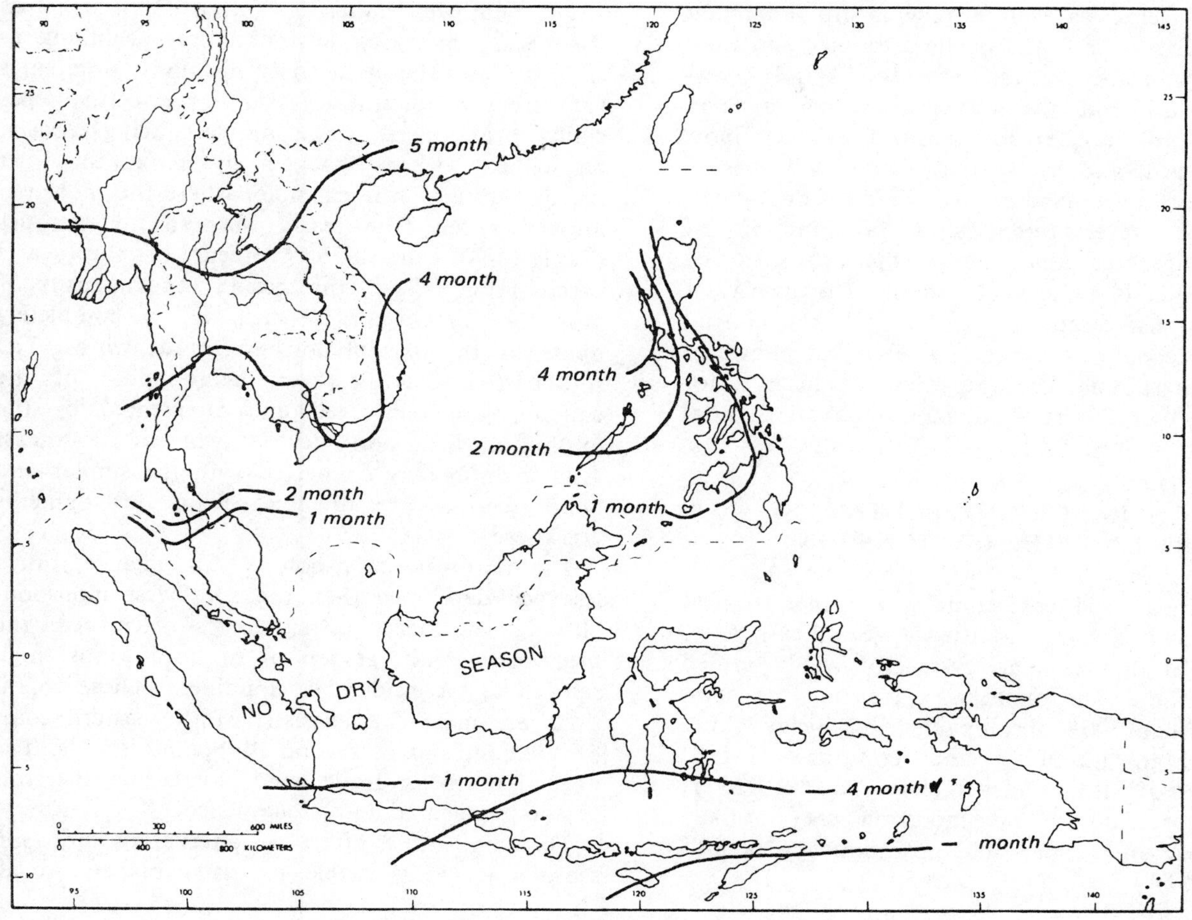

Figure 2-5. Duration of Dry Season by Month in Southeast Asia.

October through early March bringing relatively heavy rains. During the balance of the year a combination of southwest monsoon and equatorial weather contributes to moderately low rainfall.

Djakarta, situated on the north coast of Java, lies in the lee of mountain heights from April until November when the summer monsoon is best developed. Beginning in January, however, Djakarta increasingly comes under the influence of onshore, moisture laden and warm northwest winds. These winds derived from the northeast trades as they cross the equator, abruptly change direction, because of the influence of the earth's rotation, to become northwest winds.

A pronounced and protracted dry season is characteristic of the latitudinal margins of Southeast Asia (Fig. 2-5). A dry season of three months or longer is usually necessary before vegetational change, water availability, and human activity show much effect from lack of precipitation. Except for coastal fringes, mainland Southeast Asia has an annual dry season of at least four months. Interior locations experience five or more months of dry weather.

The greatest deficiency of rainfall is felt in the so-called "dry zone" of Burma centered on Mandalay. Here the seasonal effect of the southwest monsoon is lessened by topographic influences. The Chindwin and Irrawaddy valleys are situated at more or less right angles to the monsoon winds so that, even during the rainy season, Mandalay and other valley locations lie in the rain shadow of the flanking mountain ranges. With only 33 inches of precipitation per year, the Burmese dry zone is the driest part of Southeast Asia. Another "dry zone" is situated in the central part of Thailand. It also lies in a rain shadow.

A long dry season also occurs in southern Sulawesi, eastern Java, southern West Irian and the Indonesian islands which lie within the broad triangle described by these three extremes. The explanation for a lengthy dry season in these islands, surrounded by tropical seas which would normally serve as source regions for abundant moisture, is to be found in the great size and close proximity of the Australian deserts. Winds blowing outward from the high pressure centers over Australia are not greatly warmed as they blow equatorward, and in fact may actually be cooled by passage over expanses of water. Consequently, since water retention is a function of temperature, the amount of water absorbed by these winds is remarkably small. The overwater distance traversed is short and the initial moisture content is almost nil. Here, as elsewhere in Southeast Asia, dry and rainy seasons are, for the most part, the result of monsoonal wind variations.

CONTRAST EIGHT: SOUTHWEST AND NORTHEAST MONSOONS

The climatic patterns common to other tropical latitudes are greatly modified in Southeast Asia, because of the seasonal reversal of winds termed the monsoon. The remarkably constant monsoon winds usually are accompanied by heavy cloud cover, high humidity and copious rainfall. Because of the characteristic cloud cover, temperatures during the monsoon are normally lower than in the pre- and post-monsoon periods (Table 2-2).

The southwest monsoon (often referred to as the "east" monsoon in Indonesia), beginning as early as late March in some locations, dominates vast areas of Southeast Asia. Its effect is especially pronounced on southwest-facing coasts, particularly where backed by mountains. At Akyab (Burma), for example, where the monsoon impact is felt from early May to mid-October (Table 2-4), almost 98 percent of the year's precipitation falls in this period. The intensity of monsoon circulation is such as to completely obliterate the normal northeast trade winds. The southeast trades, however, being south of the equator, are reinforced and augmented by the monsoon. Monsoon development in Southeast Asia in intimately connected with the similar and better known pressure and wind developments elsewhere in Asia.

The northeast monsoon is, on balance, much less well-developed than the southwest monsoon, although northeast facing coasts often bear the brunt of a short season of onshore winds, high rainfall and considerable cloudiness. These conditions are most characteristic of the eastern coast of Vietnam and of several Philippine islands. The normal northeast trade wind circulation is at this season augmented and strengthened.

The contrasting effect of alternating monsoon seasons is easily visible in many places. At all

TABLE 2-4
Monthly Precipitation, in Inches, Southeast Asia,
Stations with Pronounced Dry Season

Station	J	F	M	A	M	J	J	A	S	O	N	D	Yearly Total
Four Month Dry Season													
Makassar	27.0	21.1	16.7	5.9	3.5	2.9	1.4	.4	.6	1.7	7.0	24.0	112.2
Rangoon	.1	.2	.3	2.0	12.1	18.9	22.9	20.8	15.5	7.1	2.7	.4	103.0
Manila	.9	.5	.7	1.3	5.1	10.0	17.0	16.6	14.0	7.6	5.7	2.6	82.0
Saigon	.7	.1	.7	1.7	8.0	13.3	12.0	10.3	13.7	11.0	4.7	2.7	78.9
Hanoi	1.0	1.3	1.9	3.6	8.4	10.4	11.1	13.9	10.5	4.3	2.0	1.2	69.6
Surabaya	12.3	11.5	10.5	7.4	4.3	3.5	1.9	.5	.5	1.5	4.6	9.8	68.3
Lashio	.3	.3	.6	2.2	6.9	9.8	12.0	12.7	7.8	5.7	2.7	.9	61.9
Bangkok	.3	.8	1.4	2.3	7.8	6.3	6.3	6.9	12.0	8.1	2.6	.2	55.0
Five Month Dry Season													
Akyab	T	.1	.3	.8	19.0	37.9	47.4	37.0	26.3	11.5	3.0	.9	184.2
Vientiane	T	.8	1.3	4.8	10.9	10.3	10.1	16.0	11.9	5.4	1.3	T	72.8
Luang Prabang	.6	.7	1.2	4.3	6.4	6.1	9.1	11.8	6.5	3.1	1.2	.5	51.5
Chiangmai	.4	.1	1.0	1.6	6.0	5.1	5.7	9.1	9.5	6.7	2.3	.5	48.0
Mandalay	.1	.1	.2	1.2	5.8	6.3	2.7	4.1	5.4	4.3	2.0	.4	32.6
Six Month Dry Season													
Kupang	22.5	14.2	4.2	1.6	.1	1.7	.1	.1	.1	7.1	4.1	10.5	66.3

monsoon-influenced locations a dry season, wet-season contrast is evident. On certain islands and peninsulas an additional contrast, geographical in nature, is encountered. While rain is occurring at one location, the dry season may prevail at another. The Kra Isthmus and Malay Peninsula offers several diverse examples. The rainfall regime at Penang is representative of equatorial stations. No month is truly dry and peaks of precipitation are experienced in Spring and Fall with the passage of the zenithial sun. Northward along the west coast, at Alor Star, the rainfall regime is still equatorial but some indication of a southwest monsoon influence is evident in the two-month dry season and the concentration of the rainfall between April and October (Table 2-3). Further north, and also on the west coast, Mergui is unquestionably a station under strong southwest monsoon influence. By contrast, the station of Kota Bharu, almost exactly opposite Alor Star but on the east coast of the peninsula, is sufficiently equatorial to have no dry month, with rainfall most heavily concentrated in the October to January period of the northeast monsoon. Perhaps the clearest geographical differentiation of monsoonal rainy seasons occurs in the Philippines where mountainous terrain often separates east and west sides of islands (Fig. 2-6).

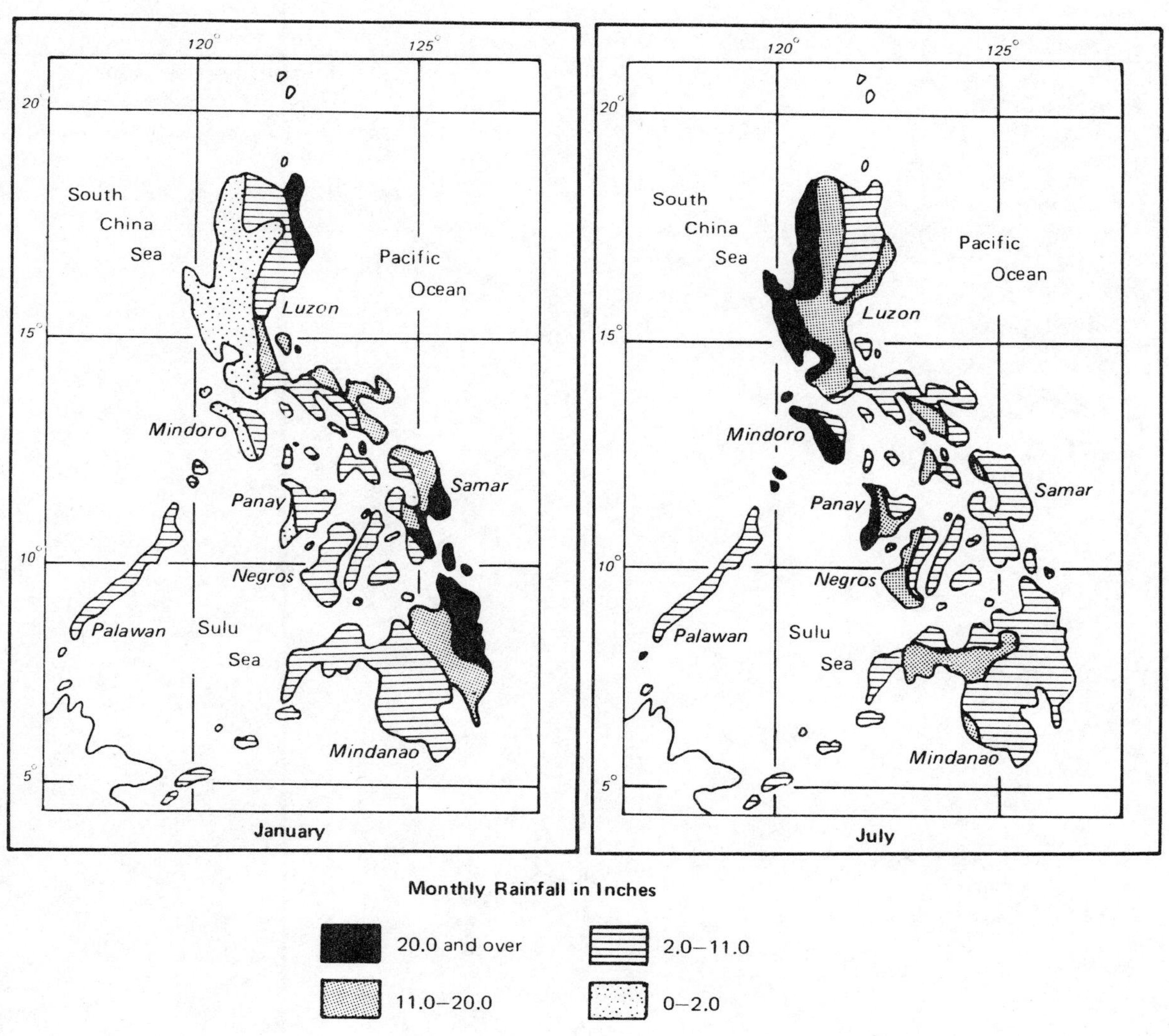

Figure 2-6. Philippines: Monthly Precipitation for January and July.

CONTRAST NINE: TYPES OF FOREST VEGETATION

The essential difference which may be noted in the vegetation of Southeast Asia is between dense tropical forest of several types (selva, mangrove swamp and monsoon forest), and the open and seasonal forest and grassland combinations which include semideciduous forest, savanna grasslands and even thorn scrubland in central Burma (Fig. 2-7). These vegetational variations resemble quite closely the rainfall patterns (Fig. 2-4).

Dense forest (except where removed to facilitate intensive cultivation) is a response to equatorial rainfall and temperature. The overall absence of high elevations contributes to the extent of dense lowland tropical forest. Although variety is the outstanding characteristic of these tropical forests, more than half of the trees belong to the family *Dipterocarpaceae*, made up of about four thousand species. Many dipterocarps are the most conspicuous trees of the forest. Large in trunk diameter, mostly unbranched except for the crown, with straight, smooth trunks, they often tower up to fifty feet above the surrounding forest canopy.[10] Also prominent are palms and bamboo grasses. More than 150 species of the former and 250 species of the latter are represented in Southeast Asian forests.

The significance of forest resources can hardly be overemphasized. Fryer suggests that perhaps as much as half of the forest cutting of the world's entire humid forest zone takes place in Indonesia.[11] In neighboring Malaysia, where nearly three-quarters of the country is still forest covered, hardwood timber exports rank third as a source of foreign exchange.

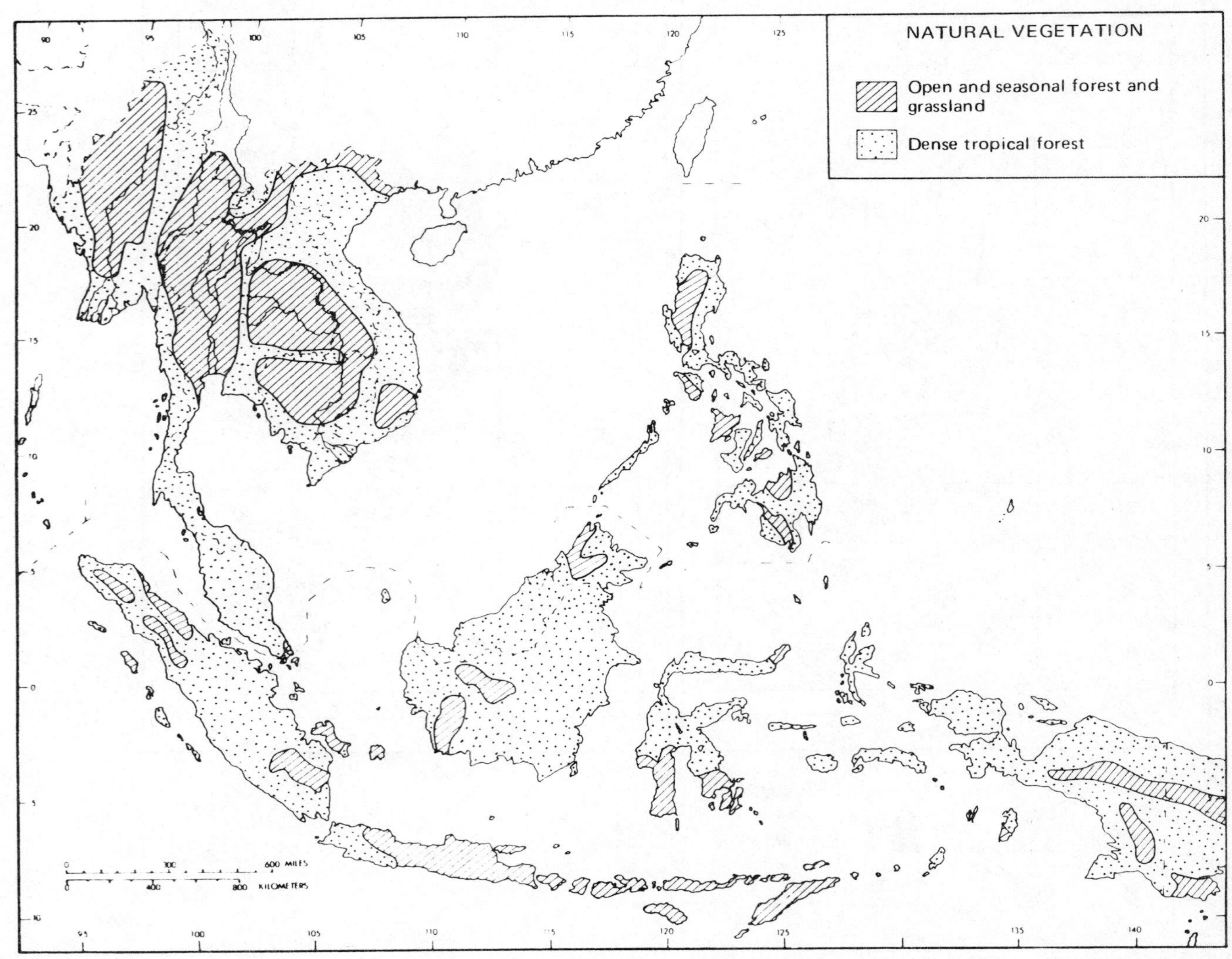

Figure 2-7. Natural Vegetation in Southeast Asia.

Economic value is not restricted to dense equatorial forest, however. Probably the single most valuable timber tree in Southeast Asia is teak, which grows best on well-drained limestone soils well within the open and seasonal forest and grassland zone. Three major areas of teak production stand out: Burma, the most important area, where over 12% of the country's forests are teak; Thailand, with a figure somewhat less, about 9%; and Java, which possess the smallest reserves. Other economically important trees of the open and seasonal forest and grassland area are sal, sandalwood, ebony and mango, the latter for its fruit rather than its wood. Within the semi-deciduous monsoon forests a greater tendency toward pure stands assists in commerical exploitation of the forest.

Open forest areas have lent themselves to greater agricultural exploitation because of the ease with which the forest and grasses could be removed to be replaced by permanent cultivation. The onslaught of pioneer farmers continues today, and even more forest has been altered by slash-and-burn (shifting) cultivation. Thus, the process of "savannization" (the creation and extension of savanna grasslands in place of forest) is aided by growing population densities. This process is especially noticeable on the heavily populated island of Java. Additionally, brush and grass fires cause further destruction of forest and consequent spread of grassland and parkland. This situation is particularly pronounced in eastern Indonesia. As Buchanan notes, the replacement of a humid-environment forest by a drought-resistant vegetation is an index of the extent to which man has affected his original environment.[12]

The central dry zone of Burma contains the sparsest vegetation. Here, relatively dense settlement, beginning as early as the eighth century, has affected vegetational evolution. "An enormous volume of Buddhist religious building in brick (Pagan and elsewhere) probably required deforestation of a wide area for kiln fuel, perhaps contributing to the present arid-land impression of the dry heart of Burma."[13]

CONTRAST TEN: ZONAL AND AZONAL SOILS

Long periods of settlement have altered not only the natural vegetation throughout Southeast Asia, but soils as well. In seasonally dry areas, destruction and removal of forest cover is a major element promoting the formation of infertile, rock-hard laterite patches. Elsewhere, where rainfall is continually high, settlement and associated clearing of forest frequently results in severe soil erosion and flooding.

The soils of Southeast Asia are complex, but a fundamental differentiation of great significance is that made between zonal soils and azonal soils. The various layers which develop within a maturing soil are collectively referred to as the soil profile. Each layer or horizon forms in response to a particular chemical and mechanical process within the soil. More or less strongly developed soil horizons are characteristic of zonal soils, while azonal soils are those so recently laid down that no distinctive horizontal layers have had time to form. Alluvial and volcanic soils, widely distributed throughout Southeast Asia (Fig. 2-8), are the most common azonal soils.

In general, azonal soils are far more significant from the point of view of agricultural productivity than zonal soils. The principal exception is found in the extensive areas of eastern Sumatra and Kalimantan where river plains and deltas frequently have coalesced to produce coastal plains. For the most part these areas are still unoccupied, swampy, and forest covered. However, along the floodplains and on the deltas of the great rivers of mainland Southeast Asia (with the sole exception of the entrenched Salween) alluvial soils support densely settled populations. In such areas, the fertility of the soils usually is renewed periodically by regular flooding.

In like fashion, soils derived largely from volcanic ash and mud receive periodic renewal from volcanic fallout transported by wind and water. Such soils occur throughout Java, in central Sumatra, the Lesser Sunda Islands, northeastern Sulawesi, and on Luzon and several other Philippine islands. For the most part, volcanic soils are derived from basaltic ejecta. However, in Sumatra acidic volcanic soils of much lower fertility occur.

Zonal soils are much more extensive than azonal soils and include both latosols and lateritic soils. Latosols occupy wetter, hotter areas, contain much organic material in surface horizons, but not elsewhere, are highly leached of mineral particles, and are deeply weathered, usually with a reddish color. Regular application of fertilizers is necessary to maintain agricultural production since these soils are naturally low in fertility.[14] Toward the drier margins of Southeast Asia lateritic soils more susceptible to seasonal movement of water predominate. It is here that the greatest extent of true laterite is found. Throughout the latosol and lateritic soil area, settlement is conspicuously lower than on the alluvial and volcanic soils.

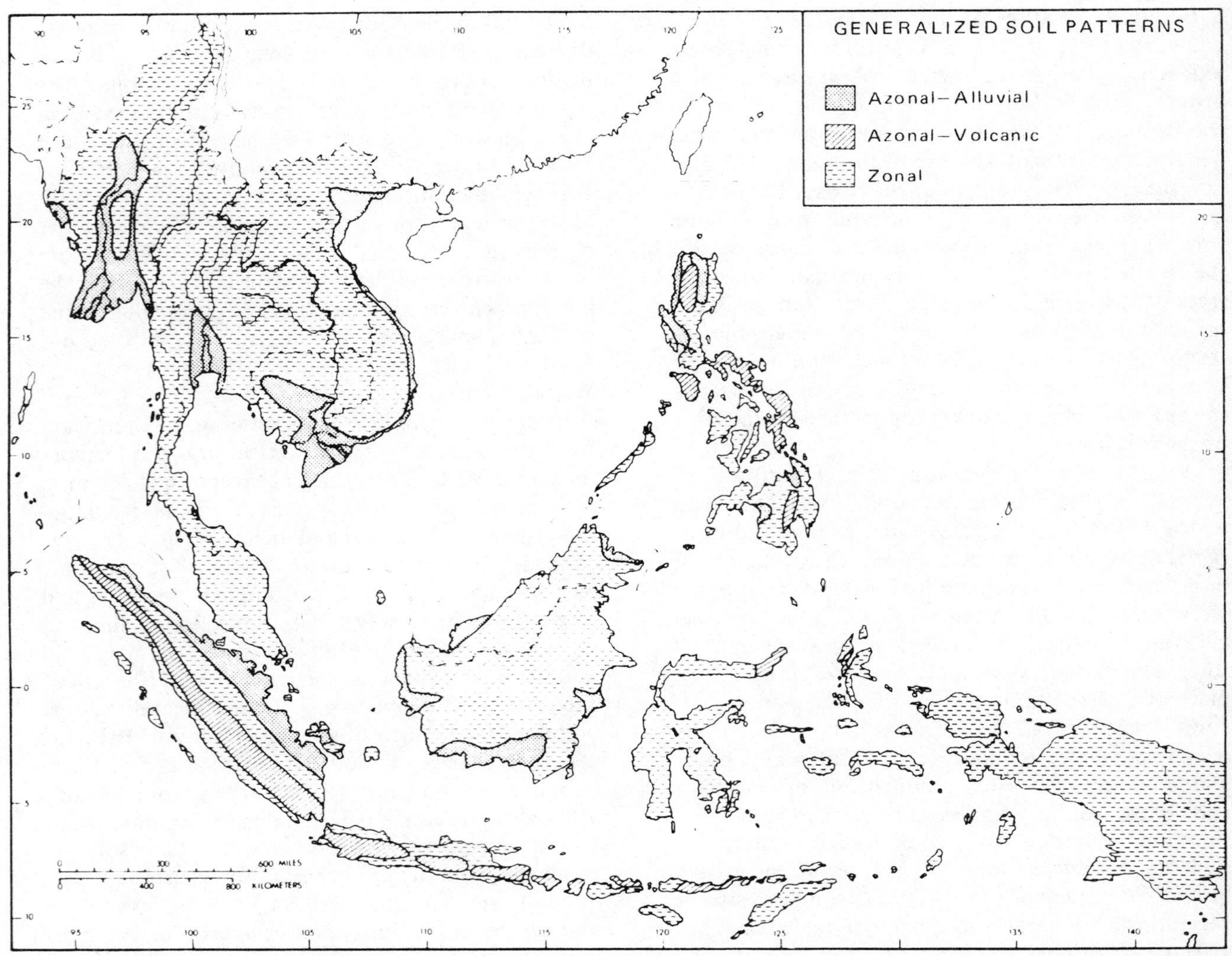

Figure 2-8. Generalized Soil Patterns of Southeast Asia.

LANDSCAPE MODIFICATION IN SOUTHEAST ASIA

Throughout the past quarter-century the physical landscape of Southeast Asia has been subjected to stress, abuse and thoughtless modification, a result of the impact of the long period of revolution and warfare in much of the area.

Beginning in 1962, aerial spraying of chemical defoliants was employed by United States military forces to reduce tropical foliage offering refuge to opposing forces. The most notorious of these is called "Agent Orange" which has been shown to have links to cancer occurrence. By 1967 the area affected by defoliation approached two million acres, and by 1969 expenditures on herbicides had reached almost 71 million dollars annually.[15] However, largely as a result of vocal concern expressed by the United States scientific community, the program was gradually curtailed. This was not, however, before the application of herbicides in Vietnam had climbed to a level nine or ten times that used for weed control in the United States.

The consequences of defoliation in Vietnam are still not fully assessed, but the possible dangers inherent in uncontrolled use of chemical herbicides are frightening indeed. Although one government-employed biologist offered the far from reassuring opinion that "herbicides used in Vietnam are only moderately toxic to warm-blooded animals",[16] other qualified biologists cite among the potential consequences: increases in human birth defects, destruction of soil fertility, proliferation of rats with consequent increases in cases of plague (6 cases in 1961 in

South Vietnam; 4,500 cases in 1965; 5,500 cases in 1967),[17] increase of other diseases such as malaria and cholera, and retention of arsenic in treated soils.

The economic consequences are staggering. Over one-quarter of a million acres of mangrove forest has been "totally destroyed". The impact in cultivated areas is even more significant. For example, within one year of use of defoliants, rubber production in South Vietnam decreased by 30%.[18] The effect upon food crops was immediate. Within days, grains and root crops die. A research team sponsored by the American Association for the Advancement of Science reported at the beginning of 1971 that "approximately enough food to feed some 500,000 people for the year is also destroyed". Less apparent but perhaps more sinister are the long-range ecological effects of defoliation. As Yale Biology Professor Galston noted, herbicides may affect a susceptible link in an important food chain. Even slightly different susceptibility to toxic agents of organisms may adversely affect the ecological evolution of the area in ways now totally unsuspected.

In addition to the devastating effects of defoliation, other abuses of the physical environment have been felt. The removal of vegetation promoted an increase in erosion and gullying and in the rapid removal of nutrients from the delicate tropical soils. Ground water levels and quality have both been adversely affected. Even such an obvious occurrence as shell cratering provides a detrimental impact not only by disturbing the agricultural land surface, but by creating a micro-environment for malarial mosquito breeding. Truly, the range of effects of a quarter-century of environmental disturbance have not yet been measured. Serious though the modifications to the physical landscape are, these are quite insignificant compared to the likely consequences of slow death, recurrent illness and abnormal gene mutation which is likely to afflict the people of Southeast Asia in future.

CONCLUSION

The physical environment of Southeast Asia may be viewed with reference to a series of contrasts, each of which offers a lesson for mankind, who must seek adjustments to the environment in order to successfully exist. But, future generations of students are likely to have to reassess the physical landscape of Southeast Asia. Technological impact has already modified the land, although it is too early to be certain exactly how extensive those changes are, and what the ultimate consequences will be for man. Advances in scientific enquiry will also reshape the thought of future generations. One example will suffice. The refinement of the geology of plate tectonics provides new explanations for the distribution of volcanic activity, earthquakes and deep sea trenches.[19] At least two plates, those of China and the Philippine Sea, occupy large areas of Southeast Asia. Their margins, along with those of other neighboring plates (Indian Ocean and Pacific), provide the key to understanding catastrophic earth movements in the area.

However exciting the changing study of the natural environment of Southeast Asia may be, that landscape represents only one facet of a very complicated realm. The cultural heritage is equally complex and fascinating as the next chapter will show.

Footnote References

[1]Norton Ginsburg, "The Political Dimension," in Alice Taylor, editor, *Focus on Southeast Asia* (New York: Praeger Publishers, Inc., 1972), p. 5.

[2]For those who desire an extended discussion of the physical features of Southeast Asia at least two excellent sources are available: E.H.G. Dobby, *Southeast Asia* (Mystic, Conn.: Lawrence Verry, Inc., 1973), and Charles A. Fisher, *Southeast Asia: A Social, Economic and Political Geography* (London: Methuen and Co. Ltd, 2nd edition, 1966).

[3]Fisher, p. 11.

[4]R.D.M. Verbeck, "The Krakatoa Eruption," *Nature* (May 1, 1884), pp. 10-15.

[5]Fisher, p. 418.

[6]Dobby, p. 301.

[7]Robbins Burling, *Hill Farms and Padi Fields* (Englewood Cliffs, N.J.: Prentice-Hall, Inc., 1965), p. 4.

[8]Benjamin Higgins and Jean Higgins, *Indonesia: The Crisis of the Millstones* (Princeton, N.J.: Van Nostrand Company, 1963), p. 15.

[9]George Rumney, *Climatology and the World's Climates* (London: The Macmillam Company, 1968), p. 585.

[10]*Ibid.*, p. 561.

[11]Donald W. Fryer, *Emerging Southeast Asia: A Study in Growth and Stagnation* (New York: McGraw-Hill Book Company, 1970), p. 301.

[12]Keith Buchanan, *The Southeast Asian World* (Garden City: Doubleday & Company, Inc., 1968), p. 55.

[13]J.E. Spencer and W.L. Thomas, *Asia, East by South: A Cultural Geography* (New York: John Wiley & Sons, Inc., 1971), p. 362.

[14]C.N. Williams and K.T. Joseph, *Climate, Soil and Crop Production in the Humid Tropics* (London: Oxford University Press, 1970), p. 124.

[15]J.B. Neilands, "Vietnam: Progress of the Chemical War," *Asian Survey*, Vol. 10, No. 3 (March, 1970), p. 221.

[16]Fred T. Tschirley, "Defoliation in Vietnam," *Science*, Vol. 163 (1969), p. 783.

[17]Neilands, p. 212.

[18]Neilands, p. 223.

[19]Thomas J. Fitch, "Plate Convergence, Transcurrent Faults, and Internal Deformation Adjacent to Southeast Asia and the Wstern Pacific", *Journal of Geophysical Research*, vol. 77, no. 23 (August 10, 1972) pp. 4432–4460.

Chapter 3

Cultural Diversity

Laurence J. Ma

Situated between India and China, two of the greatest creative early civilizations of the world, Southeast Asia historically has been an area of cultural convergence. Generally speaking, the cultural impact of India in Southeast Asia has been more widespread than that of China. The imprints of the Indian culture have been much deeper and more visible than those left by the Chinese, particularly in architecture, art forms and religion.

Indian traders came to the coast of Southeast Asia as early as the sixth century B.C. and, later, set up communities in various parts of the region. Although the earliest Chinese arriving in Southeast Asia can be traced back to the third century B.C., their number was small until after the seventeenth century when population pressure in China forced many more people to migrate to the "Nanyang" (literally, the "South Sea," meaning Southeast Asia). Today the majority of the Chineas are traders or businessmen.

Besides Indian and Chinese cultural influences, Southeast Asia has also been affected by Western culture after the Age of Exploration, particularly since the nineteenth century. This third layer of culture is today exerting a great influence in Southeast Asia, just as in other parts of the world. The Western impact, however, has been most noticeable in urban places, although increasingly it is being felt in rural areas as well.

In the late thirteenth century, Islamic missionary-adventurers came to Southeast Asia with the Arab traders, bringing with them the Moslem culture. This fourth layer of culture is particularly strong in coastal Indonesia and Malaysia where, since the fourteenth century, the previously Indianized landscape has been replaced by a Moslem one. Brunei is also predominantly Moslem.

Underneath these four great cultural layers existing in Southeast Asia are many groups of indigenous people inhabiting both hilly regions and lowland places. Tribal peoples from the southern parts of China have migrated southward under the pressure of Chinese expansion. These migrants arrived in Southeast Asia gradually, and they brought with them an immensely large variety of ethnic, linguistic, and religious traits.

EARLY CULTURAL ACHIEVEMENTS

Southeast Asia has been an area receiving different cultures from the outside since very early times. Cultural interactions between Southeast Asia and other regions have been mainly in one direction. It is difficult for one to imagine that in prehistoric times the region could have reached a cultural level which was probably both earlier and more sophisticated than that in South Asia or China.

Scholars long ago concluded that man first began to farm around 7500 B.C. in the "Fertile Crescent" area of Southwest Asia. Archaeological evidences have shown that man also engaged in agricultural activities at roughly the same time in what is now Mexico and Central America. Recent archaeological excavations carried out in the 1960s in Southeast Asia, however, have produced new evidences which may push the birth of agriculture even farther back.[1]

The idea that agriculture first began in Southeast Asia was first put forward by Carl O. Sauer, a geographer, as a hypothesis in 1952. His choice of Southeast Asia was based on six major premises: (1) Agriculture did not develop from a growing or chronic shortage of food. He argued that people on the verge of famine do not have the means nor the time to experiment with a new and different way of getting food. Only the people who lived comfortably could have had the leisure to improve edible plants by selection for better utility to man. (2) Areas of first domestication have a diversity of plants and animals. This implies well-diversified topography and possibly varied climate as well. (3) Primitive agriculturalists could not have lived in lowland areas subject to flooding. Thus agricultural origins must be sought in hilly regions. (4) Farming began in wooded lands where early farmers could easily prepare land for cultivation by removing trees and where the soils were easier to plow than grassland soils. (5) Ax-users or woodland dwellers were remote ancestors of the farmers. (6) The first farmers were sedentary people. Sauer went on and proposed that the primitive cultivators were a fishing people living in a place with mild climate and along fresh water.[2]

Little attention was paid to this hypothesis before the 1960s. Excavations made between 1966 and 1972 at Spirit Cave and Non Nok Tha located in northwestern and southeastern Thailand respectively, however, very strongly support Sauer's hypothesis.

The archaeological sites in Thailand yielded many artifacts which clearly indicate the existence of a sophisticated culture in Southeast Asia in prehistoric times. It has generally been believed that man first domesticated plants and animals in Southwest Asia some 10,000 years ago. But if the dating of the artifacts is accurate, agriculture may have begun in mainland Southeast Asia as much as 5,000 years earlier. Rice was an established cereal and humped cattle were commonly used as early as 5000 B.C., long before they were used in either India or China. An ancient socketed bronze tool was unearthed which, being buried as early as 400 B.C., predates the oldest archaeological find of a similar kind in Europe and Southwest Asia, and it may be the oldest bronze tool known to man. Solheim believes that the development of metallurgy in Southeast Asia was probably independent of the development of Southwest Asia. All these tend to point to Southeast Asia as an area of flourishing, advanced culture rather than the backward, underdeveloped culutral *cul-de-sac* it has always been thought to be.

PEOPLES AND MIGRATIONS

Indigenous Peoples

Southeast Asia is an area of geographical diversity. It forms a land bridge between Asia and Australia, and its position as a great maritime crossroads has invited invasions of both peoples and cultures. The area has experienced a succession of migrations of peoples, and the strongest of them have occupied precious fertile plains, driving the earlier occupants to less desirable areas in hilly regions; making the hill people and the plains people historically more hostile than amicable to each other.

Little is known of the origins and early migrations of peoples in Southeast Asia. The skeletal remains of Java Man (*Pithecanthropus erectus*) indicate that they were hominids inhabiting Java approximately half a million years ago, in many respects, quite similar to Peking Man (*Sinanthropus pekinensis*) found in North China. The remains of the first Southeast Asian *Homo sapiens*, which have been suggested to be of proto-Australoid race, show that early modern peoples were living in Java about 10,000 years ago. However, it is not entirely clear whether these early men preceded the Negritos who most likely migrated to Southeast Asia from India.

The Australoid people are dark-skinned, long-headed with wavy hair, and about five feet in stature whereas the Negrito is equally dark but shorter (4'5" to 5') and broad-headed with woolly hair. The mixing of these two peoples over the years has resulted in a third racial stock, the Melanesoid, which interestingly is much taller (about 5'5") and long-headed with woolly hair. The fourth important group, the Alpine-Mongoloid peoples, came to Southeast Asia from the north in the second millennium B.C. This series of migrations was triggered mainly by China's territorial expansion from the Yellow river region to the south and southwest. The migrants used primarily the longitudinal river valleys connecting China with Southeast Asia and, during the course of their movements, displaced or mixed with earlier peoples in the region. The leading ethnic groups of mainland Southeast Asia, the Vietnamese, Malays, Mons, Khmers, Pyu-Burmans, and the late-arriving Shan and Thai peoples all participated in this southward migration.[3] The result of the migrations and the mixing of these different racial groups is the extremely complex pattern of racial distribution in Southeast Asia. Several hundred groups of people are present in the region.[4] Although scholars have rightly stressed the importance of the cultures of the indigenous peoples, the fact remains that almost all the great cultural achievements is Southeast Asia were influenced by Indian civilization.

The Impact of Indian Culture

Because of the effectiveness of the almost inaccessible and rugged mountain barriers separating India from Burma, historically the diffusion of Indian culture into Southeast Asia has been almost entirely by ships.

India's initial contact with Southeast Asia was most probably motivated by trade. As early as the sixth century B.C., Indian traders were exploring the coasts of Burma, the Malay peninsula and western Indonesia, probably searching for gold and other precious metals. Around the beginning of the Christian era, India's interest in maritime trade with Southeast Asia and China increased, when a greater demand for Oriental goods, particularly Chinese silk and porcelains, developed in the Mediterranean region. Merchants from Europe and the Arab world traded actively with India, but they rarely ventured farther east. Roman gold, however, flowed continually to Asia. At the site of the ancient port of Oc Eo situated on the south side of the Mekong delta, archaeologists have found medallions of the Roman emperor Marcus Aurelius (reigned A.D. 161–180).

It was the commercial interaction between India and Southeast Asia that set the stage for the Indianization of the latter. Indianization was a long and slow process that went on for centuries. All the eastern ports of India were places of cultural diffusion, but the southern ports probably furnished most of the traders who served as diffusion agents upon arrival in Southeast Asia. The traders did business with the local chiefs and made themselves welcome by their lavish presents, the ability to heal diseases, and their gifts of amulets to ward off evil spirits. These Indians undoubtedly also posed as of royal descent to impress their hosts.[5] They established themselves locally by marrying the daughters of the chiefs. "The local girls became familiar with Hindu ways and unconsciously acted as missionaries. Being high born locally, when they asserted that Hindu ways were superior to their own, they were seldom contradicted."[6]

The introduction of Indian culture was most intensive during the Gupta Empire (A.D. 320–535) when Indian culture reached an all-time peak. At the time, Gupta India was probably the most orderly and splendid country in the world, a period of Indian history known as the Golden Age of India. It attracted cultural and political admiration not only from Southeast Asia, but also from China which during this period of time was experiencing a cultural doldrum.

Most scholars generally agree that the most important media of Indianization were Buddhism and Hinduism, both originated in India. Buddhist missionary influence first spread southward to Ceylon (Sri Lanka), which by 600 A.D. had become the center of Theravada (the so-called Hinayana or Lesser Vehicle) Buddhism, and at later times missions from Burma, Siam, and Cambodia were sent out to Ceylon to seek clarification of the faith. The Mahayana sect of Buddhism gained temporary acceptance in central Java during the eighth century and in Cambodian Angkor in the twelfth century, but eventually only the Theravada system survived in the Indianized areas of Southeast Asia.

Hinduism was imported by Southeast Asian rulers who wished to imitate the majestic style of Indian courts. The Sivaite-Hindu concept of royalty was adopted by local rulers, and Brahman priests were brought in from India to legitimize their rule, to organize their states according to the Hindu code, and to carry out the Sanskrit ritual. Indian ethical writings, political and economic treatises (*Arthasastras*), codes of law (*Dharmasastras*, particularly the so-called Code of Manu), art forms, and literary pieces were all introduced.

The complex pattern of Indian culture with a multitude of social, linguistic, and religious systems, was adopted only selectively in Southeast Asia. The caste system and the generally subordinate position of women were never accepted. But Sanskrit, the sacred language of the sacred text of Hinduism and of certain schools of Buddhism, was the first written language known to have reached Southeast Asia. "The local languages lacked not only a script, but also words for the philosophical, religious, and legal concepts which came from India. As a result, hundreds of words of Indian origin were borrowed by local languages just as Latin and French terms have been borrowed by English."[7] Sanskrit and one of its later off-shoots, Pali language, also provided the bases for developing local writing systems. In addition, the Indian astrological system and the Indian calendar were also borrowed.

In view of the fact that Indian culture diffused to Southeast Asia mainly by sea routes, it is not surprising that the earliest Indianized states emerged generally along the coast, with their individual settlement nuclei located at convenient river mouths. The earliest accounts of these states can be found only in Chinese chronicles. The first Indianized state, called Fu-nan by the Chinese, became an imperial power in the third century A.D. followed by the Khmer kingdom in Cambodia. The Chams (Lin-i in Chinese) established the Kingdom of Champa (A.D. 192–1471) along the east coast of Vietnam. By the fourth century, Siva-worship was already a court religion there.

The kingdom of Srivijaya with its capital probably at modern Palembang on Sumatra was one of the first recorded sea powers to accept Indian influence. Chinese Buddhist pilgrims, passing through there in the seventh century on their ways to and from India, described Srivijaya as a great place of Mahayana Buddhist learning. Buddhist influence was also very strong in central Java, especially during the early rule of the dynasty of the Sailendras. The most spectacular architectural monument, dating probably from the eighth century, is the Borobudur, a vast stone stupa (Buddhist relic mound) 150 feet high decorated with numerous smaller stupas and statues of Buddha.

In all these areas, Sanskrit inscriptions provided the earliest local historical records. It is clear that before the thirteenth century, all of Southeast Asia except the Tonkin region was affected by Indian culture. After that period Indian cultural influence declined and Chinese, Islamic, and Western cultures slowly moved in, further affecting the diverse cultural landscape of Southeast Asia.

In the closing decades of the nineteenth century, when Western colonialism in Southeast Asia reached a new height and the colonial powers urgently needed laborers to work in European commercial enterprises in which the local people were not interested, millions of Chinese and Indians emigrated to Southeast Asia. Because of geographical proximity, most Indians went to Burma and Malaya. In Burma, the Indians, rather than the Chinese, have controlled the retail trade; but in Malaysia they have remained in unskilled and menial occupations. In 1964, following the Burman government's nationalization programs to root out vestiges of foreign economic interest, there was heavy exodus of Indians back to India. It is estimated that over 100,000 Indians left without being compensated for nationalized property.

Chinese Migration to the Nanyang

Unlike the widespread influence of Indian civilization which had reached Southeast Asia via sea routes, Chinese impact was mainly exerted overland, and the only area affected by Chinese culture was Vietnam. The earliest contact between China and Vietnam can be traced back to China's Ch'in Dynasty (221–207 B.C.). During most of the second century B.C., North Vietnam (Tonkin) was controlled by China. North Vietnam remained a Chinese territory until almost the middle of the 10th century when it broke away from the Chinese rule and became an independent state.[8]

While the Indian cultural impact was in the main felt in spiritual beliefs which were absorbed voluntarily by the natives, the introduction of Chinese civilization into the northeastern part of Indochina was a direct result of Chinese colonization and conquest. The Chinese type of administration, the Chinese writing system, and Confucian classical studies were all superimposed on the indigenous culture. China's cultural influence persisted even after North Vietnam became independent in the middle of the 10th century. Even the dynastic chronicles were written in Chinese.[9]

The imprint of Chinese culture elsewhere in Southeast Asia is much less clear. Nonetheless, many Chinese cultural traits were indirectly brought to other parts of Southeast Asia by the Thais and the Burmans who had long been in contact with their more advanced northern neighbors before being forced to migrate southward between the seventh and eleventh centuries. Although emigration abroad, which signified dissatisfaction with the conditions at home, was officially discouraged and prohibited by imperial decrees in Ming (1368–1644) and Ch'ing (1644–1911) China, some Chinese were attracted to the Nanyang and, by the sixteenth century, Chinese trading communities were permanently established in several parts of Southeast Asia. But large-scale migration did not take place until well into the nineteenth century when internal conditions in China further deteriorated as a result of famines and rebellions. Meanwhile, there existed a great demand for manpower in modern agricultural and mining enterprises owned by Europeans in Southeast Asia. Until 1950, thousands of people from Kwangtung and Fukien provinces of China migrated to various parts of Southeast Asia to work in rubber estates or tin mines. Others came as farmers, traders, retailers (dealing particularly with rice distribution and milling), or as skilled craftsmen.

Today there are at least fourteen million overseas Chinese in Southeast Asia who are most successful in retail trade. Some dialect groups have developed occupational specialities over the years, e.g., the Hakka people usually go into agricultural work, Hainanese into coffee shops, and Teochius into the grocery trade, etc. But increasingly more and more young Chinese are abandoning the traditional occupations and going into colleges in Malaysia, Singapore, Hong Kong, Taiwan, and Western countries. These college graduates have in many places been quite prominent in such professions as education, government work, and engineering.

Friction and distrust have been developed in recent years in many parts of Southeast Asia between the Chinese and the local residents. This is due partly to the low level of assimilation by the Chinese and partly to their strong economic position in Southeast Asia which the local residents have always resented. The Chinese are seen to be different. "In Thailand they are politically second-class citizens, in that regulations for voting in both local and national elections require of Chinese voters educational and Thai-language qualifications not demanded of Thais. In both the Philippines and Indonesia there is commercial discrimination by the Governments. There has been discrimination against them, as immigrants, in Burma, Cambodia, Vietnam; in Malaysia there is the famous bargain on the proportion of government posts which they may hold, preference to Malays in government scholarships, reservations of vast areas of land as 'Malay reservations.' "[10] In the newly independent Brunei the Chinese are not even legal citizens.

LANGUAGE PATTERNS

The cultural and linguistic landscape of Southeast Asia is complex (Fig. 3-1). Hundreds of distinct languages and their dialects are spoken. The languages of Southeast Asia can be classified into four major generically different families, each encompassing several important languages:

I. Malayo-Polynesian (Austronesian) family
   Malay, Cham, Javanese, Celebes, etc.
II. Sino-Tibetan family
   Thai, Burmese, Shan, Miao, Yao, Karen
   Lolo, Chinese mandarin, Cantonese, etc.
III. Austro-Asiatic family
   Mon, Khmer, Annamese (or Vietnamese), etc.
IV. Papuan family
   New Guinea, Halmahera, etc.

Many of these languages have not been adequately studied and their generic relationships are by no means very clear. The insular portion of Southeast Asia has a simpler language pattern than the continental part because all the native languages belong to one common stock, the so-called Malayan division of the Malayo-Polynesian group. On the mainland, only the Malay Peninsula and a small enclave in southern Vietnam (Cham) belong to the same family.

The spoken languages of the mainland form a complicated mosaic developed over the centuries. Sino-Tibetan languages cover a vast area including the mountain regions of northern Vietnam and parts of the Chinese provinces of Yunnan, Kweichou, and Kwangsi. Different kinds of Chinese dialects are spoken by the overseas Chinese, including Cantonese, Hainanese, Hakka, Teochiu, and Fukienese, etc. Of course, Thai and Burmese are the national languages of Thailand and Burma, each with a large number of speakers.

Mon was the language of early kingdoms in Lower Burma, and it is still spoken by a small number of people there. Khmer is the leading language of Cambodia. Various dialects of Mon-Khmer are found in widely scattered mountain pockets throughout Southeast Asia. Annamese is spoken by most Vietnamese living in the plains of Vietnam. It is related to Mon-Khmer languages with many common basic vocabularies, but, unlike Mon-Khmer, it has a tonal system similar to that of the Thai languages. On the whole, the plain areas have relatively few languages whereas the hill regions, because of geographic seclusion, harbor most of the small groups of peoples speaking hundreds of different languages, which in most cases can be considered more accurately as dialects.

Since the eighteenth century, English has been widely used in education and administration in Southeast Asia, particularly in the Philippines, Malaysia, Thailand and Burma. But in Indochina French took the place of English. In Indonesia the Dutch language used to be quite important, but since the nation became independent in 1945, it is strongly disliked and English has gained vogue.

MAJOR RELIGIONS AND THEIR CHARACTERISTICS

The religious patterns in Southeast Asia are somewhat less complex than the linguistic ones. Indochina is largely Buddhist except along the Vietnamese plains where the so-called "Chinese religion" predominates. The insular world has largely been Islamized except on the island of Bali where Hinduism has survived the process of Islamization and in the Philippines where the people are mainly Christian in faith (Fig. 3-2). Animistic beliefs are found throughout the region's isolated and hilly places occupied by minority ethnic groups. Religion has had a profound impact upon the culture of Southeast Asia. This impact can be witnessed in the daily lives of the people, their customs, their art, and the profusion of temples, pagodas, monasteries, shrines, churches, and mosques.

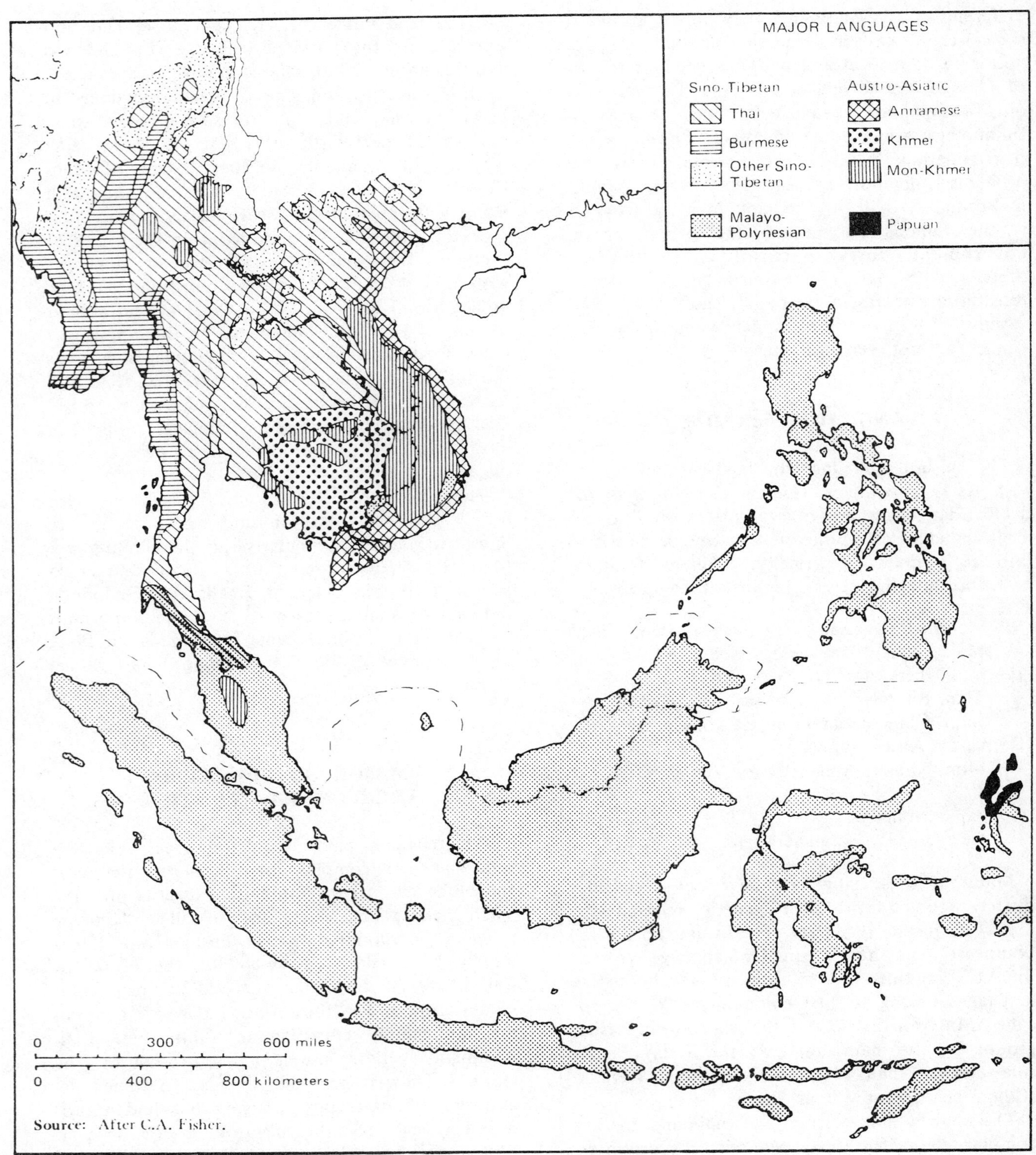

Source: After C.A. Fisher.

Figure 3-1. Major Indigenous Languages of Southeast Asia.

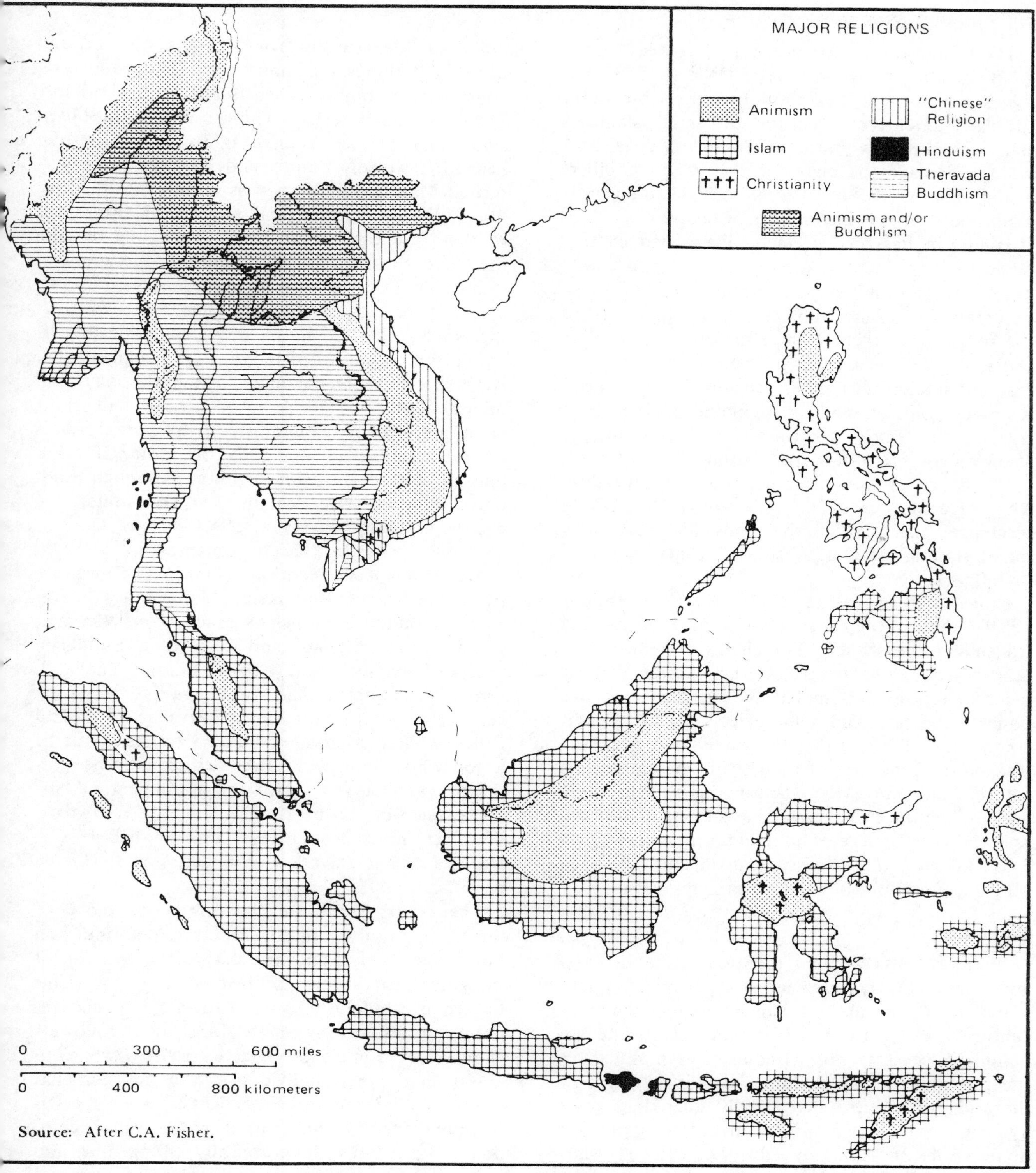

Source: After C.A. Fisher.

Figure 3-2. Major Religions of Southeast Asia.

Hinduism

Hinduism, once widespread in Southeast Asia, is now almost extinct. After the last Hindu dynasty in eastern Java had been overthrown in the early seventeenth century, the small island of Bali was the only place in Southeast Asia providing a refuge for many of the Hindu nobility. Today Bali is the only area where Hinduism is professed by a sizeable number of people.

Hinduism has an extremely diverisified character with many schools of philosophy and theology, great numbers of popular cults, and numerous sects and subsects. It attempts to be the religion for every man. Hinduism appeared in India about fifteen centuries before the Christian era, but unlike most other religions of the world, it has no founder, and its beginning is difficult to trace. The Hindu doctrines are found in the Vedas, a collection of sacred writings.

There are in Hinduism countless for worship. The diversity of gods, according to Hindu teachings, means that the gods are the many manifestations of One Absolute Reality, which is undefinable.

Concept of Karma and Dharma. The Hindus believe that life is a succession of rebirths and transmigrations to self. The chains of rebirths are determined by the law of *karma*. *Karma* literally means "action"; it implies that a man's actions done in the past had some effects on his present condition of life and that the cumulative effects of his actions in his lifetime will determine his future. Since *karma* is a continuous process, man has to control it by discipline of the mind and body, which is defined in Hinduism as his *dharma*. The word *dharma* is used to mean duty, law, religion, moral obilgations and principles.

Buddhism

Buddhism was brought to Southeast Asia from India in the early centuries A.D. by traders and travellers. It appeared in North India in the sixth century B.C. partly as a reaction against the accumulated excesses of Hinduism exemplified in the presumptions of Brahman authority, the proliferation of deities, the socially degrading caste system, and the economically growing materialism of Hindu creeds. The rise of Buddhism was partly due to the personal experience of Gautama Buddha, or simply Buddha or the "Enlightened One."[11]

Four Noble Truths. Theologically the central tenents of Buddhism were put forth by the Buddha in the Four Noble Truths. First, suffering is universal. Man suffers from sickness, old age, and death. All things are momentary in the universe, constantly becoming other things, and invariably bound to the Wheel of Change and Decay (*Samsara*). To oppose change is to cause sorrow. Secondly, worldly desires and cravings cause suffering. Man craves for power, wealth, health, long life and other existing and nonexisting things, all of them are capable of generating agony because they are all impermanent. Thirdly, the elimination of desire is the cure for suffering. This can be achieved through the fourth Noble Truth which is the Noble Eightfold Path, an ethical guide to self-discipline: right knowledge, right aspirations, right speech, right conduct, right livelihood, right mental exertion, right mindfulness and right emotional serenity. Buddhism in its pure form is a creed requiring no gods or idols. Buddha himself denied his own divinity. Although Buddhists chant a great deal in their ceremonies, the chants are not prayers directed to any God or gods but are spiritual aids to contemplation.

Mahayana and Theravada Branches. There are two branches of Buddhism—Mahayana (Greater Vehicle) Buddhism which is practiced in Vietnam, China, Korea, Japan, and Theravada Buddhism practiced mainly in Sri Lanka, Burma, Thailand, Laos, and Cambodia. Mahayana is "greater" since it claims to be more inclusive in theological concepts. It has elevated Buddha to the status of a god who, along with lesser deities, may be worshipped and prayed to for the attainment of Nirvana (escape from the Wheel of *Samsara*). However, most people have come to believe that Nirvana means salvation in a definite afterlife in paradise.

Theravada Buddhism has preserved more of the purity of the original Buddhist doctrine than Mahayana Buddhism. Buddha is the symbol of Enlightenment but is not revered as a god. This branch of Buddhism is more demanding and requires an austere way of life. Most of its followers choose to become monks, at least for a while, to aid them on their individual search for Nirvana. Theravada is monk-oriented. Thailand is especially noted for its numerous wats, a walled compound voluntarily supported by the people and normally the social, educational, and spiritual center of a town or village.

Islam

Two countries of modern Southeast Asia, Indonesia and Malaysia, are principally Islamic. Islam first gained a footing in Sumatra and Java through traders in the thirteenth and fourteenth centuries. From Sumatra it was carried by colonists and traders to the Malay Peninsula, and from Java to the Maluku. Like Hinduism and Buddhism, it was brought to the region from India by Indian and Arab traders. It spread gradually along the sea routes through the archipelago from west to east, superimposing itself on the earlier Indianized culture.

The propagation of Islam in Southeast Asia was slow and largely peaceful. On the surface at least, Moslem traders were Indians who had preached Hinduism and Buddhism and, therefore, were not viewed as total strangers by the Southeast Asians. Motivated by commerical profits, they came to Southeast Asia to seek wealth, and, contrary to common notion, the sword had little to do with the spread of Islam . Further, much of the tactics of the Moslem traders appealed to the Indonesians. Like the Hindu traders of previous centuries, they came with a new learning; they claimed to be able to heal sickness and to drive away spirits; and they married the daughters of communal chiefs and through them influenced local communities.[12]

Five Pillars. The basis of othrodox Islam is the five pillars which include the confession of faith (Moslems recite many times daily "There is no god but Allah, and Muhammed is His Prophet"), prayers (Moslems should pray five times daily—-before sunrise, at noontime, during the midafternoon, at sunset, and after sunset), charity (monetary contribution to help the poor, the needy, and the aged, and to maintain mosques), fast (during the month of Ramadan of the Arabic lunar calendar), and pilgrimage to the holy shrine of the Kaaba in Mecca at least once in a Moslem's lifetime. But not all of these are faithfully observed by the Moslems in Southeast Asia. For example, most Indonesians generally neglect the daily prayers and the rituals for purification connected with the prayers. For some people the trip to Mecca can be postponed indefinitely if they leave provision for substitutes to make the trip, although most people who have the money make the trip themselves.[13]

"Chinese" Religion

In the Vietnam plains, most people belive in the so-called "Chinese" religion, a mixture of Mahayana Buddhism, Taoism, and ancestor worship, all disseminated from China. Buddhism is a less important religious element in Vietnam than it is in other parts of Indochina. There are far fewer men becoming monks, and even fewer tend to be monks for life. Buddhist temples are not as widespread, and to the Vietnamese, the temple is only one of the many places of worship. Taoism originated in China in the sixth century B.C. as a school of intellectual thought, but it gradually developed into a religious offshoot embracing a host of mythical and magical practices accepted readily by the common folk. A number of Taoist deities together with Heaven and Earth are worshipped. Ancestor worship is not a religion but a social practice associated with Confusianism which stressed, among other things, filial piety and gratefulness to one's ancestors. In addition to these three major religious elements, a multiplicity of local cults exist, each devoted to the veneration of a protective deity, the most popular being the Guardian Spirit of each village. Moreover, artisans of all types religiously honor the founders (or patron saints) of the crafts in the same manner as in pre-1949 China.

Animism

The belief in spiritual beings and agencies is still strong among the hill tribes of Southeast Asia. Many natural objects and phenomena are considered as having souls that exist apart from their material bodies and are frequently revered and worshipped. Animals are sometimes sacrificed to satisfy the needs of the spirits. Animism, however, is not confined to the hill regions. In lowland Burma, for example, the so-called *nats* are believed to be everywhere—in the house, in the village, on the road, and in the air and water—and they are viewed as being capable of bringing harm and misfortune to people. To appease them, small box-shaped shrines containing the images of the *nats* are erected by the people outside of their houses and along the road, and food or flowers are often offered. But, as more and more places in Southeast Asia are exposed to Western cultural influences, animism and other aspects of the traditional culture are gradually disappearing.

Christianity

Nearly 80% of the people in the Philippines are Roman Catholics. The Spaniards, who governed the country for almost four hundred years, left a strong imprint of Catholicism. Churches are found in almost every city and town of any size and dominate the social life of the people. Although American missionaries came to the Philippines in the nineteenth century, the number of Protestants has never been large. At the same time, Dutch, Swiss, and German missionaries brought Christianity to parts of the tropical islands of Southeast Asia occupied by primitive peoples, particularly the peoples in Sulawesi, in West Irian in New Guinea, the Nias islanders, and the Bataks in northern Sumatra. However, the Philippines is the only country in Southeast Asia with a Christian majority.

COLONIALISM AND WESTERN IMPACT

Aside from the cultural influence of India and China, European nations also played an active role in shaping the history and cultural landscape of Southeast Asia. Prior to the arrival of the Portuguese in Southeast Asia in the early sixteenth century, Europeans had known about the great wealth of the Spice Islands centered on Malacca through their trade with the Arabs. Spices were in great demand by the Europeans who needed them for food preservation and seasoning. Vasco da Gama's voyage to India via the Cape of Good Hope in 1498 paved the way for the arrival of several waves of Europeans whose colonial rule in the next four and a half centuries was both harmful and beneficial to the nations of Southeast Asia.

The Portuguese were the first Europeans to arrive. By the early sixteeth century, they had established a series of bases in Asia that extended from the Persian Gulf to Malacca. The primary interest of the Portuguese was trade. Although there were a few Catholic missionaries in some places, their religious influence was minimal. Portugal's venture into Southeast Asia did not last long, nor did it leave any strong cultural imprints. In the early 1600s, Portugal gradually lost control of its bases to the rivaling Dutch, who ultimately defeated the Portuguese and seized all of their important bases in Southeast Asia, including Malacca in 1640. The only place that remained Portuguese until 1975 was half of the island of Timor.

The profitable spice trade attracted other Europeans to Southeast Asia, including the British and the Spanish. As the supply of spices on the European market became more abundant, their prices began to drop. The Dutch then created sugar, coffee and tobacco plantations in Java where Chinese immigrants and local Javanese worked for low wages. The small port of Batavia (Jakarta) was developed by the Dutch as their major base of operation. By virtue of their superior administrative ability and economic know-how, the Dutch succeeded in controlling the agricultural economy of Java. They manipulated supply and controlled all prices, and their high income permitted them to lead a very comfortable life in the cities. The Indonesians were not permitted to hold responsible positions in the government and this they resented. It should be pointed out that the plantation economy that the Dutch established for their own benefit later also became the mainstay of Indonesia's modern economy. The Dutch remained in Indonesia until they were driven out by the Japanese invaders at the outset of World War II. The Netherlands ceded sovereignty in 1949 when Indonesia became an independent nation.

The spice trade was the initial attraction that lured the Spanish to Southeast Asia. Under an agreement between Spain and Portugal reached at the end of the fifteenth century, the Spice Islands were granted to the Portuguese as their trade area while Spain was forced to find territories elsewhere in the region. The Spanish established a stronghold in the St. Lazarus Islands, which were later renamed Las Felipinas. By 1584, Spain controlled all of the islands of the Philippines except Sulu and Mindanao which remained Moslem territories.

Spanish trade, centered on Manila, flourished after the sixteenth century. But Spain was interested in more than trade. It wanted to create a Spanish state in Southeast Asia. From the late sixteenth century on Spain gradually introduced its administrative, judicial, and religious systems to the Philippines. Large tracts of farm land were granted to Spanish nobles, many of them Catholic priests, who collected taxes for Spain (but kept some for their own use), converted local people to Christianity, introduced such New World crops as corn and sweet potatoes, and built schools, hospitals, and churches in Spanish styles. While the heavily taxed Filipinos resented the spanish noblemen for exploitation, they were unable to do much. Spain's colonial rule in the Philippines declined in the early nineteenth century as the empire began to lose its might and as the colonial administration itself became corrupt and inefficient. After it had lost its colonies in North America, Spain's control of the Philippines further declined. In 1898, following the Spanish-American War, the U.S. paid Spain $20 million for the control of the Philippines.

The presence of the U.S. in the Philippines was by no means peaceful. A nationalistic rebellion broke out against the Americans who had just arrived to take over the islands. The war lasted two years from 1899 to 1901 in which casualties were heavy on both sides. Thereafter, the islands were ruled by U.S. essentially as a colony, although the term "colony" was rarely used at home. In many ways the Philippines benefited from American rule as Americans constructed roads in rural areas and water supply systems in the cites, built hospitals and schools, helped eliminate many contagious diseases, and invested in agricultural and mining activities. American involvement in the Philippines ended after Japan had occupied the islands from 1942 to 1945. Independence was proclaimed in 1946.

Great Britain's involvement in Southeast Asia began in the late eighteenth century after it had established trade routes to India and China. Initially the British were confined to the Malay peninsula, especially in Penang and Singapore which served as Britain's major trade bases, but in the nineteenth century the British were able to extend their control to Borneo, Sarawak, Sabah, Brunei and Burma. Like colonialists everywhere, the British, for their own benefits built transportation systems, invested heavily in local economic projects, and exported such natural resources as tin, rubber and lumber.

The French arrived in Indochina as early as the seventeenth century, but they did not establish firm control until the mid-nineteenth century. The French rule was absolute and often oppressive. They regarded themselves as culturally superior to the Indochinese who, they thought, should become more "civilized" by adopting the French culture. Frenchmen held all major administrative positions and succeeded in drawing some local elites to French culture. Economically, the French contributed heavily to water management that greatly enhanced agricultural production in the south. They also helped to build industries in north Vietnam. Industries and plantations, however, were owned largely by the French and the French-speaking Vietnamese. The majority of the rural people remained poor and isolated.

In short, the history and culture of Southeast Asia after the Age of Exploration and before the mid-twentieth century were significantly affected by European powers' involvement in Southeast Asian affairs. While the nations of Southeast Asia suffered politically and Western democracy never struck roots anywhere on the region, their economic systems underwent a fundamental transformation as a result of the establishment of plantations and mining enterprises that were organized and managed on Western models. Many great cities emerged on the coast of Southeast Asia, first as trading posts and later as seats of colonial administration. It is in such great cities as Jakarta, Singapore, and Manila that the West has left strong cultural imprints. Today these cities function as national capitals, centers of industrialization, higher education, and international trade. No one should deny that colonialism and resource exploitation went hand in hand with the construction of roads, railways, harbors, communication lines and schools that are needed for national development. It seems that, in the long run and from the perspective of future economic growth, colonialism made some positive contributions to the nations of Southeast Asia. Politically, of course, colonialism represented oppressive rule, second-class status for the local people, contempt for their culture, and, worst of all, the loss of national pride.

Footnote References

[1]For a discussion of this point, see Wilhelm G. Solheim II, "An Earlier Argicultural Revolution," *Scientific American*, Vol. 224, No. 4 (1972), pp. 34–41, and his "Late Pleistocene Horticultural Origins in Southeast Asia," Paper presented at the 68th annual meeting of the Association of American Geographers, Kansas City, Missouri, April 23, 1972.

[2]Carl O. Sauer, *Agricultural Origins and Dispersals* (Cambridge, Mass.: The MIT Press, 1969), pp. 19–39.

[3]The Mons, the Pyu, and Burmans used the Irrawaddy and Sittang valleys. The gorges of the upper Salween and Mekong rivers and the tributaries of the Menan River were used by the Malays, the Mons, and later by the Thai. The Khmer peoples followed the Mekong valley to the delta and westward to the Tonle Sap area of Cambodia. See John F. Cady, *Thailand, Burma, Laos, and Cambodia* (Englewood Cliffs, N.J.: Prentice-Hall, Inc., 1966), p. 28.

[4]For a discussion of different peoples, see Frank LaBar, Gerald C. Hickey and John K. Musgrave, *Ethnic Groups of Mainland Southeast Asia* (New Haven: Human Relations Area Files Press, 1964); Peter Kunstadter (ed.), *Southeast Asian Tribes, Minorities and Nations* (Princeton, N.J.: Princeton University Press, 1967), 2 vols; and Cady, pp. 32–36.

[5]Kenneth P. Landon, *Southeast Asia: Crossroad of Religions* (Chicago: University of Chicago Press, 1949), p. 66.

[6]*Ibid.*

[7]Robbins Burling, *Hill Farms and Padi Fields* (Englewood Cliffs, N.J.: Prentice-Hall, Inc., 1965), p. 69.

[8]For early interaction between China and Southeast Asia, see Paul Wheatley, *The Golden Khersonese* (Kuala Lumpur, 1961); Wang Gungwu, "The Nanhai Trade, a Study of the Early History of Chinese Trade in the South China Sea," *Journal of the Malayan Branch of the Royal Asiatic Society*, Vol. 31, No. 2 (1958); G. Coedes, *The making of Southeast Asia* (Berkeley and Los Angeles: University of California Press, 1966), pp. 39–49; and Victor Purcell, *The Chinese in Southeast Asia* (Oxford University Press, 1965), pp. 8–23.

[9]John K. Fairbank, Edwin O. Reischauer, and Albert M. Craig, *East Asia: The Modern Transformation* (Boston: Houghton Mifflin Company, 1965), p. 433.

[10]Guy Hunter, *Southeast Asia—Race, Culture, and Nation*, (New York: Oxford University Press, 1966), p. 50.

[11]Because the Buddha was a prince of the Sakya clan in northern India, he is sometimes referred to as Buddha Sakyamuni, or "Buddha Sage of the Sakya Clan."

[12]Landon, p. 135.

[13]*Ibid.*, pp. 144–146.

Chapter 4

Agricultural Framework

Thomas F. Barton

In many ways, agriculture remains the most important industry in Southeast Asia although manufacturing and urban populations have grown proportionately in size during the last two decades. In 1979 over four-fifths of the total population was rural dwellers.[1] Over four-fifths of the population in Thailand and Indonesia are rural dwellers who live primarily in agricultural villages. The number of rural dwellers in Burma, Kampuchea (Cambodia), Laos and Vietnam were not reported. Laos and Kampuchea might have the highest percent of their population living in the countryside. Singapore as a city-state has the highest percentage of urbanized population. Brunei, West (peninsular) Malaysia and the Philippines rank after Singapore as the most urbanized areas in the realm.[2] Growth in the predominant agricultural sector has typically slowed. This slowing has occurred after a period of relatively high rates of expansion and results in part from susceptibility to changes in weather and the supply of key inputs. A lion's share of the population is engaged in agriculture, the distribution and processing of agricultural products and in associated lumbering and forest exploitation (slash-and-burn agriculture). Agricultural exports rank high as money earners for most of the countries.

PHYSICAL ENVIRONMENTAL HABITAT

The population in this realm is increasing much faster than is the process of making arable land available. The primary restraints in providing additional cultivated land are (1) relief, (2) drainage, (3) climate, (4) soil and (5) biota. A very high percent of the area is too rugged and steep, too poorly drained, too dry or too wet, too infertile and covered with trees and grass too difficult to clear and keep cleared. A combination of two or more of these factors makes the land ecologically unsuitable for dry land cultivation and still less suitable for irrigation. To increase agricultural production the two primary potentialities are to increase yields per acre and to reclaim land from forests, swamps and grasslands.

Relief Factor

Although it does not have large areas of high relief above sea level such as that found in South Asia or East Asia, Southeast Asia is cut up with mountains, eroded plateaus or tablelands and hill lands and so divided into small areas by its peninsular and insular nature that large plains or lowlands do not exist. Arable land is confined primarily to deltas, relatively narrow floodplains, coastal plains and intermontane basins.

The largest group of lowlands is located within a horseshoe-shaped rim of mountains, eroded tablelands and hills that form the boundaries between Burma, Laos and Thailand on the west and north and continues in an arc called the Annamitic Cordillera extending to the southeast to the China Sea in Vietnam. In this large lowland is located most of Thailand, the arable land of Laos, all of Cambodia and the southern part of South Vietnam. Unfortunately, this largest lowland in continental Southeast Asia is in the rainshadow of both the summer monsoon rains coming from the southwest and the cool season monsoon rains coming from the northeast. Air moving up over the windward side of the hilly and mountainous rim of the lowland is cooled and drops most of the moisture it carries. As the air descends on the leeward or rainshadow side, it becomes warmer and its capacity for holding moisture increases. Consequently, in summer the southwest monsoon drops enough water directly into the paddy fields of the Irrawaddy delta in Burma to produce a rice crop whereas the lower and erratic rainfall of the lowland (sometimes referred to as the Great Lowland of continental Southeast Asia[3]) necessitates, if good yields are expected, the cost of adding water to the fields in Thailand, Laos, Cambodia and southern Vietnam if it is available and engineering techniques have been provided. But even this lowland is broken up into subdivisions of relief by escarpments, hills and mountains which separate the watershed of the Chao Phraya (the principal river in Thailand) from the Mekong river watershed as well as Cambodia from Thailand. The coalescing Song Koi-Bo-Ma (Red, Black and Ma Rivers) delta-coastal plain in Burma are small in comparison with the Great Lowland.

Both the mountain systems and the major rivers in continental Southeast Asia are roughly aligned in a north-south direction resulting in the core agricultural areas of (1) Burma, (2) Thailand, (3) Laos, Cambodia and southern Vietnam and (4) north Vietnam being separated from each other by mountain ranges or dissected uplands.

Drainage Constraints

In insular Southeast Asia, because of the small size of a vast majority of the islands and because of the hills and mountains on the larger ones, large plains do not exist. When considered with in the context of Southeast Asia and its agricultural potential, the Philippines has several significant lowlands such as the central plain, Cagayan Valley, and the Bicol plain of Luzon; the Cotabato and Agusan lowlands of Mindanao; the western part of Negros; and the southeastern part of Panay.

Unfortunately, the extensive coastal plains (or lowlands) of the large islands of Indonesia, fringing the Sunda Shelf, are vast coastal swamps. Here water logging slows and checks soil-forming processes, especially bacterial action. As a result, deep deposits of peat and swamp vegetation have accumulated and must be drained before the land can be agriculturally useful and healthful.

Climatic Variance

Areawise in this realm four climates may be identified. These are the Tropical Rainforest, Tropical Monsoon, Diversified Mountain and Tropical Dry Zones. The first two cover most of the area and the other two are scattered in the matrix of the first two. Most lowlands have warm temperatures which provide a year-around crop-growing season if water is available. Double, triple and intercropping is possible and practiced in some limited areas with these practices increasing. This temperature advantage is partially offset by the fact that temperature accelerates the processes of soil destruction such as weathering and erosion.

Tropical Rainforest Climate. Each month in this type of climate is moist and the average temperature stays above 64.4° F. Temperatures above 50° F. are conducive to rapid vegetation growth. Weather conditions which favor the growth of year-around agricultural crops also produce weeds and unwanted grass and brush. There is a constant battle to keep the fields cleared (Fig. 4–1).

Tropical Monsoon Climate. This type, sometimes called a Tropical Savanna, does not receive as much rainfall as the former, and there is a distinct and often extremely harsh and sometimes disasterous dry season. For example, most of Thailand's provinces are in this type of climate.[4] During the four consecutive dry months, one-third of the provinces receive less than two inches of rainfall. Furthermore, a little over one-third of additional provinces get only between two and four inches whereas about one out of every ten received between four and six inches. This shortage of rainfall creates serious water problems and often great human hardships. Cultivation is not widespread during the dry season without irrigation. The sunshine bears unrelentlessly down through cloudless skies. Hot desicating winds aid in increasing the evaporation and transpiration until unirrigated grasses become brittle and die down to the ground and trees lose their leaves. As ditches and wet-weather intermittant streams and swamps dry up some fish burrow down into the mud below. The volume of the larger rivers is greatly reduced and become very shallow interrupting former wet-weather navigation.

Diversified Mountain Climate. Such climate exist on high mountain ranges or peaks, elevated severely-eroded tablelands and/or hills where slopes of varying heights and gradients as well as

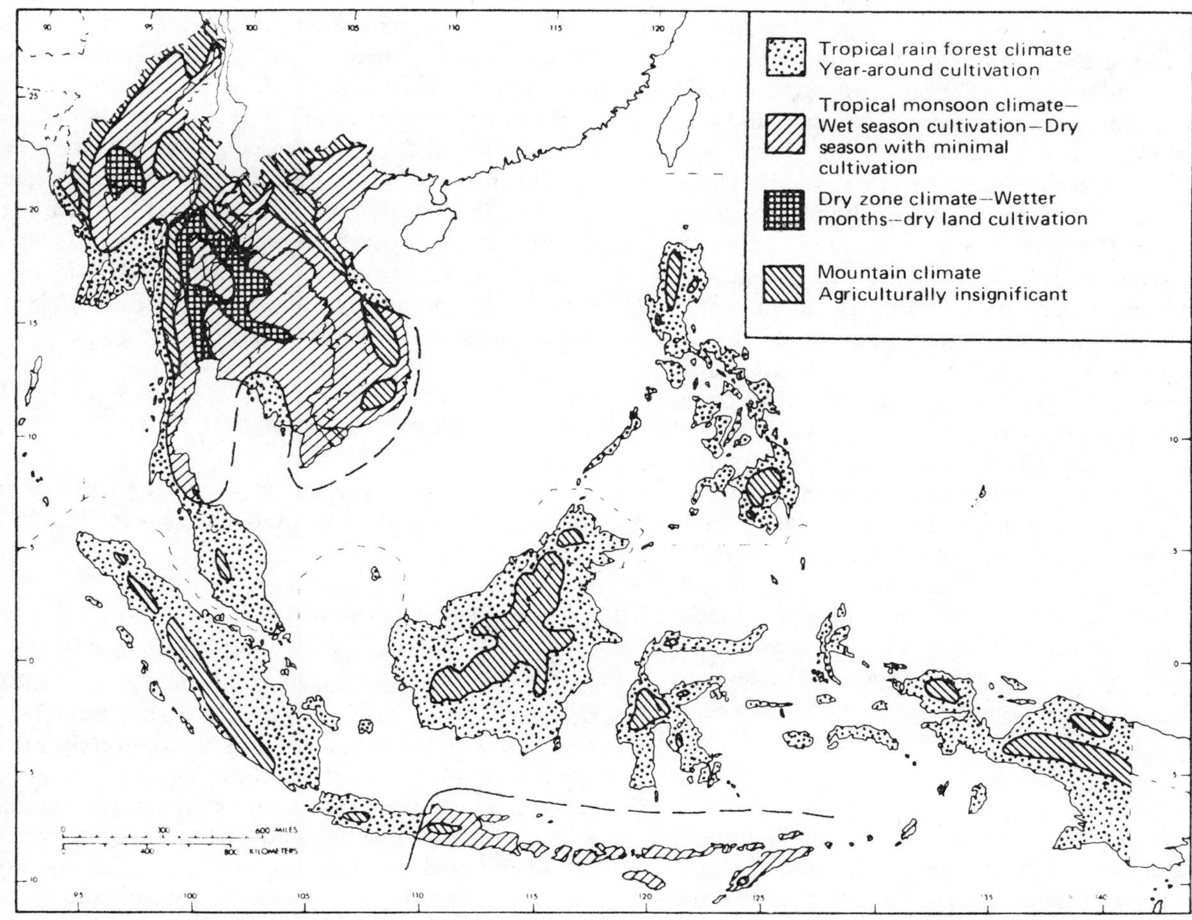

Source: For Dry Zone in Thailand, L. Ungur, *Focus*, Nov. 1970.

Figure 4-1. Climate and Cultivation Relationship.

sun and wind exposure help produce micro-climates and weather conditions of great diversity within short distances. Here temperatures and precipitation vary greatly. These areas are agriculturally insignificant.

Tropical Dry Zone Climate. This dry climate is noted for its relatively low amount of precipitation and high temperatures and drying winds also help reduce the effectiveness of 40 inches or less of rainfall. The climate is usually found in rainshadow areas where high relief nearly surrounds or encloses on three sides (especially the west and east) a lowland area. The largest areas of this type of climate are found in central Burma and the Great Lowland in Thailand. Rice cultivation without irrigation is risky in this zone, but dry-land crops can easily be grown.

Soil Resources

Except for shifting agriculture, dry farming and orchards on soils located on the lower slopes of hills and mountains, most of the cultivated fields are located on (1) alluvial soils found on deltas, narrow floodplains, and old lagoons and (2) fertile volcanic soils primarily in Indonesia. These young soils are limited in area and help place a restraint on the availablity of arable land. Soil materials are moved down slope by gravity and water by several processes such as sheet and rill erosion, and soil flow such as creeps and slides. As it is true with other young soils, these are not so highly leached and have higher quantities of nitrogen, potash, phosphorus and minor soil minerals.

It has already been mentioned in chapter 2 that mature soils, lateritic in nature, have resulted from long periods of weathering and leaching and are many times more extensive than are young soils. The processes of oxidation, biotic and chemical weathering and leaching are more accelerated in tropical rainforest climates than in any other climate. Some of the factors which help accelerate these processes are high atmospheric and soil temperatures, direct sunlight, high humidities and rainfall, presence of carbonic and nitric acids and an abundance of bacteria and surface and subsurface small animal life. Where soil temperatures exceed 75° F. the rate of accumulation of vegetable matter and/or humus is more than that offset by weathering and removal. Gourou reports that above 79° F. a rise in one degree of soil temperature "leads to an increased loss of humic nitrogen amounting to 15 to 25 pounds per acre per annum, which is equivalent to between 100 and 125 pounds of sulphate of amonia."[5] According to soil experts, because soil weathering is ten fold greater in the wet tropics as compared with temperate climates, tropical soils are poorer in plant nutrients and assimilable bases, more fragile and require greater care in order to prevent impoverishment and destruction when cultivated than those in temperate lands. Without the benefit of much humus, topsoils are not as well flocculated as in middle latitudes and the storage of soil water above water tables is limited.

Biota

It is believed that nearly all of the Southeast Asia realm was originally forest covered, the exception being primarily the swamp grasses and the nonforest vegetation at the highest elevations. Yet after being occupied for hundreds of years, it is estimated that only about one-tenth of the areas has been reclaimed for permanent cultivation. The Food and Agricultural Organization estimates that some 65%of insular Southeast Asia and 63% of continental Southeast Asia are forested. The percentage of a country covered with forests varies greatly. Of course Singapore is the least forested country. Most of the forests occupy land where relief, soil, climate and drainage are not suitable for permanently cultivated agriculture with the technology now available in the region. Moreover, the forests are noted for malaria, dysentery and other diseases and for a great variety of fauna especially biting crawling, jumping, flying, buzzing, slithering insects.

Man-made grasslands perpetuated and expanded by shifting cultivation now occupy hundreds of thousands of square miles. After repeated clearings and burnings, the original forest is unable to reproduce itself and savanna grasses and scrubs appear interspersed with clumps of horny bushes, bamboos and vines. These grasses are difficult to eradicate and are primarily useless for grazing except when they are very young because as they mature, they become coarse and have sharp cutting edges.

Potential Reclamation. The amount of potential arable land is not known. But by adopting late twentieth century technology and techniques of farm and agricultural mechanical engineering, additional land could be reclaimed from forests, swamps and man-made grasslands. But it may not be economically feasible to reclaim large areas during the next few decades.

TYPES OF AGRICULTURE

There are two general types of agriculture in this realm, shifting field and permanent field cultivation.

Shifting Field Agriculture

Shifting cultivation, sometimes called "slash and burn," is the most rudimentary, the most destructive and one of the most extensively used types in Southeast Asia. Since it is severely criticized and discouraged in some countries and illegal in most, the exact number of people making a living in this manner and the acreage cultivated or abandoned in the last twenty years is not known. According to a United Nations and Food and Agriculture Organization report in 1961, there were about 13 million shifting cultivators in Southeast Asia clearing nearly ten million acres of land each year and that the total forest under cultivation was over 112 million acres (more than under permanent cultivation).

This type of agriculture is based on rotating fields rather than rotating crops in the same field. With approximately two-thirds of the realm covered wtith forests, the cultivators have a vast area in which to operate. Although found at very high elevations and often on slopes of over 45% most of the shifting fields are on the less steep slopes, the rolling hills and even on relatively level land. Where transportation lines, such as concrete highways or railways, have cut through a formerly inaccessible area, shifting cultivation may become the pioneer use of the land before sedentary farming develops.

The first step in shifting cultivation is to remove the vegetation. Because these cultivators do not have the tools to remove tall trees with thick trunks and hard wood, a secondary forest cover is preferred where the trees, shrubs and vines have not been growing for over twenty-five years. The shorter the fallow period, the smaller will be the second growth and the easier it will be to chop off the smaller-stemmed trees and bushes and to cut off the tops and branches of larger trees. In areas with monsoon or dry zone climates, this is done during the dry season and the vegetation soon becomes brittle. Then just before the wet season, the material may be set afire where it lays or after it is stacked in small piles. In areas where the rainfall is over eighty inches and there is no dry season, the felled vegetation is left to rot and deteriorate by fungus, bacteria, worms, insects and animal life.

When the land is cleared, as soon as enough soil water is available for plant growth, the crops are planted. Some seeds are sown broadcast by hand and other dropped into holes made by a dibbling stick or hoe, and scattered at random rather than in rows. The fields are so planted that when the crops start growing none of the earth's surface is exposed to direct sunlight or falling rain. The former would accelerate the deterioration of the soil, and the latter start sheet erosion and pack the topsoil, resulting in accelerated evaporation. It is reported that dozens and scores of edible plants are grown by the shifting cultivators in one clearing. Practically all of the crops may be shared with a few farm animals such as chickens, dogs, and pigs.

There are three subtypes of shifting cultivation field farming—nomadic, sedentary and commercial. The nomadic shifting cultivators are wanderers who migrate through the jungles or who may migrate across several countries. They ignore country boundaries. These people not only abandon their fields but also the area in which their fields are located. In contrast with this type the sedentary shifting-field cultivators stay in the same general area generation after generation.

The third type, the commercial, was introduced into the area by Chinese and Europeans. At first coffee and later Hevea rubber seeds were given to the shifting cultivator to plant with his other seeds. In a few years after the clearing was abandoned, the coffee and rubber trees grew and produced. The cultivators were taught how to harvest the coffee and rubber and they became part-time or spare-time laborers.

Some major problems created by shifting cultivators are (1) permanently changing the vegetation type and cover, (2) contributing to the erratic flow of streams and rivers, and (3) accelerating the sediment load of waterways which deposit the slit where it plays havoc with man's multiple use of water and waterways. If the process of slash and burn is repeated too often with too short fallow periods between, then the forest cannot reestablish itself even as poor second growth and grasslands are established.

Permanent Field Agriculture

Permanent field cultivation may be subdivided into (1) subsistence, (2) small holding (acreage) dry-field commercial,(3) small holding irrigated commercial, (4) estate, and (5) market gardening. In 1969, fifteen cultivated field crops were grown on about 107.7 million acres, but data were not available on some crops for some countries, especially North Vietnam. The acreage of tree crops, such as rubber and palms, is not included in the 107.7 million.

Subsistence Farming. About two-thirds of the acreage in sedentary farming is devoted to subsistence farming in contrast with the one-third which involves commercial agriculture. Farmers may sell very little and they cannot sell more than half of their total production to qualify for the subsistence farming classification. These farm families grow what they need and need what they grow to sustain life. They may grow crops on both unirrigated land and irrigated land. Growing crops on unirrigated land is referred to as dry farming and is practiced where water is not available for irrigation or where the land is not ecologically suitable. Many characteristics make land unsuitable for irrigation such as having (1) limestone and sandstone too near the surface, (2) located on too steep slopes, (3) situated on elevated river terraces of older highly-leached alluvium, and (4) containing too much sand and being unable to hold water on or near the surface. By 1930, Java's acreage of dry-field cultivation approximately equalled the irrigated acreage. Nonirrigated land now far exceeds the amount irrigated.

Some dry-land crops are rice, maize, sweet potatoes and yams, sugarcane, oil seeds (such as sesame, groundnuts and soybeans) a variety of beans and peas and cassava. Of course, several of these do well if grown under irrigation but irrigation is not a prerequisite.

Subsistence irrigated farming is concentrated in area (1) adjacent to an on the submarginal fringes of natural flooded areas where water availability is precarious and erratic, (2) interspaced with commercial rice-producing farms but on the floodplain amd deltic soils which are submarginal in their ability to be irrigated, and

(3) where local families or villages have built primitive irrigation systems which at best are inefficient and often become inoperative. Consequently these areas make large contributions to the rice statistics in "acreage planted but not harvested" and in "low yields".

Generally speaking, commercial farming is carried out near the ocean whereas subsistence farming occurs farther inland. The former is associated with the best irrigated areas, has the best transportation systems leading to large cities and ports, and is adjacent to large national metropolitan regions. But it should be borne in mind that the large deltaic areas constructed by the Irrawaddy-Sittang, Chao Phraya and Mekong rivers were not commercial agricultural areas before the construction of the large water control projects under European supervision. Development of nonarable land for commercial cultivation required and still requires heavy capital outlays for (1) clearing forest, jungle and grassland, (2) railway, road and harbor construction and maintenance, and (3) often malaria and pest control.

Other differences in addition to larger crop losses, lower yields and interior spatial location which distinguish subsistence farming from commercial are that commercial farming units are often more than twice as large, the commercial farmers specialize in rice production and neglect other subsistence crops, use more draft animals and hired labor, and use small motor-driven machines both in cultivation and in pumping water.

Commerical Farming. Farm products reaching the large villages, cities, and export ports originate on small-holding irrigated fields, estates (sometimes called plantations) which manage both sedentary and shifting fields, and the market gardens located adjacent to the cities. Estate or plantation agriculture of large acreages owned or rented and managed by large corporations is the antithesis of small holding or small acreage agriculture. These estates took a relatively high percentage of the best cultivated land in a realm where the pressure of population on the arable land in some countries was as high as that in India and mainland China. In the early 1960s, nearly twenty million acres were devoted to plantation crops at a time when there were only about 100 million acres under cultivation. Over ten million acres or over half of this acreage produces rubber. Rubber uses more than twice as much land as coconuts, the second most extensively grown crop. Other estate crops are abaca, sugarcane, tea, coffee, kapok, chinchona, sisal, cassava and tobacco. Estate agriculture, however, is on the decline both in acreage and production.

Throughout Southeast Asia, the Chinese engage in and dominate the market gardening industry, both in production and sale of products. Vegetables are grown on the deltas and floodplains on man-made rounded ridges which provide excellent drainage and more square-foot space. Water may be dipped from ditches between the ridges several times a day and spread on the plots, if they are located in the monsoon climatic region which has a distinct dry season. Often the water is heavily laden with human wastes or it may originate from fishponds or pig-growing platforms built above fishponds. In the latter case, a rough platform is built above a fishpond where the hogs are fed garbage, mill brand, and other foods. What the hogs do no eat as well as their manure drops into the pond to feed the fish. Then the sediment and water from the bottom of the pond is placed on the ridged garden and small fruit plots. Both intercropping and multiple cropping is practiced on the plots. In fact, as soon as one vegetable crop is harvested another is planted. Fruits are grown under similar intensive conditions. Market gardening is the most intensive, most technical and most productive use of land in Southeast Asia. This type of farming is expanding as the cities grow, the standard of living in the cities rise and education influences city people to eat a variety of foods and not rely primarily on rice and fish. Fruits and vegetables do play a much greater role in the lives of Southeast Asians than a century ago or even before World War II.

AGRICULTURAL PRODUCTION

In 1980, the five crops of paddy rice, corn, cassava, groundnuts (in shells) and soybeans were harvested from approximately 146.5 million acres.[6] Of this total paddy rice was harvested on 113 million acres or approximately 77.2% of the total area. The second most important crop, corn, was harvested from 20.7 million acres or over 14.1% of the five crop total land area. Cassava, which ranked third in land area harvested, was grown on only 7.8 million acres. Soybeans and groundnuts were harvested from the remainder. (The statistics used here were taken from the FAO Production Yearbook, 1980, and many statistics for many countries were labelled unofficial or FAO estimates.) Other valuable crops in the economy of individual countries and the world but which occupy small areas of arable land are potatoes and yams, wheat, millet, sugar cane, cotton, kemaf and hemp, vegetables and fruits, and three tree crops: coconuts, rubber and palm oil.

Rubber, not cultivated yearly to produce a crop, is omitted from consideration in the preparation of Fig. 4–2. The acreage of coconuts, often interspersed in a single row with other land uses and also not cultivated yearly, is not reported in acres but its production in metric tons is 23 million. Indonesia and the Philippines are the giants in coconut production. In 1980 they produced over nine and ten times the amount of coconut as the third largest producer, Malaysia.

Production of meat and dairy products has increased slowly in this realm during the last decade.

Rice Economy

The importance of rice in the economy is obvious from the fact that even after three decades of stressing crop diversification, rice remains dominant.

Not only does rice occupy over three-fourths of the land devoted to the five major crops, but the amount of land devoted to its production has increased rapidly since the 1920s. This increase ranges from an average of 38.3 million acres during 1916–20 inclusive to 51.4 milion acres during the period of 1938–40 inclusive[7] and reached an average of 75.3 million acres during 1964–69 with 78.4 million acres recorded in 1969 and 113 million acres in 1980. In addition to this impressive growth in acreage, ton production has been increasing even more rapidly, which means higher yields per acre. The average annual rice production during 1916–20 was 13. 5 million tons, by 1936–40 it increased to 17.5 million, and during 1964–69 production reached 50.8 million tons. In 1980, production reached 81.5 million tons. Some of this increase is due to the Green Revolution, which will be discussed later.

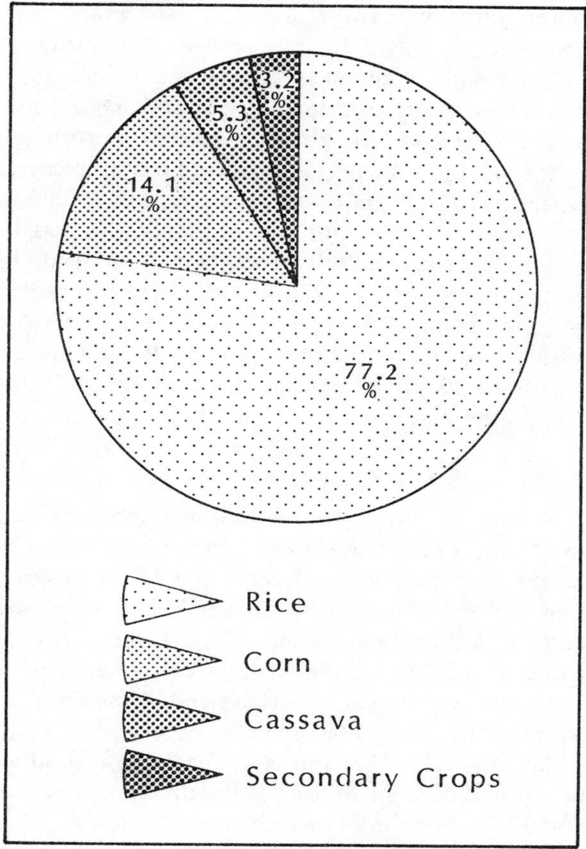

Figure 4-2. Use of Cultivated Land in Southeast Asia.

Maize

Although ranked as a primary crop along with rice, only 14.1 plus percent of the land devoted to the five principal crops was used for corn in 1980, in contrast with over 77% devoted to rice. In 1980, corn was raised on 20 million acres and the yield amounted to approximately 10.6 million metric tons. Corn has proven very popular with non-commercial farmers and is widely grown throughout the realm partly due to its topographic, soil and climatic tolerance. It is suited to a greater number of microhabitats than is rice. Moreover, it is relatively easy to harvest, store and prepare for eating. Generally, it is not preferred to rice but considered better than cassava, and always preferred to going hungry. Although more nutritious than polished rice, it plays "second fiddle" in choice as human food as well as in acreage cultivated and production. Some corn is exported.

Due in part to its large population, Indonesia in the 1960s and 1970s ranked first in corn production, but in 1980 Thailand was a close second with Indonesia producing 3.6 million metric tons, Thailand 3.15 million metric tons and the Philippines 3.11 million metric tons.

Cassava

Cassava ranks third in the big five crops utilizing the largest amount of land from which crops were harvested in the realm in 1980. In that year, cassava was harvested from 8.2 million acres. Cassava as a food is less nutritious than sweet potatoes, corn, groundnuts and soybeans. Consequently, governmental policy has generally been to stress the expansion of the latter four crops and some progress was made, especially in the 1960s. Cassava flour and gruel is consumed by both shifting cultivators and sedentary farm dwellers. Cassava can be grown on more exhausted soils than most crops, and where grown as food it is an indicator of poor soil, poor people and a twelve-month growing season. Fortunately, much of the cassava is not eaten but exported. During 1964–69 Indonesia accounted for 86% of the realm's 4.5 million acres planted to cassava and 81% of the realm's production of 14.4 million metric tons. In 1980, Indonesia harvested cassava from 3.5 million acres and harvested 39.9% of the realm's crop. But Thailand harvested 40.5% of the realm's crop in 1980 from 7.9 million acres.

Secondary Crops

Secondary crops are groundnuts (peanuts) and soybeans, each being harvested on less than 2% of the harvested area of the big five crops grown most extensively in 1980 in the realm (Fig. 4–2) and all other field crops. Groundnuts only account for 2.3% of the realm's cultivated land in 1969. In that year, Burma and Indonesia accounted for over 72% of the acreage and 37 of the yield. In 1980, Thailand was the largest producer of groundnuts, harvesting 1.0 million metric tons and 37% of the 1980 realm's production.

Tree Crops

In both acreage occupied and annual metric ton yield, rubber and coconuts are the primary tree crops. There are also some specialized crops occupying much less land and grown in fewer countries, such as palm oil, cinchona, nutmeg, kapok and cocoa. Rubber is king among the tree crops, ranking high as a utilizer of arable land after rice and maize. In 1965, Southeast Asia produced nearly 1.9 million metric tons of crude rubber. This increased to nearly 2.7 million metric tons in 1967. When one mentions Southeast Asia, people generally associate three crops with it—rice, rubber and coconut palms. Coconut palm is planted on nearly one-fifth of the total cultivated area in the Philippines where coconut oil and copra provide the largest source of export earnings[8] and this realm provides the lion's share of the world's annual import of coconut oil and copra. During the period 1964–69, the average yield of coconuts was nearly 2.14 million metric tons, and in 1980 the realm's yield was 3.3 million metric tons, with 60% of the yield in the Philippines and 29% in Indonesia. Land suitable for commercial coconut production is limited. Higher yields come from trees grown close to the area of alluvial and sandy soils which are adequately drained, and where 80 inches of rain fall occurs annually; the trees need to be a few feet above high water.

The oil palm, a native of Africa, is now grown in both Sabah (East Malaysia) and Indonesia. Malaysia, by producing 550 million metric tons in 1980, accounted for approximately 81% of the realm's production. In the same year, Indonesia produced 120 million metric tons.

THE GREEN REVOLUTION

The Green Revolution refers to growing new breed varieties of crops such as rice and maize which if properly cultivated could greatly increase yields per acre. Its potentials in this realm and the world have been presented in glowing terms. It is to end the (1) horror of famine and (2) the race between food production and population increase, thereby postponing again a Malthusian population disaster. The higher yields are to break the chain of rural poverty for farmers and free the world from hunger. The revolution is to enable agriculture to become a major economic generator of wealth, which can be used to enhance industrial development and raise the standard of living.

Perhaps the greatest limitation to the continued spread and adoption of the high yielding rice varieties in Southeast Asia, is the small amount of land ecologically suitable for their growth. Securing high yields from these miracle varieties involves more than planting different kinds of seed. Such yields are the result of a complete production package which includes (1) planting the special breed seeds; (2) strict water management of irrigation and drainage; (3) application of the right amount of fertilizer at the right time; (4) application of pesticides, insecticides, and fungicides; (5) removal of weeds by hand and machinery; and (6) harvesting as soon as ripe.

Careful water management is especially difficult in this realm. First, much of the land planted to rice is not irrigated. The high percent of land which is irrigated depends upon natural flooding and/or primititive tools used to get floodwaters from the ditches. Many small village irrigation systems are quite crude. Some of the old nationally-built ones have gravity systems and were not constructed to provide precise water control. Before land in these old systems can be used the latter must be modernized in order to provide sophisticated water controls. Even some of the governmental irrigation and/or multiple use water projects built since World War II, leave much to be desired in precise water management either in irrigation or drainage. Some irrigation engineers in Southeast Asia appear to concentrate on multiple use dams designed for delivery of water to the main canal systems, and for electricity and flood control and neglect the secondary distribution system needed to take the water to the fields and then, near the end of the growing season, to drain excess water from these fields. Moreover, high costs in constructing new irrigation projects will limit their development especially in the underdeveloped countries. Because of inadequate precision water control and the scarcity of money with which to add fertilizers, to apply insecticides, herbicides, and fungacides, to remove weeds by hand and with machinery, there are millions and millions of acres in Southeast Asia without a suitable ecological habitat for the high-yielding Green Revolution varieties. Drainage near the end of the growing season is so important because the new rice varieties are short-stemmed and, if harvesting is delayed and rains come, germination of the seeds in the panicles can result.

Other major barriers are (1) the large acreage devoted to subsistance farming, (2) many of the new rice varieties do not appeal to consumers, and (3) the new type of farming displaces or pushes aside religious beliefs and ritual practices carried on for centuries in some areas. Explicit in the instructions on how to grow the new miracle varieties are that production cannot be left to God but that man is responsible for the use of the seeds and whether their yields are successful or not.

Furthermore, small land-holding commercial farmers with land ecologically suitable for growing the new varieties may not have the farming skills and know-how to cultivate them and/or they may not be willing to retool their farming skills and practices. Or if they are, there may not be an extension educational system where they can turn for help. These new varieties require a higher order of expertise in cultivation.

By calling attention to some of the barriers to rapid adoption, and to problems involved with the new varieties the writer does not mean to imply that goals of the Green Revolution will not be attained. But to keep its aims in proper perspective it should be pointed out that during the crop year 1968–1969 less than 13 million acres of rice land in South and Southeast Asia were devoted to the new varieties and this amounted to only about 6% of the total rice land harvested. Southeast Asia has increased its total production of rice from 48.8 million tons in 1964 to 53.3 million tons in 1969. The Revolution was expected to convert the Philippines, where the new varieties were more quickly adopted, from the status of being a rice-importing country to a rice-exporting one. Its rice production did increase from near 4 million metric tons in 1964 to about 4.8 million metric tons in 1967. However, rice production dropped to 4.4 million metric tons in 1968 and to 4 million metric tons in 1969. The long-term effect of the Green Revolution remains to be seen.[8]

AGRICULTURAL PROSPECTS IN THE EIGHTIES

The last years of the 1970s provide ample evidence of two basic concepts. One generalization is that there is considerable potential for expansion of food grains production in this region and the second is that there is continuing fragility of this potential in the face of adverse weather conditions. The production gains of recent years are in part the positive results of efforts made by some developing countries of the region to channel substantially more production. One of the most successful of these rice production schemes is the Masagana/99 program which helped the Philippines to achieve self-sufficency in 1978. Malaysia in the early 1980s had almot turned to a rice self-sufficiency level. Almost 50% of Burma's rice-land is given to HYV.

However, growth of cereal output during the 1970s were below the rates of expansion recorded in the second half of the 1960s. In the future the expansion of food cereal production will have to depend more and more on the means of intensification that have become associated with the 'green revolution' which are: wider use of 1. high yielding varieties (HYV) of seeds, 2. of fertilizers and, 3. of irrigation. International authorities believe the most important single determinant of the security of annual rice production levels is the extent of irrigated land. An adequate assessment of the extent of irrigated land in individual countries is virtually impossible because a satisfactory comparable definition of irrigated land does not exist.

During the decade of the 1980s the prospects are good for wheat production to increase in Indonesia; palm oil production to expand in Indonesia and Malaysia; native rubber to increase in production in Indonesia, Malaysia and Thailand; maize production to expand in Thailand and the Philippines; and the realm's coconut palm to increase in production.

Footnote References

[1]*United Nations Demographic Yearbook*, (1979), pp. 252–254.

[2]Thomas Frank Barton, "Rural and Urban Dwellers of Southeast Asia," *The Journal of Geography*, Vol. 64 (1965), pp. 113–122.

[3]This term was applied to a regional division of the Southeast Asian realm by Thomas Frank Barton in a post-World War II regional scheme produced as a substitute for the pre-World War II colonial political division. Refer to pp. 561–562 in *World Geography*, 3rd edition, edited by John W. Morris for McGraw-Hill Book Company, New York, 1972.

[4]Thomas Frank Barton, "Thailand's Rainfall Distribution by Geographic Regions," *The Journal of Geography*, Vol. 64 (1962), p. 118.

[5]Pierre Gourou, *The Tropical World* (London: Longman, Green and Co., 1952), p. 17.

[6]United Nations *Economic Survey of Asia and the Pacific*, (1979), p. 25. United Nations *FAO Production Yearbook*, (1980), Vol. 34.

[7]E.H.G. Dobby, *Southeast Asia* (London: The University of London Press, Ltd., 1958), p. 353.

[8]A more extensive analysis of the green revolution appears in Thomas Frank Barton's , "The Green Revolution in Southeast Asia," *Journal of Bangladesh National Geographical Association*, Vol. I (1973), pp. 30–38.

Chapter 5

The Economic Infrastructure

William A. Withington

The development of a firm basic infrastructure is vital in any region or nation if it is to participate in the worldwide systems of economies, societies, and political units. A strong infrastructure is also needed for internal development as well as external relationships. The word "infrastructure" can be defined or used in many ways. In this discussion the term "economic infrastructure" is defined broadly to encompass not only the various forms of transportation but also mineral extraction, energy production, and manufacturing.

This chapter is concerned with spatial variations in the economic infrastructure of Southeast Asia since 1945. Of equal importance are the forces which have been most influential in stimulating or retarding growth of the economic infrastructure in Southeast Asia as a region and in its national or more localized subdivisions.

TRANSPORTATIONAL SYSTEMS OF SOUTHEAST ASIA

Southeast Asia is served by transportational elements which in combination provide accessibility ranging from relatively strong to very weak. These elements included sea and air routes and their nodal seaports and airports, navigable inland waterways on rivers or lakes, railways and highways, including those built parallel to oil and gas pipelines as service or access roads.[1] Transportational inaccessibility in Southeast Asia includes all areas more than about 9 miles from major transportation nodes or arteries.[2] A map of transportational inaccessibility in Southeast Asia emphasizes the dichotomy between the few areas of continuous accessibility, and broad areas having limited or no accessibility (Fig. 5-1). Although these latter areas may be served by local trails, paths, or seasonally usable roads or waterways, they are distant from seaport or airport nodes and from major year-round navigable rivers, railway lines or highway routes (Fig. 5-2 and Fig. 5-3).[3]

The Southeast Asian areas of greatest transportational accessibility, also having the most intensive networks are few in number. The principal areas are Java in Indonesia, the western plains and foothills of West Malaysia, the Irrawaddy river lowlands south of Mandalay, the central plain of Thailand, the Tonkin or Red river delta of North Vietnam, the lower Mekong river plain, and the central Luzon plain east of Manila Bay in the Philippines. Elsewhere, localized zones of moderate accessibility and lesser network intensity are the estate zone of northeastern Sumatra, the densely populated plains and uplands of West Sumatra, and the hinterlands or larger seaports, particularly Singapore, Ho Chi Minh City, Ujungpandan in the southwestern arm of Sulawesi, Kota Kinabalu (formerly Jesselton) in Sabah, East Malaysia, and Davao, Cebu, and Zamboanga in the Philippines.

The broader accessibility and more intensive networks of transportation relate partly to physical features and partly to historical or recent influences. The areas of greatest accessibility and intensity are broad plains, with deep rivers and indented coastlines, which were indigenous core areas of political development. The transportational accessibility of early core areas was reinforced by colonial establishment of trading ports and later administrative networks. For the moderately accessible areas, demand for their primary raw materials served as a stimulus to transportational development. Agricultural, fishery, mineral and forestry raw materials come from the hinterlands of the major ports noted.

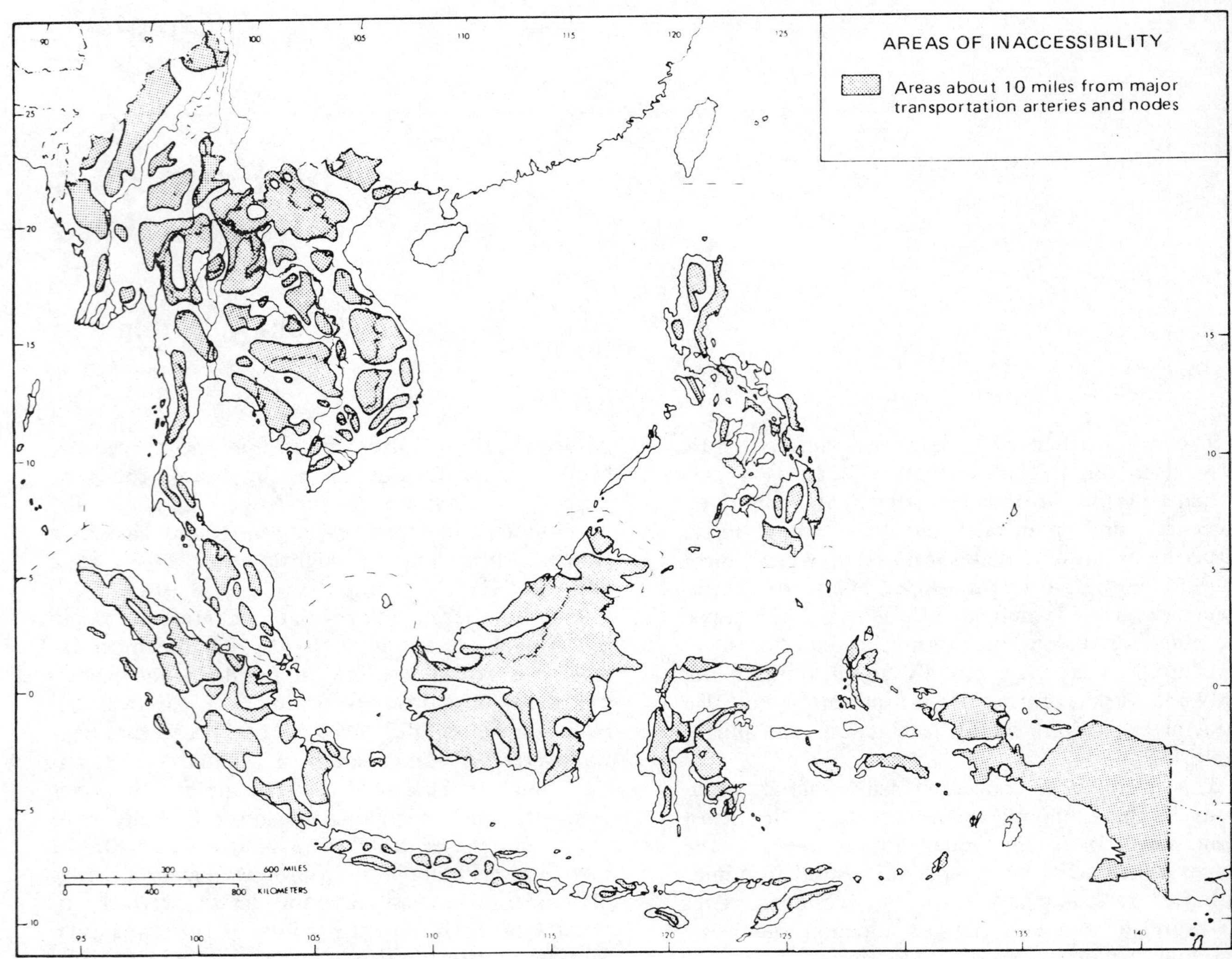

Figure 5-1. Areas of Inaccessibility in Southeast Asia.

In contrast, broad areas of Southeast Asia, including some core areas, have low or very low transportational accessibility (Fig. 5-1, Fig. 5-2, and Fig. 5-3). Even in such densely populated, political core areas as Java, western Malaysia, the Irrawaddy valley of Burma, the central plain of Thailand, the Mekong lowlands and delta in Cambodia and southern Vietnam, and the Tonkin delta of northern Vietnam, considerable areas are unserved by modern transportation. However, the typical inaccessible areas of Southeast Asia have one or more environmental handicaps. These include hill-land and mountainous districts with little level land; broad swampy areas lacking navigable waterways; heavily forested plains; and many grassland areas. Despite transportational inaccessibility, many such areas are moderately to densely populated. These areas are served by bullock carts, bicycles, or trishaws, small motor vehicles, or shallow-draft boats.[4]

Transportation Systems After World War II

Despite wartime destruction or deterioration, Southeast Asia, immediately after World War II, depended upon the transportation systems developed in previous eras. The six key elements of these transportation systems were (1) a few major seaports, plus numerous coastal, smaller ports; (2) navigable inland waterways notably including the Mekong river, the Red river, the Chao Phraya and its many tributaries, the Irrawaddy, and a number of streams and lakes in the islands of Sumatra, Borneo (Kalimantan), and Mindanao;[5] (3) airports serving the larger cities and also used as military bases; (4) several segmented railway

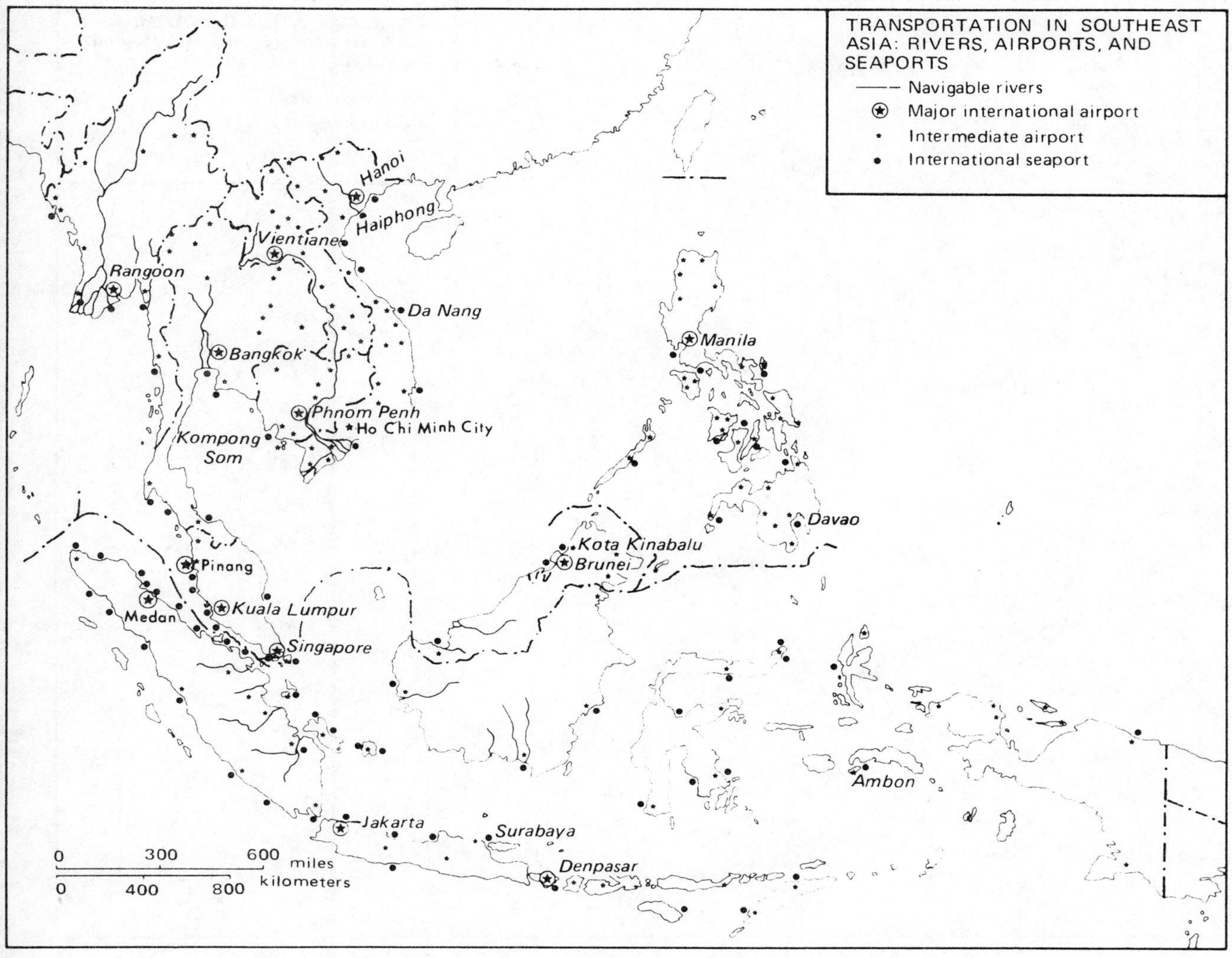

Figure 5-2. Transportation in Southeast Asia: Rivers, Airports, and Seaports.

systems;[6] (5) open networks of paved highways usable in all seasons; and (6) oil and gas pipelines connecting fields with refineries or exporting ports in Burma, Brunei, and Indonesia, Malaysia, and Thailand.

During this postwar period several problems reduced the effectiveness of Southeast Asia's transportational infrastructure. Among these were the several previous years of reduced maintenance, if not destruction, from World War II or independence conflicts; increased silting in many navigable rivers and harbor areas, as on Java;[7] antiquated equipment and a lack of spare parts for replacements;[8] and a general shortage of capital or knowledgeable planning for redevelopment or expansion of transportation.

Another critical difficulty arose during the early years of independence. Each independent state wished to control its own transportation systems. As a result, foreign companies were taken over, as in Burma, Indonesia, and the Indochina states.[9] The transition to government-controlled transportation, while desirable from the local viewpoint, resulted in reduced availability of equipment, losses of knowledgeable directors and maintenance personnel, and shortages of desperately needed capital.

The transportational infrastructure, considered sufficient for prewar needs, proved to be very inadequate for Southeast Asia's growing needs in an era of rapid technological and political change. Examples included the needs for strengthened

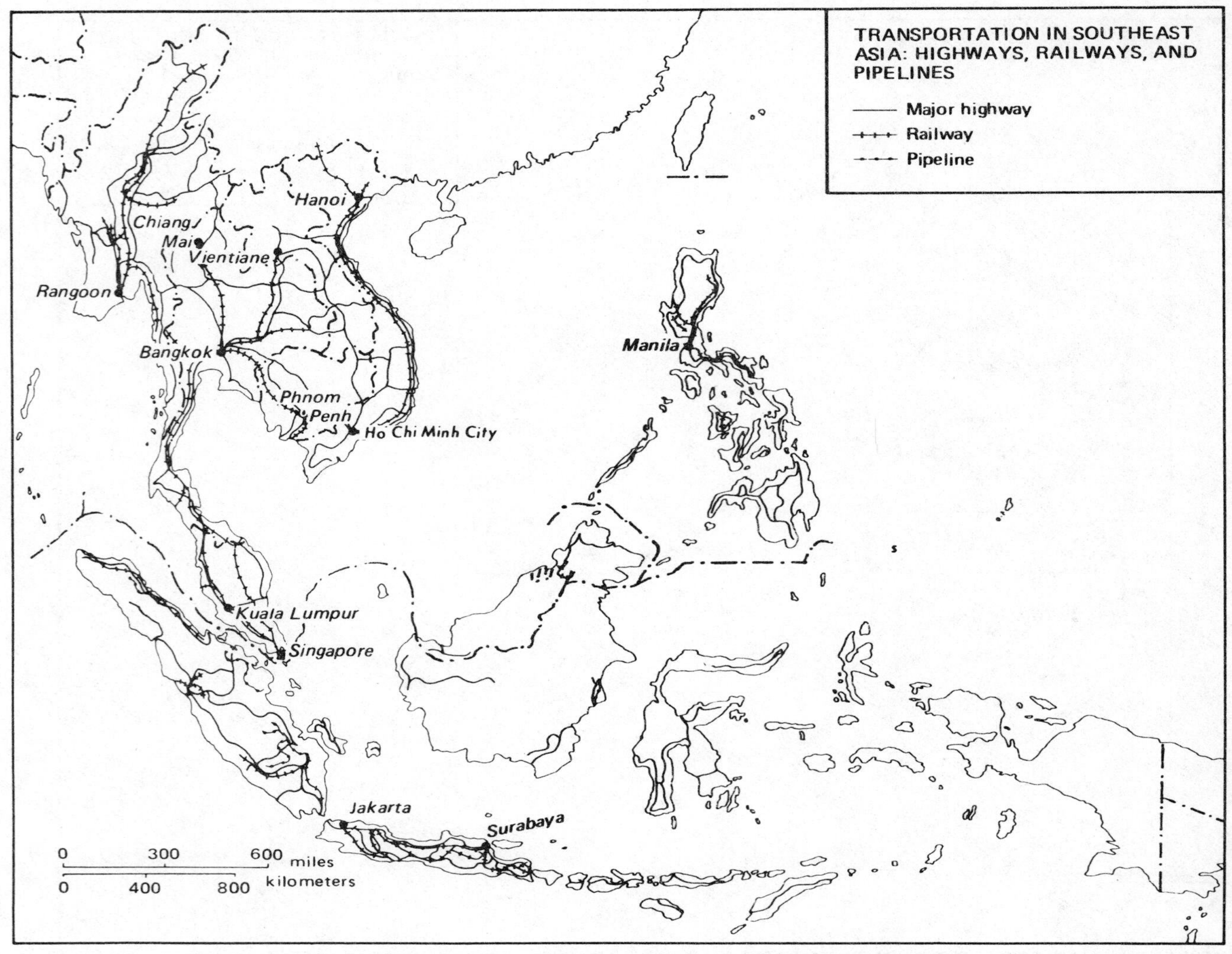

Figure 5-3. Transportation in Southeast Asia: Highways, Railways, and Pipelines.

railways roadbeds and bridges to allow use of heavier diesel-electric engines; for longer runways and improved control equipment at airports to handle the more complex, faster aircraft; for deeper harbors and more specialized equipment capable of servicing deeper-draft larger ships and containerized cargoes; and for wider highways with improved roadbeds to handle increasing volumes of heavier trucks, buses and passenger motor vehicles. Many navigable waterways became less useful, both because of downstream silting problems and of ocean vessels too large to reach upstream ports.[10]

Transportation in the 1980s

Southeast Asia's present transportational systems have several primary elements, illustrating aspects of both continuity and change (Fig. 5-2). These are:

1. The long-established system of major and minor ports along the seacoasts and larger navigable rivers is still functioning. However, international and intraregional imports and exports are increasingly handled by a few key ports. Largest among these are the national capitals or their outports: Singapore, Bangkok plus deeper water outports immediately to the southeast on the Bight of Bangkok, Manila, Tanjung Priok for Jakarta, Klang for Kuala Lumpur, Rangoon, Saigon (Ho Chi Minh City), and Haiphong. Other large ports are regional ones or those handling specialized commodities. Belawan, in Medan in northeastern Sumatra, handles estate crop exports and diversified imports, George Town (Pinang) in Peninsular Malaysia is a free port, and Batangas, south of Manila, imports petroleum for its refineries. Expanding fleets of

container-cargo ships, supertankers for oil and shipments of LNG (liquified natural gas) are further influencing trends towards specialized port facilities.

2. A limited number of international airports capable of handling the largest commercial jet aircraft serve the Southeast Asian region.[11] These airports, with few exceptions, are near national capital cities. The international airport at Denpasar, Bali, emphasizing tourist traffic, is a notable exception.
3. A number of major rivers provide upstream penetration for both oceangoing and fresh-water shipping. Projects such as that in the Mekong river basin are likely to expand those river waterways deemed most vital to the region's development. Many areas, as in much of Borneo's interior, continue to depend on water transport for most surface movement.
4. The Phnom Penh to Kompong Som rail line is one of the few new railways constructed since World War II. A continuation of the present railway systems in most areas, strengthened for newer more efficient equipment, plus a few extensions to tie in areas not now served, seems likely. Three useful new lines would be: (a) a Saigon–Phnom Penh connection; (b) a Burma–Thailand linkage, such as that attempted by the Japanese in World War II; and (c) a linkage of West Sumatra's railway lines eastward to Pakanbaru or the coast of eastern Sumatra, also attempted forty years ago by the Japanese.[12]
5. Highways have received the greatest postwar attention. These arteries have had the heaviest pressure of increased traffic volumes for both public and private use. This pressure has not been eased, even by governmental attempts to limit long-distance freight shipments solely to railways. The continuing need by governments for rapid vehicle movement by highway, of local and intercity bus and trucking lines, and of increasingly numerous private motor vehicles suggesting that Southeast Asian highway systems, including the developing Asian Highway routes in the region will require constant attention and improvement.[13]
6. The petroleum and natural gas pipelines are being extended into wider networks. A future expansion, now present in limited form, would provide petroleum and natural gas supplies within urban areas and to major electric-generating plants, at least in those nations having petroleum and natural gas resources.[14]

Developmental and Retarding Forces

A variety of forces have led to transportational improvements in some instances, or have resulted in stagnation and even retrogression of the transportational infrastructure in others. Forces favoring transportational improvement are many.

Nationalism. This force involves the desire of indigenous peoples to improve the internal linkages of their country or area and to have extra-regional linkages when these are not perceived as actual or potential threats. The expansion of railway, highway, airport, and seaport services within Thailand are examples, with extra-regional linkages southward into Malaysia, southeastward into Kampuchea, and northward and eastward to the borders of Laos.[15] Within Indonesia the peoples of several regions have attempted transportational improvements in their own areas by using central government's monetary allocations made through the Five-Year Plans.

Modernization. With increasing knowledge of other world areas, peoples and governments in Southeast Asia have begun to utilize the modern equipment and facilities in use elsewhere. In the immediate postwar years Japanese reparations contributed newer trucks and buses and other equipment; more recently, a broader range of transportational equipment has come from Japan and other producers through trade or aid agreements. Air-conditioned buses in larger cities and twinjet passenger air-craft for middle-range flights are examples.

Availability of Development Capital. This capital, from domestic, regional, foreign, and world agency sources, has allowed Southeast Asian nations to upgrade their existing transportation systems and equipment. The World Bank and the Asia Development Bank, in recent years, have made considerable funds available for transportation projects, such as Indonesia's Trans-Sumatran Highway.[16]

Competition among Major World Powers. Although some of this competition provided military equipment, much of the competition has been directed into development projects in Southeast Asian nations, including transportational improvements. Even aid originally associated with military projects, such as airport, seaport, and highway improvements, has usually expanded the transportational infrastructure of the areas where that aid was applied. The airports, highways, and new seaports of Thailand were built with American funds.

Negative or stagnating forces have also had an impact on Southeast Asia's transportational infrastructure.

Independence. With the former colonial powers no longer providing funds and personnel for transportation management and development, the newly independent national systems sometimes were inefficiently operated. In part, this low level of effectiveness also reflected several years of wartime disruption.

Nationalization and Nationalism. The intense nationalism leading to independence also led to expropriation of many segments of national transportational systems, notably railway companies, airlines, and coastal or interisland sea carrier companies. The takeover of transportation companies was complete in Burma and all of Vietnam, but only slightly less so in Indonesia. Problems arising from shortages of spare parts, of new equipment, and of inexperience in management usually resulted in periods of lessened service for the areas affected.

Limited Capital. Both of the previously mentioned forces of independence and of nationalism reduced the sources and amounts of investment capital available for maintenance or improvement of transportation. When foreign capital became available it often came from nations unfamiliar with the specific problems of the Southeast Asian nation receiving it.[17]

Internal Strife and Warfare. Since the end of World War II and also since independence for many Southeast Asian nations, localized ethnic, religious and political turmoil has resulted in destruction or interruption of transportational systems. Within Indonesia, Moslem groups demanding a theocratic state during the 1950s disrupted several areas, as did the 1958–1961 P.R.R.I. rebellion centered in parts of Sumatra and Sulawesi.[18]

All the successor nations of former French Indochina, North and South Vietnam, the Cambodian Republic , and Laos, have suffered many years of disruption and destruction, reducing transportational effectiveness within each region due to fighting, bombing and guerrilla attacks. Outlying national areas in Burma, Thailand and the Philippines have had periods of disruption, as did Peninsular Malaysia throughout the 1950s.[19]

Nondevelopmentally Oriented Leadership. Several of Southeast Asia's newly independent states were led for varying periods by leaders who emphasized political or military goals, usually at the expense of rational development planning. Indonesia's transportation systems received little developmental support until the late 1960s Burma's political situation has provided only limited developmental support for its transportational needs.

SUMMARY OF TRANSPORTATIONAL INFRASTRUCTURE

Southeast Asia has an extremely uneven pattern of transportational infrastructure (Fig. 5-2 and 5-3). The most heavily used routes are the sea routes along which large volumes of freight and some passengers moved between ports in Southeast Asia and to outside regions. The 347 million tons of trade goods loaded and unloaded in 1980 increased by more than sixfold the 1953 level of 56 million tons (Table 5-1). Leaders in sea trade are Indonesia with 32.2% and Singapore with 23.7% of Southeast Asia's tonnage. The seaports serving these trade routes form one set of nodes, scattered along the coasts and upstream on several large rivers. Besides Singapore, major ports include Bangkok, Tanjung Priok for Jakarta, Manila, and Rangoon.[20] Klang which serves Kuala Lumpur in Peninsular Malaysia, Kampong Som serving Phnom Penh in Kampuchea, and Haiphong represent new or enlarged ports.

A second set of nodes, increasing dramatically since the Second World War, are the major airports. Each nation characteristically has an international airport, plus a series of intermediate and smaller airports served by a national airline company. Southeast Asia airports handle considerable volumes of passengers and some freight (Table 5-1). Singapore had the highest per capita volume of 6,133 passenger-kilometers. Malaysia, the Philippines, and Thailand were next with 121–375; and all others were below the realm's average of nearly 115. These levels, if allowance is made for far lower figures for some of the Indochinese nations, reflect levels of economic development within Southeast Asia.

Land transportation is by highway or railway, though the increasing network of pipelines serves the specialized bulk freight needs of the major petroleum and natural gas fields. Most railway lines form internal networks, segmented as in the Philippines and Indonesia by islands or differences in gauges. The most intensive Southeast Asian network is that on Java in Indonesia with 56 miles of track per 1,000 square miles of territory, ten times Indonesia's ratio and eight times the realm's figure. The longest, international railway line extends from Singapore to Kompong

TABLE 5-1A
Transportational Elements and Use in the Southeast Asian Realm

Country	Railway Length (Km)	Paved Highway Length (Km)	Length (Km. per 1000 Sq. Km. Area) Railway	Highway	Motor Vehicles (1,000)
Brunei	19	725	3.3	126	50.6
Burma	4,345	8,206	6.4	12	82.2
Democratic Kampuchea	612(?)	2,600 ('73)	3.4	14.4	38.3 ('72)
Indonesia	6,637	57,570(?)	3.5	30.2(?)	1,145
Laos	0	622	0.0	2.6	16.5
Malaysia	2,236	21,021	6.7	63.2	949.7 ('79)
Peninsular	2,082	18,070	15.8	137.3	806
Sabah	154	1,417	2.0	18.6	83.2
Sarawak	0	1,534	0.0	12.3	60.5
Singapore	38	484	61.5	783	249.0
Philippines	1,069	17,500	3.6	58.3	890.6
Vietnam	2,806	12,075(e)	8.4	36.3	200(e)
Thailand	3,735	21,741	7.2	42.3	750
Southeast Asia	21,497	142,544	4.8	31.8	4,371.9

Source: United Nations, *Statistical Yearbook for Asia and the Pacific, 1980*, Bangkok: December, 1980.

TABLE 5-1B

Country	Ocean-going Shipping Tonnages: Total 1980 (1,000 met. t.)	Per cent of Region	Domestic and International Civil Aviation Passenger: Passenger Km. (millions)	Per Capita passenger km.
Brunei	25,044	7.2	n.d.	n.d.
Burma	1,780	0.5	259.7	8
Democratic Kampuchea	(550–1975)	0.2	42	7
Indonesia	111,539	32.2	8,680	59
Laos	0	0	22	6
Malaysia	50,696	14.6	4,290.1	300
Singapore	82,287	23.7	14,720	6,133
Thailand	31,006	8.9	5,757.4	122
Philippines	38,895	11.2	6,031	126
Vietnam	(5,073–1973)	(1.5)	n.d.	n.d.
Southeast Asia	346,870	100.0	39,802.2	112

Source: United Nations, *Statistical Yearbook for Asia and the Pacific, 1980*, (Bangkok: 1980); Far Eastern Economic Review, *Asia Yearbook 1981*, (Hong Kong: December, 1980).

Som in Kampuchea via Peninsular Malaysia, Thailand, and Phnom Penh (Fig. 5-3). Next longest is the war-shattered north-south system within United Vietnam. The Burmese railways, reaching over 600 miles from Myitkyina southward to Ye on the Tenasserim Coast, form a separate system offset to the west.

For local and middle-distance land transportation, the expanding and intensifying highway network of Southeast Asia is increasingly used. Paved highways stretch across nearly 90,000 miles, seven times the length of all railways (Table 5-1). Within the realm there are approximately 32 miles of paved highway for about every 1,000 square miles of land area as compared to less than five miles of railway. The most intensive networks of good roads serve the national core areas (Fig. 5-3). The Philippines, Malaysia, Indonesia, and Thailand have more than 150,000 motor vehicles each (Table 5-1). Vehicle concentrations are in the principal cities, usually the capital and the several largest regional centers. Only Singapore, with about one vehicle for every ten people, has a vehicle-population ratio as low as in some Western nations.[21] Public vehicles, such as buses and trucks, provide a large share of highway transportation movement within and between cities in Southeast Asia.

ENERGY AND MINERAL RESOURCES OF SOUTHEAST ASIA

Hydroelectric power, fuel minerals, and other metallic and nonmetallic minerals together constitute the mineral and energy resource sector of the economic infrastructure. From early historic times, Southeast Asia has had the reputation of being a vast storehouse of these natural resources, even though total population has been limited in contrast to many other world areas.[22] The uneven availability of known and developed mineral and energy resources in Southeast Asia continues to be a persistent theme (Fig. 5-4).

Mining Infrastructure and Mineral Resources

The diversity of Southeast Asia's mineral resources has contributed to local and regional development of the economic infrastructure. Indigenous peoples, joined later by others from outside the region, evaporated or mined salt, quarried a variety of rocks for building needs, mined precious stones and metals, and extracted fuel minerals.[23] Although at least two centuries ago, Chinese came into Southeast Asia to mine its tin, large-scale modern mining began only in the late 19th or early 20th centuries.[24] Examples of this larger-scale, industrial mining were British and Dutch tin mining operations, Dutch coal production in Java, Sumatra, and petroleum production in Java, Sumatra, Borneo, and Burma.

The presence of exploitable minerals led to rapid expansion of a local area's economic infrastructure. Networks of roads, railroads and ports, new settlements, and major processing facilities were established to search for, mine, and then export these minerals. Peninsular Malaysian cities such as Kuala Lumpur and Ipoh originated as tin mining camps, while much of Pakanbaru's postwar growth in east-central Sumatra has resulted from the large oil fields exploited nearby. This latter area, with its oil-field communities, roads, pipelines, pumping stations, and new port facilities, for massive petroleum production, refining, and export, is an illustration of the complex impact of modern mining on the previously existing landscape.[25] At another level, the sensitivity of modern mining to local and international conditions has been exemplified in Burma, through government changes, nationalization of mineral production facilities, and at times declines in most mining operations.

While Southeast Asian mineral resources are diverse, known reserves and source areas are limited for coal and iron, two of the three principal industrial minerals (Table 5-2). Only Vietnam currently mines more than a million tons of coal; only the Philippines and Malaysia have mined more than a million tons apiece of iron ore since 1950. Petroleum, the third principal industrial mineral, has been relatively abundant, with onshore and offshore indications of still more reserves. Other minerals known and mined in some quantity in Southeast Asia are tin, nickel, chromite, titanium, bauxite, gold, copper, mercury, antimony, fluorspar, tungsten, phosphates, and lesser quantities of precious metals and stones (Table 5-2).

Energy Minerals

Southeast Asia's petroleum output in the 1980s accounts for nearly 3.0% of the world's output.[26] The known oil resources of Burma, Brunei, and particularly of Indonesia comprised a major need for the oil-deficient Japanese Empire during World War II.[27] Recently increased output, discoveries, and assumed potentialities for oil in shallow offshore areas have further enhanced Southeast Asia's significance as a petroleum source.

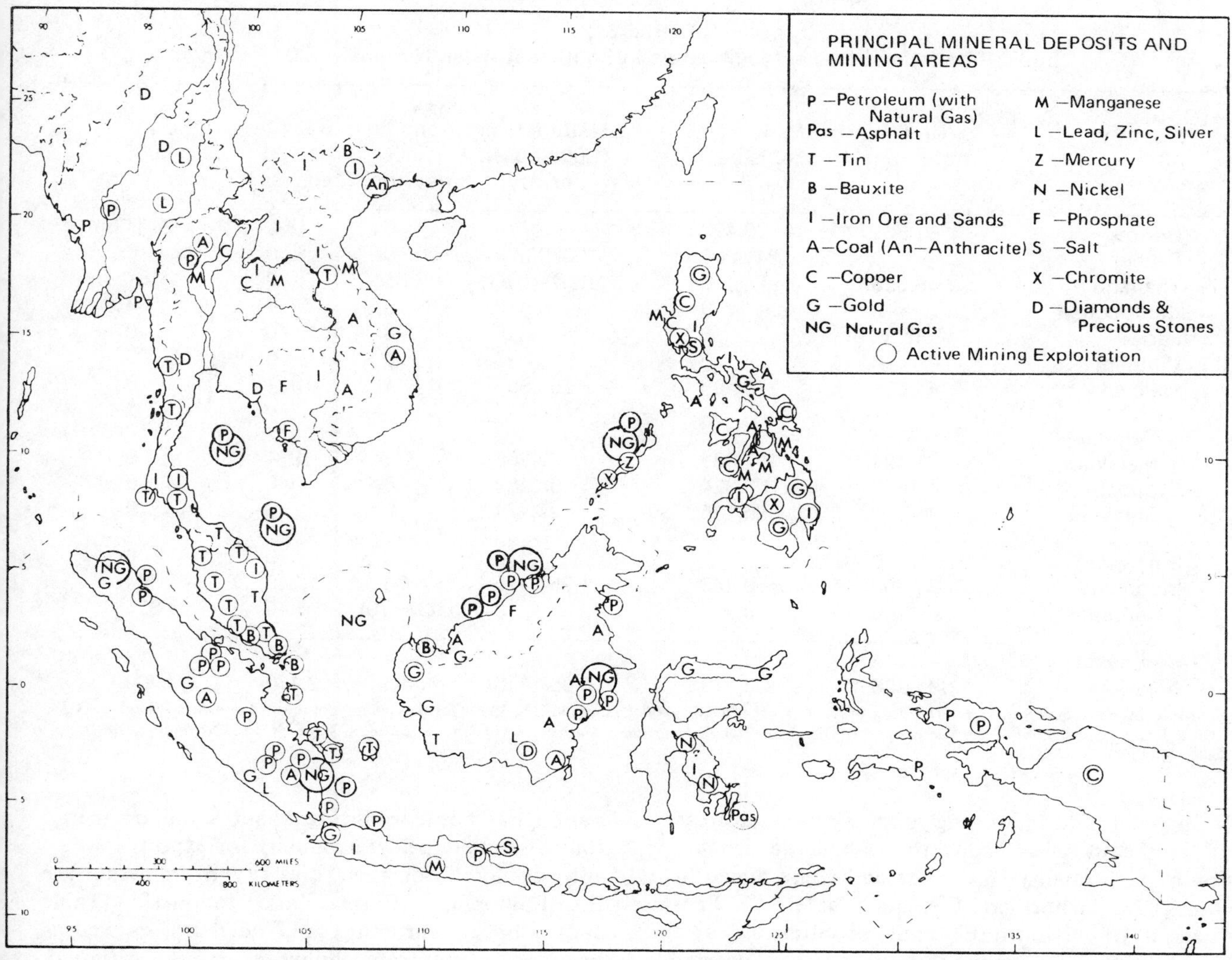

Figure 5-4. Principle Mineral Deposits and Mining Areas in Southeast Asia.

Indonesia, Brunei, and Burma are still the three principal petroleum-producing nations of Southeast Asia (Table 5-2). Sarawak, Peninsular Malaysia, and the Gulf of Thailand have recently begun to produce oil also. Fringing continental shelves of these and other nations, including Peninsular Malaysia and Vietnam, are actively being explored for petroleum, with the strong likelihood of sizeable offshore oil reserves. The leading fields are in east-central Sumatra, where the Minas Field alone produced half of the Indonesian total. The offshore fields in the Java Sea north of Jakarta is now one of the most productive area in Indonesia, behind southeastern and east-central Sumatran fields, but ahead of fields in northeastern Sumatra, eastern Kalimantan, Ceram Island, and Irian Jaya.[28] Brunei production in recent years has come increasingly from offshore fields (90% in 1981), with adjacent Sarawak (East Malaysia) sharing this new source in the South China sea. Burma's production, seriously curtailed by World War II damage to production facilities, has increased moderately in recent years to supply domestic needs.

Until recently, natural gas was produced and used largely within the Southeast Asian oil fields. In Indonesia, a large urea fertilizer factory in Palembang, southeastern Sumatra, has used gas from a nearby field for both fuel and raw material needs since 1964. A small carbon black plant uses natural gas from fields in northeastern Sumatra. Increased natural gas use has been exemplified since 1970 by Liquified Natural Gas (LNG) facilities completed in Brunei and in both Kalimantan and northern Sumatra. These facilities supply exports to Japan and South Korea.

TABLE 5-2
Production of Selected Minerals in Southeast Asian Nations, 1980

Country	Tin Ore (met. tons)	Petroleum (bbls/day)	Natural Gas (1,000 cu. ft. per day)	Iron Ore (1,000 met. ton)	Bauxite (1,000 met. ton)	Coal (1,000 met. tons)
Burma	866	28,490	n.d.	0	0	21 ('78)
Brunei	0	241,000	1,060,000	0	0	0
Thailand	46,526	0	(started '81)	85	0	1,487
Kampuchea	0	0	0	0	0	0
Laos	600 ('79)	0	0	0	0	0
Vietnam	0	0	0	0	0	5,300
Malaysia	61,404	275,498	254,893	371	921	0
Peninsular Malaysia	61,404	117,039	72,266	371	921	0
Sabah	0	63,324	55,153	0	0	0
Sarawak	0	95,135	127,474	0	0	0
Singapore	0	0	0	0	0	0
Indonesia	31,900	1,568,268	1,954,425	78	1,249	304
Philippines	0	9,917	0	3,933 ('79)	0	320
Southeast Asia	141,296	2,123,173	3,057,318	4,485	2,170	7,280

Source: United Nations *Statistical Yearbook of Asia and the Pacific 1980.* (Bangkok: UN, 1980); for petroleum and natural gas data: Fletcher, G.L., "Oil & Gas Developments in the Far East in 1981", *American Association of Petroleum Geologists, Bulletin,* V. 66, No. 11 (November, 1982), pp. 2360–2482.

Coal is found in varying grades in several areas of Southeast Asia. Today the only large production of high quality coal is the anthracite mined in Quang Yen in northern Vietnam (Table 5-2). Production of bituminous coal in Sumatra and Kalimantan has declined sharply from prewar levels when it had much greater domestic and export value.[29] Elsewhere, lignite is produced in northern Thailand and small amounts of low-grade bituminous coal, in southern Vietnam.

Metallic and Other Nonfuel Minerals

Few metallic minerals have production levels or known reserves likely to attract large-scale manufacturing. Southeast Asia is the source of 70% of the world's tin, but most is exported after smelting at refineries in Peninsular Malaysia, southern Thailand, Bangka Island in Indonesia, and Singapore (Table 5-2). In the 1970s, Peninsular Malaysia and the Philippines each mined and exported more than a million metric tons of iron ore per year, most from areas distant from their own urban-industrial centers (Table 5-2). Bauxite, the ore for aluminum, is mined from surface pits in both Peninsular and eastern Malaysia, and on the nearby Indonesian island of Bintan. Each nation has been producing about a million metric tons of bauxite per year, mainly for export.

Most noted for their diversity of minerals are the Philippines, Burma, and Indonesia (Table 5-2). Copper, chromite, gold, mercury, as well as iron ore, come from Philippine mines. Although production since World War II has been far below prewar levels, Burma still yields tin, tungsten, antimony, gold, silver, lead, and zinc. Indonesia produces small quantities of gold, silver, and diamonds. The developmental work needed to mine and export considerable amounts of copper from the highlands of Irian Jaya (Western New Guinea) in Indonesia has been yielding exports.[30]

Phosphate rock in northern Vietnam, raw materials for cement production in several nations, sulphur from the Philippines, and evaporated or mined salt, are examples of nonmetallic, nonfuel minerals also produced in Southeast Asia (Table 5-2).

The Decolonization of Mineral Production

In the years since World War II, mining as an infrastructural element has undergone many changes. Burma, in the 1950s and 1960s, nationalized all foreign mining operations. Only its petroleum output has risen to near-prewar levels. Most other nations have place restrictions on foreign mining operations. In Indonesia, a national company has overall responsibility for oil production, while international companies participate as partners, consultants, or on a production-sharing basis. Private companies in Malaysia are still the principal producers in tin, iron, and bauxite mining, though a form of production sharing is applied to potential offshore oil resources of Peninsular Malaysia.[31] The private companies in Malaysia range in size from very large corporations, based on British capital, to medium and small operating companies having Chinese or other indigenous leadership, capital, and labor. In both Thailand and the Philippines, large international corporations are participating in mining operations, but within domestic company structures where majority control is retained by either the government or nationals of the country.

Further questions of "foreign control" in Southeast Asian mining endeavors have come with increasing Japanese interest and investment.[32] The Japanese entry is a reinvolvement in Southeast Asian mining more than a generation after World War II. It reflects Japan's large and increasing consumption of mineral raw materials and fuels, as well as capital available for investment in mineral production.

POTENTIAL AND DEVELOPED ENERGY

Southeast Asia has a considerable energy base for future economic growth from hydroelectric power sources and known fuel minerals of coal, petroleum, natural gas, and some nuclear fuel minerals.[33] Varied topography and generally heavy rainfall provide the region with a large hydroelectric power potential. The discovered and anticipated fuel minerals, particularly petroleum and natural gas, also contribute energy supplies and potentials.

At the end of World War II, Southeast Asia had only limited amounts of developed energy. Except for Thailand all political units had been under prewar colonial administration and during the war were under Japanese occupation, with power resources being developed characteristically at the administrative capital and a few other centers.

In the decades between 1960 and 1980 developed energy resources increased in both installed capacity and generation of electricity (Table 5-3). By 1980, nearly one-fifth of the installed capacity was hydroelectric. Across Southeast Asia the proportional significance of hydroelectric generation varies. While Brunei and Singapore depend entirely on thermal generation, Indonesia, Thailand, Loas, Vietnam, Burma, and Peninsular Malaysia have one-fifth or more of their generating capacity in hydroelectric installations (Table 5-3).

Those nations having the highest per capita energy production are the ones most likely to have rapid economic growth.[34] On this basis, Brunei and Singapore, each with more than 1,800 kilowatt hours of generated power annually per capita, are furthest advanced in energy, Peninsular Malaysia has about one-half this level, the Philippines one-fifth, and Thailand about one-sixth (Table 5-3). All other areas of Southeast Asia have very low per capita levels of energy generation. Indonesia, the realm's largest nation in area and population, has a figure of only 48. This low figure conceals considerable regional variation in electric power generation per capita, greatest in the Java core area and in several outer island urban centers.

Despite the major expansion of energy capacity, generation, and networks of power lines, most of Southeast Asia's energy production is in its larger urban centers. Power grids are developing in some populous and well-developed areas, notably in Peninsular Malaysia. Energy development within Southeast Asia is an urgent need. Many manufacturing plants and some residences have had to install their own power sources because of insufficient or unreliable public electric generation. With considerable potential hydroelectric power and relatively abundant petroleum, natural gas, and some coal as fuel sources. Southeast Asia can greatly expand its energy production, both in the more developed core areas and in outlying national areas.

MANUFACTURING PATTERNS AND CHANGE IN SOUTHEAST ASIA

Manufacturing in Southeast Asia in the 1980s has a dualism found in most developing areas. Handicraft industry is still important in terms of employment, total output, and regional distribution. Most rice milling, much textile-making, and production of many essential household, farm and fishery items are representative of the handicraft sector. The other half of the dualism, in striking contrast, consists of the modern fac-

TABLE 5-3
Electrical Energy Capacity and Production in Southeast Asia: 1960 and 1980

Country	Installed Capacity (1,000 KW) 1960 (P = Public Only)	Installed Capacity (1,000 KW) 1980 (P = Public Only)	Percent Hydro-electric 1980	Generation (Millions of K.W.H.) 1960	Generation (Millions of K.W.H.) 1980	Per Capita Generation (K.W.H.) 1980
Brunei	21.6	150	0	64	375	1,875
Burma	251	465	42.5	432	1,433	42
Indonesia	308 (P)	2,760	16.3	1,161 (P)	7,140	48
Kampuchea	21[b]	52 (P)	n.d.	57 (P)	165	28
Laos	6.8	172	89.5	13	975	264
Malaysia	312	2,250	22.5	1,228	9,777	698
Peninsular Malaysia	284	1,360[a]	25.7	1,190	8,980	795
Sabah	11.3	90[a]	n.d.	19.4	413	345
Sarawak	17.3	103[a]	n.d.	19 (est.)	384	256
Philippines	513[b]	4,632	20.5	2,824	18,032	378
Singapore	152 (P)	1,900	0	720	6,940	2,892
Thailand	191	3,615	29.5	549	14,983	317
Vietnam	—	875[d]	± 18.4	306	3,800	71
Southeast Asia	1,928.6	± 16,000	—	7,605	63,622	178

Sources: For 1960 data, *United Nations Statistical Yearbook, 1962* (New York: United Nations, 1962). For 1980 data, *United Nations Statistical Yearbook, for Asia and Pacific, 1980* (Bangkok: United Nations).
[a]1977
[b]1959
[c]1968
[d]*United Nations Statistical Yearbook 1979/80*, (New York: United Nations, 1981), p. 824.

tories. These increasingly numerous, large industrial plants are usually located in major urban centers. Examples are textile mills, assembly plants for a broad range of consumer products marketed in Southeast Asia, and specialized heavy industries such as oil refineries, fertilizer factories, and steel and cement mills. Kampuchea in the mid-1960s exemplified this dualism with an estimated 100,000 workers in handicraft industries, but only about 10,000 in modern factories.[35]

At the close of the Second World War, Southeast Asia's manufacturing was characteristically of the handicraft or small factory variety. These small-scale industries were sited in communities ranging in size down to the village and even the hamlet, but were also plentiful in the larger cities in their commerical sections or mixed commercial-industrial areas. Artisans and workers in handicraft industries were indigenous peoples, plus ethnic Chinese and Indians.[36]

The limited modern industrial sector in 1945, with its few large factories, was an exception to handicraft workshops. These modern plants were in the chief administrative centers, in the principal regional market cities, or at locations favorable to large-scale assembly, export or import of heavy materials. A few sizable textile mills, several oil refineries, and a few cement plants, such as the one at Indarung, near Padang, West Sumatra, in Indonesia, were representative of Southeast Asia's modern industrial sector in 1945. In most cases, the factories in this sector were developed with Western capital investment associated with Western colonial administration.

Diversification of manufacturing increased greatly during the 1960s in Southeast Asia.[37] Available data from several nations indicated that by the late 1970s, proportions of workers in manufacturing were lower than in the 1950s in the necessity activities of food and beverage production, in tobacco production, and in textiles, wearing apparel and footwear. Manufacturing employment had grown absolutely and proportionately in medium and heavy industries, such as printing and publishing, metallic products and machinery, electrical goods, and transportational equipment.

The variety of modern manufacturing in Southeast Asia, as well as the clustering of manufacturing activities reflect a number of locational associations (Fig. 5–5). These include: (1) diversified light and heavy manufacturing in the larger, most accessible urban centers of national core areas which have the largest markets in terms of people and levels of income; (2) less intensive but still diversified industrial activities in the principal outlying regional centers; and (3) specialized manufacturing related to particular resource combinations. These associations occur in areas of resource exploitation and at sites having other locational advantages, such as deepwater port facilities, large-scale availability of electrical energy, or centrality in transportational costs for assembling raw materials and distributing finished products. Tin smelters, sawmills, rubber processing, and manufacturing plants, fish-processing plants, oil refineries, fertilizer works, and cement factories are among those most likely to be in this third associational category.

Planned Industrial Districts

During the past four decades, several major industrial areas have been constructed within planned industrial complexes. Among these are Petaling Jaya near Kuala Lumpur, and Klang and Penang, all in Peninsular Malaysia; the Thai Nguyen industrial complex north of Hanoi in northern Vietnam, the Jurong Estate west of Singapore City, and the industrial land between Tanjung Priok and Jakarta in northwest Java, Indonesia.

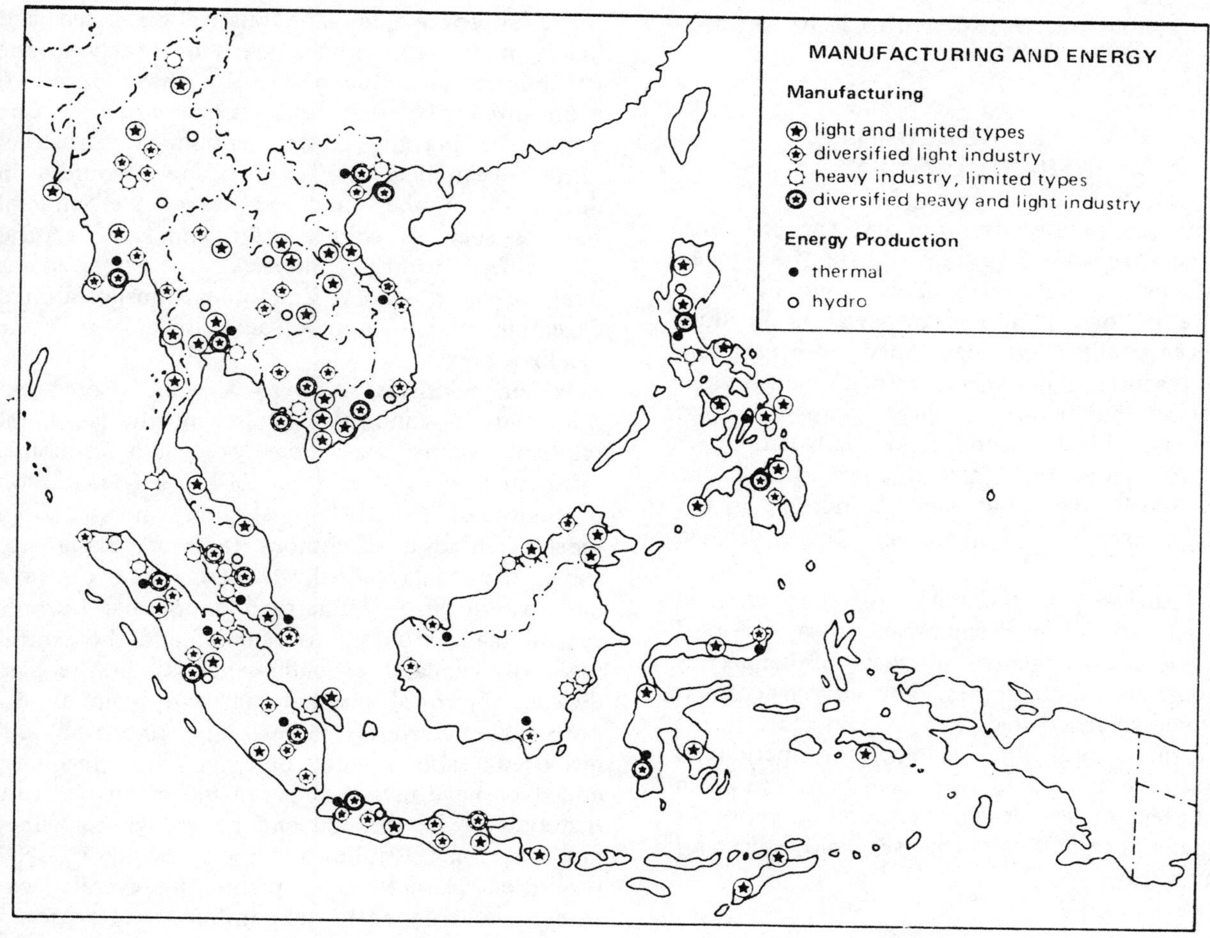

Figure 5-5. Manufacturing and Energy in Southeast Asia.

Although not formally part of named and planned industrial districts, several other clusters of manufacturing are expanding to become industrial complexes. One example is the Palembang area of southeastern Sumatra, Indonesia. Here, two old but now integrated oil refineries and several rubber mills and shipyards along the deep Musi river date from the early twentieth century. Since World War II a tire factory, a large urea fertilizer works, and a modern textile factory have been added, with other power and industrial facilities under construction or consideration.[38] Elsewhere, the Philippines has oil refineries at Batangas south of Manila, and a steel mill and fertilizer plant at Iligan on northern Mindanao near hydroelectric power; and Cambodia established an oil refinery and tractor assembly works at Kompong Som on the Gulf of Siam. When major hydroelectric power sites are developed, as on the Asahan river in northeastern Sumatra, Indonesia, or at several points along the Mekong river system, present manufacturing in nearby cities can be expected to grow into major complexes.[39]

SUMMARY OF ECONOMIC INFRASTRUCTURE

During the past quarter century, the economic infrastructure of Southeast Asia has been strengthened in most areas. This economic infrastructure is comprised of transportation facilities and accessibility; of developed mineral and energy resources; and of manufacturing activities whether of handicraft or large factory sectors. Considerable deterioration and destruction reduced this economic infrastructure during the Second World War, and warfare, notably in the Indochina nations since then, has further limited it.

The pattern of economic infrastructure in Southeast Asia is one comprised of a series of clusters joined by limited numbers of connective lines, corridors and arteries. The infrastructure is most highly articulated in national core areas around the capital cities. Linkages to peripheral national areas and across national lines, in general, remain less developed except in terms of raw material movements by sea and some air passenger travel.

The Economic Infrastructure in the 1980s

In the early 1980s, Southeast Asia's economic infrastructure showed diverse elements of growth and strengthening in some areas; stagnation and at times destruction or deterioration in others. In the Indochinese nations of Vietnam, Laos and Kampuchea (Cambodia), continuing political and economic difficulties, as well as disruptions from guerrilla warfare in some areas, has hampered broad, coherent improvement of regional economic infrastructures. Still needed are transportational routes; terminal and equipment improvements; expansion of manufacturing complexes and factories; and more effective development of known or prospective petroleum, gas, or other mineral and energy resources.

The problems slowing improvements in the economic infrastructure of the Indochina nations are present to some degree in outlying areas of northern Thailand and peripheral northern Burma as well. In these areas, dissident political and ethnic rebels have tended to retard many long-range improvements. The relatively isolated and lightly populated outlying areas of Malaysia, the Philippines and Indonesia also have localized economic infrastructural improvements. The areas receiving the most attention in infrastructural development are ones where resources in demand-of timber and of large-scale mineral reserves such as copper, petroleum and natural gas, where strategic interests are perceived as vital, result in seaport and other transportational development to improve accessibility for these localized areas.

Within Southeast Asia as a whole, some national areas stand out as having the strongest past and planned future development of economic infrastructure. Projects of ASEAN (Association of Southeast Asian Nations) have contributed in most of these areas. Among these are Singapore, Peninsular Malaysia; the Jakarta area of Java and eastern North Sumatra in Indonesia; Luzon's central plain tributary to Manila; and the central plain of Thailand around Bangkok. In the past decade, improved international and regional airports have aided air accessibility; improved and deepened seaports with container cargo facilities; added or have increased ocean movements of raw materials or freight. Oil and natural gas pipelines and necessary loading facilities, including LNG (Liquified Natural Gas) plants in several locations, have greatly expanded the region's specialized infrastructure.

Despite major national five-year plans, and of ASEAN projects as well, Southeast Asia's economic facility nodes, remain connected by sea and air but not too strongly by land transportation or navigable rivers. On land, highway transportation by truck, bus or private and public automobiles has tended to reduce the relative importance of most railway systems in Southeast Asia. The region continues to have more raw materials or partially processed products as exports than finished manufactures for domestic sub-regional, national or intraregional consumption needs. Only Brunei, Singapore and, to a limited extent, Peninsular Malaysia have advanced to intermediate or near-intermediate levels of per capita energy production and consumption or of similar per capita levels of income. Brunei's apparent high per capita production and consumption of electricity is more a reflection of its small population and relatively large petroleum and natural gas production, than of generally intensive infrastructural development.

Footnote References

[1]In Sumatra, Indonesia, some of the best roads in Riau Province are service roads for oil pipelines, such as the one from Pakanbaru northward to the Minas Oilfield, then continuing to Dumai port and refinery. W.A. Withington fieldwork, June, 1964.

[2]Airports and seaports are considered as nodes; navigable rivers, railways and major paved roads as arteries of accessibility for areas within about 9 miles of either kind.

[3]Oil and gas pipelines are specialized freight carriers and are not included in accessibility here.

[4]Trishaws are three-wheeled bicycle-like local passenger or freight carriers which compete with other small three- or four-wheeled vehicles in local, village, and city transportation.

[5]The largest Southeast Asian lake is the Tonle Sap, northwest of Phnom Penh in Kampuchea, but others in the Philippines and Indonesia are important locally in transportation.

[6]The best-publicized attempt to link up railway segments was that of the Japanese in World War II trying to connect the systems of Thailand and Burma.

[7]The silting results from erosion of the sloping volcanic lands and from modern deforestation on Java. See C.A. Fisher, *South-East Asia* (London: Methuen and Co., 1964), p. 228.

[8]In 1965, half of Java's railway locomotives and all of Sumatra's locomotives were over twenty years old. In Indonesia, 62 percent of all locomotives were 35 years or more old. Republic Indonesia, Biro Pusat Statistik, *Statistical Pocketbook of Indonesia, 1964-1967* (Jakarta, 1968), p. 287.

[9]Donald W. Fryer, *Emerging Southeast Asia* (New York: McGraw-Hill Book Company, 1970), pp. 26-29.

[10]The dramatic increase in oil tanker size is the most obvious example of larger ships. Although Phnom Penh technically remains a seaport upstream on the Mekong River, most deepwater trade of the Kampuchea now is routed via Kompong Som.

[11]Bangkok is the primary international airport, with Singapore second. A number of others are hampered by relatively short runways and outdated guidance systems for the latest jets.

[12]The Japanese completed a connection from Muara, West Sumatra, to Pakanbaru in what is now Riau Province, but few or no trains ever traveled the route, built during the Second World War, then dismantled to return equipment.

[13]UN, ECAFE *Asian Highway Routes: Indonesia; Mainland Southeast Asia*, Bangkok, 1978.

[14]The Syriam refinery near Rangoon, the refineries near Bangkok, and the Batangas area refineries south of Manila are the three serving capital city areas, but only the Syriam refinery uses domestically produced crude oil. *Oil and Gas Journal*, Vol. 70, No. 52 (December 25, 1972), pp. 89-102.

[15]Nong Khai in northeastern Thailand serves a dual role as terminus of the Thai railway system in that area and as the principal road and railway connection across the Mekong river to Vientiane, capital of Laos.

[16]Since 1970-71, the World Bank has been providing technical assistance for route studies and reconstruction of the road segments to Sumatra to be part of the highway.

[17]Much Soviet economic aid was ineffective in the countries where it was available in the 1950s and 1960s because materials supplied had not been pretreated for tropical heat and moisture.

[18]James L. Peacock, *Indonesia: An Anthropological Perspective* (Pacific Palisades, California: Goodyear, 1973), pp. 88-89.

[19]Fryer, pp. 128-129, 167, 207, 361-362.

[20]The oil-exporting port of Dumai facing the Malacca Straits in east-central Sumatra, Indonesia, has the largest export tonnage in Indonesia, although concealed under Pakanbaru. Nugroho, *Indonesia: Facts and Figures* (Djakarta: Perbitan Pertjobaan, 1967), p. 391 for 1960-1965 export tonnages.

[21]*Americana Annual 1973* (New York: Americana Corp., 1972). Western European nations now had a ration of five persons per car; East Germany about ten persons per car.

[22]P. Wheatley, *The Golden Khersonese* (Kuala Lumpur: Oxford, 1961).

[23]Fisher, p. 171.

[24]C. Robequain, *Malaya, Indonesia, Borneo and the Philippines* (Translated by E.D. Laborde, London: Longmans, 1958), p. 119.

[25]The 1930 Dutch Census did not list Pakanbaru among its 35 urban communities in Sumatra, but Pakanbaru had nearly 71,000 people in 1961 and over 186,000 in 1980. Landscape survey in field work in 1964 by W.A. Withington between Pakanbaru and Dumai, Sumatra.

[26]*World Oil*, V. 174 (February 15, 1972), p. 63.

[27]I. Swemle, "Indonesia, British Borneo, and Burma," in Wallace E. Pratt and Dorothy Good, *World Geography of Petroleum* (Princeton, N.J.: Princeton University Press for American Geographical Society, 1950), pp. 273-300.

[28]*Oil and Gas Journal*, Vol. 70, No. 52 (December 25, 1972), pp. 102-121. As of May, 1973, the Indonesian government changed the name of Irian Barat or West New Guinea to Irian Jaya.

[29]In 1940 Indonesia's coal production was about two million metric tons, with nearly 700,000 metric tons exported. R.W. van Bemmelen, *Geology of Indonesia*, Vol. II. Economic Geology (The Hague: Martinus Nijhoff, 1949), p. 44.

[30]*Indonesian News & Views* (Washington, D.C.: Embassy of Indonesia, 1973), p. 12. Exports began in December, 1972.

[31]Note in *Oil and Gas Journal*, Vol. 71 (Spring 1973).

[32]Fryer, p. 13.

[33]Some monazite sands, a source of uranium, are produced as a by-product of tin mining in Bangka, Belitung, and Singkep Islands south of Singapore in Indonesia. Bemmelen, p. 146.

[34]J.O.M. Broek and John Webb, *A Geography of Mankind*, 3rd edition, (New York: McGraw-Hill Book Company, 1978), pp. 338-343.

[35]W.A. Withington, "Cambodia," in Alice Taylor, ed., *Focus on Southeast Asia* (New York: Praeger Publishers, Inc., 1972), p. 109.

[36]Fryer, pp. 112-116. Indians are significantly involved in Peninsular Malaysia and a number of Indonesian cities.

[37]United Nations, *Growth of World Industry, 1968 and 1970 editions*, for 1958-1967 and 1960-1968 (New York: U.N., 1970 and 1972).

[38]J.C. Jackson, "Post-Independence Developments and the Indonesian City: Preliminary Observations on the Spatial Structure of Palembang," *Sumatra Research Bulletin, Vol. II, No. 2 (May, 1973), pp. 3#11.*

[39]The Mekong River Basin project, only partially complete at present and the now operational Asahan River Project near Medan, North Sumatra, Indonesia, each can greatly increase power available for manufacturing plant development beyond current levels in their respective areas.

Chapter 6

Rural-Urban Change

William A. Withington

Southeast Asia, like other developing world areas, has seen great changes in both rural and urban landscapes in the years since 1945. Many predominantly rural landscapes have become increasingly urban.[1] Most urban centers have expanded rapidly in population, in functional diversity, and in the extent of built-up urban areas, most with higher building structure profiles. However, many of the traditional Southeast Asian settlement patterns have continued with few striking changes. This chapter is an overview of changes and continuity in rural and urban landscapes since World War II.

THE RURAL LANDSCAPE OF SOUTHEAST ASIA

At the end of World War II Southeast Asia was predominantly rural. Over 77% of its 150 million people lived in the countryside in small villages and hamlets, or occasionally in dispersed farm dwellings as for some shifting cultivators. The urban nodes, containing the other 23% of the people, were scattered along Southeast Asia's long coastlines, along its navigable rivers, in several broad inland plains, and in a few upland basins.[2]

Rural settlement morphologies, both in 1945 and currently, reflect a variety of cultural and physical associations throughout Southeast Asia. Except for a few areas of modern agricultural colonization, rural settlements are nucleated. A rural village may range in population from a hundred people to several thousand people and usually is comprised of a number of smaller hamlets. An uneven pattern of houses and paths or roads is characteristic, but circular or linear patterns are also present. These latter patterns often reflect physical associations, such as hilltops or low rises of land on the one hand; streams, ancient or present beachlines, or valleys, on the other. Planned settlements, plantations, agricultural resettlement villages, or modern timber mining and fishing centers are most likely to have evenly spaced rectangular or linear morphologies.

The most widespread house type in Southeast Asia is the pile, stilt or raised dwelling.[3] The original functional reason for such a house may have been protection against seasonal flooding or animal and human enemies. The long house, used by extended families in Borneo (Kalimantan), is the most notable variant of this type.[4] Houses built on the ground are typical of recent rural settlement in many areas, and of densely settled rural areas in Vietnam, central and eastern Java, and eastern Timor Island.[5] Soaring house ridgetops, boldly raised at each end, reflect Indian cultural influences; straighter ridge lines, Chinese or Javanese influences.

Southeast Asian farm hamlets and villages have several other distinctive elements. One is the close association of a vegetable garden, usually with fruit and shade trees as well, with the farm dwelling; while rice fields and other farmlands lie beyond. Structural elements in small rural hamlets are the dwellings, their adjacent grain storage structures, and meeting house or place of worship. In the larger villages are additional buildings for the village head, police, shops, various schools or dispensaries. The Buddhist *wat* or pagoda, the Islamic mosque, the Chinese temple, and Christian church, all small in rural villages, distinguish areas of differing religions and often have associated monasteries and schools.

Most of Southeast Asia's rural villages are one of five principal types. The first three, identified by Spate in Burma, are (1) the hilltop, ridgetop or mountain village; (2) the intermediate plateau village; and (3) the larger plains village.[6] The two other types are (4) the planned agricultural settlement of the plantation or estate; and (5) the usually planned communities for agricultural colonization, rural resettlement, or refugee camps.[7]

The first village type is most often established by peoples practicing shifting cultivation in hilly or mountainous areas of Southeast Asia. The second type is found in upland basins or plateaus both in continental and insular or peninsular sections of the region. These plateau villages often are sizeable, particularly where they are in fertile basins of basaltic (basic volcanic) or alluvial soils. A number of larger villages have evolved recently into upland cities, with growth stimulated by transportation accessibility, commercial crop production, regional marketing, administrative status, industry, or tourist facilities.[8] The third type, the large plains village, is the most widespread and the most typical of all Southeast Asian villages. It is likely that two-thirds or more of all rural people in the region live in such villages.[9] Sites include the major river lowlands and deltas, narrower coastal lowlands as in eastern Vietnam, or broader lowlands of peninsular and insular areas.

The oldest form of commercially planned rural settlement in Southeast Asia is that of the plantation or estate. This is the fourth type. It dates from early Western attempts in commercial tropical agriculture, but particularly from the late nineteenth century. Central offices and processing facilities, gridiron patterns of roads, dwellings of workers and of managerial-level people distinctive in size and site, and at least one major transportation artery for import-export needs are integral elements of this rural settlement type.[10] Recent mining and forestry camps or headquarters settlements have many of the same elements, for these also involve the production and at times processing for export of primary goods.

The fifth type of rural village, usually planned if only in haste, has become a significant Southeast Asian settlement form since World War II. Agricultural colonization settlements were established as early as 1905 in the Lampung area of southern Sumatra.[11] Settlement is continuing in that area, largely by peoples from Java, Madura, Bali or other Indonesian islands.[12] Similar settlement has been taking place in northern Mindanao by peoples from the central and northern Philippines.[13] Security-oriented resettlement was a major task in Malaya during the 1950s, while Indonesia established Buru Island as a resettlement area for political detainees after the 1965 attempted coup d'etat in Java. Since World War II large numbers of rural people in Vietnam, Kampuchea (Cambodia), and Laos were forced into refugee camps by rural instability and warfare. In the early 1970s refugees in these areas represented a striking, semiurban phenomenon on the outskirts of each nations's larger cities.[14] The Khmer Rouge during the late 1970s caused urban depopulation in Kampuchea. Only in the 1980s has Phnom Penh increased again.

Changes in the Rural Landscape

Southeast Asia's changing rural landscape can be explained by a variety of influences. First, the proportion of rural population has been declining, from up to 90% in 1945 to 77% in 1982 (Table 6–1). Second, total rural population and consequent densities have been increasing, in some areas at rates faster than those for nearby cities.[15] These changes result in increasingly manmade landscapes of buildings, intensively farmed land, and more closely-knit transportation networks, particularly roads. Third, abandonment or illegal occupance of some of the large plantation lands, plus resettlement of these areas by immigrants or former employees, have resulted in more intensive, largely subsistence or petty smallholder commercial landscapes. Fourth, rural instability and related antagonisms to some "foreign" peoples, such as the Chinese, Indians, or nonindigenous people from neighboring political units, have reduced effective agricultural settlement in some areas. A fifth and positive influence has been the extension into rural areas of urban-oriented infrastructural elements such as electricity, all-weather roads, health facilities, and schools.[16] Finally, the "Green Revolution" and associated practices are tying rural areas more firmly into the urban-oriented systems developing in each of Southeast Asia's political units.

TABLE 6-1
Southeast Asia's Urbanization, 1960–1982

Area or Unit	Urban Population in percentage, Selected Years			
(1)	1960 (2)	1970 (3)	1975 (4)	1982 (5)
Brunei	42.9	46.4	48.2	76
Burma	15.8	18.5	20.0	27
Indonesia	14.6	17.2	18.6	20
Cambodia (Kampuchea)	10.3	12.2	13.3	14
Laos	10.3	15.0	18.0	21.0
Malaysia	31.9	41.2	46.0	29
West Malaysia	34.9	45.3	50.8	—
Sarawak	14.9	19.2	21.6	—
Sabah	15.0	16.9	17.9	—
Philippines	29.9	34.1	36.3	36
Singapore	65.2	80.8	84.0	100
Thailand	12.5	14.8	16.1	14
North Vietnam	14.2	18.1	20.4	—
South Vietnam	19.2	24.1	26.8	19
Southeast Asia	17.5	21.0	22.8	23
World Urbanization	33.1	37.4	39.6	37

Sources: United Nations, *Monthly Bulletin of Statistics* v. 25 (November, 1971), Special Table B for 1960, 1970, and 1975; 1982 data: Population Reference Bureau, *1982 World Population Data Sheet*, (Washington, D.C.: April, 1982). Many figures for 1970, 1975 and 1982 are estimates.

EVOLVING URBAN SYSTEMS AND SUBSYSTEMS

As a result of rapidly changing urban populations and urban relationships Southeast Asia, as a whole and within more localized areas, is following the worldwide trend of urbanization (Table 6–1). Immmediately after World War II Southeast Asia's population was about 10% urban. In 1960 this urban proportion had reached 17.5% and by 1982 the urban segment had risen to 23%. During these two decades world-wide urban levels rose from 33 to 37%. United Nations' projections indicate that by 1985 Southeast Asia will reach an urban proportion of about 25% compared with a world level of over 40% (Table 6–1).

The low levels of urbanization in Southeast Asia in 1950 resulted from several factors. Notable among these were an emphasis on subsistence production in agriculture, limited amounts of modern secondary and tertiary activities in the growing but still small urban centers, and the effects of two decades of worldwide economic depression, large-scale warfare, and postwar political and economic instability. Singapore was the only Southeast Asian area more urban than rural in 1950.

Urban ratios by 1960 ranged from 65.2% in Singapore down to 9.8% in Portuguese Timor and 10% in Laos and Cambodia. Singapore had attained self-governing status and was expanding its entrepot-related secondary and tertiary functions. With relative isolation and continuing unrest in the Indochina countries, subsistence rural livelihood activities predominated over urban development. The three moderately urbanized areas in 1960 were Brunei, with petroleum production and exports; the Federation of Malaya (Peninsular Malaysia) with increasing urbanization based on an expanding economy producing, processing, and exporting natural rubber, palm oil, tin, and iron ore; and the Philippines, also producing, processing, and exporting a variety of agricultural, forestry and mineral goods. All other Southeast Asian areas had less than one person in five in urban areas, despite the presence of major national and regional urban foci.

By 1982 Singapore had become entirely urban; Brunei and Peninsular Malaysia, more than one-half; the Philippines, greater than one-third urban; and Indonesia and Vietnam, about one-fifth urban. Primary production, manufacturing and commerce had increased in the first three above 1960 levels. In all Vietnam, Laos, and Kampuchea, disruption of the rural countryside by warfare at times has caused sizeable pseudo-urbanization when refugees have been pushed into the cities or widespread refugee camps.

The Urban Hierarchy of Southeast Asia

The pattern of urban centers in Southeast Asia is a three-tiered, pyramidal one (Fig. 6–1 and Table 6–2). At the apex in the first tier are several cities with populations exceeding 1,000,000; in the middle tier are many intermediate cities with populations between 100,000 and 1,000,000; and in the third tier are the least populous cities with fewer than 100,000 people. If all places having urban attributes or functions were included a more sizeable fourth tier might be added, consisting of most settlements having over 1–2,000 people but fewer than 20,000.[17]

The First Tier Cities. Several large and widely spaced cities make up the first tier (Fig. 6–1). Fourteen cities had at least 1,000,000 people in 1980. Seven of these are national capitals, when Manila's capital city functions are counted as well as those of its nearby suburb, Quezon City. The four Indonesian cities, Surabaya, Bandung, Medan, and Semarang, also have "million city" size. Eight of these first tier cities, notably Rangoon, Hanoi, Kuala Lumpur, and Quezon City, attained the 1,000,000 threshold after 1960.[18]

Second Tier Cities. The tier of intermediate cities includes at least eighty-three (Table 6–2). One-half of these widely scattered centers attained city status since 1960. Vientiane in Laos and Phnom Penh in Kampuchea are the only two intermediate cities which are national capitals. Kuala Lumpur's rate of growth raised it into the million city tier by the late 1970s especially after the annexation of Petaling Jaya which also increased its urban space.[19] Elsewhere, the intermediate cities characteristically are regional centers of sizeable hinterland areas at some distance from their national capitals. Among the larger cities serving as regional centers are Mandalay in Burma, Da Nang in central coastal Viet-

TABLE 6–2

The Urban Hierarchy of Southeast Asia, 1981

Country	Population Mid-1981 Est. (000's)	Percentage of Regional Population	Number of Cities Indentified: Over 1 Mill.	100,000– 1 Mill.	Under 100,000	All Cities	Expected Numbers In Proportion to National Population
Brunei	200	0.1	0	0	3	3	0
Burma	35,200	9.7	1	6	6	13	19
Indonesia	148,800	41.1	5	32	40	77	82
Kampuchea	5,500	1.5	0	1	8	9	3
Laos	3,600	1.0	0	1	6	7	2
Malaysia	14,300	3.9	1	9	9	19	8
Philippines	48,900	13.5	2	19	9	30	27
Singapore	2,400	0.7	1	0	0	1	1
Thailand	48,600	13.4	1	4	12	17	27
Vietnam	54,900	15.1	3	11	9	23	30
Southeast Asia	362,180	100.0	14	83	102	199	199

(Note: Quezon City has been counted separately, though its population is included in Manila's metropolitan total and since 1976 Manila has again become the Philippine's capital city; Bangkok in the 1970's has been extended to include the formerly separate twin city of Thonburi to the west across the Menam Chao Phraya as part of Thailand's capital district.)

Sources: Author's listing from available 1981 data or estimates in various sources including *The Americana Annual 1982* (New York: Grolier, 1982, p. 573); Biro Pusat Statistik, Republik Indonesia, *Preliminary 1980 Population Census by Kotamadya/Kabupaten* (Jakarta: May, 1981) with Tasikmalaya, Cianjur, Jember (Java); Denpasar (Bali); Prabumulih (Sumatra) estimated by author over 100,000; provincial capitals under 100,000 of Palu, Kendari (Sulawesi); Mataram, Kupang (Nusa Tenggara); Dili (Timor Timur); and Jayapura (Irian Jaya); United Nations *Demographic Yearbook, 1981* (New York: 1982); *Europa Yearbook, 1981–82* (London: Europa Publ., 1982); and Rand McNally's *Commercial Atlas and Gazetter, 1982* (Chicago, 1982).

nam, Cebu in the central Philippines, and Padang, capital of West Sumatra, in Indonesia.

Until the late 1970s, several second tier or intermediate cities were "twin cities" or "outports" of regional or national capitals.[20] Thonburi across the Chao Phraya river west of Bangkok and Quezon City in metropolitan Manila were twin cities; Johor Bahru, at Peninsular Malaysia's tip across the causeway from Singapore, is an international example. Outports include Klang (Kuala Lumpur), Haiphong (Hanoi), and Batangas (Manila), about 60 miles south but serving as an oil importing and refinery port center.

The Third Tier Urban Places. This group of cities, with less than 100,000 people in each, has many more cities than in the second tier and over seven times as many as in the first tier (Table 6-2).[21] These smaller urban places, only a few of which appear on either Table 6-2 or Fig. 6-1, are widely distributed and represent a third order of primacy in terms of hinterland size, administrative status, and functional diversity. However, this group still includes Bandar Seri Begawan, capital of Brunei; Kuching and Kota Kinabalu, capitals respectively of Sarawak and Sabah in eastern Malaysia; and many provincial capitals elsewhere.

The actual number of all cities—first tier or million size, second tier or intermediate, and third tier or less than 100,000 in population—and the expected numbers by population size of the nations in Southeast Asia at the opening of the 1980s vary widely. Only Singapore, with one city, had the same number as expected. Malaysia had 11 more cities than its population indicated; Kampuchea, 6; Laos, 5; and Brunei and the Philippines each had 3 more cities than expected (Table 6-2). By contrast, Thailand had 10 fewer cities; Vietnam, 7; Burma, 6; and Indonesia, 5 fewer. Kampuchea and Laos had more than their expected urban place numbers, but have been

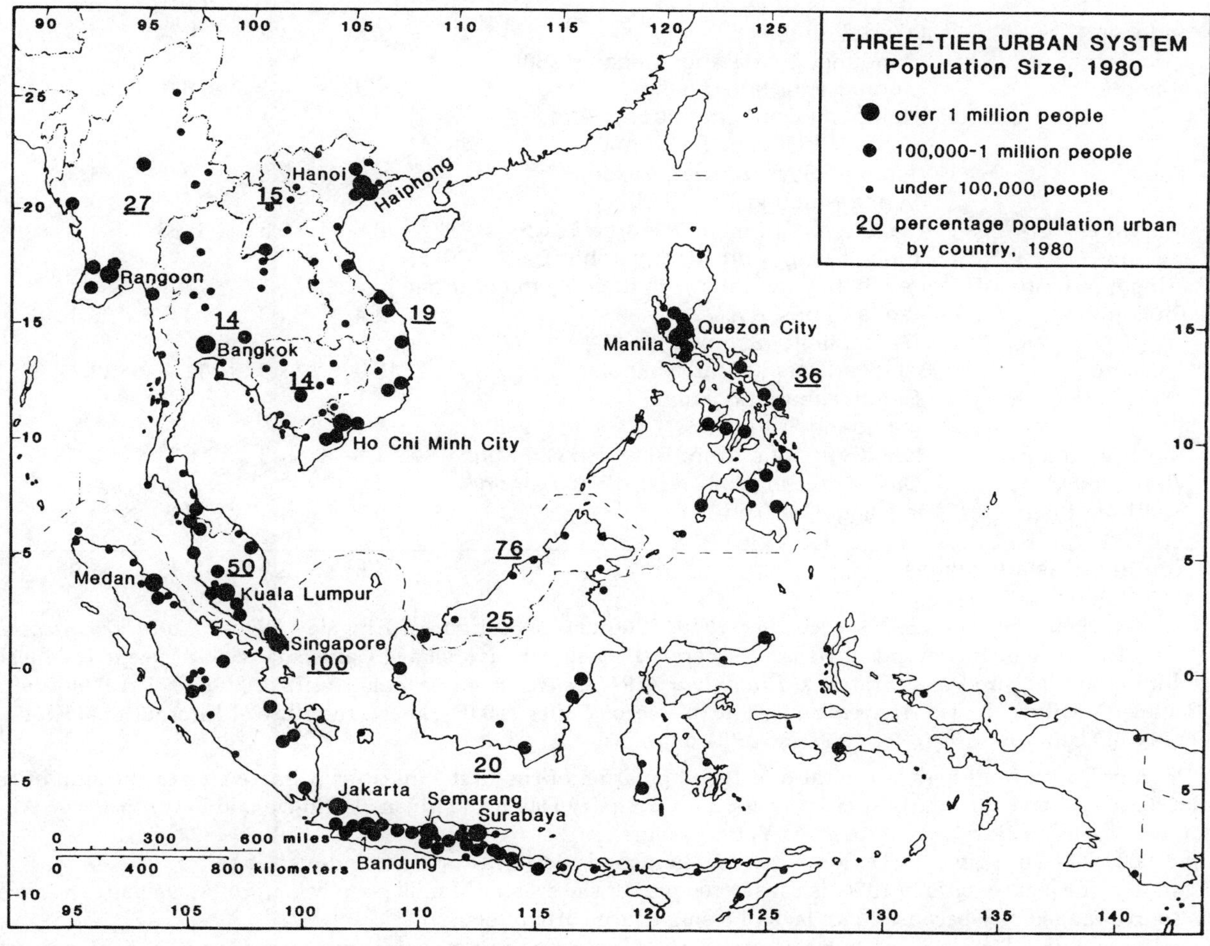

Figure 6-1. Three-Tier Urban System in Southeast Asia.

much disrupted by economic and political problems of recent decades. In general, the other nations of Southeast Asia have more or fewer urban centers than expected; a reflection of economic development strength or weakness. Thailand, with far fewer cities than expected, probably shows the predominance of Bangkok on the one hand; the lack of urban emphasis elsewhere in the nation except for a few regional nodes.

Urban Primacy in Southeast Asia

Primacy, or the size of the largest city in relation to lesser cities in a country, is an indication of the relative concentration of political, economic, and social activity and power of a nation in its largest center. In Southeast Asia, urban primacy, the ratio between the population of the largest city and the combined populations of the second, third, and fourth ranked cities, is given for 1950, 1960, 1970, and 1980 in Table 6-3.[22] The realm's urban primacy rose from 1.8 (1950 to 2.2 (1960) and 2.35 (1970), then declined to 1.9 (1980). These changes in Southeast Asian primacy indicated that the primate cities, usually political, economic, and cultural capitals of each nation, were growing faster than the next larger cities, at least until about 1970. During the 1970s other cities began to outstrip the primate city in

TABLE 6-3
Southeast Asia's Urban Primacy, 1950-1980

Country	Largest (Primate) and Second-, Third-, and Fourth-Ranked Cities	Primacy Index by Years[a]			
		1950	1960	1970	1980
Burma[b]	Rangoon/Mandalay Moulmein, Bassein	2.1	2.3	2.1 (3.1)	2.8
Indonesia	Jakarta/Surabaya, Bandung, [Semarang] Medan (1980)	0.93	1.2	1.34	1.3
Kampuchea	Phnom Penh/Battambang Kompong Cham, Kompong Som (Pursat: 1950, by 1960 4th)	n.d.	4.9	6.0	2.7
Laos	Vientiane/Savannakhet, Pakse, Luang Prabang	n.d.	2.8	2.0	1.3
Malaysia	Kuala Lumpur/Pinang (George Town) Ipoh, [Klang (Port Klang)] Johor Bahtu (80)	0.6	0.8	0.93	1.1
(Singapore, Brunei—for each, the capital city is the only major urban place.)					
Philippines[c]	Manila/Cebu City, Davao, Iloilo [Zamboanga-'80]	4.4	4.3	4.6	4.1
Thailand[d]	Bangkok/Chiang Mai, Nakhon Ratchasima, Songkhla (Lampang 3rd in 1960)	15.0	11.9	12.4	11.7
North Vietnam Vietnam (80)	Hanoi/Haiphong, Nam Dinh, Ho Chi Minh City, Hon Gai (Vinh-1950, 1960) Saigon/	1.1	1.3	1.7[e]	0.8
South Vietnam	Da Nang, Can Tho	4.7	4.5	2.8	
Southeast Asia Averages		1.8	2.2	2.35	1.9

Sources: For 1980, see Table 6-2 sources, for 1970, 1960 and 1950 figures, Kingsley Davis, *World urbanization, 1950-1970,* Institute of International Urban Research (Berkeley: University of California, 1969); except Indonesia: Republik Indonesia, Biro Pusat Statistik, *Preliminary 1971 Census Figures* (Jakarta, 1972), for 1971 (1970) figures, and Pauline D. Milone, *Urban Areas in Indonesia, Research Series* #10 (Berkeley: Institute of International Studies, University of California, 1966), for 1950 and 1961 data.

[a]The Primacy Index used here is the ratio of the population of the first ranked or primate city to the sum of the population of the next three largest cities as used by Kingsley Davis and given also in Donald Fryer, p. 32, in Alice Taylor, ed., *Focus on Southeast Asia* (New York: Praeger, 1972).
[b]If the 1,800,000 figure given in Taylor, p. 32, for Rangoon is used, the primacy index rises to 3.1.
[c]Quezon City, the legal capital in 1970, is considered part of the greater Manila population, while Basilian is not used as the fourth-ranked city because of its lack of a single large urban focus.
[d] The figure includes Thonburi's population across the Menan Chao Phraya, incorporated after 1970 in Bangkok.
[e]It is probable that the primacy index is misleading due to population dispersal from Hanoi and most other major cities.

population growth (Table 6-3). For most Southeast Asian countries the variable primacy reflects processes of development and of instability in the years after independence.

Primacy declined from the very high 15.0 in 1950 to about 11.7 in 1980 in Thailand (Table 6-3). The decline in primacy of Bangkok indicates that Thailand's transportational network is increasingly effective, together with regional development, so that the lesser outlying cities are now growing faster than Bangkok. Only the Philippines among other Southeast Asian nations had a primacy level greater than 4.0. In Kampuchea, unsettled conditions of strife in recent years have greatly reduced Phnom Penh's primacy; Manila, including Quezon City, has grown at a rate which keeps its primacy about the same as in 1950. The distinctive decline in primacy in Vietnam reflects the 1976 unification of the two parts and resultant larger 2nd, 3rd, and 4th level cities (Table 6–3).

Low primacy in Burma reflects a combination of large regional centers and nationwide economic stagnation. For Indonesia, primacy is lower and still decreasing as major outlying cities are growing slightly faster than Jakarta. Malaysia was the only nation with a primacy below 1.0, but when Kuala Lumpur merged with its nearby planned satellite community, Petaling Jaya, its primacy level over slower-growing secondary cities has now risen above 1.0. Even without the city's areal expansion, Kuala Lumpur's primacy ratio increased about 0.6% in the thirty years between 1950 and 1980 (Table 6-3). Without reasonable stability of political, economic and social conditions, many nations of Southeast Asia will show sharply divergent primacy levels for at least the short term, before outlying or core area secondary cities grow rapidly in population and infrastructure as compared to the primate city.

Traditional and Current Urban Functions

The cities of Southeast Asia's urban system in 1945 had functions resulting from diverse historical circumstances. Other than the ever-present residential one, most long-lasting were commercial and administrative functions; most coastal and inland cities included both functions. Surakarta and Yogyakarta, ancient inland sultanate capitals on Java, with considerable handicraft industry as well. Ports along Java's northern coast, were well-established entrepots in commercial trade before the arrival of Westerners.[23] Since the Siamese royal capital was moved there in 1782, Bangkok (Krung Thep) has combined governmental and many other functions. A few cities, notably Palembang in southern Sumatra and Pagan in central Burma, in this earlier era were major religious, as well as political and military centers.

Following the arrival of Western influence, new urban centers and new or altered functions in existing centers were established.[24] A series of widely spaced coastal ports were developed for commercial activity at first; then for colonial administrative control as well. Among these were all of the largest present cities of Southeast Asia except for Bangkok and Hanoi, two cities of indigenous, pre-European vitality. Jakarta (Batavia) was a Dutch creation; Manila, expanded from its fishing focus by the Spanish, then further changed by Americans; and Ho Chi Minh City (Saigon), by the French. Singapore was established in 1819 by the British, who also greatly altered the indigenous character of Mandalay and Rangoon in Burma.[25]

Some of today's cities began as mining camps for tin, as at Kuala Lumpur in Peninsular Malaysia. Others, as at Bukittinggi (the Dutch Fort de Kock) in the west Sumatran uplands, were military garrisons. A few of Southeast Asia's cities received their impetus from Western demands for upland weekend or recreational places (hill stations) and for Western foodstuffs which grow better in the cooler uplands. Bandung and the surrounding Preanger Uplands of western Java, Indonesia, received Western stimuli, as did Baguio in the Philippines, beyond indigenous influences.[26]

Administrative Function. Several urban functions, individually or in diversified combinations, predominate today in Southeast Asia. National capital administrative functions are vital in six of the ten largest cities, with Ho Chi Minh City (Saigon) an earlier capital and largest regional center; and Bandung, Surabaya and Medan in Indonesia, major regional capitals also having some national administrative agency functions as well. The four other cities over 1,000,000 include Quezon City with several national capital functions close to central Manila; Kuala Lumpur as a national capital; Haiphong as a capital city outport; and Semarang as a port and major regional capital on Java. All larger and many smaller cities have sizeable squatter populations, as high as a third of the total for Quezon City. Such squatter populations reflect rural instability, rapid urban growth and "attractiveness", and shortages of available land and housing in the receiving cities.[27]

Commercial Function. This function, which includes foreign and inter-island import-export trade, is characteristic of most large cities. These commercial functions service national, regional and local marketing demands. Among the fourteen largest cities, only Hanoi, Bandung, Kuala Lumpur and Quezon City are not ports directly handling ocean-going ships. Of these, only highland Bandung lacks an outport nearby, with Haiphong functions as an outport for Hanoi, Manila for Quezon City, and Klang for Kuala Lumpur. The great majority of second tier, intermediate size cities are commercial centers for regional if not national markets.

Manufacturing Function. An increasingly important function of Southeast Asian cities is that of manufacturing. Except for hand-stamped Batik cloth, urban industry no longer has a handicraft basis, though some necessities continue to be produced in household industries within urban commercial and residential districts.

Larger manufacturing plants, using powered machinery and involving sizeable work force, increasingly are replacing the craft workshops as sources of manufactured goods in most Southeast Asian cities.

Recent private and public planning has emphasized industrial estates near the larger cities in Southeast Asia. The Jurong Estate (Singapore), the Petaling Jaya district (Kuala Lumpur), and the Tanjung Priok district (Jakarta) are major examples. the Thai Nguyen steel mill and associated works in northern Vietnam, prior to devastation in the early 1970s, formed an integrated, planned industrial complex. Many other, less specifically planned, industrial zones have also evolved. Downstream from Palembang's urban core, a tire factory and large urea fertilizer plant border the Musi river's north bank, facing rubber remilling plants, boatyards, and two integrated oil refineries along the south bank. To the northeast, a large textile plant is set in the city's urban spread toward its airport.

Other cities known for their manufacturing have grown to importance through gradual accretion of industrial plants. Some have enlarged one particular specialty, such as rice remilling, textile weaving, or silver and metal working. Medan, in eastern North Sumatra, initially processed estate raw materials as these funneled through on transportation enroute to overseas export from Belawan Harbor. Today, Medan leads in industry and population among cities outside of Java in Indonesia. Here, light industries include textiles; kretek cigarettes; books, magazines, and newspapers; assembly of vehicles; leather goods and furniture. Nearby, the Asahan Falls power project, the largest hydroelectric source in Indonesia, has begun to support heavy industry with aluminum refining as the first major producer.

Transportation Function. This function has become increasingly vital. In most Southeast Asian areas, city size and transportational accessibility, measured by seaport and airport nodes, and by river, railway and highway routes, correlate at significant statistical levels.[28] Well-constructed hard-surface, all-weather highways in more closely-knit networks are especially important in present and future urban development, helping to link cities and integrate them with their rural hinterlands as well.

Cultural and Recreational Functions. Additional functions associated with Southeast Asian cities include culture, religion, higher education, and recreational or tourist elements. Examples are Mandalay, Surakarta, Yogyakarta, and Hue as cultural focuses; Cirebon and Siem Reap in religion; Bandung, Bangkok, or Hue in higher education; and Singapore, Pinang, Bogor, or Baguio for local or general tourist recreational activities. The largest cities incorporate most of these functions, in addition to those of administration, commerce, industry, transportation, and police and military roles.

Functional diversity of urban places in Southeast Asia, as elsewhere, tends to be more pronounced in the largest cities. Specialization is far more likely to be found within the third tier, smaller-sized cities of under 100,000 people. In many of these cities one function or even one particular factory or activity may predominate, with marketing and some transportational accessibility as the most common functional combination.

MAJOR FACTORS OF CHANGE AND CONTINUITY

Southeast Asia's rural and urban areas have been influenced by many forces since World War II. Continuity, however, remains exceedingly strong in many traditionally-oriented cities and rural areas. Among intermediate cities, Yogyakarta in Indonesia, Hue in central Vietnam, and Mandalay in Burma are notable examples of long-term cultural contnuity.[29]

Factors which have been most influential in rural and urban change can be summarized under six headings:

1. The transition to national independent status usually resulted in increased population mobility, only part of which is rural to urban in direction. Many people from overcrowded rural areas have moved to less densely occupied rural areas, such as the Lampung and Riau lowlands of southern and eastern Sumatra, or the northern parts of Mindanao in the Philippines. Others have moved into cities or city-fringe areas, either as legal owners or as squatters. Still others have formed the first thrust of Southeast Asian suburbanization, if not exurbanization, outside major cities.[30]
2. The perception of greater opportunities in cities has led to a large in-migration to urban areas by people seeking employment, education and housing, among other benefits. Those immigrants, not finding space within the political city boundaries, swell the populations of the real or pseudo-suburban fringe areas.
3. Warfare and local rebellions continue to be distruptive in rural and urban areas in the decades since 1945. The cities and surrounding rural areas in Vietnam were most devastated up to 1975. Kampuchea (Cambodia), Laos, and areas of Peninsular Malaysia and Indonesia earlier had similar disruptions. Any predictions, thus are hazardous as to stability in either rural or urban areas.
4. Out-migrations of particular national or ethnic groups have been sizeable from both urban and rural areas. Among those departing have been former Western colonial administrators and businessmen; ethnic Chinese from several areas; all Indian residents in Burma's rural or urban areas; and, before 1975, Vietnamese from Kampuchea (Cambodia). Plantation and commercial rice-growing lands have been the chief rural areas affected by such out-migrations, as in eastern North Sumatra and Burma. Indigenous directors and managers have come to both urban and rural areas, replacing departing migrants in most activities.
5. Worldwide urbanization trends are reflected in Southeast Asia. These trends are most noticeable in taller and more varied urban building profiles; the outward spread of most urban areas from earlier, restricted limits; wider highways and all-weather roads to handle increased traffic; and, at least in the larger cities, a more cosmopolitan, educated populace whose interests and outlooks are increasingly similar to those found worldwide. The increases in branches of transnational enterprises—banks, airlines, hotels, and other businesses or industries—reinforces this world outlook. However, despite large-scale urban planning, most urban areas change as a result of varied processes besides those anticipated planned.
6. The increasing pressures of population, both urban and rural, will continue. More effective and efficient use of land and human resources will be even more crucial needs in the years ahead than in the nearly four decades since 1945. With increasing population densities, the "plural societies" of urban areas will be under still greater stress, with their functional sectors segregated in terms of ethnic, religious, linguistic, political, and economic associations.

RURAL–URBAN TRENDS IN THE 1980S IN SOUTHEAST ASIA

The major factors of change and continuity already discussed provide a background for emphasizing a series of trends in the 1980s already affecting or likely to affect rural–urban change. These are:

1. *Continuing rural–urban instability in some areas, notably Kampuchea (formerly Cambodia).* In Kampuchea, where the Khmer Rouge government of the mid-1970s was replaced by another supported by large Vietnamese military forces, active and guerrilla-level warfare will continue to destabilize both rural and urban landscapes. In these areas any coherent planning for rural and urban development remains difficult or impossible until such warfare ceases.
2. *A shift from pre-1975 conditions often leading to rural depopulation and over-rapid urban growth, including squatters or refugees.* This shift has been to a more even rural–urban growth pattern, both in population and of supporting economic activities with the necessary social-transportational infrastructure. Several national plans, in Malaysia, Indonesia and Thailand, have among their major goals improvement of both rural and urban qualities of life through improved water, health services, transportation linkages, and economic activities.
3. *Slower urban growth, at least in the larger (million plus) cities, though not necessarily in the intermediate (100,000–1 million) or smaller (under 100,000) cities.* The largest cities already have more people than housing, employment

and social or transportational infrastructure can support at reasonable quality of life levels. Most of the lesser cities which grow rapidly will do so on the strength of developing nearby raw materials of waters, forest, soil, or mineral elements; of processing and manufacturing plants; and of improved transportation facilities.

4. *For several cities or city clusters a trend to megalopolis-like expansion*. Such expansion will result in broader urban "regions". Included among those urban centers having this trend are the Kuala Lumpur-Klang zone; Greater Manila with Quezon City and others; Greater Bangkok which since the 1970s has included Thonburi formerly a separate twin city across the Menam Chao Phraya; Jakarta, Indonesia's and Southeast Asia's largest city, expanding away from its earlier core in all directions and southward toward Bogor; Hanoi-Haiphong on the lower Red river in Vietnam's northern Tonkin plain; Pinang (George Town) on its island and on the facing western coast of Peninsular Malaysia; and the two-nation conurbation of Singapore (city and the island) with Johore Bahru in southernmost Peninsular Malaysia, linked by road and railway transportation.

5. *In urban centers, continuance of developmental stresses in the 1980s*. These are between indigenous or colonial cultural patterns established much earlier and the worldwide urbanization patterns, such as high rise buildings reflecting introduced western, Japanese or other influences on construction, city silhouettes, and diverse functional elements.

6. *Finally, rural–urban changes strongly dependent on the combination of domestic, regional and worldwide economic trends*. These include on the one hand, the strength of local or regional demands for commercial crops or raw materials for consumption as well as for foreign exchange-earning exports; on the other, the sharp fluctuations in prices and foreign demands. The latter aspect has been crucial as prices have decreased rapidly for many raw materials, such as rubber, timber and crude oil in the early 1980s. National and regional planning goals affecting rural–urban change usually are highly susceptible to any international economic fluctuations.

The effective dealing with the ongoing stresses of rural–urban change to Southeast Asia's landscape and fabric of life represents the greatest challenge for Southeast Asia's nations and leaders if their peoples are to live together in any kind of harmony.

Footnote References

[1]Thomas Leinbach and Richard Ulack, Chapter 10 "Southeast Asian Cities", pp. 371–407, in Stanley J. Brunn & Jack F. Williams, *Cities of the World*, (New York: Harper & Row, 1983).

[2]Joseph E. Spencer, Oriental Asia: Themes Toward A Geography, (Englewood Cliffs, NJ: Prentice-Hall, 1973), discussion of rural and urban landscapes throughout text.

[3]Jan O.M. Brock and John Webb, *A Geography of Mankind*, 2nd edition (New York: McGraw-Hill Book Company, 1973), p. 381.

[4]Derek Freeman, *Report on the Iban*, (New York: Humanities Press, 1970), pp. 1–4.

[5]Brock and Webb, 3rd ed. (1978), p. 329.

[6]O.H.K. Spate, "The Burmese Village," *Geographical Review*, Vol. 35 (1945), pp. 523–543.

[7]Examples of refugee camps in the 1980's are in border areas of Thailand adjacent to Kampuchea (Cambodia).

[8]Robert Reed, *City of Pines: The Origins of Baguio as a Colonial Hill Station & Regional Capital*, (Berkeley: Univ. of California, Center for South & Southeast Asian Studies, 1976).

[9]J.E. Spencer & William L. Thomas, *Asia, East by South*, 2nd Ed., (New York: John Wiley & Sons, Inc., 1972), pp. 65–72.

[10]Spencer, pp. 80–84.

[11]Karl Pelzer, *Pioneer Settlement in the Asiatic Tropics* (New York: American Geographical Society, 1945), pp. 190–193.

[12]William A. Withington, "Sumatran population changes, 1961–1980", *Indonesia Circle*, No. 27 (March, 1982), pp. 11–25.

[13]Peter C. Smith, "The changing character of interregional migration in the Philippines", *Philippine Geographical Journal*, Vol. 20, no. 4 (Oct.–Dec., 1976), pp. 146–162.

[14]*The Far Eastern Economic Review* (weekly, Hong Kong), has carried the most comprehensive coverage of city-oriented refugee resettlement in South Vietnam, Laos and Kampuchea.

[15]William A. Withington, "Growth, Change and Tradition in Sumatra's Major Cities, 1961–1971," *Sumatra Research Bulletin*, Vol. III, No. 1 (1974), pp. 3–17. Population growth in the country-like areas around the cities was more rapid than within ten of the twenty cities, suggesting an increasing "suburbanization" in many of these urban areas.

[16]"Infrastructure" is defined here to include transportation and communication elements—roads, railroads, airports, seaports, telephone services—plus energy supplies, especially electricity, and social services of health and education. See Chapter 5.

[17]Hamzah Sendut, "Contemporary Urbanization in Malaysia," *Asian Survey*, Vol. 6 (September, 1966), pp. 484–492. The 20,000 person lower threshold is that used by the United Nations.

[18]Due to bombings and dispersal policies for persons and activities in the city, Hanoi only later reached the million size credited to it in 1970 by Davis. Phnom Penh's estimated refugee-induced size of 1,200,000 declined after 1975, then grew to 400,000 in the early 1980s.

[19]With Petaling Jaya, a planned outlier community incorporated with Kuala Lumpur in Malaysia's capital city. That city's population by the late 1970s exceeded 1,000,000.

[20]A "Twin city" is defined as one immediately adjacent to another larger city; and "outport" is a deepwater port serving a nearby city which may or may not have its own port (sea or river). The most distant "outport" is Dumai on Sumatra's eastern coast 100 kilometers (150 kilometers by road) north of Pakanbaru, usually listed as "port", Dumai now has over 50,000 people, a large oil storage and refinery area, and airport and refinery.

[21]For discussion purposes and as shown in Table 6-2, W.A. Withington identified 199 "urban nodes" in Southeast Asia as of 1982, including Bandar Seri Begawan (Brunei Town) and Dili, now capital of Indonesian Timor (Timur province rather than of colonial Portuguese Timor). Lack of census or other reliable sources of urban population data means that many smaller urban centers in most Southeast Asian nations have not been included, such as most of the *kabupaten* (county-level) capitals of Indonesia.

[22]Donald W. Fryer, "The Primate Cities of Southeast Asia and Their Problems", Alice Taylor, ed., *Focus on Southeast Asia*, (New York: Praeger Publishers, Inc., 1972).

[23]D.G.E. Hall, *Atlas of Southeast Asia*, (Amsterdam: Djambatan, 1964), pp. 68–72.

[24]Rhoads Murphey, "Traditionalism and Colonialism: Changing Urban Roles in Asia," *Journal of Asian Studies*, Vol. 29 (1969), pp. 67–84.

[25]William Kirk, "The Road from Mandalay...", *Transactions, Institute of British Geographers*, New Series, Vol. 3, No. 4 (1978), pp. 381–394.

[26]William A. Withington, "Upland Resorts and Tourism in Indonesia: Some Recent Trends", *Geographical Review*, Vol. 51 (July, 1961), pp. 418–423; and Robert Reed, *op. cit.*, *City of Pines: The Origins of Baguio....*

[27]Fryer, 2nd ed., urban development discussion.

[28]Computations of W.A. Withington for intermediate and larger (first and second tier) cities using 1980–82 population and transportational data estimates.

[29]Kirk, pp. 384–386.

[30]For migration to other rural areas see footnotes 5 and 6; for city-ward mobility, footnote 18; for suburbanization, footnote 14; and for movements into planned outlier communities, footnotes 7 and 10.

Chapter 7

The Role of National Planning

Ashok K. Dutt

National Planning became an accepted part of government organization in all Southeast Asian countries after World War II. Singapore and Malaysia have had a great success with planning partly because they already had a more progressive economy and adopted more realistic approaches to planning. North Vietnam had also registered overall economic progress under the aegis of socialist planning, but war has worked out as a great deterrent and the united Vietnam Republic, since 1976, is finding it difficult to make an economic take-off. Thailand's reaction to planning has been mixed, but on the whole some legitimate progress has been attained. Indonesia, on the other hand, deteriorated up to the mid-sixties because of ill conceived and poorly directed planning, but with a change in policy her economy has reacted positively to the efforts of planning. Burma followed a dogmatic, unrealistic socialistic policy and tried to generate development while remaining in virtual isolation from the rest of the world, but starting from the mid-seventies it attempted more realistic policies which infused some progress in the economy. The Philippines started its national planning in 1974, but it was facing a great deal of investment problems right from the start. In 1978 Laos was the last country in Southeast Asia to initiate national planning . Kampuchea has had successess in planning, but they have been totally overshadowed in the quagmire of civil war that started in 1970. Brunei, a country with surplus balance of payments, remains in an advantageous position, and has organized its investments under the aegis of national planning since 1962.

Planning became a part of national operations soon after the independence of most Southeast Asian countries because it was widely believed that if the developing nations grew without any state planning their pace of growth will be slow and the difference between the developed and underdeveloped (developing) nations will widen drastically. The nations of Southeast Asia, all of which fell in the 'developing' category in the fifties, thought it to be most appropriate to embark on national economic planning and to infuse economic growth by making investments in those sectors and projects which were likely to generate sustained growth. It was also thought that if by such accelerated growth, the developing nations could progress at a greater pace compared to the developed nations, eventually the development gap between the "have" nations and "have not" nations could be narrowed. Thus, national planning was introduced with a great deal of hope in Southeast Asia.

In the case of communist countries, the necessity of national planning increases with the increasing pace of nationalization of services, means of production, and the transportation system. It is for the survival of the system that planning is essential in communist countries. In North Vietnam, the decades old communist government, had been able to nationalize most aspects of production, transporatation and services and, therefore, the centralized national planning there has attained a great deal of maturity. The southern part of Vietnam and Laos, where communist governments have only emerged since 1975 and where private property and services had not been abolished to a large extent (at least until the beginning of the eighties), the national planning or some kind of an integrated planning strategy was in an incipient stage.

EVALUATION FRAMEWORK

A framework for evaluating and comparing national planning programs has been developed in this chapter. The following elements may be considered

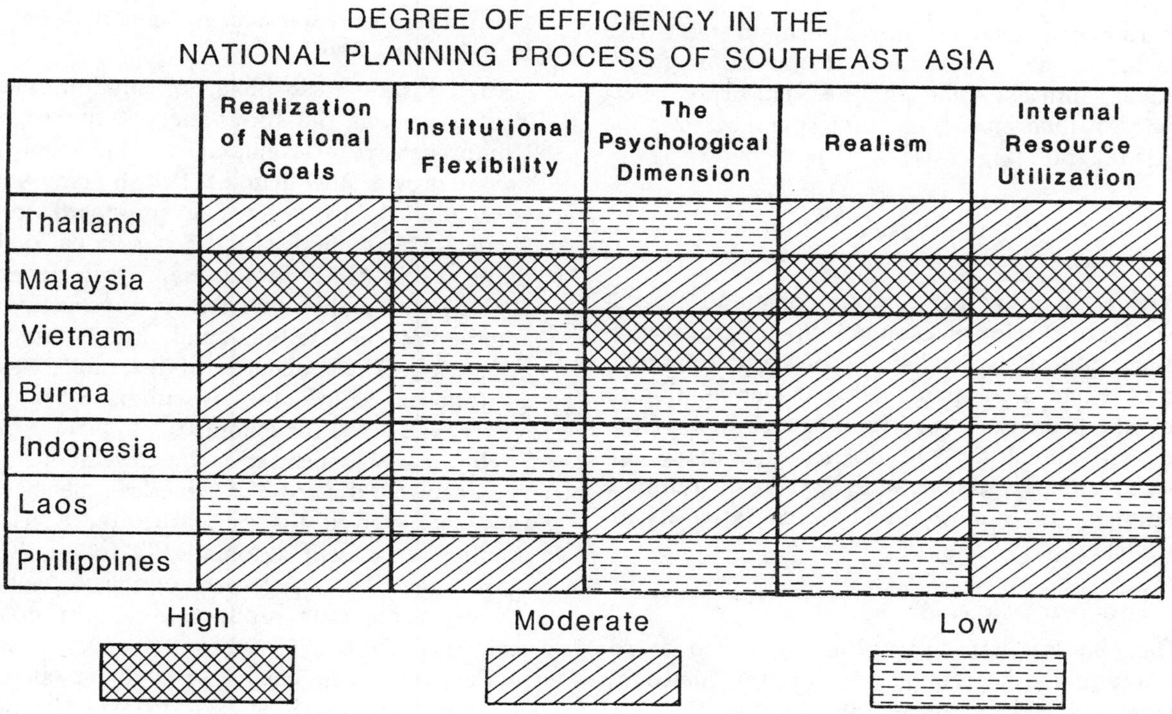

DEGREE OF EFFICIENCY IN THE NATIONAL PLANNING PROCESS OF SOUTHEAST ASIA

	Realization of National Goals	Institutional Flexibility	The Psychological Dimension	Realism	Internal Resource Utilization
Thailand	Moderate	Low	Low	Moderate	Moderate
Malaysia	High	High	Moderate	High	High
Vietnam	Moderate	Low	High	Moderate	Moderate
Burma	Moderate	Low	Low	Moderate	Low
Indonesia	Moderate	Low	Low	Moderate	Moderate
Laos	Low	Low	Moderate	Moderate	Low
Philippines	Moderate	Moderate	Low	Low	Moderate

High Moderate Low

Figure 7-1. Author's Perception of Degree of Efficiency in the National Planning by Countries of Southeast Asia. Based on the Analysis used in this chapter.

for the purpose.

1. *The role of planning in the realization of national goals.* National planning ought to reflect a cohesive and integrated set of national goals and priorities based upon the most efficient and equitable use of national resources. The programs should be oriented toward general societal improvement or an attempt should be made to satisfy existing pressures for reform before they become explosive.
2. *Institutional flexibility and the planning process.* Provisions must be made for popular participation in both the planning and implementation stages of the national planning program. The institutions should be developed readily through the programs so that it might respond to new concepts relative to their own organization, changes in intermediate goals, and the administrator–client relationship.
3. *The psychological dimension.* The political orientation of the clients needs to be assessed. The degree to which they feel integrated into the general society and how well they identify with national goals must be ascertained. The cooperative efforts acceptable to the clients has to be generated. People's attitudes toward government intervention must also be fathomed. Attitudes toward community development resulting in social change needs to be measured. Variation in educational levels has to be gauged.
4. *Realism.* In order for any plan to succeed, it must accurately predict what the country is capable of achieving. The biggest mistake a nation can make is to attempt to grow too soon. Economic and social development is a long, hard and continuous process and any nation that attempts to develop instantaneously will find its people exasperated rather than its conditions ameliorated. This is particularly true in the case of industrialization. Many nations are simply not capable of industrializing and would actually be better off investing in agriculture for the purpose of becoming self-sufficient in food production, at least for the time being.
5. *Internal Resource Utilization.* It is extremely important that developing countries put to work all of the energy and materials available at their disposal. This will include both natural and human resources. When such resource utilization is associated with foreign economic and comparatively advanced technological inputs, it can bring about most desirable returns. Where there are few resources to begin with, inefficiency, mismanagement and wastefulness can be suicidal to a nation.[1]

The following analyses hovers around these five elements in the context of their application to individual Southeast Asian countries. The degree of efficiency of the elements has been summarized in the matrix diagram (Fig. 7-1).

BURMA

Burma has a low per capita income and has not been able to develop an economically progressive nation in spite of the availability of sizeable internal resources and a comparatively small population to feed. The primary reasons for this lack of development are unrealistic and dogmatic planning approaches and perspectives adhered to by the Burmese government for almost three decades after its independence.

The Two-Year Plan (1948–50)

The two-year plan was primarily aimed at rehabilitation of the economy which was ruined by Japanese occupation during World War II. Agricultural development was greatly emphasized in the plan which called for: (1) the abolition of landlordism, (2) land to the cultivators, (3) scientific cultivation, and (4) recovery of the prewar level of rice production. The aim was to make the nation self-sufficient in all other agricultural products with rice serving as the main foreign exchange earner. In the industrial sector, the plan recommended nationalization of light industries, but stipulated mandatory nationalization of basic industries.[2] All electric power generating facilities were nationalized and operated by the new Electric Supply Board.

Most elements of the plan were only partially realized. Implementation was interrupted by civil insurrection; Communists and rebels forced a drop in the production of rice resulting in a decrease of funds available for plan implementation. Also many of the goals were vague with no specific means of fulfillment. The plan was more a statement of national objectives than a technical guide for national development. The positive aspects of the plan have been best summarized by Walinsky.[3]

> While neither comprehensive nor thorough, the Two-Year Plan of 1948 is significant in a number of ways. It was, until 1960, the only attempt at comprehensive economic planning made by independent Burma without the assistance of foreign advisors. It was a first attempt to formulate specific ways and means of achieving the principles and goals stated in the Constitution. It defined the current thinking about economic policies and projects. And it in fact shaped basic agricultural and industrial planning and policy for a number of years thereafter.

Comprehensive Development Plan (1951–60) or Pyidawtha Plan

In terms of basic policy orientation, the Two-Year Plan was the forerunner of the Eight-Year Comprehensive Development Plan which was prepared with the help of British and American consultants. This latter plan proposed to spend Kyats 3525 million (5.45 Kyats equaled United States $1 in 1972) in the eight year period with 50% of this money invested in transportation and communication facilities and 27.3% for power generation. The remainder of the funds was spent as follows: 12.8% for irrigation, 6.5% for industry, and 3.3% for mining.[4]

The heavy concentration on development of infrastructure reflected the American belief at that time that "given the infrastructure, development in other areas will automatically follow." At the outset, the plan was overly optimistic calling for the gross domestic product to almost double in real terms from 1950–51 to 1959–60.[5] In addition to this, per capita income was to be raised from 201 Kyats to 340 Kyats. A drop in the price of rice in the international market following the Korean War, however, brought a sobering effect upon the planning process when it became more difficult to raise resources for investment. Therefore, the remaining half of the Eight-Year Plan was designated as a Four-Year Plan (1956–60) with revised and more modest targets.

The agricultural sector of the Eight-Year Plan was implemented in conjunction with the Land Nationalization Act of 1948. It outlined the way agricultural land would be distributed and declared that "The state is the ultimate owner of all lands."[6] It provided for a central committee for land nationalization, with district and local staffs. Maps and information were to be gathered to aid in equal distribution of nine million acres[7] among the landless peasants. Newly landed farmers were to be organized into agricultural cooperatives and collective farms modeled after earlier experimental mechanized cooperatives. Details of this massive task were vague or non-existent. The size of free farms was not stipulated, compensation for the former owner was not determined, and how the land was to be transferred or the status of ownership was not defined. Consequently, by 1958 only 3.5 million acres were nationalized and the legislation did not contribute significantly to agricultural reconstruction or to an increase in production. Both in terms of agricultural acreage sown and income generated, even the prewar level could not be reached by 1960. Eighteen million acres sown and Kyat 1833 million income from agriculture and fishery in 1959-60 ran short of the 1938-39 level.

In the process of implementation of the Eight-Year Plan, industrialization was over-emphasized. At the insistence of the Burmese leaders, a steel mill was incorporated in the plan though iron was not mined in Burma, coking coal was not available in the country and local technical know-how was scarce.

Industrialization was one of the foremost goals of the government since industrial development, it was thought, was more productive than agriculture; it would create more employment, and help diversify and stabilize the economy as well as coordinate economic self-sufficiency with political independence. Development of heavy as well as light industry, all implemented by the state to the exclusion of the private sector, was elemental to the industrialization policy. Sixty-five industries were proposed without consideration of cost, and consequently exhausted the funds of the Eight-Year budget as early as 1955. The steel, pharmaceuticals, jute, sugar, brick, and tile plants came first, followed by the establishment of cotton, paper, fertilizer, rubber, and glass factories.

Examples of unrealistic and uneconomic ventures can be cited. The erection of a steel mill in Insein, an industrial suburb of Rangoon, at a cost of Kyat 44 million was a 'prestige' issue. The plant, equipped with an electric furnace, was designed to produce 20,000 tons of steel products, such as bars, sheets, and wire. It went into production in 1957 based on scrap originating from World War II. However, the limited supply of scrap lasted only a few years, after which the plant had to run on imported raw materials. Moreover, the products were so uneconomic that some sections had to close down.[8] Equally unrealistic and uneconomic were other factories including the Kyat 67 million pharmaceuticals plant started at Gyogan, near Rangoon.

In the transportation section, rehabilitation was the key note with the railways receiving greatest attention. Public health, mass education, higher education, and housing were also given attention in the Plan.

In the final analysis, the Plan could hardly generate a significant headway in the economic take-off of the country for the following reasons:

1. The two erroneous assumptions, that (a) the export price of rice would remain at 1951-52 level and (b) internal insurgency would be over by 1954.
2. Mobilization of capital either from internal or external sources was ineffectual because (a) private capital was already frightened by the specter of nationalization, and (b) the rice-export price declined.
3. Neglect of the agricultural sector, which had produced about 60% of the Gross Domestic Product.
4. Adventurism with industrial experiments was evident when dogmatic policies superseded the realities of the country's natural and technical resources.
5. Administrative and business inexperience of the Burmans emanated from the fact that prior to Burma's independence, (a) the entire civil service was manned primarily by British or Indian officials and (b) Indian, Chinese, and British investments predominated, thus preventing growth of Burmese entrepreneurship.
6. Corruption in the officialdom, inherited from the colonial system, made any implementation of plans difficult.

Second Four-Year Plan (1960-64)

The Second Plan was never even properly initiated because of political instability, which finally culminated in a military *coup d'etat* led by Ne Win in 1962. The elected parliament was prorogued; prime minister U Nu was put into prison. Comprehensive planning was guillotined in the name of leading the country to "The Burmese Way to Socialism."

"The Burmese Way to Socialism"
Since 1962

The Socialist Economic Planning Committee drafted the plan "The Burmese Way to Socialism", which was in reality a policy, not a detailed plan, adopted by the Revolutionary Council. By 1965, Burma's government had nationalized all of the important industries and commerce, including banks, and had a monopoly in agriculture.

Twenty-two government departments replaced the previous development agencies and private enterprises. The economy remained centrally organized through these twenty-two corporations, whch were put under direct command of the ministers of the military government and special duty officiers.[9] A command economy was instituted with directions given by the Revolutionary Council of the Socialist Military government. Commands were issued without any planning or systematic comprehension, and yet it was claimed to create a socialist economy where "planned proportional development" would prevail.[10]

The New First Four-Year Plan (1971–75)

In March of 1971 the government presented the draft of Burma's First Four-Year Plan (1971–75) as a part of the "Guide to Economic Planning for the Union of Burma" to be approved by the first National Congress of the Burma Socialist Program Party in June 1971. It planned to increase the Gross National Product by 10% in four years and the per capita income by 8%. It emphasized the development of agriculture, meat and fish production, and forestry for export, the establishment of industries for manufacture of consumer goods, increased production of minerals, and development of heavy industry.[11] The deficit balance of payments, the decrease in gold and foreign exchange reserves and lack of funds for state enterprises were Burmese economic problems.[12]

The gross domestic product, which rose only 2.7% per year, partially represents the failure of the First Four-Year Plan. In its first two years, the plan showed a disappointing annual growth rate of 2.2%, while the population rose by 2.3% annually; indicating a negative rate of growth.[13]

While evaluating the performance of the Ne Win government, the World Bank asserted that although Burma provided universal basic education and the malnutrition problem was basically eradicated, its forcible 'drive for equalitarianism and rapid industrialization through import substitution' led to a neglect of agriculture. For instance, rice, the country's staple food and a significant export earner, suffered.

> From about 1.5 million tons annually in the early 1960s—making the country the world's largest rice exporter—Burma's exports shrivelled to about 200,000 tons a decade later. As a result, the share of total exports in the gross domestic product (GDP) during the period also fell, from 16% to 7%.[14]

New Second Four-Year Plan (1974–78)

The First Four-Year Plan was truncated shortly before its completion because of its dismal performance. Therefore, a second plan was introduced which contained more modest economic goals and proposed to rectify the previous decades' economic debacles.

A 4.5% annual growth of GDP was to be secured in the Second Four-Year Plan. This was to be accomplished by emphasizing agriculture, forestry, mining, and transport. Such a realistic approach was the first of its kind since the Two-Year Recovery Plan of 1948–50.

By increasing acreage and the swift adoption of green revolution techniques, an improvement of rice production was envisioned. Forestry output was to rise by stepping up conservation, mechanization, and to minimize wastage. Mining improvement was mainly directed to accentuate oil production and exploration. Various small scale as well as private investors were encouraged; a significant departure from previous plans.[15]

This revised plan was a success and exceeded its targeted GDP with a 4.8% annual growth rate. The performance of agriculture also was ameliorated in the Second Plan (1975–78), registering a 3.6% annual growth rate, in contrast to the previous ten years' (1964–74) growth rate of 2.4%.

The introduction of high yielding variety (HYV) rice, which constituted a part of the green revolution technique, was one major factor in the agricultural recovery. Table 7-1 shows how HYV caused Burma's rice yields to improve during the plan period.

Although HYV seeds were first introduced to Burma in 1966, it took a decade before the Burmese National Agricultural Corporation was able to develop sixteen new effective varieties of seeds. Thus, by 1978–79, one of every seven acres was given to HYV.[16]

In reviewing the sluggish new investments during the previous decades, the Burmese Assembly passed a Right of Private Enterprise Act in 1977, which listed twenty-seven economic categories wherein the private sector was permitted to operate. At the same time, the Act guaranteed that manufacturing and transportation enterprises would not be nationalized until 1994.[17] This opening of doors to private enterprise by Socialist Burma was another pragmatic relaxation for economic progress. As early as 1976, Harriman had predicted "Burma's first steps to capitalism."[18] Offshore oil drilling contracts were signed with the Japanese National Oil Company in 1981. However, French and other companies had already negotiated drilling rights before 1977. In 1977, Burma became an oil exporter and by 1980 Burma produced 12 million barrels, i.e., 2 million barrels over her domestic consumption. Most of the surplus was purchased by Japan.[19]

Thus, improved rice production and greater export earnings from rice and oil provided a sound

TABLE 7-1
Rice Production in Burma

Year	Million Acres Sown	% High Yielding Variety	lbs/acre	Million US (2000lb) tons
1950-55	9.75	—	1316.55	6.1
1956-60	10.50	—	1401.57	6.6
1961-65	12.00	—	1474.96	8.2
1966-70	12.50	1.3	1466.91	8.4
1970-71	12.50	4.0	1518.82	8.8
1971-72	12.50	3.9	1535.82	8.8
1972-73	12.25	4.4	1453.48	8.0
1973-74	12.75	5.0	1576.99	9.4
1974-75	13.00	6.8	1572.52	9.3
1975-76	13.00	7.9	1637.85	10.1
1976-77	12.75	8.9	1697.82	10.2
1977-78	12.75	10.0	1740.78	10.3
1978-79	13.00	14.8	1880.40	11.5

Source: John McBeth, "The Party Aids the Paddy", *Far Eastern Economic Review* (October 16, 1981), p. 91.

fiscal base for the Second Four-Year Plan's success.

The Third Four-Year Plan (1979–82)

The achievement of the Second Plan indicated that the economic decline and stagnation of 1962–74 was heretofore remedied. The nation was moving forward.[20] Therefore, the Third Four-Year Plan not only started with optimism, but its targets were more optimistic: 6.6% annual growth rate of the GDP and 5.8% for agriculture. The plan also projected private domestic investments to quadruple and total investment to double over the previous plan levels.[21] Exports were projected to rise 24% per annum.

Certain obvious problems about the growth of the private sector were foreseeable. The private sector is partly plagued by the small size of its operations. Of the 490 factories employing more than 100 workers in 1978, only 19 were privately-owned. In sharp contrast, 98% of the 34,574 factories with less than 10 workers were in the private sector. What the "private sector" means in Burmese industry is a dingy, dilapidated hut with a few tools and smuggled spared parts, and selling either some repair services or some very simple metal goods. It is questionable how financial incentives can be extended to these small-scale enterprises.[22]

The Third Plan can be viewed as successful because during three years of its four-year span the country's annual growth rate of GDP registered an average 6.7%, a little more than was originally targeted for. Agriculture's (mainly rice) grand achievement may be accredited for pushing the GDP to such a satisfactory level.

> Agriculture's fine performance was explained as the result of a vigorous programme of official assistance to and supervision of farmers, especially rice farmers, as rice is Burma's main food and export crop. Farmers were required to grow high yield varieties on 2.4 million hectares (or 45% of the total area under rice) while fertilizers and pesticides were provided at subsidized prices. At the same time, mass voluntary labour was mobilized at critical stages of the farming process, such as transplanting and harvesting, to speed up operations and overcome a farm labour shortage.[23]

As a result, the rice yield rose 41.5%, from about 1650 kilograms per acre in 1977 to 2300 in 1981.[24] In a country where agriculture accounts for over two-thirds of employment and where over 60% of the raw materials needed for the country's industries are agro-based, this outstanding rise in agricultural productivity brought about prosperity in general. However, such prosperity stimulated an increase in domestic oil consumption, thereby curtailing oil exports which are an important foreign-exchange earner.

Burma has been mismanaged in terms of economic planning ever since her independence. In her overreaction to decolonize her economy, the leaders of Burma not only did not allow any local entrepreneurship to emerge, but in the name of nationalization and socialism, put the management of all means of production in the hands of inexperienced, currupt and dogmatic politicians and bureaucrats. This naturally led to failure of economic growth and is responsible for a stagnation of the economy. But since the mid-1970s, pragmatic and open door policies have brought about significant economic gains in the country.

INDONESIA

Indonesia, a country which has shown signs of progress only in recent years, has had its own ups and downs and major shifts in planning policy. Those policies may be divided into: (1) Sukarno's Planning Adventurism (1951-66) and (2) Suharto's Planning Realism since 1966. The Adventurism caused a debacle of the national economy, whereas, Realism has started to generate some progress.

Planning Adventurism (1951-66)

This had three planning periods: The Five-Year Plan (1951-56), The Four-Year Plan (1956-60) and The Eight-Year Plan (1960-68). The first one was not effectively implemented and hence, did not severely damage the economy, whereas, the second and third ones were vigorously operational resulting in an untold economic dislocation.

*The Five-Year Plan (1951-*56). This was a combination of "urgency programs," and not a well conceived Five-Year Plan. Agricultural output was expected to be increased by application of fertilizers, irrigation, and by undertaking reclamation of new fields for paddy. Very little of this was achieved. Though labor was plentiful, mechanization of small farms was attempted. Some new goals and funds for the plan were modest. As the budget and the production targets were fixed annually,[25] there was not much true planning, but rather a year to year extension of economic goals. During this period, economic conditions showed signs of deterioration: (a) an imbalance occurred in export-import trade resulting in loss of foreign exchange at a faster rate than any other country in the world,[26] and (b) financial "paralysis" affected the organs of the state itself.[27] The only sector of economy which maintained some economic viability was petrochemical; but even that was facing increasing problems.

*The Five-Year Plan (1956-*60). This plan proved to be a bitter failure. Unrealistically oriented to industry and infrastructural development, this plan allocated only 13% of its total budget of million Rupiah 12,500 (347 Rupiahs equaled United States $1 in 1972) to agriculture with an additional allocation of 9% for irrigation. Industry, transport, and power accounted for two-thirds of the budget. This was done in spite of the fact that about 50% of the national income was generated from agriculture with the overwhelming majority of Indonesians being subsistance farmers. Though the goals of 3% annual increase of national income and 1.3% increase in per capita annual income were modest, the assumption that 40% of the increase in national income should be invested in capital formation seemed unrealistic. Rubber, the second most important foreign exchange earner was particularly neglected and the situation became much worse when the Dutch-owned plantations were nationalized in 1957, only to be run inefficiently by inexperienced local management. In spite of so much emphasis on government leadership in industrialization, the only substantial success was realized in the privately owned petroleum industry. Neglect of agriculture, on the other hand, brought about a stagnation in rice production. Since the population continued to grow at an annual rate of over 2% during this time, it became necessary to import foodstuffs, further offsetting the import-export balance. Futher criticism of the plan has aimed at the unsuccessful attempt to move people from the populated areas of Java to the less populated outlying areas. Finally, Higgins comments that the plan paid insufficient attention to the problems of entrepreneurship and management.[29]

The Eight-Year Development Plan (1960-68). The general goals of this plan were to make Indonesia a self-sufficient nation and to upgrade the people economically, culturally, and militarily. These goals were to be fully achieved by the end of the eight year period. The resources were to be directed toward increasing the production of consumer goods and preparing grounds for capital development for the first three years of the plan. The last three years were to be devoted to the creation of major industrial projects which would make steel, aluminum, petrochemical products, rayon and also to extend light industries. The cultural goals were the development of a "collection of cultural hertiage," a "national museum," "cultural gardens," an Indonesian language, and many similar projects. Military goals were termed "special projects," and were secret.[30]

The basic concept of the plan was simple; it was divided into two separate parts. The "A" projects, 335 in number, were the *core* development program and intended to contribute to the country's overall national development. "A" projects had 77% of their total planned expenditure as the foreign exchange component. The "B" projects, 8 in number, were earmarked for providing additional local financial resource and increase foreign exchange revenues sufficiently to finance all the "A" projects.[31] The "B" projects included oil, rubber, timber, and tourism.

The unrealistic transport-and-industry bias of the "A" projects can be assessed from the fact that 58.8% of the total Eight-Year allocation was for transport and industry including clothing. To meet the expenses of "A" projects the monetary exchange rate of the Indonesian rupiah was artificially raised in the international market, which prompted large-scale black market currency exchanges and smuggling. In the absence of expected monetary support from the "B" projects, financing of "A" projects prompted soaring inflation which forced the economy into a virtual collapse by 1965. Since the majority of the people were farmers and did not need to purchase their subsistence necessities, the inflation did not really hurt them. The urban dwellers and the salaried employees were hit hardest and they were the people who were starving. The cost of living index jumped. This meant for example, that a dress purchased for ten dollars in 1958 cost over $360 in 1963. In 1965, prices had risen more than 500% in one year.[32] This inflation during the 1960s was probably one of the worst experienced in modern history. Corruption of government officials was another result of inflation since they were paid by contract and could not continue to meet their own expenses. The government made attempts to stop inflation. Taxes were increased to bring in more revenue and stabilize the rupiah. This was unsuccessful because the tax collectors were bribed for an amount less than the tax, and the government received even less tax revenue than before. Even when the government introduced a price freeze, the law could not be enforced because of corruption.[33]

In the process of implementation, development projects were weighted down by such non-developmental projects as defense and cultural activity. Confrontation with Malaya caused defense expenditures to consume a good proportion of the budget in 1963. The pompously celebrated Asian Games of 1962 also drained considerable money.

The inexperienced state officials not only mismanaged the nationalized enterprises but hastily launched uneconomic business projects, to enhance "prestige." The largest source of internal funds, which came from the Chinese minority, as they controlled 70% of the country's economy,[34] was alienated only to satisfy narrow nationalism. Food imports increased. Capital became scarce. The country was in real distress by 1966, when President Sukarno was replaced by Suharto. Thus, not only the plan failed, but the man behind it also failed.

Planning Realism (1966-)

President Suharto, preoccupied with the necessity of consolidating political power let the Eight-Year Plan complete its term, but instituted a new planning policy of economic recovery and development.

The Five-Year Development Plan (1969–74). Under Suharto's leadership a new Five-Year Plan (Repelita I) was started in 1969. "In official terms the only emphasis in the First Five-Year Plan is on the agricultural sector and the rehabilitation of the infrastructure."[35] Agricultural development has been achieved by increasing crop production, (particularly rice) and by supplying fertilizers and better agricultural tools.

In the industrial sector, private enterprise, of both national and foreign origin, has been recognized as a major element of development. Two laws were promulgated: the Foreign Capital Investment Law of 1967 and the Domestic Capital Investment Law of 1968. "Both laws contain incentives, facilities and guarantees by the government to new investment..."[36] Economic stability was restored. Inflation was already down to 112% by 1967 and 65% in 1968 and was expected to be reduced to only 20–30% in 1972.[37] Currency and prices have also been stabilized since 1967. Political stability was restored when the 1971 elections, the first in 16 years, supported the government in power. All those encouraging signs were responded to by 500 foreign investment projects involving committed capital of U.S. $1,700 million and by 800 domestic projects involving an investment of $1,200 million from 1967 through 1972. A $300 million investment in oil exploration was additional.[38] These investments provided great incentive for the expansion of industries, particularly textiles and chemicals. They also created new jobs.

However, the ills of foreign investment started to surface. "...recently...many domestic textile enterprises had been forced to close down because they were unable to compete against the greater capital and higher technical skill of foreign (mainly Japanese) textile manufacturers."[39] This has resulted in government prohibition of foreign investment in certain industries in 1972. Nonetheless, it cannot be denied that foreign aid, mainly from the United States, constituted the major part (58.7%) of the total funds allocated for the Five-Year Development Plan.

Signs of Progress. The following facts clearly indicted the progress registered by Indonesia during Five-Year Plan period (1969–74):

1. Private savings had shown optimistic trends; time deposits in state banks increased from Rps. 4,500 million in December 1968 to Rps. 85,800 million in 1971.[40]
2. Exports surpassed the imports.
3. Per capita income in the first three years of the plan increased from $70 to $90.[41]

Although a substantial increase in the export sector was noticed during this five-year plan (Repelita I), it overfulfilled its targets only because they were modestly set by the Suharto Government. For instance, Repelita I targeted an annual growth rate of 5%, however, throughout 1969–73 the gross domestic product rose by 8.4% per annum. Also manufacturing (9.4%), mining (17%), transportation (12%), and banking/finance (30%) showed significant annual rates of growth during the five-year plan, but the actual annual growth rate of agriculture fell short of the planned target.[42]

Signs of Weakness. Even though Suharto's first five year plan proved unexpectedly successful, it showed certain weaknesses. Rice, which is the staple food, could not keep pace with its targeted growth rate of 5.7% per annum. Instead, production rose at a modest rate of 4.3%, but the demand for rice rose more speedily because of the rise in real incomes. Indonesia was, thus, forced to augment its rice import from .24 million tons in 1969 to 1.9 million tons in 1973.

The government tried to rectify the situation by expanding farm lands and using green revolution techniques, however, these programs proved to be inadequate for any dramatic increase in rice production. In order for Indonesia to become self-sufficient, it was essential that the country significantly improve its output of rice. Also, it was noticed that in 1974 manufacturing production began to show signs of stagnation, even though in the first three years of Repelita I marked increases in manufacturing production were registered.[43]

The Second Five-Year Plan (Repelita II, 1974–79). Repelita II was put in motion to lay the foundations for long-run economic and social development of the country. The plan was introduced during the time when the price of primary commodities was sharply accelerating on the world market, resulting in greatly augmented Indonesian export earnings, particularly from crude petroleum, which rose 314% during the years of 1972–74.

Repelita II was targeted for a 50% increase in real gross domestic product. Thus, the annual growth rate was projected at 7.5%. The Suharto government set these goals with the expectation of a boom in the extractive exports. The annual growth rate of agriculture was set at a modest 4.6% while industry was put at 13%. Although there were signs of increased earnings from exports, its growth rate was actually underestimated at 10.5%. On the whole, not only did the plan start on an optimistic note, but also accomplished a satisfactory performance.

The acutal growth rate of the gross domestic product fell only a little short of the 7.5% target, registering a 6.9% per annum during the second five-year plan. Whereas the manufacturing sector grew as projected, the annual growth rate of agriculture was 40% less than what was predicted.

Though export earnings rose substantially during the plan period, the plan's performance can articulately be summarized as follows:

> Even though the extra export income meant a healthier fiscal year, most of the increase came from higher prices rather than increased production. The available data shows commodity production for export and domestic markets generally below targets outlined in the Second Five-Year Plan (Repelita II), and in many cases production decreased.[44]

Moreover, because the Indonesians are predominantly Moslem and as the country has a labor-surplus economy, large numbers of them have been attracted to the oil-rich Middle Eastern countries, from which a good deal of money is sent back to Indonesia. This in turn stimulates the Indonesia's national income and strengthens the foreign exchange balance. It was estimated that by the end of the 1970s there were 20,000 Indonesian workers in Saudi Arabia who remitted about U.S. $132 million every year to their home.[45] However, it should be noted that any instability in the Middle East oil economy will have repercussions in Indonesia. In addition, foreign aid financed "... 54.3% of the develpoment budget, as opposed to the Repelita target of 22.3% for fiscal 1977–78."[46] This type of dependence on foreign resource is economically dangerous.

Family planning was accentuated during this plan period, which showed encouraging results. For instance, the annual population growth dropped from 2.2% in 1971 to 2% in 1976. Therefore, the original population projection of 250 million was lowered to 210 million for the year 2000.[47] Any significant real rise in the standard of living was doubted during the plan period.

Although the development budget (Rps 2, 168 billion) is 81% more than the original target expenditures under Repelita II, the cost-of-living index has risen nearly 75% and population increased 9 million since the targets were drawn up. The amount this development contributes to raising the real standard of living of the Indonesian people is one of the major debates currently running through Jakarta's planning bureaux.[48]

Repelita III (1979–84). This five-year plan was launched when the annual population growth rate had declined to less than 2% and increased earnings from petroleum exports were occurring. Like the previous two plans, Repelita III aimed at increased food production, greater employment, equitable income distribution, and relieving Java's overcrowdedness.[49] Furthermore, "eight paths towards the equitable distribution of the fruits of development were devised."[50] Also, six million new jobs were planned by 1983,[51] and a 6.5% annual growth rate of the gross domestic product was projected. Investments were projected to rise from Rps. 4,915 billion in 1978–79 to Rps. 11,145 bilion in 1983–84. During this same period, consumers' import goods were to drop from 21.1% to 15.6% of total imports.[52]

In 1981, Indonesia's foreign exchange reserves hit an unprecedented high, bursting through the U.S. $12 billion mark.[53] Although this situation was more favorable than the previous Repelitas, it began to change in 1982. The oil glut and decreased consumption, resulting from worldwide recession and conservation, were responsible for the export earnings to dwindle in 1982. Such a situation put a lid on the technocrat's dream of accelerating the country's economic base by creating capital-intensive projects. The Indonesian economy started to show signs of weakness.

A new policy during this period was devised to distribute the fruits of development more equitably by providing special favors to indigenous Indonesians (*pribumi*) to invest in small businesses. If the *pribumi* investors were available for small contracts, they were preferred over others. The policy, in effect, was politically motivated and had little economic consequences.

The ethnic Chinese community, consisting of 2% of the population had traditionally dominated the business sector and contolled over half of the country's economic activity.[54] Many local Indonesians are unhappy with such a situation. Suharto's Government, by its pro-*pribumi* stand, was able to take advantage of the political issue without realizing the economic consequences of encouraging inexperienced *pribumi* entrepreneurs.

THAILAND

Thailand had begun to show signs of national development in the 1960s. It was at this time that certain factors from within the country combined with external conditions to upset the equilibrium. These conditions seriously threatened any future growth in Thailand. However, starting from late 1970s, its economy has shown signs of progress.

The Six-Year Plan (1961–66)

In 1958, the government announced its intentions to disassociate itself with large-scale industrial investments. This was almost a complete reversal for the Thai government. Prior to this time, it dominated industry with its ownership of factories, producing cotton textiles, gunny sacks, glass, chemicals, sugar, and other products. All government enterprises were turned over to private investors with the exception of the public utilities, cigarette production, and armament manufacturing.[55] Thus, the Six-Year Plan, initiated in 1961, proposed to spend $1575 million of which only 7.94% was earmarked for industry and mining. Of the remaining funds, 14.15% was allocated for agricultural development, but approximately three-fifths of the full amount was invested in transport and social development.[56] The aim was not to bring immediate economic improvement, but to build the social and economic foundation upon which substantial development could be realized later. In spite of this intention, the country experienced great economic success during this period of time. The GNP increased 8%, rice production increased from 7,834 thousand metric tons in 1960, to 13,500 thousand in 1966.[57]

The Second Five-Year Plan (1967–71)

The Second Plan was designated to increase government spending by 72% over that of the First Plan but with some shifts in emphasis. For example, the position of agriculture was rightfully improved, but it still consumed only 20.23% of the total plan allocation. Industrial development was relegated to a mere 1.58% thus, leaving industry almost totally dependent upon private capital, both internal and external. Transportation and social development continued to hold the strongest position in the plan with 30.58% and 34.62% of the total allocation respectively.[58] Policies relating to the implementation of the Second Plan included:

> ...emphasis on development of rural areas to increase income in that sector, expansion of employment opportunities and the upgrading of skills, encouragement of accelerated private industrial investments through government inducement, an increase in agricultural productivity, and enhancement of the role of science and technology. The government accepted as its major functions the implementation of economic and social infrastructural programs and the provision of maintenance of a climate conducive to increased private investment, both domestic and foreign.[59]

Although annual per capita income increased from $146 to $184 during this time, the Second Plan was not the overall success that the First Plan was. The balance of payments deficit continued to widen. Though several dams and irrigation projects were completed, bad weather conditions—mainly drought—prevented rice production from rising. Continued growth of population at about 3% per annum consumed the otherwise exportable rice surplus of the country. The National Economic Development Board admitted the following pitfalls of the Second Plan:

1. There has been a wide regional disparity of wealth distributions; Northeastern region, endemically a depressed area, had less than one-third of the average of the central region (around Bangkok).
2. Agriculture, the principal source of Thai livelihood, continued to be left largely at the mercy of unpredictable weather, particularly drought.
3. Two principal export items of Thailand, rice and rubber, have traditionally faced price fluctuations in the world market. During the plan period, world prices for both went downward, causing problems in balance of trade and depression in the agricultural sector.
4. Thai farmers' ignorance of the internal and external marketing situation has been taken unnecessary advantage of by the middlemen.
5. "...American military presence contributed to the instability of Thailand's economic foundation. American expenditure in Thailand in support of the Vietnam War averaged $218.75 million during the plan's five-year period, causing rapid growth in certain sectors of the economy, particularly services and construction. But this noneconomic factor...was unable to create firm foundations for future development."[60]

Third Five-Year Plan (1971–76)

The gross domestic product (GDP) during the plan period was targeted to rise at 7% annually. Rural development constituted a major proportion of the plan policy, which also envisioned a reduction of rural-urban income disparity. Also part of the plan were regional development strategies, which aimed at increased agricultural production and an integrated family planning to lower the population growth rate from 3.0% to 2.5% per annum. The depressed Northeastern region was earmarked principally for expansion of infrastructure and rural employment opportunities.[61]

During the Third Plan mid-years, the economy showed sluggish trends, mainly because of declining exports resulting from the worldwide recession after the 1973 Arab oil embargo. Total rice exports decreased sharply, from 1.57 million metric tons in 1971 to .84 million in 1973. However, by 1975 total rice exports rose to .94 million metric tons. The balance of payments deficit for 1975 reached a distressed Baht 2,000 million. But the most serious economic casuality was the 30% drop of public expenditure in 1974.[62]

In 1976, an economic recovery was registered along with the cessation of the worldwide recession. The recovery was backed by a continuingly strong agricultural base of the country for which the foundation was laid in the late 1950s, whereby export diversification of commercial crops was specifically emphasized.

> The government invested in agricultural infrastructure but left industry to the private sector, which responded with high investment ratios of near 16% of gross domestic product. Moreover, the official road-building projects, together with malaria eradication, opened the "upland frontier" to cultivation of maize, kanaf, sugar and tapioca, and moved the economy out of its previous excessive dependence on rice.[63]

Rice exports climbed to 1.9 million metric tons in 1976. Nevertheless, it should be noted that production of maize, tapioca, and sugarcane rose over 100%, while rice production rose only 40% from 1972 to 1976.[64] Also noteworthy is that in 1976, both maize and tapioca together earned approximately 50% more in export revenue than rice, while the export revenue from sugar was only slightly less than rice.[65] Thus, diversification of Thailand's agricultural export base proved to substantially improve the country's earning power and decrease its dependence on rice during the Third Plan.

The GDP fell just short of the Plan target, averaging an annual rate of 6.2%. In terms of regional distribution, the central region situated around the metropolis of Bangkok and the heart of the productive Chao Phraya delta, grew at an annual rate of 7.1%. The Northeast, which had been particularly neglected, grew only at a rate of 5.4% during 1971–76, but the central region produced 57% of the GDP in 1971, and this reached 60% in 1976.

> The northeast has received the smallest share of the development budget in the past. Funds for the agricultural

sector in the northeast amounted to only Baht 238.4 per capita during the Third Plan. The figure for the central region was almost double that.[66]

The higher growth rate of the central area negated the plan strategy of reducing rural-urban disparity because the urbanized Bangkok area (the main hub of the central region) developed at a pace greater in comparison to the other regions. Thai planners not only recognized the neglect of the predominantly rural Northeast area, but realized its potential threat to the national stability. Such a realization is also expressed in the Fourth Plan:

> The regions with the most serious insurgency problems tend to be the regions which are the least developed. In 1975, the northeast region had a per capita gross regional product of only Baht 3,036 (U.S. $150), and the number of people living in the areas classified as insurgents is equivalent to 52.29% of the total number of people living in insurgency throughout the country.[67]

Fourth Five-Year Plan (1977–81)

This plan (also known as the Fourth National Economic Development Plan) in its first year started with a thriving export sector and expanding domestic economy. It targeted an average annual growth rate of 7.3% for the GDP; 3% for agriculture; and 9% for industry and; 11.2% for mining. Population's annual growth rate was projected to decline by 1981 to 2.1%.

A link between poverty and communism was highlighted in the Plan document, which shifted emphasis from the 'heavy' strategy (development of power, transport, and communications) to 'soft' social programs, stressing on-farm development, whereby marketing and credit were extended to regional industries and to farmers' organizations.[68]

The problems of the development of the Northeastern region were acknowledged as the area stood at the bottom of the national income scale with 41% of the families earning less than Baht 6,000 per year. According to Thai standards, this income is at a real poverty level. The Northeast's problem is not in its land tenure system because the region does not suffer the extremes of landlords' exploitation as the farmers generally own their land. These farmers, however, practice small-scale subsistance farming without incentives generated from commercialization. The highly porous soil, mainly of leteritic origin, not only make irrigation difficult in the region, but also is responsible for low crop yields.[69]

Responsible for the success of the Fourth Plan were the expansion of exports, agriculture's significant performance and the beginning of gas exploitation in the Gulf of Thailand (Fig. 7–2). Although in 1977 the GDP registered a low growth rate (6.2%), it eventually picked up in 1981 (7.6%). Thus, the GDP grew almost in accordance with the Fourth Plan expectation. The agricultural sector grew at an annual rate of 3.9%, which surpassed the Fourth Plan target. Domestic natural gas supplies reached 200 million cubic feet per day. Population growth rate declined to 2.1% as projected, in 1981.

As countries progress and turn to commercial agriculture and industrialization, new problems surface. In Thailand the problem was petroleum imports, which in 1979 supplied 83% of the country's energy requirements. Moreover, in 1979 alone, Thailand's expanding economy accrued an additional demand for petroleum products by approximately 14%.[70] Therefore, when oil prices rose in 1979, the Thai economy felt its effect. Even though the Thai planners found it relatively inexpensive to import crude petroleum and then refine it in the country, the refinery capacity (both existing and projected) was seen to have increasing difficulty in keeping pace with sharply rising demands.

It is evident from Table 7–2 that agricultural production rose significantly during this five-year period (1977–81). The most spectacular progress was recorded by maize, tapioca, sugarcane and cotton. Also rice production registered a moderate increase. It was also noticeable that by 1981 the Thai agricultural base was reasonably diversified and therefore stood on a sound progressive foundation.

Fifth Five-Year Plan (1982–86)

The Fifth Five-Year Plan (also known as the Fifth National Economic Development Plan) set ambitious targets which included the following:

i) decreasing dependence on petroleum for energy needs from 75% to 46% by replacing imported oil with domestic gas and hydro-electric projects;
ii) increasing exports by 15% annually, with manufactured commodities achieving 45% of the total exports in 1986;
iii) Fiscal balance to be reached in budgetary allocations;
iv) gradual correction of export-import balance;
v) reduction of rural-urban disparities and;
vi) advancement of Thailand to the rank of a new industrial country.[71]

TABLE 7-2
Index of Agricultural Production in Thailand

	Weights	1972	1975	1976	1977	1978	1979	1980	1981	1982
Crops	63.80	100	128	141	137	158	149	162	179	182
Paddy (rice)	28.02	100	121	120	111	135	136	135	143	147
Rubber	4.23	100	104	117	128	139	158	149	151	160
Maize	3.03	100	218	203	141	230	251	240	304	319
Jute and kenaf	2.32	100	72	43	56	72	61	49	58	63
Tapioca roots	4.95	100	179	257	298	442	279	416	447	403
Coconuts	2.11	100	121	129	132	123	99	105	119	134
Sugarcane	3.49	100	209	274	199	213	131	196	304	284
Tobacco leaves	3.60	100	130	134	132	135	138	130	147	151
Kapok and bambax fiber	0.47	100	111	104	97	70	88	78	90	104
Groundnuts	0.80	100	93	99	69	83	71	84	103	103
Cotton	0.57	100	58	54	184	151	289	390	466	506
Other	10.21	100	115	117	116	120	119	119	126	142
Forest products	7.45	100	92	101	95	79	90	72	58	52
Animal products	13.50	100	98	103	115	117	123	133	141	151
Fish catch	15.25	100	93	101	130	125	132	119	107	101
Total	100	100	118	129	131	145	141	148	159	162

Source: Based on Bank of Thailand data. The rice continued to be the most significant crop in the 1970s and early 1980s, though the rate of production (growth) was higher for most other agricultural products.

Thus, Thailand embarked on a major policy reform on the economic front by redressing imbalances, bringing about equitable growth, and uplifting itself to the ranks of a new industrial nation.[72]

During the Fifth Plan period, the GDP was targeted to increase 6.6% annually; 4.5% per annum for agriculture and; 16.4% per annum for mining, thereby these sectors were projected to grow more rapidly than in the previous plan. By 1986, natural gas production was targeted to reach 525 million cubic feet per day. The average annual value of exports was aimed to rise from Baht 153 million in the Fourth Plan to Baht 388 million during the Fifth Plan.

This plan also unfolded policies for restoring economic and financial stability, which are most important for sustained long term growth.[73] In 1982, Niksch raised doubts about the possibility of achieving the aforementioned opitimistic goals in an atmosphere of domestic political uncertainty, international pressures for economic reform, amid depressed economic growth in the industrial nations.[74]

PHILIPPINES

The Philippines was one of the last countries in Southeast Asia to embark on national planning.

Four-Year Development Plan (1974–77)

After an emergency was proclaimed in 1972, President Marcos proposed to launch a Four-Year Plan for the Philippines. The Plan targeted to increase the gross domestic product (GDP) from an average annual growth rate of 5.5% to 7.5%, while reducing the population growth rate from 3.1% per annum (1960–70) to 2.4% by 1977. The plan also envisaged to raise the standard of living mainly by augmenting rural income. Other goals included the achievement of self-sufficiency in food production, rationalization of industries, equitable income distribution, and the reduction of regional imbalances in economic development. Agricultural and industrial developments were planned in harmony with an emphasis on the expansion of infrastructure.[75]

The Plan failed to achieve its overall proposed target of 7.5% annual economic growth. In its first two years the economy grew at an annual growth rate

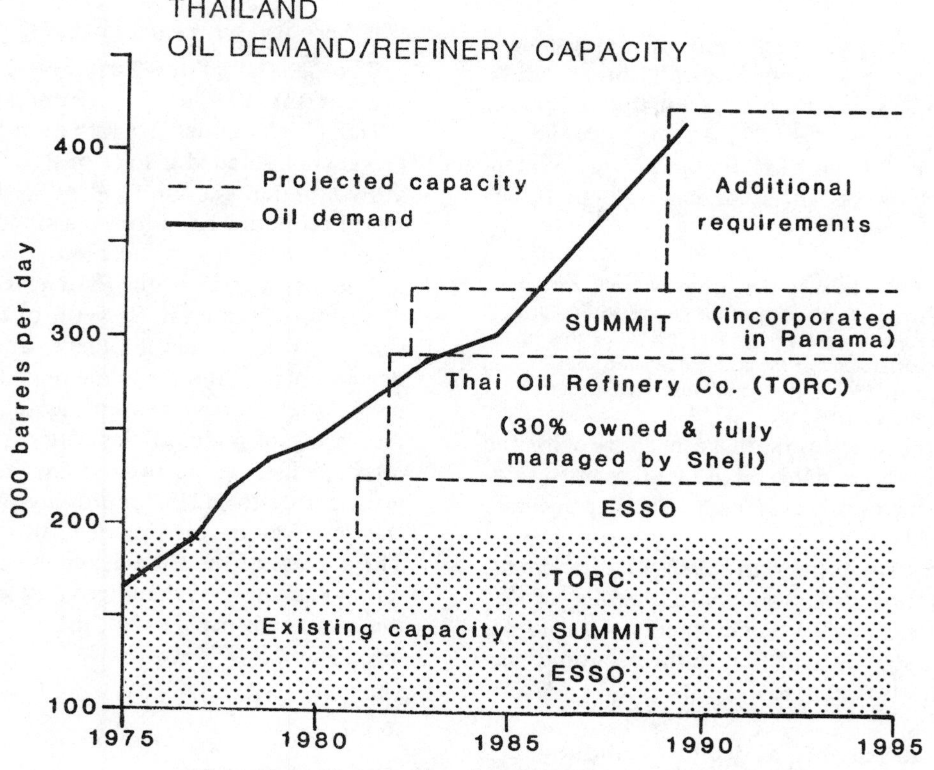

Figure 7-2. Oil-demand and Refinery Capacity in Thailand.

(**Source:** *Far Eastern Economic Review*)

between 5 to 6%, while during its last two years the annual growth rate was between 6 to 7%. Imported oil price increases not only caused higher inflation, but also strained the balance of payments. Agricultural profits were adversely affected by declining sugar prices in the world market. Nonetheless, domestic rice and corn production improved.

Though equitable income distribution was one of the basic goals of the Plan, the 1975 official data revealed that, according to Philippine standards, 85% of all households in the country fell in the low income category, while 10% and 5% were in the middle and high income groups, respectively. The data also indicated that the wealthy were advancing economically at a faster pace than the poor. For instance, family income was up by 53% for the high income group, 32% for the middle income group and 15% for the low income group.[76] Thus, the gap between the rich and poor was widening. Reversing such structural trends already established in the economy placed a tremendous burden upon the planners.

The First Five-Year Plan (1978–82)

This plan identified the crucial problems in the country and, of course, aimed to remedy them. The problems were found to be high population growth, balance of payment deficits, income inequality, price instability, energy supply problems and unemployment. Furthermore, in the plan, foreign investments were to be promoted and new industries were planned in southern areas for better economic and regional balance within the country. However, in order for the country to move towards industrialization, the Plan aimed at a further contraction of agriculture's share in the GDP.

The average annual growth target was set at 5.5% for agriculture and 9.7% for industry during the plan period.[77] The plan also projected an average annual increment of 7.5% in the production of goods and services.[78]

From its beginning the Plan was plagued with financial difficulties. The World Bank, who provided much of the financing for the Plan (the foreign exchange component was estimated at $11.7 billion during 1978–82), recommended to cut the Philippines' borrowing by half.[79] Further, 95% of the nation's energy was provided by oil and the oil price rises of the late 1970s meant that the cost of imported oil accounted for 40% of the country's total import bill. Inflation rose to 19% in 1980 although reduced to 13% in 1981. Further, the nation's foreign debt increased to a dangerous level of $15.37 billion. The aforementioned factors resulted in budget cuts and a slowdown in the implementation of development projects. In 1981, plans for the establishment of 11 industrial projects, costing an estimated 6 billion U.S. dollars, were shelved.[80] Inflation and the accompanying rise in cost of living hit the underprivileged the hardest. An estimate of 1979 by Neher states:

> The poor suffered most severely from the rising cost of living. The national income share of the poorest 40% of the population dropped from 11.7% to 11.2% while the top 20% increased their share of the national income to 55.5% and the wealthiest 5% of the population increased their share from 24.8% to 32%.[81]

The GDP failed to grow in accordance with the planned target. Its annual growth rate remained sluggish at 5.5% during 1978–81 and it further declined to 4.1% in 1982.

The Second Five-Year Plan (1983–87) document, however, did not dwell on the shortfalls of the previous plan as only its achievements were noted. The document summarized that in the economic sector, the country was able to:

> a) sustain increases in agricultural output and maintain self-sufficiency in rice;
>
> b) reduce the dependence on imported oil from more than 90 percent of total consumption in 1978 to around 84 percent by 1981;
>
> c) expand infrastructure support such as transportation, electrification and irrigation;
>
> d) sustain industrial growth through the continued promotion of industrial peace and a favorable investment climate. This resulted in the expansion of industry's share to overall output from 35.7 percent in 1978 to 36.4 percent as of 1981;
>
> e) accelerate export growth, notably in non-traditional manufactures which averaged 34.3 percent annually in 1978–81; and
>
> f) moderate inflation to a tolerable level.[82]

Inspite of these proclaimed accomplishments by the Philippine government, the fact remained that the country had reached a temporary phase of a lesser growth rate because of the world recession which resulted in declining exports. The International Monetary Fund, another lender to the Philippines, made it clear that middle income countries such as the Philippines may now be forced to cutback on growth targets rather than simply keep borrowing in order to maintain growth.[83]

The Second Five-Year Plan (1983–87)

The debacle of the First Five-Year Plan did not prevent the Second Plan from setting an unrealistically high annual growth rate target of 6.5%. This target was pursued inspite of a 5.1% annual rate of growth in the 1960s and a 6.2% in the 1970s when the world economic situation was much better than what might be expected in the 1980s.

The major goals of the Plan have been described as a) sustained economic growth, b) equitable distribution of fruits of development, and c) total human development.[84] It aims at the reduction of unemployment, the improvement of agricultural yields, the redressing of regional disparities, reducing imported oil dependence, decreasing the annual population growth rate to 2.2%, improving infrastructure, and the removal of existing institutional bottlenecks.[85] The success of the Plan depends not only on the better management of the internal economy, but also on the general prosperity of the world market in the middle and late 1980s.

MALAYSIA

Malaysia embarked on a National Plan in 1955, when it was still a British colony. Thereafter, it has had two successive Five-Year Plans. The third (1965–1970) was named the *First Malaysian Plan*. The independence of the country in 1957, inclusion of Sarawak and Sabah in Borneo into the Malaysian Federation, and the separation of Singapore from the Federation in 1965 demanded a new framework for the developmental aspects of the country. The plans in general were greatly successful in fostering economic growth and have resulted in raising the per capita annual income, which is surpassed by only two other countries in the Southeast Asian Realm: Singapore (a city state) and Brunei (a small but oil rich sultanate).

The First Five-Year Plan (1955–60)

This plan involved an expenditure of U.S. $340 million in the five-year period and was framed in accordance with the recommendations of the International Bank. The main thrust of the planning was aimed at agricultural and transportational development. On the agricultural front two major steps were taken: (1) projects to replace the older uneconomic rubber holdings with new ones to increase productivity and (2) clearing of large blocks of virgin land for settlement by pioneer-colonists with ten-acre family holdings[86] to produce commercial as well as subsistence crops.

However, true to the colonial interests of the British regime, the economy of Malaysia was planned so as to provide raw materials (rubber and tin primarily) to the industrialized West. Hence, the country needed to produce those raw materials more efficiently; this involved the development of transportation infrastructure to supply the materials to the port-locations for shipping. In actual terms, a great deal of economic progress was registered in the country. From 1945 through 1960, the economy grew at a commendable annual rate of 4.7%, in spite of internal insurgency, but during the same period the high annual population growth of 2.7% minimized the amount of progress the country could have achieved. Though education received some prominence, the First Five-Year Plan was little more than an extension of a colonial scheme.

The Second Five-Year Plan (1961–65)

The Second Five-Year Plan also did not alter the colonial character of the First. This Plan not only more than doubled the public expenditure compared to the First Plan, but two-thirds of its total investments were earmarked for agriculture and infrastructure development. In the field of highway development alone, the Second Plan expenditures amounted to 25% of the entire plan investment. The Plan document realized the depressed conditions of the rural areas,[87] which are primarily inhabited by the Malays with a high rate of tenant farming.

> Tenancy in itself would not be alarming if the farmer were sure of his livelihood, but insecurity to tenure is a great problem. The length of tenure is only three to four years on the average in the Rice Bowl, and only one year in Kelantan....the plots of land are too small to be economical....Insecurity of tenure is a major factor in low agricultural productivity....Fertilizers are little used on Malay lands, tools are still primitive....[88]

Realizing the rural problem, the Second Plan advocated a program of "Land for the Landless," in which plots of 4,000 acre size were cleared of forest to be distributed to individual landless farmers in 8-acre lots for rubber production. When the rubber tree goes into production after seven years, each farmer would be capable of earning M$1,700 a year, which would also enable him to repay the development cost back to the government.[89] Compared to the return, the program was costly and had to run under the canopy of governmental paternalism. Rural life stagnated and farmers were not sharing equitably in Malaysia's economic growth.[90]

However, efficient administration of the development programs and favorable economic conditions nationally as well as internationally, generated an accelerated pace of economic growth of 6.5% per year during the Second Five-Year Plan.

The First Malaysia Plan (1966–70)

This plan encompassed not only West Malaysia (the Malay Peninsula or formerly British Malaya), but also the newly federated territories of Sabah and Sarawak known collectively as East Malayia. This was the first plan where decolonization trends were visible. Heavy emphasis in infrastructural development was replaced by more meaningful development in agriculture. In terms of Plan expenditure, the five top priorities were: (1) agriculture and rural development: 23.9%, (2) utilities including electricity: 17.2%, (3) defense: 13.1%, (4) transport: 12.0%, and (5) education: 9.7%.[91]

The First Malaysia Plan proposed the creation of 461,000 new jobs while at the same time it lowered the unemployment rate from 6% to 5%. It also instituted a National Family Planning Board to deal with Malaysia's rapid growth in population. Of equal importance was the call for diversification of the economy. Paragraph 21 of the Plan states:

> ...as exports of tin and rubber will not expand fast enough, other products which will earn the needed foreign exchange must be sought. In addition, Malaysians must produce for themselves more and more of the items that are at present imported.[92]

The plan listed palm oil and timber as the new products offering increased export potential. While the First Malaysia Plan called for economic growth through diversification, it maintained a firm stance with regards to a favorable balance of payments. In fact, a strong balance of payments was one of the underlying concerns of the Plan. The "strategy" of the Plan was "...if there is to be an excess of imports over exports, the gap should not exceed the expected amount of capital inflow to pay for such deficits."[93] As a result, as Lee Soo Ann has pointed out, "the development of growth potential is thus limited to those lines of production which will result in a net gain of foreign exchange in the economy, either in the form of new exports or as import substitues."[94] It is within this framework that the Malaysian Gross National Product was projected to increase by 4.8% annually. The growth of the Malaysian economy was expectred to depend heavily upon foreign assistance.

An analysis of the levels of achievement of the Plan reveals that it was the first truly national economic plan and was more comprehensive than any Malayan plan in the past. However, as Harvey Stockwin points out, "it is a plan in the style of a 'five-year budget' and an economic review (rather than a totalistic plan for a wholly-planned economy)....''[95]

Little has been done to diversify export products, as Milton Esman has pointed out:

> Four primary products, rubber, tin, oil palm, and timber contribute about 70% of the export earnings in 1967... Pressure to diversify has been less pronounced than in most countries because the traditional products, rubber and tin have remained profitable over long periods of time.[96]

The timber industry, which had become the victim of excessive exploitation, suffered a setback. The industry lacked any sort of planned development for the future, as it was pointed out:

> High rates of extraction have contributed to the present situation, and here the difficulties have been compounded by the lack of coordination between the various state governments who have pursued their own exploitation policies without due regard to the long-term potential of the industry.[97]

This slowdown in the timber industry dealt a blow to the diversification efforts sought under the First Malaysian Plan. It is, nonetheless, true that the efforts at diversification are gathering slowly, but with a steady momentum. Rubber and tin, which accounted for 70% of Malaysian exports in 1960, declined to comprise 54% in 1970; thus showing signs of diversification.

Many of the Plan's targets had been too conservative. In terms of growth in Gross National Product, the original Plan had sought a rate of 4.8% annual growth; the average for the first four years was 6.6%. In 1970 it was 6%. Likewise, the per annum growth of exports of goods and services was proposed to be less than 1% while it actually reached 6.3% annually.

Despite these over-fulfillments of planned targets, it became evident in 1969 that certain targets were not being met. One of the most important of these is education. Expenditures on education in 1969 dropped 17% from the 1968 level. Because Malaysia deperately needed trained personnel, this decline in the expenditures in education was serious. V. Kanapathy has pointed out:

> In the agricultural sector alone, the output of agricultural scientists and technologists has to be about 300%, if the objectives of the First Malaysia Plan and the Malaysianization programme are to be successfully implemented.[98]

Such an increase in educated personnel was virtually impossible with the cut in educational expenditure. A second major target, which was evidently not being fulfilled, was the lowering of the unemployment rate in West Malaysia, the most developed sector of the country. This had reached a level of 6.8%. A breakdown of these figures reveals the fact that the rate for the 15–19 age group was 20.5% and that of the 20–24 age group was 11.5%. As the 1969 *Colombo Plan* pointed out, though much progress was achieved in the four years of the First Malaysia Plan, the problem of unemployment remained largely unsolved.[99]

The Second Malyasia Plan (1971–75)

The Second Plan investments were equally shared by public and private sectors. This plan went a step further in decolonizing Malaysia's economy by putting forth the target of doubling industrial production by 1975, so that this sector might account for more than 25% of the Gross National Product. The following industries have been particularly specified for growth in the plan: food products, metallic and nonmetallic products, electrical and nonelectrical machinery and transport equipment. Though Malaysian planning has a socialistic coating, it is very realistic about private investment; capital is encouraged from internal sources, and foreign capital is welcomed. "Total foreign financing for the private sector in 1971–75 period is expected to reach $1,150 million out of a total expenditure by the private sector of over $7,800 million.''[100] Malaysia provided one of the best preconditions for foreign investment in Southeast Asia. In 1971, the government gave further incentive to 'priority industries,' such as, electronics; and through these, investors may obtain an eight-year tax holiday and duty-free import of raw materials. If such investment is for production of those goods, which are supposed to be wholly for exports, a foreign entrepreneur may operate even without the traditional rule that 51% of the capital should be Malaysian.[101] However, the Plan realized that the great industrial potentialities created in the country will have to be dependent partly on export market. This will necessitate doubling of manufactured goods exported in 1975 compared to 1970. This is another step in the diversification of the nation's economy.

Combating unemployment was yet another goal of the Plan. In the previous plans economic development had always been geared to a "growth first" basis. But, the Second Plan made it clear that "creation of job opportunities is [was] a major aim.''[102] The first three years of the Second Plan had witnessed declining unemployment. The Plan aimed at creating 600,000 new jobs. Such an aim was made operational by creating labor-intensive industries, where the cost of a new job was only about $8,000 per place as opposed to over $20,000 in the past.[103] (The problem was that the diminutive size of capital available to a worker of such industries depressed his productivity.)

During the Second Malaysia Plan the Gross National Product (GNP) was projected to rise to a rate of 6.8% per annum; however, the GNP exceeded this target and actually grew at a rate of 7.4% per annum. This undoubtedly was an impressive performance. The growth rate resulted largely from an increase in public investment at 17.6% per annum, compared to the First Malaysia Plan's 1.9%.

The manufacturing, utilities and transport sectors showed substantial growth rates of 10.9%, 10.4% and 12.6%, respectively. The agriculture sector, on the other hand, grew only 5.9% per annum during 1971-75. It should be noted that as a larger input of capital was made in the non-agricultural sector, it was not unreasonable for that sector to progress more rapidly. Agricultural development included a noticeable increase in palm oil production, resulting from greater export demands. The adoption of the green revolution techinque (the use of high yielding seeds) and an expansion of planted acreage by more than a million acres resulted in a significant increase of rice production: 25% rise during 1971-75. Therefore, by 1975 Malaysia produced approximately 87% of its domestic rice needs; almost reaching self-sufficiency.

Since the export sector is very important to the Malaysian economy, its diversification—i.e., loosening the country's dependence on rubber exports, is recognized as a crucial objective of the Second Plan.

> Changes in the sectorial growth in the Malaysian economy were reflected by changes in the structure of the export sector. In 1970 rubber accounted for 33 percent of the total export earning and palm oil 5 percent; by 1975 these shares were 22 and 15 percent. Over the same period the share of manufactured exports rose from 8 percent to 21 percent; the highest growth rates were registered by the electrical machinery industry (42 percent per annum) and the industrial machinery industry (22 percent per annum)."[104]

New Economic Policy (NEP). In 1971 a New Economic Policy was launched as a twenty-year Perspective Plan, which is to be completed by the four successive five-year plans ending in 1990. Although the details of the policy has been explained in Chapter 14, its broad objectives may be summarized as follows:

a) eradication of poverty among *all* Malaysians and
b) reduction and elimination of local Malay (*bumiputra*) economic inequality in relation to other Malaysians who are of Chinese and Indian ethnic orgin.

In operational terms, the Perspective Plan sets forth two specific quota goals.

> The first is that employment by sector should approximate the ethnic composition of the population, which in 1970 was 55 percent Malay and other indigenous peoples, 34 percent Chinese, 9 percent Indian and 2 percent others. The second is that by 1990 Malays and other indigenous people would own and manage at least 30 percent of the share capital of the corporate sector, as compared to 2.4 percent share in 1970. The share of other Malaysians [Chinese and Indians] is to increase from 34.3 percent to 40 percent, while that of foreigners is to decline from 63.3 percent to 30 percent.[105]

It is evident from Table 7-3 that both mean and median income of Peninsular or West Malaysians have increased significantly between 1970-76, indicating a reduction in the incidence of poverty. However, a progressive increase in the mean/median ratio from 1970 through 1976 reflects increased inequality in income distribution among all Malaysians in general.[106] Although ethnic Malays remained the lowest in terms of mean monthly household income, they show the sharpest percentage increase during the six-year period; while the Indians' income registered the lowest rate of growth. Thus, during the Second Malaysia Plan, NEP succeeded in infusing a greater pace of economic growth among *bumiputras*.

The Third Malaysia Plan (1976-80)

The Third Malaysia Plan projected a GNP target of 8.4% annual rate of increase. Like the previous plans, the objective was to reduce poverty and infuse more economic growth among *bumiputras*. Direct development expenditures were targeted at 18,555 million Malaysian dollars (M$) of which transport was to receive about 30%, agriculture 25%, and industry and commerce 10%.[107]

With an impressive 8.6% annual growth rate of the GDP, the Third Plan target was surpassed. Two favorable circumstances were responsible for the success: first, as petroleum exploration successfully found additional oil during the period, the oil export rose ten-fold to U.S. $3.2 billion, also accounting for 15% of government revenue thereby enabling a similar rise in public spending; second, prices of other major exports (except palm oil) registered significant increases, which in turn improved national income.[108]

The meager 3.9% annual growth rate in agriculture during the plan period was recognized as a notable shortfall. Agriculture is the mainstay of the population and accounted for about one quarter of the GNP in 1980. It is in this sector that poverty was largely concentrated and thereby an increase on "manufacturing output

TABLE 7-3
Real Monthly Household Income in Peninsular Malaysia
(1970-76) in $M at 1970 Prices

	Peninsular Malaysia	By the three ethnic groups Malay	Chinese	Indian
1970				
Mean	264	172	394	304
Median	166	120	268	194
Mean/Median ratio	1.59	1.43	1.47	1.59
1973				
Mean	313	209	461	352
Median	196	141	296	239
Mean/Median ratio	1.60	1.48	1.56	1.47
1976				
Mean	375	246	612	378
Median	209	157	330	246
Mean/Median ratio	1.79	1.57	1.85	1.54
1970-76				
Percentage change in mean	42	43	35	24

Source: Malaysia, *Mid-term Review of the Third Malaysia Plan, 1976-1980*, (Kuala Lumpur, 1979), table 3-1, p. 44 (adapted).

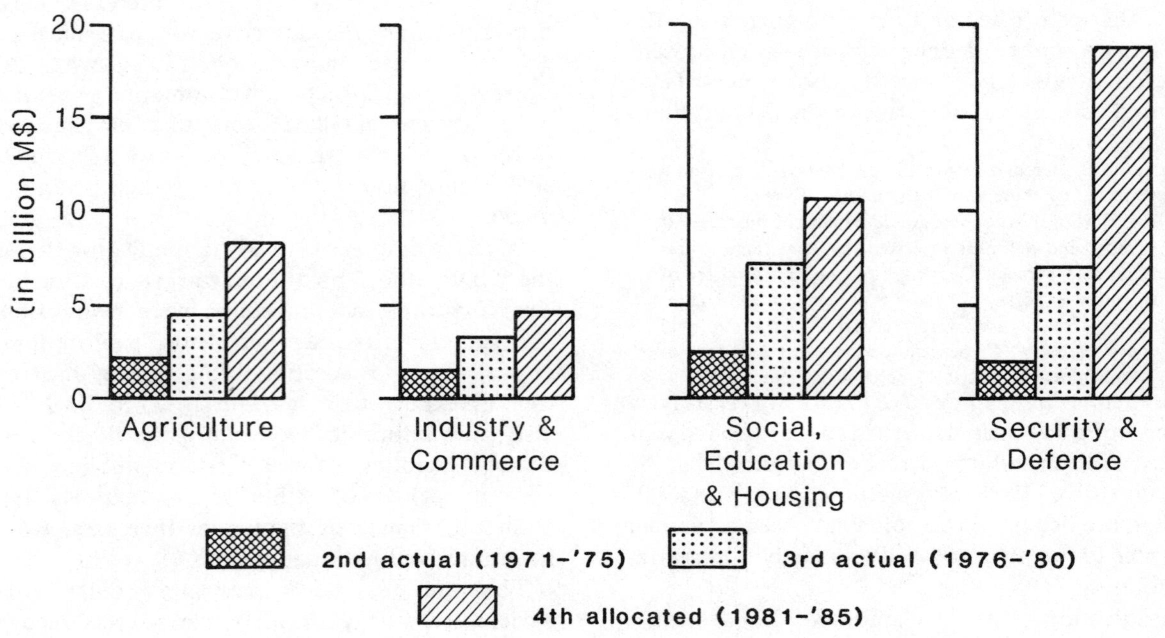

Figure 7-3. Development Spending under Four Malaysia Plans (1971-85).
(**Source:** *Far Eastern Economic Review*)

without corresponding improvement in agriculture could distort economic development and accelerate rural-urban income disparities and migration."[109] This deficiency in agricultural growth was accredited to the slow implementation of government schemes, which were designed to clear and replant new land, extend agriculture and credit services, and construct irrigation and drainage systems. Further, the schemes were also aimed to increase the productivity of small farmers, who were responsible for over 50% of the country's agricultural exports.[110]

NEP's Impact on the Third Malaysia Plan. The NEP had already reached its midpoint by the end of the Third Malaysia Plan.[111] By this time the government's massive 'affirmative action' spending on behalf of the *bumiputras* was taken for granted.[112] During 1971-80 the *bumiputras'* (ethnic Malays) general economic situation advanced more rapidly than the Chinese and Indian ethnic communities. The Malay percentage of administrative and managerial workers rose from 24% to 32%; local university degree course enrollments from 40% to 67%; control of corporate capital from 4% to 12% and; bank advances from 12% to 20%. Similarly, *bumiputras'* standing in industrial employment has been enhanced because of the preference received in government enterprises.

Thus, the aforementioned advances resulted in *bumiputras'* migrating to urban areas in a larger proportion than ever before. For instance, in 1970 14% of the Malays constituted urban dwellers, but in 1980 this figure increased to 21%.

However, the Fourth Malaysia Plan launched in 1981 noted that a) *bumiputras'* advancement was relatively slow in higher paid professional fields as Malays accounted for only 8% of accountants, 9% of doctors and 12% of engineers in 1979.[113]

Neither the Chinese nor the Indian ethnic groups are entirely pleased with the NEP, but any noticeable opposition to the policy did not surface mainly because during the 1970s the Malaysian economy rapidly progressed and therefore, the bigger pie was shared, at least partly, by the non-Malays as well. However, the Indian estate workers, the Chinese new village inhabitants and the non-*bumiputra* landless workers were not only left out, but continued to remain in poverty.[114]

Fourth Malaysia Plan (1981-85)

The Government proposed to spend a total of U.S. $19 billion for development during the Fourth Malaysia Plan. A little over half of the spending was earmarked for economic development, whereas, the remaining amount was reserved for meeting social, education, housing and security goals. Moreover, agriculture accounted for 20% of the spending, a much higher percentage compared to commerce and industry (Fig. 7-3). Reduced public spending in industry was guided by the idea that the private sector should become the main lever of economic growth in the country. Even though such a goal did not produce any meaningful results in the Third Malaysia Plan, the Fourth Plan proposed to accelerate the pace of private investment by 9% annually; accounting for 72% of the national investment at the end of the Plan. At the end of the Third Plan the share of private investment in total national investment stood at 63%.[115]

Economic growth rates achieved during the 1970s were projected to be sustained during the Fourth Malaysia Plan. The GDP was targeted to grow at 7.6% per annum, while manufacturing was projected to grow by 11% annually in constrast to agriculture's 3%.

The Plan proposed a decline in agricultural commodities' share of the gross domestic product from 22% to 18% by 1985.[116] Thus, the stage had been set to accelerate the tempo of transformation from a primary commodity-production-and-export based economy to an industrial nation with an increasing emphasis on the application of higher technology.

Crucial to the plan was a balanced development of regions: particularly, for fighting regional poverty, by creating employment in the northern and eastern part of the peninsula, which were identified as the traditional areas of out-migration. "An important part of the plan is the decentralisation of industry away from the traditional growth centres of the west and south and the development of industry in growth centres on the east coast and in the underdeveloped north." (Fig. 7-4).[117]

Falling revenues from the vital export sector severely constrained the success of the Fourth Plan in its first year. Crude oil exports declined along with rubber, lumber, and other minerals mainly because of a recession in the Western markets. The picture on the domestic economy was also grim: imported inflation, sluggish growth in output, declining savings and investment, and a public sector taking an increasingly dominant role as private business weakened.[118]

As Malaysia has an open economy, it is vulnerable to the ups and downs in the world market. The success of the Fourth Plan depends on the health of an external economy, which is obviously beyond the control of any single nation.

NEP's Impact on the Fourth Malaysia Plan. In the 1970s, when the economy was growing at a rapid rate sharing with the poor and ethnically disadvantaged Malays was not *too much* of a strain on the ethnic Chinese or Indian communities. The depressed economy of the 1980s, however, made it difficult to advance the goals of the NEP. In 1981, *bamiputra* corporate ownership was trailing way behind the twenty-year Perspective Plan goal, which projected that by 1990 30% of the corporate sector would be owned by the *bamiputras*. "As a result, the Fourth Malaysia Plan is aimed for a massive boost, particularly through the acquisition of shares by the government-funded institutions which act in trust for the *bamiputra* community."[119]

SINGAPORE

In the early 1960s, the leaders of Singapore were primarily faced with the problems of decolonizing its economic base through diversification of its economy and by making the city livable. The first real plan of Singapore, initiated in 1961, reflected the effort to cope with these problems.

First Five-Year Plan (1961–65)

The First Four-Year Plan was extended an extra year and labelled the First Five-Year Plan (1961–65). There were two principal economic objectives of the Plan:

1. to increase the national income to match the natural growth of population, estimated at 3.6% between 1947–57, and
2. to create additional employment opportunities.

Of the M$946.06 million (M$2.86 equalled U.S. $1 in 1972) expenditure for the Plan, 62.3% went to economic development.[120] The principal economic measure was for industrial development through the enactment of a Pioneer Industries Ordinance and establishing industrial estates. The Ordinance allowed the "pioneer industries," (i.e., industries producing those goods not produced earlier in the Republic or 100% for export), a five-year tax holiday along with other concessions. Though Singapore's republican form of government was socialist-oriented it went as far to give the employers the right to hire, fire and transfer at will with the non-negotiable holidays and severe limitations on sick pay and sick leave.[121] Creation of such an "employers' market" was essentially a desperate move to reduce unemploy-

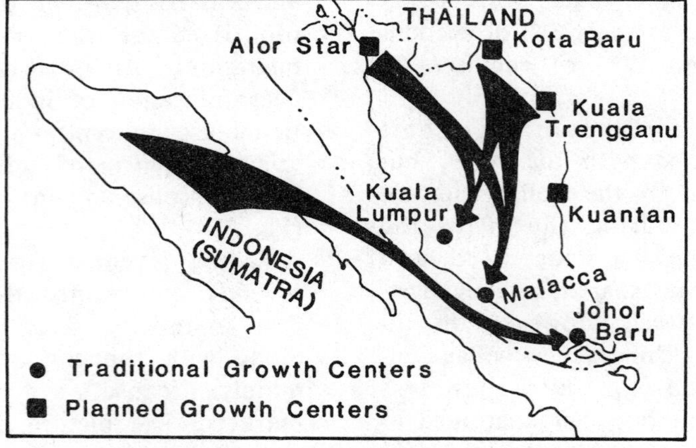

Figure 7-4. The Three Growth-centers of Peninsulan Malaysia (Kuala Lumpur, Malacca and Johor Baru) attract Labor Migration from the North and Sumatra.
(**Source:** *Far Eastern Economic Review*)

ment through industrialization.

Industrial Estates or New Towns (at least three of these were planned) were intended not only to provide jobs for more people, but also to help decongest the city. The three industrial estates referred to are located at Jurong, Toa Payoh, and at Kallang Basin. All are well planned with provisions for jobs and housing in each subsidiary developments including shops, community centers, schools, parks, and open spaces.[122] The comprehensive nature of this planning can be seen from its emphasis on the social as well as the economic and physical aspects of planning.

In the social area the Plan expenditure totalled 36.3% and mainly emphasized building 54,500 housing units, which together with 23,000 units built previously by the Improvement Trust,[123] housed nearly 25% of Singapore's population.[124]

The Second Five-Year Plan (1966–70)

The Second Plan continued the economic thrust established in the First Plan but with an emphasis on industrial development so as to increase exports. The Plan contained provisions for Phase I of the Urban Renewal Program to redevelop the central area along the river. Its objectives were based fundamentally on land clearance to pave the way for a better economic use of the land. A total of sixty thousand new housing units were called for. By the end of the Second Plan one-third of Singapore's population lived in public housing units. In 1973, almost 40% lived in public housing. During this time, the Government also created a Family Planning and Population Board to "initiate and undertake population control programmes."[125] By the end of the Plan, the population growth rate had already dropped to about 2%.

The proposed expenditures in this Second Plan amounted to M$1,521.1 million, a substantial increase over the First Plan. Once again, economic development programs accounted for the majority of expenditures (over 64%). Social development costs decreased slightly to 31.8% and administration increased to 4%.

The Third Five-Year Plan (1971–76) and the Achievements of Planning

The Third Plan continued the major trends of the First and Second Plans. One hundred thousand new housing units were planned. Private ownership of houses was particularly encouraged.[126] Industrial enterprises continued to be encouraged to produce goods for export. In the early 1970s the United Nations-assisted state and city planning project prepared a long-range *Concept Plan*, a key element of which is known as the Ring Plan. The following facts taken from the Annual Budget Statement for 1972–73[127] clearly state the progress registered by Singapore in her planned efforts since the inception of the First Plan:

1. The *entrepot* trade showed a small decline trend between 1960–71 with only 3% gross increase, whereas, the domestic trade sector increased by 20.2% in 1970 and 13.8% in 1971.[128]
2. Manufacturing growth is primarily responsible for the rise in the domestic trade sector. The success of the industrialization program can be judged from the fact that the share of the manufacturing sector of the total Gross Domestic Product (GDP) rose from 9.2% in 1960 to 23.0% in 1971.[129]
3. The efforts for lessening dependence on trade and services, particularly those based on *entrepot*, can best be reflected by a decline of their total share of GDP from 70.7% in 1960 to 55.5% in 1971.[130]
4. One of the most progressive industries of the sixties and seventies, a petroleum refinery, constitutes the main base (33.4% of the total output of the manufacturing sector in 1971)[131] of Singapore's industrial investments. This assured a bright industrial future of the country. Moreover, as a result of the large-scale industrialization, the unemployment percentage was reduced from 10% in the early sixties to 6.7% in 1969 and to 4.8% in 1971.[132]

Plans after 1976

Starting in the early seventies, Singapore did not have any set of established national plans which really directed its economic progress. Some national policies, however, do combine socialist principles within a capitalist setting. Poon-Kim pointed out that it had developed a unique economic structure with direct involvement of state enterprises within the capitalistic economic system. He says that the government does not nationalize private industries,

> but has created so far about 52 directly or jointly owned state enterprises, such as the Development Bank of Singapore, Post Office Savings Bank (POSB), State Housing Development Board, Housing and Urban Development Company, Jurong Shipyard, etc., which are in direct competition with private enterprises. The Government's involvement in these areas provoked complaints from the private sector, which considered itself in a disadvantageous position to compete with these dynamic government enterprises. The Government, however, has no intention of

abandoning these ventures for, in the words of Deputy Prime Minister Goh Keng Swee, the establishment of these new enterprises is "creating new wealth, providing new jobs and adding to the growth of the GNP."[133]

Though Singapore's economy grew consistently from 1968 through 1973 with the gross domestic product rising at an annual rate of between 10% to 15%, this rate declined sharply to 7% in 1974 and 4% in 1975 as a result of the world oil crisis.[134] The growth rate increased with economic recovery in the second half of the seventies reaching about 10% in 1981, but the worldwide recession of the early eighties further depressed the growth rate of gross domestic product to 7.3% for the first three months of 1982. Thus, Singapore's open economy reacts sharply to ups and downs of the world market, and therefore, the lack of a large domestic market makes its otherwise progressive economy vulnerable.

BRUNEI

Brunei has had Development Plans since 1962. This oil-rich country, with a very large, annual balance-of-payments surplus, had problems in channelling its investments. It is fortunate, though, that it has not had to seek external aid. In 1962, of the total revenue of the country (M$115 million), 33% was derived from interest investment, mainly made out of oil income; 32% was from income tax, predominantly from the profits of the Shell Oil Company; and 23% from oil royalties. The 1962–66 Development Plan recommended diversifying the economy; lessening the country's dependence on crude oil exports; and establishing petroleum and natural gas based secondary industries such as fertilizers, petrochemicals and plastics. The diversification policy is still followed in setting national economic goals. Though a great deal of expenditure was directed towards the expansion of education, it was realized by the mid-seventies that 7000 school graduates needed employment. Most of them sought work in the non-agricultural sector and were reluctant, like other native Bruneians, to join the menial/manual work force, which was filled by both legal and illegal immigrants from Sarawak (East Malaysia) and Indonesia during the sixties. Though a little late according to the Plan schedule, the world's largest liquified natural gas (LNG) plant was opened in 1973, providing a diversification in an economy which was, until then, so intrinsically dependent on oil. With the Brunei government, two foreign companies, Mitsubishi and Shell Oil, own the LNG plant.

The 1975–79 Five-Year National Development Plan was intended to create a 'rugged, united and properous society'; to redistribute income; reduce dependence on oil for employment; provide a high level of employment (10,000 new jobs); offer incentives to the private sector to establish industries in the Muara Industrial Estate, north of the capital; develop the neglected forestry sector; and establish a newspaper pulp mill. The total amount earmarked for expenditure for the plan was 5,200 million British pounds. Although the Plan's intention was to create a 'united' society, the Chinese ethnic community, over one-fifth of the country's population, remains in a second-class level compared to the first-class status enjoyed by the native Malay-speaking ethnic group. Today the Chinese are still non-citizens. The Plan did succeed in making significant progress in health, education, communications and agriculture.

The 1980–85 Five-Year Plan basically continued to implement the aims set forth in the previous plans. Along with the development of oil and natural gas extraction, the service sector was greatly emphasized. A new seven-story, $4 million shopping center was opened in the capital in 1982; a $400 million palace was completed for the Sultan in 1984, as was a 530 bed hospital and a sports stadium. In addition, a local private investor, Yusof Holdings, completed a $200 million hilltop hotel. Thus, the construction sector absorbed a great deal of new employment. The Bruneians hate to take the blue collar jobs of this sector in particular, which, in the early eighties, were mainly filled by Filipinos and Indonesians.

Brunei, in 1983, continued to enjoy an economy in which government revenue greatly exceeded expenditures. Oil and gas continued to be the main base of economic prosperity. Brunei's 1.8 billion barrels of oil and several billion cu. ft. of gas reserves along with its national depletion policy, aimed at conservation, are expected to maintain this high level of economic prosperity at least through the first decade of the 21st century.

VIETNAM

The planning in Vietnam may be divided into two phases: the North Vietnam period (1955–75) and United Vietnam period (1976–). Nationalization, industrialization and collectivization had been the running theme of North Vietnamese planning. However, in spite of its drive for industrialization North Vietnam is still a predominantly agrarian society. The new United Vietnam is marked by a dual approach in planning, one for the more mature socialist economy in the North and the other for an incipient socialist system in the South.

Plan of 1955

The economy of the country had suffered extensively as a result of civil war in the early 1950s. Industries and railways were destroyed and farms were damaged. Thus, in 1955, the National Planning Board was established and the first plan drawn up. The aim of this plan was to revitalize the economy and restore industrial and agricultural production to levels achieved prior to World War II. Financial investment was as follows: 38% for industry, 23% for transportation and communication, 20% for agriculture and irrigation, and 19% for education and social services. Such a lopsided bias for industrialization (heavy industry particularly) has been fashioned for most socialist countries. North Vietnam simply joined the bandwagon.

Of major significance during the time that this plan was carried out was the appreach taken by the government towards crop lands. Lands were taken away from the rich farmers for distribution to tillers, which sometimes resulted in unnecessary terror and brutality. Shabad comments:

> The terror and confusion reigning throughout the country not only upset farming but caused a serious setback in the implementation of the program of rehabilitation and industrial reconstruction.[135]

The Three-Year Plan (1958–60)

In spite of the fact that the political goals of land redistribution had been met to a great extent (i.e., nearly one-half of the agricultural land had been turned over to the tillers), the country was in such turmoil that it became necessary to relieve the pressure of forced development.[136] Thus it was announced that three years would be earmarked for "consolidation." This, however, did not mean slowing down the rapid pace of economic development. Investment in the agricultural and industrial sectors were doubled with the goal of raising overall production by 82%. By 1960 it was clear to officials that this figure was extremely high and so it was revised and reduced to 50%. Even this was not enough, however, for when the results were observed at the end of 1960, they showed that not even the revised targets were reached by all sectors of the economy. Such target-oriented planning is quite common to socialist planning.

The political goals of the North Vietnamese were not really relaxed during these three years either. The public sector was expanded even further with more collective farms and transfers of private industries to the "socialist economy."

First Five-Year Plan (1960–65)

By 1960, North Vietnam was suffering from a real food crisis. The situation has been described by Honey:

> Since the relatively plentiful harvests of 1959, North Vietnamese agriculture has moved from crisis to crisis with the Communist leaders laying the blame on bad weather conditions, poor cooperative management, unwillingness to work on the part of the peasants, etc. Collectivisation, however, and compulsory State purchases are the real causes of the deterioration.....[137]

Consequently, when the Five-Year Plan was devised, more emphasis was given to agricultural development and meat production (mostly pork). The five principle objectives of the plan were: (1) to develop agriculture and industry, (2) to complete socialist consciousness of the people, (4) to bring about further improvements in the material and cultural life of the working people, and (5) to combine economic development with the consolidation of national defense, the strengthening of public order and security and the protection of socialist construction.[138]

The North Vietnamese had begun to make considerable progress in food production during the 1960s. Then came the flood of 1971. The second, and normally largest, harvest of October was a disaster. Fields were inundated and it is estimated that one-half of the crops were lost.[139] With this major setback, North Vietnam was once again struggling to feed its people. Mechanization, greater use of fertilizer, and new varieties of seed are needed to make the land more productive.

As for industry, there was no true measure of production output; reliable figures were unavailable. The goals set forth by the Lao Dong Central Committee's 19th Plenary session held in January of 1971 seem to emphasize development of light industry which it is felt will have the greatest potential for economic growth. There still is very little heavy industry in North Vietnam in spite of earlier emphasis given to it in planning.

Three-Year Plan (1972–75)

After the first Five-Year Plan with the intensification of war activity, North Vietnam disposed of its medium-term planning and resorted to an annual planning process. Then with the emergence of peace prospects in 1972, the country returned to a medium-term three-year plan. The planners, however, basically followed a short-term year-to-year planning process. In 1972, for example, the State Economic Plan was operational for the year, which continued to place a heavy emphasis on rationalization of agriculture to increase productivity.[140] The 1975 Plan aimed at a restoration of the economy to the level of 1965 (when the U.S. bombing began). Planning activity was primarily centerd around the idea of introducing the peasantry and agriculture to socialism without waiting for a developed industry. Lee Duan, First Secretary of the North Vietnamese Worker's Party, articulately summarized the planning strategy in the following words:

> Give primacy to the development of heavy industry on the basis of the development of agriculture and light industry; build the centrally-run economy along with developing the regional economy; coordinate economic development with national defense.[141]

In practice North Vietnam, however, gave priority emphasis to the power industry; which was largely destroyed by the U.S. bombings. The U.S. air strikes upon North Vietnam were overwhelming; some 33,000 air strikes occurred from April through August 1972 alone. Communications and the transportation network were the main targets of these attacks.[142] Also, it was estimated that as a result of the bombing between 1965–72, 70% of North Vietnam's industry was destroyed.[143]

Although the Vietnamese government claimed that the Three-Year Plan succeeded in repairing the physical damage caused by the war and achieved the production levels of 1965,[144] a few major industial works, such as Haiphong Cement Works, were still not fully operational at the end of 1975.[145] In the agricultural sector, where approximately 10% of farm work was done by machinery,[146] the total rice production improved in the first four years of the 1970s and then declined in 1975; 4 million tons in 1971, 5 million tons in 1972, 6 million tons in 1974 and, 4.7 million tons in 1975. Heavy rains were responsible for the lower production of 1975. Compared to the rice production of 1965 (4.3 million metric tons), the Three-Year Plan average (5.2. million metric tons) was higher than the target. The success of exceeding the target provided no comfort to the Vietnamese planners, as the country was already beset with a baby boom, which caused per capita share of rice to decline from 233 kilograms in 1965 to 192 kilograms in 1975.[147]

Thus, the main goal of restoring the economy back to its previous level of 1965 was generally accomplished, despite the diversion of an enormous amount of manpower and resources for the 'liberation' of South Vietnam. In 1975, output of the most important commodities either reached or surpassed the 1965 level, except for a few products, such as timber, cement, paper and sugar.[148]

Second Five-Year Plan of The Republic of Vietnam (1976–80).

This plan began only a month after the reunification of North and South Vietnam and therefore, the possibility emerged for the rational development of the country's specialized potentials; the South's agriculture and light industry and the North's minerals, power resources, and heavy industry. It should be noted that the South was at one time a rice exporter and in 1960, before the start of the intensive civil war, it exported 300,000 tons annually. Therefore, it was believed that within a few years when full recovery was attained, the South could make the new Republic of Vietnam self-sufficient in food.[149]

There were, however, certain constraints. For instance, apart from war damages crippling the economic structure in both the North and South, the North had already passed through two decades of socialism, while the South still had a capitalist-feudal structure. Thus, two different agricultural strategies had to be devised, one for each region. First, initial plans to consolidate the communes of the North into larger operational units, in order that mechanization could be implemented efficiently, had to be delayed until the later stage of the Five-Year Plan because of the lack of an effective management capability in the countryside.

Secondly, although there was no dispute over the fact that the South's agriculture would eventually be collectivized, the time and pace of such collectivization was not settled. The Second Plan had projected initially to establish cooperatives by 1978 and to assemble all southern farms under a cooperative system. This strategy was resisted by the southern farmers. For example, individual farmers of the Mekong delta were reluctant to grow any surplus because of the requirement for all the surplus to be sold at low prices to the State. However, these farmers used a number of tactics to avoid selling the surplus to the State. Some used their excess rice for making wine or for cattle feed. Others concealed the surplus rice then sold it to Ho Chi Minh city for a profit in the 'open market'.[150] Also, many farming families divided their landholdings among relatives and transformed rice paddies into ponds and orchards in fear of being collectivized. These schemes subsequently led to lower farm production and fewer available food grains through the government channel. Thereby only 40% of the targeted food surplus was collected from the South by the Government in 1979.[151]

With the failure of ideological motivations to augment desired food production, the procurement by material incentives, such as better grain prices and additional supplies of consumer goods, were provided to peasants in both the North and South.[152] The incentive policy worked and it was estimated that government rice purchases in the Mekong delta increased from .5 million tons in 1979 to 1.1 million tons in 1980.[153] Also, more rice was available to the government in the North.

The Second Five-Year Plan changed its strategy from an earlier Soviet-style emphasis on heavy industry to a Chinese-style emphasis on agriculture, which earmarked a record 35% of its financial allocations to agricultural development. Due to premature collectivization efforts in the South, a lack of competent management, corruption and impractical tactics, the Second Five-Year Plan failed to meet its agricultural targets. The projected grain production target of 22 million tons, (18 million tons of rice and 4 million tons of secondary crops), was revised to 15 million tons for 1980, but this mark was also missed by a million tons.[154] Imports partially rectified the deficit. Also, reductions in food rations resulted from the deficit. In the time of war the basic ration in the North was 15 kilograms per person per month, which dropped to 8–10 kilograms during 1978–80.[155] Because food riots and peasant unrest surfaced in the North late in 1980, the Hanoi regime went back to rethink and made efforts to improve its performance and popularity.[156]

Heavy industry was ranked third in terms of the Plan's priorities. Light industry, intended to meet the demand for consumer goods, such as clothing, bicycles, radios and plastic goods, was ranked second after agriculture.[157] In general, however, the industries suffered from a deficiency of raw materials, spare parts and disorganized transport management; which were severely handicapped by the Chinese cut in aid and the diversion of scarce foreign exchange for the import of food grains. For example, in 1978, industrial output only grew by 7% compared to the target of 21%. Thereby the target was lowered to 12% in the following year, but barely half of that growth rate was attained.[158] Furthermore, during the second half of the 1970s and the early 1980s, the

TABLE 7-4
VIETNAM'S PRODUCTION, AND FIRST, SECOND AND THIRD PLAN TARGETS

	1965 target (1961-65 Plan) for north	1973 production in south	1975 production in north	1976 production (whole country)	1980 target (1976-80 Plan)	Actual production in 1980	1985 target (1981-85)
Unmilled rice (m. tons)	5	7	4.7	12	17.5-18	15	—
Subsidiary crop (m. tons)	2.5	n.a.	n.a.	2.0	3 -3.5		—
Fish ('000 tons)	n.a.	713	n.a.	780	1,300 -1,500	—	—
Meat (('000 tons)	n.a.	n.a.	n.a.	348	1,000	—	—
Coal (M. tons)	5	n.a.	5	5.4	10	6	10
Steel ('000 tons)	105	n.a.	5 0	n.a.	300	—	—
Cement ('000 tons)	800	265	300	722	2,000	1,000	3,500
Chemical fertilizer ('000 tons)	500	n.a.	n.a.	438	1,300	—	—
Paper ('000 tons)	35.5	44	n.a.	n.a.	130	—	—
Textiles (m. sq. metres)	134	107	95	n.a.	450	—	—
Electricity (m. kwh.)	700	1,600	1,400	3,027	5,000	—	—
Wood ('000 cu.meters)	n.a.	746	n.a.	1,570	3,500	—	—

Source: Partly based on *Far Eastern Economic Review* (February 4, 1977).

availability of consumer goods dropped by 50%; for instance, in 1980 the supply of soap dropped by 40%.[159]

Thus, the Plan proved to be a dismal failure. The Soviet bloc aid to infuse economic growth was available, but only in small amounts. Aid and industrial collaboration were initiated with the Free World, but stayed at minimal levels. Also, the generation of an internal surplus for additional investments remained disappointingly low. Pike summarized the bleak situation of 1980 in the following words:

(1)Poverty that steadily deepens, defying all remedial measures and slowly pushing Vietnam to the edge of malnutrition.

(2)Economic stagnation, the culmination of an economic decline that began at the war's end and, chiefly the result of a series of extraordinary bad decisions by the 17 men of the Politburo who run Vietnam.

(3)An unhealthy and unwanted dependence—for food, oil, armaments, raw materials—on the Soviets, whom the Vietnamese neither trust nor particularly like.

(4)Lack of a development strategy, or, more precisely, a collapse of faith in the previous strategy for economic development.[160]

The political picture which emerged at the end of the Plan period was ominous. The quagmire of the Kampuchean War and the enmity with China led Vietnam to allocate a considerable amount of its budget for military expenditures, which otherwise could have been diverted to development projects. The military budget of 1980 was $3.8 billion, approximately 47% of the total state budget and about 28% of the national income.[161] Moreover, Vietnam lived in trepidation as it was surrounded by hostile neighbors and its only two "dependable" friends (U.S.S.R. and Cuba) were in distant lands.

Third Five-Year Plan (1981–85)

The Third Plan continued to stress agriculture and light industry, while heavy industry was geared to support them. This idea was employed in order to improve the farm production and to attain self-sufficiency in food by 1985. Capitalistic incentives also continued, so that the farmers would produce more and with their relatively high grain sales to the government they could then purchase more consumer goods. Thus, the development of light industry was tied to the

VIETNAM'S FOOD DEFICIT DURING SECOND FIVE-YEAR PLAN

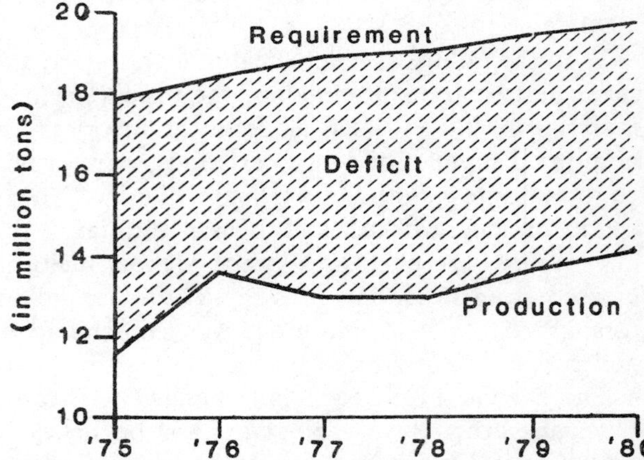

Figure 7-5. As Food Productions in the Vietnam Republic Leveled the Requirement During the Second Five-Year Plan (1976–80) Widening the Deficit. (**Source:** *Far Eastern Economic Review*)

farmers' incentive to produce a surplus. Such incentives were introduced in 1979 and their full repercussions could be seen from a record grain harvest in 1981 of 15 million tons. Furthermore, in 1981, only .3 million tons of grain were imported compared to over 1.6 million tons in 1979.[162] Therefore, it was felt that the first year of the Plan began with optimistic signs. However, the high population growth rate (officially 2.4%) and with only 20% of the women of child-bearing age using contraceptives, the per capita food availability may not gain significantly. The Plan targeted a population growth rate of 1.7% by 1985;[163] a target impossible to achieve without more vigorous efforts, such as greater use of contraceptives, delayed marriages and disincentives for families with more than two children.

Hydro-electric power generation was planned to be improved, partly to augment agricultural production. Coal production was targeted to increase to 10 million tons by 1985, compared to 6 million tons in 1980. Cement production was to be stepped-up to 3.5 million tons in 1985, compared to less than a million tons in 1980. One Vietnamese leader remarked that "with larger amounts of cement available...Mekong Delta peasants" could be offered "brick houses in exchange for bigger supplies of rice."[164] It should be noted, however, that in the South as late as 1981, only 9% of the peasant families and 7% of the cultivated land were brought under collective farming.[165]

The post-unification planning phase of Vietnam remained constrained not only by the regional inequalities of the north and south, but by the excessive expenditure in defence, poor management and structural problems of the communist system.

New investments remain the basis for accelerated development in the country. They could either be generated from internal or external sources. An impoverished and agrarian country like Vietnam has been geared to generate a "surplus" from agriculture for investments in industrial and other nonagricultural sectors. This not only slows down rural development but falls hard on the peasantry. However, the aid received from the Soviet Union and other communist countries came as a relief as it formed a sizeable volume of new investments. A highly centralized planning hierarchy together with well-defined socialist principles allows for the possibility for successful planning.

KAMPUCHEA

When Cambodia gained her independence from France in 1954, the first task at hand was to decolonize the economic and political structure. A two-year plan was devised to perform this task.

Two-Year Plan (1956–57)

The Plan emphasized the expansion of education, health care, transportation, and communication. Secondary objectives included projects for irrigation and flood control, community development projects, and encouragement of private enterprise.[166] Because the goals were not met to the satisfaction of the government, the Plan was extended an extra year, through 1958. However, even by the end of this time only two-thirds of the proposed expenditures had actually been spent. Between 1956 and 1958, a total of 2455 million riels (120 riels equaled United States $1 in 1972) were spent, 70% of which were spent for the development of Cambodia's infrastructure. The reason for this particular allocation was because the United States' aid to Cambodia amounted to 70% of its total budgeted funds and this money was earmarked for building roads, railroads, and airports. Social development received 12% of the funds and agriculture ended up with a mere 7%. Private enterprise, which was largely in the hands of a Chinese minority was not sufficient to meet the needs of industrial investment.

> Private investment capital continues to be in short supply, and in Cambodia, as in other undeveloped countries, the rate of capital accumulation continues to be low. In this situation, the government appears to be the only possible source of funds and entrepreneurship for large projects, such as the textile, cement, plywood, and paper mills and for any other prospective pioneer large-scale manufacturing industries. Because of the limited capital market, the government must also devise ways and means of providing financial assistance to small businessmen, farmers, and even to corporations.[167]

The Two-Year Plan encountered some difficult problems which deterred success. Exports were priced out of the international market, citizens evaded taxes, skilled labor was lacking, and complications forced delays in the improvement and repairs of communication and transportation systems.[168] Trained technical and administrative personnel were also lacking; the incompetence of these administrators was made obvious in 1956. For example, when China gave Cambodia money to equip its factories for the production of plywood, cement, and paper,[169] the officials were so eager to industrialize that they proceeded without any consideration of the market demand for these products; thus, the whole project failed miserably. Cambodia's effort to rid itself of French colonialism and substitute self-sufficiency was only started during the three years of this Plan. Cambodia did in fact remain dependent upon France for many consumer goods, although it was quite successful at building an economic infrastructure.

First Five-Year Plan (1960–64)

The First Five-Year Plan was a suggestive comprehensive plan with emphasis on increasing the gross national product (GNP) to 3% per capita, if the population increased at a rate of 2% per year.[170]

To accomplish the rise in the GNP the government needed a capital outlay of which 66% was to come from the national budget, and the remaining was to come from private sources. The capital, according to the Five-Year Plan, was to be divided into four main categories. First, agriculture (8%), industry, and mining activities were to receive 40% of the allotment. Second, infrastructure developments were to be appropriated 28% of the money. Third, social needs such as education, public health, and the extension of resettlement for frontier development were to get 24.5% of the outlay. Fourth, the remaining 7.5% would go for administrative purposes.[171]

The results of the Five-Year Plan may be seen in light of population growth. The population grew faster than was anticipated, at a rate of 2.2%.

Because of this, per capita GNP rose only 2.5% instead of the desired 3%.[172] In 1963, Cambodian per capita income was $117.

Instead of maintaining the planned proportions of expenditure, the leadership altered the direction of allocations which in turn caused a problem in fulfilling the planned objectives. Money allocations were taken from agriculture, industry, and mining and social sectors and diverted to infrastructure and administration. Instead of 40% going to agriculture and other productive activities, only 35% went in that direction. However, the infrastructure received 33% of the funding rather than 28%.[173] Administration consumed 10%, which seems to be out of proportion. Nonetheless, there were improvements in some areas. Manufactures began to rise. Also, the infrastructure was still being improved.

The Second Five-Year Plan (1967–71)

The Second Five-Year Plan did not go into effect until late 1967 because of power struggles within the government. However, when it finally was initiated as a suggestive comprehensive plan, it took into consideration the mistakes and pitfalls of the previous Five-Year Plan. In this sense, the Second Five-Year Plan had a more rational emphasis with the pace of change dependent on the population's ability to assimilate to the changes.

This Plan emphasized agricultural diversity and industrialization at a more moderate pace than the first plan. There were portions of the plan devoted to infrastructure improvements with special emphasis on waterways and wateruse, highways and airports. The educational segment of the plan was designed to seek a balance between trained workers and managers. In other words, education was to be of immediate use and was concentrated on vocational training. The Plan was aimed at economic change through encouragement of local production while decreasing the importation of luxury items and excessive nonluxury items.[174]

The Plan, however, had a premature death because its initiator, Prince Sihanouk, was ousted by his military general in 1970, starting a crippling civil war, which continued on through 1975.

Norton pointed out that Cambodia's Second Five-Year Plan operated under Prince Sihanouk's "wooly-headed Buddhism-cum-socialism," whereby the state took control of banks, certain manufacturing products and foreigh trade.[175] Moreover, Sihanouk's capricious shifting of priorities and interference in economic affairs made the situation more severe. Thus, the country's economy stagnated and this can be seen by a growth in gross domestic product of only 2.2% in 1969.

In 1970, Lon Nol led a successful coup against Sihanouk and soon thereafter the communist countries severed diplomatic and trade relations. Such action did not affect the Cambodian economy much because trade with communist nations amounted only 7% of Cambodia's total.[176] Moreover, the internal strife destabilized the overall economic base and rice production as well as exports declined. In 1970 alone, Cambodia was expected to export .45 million tons of rice, but only .17 million tons were actually exported.

The Plan virtually collapsed with the increase in insurgent activites inside the country, which turned the Cambodian economy into such shambles that it turned into a rice importer and entered a new era of economic dependence on the United States.

Kampuchea After 1975

With communist taking control of Kampuchea in 1975, a new ideology to convert the nation into a "hermit country" emerged. Also, inhabitants from the refugee-swollen Phonm Penh were forced to march to villages in order to augment rice cultivation. This unrealistic and unplanned march resulted in thousands of lost lives. A new civil war began in 1979 and the country's economy reached a record economic low. From 1975 to the early 1980s no National Plan was implemented, other than some policies which were devised year to year.

Although realizing the dire nature of the economic situation, President Samrin was in no position to design a Five-Year Plan; however he cautioned that only "transistional steps towards true socialism" çould be taken because "impatience, haste and failure to keep in touch with the actual situation" would jeopardize the revolution.[177] Futhermore, Samrin admitted that the free market, which played an active role, should be maintained and that for the next few years private enterprise would be important to the economy. The realities of Kampuchea forced its political leaders to put their rigid ideology, at least for the time being, on hold.

LAOS

Soon after the communist Pathet Lao rose to power in 1975, strategies were being devised by government officials in Vientiane. Their priority consideration was the development of agriculture and related industries to achieve self-sufficiency in food.[178] In 1975, Laos was running a food deficit of only 70,000 tons per year, constituting approximately 10% of its national requirement.[179] It was thought that such a deficit could be overcome by an extension of irrigation and improving cultivation practices. The Pathet Lao government, in the beginning, was very prudent in not taking any immediate adventurist action motivated by "pure" Marxist ideals.

> All along, the Pathet Lao has been very careful not to antagonise the peasantry. While the property of big absentee landlords was nationalised and distributed to landless peasants, plots of land were preserved for any members of the landlords' families who chose to stay in Laos.
>
> A 10-point declaration made public after the Pathet Lao takeover of Vientiane insisted that the right to own land would continue to be respected, but that landlords must relinquish their control over water resources. Patriotic landlords, it added, would be given Government assistance to promote mechanised farming.[180]

First Three-Year Development Plan (1978–81)

This Three-Year Plan continued to emphasize the goal of attaining self-sufficiency in food and during its duration Pathet Lao managed to regain some of the international aid, which it had lost earlier. Self-sufficiency was to be achieved by stressing the expansion of irrigation, intensive cultivation in permanent rice fields, and by discouraging mountain tribesmen (ethnic minorities who farmed about 50% of the country's land under cultivation) from continuing their traditional slash-and-burn agriculture in favor of sedentary farming.[181]

Collectivization of farmlands was always the ultimate aim of the Laos planners. To them collectivism was no problem because the country not only had an abundance of cultivable land and a relative small population to feed, but also there had "never been much 'landlordism' that would call for land reform or redistribution of land."[182] Possession of cattle by farmers was also relatively even. The main problem of collectivization, however, rested on one fundamental question: "How to collectivise the labour?"[183]

In order for Pathet Laos to directly advance collectivization four steps were outlined in the Plan.

> The first stage would be to form solidarity groups in villages based on the age-old samukhi—the Lao tradition of mutual help. The second step would be to organise this cooperation on a regular basis of exchange of labour with different groups specialising in certain tasks.
>
> In the third stage—the initial formation of cooperatives—peasants would retain their individual ownership of land but would collectively use tools and draught animals.
>
> The fourth and highest stage of cooperatives would involve common ownership of land and tools of production.[184]

It was targeted that two-thirds of the farms were to be organized into cooperatives by the end of the Three-Year Plan.[185] In the first half of 1979, the number of cooperatives rose 64%.[186] This over-zealous endeavor not only caused considerable human hardship which resulted in the exodus of thousands of refugees,[187] but also caused rice production to decline. Moreover, private trade was so sharply curbed that markets closed and a crisis beset the economy.[188] Hence, the target for the creation of additional cooperatives was cut in half in 1980 and the existing cooperatives were consolidated. The bright side of the Plan performance was that 25% of the rice fields of Laos was irrigated by the end of the Plan compared to 10% in 1976. The food deficit was reduced from 80,000 tons in 1979 to 60,000 tons in 1980.[189]

First Five-Year Plan (1981–85)

The First Five-Year Plan realized the mistake of advancing too fast toward socialism. The Plan's strategies were based on a long process of transformation to socialism and the use of coercion to accelerate collectivization was not employed.

> the rush into cooperatives without proper managerial ability was an error, the plan strongly emphasised the need to train sufficient cadres and economic managers and to provide the material and technical assistance required to make cooperatives attractive. The plan urged cadres to use bureaucratic measures and decrees less and economic levers of high prices and material incentives more so as to stimulate agriculture development.[190]

The Plan targeted to increase internal revenue by 88%; rice production by 21% (so that the country would be self-sufficient in food); achieve a balance in trade; and increase the volume of passenger transport by 44%.

Much of Lao's success depends heavily on its management of food production and successess in exploiting other primary goods such as timber and metals.

SUCCESSES OF SINGAPORE'S PLANNING COMPARED WITH BURMESE FAILURES

Singapore has progressed considerably ever since its independence in 1961 and this is due in part to its comprehensive National Planning. The First (1961–65), the Second (1966–70), and the Third (1971–76) Five-Year Plans have brought about tangible results in the country in terms of uplifting the general economy and ameliorating a principal problem of the city: housing. In the following parargraphs Singapore's success in planning have been compared with those of Burma.

National planning has been practiced in both countries ever since independence with different policy orientations and approaches. The Burmese attitude toward national development is best characterized by a "closed-door policy," while Singapore has adopted an "open-door policy." The net result of these two perspectives has been quite different. Burma is stagnating economically while Singapore enjoys increasing prosperity. The following contrasts may be summed up:

1. A *comprehensive* planning attitude has been lacking in the planning of both countries for well over a decade. By comprehensive planning the author means; a balanced approach, and interdisciplinary attitude and a well-coordinated apparatus to implement the planning.[191] In the case of Burma, an overemphasis has been given to organizational control from the center while in the case of Singapore, economic goals have superseded all others.
2. The *Closed-door* policy of Burma has prevented her from taking advantage of foreign investments even though the availability of capital within the country is limited. The result has been a lack of extensive infrastructural investments, so very necessary to foster progress in any kind of an economy but most especially in an underdeveloped economy like Burma. The *Open-door* policy in the case of Singapore has been so successful that foreign capital particularly from Japan and the United States has poured in millions for industrial development. Such investments have significantly accelerated economic growth.
3. *Dogmatic socialism* as adopted and practiced in Burma has been so mentally rigid that even a decade of economic stagnation in the 1960s failed to impel the political leadership to adopt more *open-minded* and *flexible* economic policies. The leaders of Singapore on the other hand, have found it most useful to provide flexible responses to changing needs.
4. Being a *traditional agricultural* country, the progress of rapid modernization in Burma is difficult, if not impossible, while Singapore, which was already exposed to more highly developed forms of trade and commerce, has had little difficulty in accepting modern scientific methods. In spite of the great emphasis given to industrial planning in both countries, Singapore's rate of modern industrialization has been spectacular, while that of Burma has been very disappointing.
5. *Per capita income* in Burma is so *low* that only a small rate of internal investment can be expected, whereas, the higher per capita income of Singapore is capable of generating more surplus for developmental investments. Moreover, better and more practical use of such investments in Singapore has brought her to a position where her rate of national economic development is much higher than that of Burma.
6. The geographical fact of Singapore's *crossroads location* has always placed it in an advantageous position in terms of trading and diminishing trans-shipment costs. Burma, on the other hand, occupies an out-of-the-way location making it less attractive for investments meant primarily for markets abroad. Therefore, when the planners in Singapore decided to convert it into an industrial nation, they had no difficulty in attracting really progressive industries which marketed their products in Asia, Australia, Africa and Europe.
7. In the name of "Burmanization" the pre-existing entrepreneurs, Indians and Chinese, were displaced thereby causing a great vacuum in the field of entrepreneurship; whereas, in Singapore neither the Chinese nor the Indian entrepreneurs were ever discouraged and thus, the stream of new ideas and entrepreneurship has flourished unobstructed. Such enlightened entrepreneurship has been the backbone of Singapore's development.
8. One of the prerequistes for the success of any development planning is internal peace, which has been non-existent in Burma since she achieved her independence. Singapore, on the other hand, thrived consistently in the midst of well-established internal peace.

Since the mid-1970s the Burman planners have become more pragmatic and opened their doors to foreign investments as well as to collaboration with foreign companies. Their own national policies also relaxed the tight rope of 'Burmese Way to Socialism.' All these resulted in an infusion of economic stimulation, which nevertheless, stayed in an incipient stage of 'take off' in the early 1980s. Singapore, on the other hand, turned more to stress the formulation of pragmatic national policies instead of sticking to target-oriented planning. In the early 1980s Singapore's economy was booming though the filtering effect of the worldwide recession affected its rate of growth.

COMPARATIVE ANALYSIS OF NATIONAL PLANNING

There are primarily three factors inherent in the planning process which have been used as criteria for comparing national planning among the Southeast Asian countries. The first is *realism*. In order for any plan to succeed, it must accurately predict what the country is capable of achieving . The biggest mistake a nation can make is to attempt to grow "too quickly." Economic and social development is a long and hard process and any nation that attempts to develop instantaneously will find its people exasperated rather than its conditions ameliorated. This is particularly true when it comes to industrialization. Many countries are simply not capable of industrializing and would actually be better off investing in agriculture for the purpose of becoming self-sufficient in food production, at least for the time being.

The second factor to be used as criteria in comparative analysis is the willingness or *ability to utilize* all possible *internal resources*. Most of Southeast Asia (except Malaysia, Singapore and Brunei) can be considered underdeveloped. Therefore, it is extremely important that these countries put to work all the energy and materials available to them. When there are few resources to begin with, inefficiency and wastefulness are suicidal.

Among the countries discussed in this chapter, three countries stand out as having the best prospects for development as a result of their planning processes. Malaysia, in particular, can be cited for awareness of its needs. The nation was weak in the agricultural sector and so it devoted its resources to improve this sector of the economy. Singapore, likewise made use of its location to attract foreign entrepreneurs. Officials in Singapore recognized that urban congestion was creating a problem in the city, with serious side effects. Industrial estates that were built not only helped decongest the city, but added further employment and economic growth. As for Vietnam, it has not only sizeable primary resources, but its rigorous, sometimes painful socialist planning has boosted the economy. Vietnam relies on foreign aid, primarily from the U.S.S.R. Also, comprehensive long-range plan, have been implemented by the National Planning Board in since 1958 which at least shows an effort to add maturity and depth to the planning process. When North and South Vietnam became one nation and Chinese support ceased, the Republic of Vietnam had to rely on Soviet-bloc countries for aid and technology. Vietnam's national planning had to adjust with two different economic systems that were prevalent in the North and the South. North Vietnam's earlier planning successess were retarded by the problems of unity. Further, the South had problems of attempting to advance too fast towards socialism.

The third factor is the application of a comprehensive approach to planning on the basis of social equality. Social planning, which has been added to physical and economic planning in Singapore deserves credit because the low income people have certain minimum economic and housing guarantees. Truly comprehensive, planning involving social as well as economic and physical aspects is planning in its most advanced form and is practiced best in Singapore.

Thailand has been unable to start her economic "take-off' in spite of large-scale foreign aid. Burma, Cambodia, and Indonesia have all, conversely, shown ill judgement in national planning. Until the mid-sixties, Indonesia was very unrealistic in its emphasis on industrial development. Burmese officials have displayed poor judgement and in some cases corruption. Cambodia has not even been able to capitalize on foreign assistance as exemplified by the waste of Chinese aid. Planning in the Philippines has brought mixed results because it has infused development by loans from international sources and thus, in 1984, its foreign debt was the largest compared to all other Southeast Asian countries.

Footnote References

[1]Frank J. Costa and Ashok K. Dutt, "Framework for Evaluating National Planning in Southeast Asia", *Asian Survey*, Vol. 3, No. 3 (1975), pp. 331-332.

[2]Louis Walinsky, *Economic Development in Burma 1951*-1960 (New York: The Twenieth Century Fund, 1962), p. 65.

[3]*Ibid.*, p. 64.

[4]*Ibid.*, p. 135.

[5]Cranby Onslow, *Asian Economic Development* (London: Weindenfield and Nicolson, 1965), p. 7.

[6]Frank N. Trager, *Burma: From Kingdom to Republic* (New York: Fredrick A. Praeger, Inc., 1966), p. 151.

[7]In 1940-1941, when maximum acreage was under agriculture in the pre-war Burma, the total agricultural land accounted to about 19 million acres: ⅔ given to rice. J. Russell Andrus, *Burmese Economic Life* (Stanford, California: Stanford University Press, 1956), p. 42.

[8]Walinsky, pp. 305-306.

[9]Mya Maung, *Burma and Pakistan: A Comparative Study of Development* (New York: Praeger Publishers, Inc., 1971), p. 59.

[10]Josef Silverstein, "Ne Win's Revolution Considered," *Asian Survey*, Vol. VI, No. 2 (February, 1966) pp. 96-97.

[11]Henderson & others, *Area Handbook for Burma* (Washington, D.C.: U.S. Government Printing Office, 1971), p. 6.

[12]*Ibid.*, p. 218.

[13]Nayan Chanda, "Loosening The Grip On Burma's Tiger," *Far Eastern Economic Review*, Vol. 83, No. 11 (March 18, 1974), p. 38.

[14]Ho Kwon Ping, "The Cautious Search For Success," *Far Eastern Economic Review*, Vol. 107, No. 3 (January 18, 1980), p. 36.

[15]M.C. Tun, "Burma: Sobering Up," *Far Eastern Economic Review*, Vol. 84, No. 15 (April 15, 1974), pp. 48-49.

[16]John McBeth, "Paranoia of Progress," *Far Eastern Economic Review*, Vol. 114, No. 43 (October 16, 1981), p. 91.

[17]Peter Weintraub, "Rangoon Spells It Out For Business," *Far Eastern Economic Review*, Vol. 98, No. 41 (October 14, 1977), p. 51.

[18]James Harriman, "Burma's First Steps to Capitalism," *Far Eastern Economic Review*, Vol. 94, No. 52 (December 24, 1976), pp. 100-103.

[19]Josef Silverstein, "Burma In 1980: An Uncertain Balance Sheet," *Asian Survey*, Vol. XXI, No. 2 (February 1981), p. 214.

[20]*Ibid.*, p. 213.

[21]Ping, p. 38.

[22]*Ibid.*, p. 41.

[23]*Asia 1982 Yearbook* (Hongkong: Far Eastern Economic Review Limited), p. 125.

[24]*Ibid.*

[25]Kwat Soen Sie, *Prospects for Agricultural Development in Indonesia* (Wageningen: Center for Agricultural Publishing and Documentation, 1968), p. 66.

[26]Benjamin Higgins, *Indonesia's Economic Stabilization and Development* (New York: Institute of Pacific Relations, 1957), p. xii.

[27]D.W. Fryer, "Economic Aspects of Indonesian Disunity," *Pacific Affairs*, XXX, No. 3 (1957), p. 202.

[28]*Ibid.*, p. 207.

[29]Higgins, p. 123.

[30]United States Economic Survey Team to Indonesia, *Indonesia: Perspectives and Proposals for United States Economic Aid* A Report to the President (New Haven, 1963), p. 86.

[31]*Ibid.*, p. 85.

[32]J. Panglaykim and H.W. Arndt, *The Indonesian Economy: Facing a New Era?* (Rooterdam, 1966), pp. 28, 30.

[33]Rossal J. Johnson and Dale L. McKeen and Leon A. Mears, *Business Environment in an Emerging Nation* (Evanston, Illinois, 1966), p. 82.

[34]Business International Corporation, *Doing Business in the New Indonesia* (New York, 1968), p. 4.

[35]A.R. Shoehoed, "Indonesian Investment Private Enterprise Challenge," *Far Eastern Economic Review* (August 19, 1972), p. 18.

[36]*Ibid.*

[37]Business International Corporation, p. 27.

[38]Shoehoed, p. 18.

[39]S. Iskander, "Indoesia: Polarized Progress," *Far Eastern Economic Review* (April 1, 1972), p. 141.

[40]*Ibid.*, p. 142.

[41]*The Americana Annual 1972* (Americana Corporation, 1972), p. 349.

[42]Douglas S. Paauw, "The Indonesian Economy In the 1980s," *Economic Bulletin For Asia And The Pacific*, Vol. XXXI, No. 2 (December 1980), pp. 31-33.

[43]*Ibid.*

[44]*Asia 1978 Yearbook* (Hong Kong: *Far Eastern Economic Review Ltd.* 1978), p. 200.

[45]"Island of Stability," *Far Eastern Economic Review*, Vol. 107, No. 2 (January 11, 1980), p. 36.

[46]Asia 1978 Yearbook, p. 200.

[47]Rodney Tasker, "Exceeding All Expectancies," *Far Eastern Economic Review*, Vol. 101, No. 34 (August 25, 1978) pp. 23-25.

[48]Asia 1978 Yearbook p. 200.

[49]*Asia 1980 Yearbook* (Hong Kong: *Far Eastern Economic Review Ltd.* 1980), p. 190.

[50]Asia 1981 Yearbook (Hong Kong: *Far Eastern Economic Review Ltd.* 1981), p. 153.

[51]Guy Sacerdoti, "Overdraft of Inefficiency," *Far Eastern Economic Review*, Vol. 112, No. 23 (May 29, 1981), p. 44.

[52]Guy Sacerdoti, "Jakarta Takes More Time,'" *Far Eastern Economic Review*, Vol. 103, No. 3 (January 19, 1979), p. 67.

[53]Sacerdoti (1981), p. 44.

[54]*Asia 1981 Yearbook*, p. 154.

[55]George L. Harris and others, *Area Handbook for Thailand* (Washington, D.C.: U.S. Government Printing Office, 1963), p. 423.

[56]Transport and Communication was allocated 31.42% of the budgetary allocation, Community Facilties 16.7%, Health 4.18%, and Education 7.63%. Katsumi Mitani, "Key Factors in the Development of Tahiland," in *Economic Development Issues: Greece, Isreal, Taiwan, Thailand* (New York: Committee for Econimc Development, 1968), p. 196.

[57]Alek A. Rozental, *Finance and Development in Thailand* (New York: Praeger Publishers, Inc., 1970), p. 33, Table 2.1.

[58]Figures have been taken from Mitani, p. 196 (Table 14).

[59]Henderson & others, *Area Handbook for Thailand* (Washington D.C.: U.S. Government Printing Office, 1971), p. 233.

[60]"Behind Thai Woes," *Far Eastern Economic Review* (June 24, 1972), p. 31.

[61]R.J. Pryor, "Population Redistribution and Development Planning in South-East Asia," *Proceedings of the International Geographical Union Regional Conference and Eighth New Zealand Geography Conference*, New Zealand Geographical Society: Conference Series No. 8 (Hamilton: Rice Printers, 1975), p. 73.

[62]Richard Nations, "Thais Rely On An Old Formula," *Far Eastern Economic Review*, Vol. 95, No. 5 (February 4, 1977), pp. 36-39.

[63]*Ibid.*, p. 38.

[64]Philip Bowring, "ASEAN Dark Horse," *Far Eastern Economic Review*, Vol. 118, No. 43 (October 22, 1982), p. 88.

[65]Nations, p. 39.

[66]Richard Nations, "Drought Hits Thai Trouble Zone," *Far Eastern Economic Review*, Vol. 98, No. 50 (December 16, 1977), p. 93.

[67]*Ibid.*, p. 89.

[68]*Ibid.*

[69]*Ibid.*, pp. 90-93.

[70]Richard Nations, "Bangkok Is Caught In A Squeeze," *Far Eastern Economic Review*, Vol. 105, No. 38 (September 21, 1979), p. 104.

[71]Larry A. Niksch, "Thailand In 1981: The Prem Government Feels The Heat," *Asian Survey*, Vol. XXII, No. 2 (February, 1982), p. 196.

[72]Paisal Sricharatchanya, "Change Of Gear For Thailand," *Far Eastern Economic Review*, Vol. 113, No. 40 (September 25, 1981), p. 68.

[73]Bowring, pp. 85-86.

[74]Niksch, p. 196.

[75]R.J. Pryor, pp. 74-78.

[76]Leo Gonzaga, "Philippine Planners at Work," *Far Eastern Economic Review*, Vol. 97, No. 31 (August 5, 1977), p. 39.

[77]*Ibid.*

[78]Leo Gonzaga, "Batten Down Hatches, Turbulence Ahead," *Far Eastern Economic Review*, Vol. 102, No. 46 (November 17, 1978), p. 50.

[79]Kit Machado, "The Philippines in 1977: Beginning a 'Return to Normalcy'?" *Asian Survey*, Vol. XVIII, No. 2 (February 1978), p. 209.

[80]Robert L. Youngblood, "The Philippines in 1981: From 'New Society' to 'New Republic'," *Asian Survey*, Vol. XXII, No. 2 (February 1982), p. 232.

[81]Clark Neher, "The Philippines 1979: Cracks in the Fortress," *Asian Survey*, Vol. XX, No. 2 (February 1980), p. 163.

[82]*The Second Five-Year Plan (1983*-87) (document), parts of which were supplied by the Philippine Embassy, Washington, D.C., p. 1.

[83]Richard Nations, "A Chilles for Manila," *Far Eastern Economic Review*, Vol. 116, No. 18 (April 30, 1982), p. 40.

[84]Jose E. Romero Jr., "The First Decade," *Philippine Finance/ASEAN Perspectives*, Vol. 2, No. 1 (September 1982), p. 3.

[85]Footnote 82, pp. 3-5.

[86]J. Kennedy, *A History of Malaya*, 2nd edition (London: The Macmillan Company, 1970), p. 329.

[87]*Malaya Second Five-Year Plan, 1961*-1965 (Kuala Lumpur: Government Printers, 1961), para. 50.

[88]James W. Gould, *The United States and Malaysia* (Cambridge, Mass.: Harvard University Press, 1969), p. 157.

[89]*Ibid.*, pp. 158-159.

[90]Milton J. Esman, *Administration and Development in Malaysia (Ithica, New York: 1972), p. 52.*
[91]Harvey Stockwin, "Back from the Brink?" *Far Eastern Economic Review* (December 30, 1965), p. 592.
[92]Lee Soo Ann, "Financing Planning of Investment in Malaysia," *Malaysian Economic Review* (April, 1969), p. 48.
[93]*Ibid.*, p. 48.
[94]*Ibid.*
[95]Stockwin, p. 592.
[96]Esman, pp. 51-52.
[97]*Quarterly Economic Review of Malaysia, Singapore, and Brunei* (No. 2, 1970), p. 6.
[98]V. Kanapathy, *The Malaysian Economy* (Singapore: 1970).
[99]"Malaysia," *The Colombo Plan 1969*-1970 (London: 1972).
[100]"Malaysia's New Phase," *Far Eastern Economic Review* (Sept. 2, 1972), p. 39.
[101]*Ibid.* This rule has been breached quite often to attract foreign investment particularly for creating new jobs.
[102]James Morgan, "Satisfying Malay Aspirations," *Far Eastern Economic Review* (August 26, 1972), *Focus*, p. 10.
[103]James Morgan, "Malaysia's New Phase," *Far Eastern Economic Review* (Sept. 2, 1972), p. 38.
[104]David Lim, "Malaysian Social And Economic Development Strategies for the 1980s", *Economic Bulletin For Asia And The Pacific*, Vol. XXXI, No. 2 (December 1980), p. 61.
[105]*Ibid.*, p. 59.
[106]*Ibid.*, p. 65.
[107]HoKwon Ping, "Planning With a Cosmetic Touch," *Far Eastern Economic Review*, Vol. 102, No. 42 (October 20, 1978), p.49.
[108]Philip Bowring, "Half-way to Maturity," *Far Eastern Economic Review*, Vol. 112, No. 16 (April 10, 1981), p. 72.
[109]Ping, p. 49.
[110]*Ibid.*
[111]It may be noted that the NEP is expected to be completed in 1990.
[112]Bowring, p. 70.
[113]*Ibid.*, p. 75.
[114]*Ibid.*, p. 71.
[115]*Ibid.*, pp. 70-71.
[116]Patrick Smith, "Malaysia's Labour Pains," *Far Eastern Economic Review*, Vol. 114, No. 44 (October 23, 1981), p. 83.
[117]*Ibid.*, p. 84.
[118]Jeffrey Segal, "Malaysia's Vulnerability Shows," *Far Eastern Economic Review*, Vol. 116, No. 15 (April 9, 1982), p. 59.
[119]Bowring, p. 77.
[120]*First Development Plan 1961*-1964: Review of Progress for the Three Years Ending 31st December, 1963 (Singapore: Economic Planning Unit, Prime Minister's Office, 1964), p. 37.
[121]Peter Simms and Rush Loring, Jr., "New Tide in an Island Nation," *Fortune* (August 15, 1969), p. 82.
[122]Marvin L. Rogers, "Malaysia and Singapore: 1971 Development," *Asian Survey* Vol. 12, No. 2 (February, 1972), p. 174.
[123]Rolf Jensen, "Planning Urban Renewal and Housing in Singapore," *Town Planning Review*, Vol. 38, No. 2 (July 1967), pp. 123-126.
[124]Being a socialist government, the provision of housing for the general public was one of the most important objectives of government policy.
[125]Gayl D. Ness, *The Sociology of Economic Development: A Reader* (New York: Harper & Row Publishers, 1972), p. 358.
[126]Yue-Man Yeung, "Singapore," *Focus* (April, 1971), p. 10.
[127]*Annual Budget Statement* moved to the Parliament of Singapore for financial year 1st April, 1972, to 31st March, 1973, (mimeographed), supplied by the Embassy of the Republic of Singapore, Washington, D.C.
[128]*Ibid.*, pp. 13-16.
[129]*Ibid.*, p. 10.
[130]*Ibid.*
[131]*Ibid.*, p. 11.
[132]*Ibid.*, p. 15.
[133]Shee Poon-Kim, "Singapore in 1977: Stability and Growth", *Asian Survey*, (February, 1978), p. 197-198.
[134]Anthony Rowley, "Stabilize Wages for more investment from abroad", *Far Eastern Economic Review* (August 12, 1977), p. 35.
[135]Theodore Shabad, "Economic Development in North Vietnam," *Pacific Affairs*, XXXI (1958), p. 36.
[136]William Kaye, "A Bowl of Rice Divided: The Economy of North Vietnam" in P.J. Honey (ed.) *North Vietnam Today* (New York: Frederick A. Praeger, Inc., 1962), p. 108.
[137]P.J. Honey, "Food Crisis in North Vietnam," *Far Eastern Economic Review*, 41 (August 15, 1963), p. 494,
[138]Kaye, p. 110.
[139]Douglass Pike, "North Vietnam in 1971," *Asian Survey*, XIII, No. 1, (January, 1972), p. 22
[140]Douglas Pike, "North Vietnam In The Year 1972," *Asian Survey*, Vol. XIII, No. 1 (January 1973), p. 50.

[141]*Asia 1976 Yearbook*, (Hong Kong: Far Eastern Economic Review Limited), p. 319.

[142]Pike, p. 52.

[143]*Asia 1976 Yearbook*, p. 319.

[144]Massimo Loche, "Foundations For The Year 2000," *Far Eastern Economic Review*, Vol. 94, No. 52 (December 24, 1976), p. 23.

[145]*Asia 1976 Yearbook*, p. 319.

[146]*Ibid.*

[147]Nayan Chanda, "Rebuilding Shattered Vietnam," *Far Eastern Economic Review*, Vol. 91, No. 7 (February 13, 1976), pp. 93–94.

[148]*Ibid.*

[149]*Ibid.*, p. 94.

[150]Nayan Chanda, "Hanoi Comes Down To Earth," *Far Eastern Economic Review*, Vol. 111, No. 8 (February 4, 1977), p. 30.

[151]Nayan Chanda, "Vietnam's Economic Post-Mortem," *Far Eastern Economic Review*, Vol. III, No. 3 (January 9, 1981), p. 40.

[152]*Asia 1978 Yearbook*, p. 33.

[153]Nayan Chanda, "A Last-Minute Rescue," *Far Eastern Economic Review*, Vol. III, No. 10 (February 27, 1981), p. 30.

[154]Nayan Chanda, "Vietnam's Economic Post-Mortem," (1981) p. 40.

[155]Douglas Pike, "Vietnam In 1980: The Gathering Storm?," *Asian Survey*, Vol. XXI, No. 1 (January 1981), p. 86.

[156]Nayan Chanda, "A Last-Minute Rescue," (1981), p. 28.

[157]Nayan Chanda, "Vietnam's Economy: New Priorities," *Far Eastern Economic Review*, Vol. 94, No. 47 (November 19, 1976), p. 40.

[158]*Asia 1980 Yearbook*, p. 303.

[159]Douglas Pike, (1981), p. 87.

[160]*Ibid.*, pp. 84–85.

[161]*Ibid.*, p. 87.

[162]Michael Morrow, "Ready For A Rebound," *Far eastern Economic Review*, Vol. 115, No. 5 (January 29, 1982), p. 48.

[163]Paul Quinn-Judge, "The Threat In The Cradle," *Far Eastern Economic Review*, Vol. 118, No. 48 (November 26, 1982), p. 40.

[164]Nayan Chanda, "A Last-Minute Rescue," (1981), p. 31.

[165]Nayan Chanda, "Cracks In The Edifice," *Far Eastern Economic Review*, Vol. 114, No. 50 (December 4, 1981), p. 84.

[166]U.S. Dept. of the Army, *Area Handbook for Cambodia* (Washington, D.C.: U.S. Government Printing Office, 1963), pp. 253–254.

[167]*Ibid.*, p. 259.

[168]David J. Steinberg, *Cambodia* (New Haven: Hraf Press, 1959), p. 171.

[169]Michael Leifer, *Cambodia: The Search for Security* (New York: Fererick A. Praeger, Inc., 1967), p. 7.

[170]Frederick Munson, *Area Handbook for Cambodia* (Washington, D.C.: U.S. Government Printing Office, D A Pam. No. 550–50, 1968), p. 216.

[171]*Ibid.*, p. 217.

[172]*Ibid.*, p. 216.

[173]*Ibid.*, p. 217.

[174]Donald Kirk, "Cambodia's Economic Crisis," *Asian Survey* XI (March, 1971), p. 243.

[175]R.P.W. Norton, Doing It Their Way," *Far Eastern Economic Review*, Vol. 71, No. 13 (March 27, 1971), p. 80.

[176]*Ibid.*

[177]*Asian 1982 Yearbook* (Hong Kong: Far Eastern Economic Review Limited), p. 130.

[178]*Asia 1976 Yearbook*, p. 206.

[179]*Ibid.*

[180]*Ibid.*

[181]Nayan Chanda, "Laos Back To The Drawing Board," *Far eastern Economic Review*, Vol. 101, No. 36 (September 8, 1978), p. 32.

[182]*Ibid.*, p. 33.

[183]*Ibid.*

[184]Nayan Chanda, "Laos Gears Up For Rural Progress," *Far Eastern Economic Review*, Vol. 96, No. 14 (April 8, 1977), p. 125.

[185]McAlister Brown and Joseph J. Zasloff, "Laos 1979: Caught In Vietnam's Wake," *Asian Survey*, Vol. XX, No. 2 (February 1979), p. 108.

[186]*Asia 1980 Yearbook*, p. 222.

[187]Stanley S. Bedlington, "Laos In 1980: The Portents Are Ominous," *Asian Survey*, Vol. XXI, No. 1 (January 1981), p. 110.

[188]Nayan Chanda, "Softy-soft Socialism," *Far Eastern Economic Review*, Vol. 116, No. 22 (May 28, 1982), p. 21.

[189]*Asia 1981 Yearbook*, p. 184.

[190]Nayan Chanda, "Softy-soft Socialism," (1982), p. 22.

[191]Ashok K. Dutt, "A Comparative Study of Regional Planning in Britain and The Netherlands," *The Ohio Journal of Science* Vol. 70, No. 6 (November, 1970), pp. 321–322.

Part II

Case Studies

Chapter 8

Indonesia: Insular Contrasts of the Java Core with Outer Islands

William A. Withington

Indonesia now, as throughout Southeast Asia's long history, is of vital importance in area, character, and population. In location it commands major land, sea, and air passageways. The Indonesian archipelago, extending over 3,000 miles from east to west, is the largest nation of Southeast Asia. Indonesia's area is 736,000 square miles; its 1980 population, 147.5 million. The principal chain of islands, from northern Sumatra to eastern Irian Jaya in mid-New Guinea, is an almost continuous barrier to any north-south transportation and trade.[1]

The Indonesian archipelago has always occupied a bridge position (Fig. 8-1). Continental and peninsular Asia to the northeast; Australia, to the south; and the Pacific Island world, to the east. The larger western Indonesian islands, fringing the ancient rocks of the Sunda Platform, continue Asiatic patterns of physiography, flora and fauna southeastward. Similar Australian patterns of flora and fauna extend northwestward on the Sahul Shelf underlying western New Guinea or Irian Barat and the eastern Lesser Sunda (Nusa Tenggara) Islands. This chain of islands, has only a few deep and wide passageways for shipping.

The bridge and crossroad conditions are reflected in the diverse peoples of Indonesia. Malay stock of earlier proto-Malay or later deutero-Malay types from Asia predominates.[2] Other 'Indonesians' are the eastern Papuans and scattered small Negritoid groups, plus Indians, Chinese, Arabs, and Westerners, particularly in urban centers. Indonesia is part of the widespread Malayo-Polynesian world reaching far northeastward to Hawaii, southeast to New Zealand, and southwestward to Madagascar.[3]

Other important attributes of Indonesia are its very large population; its striking contrasts between core and outer islands; and its great diversity of cultures, resources, and economic activities. Indonesia's population is exceeded only by those of China, India, the Soviet Union, and the United States. It is three times as populous as the Philippines or Thailand, the next largest nations of Southeast Asia. Within Indonesia the concentration of people and their activities are in sharp contrast between Java, Madura, and Bali on the one hand, and the outlying islands on the other. Java (always in this discussion including administratively allied Madura) with 90,000,000 people living within 50,000 square miles, is among the world's most densely populated areas.[4] Only Bali and a few, primarily urban-oriented areas elsewhere in Indonesia have similar densities. Indonesia's diversity has been further accentuated by uneven economic development. Java and Bali very early evolved a wet rice *sawah* cultivation system.[5] A few outer island areas, notably upland northern and western Sumatra and northeastern Sulawesi, also have had intensive sawah agriculture for centuries. Western influence, largely through the Dutch focus on Java, increased these differential developments. Since Indonesia became independent in 1949 the intensive occupation of Java and Bali has continued to contrast with outer islands, except in nodes of localized development—'developmental islands' within a broad 'sea' of more extensive occupance.

POLITICAL, HUMAN, AND ECONOMIC RESOURCES OF INDONESIA

Since independence, the Republic of Indonesia has evolved a pattern of major and minor internal ad-

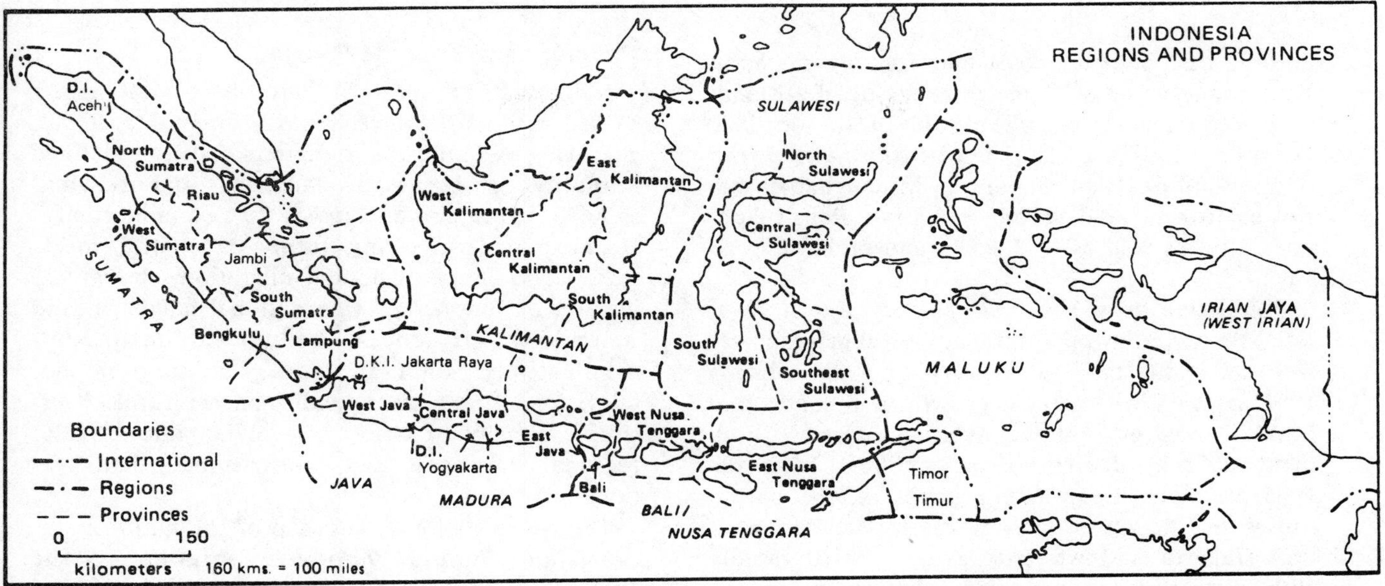

Figure 8-1. Indonesia: Regions and Provinces.

ministrative units within seven distinctive island regions.[6] Twenty-seven areas are provinces (Fig. 8-1).[7] The focus of government is on the northwest coast of Java in D.K.I. Jakarta (also referred to as Djakarta), the Special Capital District of Jakarta, analagous to the District of Columbia in the United States. In addition, Indonesia has about 300 second level areas, most *kabupaten* similar to counties and 50 *kotamadya* or autonomous municipalities.[8]

Population Growth

The population of Indonesia has risen from 60.4 million in 1930 to 147.5 million in 1980.[9] In 1930 the populous core of Java had 41.7 million people, 69% of Indonesia's total. This core population grew to 91.3 million by 1980, 61.9% of the national total. Java thus has a slower rate of growth, despite a huge increase in numbers, than the outer islands or the nation as a whole. The relatively slower rate of population increase in Java is causally related to a combination of factors. 'Transmigration,' the movement of people from intensively populated rural areas of Java and Bali to outer islands, particularly to southern Sumatra since 1905, has somewhat lowered the core area population growth. Modern rural to urban population movements have made the Java core area more highly urbanized than peripheral areas. This higher urbanization, much greater rural population densities than in outer islands, and family planning programs have resulted in lower increases in the central area, 2.0% versus 2.9% annual rise elsewhere. Deaths in the wake of the 1965 attempted *coup d'etat* had a greater impact on Java—and possibly Bali—than in outer island areas.[10]

Outer island population grew from about 19 million, 31% of Indonesian population, in 1930 to the 1980 total of 56.2 million, 38.1% of all Indonesians. Annual rates of natural increase in 1971–80 were 2.3% for Indonesia; about 2.9% for the outer islands, and 2.0% for Java.[11] The more rapid population increases in the outer islands reflect such conditions and influences as lower densities of population and more space for additional people; larger natural increases typical of many less-urbanized outer island ethnic groups as compared to the central area peoples; and sizeable transmigration from Java, Madura, and Bali, mainly to Sumatra, but also to northern and eastern islands, including politically-influenced growth in the Maluku area.[12]

Among the outer island areas, Sumatra grew most rapidly, from 8.3 million (13.7% of all Indonesians) in 1930 to 28.0 million (19.0% in 1980). Factors contributing to Sumatra's very rapid growth have been the comparative economic health of plantation and smallholder agriculture, most concentrated around Medan (eastern North Sumatra), exporting natural rubber, palm oil, cigar wrapper tobacco, coffee, and tea; large-scale transmigration into the Lampung and other southern areas; increased manufacturing; and expanding production of minerals (petroleum, tin, natural gas, bauxite, coal) and forestry materials from many areas of Sumatra or its nearby islands (Fig. 8-2). Data from the 1961, 1971, and 1980 censuses indicate the traditional *merantau* (migration) of West Sumatran Minangkabau has flowed to rural and urban, Sumatran areas of opportunity, as well as to Jakarta and other cities of Java.[13]

Population growth in central and eastern Java, Bali, South Sulawesi, and South Kalimantan was well below the national average of 51.9% during 1961 to 1980, while recent growth of Sumatra and Maluku was well above average. Already high densities, plus disruptions and killings after the 1965 attempted *coup d'etat* appear to be partial causes of the lower growth rates. Population in both Jakarta and western Java increased rapidly with diversified economic developments. In the case of Sumatra, the transmigation (encouraged migration) policies begun by the Dutch colonial government in 1905 have been continued by the Indonesian government since 1945, though with uneven numbers migrating, as an attempt to relieve population pressures in parts of Java, Madura, and Bali.[14] Most of the migrants have gone to the Lampung province of Sumatra, with smaller streams directed to several other Sumatran, Sulawesi, or Kalimantan settlement areas. Maluku Province has gained population as a result of two divergent processes. The Central Government moved at least 80,000 political detainees from Java to Buru Island in the central Maluku area in the late 1960s with the aim of agricultural settlement away from their former homes. In addition, some of the many peoples born in Indonesia who went to the Netherlands in 1957 and 1958 have returned to their original home areas in Ambon and in other parts of Maluku Province.[15]

The patterns of population densities reflect diversity in people, developed or undeveloped resources, and pressures on the land (Fig. 8-3). Population densities in Bali and Java nearly everywhere exceed 1,000 persons per square mile and over most areas of Java exceed 1,500 persons per square mile. The lowest densities found in Indonesia are under 8 persons per square mile in most of Irian Jaya, and 10 to 20 per square mile in East and Central Kalimantan. By comparison, Indonesia has a national average of 203 persons per square mile (78 per square kilometer), more than threefold that of the United States in 1980.

Culture, Language, and Religion

Indonesia's cultural diversity is a vital aspect of its national, as well as its internal regional, character. Culture in Indonesia can be defined primarily in terms of language and religion, though customary law (*adat*) is also important.[16] Because of increasing inter-island and inter-regional mobility, including migration, the widening use of Indonesian as a national language, and increasing influences through modern communications, such as radio, newspapers and television, Indonesia's traditional cultural diversity, especially in cities, is evolving into broader regional, national, and international identifications.

Today the national language of the nation is Indonesian (*Bahasa Indonesia*), similar to the Malay of Malaysia, both derived from the widespread earlier Malay of peninsular and insular Southeast Asia.[17] Though local languages are spoken by many peoples, Indonesian is the school language beyond second grade, with English taught as the second language.

The three largest cultural groups and languages are Javanese in central and eastern Java, Madurese in Madura and eastern Java, and Sundanese in western Java. Several other relatively large linguistic and cultural groups have their hearths in Sumatra. Among these are Acehnese in the north; East Coast Malay along the entire eastern Sumatran plains; Batak groups of North Sumatra areas; Minangkabau in the west; Rejang-Lebong in the southwest; and Lampung in the south.[18] Banjarese, and various Dyak and Borneo Malay tongues predominate in Kalimantan. In Sulawesi there are Minahasa (Manadonese) in the north, Toraja in the central areas, and Buginese and Makasarese in the southwest arm. Balinese on Bali and western Lombok, Ambonese in Central Maluku, and Sumbanese on Sumba Island are a few of the many distinctive languages and peoples in the eastern islands. A diversity of Papuan languages and groups makes for extreme complexity within Irian Jaya. Some of these languages and groups blend with others in nearby eastern islands of Indonesia.[19]

About 85% of all Indonesians are identified as Islamic, or think of themselves as Islamic, in religion. Syncretism of varying degrees among many Islamic peoples reflects past Animistic, Hindu, and Buddhist influences.[20] Eight percent

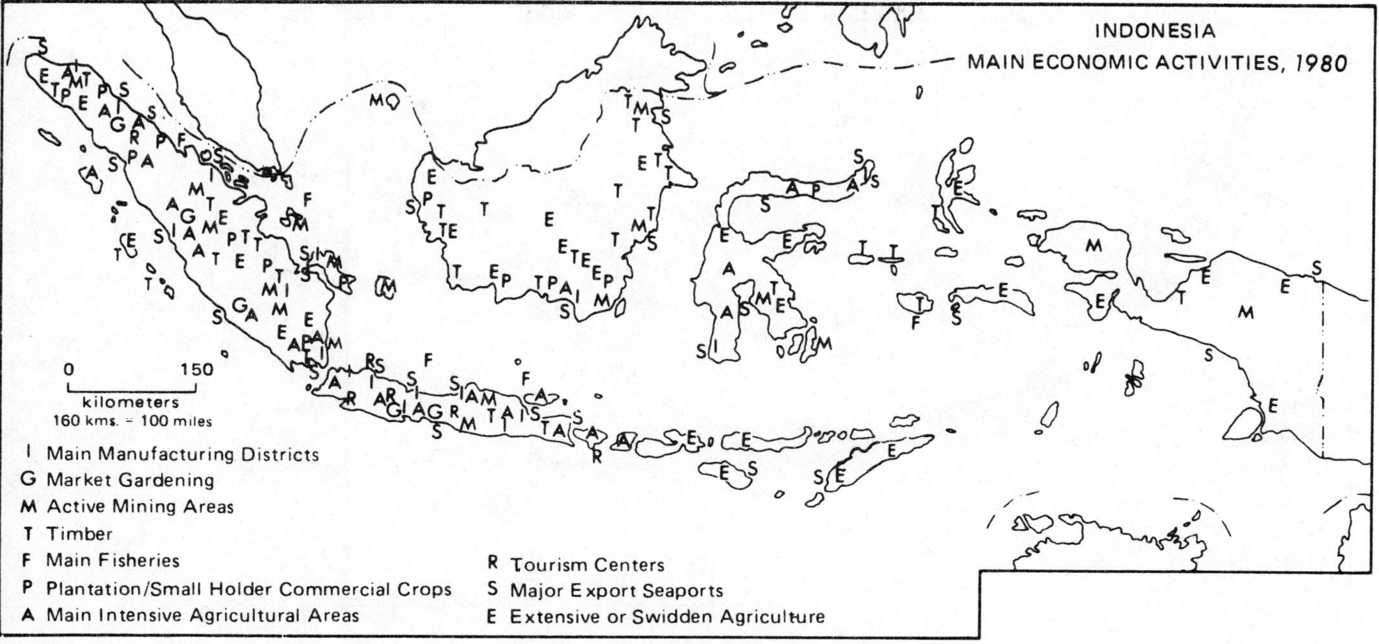

Figure 8-2. Indonesia: Main Economic Activities, 1971.

of the Indonesian population is Christian, either Roman Catholic or Protestant. These Christians are most concentrated in North Sumatra, central and northern Sulawesi and in several islands, including Timor, of the Lesser Sunda (Nusa Tenggara) chain. Missionary activities by Christians have been confined to non-Moslem peoples in most of Indonesia, with some evidence that Christianity has been increasing through conversions since 1961.[21] Many of the four million Chinese in Indonesia practice forms of ancestor worship. Scattered indigenous groups, especially in Indonesia's more isolated forested plains, uplands or island interiors, are still Animistic.

Urban Nodes and Rural Predominance

Despite rapid growth in most of its urban centers, Indonesia's population remains overwhelmingly rural at about 79%.[22] Rural predominance is evident in every province except Jakarta in northwestern Java, listed in 1980 as entirely urban.[23] Elsewhere, rural population proportions were as low as 60% in East Kalimantan; more than 90% in East Nusa Tenggara. Among the major regions, Kalimantan, Sumatra, and the Java core area are slightly less rural; Sulawesi and eastern island areas are more rural than the 79% national average.

In spite of its rural emphasis, Indonesia has more, and generally larger, cities than other Southeast Asian nations. Only part of this abundance of cities is accounted for by Indonesia's large area or population. The division into several major island clusters, each at some distance from the others, has been one city-forming and city-stimulating influence. The large number of separate ethnic groups, each with its own principal cultural center, also has contributed to the numbers of urban places, as has insular and river valley separation of settled areas.

As a group, Indonesia's larger cities, known as *Kotamadya* (autonomous municipalities) between 1961–80, have had a very rapid growth in population, averaging 92.6%.[24] This rapid large city growth results from such recent influences as immigration from nearby or upland rural areas, overcrowding and lack of agricultural land in rural areas, and a perception by many Indonesians that greater opportunities for employment, education, and amenities are available in urban rather that rural areas.[25] In 1980 Indonesia had five cities—Jakarta, Surabaya, Bandung, Medan, and Semarang—in the million population category, with Jakarta's 6.5 million the largest city in Southeast Asia. Another thirty-two centers were intermediate cities of 100,000 to 1,000,000 people (See Fig. 6-3). At least 100 other places were small urban centers of 20,000 to 100,000 and many more places considered urban by Indonesia had fewer than 20,000 people. These city figures

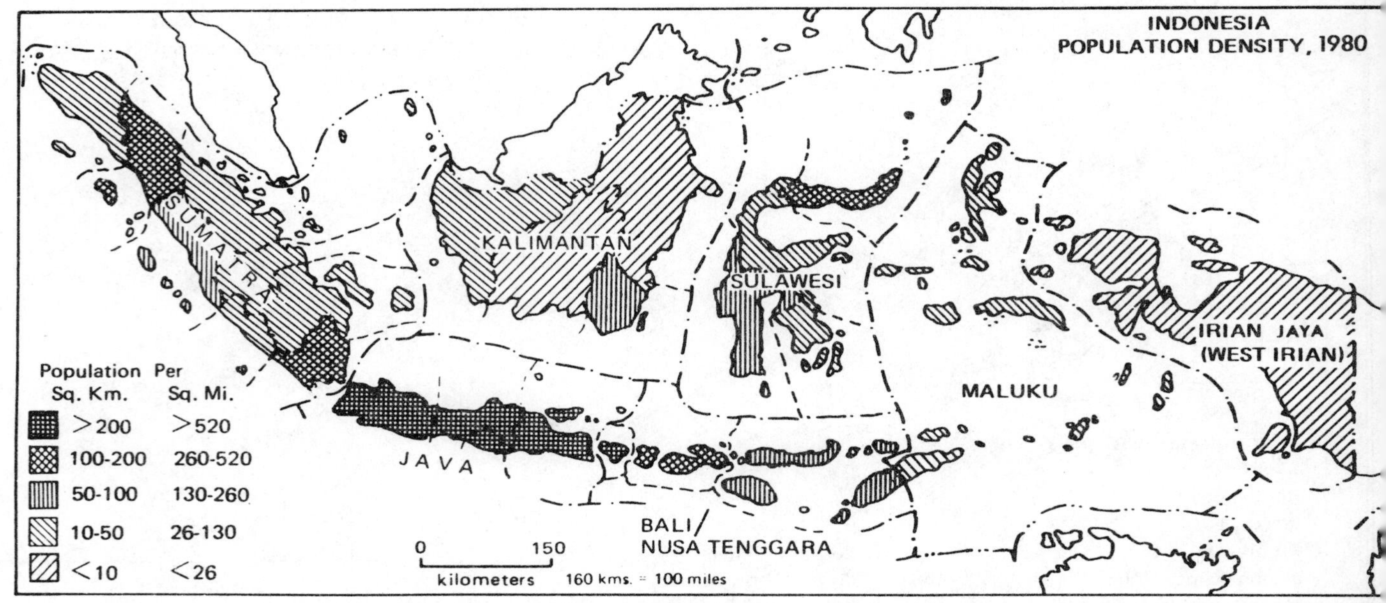

Figure 8-3. Indonesia: Population Density.

reflect growing numbers and proportions of cities over one million, over 100,000, and above 20,000 people, though many are smaller.[26]

Indonesia has a series of major and lesser urban clusters (Fig. 8-4). Nineteen large and intermediate cities of Java form the largest cluster. One city of a million size, seven intermediate cities, plus many smaller ones, make up a second, western cluster on Sumatra. Elsewhere, Kalimantan has four and Sulawesi two intermediate cities. In eastern Indonesia, Ambon in Maluku with over 200,000 people is the largest city. Denpasar on Bali is also intermediate in size, with an international airport, tourist hotels, and nearby seaport as an extension of Jakarta's tourist/cultural attractions. Kupang on western Timor, Ternate, Dili, and Jayapura (formerly Hollandia, then Sukarnapura) are other eastern urban nodes.[27]

Urban places in Indonesia are defined in three ways: first, as *Kotamadya*; second as administrative capitals of provinces or *Kabupaten*; and third as specific urban centers without the status of the first two types.[28] Of the fifty *Kotamadya*, thirty are intermediate or large cities, and twenty-four are provincial or national capital cities. Most of the smaller *Kotamadya* are on Sumatra, the result of granting autonomous municipality status earlier to politically and economically important places which have not grown to intermediate or large size. Similar lesser *Kotamadya* or other small cities are found on Java, Sulawesi, and Kalimantan, and on smaller islands to the east. Of the many other, smaller urban places noted earlier, six are provincial capitals and most of the remaining ones are also in the second or administrative category of *kabupaten* capitals. If urban places in Indonesia were defined by population size or functional diversity, rather than by administrative status, numerous additional communities would qualify. Included would be several outports, such as *Dumai* fifty miles north of Pakanbaru on Sumatra's eastern plain, and many market towns.[29]

ECONOMIC ACTIVITIES IN INDONESIA'S CORE AND PERIPHERIES

Despite the rapid recent growth of urban centers, Indonesia remains strongly in agriculture and other primary economic activities (Table 8-1). Estimates for 1981 indicate a marked decline in the proportion of agriculture, forestry and mining, but increases in manufacturing and tertiary services. Economic hardships of the middle 1960s reduced manufacturing activity. Since 1967 this low level has risen with improving internal and external markets and sizeable foreign investments for new manufacturing facilities and associated work forces.

Core area/outer island dichotomies are indicated by strong regional differences. First, two-thirds of the labor force is concentrated in Java,

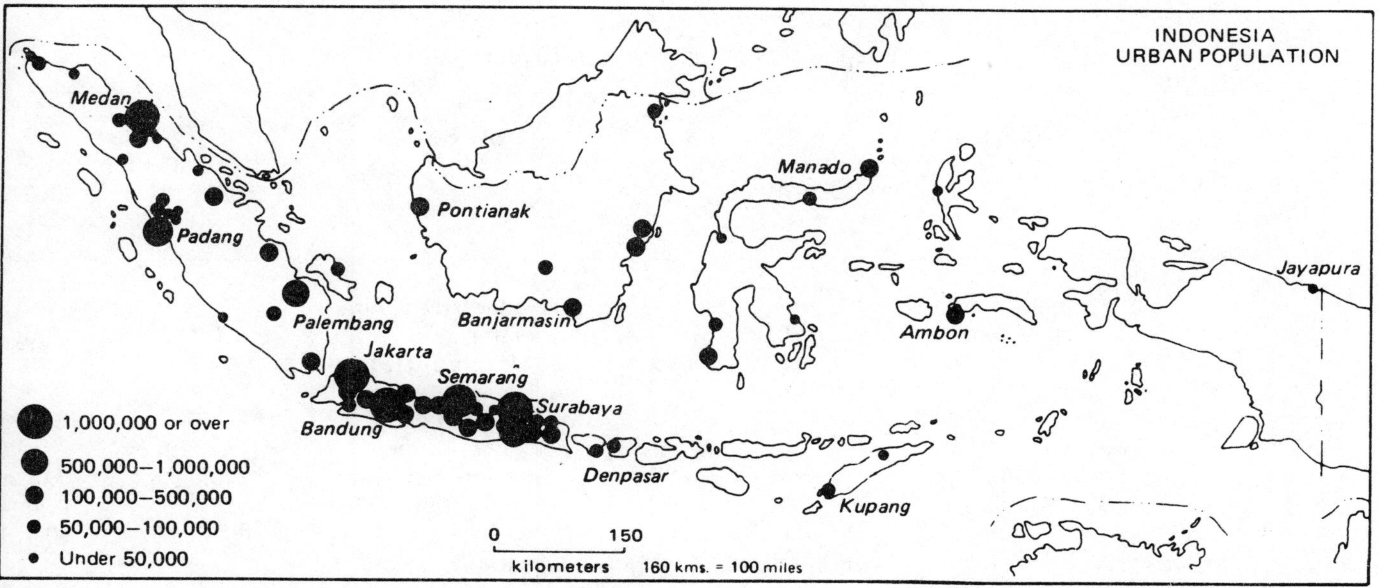

Figure 8-4. Indonesia: Urban Nodes.

about one-sixth in Sumatra, and the remaining sixth almost equally divided among Kalimantan, Sulawesi and the eastern islands. Second, primary sector activities account for less than 60% of all employment in the Java core area, but about 70% in the outer islands. Four-fifths of all manufacturing and construction workers are in Java, representing 9% of all core area employment. Outer island secondary activities employ less than 5% of all workers. Likewise, the core area has about 33% of its work force in the tertiary activities, but these figures average only 20% in the outer islands.

Agriculture, Forestry, and Fishing

These three activities involve almost six of every ten Indonesians (Table 8-1). Large numbers of Indonesians are part-time foresters and fishermen as well as farmers. Only small numbers are commercially active full time in forestry and fishing. The large majority of Indonesians are subsistence farmers. Most of them grow irrigated rice and subsistence crops, with many outer islanders depending on shifting cultivation or unirrigated rice and several smallholder crops such as coffee, rubber, and pepper.[30] Six-tenths of Indonesia's rice crop of 31 million metric tons (20 million metric tons of milled rice) is raised on Java where over six-tenths of Indonesia's people live.[31] Similar proportions of the nation's maize (corn), cassava, peanuts, vegetables, soybeans, and fruit also are grown on Java. One of Indonesia's dilemmas is that the core area, with six-tenths of the people, produces only one-half of the necessary food crops, while available inter-regional and interisland transportation is inadequate to move the supplies from surplus to deficit areas. Drought in 1972–73 and years of reduced yields requiring extra food imports, place even greater strains on Indonesia's agriculturally-oriented domestic economy.[32]

The Type and Intensity of Land Uses. Most of Indonesian rice is grown in the *sawah* or irrigated/flooded field system. Although agriculture on Java is the most intensive, similar *sawah* landscapes are also found on Bali, Lombok, southern, western and northern Sumatra, and southwestern and northeastern Sulawesi.[33] In Java the average farm size is under three-fourths of an acre (1.3 ha.).[34] Here farmland usually has a three-fold division of *sawah*; *tegelan* or dry fields; and *pekarangan,* the vegetable and fruit gardens next to farmhouses, in the *desa* (small village).[35] Intensity of land use in Java can be epitomized by the fact that the total land harvested annually is between 120 and 150 percent, possible only by using many fields for two and sometimes three crops. The extra crops may be additional irrigated ones if sufficient water is seasonally available, but usually are unirrigated crops such as maize, peanuts, or cassava. The in-

TABLE 8-1
Employment in Indonesia, 1976 and 1980

Activity Section (1)	Workers (Percent) 1976 (2)	1980	Activity Section (cont.)	Workers (Percent) 1976 (cont.)	1980
A. **Primary**			C. **Tertiary**		
1. Agriculture, forestry, fishing	61.6	58.7e.	5. Electricity, gas water	0.1	(a)
2. Mining, quarrying	0.2	0.3e.	6. Transportation	2.7	(a)
Subtotals	61.8	59.0	7. Trade, finance, Real Estate	14.6	23.0[a]
B. **Secondary**			8. Public Administration, Services	10.6	5.0[a]
3. Manufacturing	8.4	11.0	Subtotals	28.1	28.0
4. Construction	1.7	2.0	Totals	100.0	100.0

(Work force in 1980: 56.5 million)

[a]The mining, quarrying segment of primary workforce was estimated by William A. Withington; under Terriary, 1980 data were for Commerce, services–23.0; Government & Public Authorities–5.0' thus not strictly comparable with 1976 categories.

Sources: For 1976, Biro Pusat Statistik, *Statistical Pocketbook of Indonesia, 1977/1978* (Jakarta: December, 1978), pp. 80–81; for 1980, Far Eastern Economic Review, *Asia 1982 Yearbook* (Hong Kong: 1981) pp. 8–9.

tensive landscapes of Java are increasingly noticeable elsewhere, as in Lampung, where large numbers of transmigrants from Java have brought their agriculture system with them, and in other areas of the outer islands where *sawah* rice landscapes are replacing shifting cultivation as population densities rise.

Shifting Agriculture

Subsistence agriculture outside the core area and away from the more intensively farmed *sawah* areas is shifting cultivation of either the dry field (*ladang*) or wet field (*paya)* type. Fifty percent or more of the land used for agriculture in outer island areas has been in shifting cultivation.[36] Much additional forest land has also been used. In shifting cultivation rice, soybeans and other crops are grown, usually on nonirrigated *ladang* during a one to three year cycle in cleared forest land, before new land is cleared and the former plots abandoned. The wet or *paya* form of shifting cultivation uses natural irrigation by small streams in coastal plains and valleys, keeps down other plant growth by burning during a short dry season and gives a higher yield in most years than on *ladang*. Some commercial crop production often accompanies shifting cultivation, typically natural rubber, pepper, and coffee.[37] Several forms of shifting cultivation in Indonesia, once declining have begun to expand again, and produce several crops effectively for the rising population densities and urban markets in outer islands away from areas of more intensive farming practices.[38]

Commercial Agriculture. In Indonesia this type consists of three principal subgroups. These are: (1) the large estate or plantation; (2) the smallholding yielding both estate and other crops; and (3) the market garden supplying vegetables, fruit, and flowers. The increasing amount of commercial dairying and livestock raising oriented to urban or tourist resorts markets represent a variant of this latter subtype. Estate agriculture is concentrated in eastern North Sumatra and nearby eastern Aceh, with rubber, palm oil, tea, and cigar wrapper tobacco as leading crops. Medan serves as the primary commercial entrepot, nearby Belawan as the port, for these products and their estate areas. A limited amount of estate agriculture continues on Java, with tea, natural rubber, and some cinchona trees whose bark yields quinine. A few other Indonesian areas, mainly on Sumatra, also have some estate agriculture. Since independence, estate agriculture has been carried out by foreign corporations, such as Goodyear; by the Department of Agriculture on nationalized lands; and by Indonesian citizens or corporations.

Small-holdings yield many of the same products as the estates, but in Indonesia also produce sugarcane, cigarette tobacco, copra, pepper, and other spices. Except for sugarcane, tobacco, and some coffee areas of Java, most commercial smallholdings are on the three large outer islands of Sumatra, Kalimantan and Sulawesi. The increasing proportion of commercial crops grown on small-holdings, notably natural rubber, poses questions as to the future of estate agriculture in Indonesia.

Market or truck gardens are located around major cities in Indonesia and also are situated on fertile volcanic soils in several accessible uplands. The Preanger Plateau of West Java; the Karo Batak highlands west of Medan in northeastern Sumatra; and the southwestern Sumatran highlands around Pagaralam are examples of uplands supplying produce to nearby and more distant urban areas.[39]

Fishing. For Indonesia as an archipelagic nation, fishing is vital for the country's livelihood. Fish from inland or sea waters supply most of the animal protein consumed by Indonesians. Nearly 700,000 hectares of farm ponds, saltwater lagoons, rivers and lakes in Indonesia yield over 400,000 metric tons of fish a year, about four-tenths the sea fisheries amount.[40] Fishing is both an adjunct to farming and a full-time occupation for others. One-third of the nation's fishermen live in Java. The other two-thirds of Indonesia's fishermen are in the outer islands, and account for 30% of the inland and 75% of the sea fish catch tonnage. In the outer islands, shores, nearby shallow banks and deeper waters, and more numerous lakes and streams, provide a greater diversity of fishing opportunities than in the central core area of Java with its silted, relatively smooth shoreline.[41]

Forestry and Lumbering. Indonesia's core area (i.e., Java) was until recently dominant in forestry, both in the part-time type carried on with farming and in commercial forestry of teak and other wood.[42] Since World War II, Java has had limited virgin forest areas which could be cut only at the risk of seriously endangering watersheds vital to agriculture and urban areas. Wood for papermaking , railway ties, household cooking and construction needs in Java has been cut in abandoned estate lands, a few remaining forest reserves, and from trees shading the villages. Huge commercial timber operations use the forests of Kalimantan and Sumatra as main sources. These areas by the late 1970s became the world's largest sources of tropical hardwoods.[43]

Mineral Production

Historically, Indonesia has been identified as rich in precious minerals.[44] While much building stone was quarried and some precious minerals or stones were mined, in 1940 most production was in petroleum, tin, coal, manganese, bauxite, and nickel (Table 8-2). Mining was concentrated in several districts of Sumatra: on or near Bintan, Singkep, Bangka and Belitung islands south of Singapore; in eastern Kalimantan; in southern and eastern Java; and in south-central Sulawesi (Fig. 8-2).

By 1980, natural gas was a notable new commercial energy resource, processed to LNG (Liquified Natural Gas) from the Arun Field in Aceh, northernmost Sumatra, and the Bintang Field of eastern Kalimantan. Recent finds indicate the Natuna Island area in the South China Sea may become the largest Indonesian gas field. Production of 1940 minerals rose by a factor of six for oil; five for bauxite (aluminum ore); and twenty-one for nickel. Manganese output has changed little. Tin extraction, rising rapidly, is still only 72% of 1940 output; and coal is even lower at 15% of 1940 output (Table 8-2). Production of iron sands in southern Java and copper concentrates from Irian Jaya highlands are post-independence developments peaking in the mid-1970s. Asphalt rock production on Buton Island off southeastern Sulawesi has recently increased.

Until commercial natural gas production began in the 1970s, the growth in crude oil production was the most dramatic among Indonesian minerals. Minas and other east-central Sumatra fields have been leading producers. Smaller fields are in eastern Kalimantan, southeastern and northeastern Sumatra and lesser ones in Java. Increasing extraction from offshore fields, as in the-Java Sea northwest of Jakarta, suggests a future trend. The basic National Minerals Control and Mining Law of 1963 reaffirmed national ownership of all mineral resources under Indonesian lands or waters. Petroleum operations are coordinated by PERTAMINA, the government company, carrying out distribution itself and supervising exploration, production, and refining by national or foreign companies under contract.

TABLE 8-2
Indonesia Mineral Production, 1940-1980

Minerals (1)	Units (2)	1940 (3)	1970 (4)	1980 (5)
Petroleum	Barrels (Mil.)	± 96	311.5	577.0
Natural Gas[a]	Cubic Feet (Mil.)	—	—	1,045,748
Coal	Metric Tons (000)	2,001	176.5	304.0
Tin	Metric Tons (000)	44.4	19.1	26.1
Bauxite	Metric Tons (000)	274	1,229	1,249.1
Nickel Ore	Metric Tons (000)	55.5	600.0	1,153
Manganese	Metric Tons (000)	11.9	10.8	n.d.
Iron Sands	Metric Tons (000)	—	—	74.7
Copper Concentr.	(DMT) (000)	—	—	186.1
Asphalt Rock	Metric Tons (000)	8.0	61.5	n.d.

[a]First recorded production in 1976.

Sources: 1940 data from Republic of Indonesia, Biro Pusat Statistik, *Statistical Pocketbook of Indonesia, 1957*, and *1964-1967* (Jakarta); 1970-1980, Republic of Indonesia, *Indonesia Development News*, V. 4, No. 11, (July, 1981), p. 7.

Manufacturing

Manufacturing in Indonesia has three principal sectors. First is a processing sector for primary raw materials from agriculture, mining, forestry or fishing; second is a handicraft and small workshop sector; and third is the modern, intermediate, to large factory sector.

Employment and production in manufacturing continues to be concentrated primarily on Java. Since independence (in 1949) Indonesian manufacturing rose to its highest level early in the 1960s, declined drastically with political and economic problems in the mid-1960s, and since 1968 has greatly improved in most sectors. In 1980 the industrial segment of the economy contributed 38% of Gross National Product, a significantly higher segment in 1980 than the 28% for agriculture.[45]

Processing Sector. This sector is widely distributed, being closely associated with raw materials. The processing of commercial estate products is most concentrated in eastern North Sumatra, but rice milling is found wherever rice is harvested. Other processing facilities include eight oil refineries in Sumatra, Kalimantan, and Java; several cement plants near raw materials and major ports or urban nodes; a urea fertilizer plant in Palembang near a naturaı gas field; and LNG (Liquified Natural Gas) plants in Aceh and east Kalimantan; an aluminum smelter near the Asahan Hydroelectric Power Project in eastern North Sumatra; and a tin smelter at Muntok near the tin fields of Bangka and other islands.[46]

Modern Manufacturing. Most of this manufacturing is concentrated in Java.[47] More than 80% of all of Indonesia's manufacturing, including its heavy and medium industries, are in Java. These two levels of industry employ an estimated 800,000 workers in Java. Modern manufacturing in Java is further concentrated in or near the several largest cities, notably in and around Jakarta. Here many factories are in the city's central part, some are in the northeast industrial district near Tanjung Priok; and others are sited along the expressway leading south to Bogor and Bandung. The Jatiluhur Power, Flood Control, and Irrigation Project, when completed in 1966, about 70 miles east of Jakarta, contained 50% of Indonesia's installed public power capacity. Most of this is sent to metropolitan Jakarta. Also in western Java are texile mills producing two-thirds of Indonesia's cloth. Major industrial nodes elsewhere in Java are Bandung and Bogor in the west; Semarang and Yogyakarta in the center; and the Surabaya area on the east. By comparison with the rest of Indonesia, Java's manufacturing is highly diversified. Products include processed food, vegetable oil, and beverages; clothing, household and farm supplies; bicycles, motorcycles, cars and airplanes, radios and television sets, and chemical or pharmaceutical products.

Outer island manufacturing emphasizes the processing and small workshop sectors. Most of the processing plants are oriented to primary resources even when the plants are in or near cities. The small workshops are in urban areas of all sizes. Modern industrial factories are being erected in the outer islands particularly in the leading regional centers. The largest outer island manufacturing nodes are Medan, Palembang, Padang and Tanjungkarang on Sumatra; Pontianak, Banjarmasin and Balikpapan on Kalimantan; and Makasar and Manado on Sulawesi. Manufacturing in the eastern islands is at the principal ports and processes fish and varied local necessity goods. Each of the outer island industrial nodes serves a local market hinterland, but is limited by distance or poorly developed transportation from most other industrial nodes or market areas.

Transportation

Due to the archipelagic character of Indonesia the most crucial linkages are those of ocean and air transportation at the principal sea ports and airports (Fig. 5-2). In the three largest outer island areas of Sumatra, Kalimantan, and Irian Jaya navigable rivers and lakes are important. Railways are found only on Java and Sumatra, while improved highways carry increasing volumes of passenger and freight traffic within each island.

After a period of reduced service following independence and the departure of Dutch shipping services in the 1950s and 1960s, Indonesia has redeveloped its inter-island system of ports and routes. Air travel has also improved, with more effective airports, jet aircraft, and routes in an integrated domestic system. New airports and higher passenger and freight volumes have resulted in further intensification of air travel. Indonesia's international and inter-island linkages are comprised of a series of primary and secondary nodes. These have domestic and international air and sea connections.

The largest and most close-knit transportation network in Indonesia is in the core area of Java. Even here, approximately one-third of its land area is inaccessible, being more than 10 miles (15 km.) from the nearest route or port (Fig. 5-1). The transportational predominance of the Java core area, however, is notable since it has more than 70% of Indonesia's 4,123 miles of railway; over 91% of passenger traffic; and 72% of freight traffic handled by rail (Table 8-3). About three-fourths of Indonesia's paved highways, totaling 9,672 miles, are on Java, though Java has few airports or seaports. About ten of Indonesia's 40 large airports and about ten of its 62 seaports are major nodes in foreign trade.[48]

In transportational development and accessibility Sumatra is superior to other outer island areas (Table 8-3). Sumatra has three major railway systems in the south, west, and north, plus many narrow-gauge estate systems; one-fifth of Indonesia's paved highway mileage; almost one-third of the commercial airports; nearly half of the exporting seaports; and over half of the importing seaports in foreign trade. The transportation systems of Sulawesi and Kalimantan are comparable except for the much greater length of navigable rivers in Kalimantan. The eastern Indonesian areas have a number of small seaports and some airports linking their scattered island areas. Several of the outer islands have considerable stretches of navigable rivers, some deep enough for oceangoing vessels, as on the Musi River to Palembang, and the Batang Hari to Jambi in Sumatra. Oil pipelines on Sumatra, Kalimantan, and a few on Java provide specialized freight transportation between producing fields, export ports, or refinery sites.[49]

International Trade

Indonesia's four leading export commodities in 1980—petroleum, forest products, natural gas, and natural rubber-together account for 92.0% of the nearly US $21 billion in exports (Table 8-4). Two decades earlier in 1960, the four leading items were natural rubber, petroleum, tin, and copra, together representing 81.1% of all exports by value. These same four were the most important ones, in the ten years prior to World War II. The changes have resulted from a great expansion of oil and natural gas produced for export; the opening of extensive timber-producing areas in Sumatra and Kalimantan; and the relative decline of both natural rubber and tin in production and export amounts. Agricultural exports of copra, tea, sugar and tobacco shared natural rubber's decline between 1939 and 1980. Some of this decline reflects disruption of production systems within Indonesia. It also results from a combination of greatly increased production in other export commodities and low prices for most agricultural raw materials.

In 1980 Indonesian imports had a value of

TABLE 8-3
Indonesia: Transportation Systems & Trade By Regions, 1980

Transportation Elements (1Km = 0.621 Mi)	Java and Madura	Sumatra	Kali-mantan	Sula-wesi	Eastern Islands	Indonesia Total
Railways[a]						
(Length (Kilometers)	4,684	1,953	0	0	0	6,637
Ton-Km Freight (Mill.)	507	196	0	0	0	703
Passenger-Km (Mill.)	3,211	311	0	0	0	3,511
Paved Highway[b]						
(Km., 1979)	18,422	18,883	3,857	9,154	7,254	57,570
Motor vehicles[c]						
(cars, trucks, buses)	1,828,044	449,900	74,983	121,525	111,182	2,585,634
(motorcycles)						(5,463,533)
Commercial Airports[d]	6	22	15	12	46	101
Passenger-Km (Mill.)[e]	nd	nd	nd	nd	nd	5,904
Freight Ton-Km (Mill.)[e] ('77)	nd	nd	nd	nd	nd	396
Seaports, Major[f]	4	6	4	4	2	20
Sea exports (1,000 metric tons						99,972 ('79)
loaded (regions)[g]	12,940	46,624	29,844	1,338	4,556	95,302 ('77)
Sea imports (1,000 metric tons						14,880 ('79)
unloaded (regions)[g]	10,341	2,235	610	633	106	13,925 ('77)
Sea exports value (US $ Mill.)[g]						21,909 ('79)
(regions)	1,674	5,753	2,792	118	516	10,853 ('77)
Sea imports value (US $ Mill.)[g]						12,608 ('79)
(regions)	4,836	895	254	206	45	6,230 ('77)

Sources:

[a]United Nations, *Statistical Yearbook for Asia and the Pacific, 1980*, (Bangkok, 1980); island division as of 1977 from the *Statistical Pocketbook of Indonesia, 1977/1978* (Jakarta; Biro Pusat Statistik, Dec., 1978).

[b]*Ibid.*, island region totals proportional to 1977 distributions.

[c]*Ibid.*, island region totals proportional to 1977 distributions.

[d]*Indonesia Development News*, "Pioneer Airports, Air Route Map," v. 1, no. 6 (June, 1977), p. 3, with some additions by W.A. Withington.

[e]source in footnote a.

[f]*Statistical Pocketbook of Indonesia, 1977/1978* (footnote a), and W.A. Withington additions. Most lesser seaports uncounted.

[g]*Statistical Pocketbook, 1977/1978* for the 1977 data by regions; United Nations, *Statistical Yearbook for Asian and and Pacific, 1980*, (foonote a), for 1979 data.

developmental activities and infrastruture as well as materials associated with the oil, gas and forestry industries. These changes, from a different perspective, can be regarded as a partial decolonization of Indonesia's economy. Indonesia, however, has remained highly sensitive to worldwide alterations in demand or prices of either export or import goods.

The core-outer island differentation in Indonesia has been illustrated strongly in both ports and export-import amounts and values (Table 8-3). During the 1960–65 period, more than about US $12.8 billion (Table 8-4). Consumer goods, raw materials, and capital goods together accounted for about 85% of all imports by value, with an additional 14% in oil or other products.

The principal changes since independence in 1949 have been the decreasing percentages of consumer goods and the considerably increased proportions of capital goods imported (Table 8-4). These changes reflect greater domestic production of consumer goods, including cloth or finished textile materials, plywood and processed wood, using the greatly increased investment in

TABLE 8-4

Indonesia's Principal Exports and Imports by Percentage of Total Value, 1939-1980

Commodity or Category (1)	Percentage of Total Value 1939 (2)	1950 (3)	1960 (4)	1970 (5)	1980 (6)
Exports:					
Petroleum	20.1	18.4	26.3	36.9	72.4
Rubber, Natural	27.9	42.8	44.9	23.0	5.4
Lumber	—	—	—	10.7	8.3
Coffee	1.5	1.9	1.6	6.1	3.0
Tin	7.7	6.1	6.5	5.3	1.8
Palm Oil, Kernels	2.0	3.4	2.4	3.6	3.6
Copra, cakes	3.3	7.2	3.4	3.2	0.3
Tea	7.4	3.4	3.3	1.6	0.5
Tobacco	3.4	5.1	1.7	1.0	0.5
Tapioca	1.3	0.4	0.4	0.8	n.d.
Natural, manufactured gas	—	—	—	—	5.9
Hides	—	—	—	0.5	n.d.
Pepper	1.3	2.7	1.2	0.3	0.2
Other	24.1	8.6	8.3	7.0	0.7
Total Percent	100.0	100.0	100.0	100.0	100.0
Value: U.S. $ Million				1,173.0	
Imports:					
Consumer Goods	45.9	43.2	37.1	29.1	23.9
Raw cotton, thread, textile materials	8.9	14.3	22.0	6.8	—
Raw Materials	35.1	32.2	36.5	30.5	23.3
Rice, wheat flour & other foodstuffs	9.7	13.7	22.0	15.0	—
Capital Goods	17.3	7.2	21.9	30.1	38.7
Imports for Petroleum Companies/	1.7	17.4	4.5	8.1	
Petrol. Products					14.1
Unclassified(est.)	—	—	—	2.2	
Total Percent	100.0	100.0	100.0	100.0	100.0
Value: U.S. $ Million				1,262.7	

Sources: 1939 and 1950: Republik Indonesia, Biro Pusat Statistik, *Statistical Pocketbook of Indonesia, 1957* (Djakarta: 1957), pp. 107, 135; percentages by author: 1960. Republic Indonesia, Biro Pusat Statistik, *Statistical Pocketbook of Indonesia, 1964-1967* (Djakarta: 1968), pp. 212, 246; percentages by author: 1970. Lawrence White, "Problems and Prospects of Indonesian Foreign Exchange System," *Indonesia*, No. 14 (Oct., 1972), pp. 137-138: 1971. H.W. Arndt, "Survey of Recent Developments," *Bulletin of Indonesian Economic Studies*, Vol. 8, No. 2 (July, 1972), p. 3. 1980: *The Europa Yearbook, 1982*, Vol. II (London: Europa Publishers, Ltd., 1982).

of available exports and increased Java's imports of a broad range of goods. In recent years the Central Government has sought to reduce tensions of outer island peoples, who feel that they are supporting the core area population, by returning to the outer islands a larger share of the export earning for regional-development needs.[50]

three-fourths of all Indonesian imports by value were received in Java's few ports. In contrast, the Java ports used for exports shipped only 13% of Indonesian materials by value. Thus, by value the outer islands were exporting 87% of Indonesian materials and receiving only 22% of the imports. Since independence, and even earlier, the pressure of population needs in Java has reduced amounts

PROGRESS AND PITFALLS: INDONESIA

For the twenty years between 1945 and 1965 Indonesia was evolving as a nation, first by its independence declaration of August 17, 1945, and then by the mutual independence agreement of 1949 between Indonesia and the Netherlands. During these two decades President Sukarno led the nation. He placed primary emphasis on political leadership in the developing world, rather than on domestic economic development.[51]

National development for Indonesia since 1965 can be epitomized as follows:

1. After a period of economic crisis, Indonesia became more politically and economically stable after 1965. Governmental power has remained centralized in Jakarta with a large proportion of high government posts filled by military officers.
2. Production in most regions and economic sectors increased. In agriculture, mineral production, forest products, and manufacturing the result was broader availability of a wider range of necessity and amenity goods. The 'Green Revolution' aided in expanding agricultural production in rice, so that despite droughts or other natural hazards and cultural conservatism hampering efforts, domestic self-sufficiency can be reached.
3. The Five-Year Plans, known as REPELITA I, II, and III (1969–73; 1973–78; 1979–83), have focused on rehabilitation of agricultural and transportational sectors of the economy, but establishment or expansion of enterprises capable of generating foreign exchange earnings, such as timber operations, also were encouraged.[52]
4. The core area-outer island dichotomy has continued to be a strong factor in national evolution. Java's massive population, occupying Indonesia's political and economic core, required the support of outer island production of primary and other materials for export earnings or transfers of surpluses to Java. Sumatra, the largest generator of materials for foreign exchange earnings, in 1980 had over 28 million people, but this total was less than one-third that of Java. The other outer island areas were much less populous despite localized high population densities, notably in Bali and Lombok.
5. Broad areas of outer Indonesia, particularly in Kalimantan and the eastern islands, remained at low levels of subsistence, accessibility and development, only weakly integrated into Indonesia's extensive political and economic systems.
6. The neo-Malthusian dilemma of intense pressures of people upon the land and its resources, particularly in Java, seems likely to dominate Indonesian development plans and potentialities regardless of further development in Sumatra and other outer island areas.
7. While Indonesia is not among the most rapidly developing or economically strongest nations in Southeast Asia, its great number of people, size of territory, and resources makes it a crucial southern third of the Southeast Asian realm.

Footnote References

[1]After the early 1970s Irian Jaya became the new name for Irian Barat (*Indonesian News & Views*, Embassy of Indonesia, Washington, D.C., June 1973, p. 12).

[2]C.A. Fisher, *Southeast Asia* (London: Meuthen, 1964), pp. 239-245.

[3]Also called Austronesian linguistically. See E.B. Espenshade, Jr., editor, *Goode's World Atlas*, 16th edition (Chicago: Rand McNally & Co., 1982), p. 29.

[4]Republic of Indonesia, *Census of Population 1980* (Jakarta: Biro Pusat Statistik, May 1981), Population of Provinces and *Kotamadya/Kabupaten*.

[5]C. Geertz, *Agricultural Involution, The Process of Ecological Change in Indonesia* (Berkeley: University of California, 1963), p. 16.

[6]W.A. Withington, "Indonesia's Significance in the Study of Regional Geography," *Journal of Geography*, vol. 68 (April, 1969), pp. 227-237.

[7]Of these, twenty-four are actual provinces (*propinsi*), two are Special Autonomous Regions (D.I. or *Daerah Istimewa*, Aceh & Yogyakarta), and one is the Special Capital District of Jakarta (D.K.I or *Daerah Kusus Istimewa*). The regional distribution of these 27 provinces are: Java-Madura, 5; Sumatra with adjacent islands, 8; Kalimantan and Sulawesi, 4 each; while Bali, west Nusa Tenggara, east Nusa Tenggara, Timor Timur, Maluku, and Irian Jaya are each a single province.

[8]Republik Indonesia, Biro Pusat Statistik, *Indonesia: 1980 Population Census, Population by Province and Kotamadya/Kabupaten* (Seri L No. 2) (Jakarta: 1981).

[9]*Ibid.*, and P.D. Malone, *Urban Areas of Indonesia*, Research Series No. 10, Institute of International Studies (Berkeley: University of California, 1966).

[10]Harold Crouch, "Another Look at the Indonesian 'Coup'," *Indonesia*, No. 15 (April, 1973), pp. 1-20.

[11]Biro Pusat Statistik, *Indonesian 1980 Census of Population by Provinces* (Jakarta: 1981), p. 5.

[12]Since 1965 Buru Island, Maluku Province, has been the Government's resettlement area for at least 80,000 political detainees and their families after the 1965 coup d'etat attempt. At least some of the Ambonese, who originally left Indonesia for the Netherlands in the late 1950s, have returned to their original Maluku home area.

[13]Tsuyoshi Kota, "Change and Continuity in the Minangkabau Matrilineal System," *Indonesia*, No. 25 (April 1978), pp. 1-16.

[14]Karl Pelzer, *Pioneer Settlement in the Asiatic Tropics* (New York: American Geographical Society, 1945), Chapters 4–5 and Nugroho, pp. 82-83.

[15]See footnote 11 and articles in *Far Eastern Economic Review*.

[16]B. Ter Haar, *Adat Law in Indonesia*, edited and translated by E.A. Hoebel and A.A. Schiller (Jakarta: Bhratara, 1962).

[17]W.F. Wertheim, *Indonesian Society in Transition*, 2nd rev. edition (The Hague: W. van Hoeve, 1959), pp. 9-10.

[18]W.A. Withington, "The Major Geographic Regions of Sumatra, Indonesia," *Association of American Geographers, Annals*, 57 (September 1967), pp. 534-549.

[19]Fisher, pp. 239-245.

[20]Hildred Geertz, "Indonesian Cultures and Communities," in Ruth McVey, editor, *Indonesia* (New Haven: Human Relations Area Files Press, 1964), pp. 24-96.

[21]Although no recent data are available, knowledgeable authorities have written to the author that large numbers of Karo Batak in North Sumatra, listed as predominantly Animist in 1961 (*Agama Lain*), converted to Catholic or Protestant Christianity in the 1960s and 1970s.

[22]Percentages computed by W.A. Withington from the 1980 Census data.

[23]In 1961 Jakarta still had 4.8% of its working population listed in primary occupations, mainly agriculture, as given in Republik Indonesia, Biro Pusat Statistik, *Popualtion Census 1961*, D.C.I. Djakarta, (1963).

[24]Computed by W.A. Withington form Indonesian censuses of 1961 and 1980.

[25]W.A. Withington, "Sumatran Population Changes, 1961–1980," *Indonesian Circle*, No. 27 (March 1982), pp. 11-25.

[26]*Indonesian 1980 Census of Population* for Kotamadya. Estimated for others by W.A. Withington in lieu of urban census data.

[27]Estimate made by the author.

[28]Milone, p. 82.

[29]Milone, Chart XII, pp. 190-225, for 1961 places; *1971 Indonesian Census (Preliminary Data)*, Kabupaten & Kotamadya (Jakarta: Biro Pusat Statistik, 1972) for 1971 data, but with not urban names for *kabupaten* capitals. Dumai and Pakning, Riau Province, on the Malacca Strait, now have oil refineries and port facilities. Balige, on Lake Toba's south shore in North Sumatra, is a sizeable market town. (See also *Indonesia Development News* issues, 1977–1984.

[30]Ulrich Scholz, "Decrease and revival of shifting cultivation in the tropics of Southeast Asia—The Examples of Sumatra and Thailand," *Applied Geography and Development* (1982, Germany), pp. 32-45.

[31]Far Eastern Economic Review, *Asia 1982 Yearbook* (Hong Kong: 1981), pp. 165-6.

[32]*Indonesia Development News*, various issues, 1977–84; and Far Eastern Economic Review, *Asia 1982 Yearbook* and earlier yearbooks (Hong Kong, 1981, or earlier years), for agricultural food production and import figures.

[33]Plate on agricultural land use (*Agrarlandschaften*) in H. Uhlig, "Sudostasian-Lander-Volker-Wirtschaft," *Information Zur Politischen Bildung*, 148 (1972), following p. 16.

[34]From Republik Indonesia, Biro Pusat Statistik, *Agricultural Census, 1963, Republic of Indonesia, Preliminary Figures* (Jakarta: October, 1964, Report No. 1), p. 10.

[35]Karl Pelzer in Ruth McVey, editor, pp. 124-126.

[36]Karl Peltzer, in McVey editor, p. 122.

[37]Ibid., pp. 122-124.

[38]Scholz, pp. 32-41.

[39]Each of these uplands has fertile basic volcanic-derived soils on which the intensive cultivation of vegetables and other crops is carried out.

[40]Republik Indonesia, Biro Pusat Statistik, *Statistical Pocketbook of Indonesia, 1977/78*, (Jakarta: 1978), pp. 226-228.

[41]Fisher, pp. 334-336.

[42]*Ibid.*, pp. 330-331.

[43]Far Eastern Economic Review, *Asia 1982 Yearbook* (Hong Kong: 1981), p. 165.

[44]"Land of Gold," was a frequent historical term as noted by Paul Wheatley, *The Golden Khersonese* (Kuala Lumpur: 1961), pp. xxi-xxiv.

[45]Far Eastern Economic Review, *Asia 1982 Yearbook* (Hong Kong: 1981), p. 8.

[46]The Indonesian oil refineries are at Plaju and Sungeigerong, on the southside of Palembang, South Sumatra; Pakning and Dumai on Riau's coast in east-central Sumatra; Pangkalanbrandan in eastern North Sumatra; Balikpapan in eastern Kalimantan; and at Cepu and Cilacap (Tjepu, Tjilatjap), east and south Java.

[47]Donald W. Fryer & James C. Jackson, *Indonesia*, (Boulder: Westview Press, 1977), p. 225.

[48]Nugroho, pp. 373, 391-398; 1980 estimates by W.A. Withington.

[49]See replacement.

[50]See *Indonesia Development News*, volumes 1-6, 1977-1983.

[51]Sukarno's political focus was notable in the Bandung Conference of 1955, the West Irian confrontation with the Dutch and United Nations during 1957-1962, and his policy of Konfrontasi with Malaysia from 1963 until 1966, at a time that the internal economy of Indonesia was becoming increasingly weak.

Chapter 9

Burma: From Colonialism to Socialism

David G. Dickason

The western and northernmost of Southeast Asia's nations, Burma has been known as a golden land through most of its history.[1] As compared to life elsewhere before the western colonial era, the wealth of the Burmese earth as curried by its peoples provided amply for their material needs. During the nineteenth century, when the British successively came to control the region starting from the coast and finally acquiring upper Burma after 1885, the country's primary resources of land, forests, and minerals were progressively commercialized under an exploitative colonial system. That Burma actually possessed great resource development potential is clear, for substantial profits and taxes were taken and transmitted to India, England, and China and also the standard of living of many indigenous peoples may have improved during this period. (Herbert Hoover noted early in the twentieth century that the Burmans were the "only genuinely happy people of all of Asia.") By the eve of World War II Burma reached the zenith of its material development as measured in objective economic terms like per capita income and exports.

The commercial development of Burma under British rule, however, constituted growth without true modernization; important social and cultural issues were never directly resolved. As a result, the post-World War II period has been filled with internal turmoil as these issues have been worked through. The Burmans (the dominant lowlands peoples who today constitute about 60% of the country's population) never reconciled themselves ideologically to subjugation under British colonialism, which lasted in Burma for about 75 years. The short period of Japanese rule during World War II served as an opportunity for the young nationalist movement to organize op-

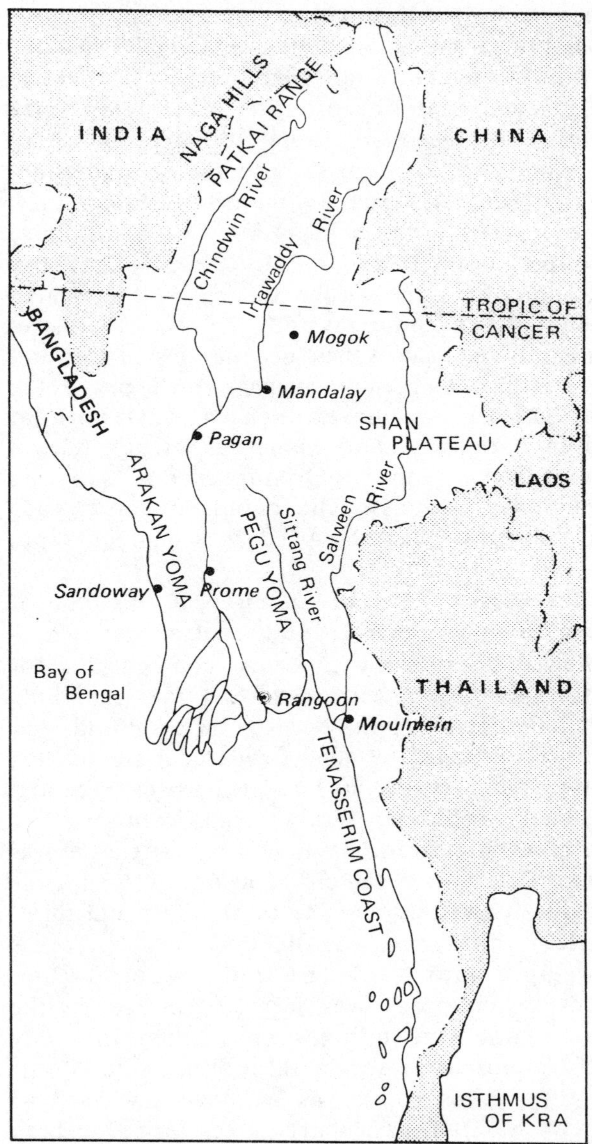

Figure 9-1. Burma: A General Map.

position to the re-establishement of British rule; and in the face of probable resistance to Burma in 1948. At that time, the issues tabled throughout the colonial era developed into sharp conflicts.

One of the most important sets of issues focused upon interethnic competition, wherein minority communities aimed to establish the principle of political autonomy for themselves, whereas the majority community, the Burmans, aimed to be the first among many ethno-linguistic groups in a unitary state. To the Burmans, Independence implied a number of consequences. First, the country was to be Burman-dominated as it had been before colonial rule. Second, and related, self determination would create a society governed by Theravada Buddhist values and norms.[2] Third, liberation from colonialism would end economic exploitation, and therefore, produce a vastly heightened material prosperity. To empathize with these perceptions is not difficult, but sharp opposition to these views (also readily understandable) was registered by minority communities. The Karens, the largest family of minority groups, aimed for their won politically autonomous state within Burma to be located preferably in the Irrawaddy delta (or with an outlet to the sea). When negotiations proved unsuccessful, insurgency ensued which pitted the Burman-oriented government against militant Karen nationalist and numerous other political opposition groups (including several separate communist groups). The details of insurgency have already been discussed in Chapter 1 (pp. 24–25).

The central government survived this test of strength, but the war and civil unrest which followed it produced important consequences for Burma's more recent history. First, economic rehabilitation from the devastation of World War II was postponed by almost a decade; second, the ruling party (the Anti-Fascist Peoples Freedom League) functioned without significant pressure for internal reform, because much attention was diverted from it because of concern over both the operation and the outcome of the war; and third, in less than a decade Burma's armed forces developed into a modern military institution. Thus, when peace was largely restored to the countryside, the military constituted the only major reformist force in the political life of the country. Thus force was employed twice, first when the dominant party's leadersip seemed unable to run the country effectively in 1958 and second when negotiations with dissident Shans (another major ethnic group) had badly deteriorated. Since the latter experience in 1962, the military has controlled the country. After over two decades of rule by General Ne Win, the Union Revolutionary Council (mainly composed of military officers), and the armed forces, the regime is carefully nurturing a one-party (Burma Socialist Program Party) system of limited democracy.[3]

The remainder of this chapter traces the physical and social setting of life in Burma, the manner in which Burma came to be commerically developed during the colonial era without experiencing true development, and the tactics employed during independent rule both to cope with internal problems and produce economic growth in a multinational state.

THE PHYSICAL AND SOCIAL SETTING

The physical configuration of Burma has been significantly related to the life of its populace, who for most of history have possessed a limited technological base with which to cope with nature.[4] Laid out in a kitelike shape on the eastern coast of the Bay of Bengal the country is nearly the size of Texas, and shows a highly varied landscape.

The Irrawaddy-Sittang Lowland Core

The main core of the region focuses upon the central lowland of the Irrawaddy and Sittang rivers, the two being separated by the Pegu Yomas no more than several thousand feet high. In these valleys Burma and Shan Kingdoms, and later British Burma, were most firmly based. The Irrawaddy river itself is the most important feature of the lowland, being navigable for almost 900 miles from the sea to Bhamo nearly on the China border. In fact, the wealth of the early kingdoms sited on the river from Prome to Pagan (an archeological equivalent of Angkor in Cambodia) to the Ava-Mandalay region stemmed from the accessibility which this major river afforded. The single most important tributary of the Irrawaddy, the Chindwin, converges upon the main stream below Mandalay; this stream has been of little significance to human occupance of the lowland, largely because the river is highly seasonal in flow (providing only 2-3 foot drafts during the dry season) and because the mature gradient of the stream coupled with the climatic character of the valley made it a highly malarial tract historically. The delta of the lower Irrawaddy appears obviously attractive to human settlement; through much of history, however, its productive soil has been compensated for by its susceptibility to alien intrusion. Until the last half of the nineteenth century its agricultural potential remained largely undeveloped. The Sittang river, an old course of the Irrawaddy, is a small stream navigable for only a short distance from its mouth; the valley's relative isolation despite its potential productivity accounts for the Sittang valley's secondary importance as a seat of culture until the railroad was extended northward to upper Burma by this route at the end of the nineteenth century.

Arakan and Tenasserim

Cut off from the central core are the Arakan and Tenasserim coasts. Arakan on the west has supported a marked regionalism in its semi-isolation from both "Burma Proper" and Bangladesh. Tenasserim, the southern tail of the "kite" is also marked by semi-isolation from the core lowland, for the Salween river interrupts overland links and in the coastal waters further south near the Isthmus of Kra the many islands of the Mergui Archipelago have made navigation difficult. South of the Salween's mouth are located many of Burma's Mon-Talaing population—who fled the Irrawaddy delta when persecuted by Burmese kings.

The North and Eastern Hills and Shan Highlands

The remainder of Burma is made up of mountain and highland regions. On the west the Patkai-Naga-Chin Hills—Arakan Yomas complex of ranges extend southward from Tibet, declining in altitude as they progress toward the sea; all along their extent they constitute a major barrier to movement, and in these ranges are located some of Burma's more isolated societies—protected by their very inaccessibility from external cultural influence. The northern hills and the Shan Highlands have constituted a permeable barrier through history; the ancestors of most of Burma's population at one time filtered southward through these mountains. Today the northern hills are dominated by Kachin tribes and the Shan (akin to the Thais) dominate in the eastern highlands, although considerable ethnic heterogeneity remains. The Shan Highlands are sharply demarcated from the central lowland by an escarpment rising more than 2,000'. Except for the gem-stone mines around Mogok, Burmans have seldom penetrated the highland for permanent settlement. The Salween river, virtually a canyon through most of its course, bisects the highlands which increase in altitude towards China. The zone to the east of the river has never been strongly integrated into the state.

Effects of Monsoon

The full effects of the Asian monsoonal system are felt in Burma, producing rainfall characteristically during the "summer" months (the wet season) and drought (the hot season). On windward slopes air mass movement in combination with orography produces heavy rainfall in such areas as Moulmein (188 inches)—where Kipling's pagoda, incidentially, looks "westward" to the sea. In the northern hills and Shan Highlands, precipitation is substantial, although lower than on the windward slopes of the Arakan Yomas.

Correlative vegetational zones extend throughout the country. Rainforest was observed by Ward well north of the Tropic of Cancer in areas receiving more than 80 inches of precipitation per year. In drier regions, monsoon deciduous forest famous for its teak and other equally useful hardwoods is to be found, particularly in such areas as the Pegu Yomas. Considerable modification of the vegetative landscape has been made by man, not only in the lowlands where sedentary agriculture is practiced but also in the highlands where shifting cultivation practices interrupt the natural succession of vegetation.

COMMERCIALIZATION UNDER COLONIAL STATUS

The initial commercial transformation of Burma occurred with change in its political status, for British colonial rule (which by 1850 controlled lower Burma and by 1885 upper Burma also) introduced fundamental changes in the political, social, and economic fabric of the country. The changes themselves can largely be categorized as follows: (1) creation of a stable system of public administration, reinforced by a police system for maintenance of civil order; (2) introduction of a standard monetary system; (3) introduction of skilled traders and establishment of credit and banking systems; (4) incentives to commercialize production; and (5) construction of modern transport and communications facilities. Each of these new features was important in its own right, but no single change alone was sufficient to induce commercialization; the combined effects of all of them, however, provided a strong (almost overpowering) stimulus for change. From the geographic viewpoint, given the frame of reference of the first four features above, study of the modern transport and communications introduced in the colonial era aids greatly in comprehending why commerical activities became located where they did.

A New Trade Pattern

Stable public administration and standardized coinage system were fundamental prerequisites to the growth of trade. Internal unrest and civil disorder generally are perceived as disincentives to trade. Peasant farmers inclined to trade would be vulnerable to robbery and other possible violence where unprotected by government authority. Further, British administration brought with it western legal notions regarding property rights; this contrasted sharply with traditional Burma, where farmers had rights to the produce of the land but possessed no absolute sovereignty over the land itself. The new legal concept helped to separate the farmer's decisions about production from the older system of social obligations which previously had affected his economic decisions about cultivation. A standardized monetary system, of course, meant that the farmer was no longer limited in his trading patterns as previously, when he bartered some of his produce for other locally available goods and services; further, the monetary system permitted him to store up his wealth (at least hypothetically) in "nonperishable" form for later use when he needed and desired other goods and services. During the latter half of the nineteenth century, British industrial goods sold in local markets, together with locally-produced luxury goods and services, provided the principal stimuli for commercializing rice production; prior to that time, producing a surplus was not valued greatly by the farmer because of the few uses to which surpluses could be put. Trade goods were made available through new transportation and market systems. The trading network which previously had been casual and unsophisticated was progressively modernized through a simple stratagem; British authorities tacitly encouraged the immigration of trading classes from other parts of Asia under British control. Indian traders needed no immigration papers since Burma was a part of British India until 1937, and Chinese traders came from Yunnan and the coastal provinces of South China (where British and French influence was strong). Consequently the indigenous peoples, who had been prohibited earlier from active trading by policies of the Burmese kings, were forced to occupy a minor economic role in the colonial trading system. Thus, from the beginning British policy encouraged the competitive Indians and Chinese over local peoples, for the *laissez faire* economic philosophy of the time did not justify sacrificing short run profits in favor of improving the economic status of the native Burmese.

Effects of Modern Transportation

Not until the last three decades of the nineteenth century did the pace of commercialization sharply accelerate, when modern transportation facilities were extended throughout the central lowland core. The impact of these new systems within Burma was heightened by transport developments linking Burma with the global economy. First, steam-shipping services linked Burma (particularly Rangoon, and secondarily Moulmein and Bassein) with nearby ports in India and Southeast Asia, providing both improved communication and declining freight charges. Particularly as steam shipping extended into the long distance trades after the Suez Canal was completed (1869), Burma became better linked to the world economy owing to the increasing availability of large sailing vessels, which progressively lost high unit-value cargoes to steamships and were forced to rely increasingly upon the carriage of lower unit value products such as rice in order to remain in business.

Modern transport facilities were not extended within Burma before the 1870s not only because of international transport limitation but also because much of southern lower Burma lying in the central lowlands was thinly populated. The last kings of Burma had oppressed the minority communities of the region so that many migrated to Tenasserim. Reportedly, much of the Irrawaddy delta region registered population densities as low as four people per square mile at the time of British accession in 1852.[5] British control of Burma was not established without waging significantly expensive wars; ultimately military and administration reasons were used as the prime justification for introducing railroads. In the 1870s rail lines were built with the aim of

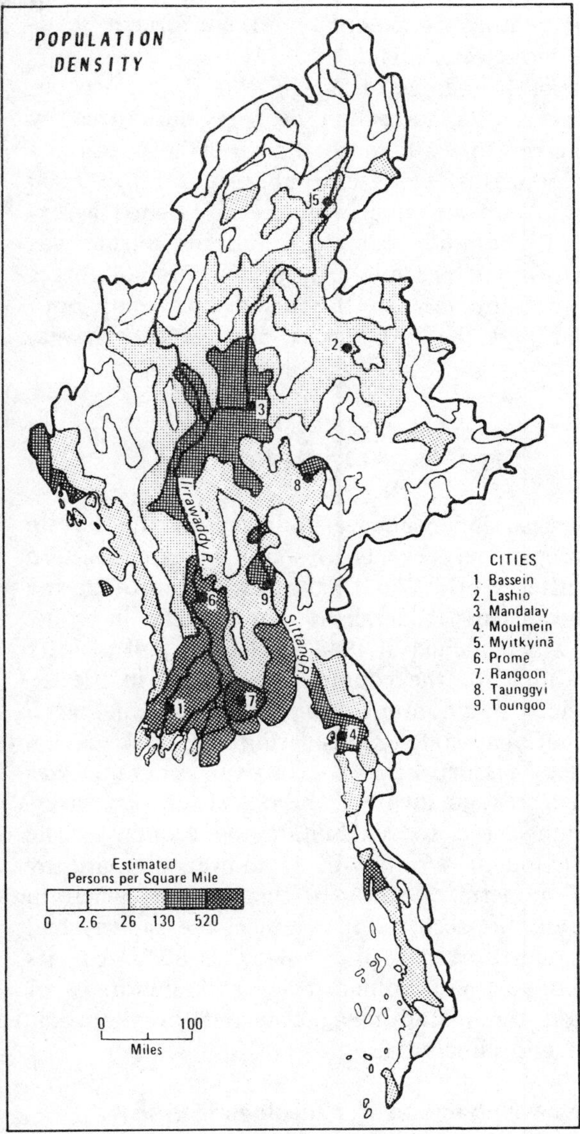

Figure 9-2. Burma: Population Density.

rendering troops much more mobile, and therefore producing a reduction in military costs of occupation.[6] Earlier, in India, the Sepoy Mutiny of 1857 (as it was called by the British though the Indian's call it India's First War of Independence) demonstrated clearly to the British the need for ready spatial accessibility between garrisons. Initially railroads were extended to Prome and Toungoo (on the British Burma frontier) to permit both border defense and penetration into upper Burma, if necessary. Railroads were meant to open up areas relatively inaccessible by trading water routes; thus rail and water transportation systems were intended to complement each other.

Trade motives were much less important in deciding to build a railroad system, for little traffic would be generated in areas as sparsely settled as lower Burma. The main economic justification of the new transport system was that when the beneficent effects of British colonial rule became known to the peasantry of upper Burma, railroads would facilitate their migration southward to settle on the fertile lands of lower Burma and Irrawaddy delta. Thus, it was argued, in the long run commerical traffic would develop to make railroads profitable.

With the takeover of upper Burma in 1885 following the Third Anglo-Burmese War, the rail system was extended northward via the Sittang valley and onward toward the China frontier by several routes. At this time trade motives were important, for many western traders believed China to be rich in primary resources and a good potential market for industrial products. A route into China from west of the Malacca Straits would provide marked advantages to British trade interest; although these perceptions of China were largely romantic overestimates except for mines in the Shan Highlands[7], the network's outline in Burma stabilized with these frontier lines.

The waterways, too, were transformed by introducing shallow-draft steamers in addition to the "country boats" powered by currents and tides, wind and men. Rangoon, the colonial capital, was linked with the Irrawaddy river system by the Twante Canal. Together these transportation changes and attractive freight rate structures combined with the other new institutional features of colonial rule to dramatically change the spatial and economic configuration of the country. A wholesale redistribution of population resulted; where upper Burma had constituted the core of the country both demographically and culturally during the precolonial period, lower Burma became the modern demographic focus of population.

Monoculture of Rice in Lower Burma

In lower Burma the population was largely occupied in the monoculture of rice, surpluses of which were readily marketed and transported to mills near the major cities and towns and subsequently sold abroad by export firms. Much land was available, and British rule prohibited foreigners from developing rice plantations such as developed in Indochina. (Note that Indians were not considered foreigners, however.) Until 1907 world prices for rice rose steadily; lower Burma enjoyed prosperity, for all sectors of society benefited (although unequally). During this period, however, easy credit was often extended to peasant farmers by Indian moneylenders mainly, a situation which provided no social distress until the world price for rice began to fluctuate markedly in the twentieth century. A traumatic period followed as peasants lost their land when loans could not be repaid. Evidence of social distress was manifested by increasing rates of violent crimes in lower Burma. By the mid-1930s more than one-half of the cultivated land of Irrawaddy delta, the best in the country, had passed into the hands of indigenous and foreign (mainly Indian) moneylenders. Many peasant farmers had no immediate alternative but to remain on the land as tenant farmers rack-rented by exorbitant year-to-year leases. Thus the deep-seated animosity of Burmans for Indians and their preferred economic status, reinforced by a color and race bias, was built in precisely the period which showed Burma's economy to be healthiest in terms of objective measures of output.[8]

Diversification of Crops in the Dry Zone

The Dry Zone and upper Burma did not experience the same degree of commercialization or alienation from foreigners that lower Burma did. This resulted largely because the environmental character of the region did not permit the cultivation of rice except by irrigation, a much more expensive method of cultivation (aside from the additional transport cost on produce to southern markets) than rice production in the delta which never required irrigation works because of adequate supplies of monsoonal rainfall or floodwaters. The Dry Zone maintained considerable diversity in dry crop cultivation (millets, pulses, cotton, tobacco, sesamum, and cattle raising, for instance) instead of developing a commerical monoculture of rice. Doubtlessly traders and brokers perceived profit margins to be significantly lower there than in lower Burma. Thus, central and upper Burma were better preserved from the delta society. Commercial influences extended into the region with regard to other primary products, however; timber and minerals like lead, zinc, and petroleum (together with gemstones) were developed into major industrial ventures. These activities were not territorially extensive or as labor absorbing as agriculture, and did not form a significant basis for generating anticolonial and antiforeign sentiment among the people.

Burma on the eve of World War II and occupation by the Japanese had been revolutionized by commerce. In 1938 more than 3,000,000 tons of rice, 250,000,000 tons of timber, and 170,000,000 tons of lead and zinc ore were dispatched as exports. By common colonial standards Burma was a healthy and profitable property. Internal forces worked ultimately to the disadvantage of both Britain and the indigenous peoples themselves, however.

THE INDEPENDENCE ERA

Burmese independence followed in the terrain of independence events in south and southeastern Asia after World War II; the new Union of Burma (neither clearly federalistic nor unitary in structure) was launched in 1948, its leaders full of lofty aspirations for the country but limited in the experience of administering and organizing a multinational state. Considering this lack of expertise, a surprisingly effective program was created. Pragmatically, there existed an overwhelming need to rehabilitate the economy. The destruction of World War II showed dramatically in the modernized sector of the economy where in the transport sector, for instance, the railway had lost one-third of its mileage, 80% of its locomotives and rollingstock, and hundreds of bridges; the inland navigation fleet was proportionately decimated also.

The New Nation and Her Ideological Basis

The ideological bias of the new nation emerged in the first few years after independence and was strongly anticolonial, but development oriented. Because it was generally perceived that the colonial experience had been fundamentally exploitative of Burma's human and natural resources, a socialistic philosophy aimed at creating a welfare state was espoused. Basic to this mind-set was the control of private businesses. Accordingly, private enterprises were either nationalized or regulated by new government-owned corporations or agencies. Absentee landlords (mainly Indian) found their lands nationalized, as were pawnshops (mainly Chinese owned); more formally organized firms either became joint ventures between the government and private business or were coordinated by the State Agricultural Marketing Board (responsible for rice exports), the Civil Supplies Management Board (responsible for all imports), and several other agencies which controlled timber and mineral exports, and other industrial activities.

A second feature of Burmese anticolonial sentiment was expressed in the policy of "Burmanization," wherein significant efforts were made to employ citizens of Burma in preference to noncitizens (particularly the overseas Indians and Chinese). Further, close control was placed on the conditions of entry and exit of noncitizens into and out of the country. Correlatively, fluency in Burmese (the majority language) and some evidence of acculturation into Burmese society (a name change, or adherence to indigenous standards to dress and behavior) came to be overtly or covertly required for admission to positions of prestige.[9]

The economic development aspect of the independence ideology focused particularly upon industrialization, since most industrial activities (excepting rice milling) upon which Burma had become dependent during the colonial era were located outside the country. Economic growth was perceived as a natural correlate of Burmese independence and in the early years after World War II politicians promised vastly heightened standards of living to the people. In large measure, new industry was expected to provide these improvements in well-being.

The Slow Pace of Economic Rehabilitation

Actually, rehabilitation of the economy took place rather slowly. U Aung San (Burma's first prime minister) and his cabinet were assassinated early in the new country's history; insurrection and banditry spread widely making it most difficult to rehabilitate rural areas (and even to maintain control of the major towns). As a result, rehabilitation efforts were drawn out over almost a decade. The slow pace of reconstruction was not as evident as it should have been, owing to new features in the transport and communications system of the country. At the end of World War II departing occupationary forces (both Japanese and Allied) left behind a seemingly inexhaustible supply of highway vehicles. Many individuals filled the country's land transport gaps from this equipment bonanza. Further, war surplus aircraft augmented by some new airplanes linked major towns and points of control by air. The Union of Burma Airways Corporation provided vital services during the intense insurgency years, and has continued to play an important role in spatially integrating the nation to this day.

After the peak of the insurgency in 1952 the first social and economic development plan was articulated in consultation with British and American economic and engineering consultants. Entitled the Pyidawtha (literally, "Happy Land") Plan, it envisaged creating an socialist economy and welfare state over an eight-year period. The plan aimed to increase Burma's gross domestic product by about one-third over the 1939 level (more than two-third over the debilitated 1952 levels). In terms of economic growth, it was expected that agricultural output would increase by 80%. The bulk of the plan was avowedly oriented towards creating a welfare state with social and welfare institutions and programs (including manpower development). In terms of the growth of productive capacities, however, the plan tilted towards the modern industrial sector. Overall the investment projection implied a very considerable increase in tertiary and quaternary economic sectors, since the government assumed primary responsibility for social welfare and manpower development. Other details relating to the economic aspect of the Plan have already been covered in Chapter 7.

The plan itself contained no heavy spatial bias within it. Many projects were slated for devlopment in disparate parts of the country. Some of these were not implemented either because of technical difficulties or erroneous cost-benefit estimates (such as the Kalewa coal mining project); other projects could not be implemented because of continuing civil unrest in the project region. As a result, about 90% of plan outlays were expended on projects located in Rangoon or closely adjacent areas. A primate city before World War II and one of the few areas firmly under government control in the early years of independence, Rangoon swelled from a population of 500,000 in 1941 to an estimated population of almost 740,000 in 1953. (By the early 1970s Rangoon's population was estimated at about 1,700,000[10]—indicative of continuing spatial processes subsequently.) Mandalay, which was located in the cultural core of the country, grew by only a little more than 20,000 people in twelve years to a size of 185,000 in 1953. (By the early 1970s Mandalay's size was estimated at 215,000.) All of Burma's other towns—Moulmein, Bassein, Henzada, Pegu, Akyab, Tavoy, and other centers—were considerable smaller than 100,000 people in 1953, excepting Moulmein at nearly that size.

One of the most successful parts of the plan lay in agriculture, where some irrigation projects were completed and during the late 1950s large tracts of land were cleared for rice cultivation subsequent to pacification of much of the countryside. However idealistic or inadvisable various features of the plan appear by hindsight, its full implementation became impossible when the main basis for its financing, the international sale of rice, could no longer be relied upon to provide adequate revenues. During the 1950s world prices for rice fell more than 25% below the consultant's minimum price projections. Alternate measures such as bilateral barter-trade agreements with East European countries were arranged in hopes of surmounting the problem, only to discover later that Burmese rice was being sold by these same nations on the open market and acted as a further depressant on international rice prices. Foreign aid was also rejected as a plan financing alternative, for it would violate Burma's foreign policy of strict nonalignment and render the country vulnerable to political pressure from donor nations, and it would probably mean the presence of many foreigners as a new technological elite, influencing indigenous values and behavior.[11]

Burma's decision-makers seemed not to appreciate the need for flexible pricing policies domestically and internationally as tools of modernization. Domestically, state corporation employed pricing systems which did not differ significantly from those employed by their colonial capitalist predecessors who wanted to maximize short-run profits. Prices for domestic manufactures and transport services (excepting air and private road transport) stimulated neither consumption and import substitution nor regional interdependence. In procuring rice domestically for export, the government offered such low prices that little stimulus was given for farmers to intensify production. Internationally, the pricing of Burmese rice was for a long time generally reactive to, rather than anticipative of, the trend of market conditions; revenues, thus, were smaller than they could have been.

That targets for growth were not met by the end of the plan period should come as no surprise. In fact, by the end of the plan the economy remained below its 1939 level in terms of output. Correlatively, with an increasing population the government found itself under mounting pressure to provide employment in the modernized sectors of the economy. Whether deliberate or not, many new positions were created in government without accordingly increasing the volume of services or output from the agencies; this "featherbedding" was also combined with efforts to slow the rate of progress of students through the educational system. The net effect of this situation was either alienation or politicization of much of the educated elite. Attention was diverted from the more immediate priorities of realizing economic growth in the face of unfavorable domestic and international conditions.

General Ne Win's caretaker government of 1958–59 may thus be understood as an attempt to redirect Burma's priorities towards fundamental issues of economic growth. Replacing civilian politics with authoritarian decisions of the military, the most modern institution in the country by that time, provided temporary relief from these problems. Following general elections in which most of the established politicans were returned to office, it soon became clear that conditions were returning to their pre-1958 status. On the grounds that Shan separatism threatened national viability, General Ne Win and the military again came into power in 1962.

BURMESE SOCIALISM

Shortly after the Revolutionary Government established itself in 1962, it produced a policy statement of its philosophy entitled the "Burmese Way to Socialism".[12] A brief reference to their kind of *Socialism* has already been made in Chapter 7. Marxist socialism adapted to Burmese conditions was its message, which incidentally did not appear very revolutionary in a country that had been basically committed to socialistic principles since its independence. Total nationalization of production and exchange was its aim, as became clear in the following three years. The banking system, the retail and wholesale distribution systems, and private lands were almost entirely removed from private ownership. Initially, these measures were welcomed by many and helped to legitimize the military junta (the Revolutionary Council) government, for almost immediately nationalization gutted the economic base of the Indian and Chinese communities. More than 100,000 Indians and Pakistanis emigrated to their mother countries after the takeover of retail trade; ultimately only about 125,000 South Asians (Indians, Pakistanis, and Bengalis) remained in Burma. The Chinese were less inclined to emigrate to mainland China not being open to private enterprise, and Taiwan, Hong Kong, and Singapore being intensely competitive economic and political arenas. Further, as Burma was to be transformed into a classless economy, the government demonetized its currency down to the equivalent of the ten dollar bill. Bumans had the satisfaction of knowing that foreign capitalists had at long last lost their hold on the country. Later the effects of nationalization tended to alienate many, particularly urbanites, as both daily necessities became progressively more difficult to purchase through the People's shops and people were laid off as their old employers could no longer afford to pay them.

Difficulties in the Economic Front

In agriculture, the new government enacted a law which made it impossible for a farmer to lose his material possessions to creditors. With land already nationalized, farmers no longer had collateral with which to ensure loans from illicit moneylenders, and government abolished agricultural rents only to discover subseqently that the incidence of default on government loans increased greatly from year to year. In part, these higher rates occurred because the government possessed no real punitive measures with which to treat defaulters, and in part the higher rates may have occurred in compensation for the low prices which the government paid for rice. Even though lenient policies were extended to the agricultural sector, marketable surpluses progressively declined (despite an increase in cultivated acreage to 6% above the 1938 level) for a number of reasons, such as: (1) redistribution of land into relatively small, perhaps uneconomic, units (averaging about 5.4 acres per holding); (2) fixed but low prices for rice (similar to the planned purchased and planned supply system of China in the 1950s); (3) increasing demand for agricultural produce because of population growth in the countryside; and (4) the general unavailability of luxury and other produce upon which to spend earnings from the sale of agricultural commodities. Although production doubtlessly supplied the subsistence needs of farmers, Burma's exports of rice declined precipitously in the 1960s to a proverbial trickle. Prior to the Revolutionary Government rice exports amounted to 1,840,000 tons in 1961–62; by 1967–68 Burma's exports of rice had fallen as low as 350,000 tons, despite substantial external demand for Burmese rice. By the latter 1960s the railroad system, which since its inception had channeled agricultural surpluses southward to Rangoon, experienced reversal in its dominant flow pattern on the trunk line; north-bound traffic now predominated and was mainly constituted of rice moving to the Dry Zone.

In the late 1960s improved strains of "Green Revolution" rice were adapted to Burmese conditions and spread widely throughout the irrigated acreage of the country.[13] The promise of hybrid species for relief of the problem of declining surpluses depended crucially upon the capacity of the government to provide a technological package of fertilizers, pesticides, and irrigation water to farmers in quantities large enough and at prices low enough to stimulate increased yields. Furthermore, increased prices for *paddy* together with a supply of consumer goods will probably be important additional elements in stimulating intensive farming practices by farmers. Starting from the early 1970s new Four Year Plans (for details see Chapter 7) were operational. They are aimed at increased output without significant new investment; presumably the plans focused upon organizing productive capacities in a more efficient manner than had been characteristic of the post-1962 period.

Industrial production has likewise suffered not only from industrial relations difficulties but also because imported raw materials are either in short supply or are distributed inefficiently within the country. As a result, the economy of Burma had progressively diminished in size since 1962, and the standard of living of the great bulk of the populace had declined to the point that basic necessities are rationed and an illicit black market trade flourishes. Economic progress has been registered only since the mid-1970s with the change in attitude in organizing the productive capacities of the country.

The Nature of Political Centralization

Politically, the Revolutionary Government sought to stifle all opposition to its policies. In the middle 1960s many of the more influential, better educated people who were not on the government's side were placed in detention camps, including politicians from the pre-1962 period who were under house arrest. An atmosphere of fear and mutual suspicion pervaded public life, for charges were not generally brought against detainees. Ultimately most of them were released and were permitted to leave the country if they remained a threat to the domestic polity;

otherwise, they were permitted to reenter civilian life, well aware of the consequences of having appeared to offer opposition to the regime. Control over any potential opposition movement within the country has been established by reorganizing public administration. Security and Administration Committees (SAC's) have been established for each administrative district and maintain close control over the activities and movements of their resident populations. Interregional movement within the country is controlled through a travel permit system issued by SACs at places of origin and destination, and travel is monitored by the Military Intelligence System. The government has never attempted at any time to interfere with the practice of Buddhism; other organized religious groups have been required to register with the government and some of their formal activities have been curtailed (such as the operation of charitable hospitals), although the practice of personal religion has not apparently been affected. Thus, there is today no significant organized source of opposition to Burmese socialist ideology within the country. In this quiescent atmosphere a single party, the Burma Socialist Programme Party (BSPP), was firmly founded by the Revolutionary Government. In 1973 the military junta was preparing to hand over power to the BSPP, although in fact many of the major figures in the party were ex-military officers who played important roles in the earlier government. A 'limited democracy' has returned to Burma since 1974 (also see p. 6).

BURMA IN THE 1980s

Thirty years of turmoil and experimentation in national self-development have left their mark. The legacy of the past continues to plague Burma in terms of its ethnic divisions and the nature of its politics. Despite efforts to remove to accommodate insurgent ethnic forces in the 1970s, the government has not successfully consolidated its hold over the entire country. Perhaps one-third of its area remains beyond government control; in these areas insurgent forces live, generate revenues and foster counter-economies (producing for, or trading in, illicit international or domestic Burmese trade). The difficulty of incorporating Burma's ethnic minorities into the fabric of the state is reflected in recently enacted citizenship laws. The category of 'Associated Citizen' may be extended to children of Burma's indigenous minorities; full citizenship may be extended to the grandchildren of these minorities. However, the associate citizenship of any individual is revocable. Thus, the systematic process for legal assimilation of minority peoples reflects the continuing dominance of a Burman Burma concept.

Burma's experiment with radical socialism as operationalized politically in the form of constitutional dictatorship through the Burma Socialist Programme Party (BSPP) have produced mixed effects. Recurrent problem has developed as the party has build a wider base in civilian membership. Divergence of opinion has produced repeated restructuring of the party, including expulsion of many members. In the 1980s the core of the party membership is drawn once again from Burma's military forces. Thus, while the Party and government continue strong, the process model for demilitarizing political participation has proven elusive. The government has acknowledged the importance of Buddhism in the history and culture of Burma by creating a Ministry of Religion. At a conference for 'Purification, Perpetuation and Propagation of Buddhism' agreement was reached with representative monks that a central authority should be created to control the 'sangha' (organization of monks and nuns), and that monks should carry identity cards. Subsequently, religious courts were also revived.

To great extent the difficulties of the government in gaining popular acclaim and widespread support stems from the indifferent performance of the economy through the mid-1970s in the face of rapid inflation of prices by 250% in about 10 years. The economic and bureaucratic rigidities brought about by regulation 'en route' to Burmese Socialism produced an economy of scarcity (though maldistribution and slow growth). Throughout this period, population has continuously increased, producing an obvious demand for economic expansion. (Detailed results of Burma's national consus in the mid-1970s have not been circulated). Substantial popular discontent with the regime was registered in the 1970s, including an attempt at government overthrow by dissident army officers. The net effect produced a liberalizaion in Burma's economic policies; these were to deal more pragmatically with the nation's needs. A substantial share of the economy remained under private control, and private enterprise seemed accepted as part of Burma's longer-term economic environment. Review of national assets showed that policies aimed at encouraging agriculture, forestry, and mining could produce significant growth.

It has already been stated in Chapter 7 that, in agriculture, the new variety of high-yielding rice was introduced successfully into rural Burma, with more than 6 million acres of the new HYV under cultivation in 1981. Substantial investment in fertilizer manufacture and irrigation development is part of the plan for stimulating agricultural growth further. Gains in output have been achieved with the new rice producing 1086 kg./acre (an increase of 448 kg.). However, the policy tools of a flexible pricing system for rice purchase, agricultural credit programs, and security of tenure to farmers have not received heavy emphasis. (A World Bank study indicated that more than 400,000 acres of paddy were abandoned in the decade before 1974 because of inadequate pricing and flood control/drainage facilities.) Average farm sizes remain small, about 4.76 acres in 1978, with about 10 acres required to produce an income above poverty level without cultivating the new rice; farm sizes were smaller in upper Burma than lower Burma. Thus, nearly five farm families in six remained in rural poverty. Official procurement prices for rice have offered farmers characteristically about one-half that which their counterparts elsewhere in Southeast Asia receive; to discover that substantial rice output may have been channeled to the alternative 'parallel' economy in return for higher prices is no surprise.

Development of products of mines, particularly oil and natural gas reserves, has been significant. In this respect, Burma has extended its nautical boundary to 200 miles off-shore, and extensive exploration has been taking place. Development of forest products, particularly teak extraction for export, has also increased greatly in recent years. With perhaps 75% of world teak supplies, Burma possesses substantial growth potential for teak exports. Whether continued emphasis on primary products can provide long-term national economic growth is not clear; however, this is the sector towards which much of the recent investment has been funnelled. In recent years manufacture has increasingly become dependent upon foreign imports; the domestic economy provides textiles and food processing principally. Products of high technology come from abroad.

The distribution system of wholesale and retail trade (together with transportation) remain heavily in the private sector. The government has made significant attempts to curtail parallel (or 'Black') economies. A specific variant of this has been the illicit opium trade from the "Golden Triangle" of northeast Burma and Laos. The government (with the support of the U.N. and U.S.A.) has attempted to deny supply of opium into the global 'pipeline' by using helicopters and aircraft to destroy poppy crops before they mature. Other efforts have been made by the government to stimulate the formal domestic economy, in order to diminish the impetus of the "parallel" economy which spread throughout Burma. The growth of a "Black Market" throughout Burma was not produced by dissident ethnic groups, although the regions controlled by them may have constituted the 'port-of-entry' for import and export products distributed through that system.

The single largest barrier to the rapid growth of the domestic economy (beyond any factors previously noted) is the lack of adequate national transportation system. Limited highway and rail networks do no make possible the benefits that 'time-space convergence' has conferred on other economic regions of the world. The rail system carries today only about the same freight volume it carried in 1962 before the revolution. The inland navigation system is antiquated; and the commerical air transport network is little developed beyond its capacities in 1960. It continues as the modern means of linking the disparate parts of the country into one political unit. Rangoon remains Burma's pre-eminent center of transport and private city. (Most flights either originate there, or link with it as national capital and hub city.)

Much of Burma's recent growth has veen induced by deficit financing through international loans. Because Burma did not heavily depend on such loans in the earlier years, its indebtedness should not create the fiscal problems numerous other less developed nations have encountered. However, long-term dependency on such means of stimulating domestic economic growth may undermine the national autonomy that the Burmese have so long sought to maintain.

PROSPECTS

Over thirty years of turmoil and experimentation in national self-development have cost Burma much of its great economic development potential. It can only be hoped that in ensuing years a critical evaluation of policies of the 1950 and 1960s may be openly and constructively reviewed. Certainly one conclusion which seems warranted is that any government (colonial or indigenous) can violate the best interest of a region's resident population if it insensitively imposes policies based on ideological premises not shared by a majority of that population. Certainly Burmans are the ones who are best equipped to ascertain the fundamental desires of their own people, and to devise appropriate policy. In this writer's view, however, responsibility for decision-making in many areas will have to be returned to all of the common people, for a strong sense of individual liberty is one of the basic features of the dominant Burmese Buddhist society. Government, instead of acting as the arbitrator and controller of public behavior, will have to reorient its efforts to become an enabling institution, sensitive to and supportive of the actions of individuals. Now that alien influences have been largely expunged from Burma's national life, such a development should be more readily feasible. Only with such strong medicine as this can the plural society of Burma recoup its losses and rebuild a Golden Land for all of its citizens. Though, starting from the mid-1970s, pragmatic approaches have been introduced in the economic sector, the political system remains essentially undemocratic.

Footnote References

[1]See Maung Htin Aung, *A History of Burma* (New York: Columbia University Press, 1967); D.G.E. Hall, *A History of Southeast Asia* (London: The Macmillan Company, 1964); John F. Cady, *Southeast Asia: Its Historical Development* (New York: McGraw-Hill Book Company, 1964); and B.R. Pearn, *Burma Background* (Calcutta: Longmans, Green & Co., Ltd., 1943) for explication of Burma's historical evolution.

[2]This chapter makes no real attempt to portray the religious and cultural fabric of Burmese Buddhist society. For excellent, readable introductions to these topics see R. Burling, *Hill Farms and Padi Fields: Life in Mainland Southeast Asia* (Englewood Cliffs, N.J.: Prentice-Hall, Inc., 1965); Shway Yoe, *The Burman: His Life and Notions* (New York: W.W. Norton & Company, Inc., 1963); Mi Mi Khaing, *Burmese Family* (Bloomington: Indiana University Press, 1972); Robert C. Lester, *Thervada Buddhism in Southeast Asis* (Ann Arbor: The University of Michigan Press, 1973).

[3]Jon A. Wiant, "Burma: Loosening Up on the Tiger's Tail," *Asian Survey*, Vol. XIII (February, 1973), pp. 179–186.

[4]See particularly for this section O.H.K. Spate, *Burma Setting* (Calcutta: Longsmans, Green & Co., Ltd., 1943); Charles A. Fisher, *Southeast Asia: A Social, Economic and Political Geography* (London: Methuen & Co., Ltd., 1966); Donald W. Fryer, *Emerging Southeast Asia: A Study in Growth and Stagnation* (New York: McGraw-Hill Book Company, 1970).

[5]Maung Shein, *Burma's Transport and Foreign Trade* (Rangoon: Department of Economics, University of Rangoon, 1964).

[6]J.S. Furnivall, *Colonial Policy and Practice: A Comparative Study of Burma and Netherlands India* (Cambridge: Cambridge University Press, 1948).

[7]One of the richest lead and zinc complexes ever discovered lay close to the railroad. Much of it consisted of tailings from centuries old Chinese silver mining. It was developed at the direction of Herbert Hoover, before he became active in American politics. For details see J.C. Brown and A.K. Dey, *India's Mineral Wealth*, 3rd edition (London: Oxford University Press, 1955).

[8]J.S. Furnivall, *An Introduction to the Political Economy of Burma*, 3rd edition (Rangoon: Peoples' Literature Committee & House, 1957). See also Ching Hsiok-Hwa, *The Rice Industry of Burma: 1852–1940* (Kuala Lumpur: University of Malaya Press, 1968).

[9]Government representatives even debated constituting Buddhism as the state's official religion. The bill was modified under pressure from non-Buddhist representatives, so that no formal discrimination on grounds of religious preference was to be permitted. Even so, the government underwrote a considerable portion of the cost of convening the Sixth Buddhist World Council in the Rangoon suburbs during 1954–56.

[10]U.S. Department of State, *Union of Burma*, Background Notes (Washington, D.C.: U.S. Government Printing Office, November 1971). Note that the only post-war was census was taken in 1953, and included 252 towns with the country. Other useful resources for this period include: Hugh Tinker, *The Union of Burma: A Study of the First Years of Independence* (London: Oxford University Press, 1961); and Louis J. Walinsky, *Economic Development in Burma, 1951–1960* (New York: Twentieth Century Fund, 1962).

[11]A case in point was that of American technical experts, who inundated the life of the capital with their presence in 1950–1951.

[12]See F.S.V. Donnison, *Burma* (New York: Praeger Publishers, Inc., 1970); Mya Maung, *Burma and Pakistan: A Comparative Study of Development* (New York: Praeger Publishers, Inc., 1971); N.R. Chakravarti, *The Indian Minority in Burma: The Rise and Decline of an Immigrant Community* (London: Oxford University Press, 1971); and U.S. Department of State bulletin noted in footnote 10.

[13]Robert E. Huke, "Burma" in A. Taylor, editor, *Focus on Southeast Asia* (New York: Praeger Publishers, Inc., 1972), p. 80.

Chapter 10

Indochina: Physical Setting and Evolution of the Tonkin Core Area

Ashok K. Dutt

Indochina occupies a crossroads location where the two great Asian cultural traditions—Chinese and Indian—have clashed head-on, giving rise to a new Indo-Chinese culture. Indochina as a political unit, however, was the creation of French colonial administrators in the 19th century.[1] The cultural, historical, and political separatism within this unit has remained so strong that the imposed French unification, which lasted for almost a century, has fallen apart into separate and independent political units. This separation occurred in 1954 as a result of the Geneva Agreements. At that time the four countries of Cambodia, Laos, North Vietnam, and South Vietnam were created out of former French Indochina. In 1976, North and South Vietnam were united into one country.

GEOGRAPHICAL BASIS

Geographically, Indochina is a peninsular region bordering the South China Sea to the east and the Gulf of Siam to the west. Although plains cover almost the same amount of area as mountains, the plains support the majority of the people.[2]

Land-Forms and Surface Configuration

The northern highlands and the Annamite Cordillera are the most noteworthy mountainous areas of the peninsula. One of the highest points lies in the central region of the Annamite Cordillera in southern Vietnam; here the peak of Quang Ngai reaches an altitude of 10,761 feet. In the Central Highlands deforestation resulting from shifting agriculture has led to the exposure of bare rock in many places; otherwise the entire region is rugged and heavily forested. East-west travel across the Cordillera is not impossible, but difficult. The Cordillera steps down gradually in the west towards the Mekong valley making access easy from this direction. However, the Cordillera rises precipitously from the east making access difficult.[3] Travel between east and west, however, is made a little easier because of the presence of many low passes with altitudes of 2,000' to 3,000'. The plains and valleys that surround the Cordillera in an elliptical shape allow easy access. Therefore, the principal cultural, political, population movements have occurred longitudinally in this peninsula, following the landwise connections provided by the plains.

Climate and Drainage

The northern part of Indochina has a climate dominated by tropical and polar air masses with a marked winter season. Although Hanoi averages a January temperature of 62 °F, the winter temperature in the north can sometimes reach as low as 45 °F making "the cultivation of low-latitude perennials economically impossible"[4] (Fig. 10-1). Climate in southern Indochina is dominated by equatorial and tropical air masses causing a year round warm season. Equatorial influence in Saigon (Ho Chi Minh City) is quite evident because of three factors: (1) the annual range of average monthly temperature is less than 4 °F[5], (2) maximum rainfall occurs twice a year—in June and September—with the passing of the sun towards the Tropics of Cancer and Capricorn, and (3) the average annual rainfall is 80 inches. In contrast, Hanoi has a monthly temperature range of 21 °F and a rainfall maximum occuring only in August. Because Hanoi is under tropical influence in the summer months, its average summer temperature is around the 80 as is Saigon's.

Among climatic factors, volume and seasonal incidence of rainfall are the two most responsible for

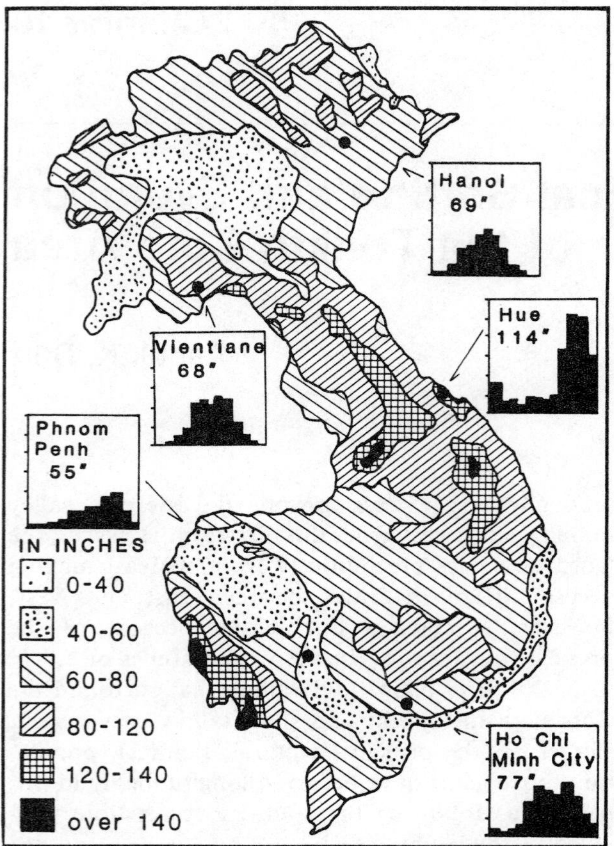

Figure 10-1. Annual Rainfall in Indochina and Bar-charts Showing Rainfall by Months for Fire Cities.

agricultural intensity, patterns, and constraints. Rice, the main crop of the peninsula, is cultivated in all areas; its success, however, is not quite secured in the western Tonle Sap basin where the rainfall is less than 50 inches per annum. In tropical climates, approximately forty-five inches of rainfall is the minimum amount required for rice cultivation without irrigation. Generally, the monsoon climate produces a great deal of uncertainity in terms of total annual precipitation causing rainfall to vary possibly several inches in any one particular place. Therefore, areas with rainfall varying from 40 to 50 inches are always in serious danger of having unsuccessful rice production in certain years. However, most areas of Indochina have rainfall and summer temperatures ideal for rice. Areas in the Red River delta and parts of the coastal plains have a winter rainfall or drizzle which makes the production of a second or third winter crop possible. The winter rainfall in the Cardamom Hills, however, does not contribute to winter cropping since the hilly and forested terrain precludes the possibility of effective agriculture.

Typhoons. Tropical cyclones, or typhoons, which are similar to the hurricanes that invade the southeastern parts of the United States, are regular occurrences in much of the Southeast Asia, particularly in the Philippines and in Vietnam.

"A fully developed tropical cyclone is a warm coned, energy-exporting system which usually remains intense for many days over the ocean."[6] Because these cyclones quickly lose their intensity and violence as they move over land, the coastal areas of Vietnam are the most devastated. Winds may exceed 80 knots, and the area covered by a typhoon may extend outward to a radius of about hundred miles from its eye,[7] the low pressure center of the typhoon. As the storms move westward from the South China Sea, they often take a heavy toll in lives and property along the eastern coast of Vietnam.

NATURAL REGIONS

There have been several attempts made to divide the Indochinese peninsula into regions (see Fig. 10–2). Dobby, Fisher, and Fryer have, for example subdivided the peninsula in such a way as to stress physical divisions. The author (Dutt) in this chapter, however, has attempted a regional division taking a composite view, such as, (a) the historical attractiveness or repulsion of areas for human settlement, (b) the core areas of political power during different historical periods, and (c) physical characteristics (Fig. 10–2D). It is also these three factors which are mainly responsible for cultural diffusion in the peninsula. This scheme results in two major regions and seven subregions:

1. Highlands
   a. Annamite Cordillera and Northern Mountains and Plateaus.
   b. Cardamom and Elephant Mountains.
2. Plains
   a. Red River delta.
   b. Mekong delta and Funan.
   c. Coastal plains and Champa.
   d. Tonle Sap, Mekong Lowlands, and Angkor.
   e. Upper Mekong valley and Laos.

ANNAMITE CORDILLERA AND NORTHERN MOUNTAINS AND PLATEAUS

The Annamite Cordillera and Northern Mountains and Plateaus (henceforth referred to as A.C.N. Mountains) is an upland area located in parts of Vietnam, Laos, and Cambodia that has been used over the centuries as a place of refuge from expulsion. For over 2,000 years, the all-too human instinct that

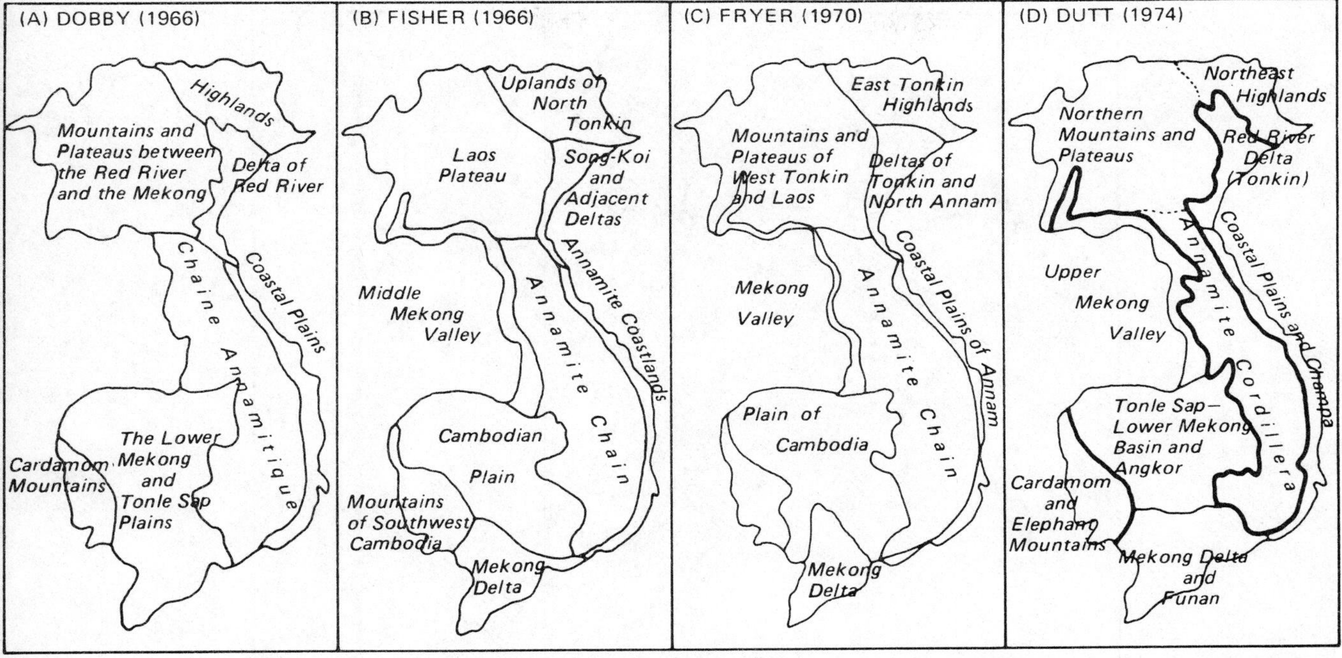

Figure 10-2. Regions of Indochina as Delineated by Dobby, Fisher, Fryer, and Dutt.

"Might Makes Right" has been very evident in Indochina. The powerful and culturally superior peoples have always occupied the plains areas since these areas were best suited for agriculture; the weaker and numerically smaller groups have always been driven upward into the infertile hills and plateaus and hence, have a lower population density (Fig. 10-3). Since the French occupation of Indochina, such forced migration has largely been stopped; however, the results of past deeds can be seen in the segregation of the plains people from the *montagnards* in the A.C.N. Mountains.

The *montagnards* are not a homogeneous people. They have little contact with the numerous plains people, and they also live in relative isolation from each other. Because of *montagnard* disunity, and the poor agricultural potential of the A.C.N. Mountains, no political core area of any significance was ever centered in this region during the entire course of Indochinese history. Thus, the A.C.N. Mountain area has always been relegated to poverty and cultural backwardness.

Racially and ethnically, the *montagnards* are no different from the plains people; most of them too came from Malayo-Polynesian (like the Chams) and Mongoloid (like the Khmers, the Viets and the Laos) stocks. Despite their common ancestry, though, the plains people have always regarded the *montagnards* as inferiors and savages. The *montagnards* of Mongoloid stock generally occupy the northern third of the A.C.N. Mountains, while those of Malayo-Polnesian stock generally inhabit the southern two-thirds. The latter group are apparently among the oldest natives of Indochina and were driven into the A.C.N. Mountains by ruling Viets, Chams, Funanese, and Khmers. Beginning in the fifteenth century, the Chams were driven by the Viets to this area from the coastal plains. These mountain-dwelling Chams have adhered to Hindu and Moslem beliefs. They now live on both sides of the southern Cordillera. In addition to the Chams, the southern *montagnards* consist of Rhade, Jarai, Bahnar, Tai, Meo, and Stieng tribal groups. Of these groups, the Tai are Mongoloid, while the Meo are relatives of the wooly-haired Negrito.[8] These groups practice shifting agriculture and adhere to animistic spiritual beliefs.

The northern *montagnards* show a greater influence of Chinese culture; they practice elements of Confucianism and Buddhism as well as animism. They are made up both of groups who were driven from the Tonkin delta and the upper Mekong valley and groups who more recently migrated from South China. The Meos were the latest of these Chinese migrants, arriving in Indochina around 1850. Other groups in this area include the Tai, Muong, Man, Lao, Ho, Lolo, and Kha.

Although many of the northern *montagnards* sustain themselves in small villages by shifting agriculture and perhaps some herding and hunting, two of the largest groups, the Thai (Tai) and the Muong are skilled wet-rice farmers.[9] Villages are apt to be larger than those of the

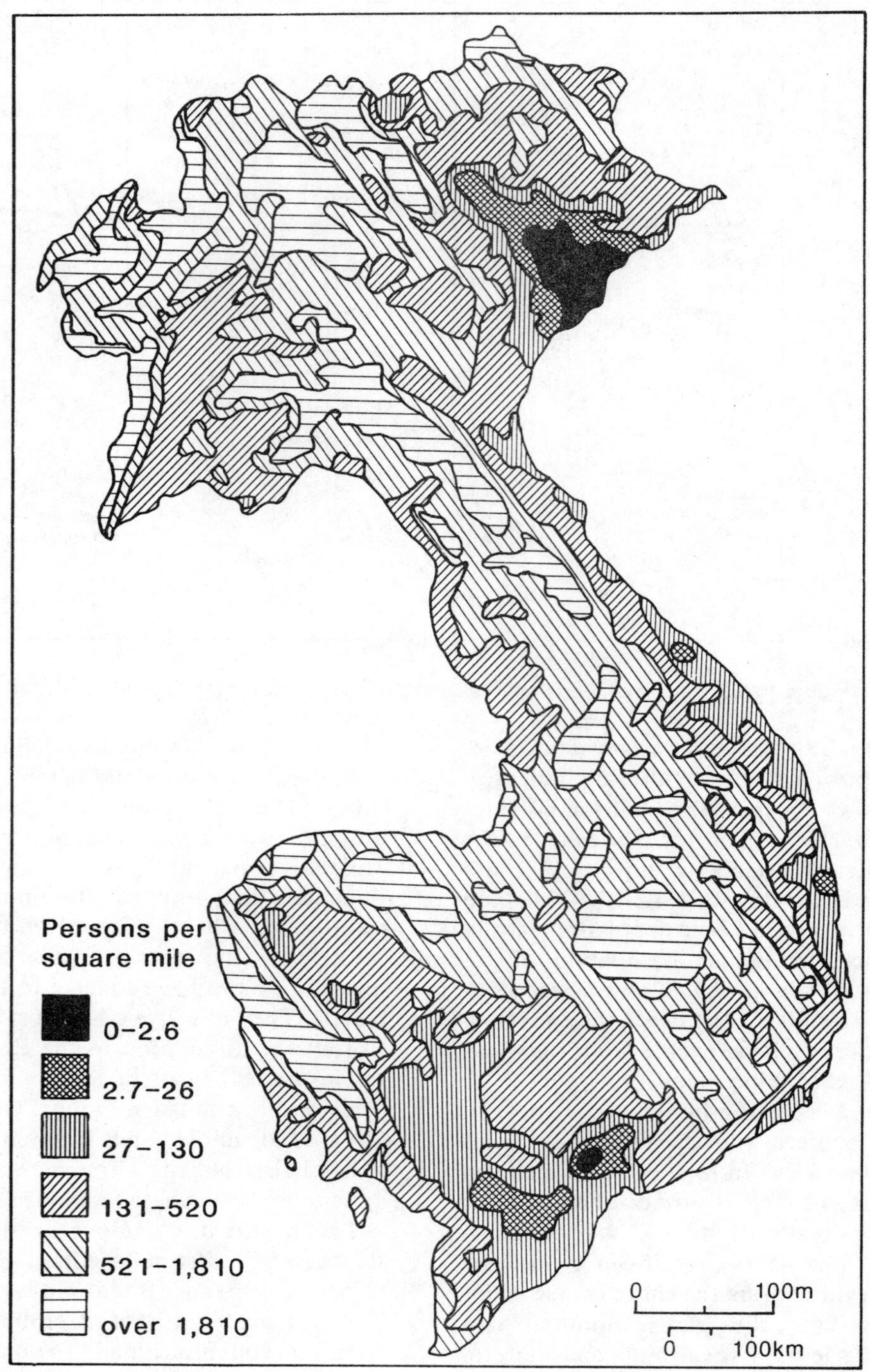

Figure 10-3. Density of Population in Indochina (about 1965).

economically less advanced groups in the South.[10]

The A.C.N. Mountains had been the region most susceptible to a communist guerrilla activity for two principal reasons: (1) the *montagnards*, who had been suppressed and looked down upon by the plains people for centuries, often looked to the Communists for sympathy and the promise of a better future, and (2) the terrain of this area is an ideal operations ground for guerrilla groups because it is hilly and forested and provides difficulty for transportation. The intensity of communist guerrilla activity in this area was especially evident in 1954, just before the Geneva Convention, and also in early 1973, at the time of the cease-fire (see also Introduction and Chapter 1).

The future of Indochina lies not only in the increased productivity of wet-rice cultivation in the plains, but also in more effective use of the timber and mineral resources located mainly in the A.C.N. Mountains (See Fig. 5–4). In 1940 the French estimated that 95% of Indochina's mining interests were in its northern area, especially in the mountains of northern Vietnam. Quang Yen is the primary mining site of Vietnam's good quality anthracite coal (estimated reserve totals 20 billion tons). Tin, iron ore, phosphate, lead, zinc, and gold are also mined in Vietnam. Laos also has significant deposits of tin, iron ore, and lead, whereas mineral deposits in Cambodia are relatively poor. Thus, the A.C.N. Mountain area seems to have a brighter future since it has sizeable economic potentialities and its political importance has been realized in all the countries of Indochina.

Islands of basaltic "terres rouges," which are particularly suitable for rubber cultivations are found at the southern part of the A.C.N. Mountains. The semiequatorial winterless climate is most suitable for rubber plantations, which began under the ownership of the French *colons*. These plantations produced almost 75,000 tons of rubber a year at the beginning of World War II, meeting the needs of industries in France. Before 1930, the conditions under which the plantation laborers worked and lived were exacting, inhuman, and rather unattractive to the natives; however, with improved labor legislation, work in the plantations did become very attractive in the thirties. During the 1960s it is in these rubber plantations where some of the most bitter battles were fought between the Saigon and Viet Cong forces. With the peace, however, the area's potential for rubber has been revived.

The Laotian part of the A.C.N. Mountains in the 1960s was one of the world's major centers of opium production. Because of the huge profit involved the natives eagerly cultivated the opium poppy, combining their hard labor with shifting agriculture, which is apparently the most suitable basis for poppy cultivation.

> Opium poppy cultivation requires freshly burnt clearings, and laborious and meticulous cultivation; about one acre of poppies is necessary for the production of a pound of raw opium, the processing of which is also very laborious undertaking.[11]

Since the Laotian A.C.N. Mountains probably produced 400 tons of raw opium annually, it was no wonder that the cities of the upper Mekong valley (such as Vientiane) were crowded with drug addicts from the United States and Western Europe until the early 1970s. Although the poppy grower earned only $10 per pound of opium, the same pound sold at final points of consumption in Europe or the United States at around $30,000.[12] After 1975 with the communist take over, Vientiane is no longer the heaven of the western opium addicts. Instead the 'golden triangle' bordering Burma and Thailand turned into one of the leading opium producers in the world during the 1980s.

CARDAMOM AND ELEPHANT MOUNTAINS

This area has been the most unattractive in history from a settlement point of view. It is rugged, agriculturally unproductive, and heavily forested in most places. The very few people who live here are the tribal Pears who have Negro-like features. They have largely assimilated into the Khmer Buddhist culture of present-day Kampuchea.

RED RIVER DELTA OR TONKIN

Geologically, the two Vietnamese deltas (Red River and Mekong) are the most recent of all the landforms in Indochina. Both were built from sediments brought down by the rivers from their headwater regions in recent geologic times. Actually, both the Red (Song Koi) and Mekong River deltas are even now growing seaward at the rate of 200 and 300 feet per year respectively.

Bronze Age Culture

The overwhelming majority of Tonkinese have descended from the Mongoloid race which migrated to Tonkin from South China; these migrants absorbed the local aboriginals, who were probably of Melanoid and Malayo-Indonesian origins, both by conquest and intermarriage.[13] These newly assimilated Austro-Indonesian and Mongoloid

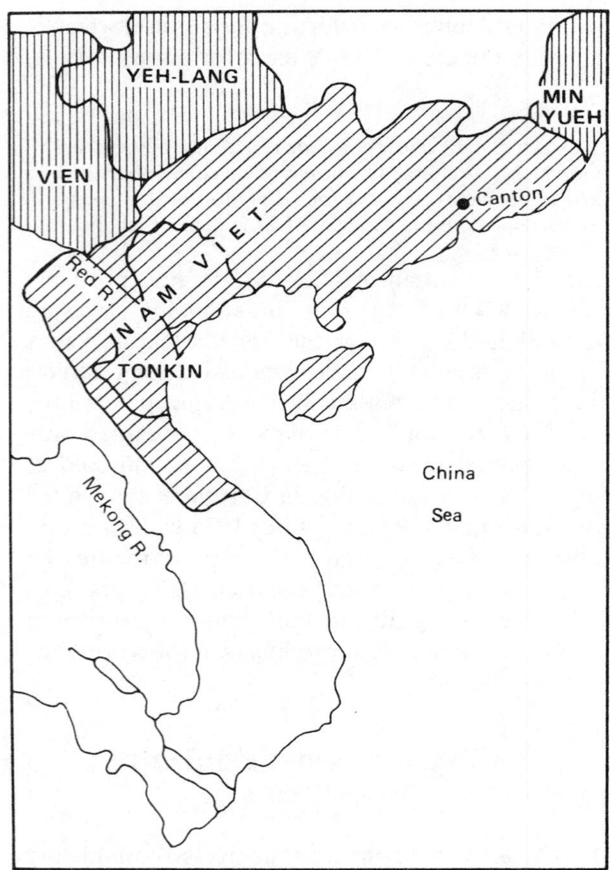

Figure 10-4. Nam Viet (before conquest by the Han in 111 B.C.).

elements gave rise to a Bronze Age culture in Tonkin between 300 B.C. and 100 B.C. The way of life at the time was based on "primitive agricultural practices, supplementing their cereal diet by hunting and fishing. The tool these people used was a hoe made of polished stone...bronze...being used for the points of their poisoned arrows."[14] According to both legend and factual evidence, there existed at that time the two Kingdoms of Van Lang and Au Lac which were Vietnamese in culture and were made up primarily of sedentary peasantry. The farmers had to work hard under the primitive agricultural system since returns mainly depended on the amount of labor. A new system of law and order also evolved.[15]

Chinese Influence

The year 207 B.C. marked the beginning of Chinese rule in the area. In that year the Tonkinese Kingdom of Au Lac was overpowered by the Chinese general Trieu Da. During the Ch'in dynasty, Trieu Da seceded from the Chinese Empire to form a new kingdom, Nam Viet, consisting of Southeast China and Tonkin. His capital was near Canton in present-day China. However, when the central power of China regained its strength under the Han Emperor Wu-ti, all of the Nam Viet territory including Tonkin and parts of the northern coastal plains of Indochina were brought under Chinese Imperial control. The Imperial Chinese rule in Tonkin lasted from about 111 B.C. to A.D. 939; this area was then known in Chinese annals as the province of Chaio Chih (Fig. 10–4).[16]

The long Chinese subjugation cast far reaching influences over the Tonkinese life and landscape. First, the Chinese civilization centering around the Yellow River was over 2,000 years old at the time Tonkin was conquered; Tonkin's Bronze Age civilization was thus lifted to a higher level of civilization and significant socioeconomic and political changes were sparked.

Secondly, the Chinese introduced their more advanced agricultural methods to Tonkin. These innovations were greatly welcomed by the local population because the new methods helped support a greater number of people without any serious dislocation. One of these new techniques was "hydraulic civilization,"[17] meaning effective control of both riverine and oceanic waters by dyking. The only parallel to such a technique in the pre-Modern Western world existed in Holland where people have reclaimed lands from the bed of the sea since about A.D. 1200.[18] Irrigated water from the hydraulic civilization, the use of human excreta for manure, the replacement of the primitive stone hoe with metallic ploughs, the use of water buffalos, and better use of land were the essential contributions of the Chinese agriculture. The Red River delta was the only extensive fertile alluvial plain south of the Yangtze plain within the Chinese Empire. Thus, it offered excellent opportunities for adopting such productive agricultural techniques. Since these methods had such a far reaching effect, the Tonkinese (also referred to as Annamites) acquired an overriding agricultural advantage over the other Indochinese populations in the years that followed.[19]

A third Chinese influence was the use of Chinese characters in the writing of the Vietnamese language; a practice that continued until the seventeenth century. "*Chu nom*, a popular form of Chinese calligraphy, is still in use today for certain types of scholarly writing."[20] The dominant Chinese influence on the Annamese (or Vietnamese) language has so enriched it that it stands out in the literature of the peninsula.[21]

Some other influences are related to religion. First, Confucian, Mahayanan, and Taoist traditions emanated southward from China and became rooted in the minds of the average Tonkinese. Also, two first-century Chinese governors, Tch Quang and Nham Dien, were still honored for teaching the Tonkinese people Confucian ethics along with the use of improved farm inplements.[22]

Finally, the Chinese introduced a more efficient administrative system (known as Mandarin) to replace the old, often inefficient, hereditary one. The Mandarin was the "prototype of the bureaucrat, durable as the Chinese empire itself, and combining within itself something of the peasant, vagabond, pirate, warrior, and philosopher."[23] In the Mandarin system the officials (or Mandarin), appointed by the ruler for local administration, were chosen on the basis of their training and education.

However, no matter how deeply Chinese influences were entrenched in Tonkin, Tonkin never lost its identity and culture. Although the average farmer adopted many Chinese customs and ways of thinking, he still continued to cling to many of his pre-Chinese traditions inspired by legends and myths surviving from Au Lac. Such a deep-rooted feeling for the past prevented a total Chinese assimilation of Tonkin.

Under the impact of the "hydraulic civilization" and its advanced agricultural techniques, Tonkin became wealthy, agriculturally productive, and new areas were reclaimed for agriculture. However, the Chinese rule did not bring any significant material well-being to Tonkin's general peasantry. This was due to the fact that the Chinese emperor, his local Chinese governor, feudal lords, Mandarins, and other administrators were the principal beneficiaries of the new techniques. As a result there were a dozen uprisings between A.D. 39 and A.D. 939 against the Chinese. The last one turned into a mass rebellion because participation was no longer restricted to members of the upper class. This rebellion in 939 was so effective that it succeeded in ridding Tonkin completely of Chinese rule.

The geographical location of Tonkin was an important factor to the success of the 939 rebellion. During the ancient and medieval Chinese Empires, peripheral and frontier states as a rule declared their independence whenever the central government became weak and disorganized. Being a peripheral Chinese province, not only did Tonkin remain least assimilated, but it also was able to take advantage of the decaying T'ang Dynasty in the tenth century and drove the Chinese army from its soils.

As a direct result of Chinese rule, Tonkin amassed a great deal of knowledge relating to technical advancement in agriculture and administration. This knowledge constituted the main lever for the formation of a persistent and unbreakable core area in the years that followed. The "grass-root level" agricultural techniques such as dyking, fertilizing, and irrigating, provided a stable economic base for the Tonkinese core. "Grass-root level" here refers to those average farmers who maintained the dykes with community effort, manufactured their own manure, and controlled water allotments. Thus was established an enduring economic well-being based on decentralization whose effectiveness and efficiency depended primarily on the basic human instinct for survival.

The Solidification of the Tonkinese Core Area (939–1883)

The strong and stable core area created in Tonkin after 939 continued to be an independent and powerful centralized kingdom until A.D. 1883. However, there were minor disruptions during this period: (a) the 20 years between 1407 and 1427 when Tonkin was temporarily reoccupied by the Chinese Imperial Armies, and (b) the years 1550 and 1620 when the country was twice divided into two parts, North and South.

Kings or rulers of dynastic heredity determined the legitimate heir to the throne. Sometimes, however, these determinations were contested and resulted in civil wars and dynastic changes. Thus, during its 944 years of independence Tonkin had a total of six dynasties, the last and the greatest of which was the Later Le Dynasty. This dynasty began in 1427 and lasted until the French took over the region in 1883. In 1428 the Les established their capital at Hanoi, the city which previously had been chosen by the Tonkinese to be the rebel capital in A.D. 599.[24] Since 1428 Hanoi has remained the national capital except for the periods (to be mentioned in the latter part of this Chapter) when it was relegated to the status of a provincial center.

As soon as people of a region develop individuality through various experiences, their experience of independence often makes it difficult and sometimes impossible to be resubjugated by any foreign power. Therefore, three massive attempts to resubjugate Tonkin failed—two at the end of the thirteenth century. In 1276, after conquering the Chinese Empire and creating probably one of the world's greatest empires, Kublai Khan advanced on Tonkin with 500,000 Mongol troops. The Tonkinese people (also known as Viets or Vietnamese) fought diligently to defend their independence, and with only 300,000 troops, they were able to repulse the attack. Eleven years later the Mongols tried again but were once more driven back by the spirited Viets. The third major attempt to subjugate Tonkin, made by the Chinese

Ming Imperial Armies in 1407, did succeed in overpowering Tonkin. But an unprecendented guerrilla struggle which started in 1417, and lasting a decade, drove the Chinese away from the Red River valley in 1427. Thus, the independence of the Tonkin region was regained and Tonkin was strengthened as a political core.

The stability of Tonkin as a political unit depended to a great extent on the efficiency of the administrative system it employed. The Chinese departure in A.D. 939 did not mean the extinction of the Chinese administrative system; rather, the Mandarin system was further strengthened, much to the displeasure of the local feudal lords who wanted a free hand in local administration. Tonkinese monarchs maintained a strong and unified central government based on the Chinese model. As early as 1076, "a fixed hierarchy of state officials with nine degrees of civil and military mandarins" was established; examinations for public service were introduced along with the introduction of Chinese classical writings.[25] In 1225 an officers' training school was established. Thus a strong organizational framework became the base for the existence and continuation of the Tonkin core area.

As the population grew, there was a need for increased crop production. The Viets had open to them three possible ways to attain such an increase: (a) greater productivity per unit cultivated, (b) extension of arable land, and (c) colonization of foreign territories. Because the population was growing so rapidly, the Vietnamese used all three methods simultaneously.

Increased productivity was attained by extending irrigation and, from the eleventh and twelfth centuries on, allowing soldiers to work their village farms six months a year. Probably one of the most effective means of increasing productivity was the effort made to give land to landless peasants who would thus acquire greater incentive by working their *own private* farms. This idea was implemented by the strong monarch Le Thai after he drove away the Chinese in 1427. Every person in the country—men, women, children, from Mandarin down to the poorest peasant—received some land; the land, however, was never equally distributed. Members of royal families, princes, landlords, and officials continued to own large individual shares of land.

The principal technique for the expansion of arable land was dyking, deforestation and the use of cultivable wasteland. Basically, dykes are embankments along the rivers and coast which not only protect the land from the invasion of salty seawater, but also control floods and divert the needed water through a system of canals for irrigation. The construction of dykes reached a peak in 1224 under the rule of Thai Ton, an innovative sovereign who ordered the expansion of the dykes to the Gulf of Tonkin. Thai Ton also established a system of ten-family peasant cooperatives, a measure designed to ensure lasting inspection and maintenance of dykes.[26]

The fast growing population caused the Tonkin core area to resort to the tactics of "lebensraum." The only directional option open to the Tonkinese expansion was to move toward the south since that was the only direction in which extensive plains contiguous to Tonkin were available. Except to the south, the Tonkin delta is surrounded by hilly and mountainous land which was not only bad for crops, but was also incapable of supporting any sizeable number of peasants. The "March to the South" was accomplished in stages by means of infiltration and conquest. Infiltration took the form of migration in small groups to the coastal kingdom of Champa where the Viets settled on unoccupied land that was virtually waiting for them. This migration was encouraged by the Mandarins and landlords of Tonkin since it lessened pressure on their land. However, the real southward conquest began in 1427 after Tonkin was secured from the Chinese and was able to continue its existence as a powerful core area. It was also around this time that landlessness among the Tonkinese peasants had reached serious proportions, necessitating the capture of new lands outside of Tonkin. The victory over Champa was decisive in 1471 (Fig. 10-5). Then, in the eighteenth century, inroads were made into the Khmer realm of the Mekong delta. As the Viets spread into the coastal plains and the Mekong delta, their cultural as well as political penetration was massive and enduring. Therefore, the cultural pattern as seen today is the result of the southward expansion of the Tonkin core area along a relatively thin 600 mile-long strip whose northern apex was the Red River delta and whose southern limit was the Mekong delta.

French Assimilation of Tonkin

The French conquest of Tonkin occurred in 1882, i.e., twenty years after their occupation of the Mekong delta. Earlier, they had hoped to use the Mekong River for regular water-borne trade with China. Such a backdoor route would have given the French easier trade access to China, whose trade at that time was confined to the East China Sea ports. However, the Mekong proved to be useless for long-distance navigation because of the presence of many rapids; a journey to Lauang Prabang from the mouth of the Mekong required 37 days in the dry season and

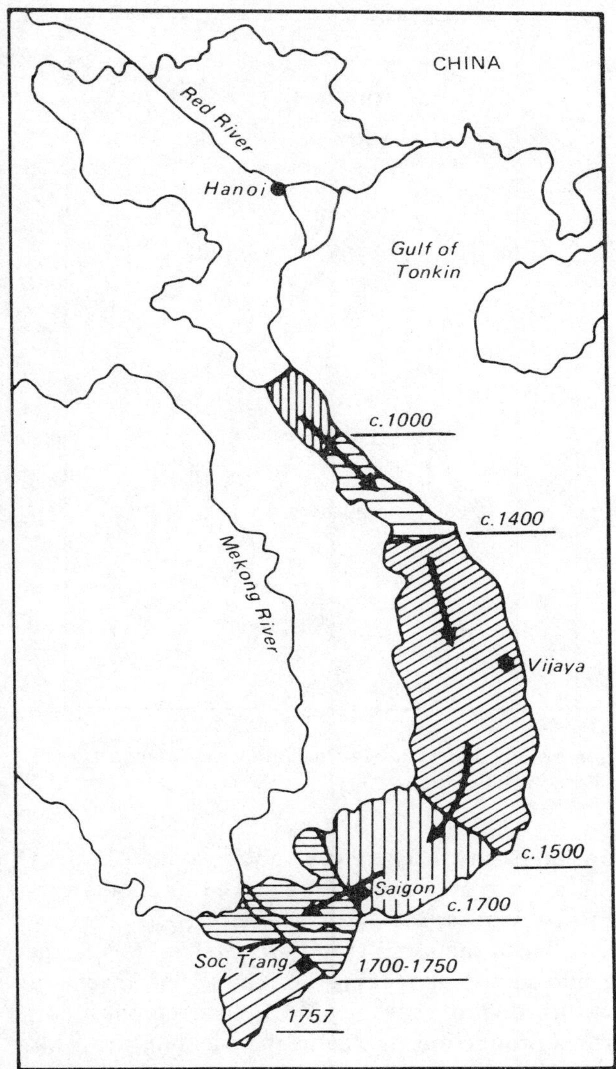

Figure 10-5. Vietnamese "March to the South" from the Tonkin Delta to the Mekong Delta.

27 days in the wet season.[27] Thus the French began to explore access to China by means of the Red River. This made it necessary to conquer Tonkin which at that time was under the kingdom of Hue. So, using the pretext of the King of Hue's sending embassies to the China and his inability to protect French traders from rebels and pirates, France initiated the conquest of Tonkin. The first target of attack was Hanoi since it was the seat of the Vietnamese viceroy of North Vietnam and housed a military citadel controlling the entire region. It fell into French hands on April 24, 1882. By 1884 the King of Hue was so weakened and helpless that he acknowledged a French protectorate status not only over Tonkin and North Vietnam, but also over his own remaining territories east of the Annamite Cordillera. Although the French dream of finding a navigable route to China by means of the Red River proved to be futile, but they were more than satisfied with their newly acquired territorial gains.

French Policy. The French policy discussed below is applicable not only to Tonkin, but is also true for the entire colony of Indochina. Since the French felt that natives of Indochina were "barbarians" who needed civilization in the French style, they thought it their humanitarian duty to rule the colony. French rule was absolute, unchallengeable, and often brutal. They consistently repressed the native Indochinese; Buttinger says, "The natives by and large remained unprotected, subject to economic exploitation and humilitating treatment, under a political dictatorship aggravated by foreign rule."[28]

Economically, the French endeavored to structure Indochina along the traditional colony-metropolitan country model in which the colony produces primary goods (agricultural, forest, and mineral products) and the metropolitan country builds its industries on the colonial plunder and raw material. Then, a portion of the manufactured goods are marketed in the colony. To accomplish this in Indochina, France encouraged the production of rice, rubber, coffee, tea, coal, zinc, and tin for export; France was never interested, however, in building industrial bases in the colony except to cater to the limited local market.

French political and economic policy was mainly guided by the *colons*, who were Frenchmen living in Indochina and working as merchants, speculators, bankers, and large landowners. Although they were few in number (only a few hundred), they held the key to the Indochinese economy and French policy was generally subservient to their interests. Many Governors General were called back to Paris if they happened to conflict with the *colons*. As in other colonies, France considered Indochina to be a humanitarian responsibility as well as an economic asset.

Socially, the Indochinese were second-class citizens in their own lands. The law was often brutal to the natives and permissive to French citizens; the French paid no taxes while the natives paid both direct taxes and heavy indirect taxes levied on alcohol, opium, and salt. Also, the natives were especially discouraged by the French to undertake secondary and higher education since *one educated native meant one less coolie*. Only lower level administrative jobs were open to the natives. The degrees for these jobs and others were obtained from the University of Hanoi, but were not recognized in France. To make matters more difficult, the French used their own language for higher education and romanized the Vietnamese script.

The true exploitative and inhuman colonial designs were always camouflaged by so-called policies of *assimilation* and *association*. While the *assimilation* policy began being advocated toward the last quarter of the 19th century, it was first strongly proclaimed by Dumer (1897–1901), the dynamic Governor General of Indochina. The policy of *association* was initiated by Governor General Sarraut in 1909. Neither of these policies presented any new ideas; they were merely old wine in new bottles.

Vietnam Divided Into Three. The long strip of Vietnam, which had a common language, heritage, and racial origin was illogically divided into three parts—Tonkin, Annam, and Cochin China—for the administrative convenience of the French (Fig. 10–6). Although Cochin China was the only legal colony, the French Governor also directly ruled the protectorates of Tonkin and Annam. Similar direct rule was also employed when Cambodia and Laos were brought under French "protection."

French Influence in Tonkin. For almost two decades, the French did not disturb the ancient Mandarin system of administration in Tonkin and Annam. Soon after Governor Dumer began to centralize the administrative functions by orienting the entire structure around French colonial interests, the scholarly and justice-oriented role of the Madarins deteriorated into corruption and decadence. Although Mandarins continued as the legal head at the village level, they were also chosen to do the dirty work for the French.[29] There were no tests used to choose them; rather their appointment depended on "service rendered to, or evident willingness to perform for, the colonial regime."[30] Such a change demolished the legal and administrative structure of the villages that had crystalized in the last 2,000 years.

In 1902, Hanoi was chosen to be the capital of French Indochina, which meant that the Tonkin core for the first time had administrative jurisdiction over the entire peninsula. Hanoi was chosen by the French because of its cool winter climate and because its surrounding region had a maximum concentration of people. Thus, many Frenchmen settled in the city who never associated with the native Vietnamese, causing a wall to develop between the Viet and French cultures. The main capital functions were later shared by Saigon.

Economically, the French strengthened the hydraulic system of Tonkin after the system had been devastated in the floods of 1926. They rebuilt the old dykes and supplemented the irrigation works with a series of new dams and canals which allowed for more efficient control of the water level on the rice-

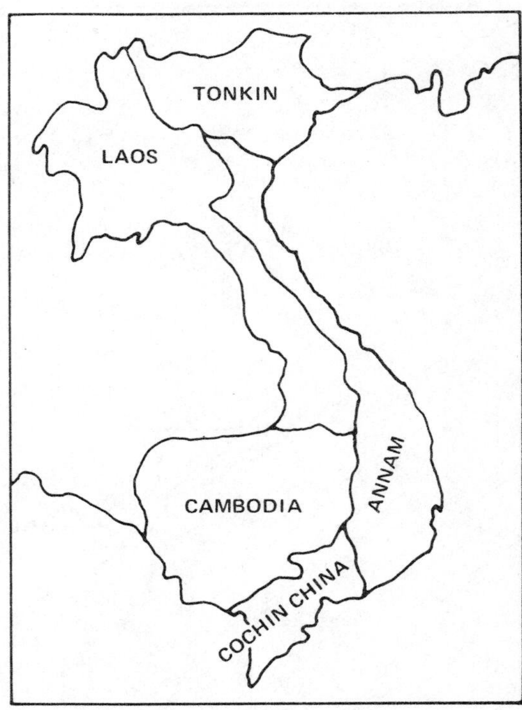

Figure 10-6. Administrative Divisons of Indochina During the French Rule.

growing basins.[31] Therefore, about a one-third of Tonkin's rice area came to be served by modern irrigation works.[32] All of these efforts further strengthened the multi-crop basis of Tonkin's farming and aimed at making Tonkin self-sufficient in agriculture. Furthermore, the French emphasis on surplus production of rice in the Mekong delta for export rather than for internal consumption, forced Tonkin to become self-sufficient as far as possible.

Beginning in Dumer's regime at the end of the nineteenth century, a vigorous effort was made to spread the network of railways into the populated areas of Vietnam—the motive being economic benefit to the colonial interests. Dumer mistakenly thought that the spread of the transport-net would automatically bring prosperity to the people, increase the supply of food and raw materials shipped to France, and facilitate the distribution of manufactured goods from France. The French made railroad connections with Long Tcheon and other areas deep in China such as Kunming only to discover that this part of China was commerically unattractive. Because of the lack of any sizeable economic gain from the railways, construction slowed down after 1910. This delayed Dumer's dream of connecting Saigon with Hanoi until the thirties.

Although the French were very cautious about not permitting Indochina to develop her own industries, they did allow a few industries to develop as long as they did not conflict with French interests. For example, cement and cotton industries were permitted. A cement factory based on nearby limestone and coal was established in Haiphong since the French felt that cement was too bulky to be imported economically from France. Because the local people were too poor to buy imported French textiles and cheap Indian textiles were flooding the local markets, the French *colons* set up large spinning mills in Hanoi, Haiphong, and Nam Dinh.[33] Tonkin could provide the needed raw cotton and men trained in textiles handicrafts for the mills. In addition, Tonkin developed as a center of other light industries such as glass bottles, pottery, rugs, rice milling, and distilling, none of which competed with French goods in the local market.

It is estimated that at the time of French occupation in 1882, Tonkin had a density of 500-600 people per square mile. After fifty years, the population density doubled because of the declining death rate which resulted from the modern health care facilities introduced by the French. This also led to additional pressure on the cultivated land and fragmentation of agricultural plots during the French rule. More than 70% of holdings were less than one acre;[34] small landholders in Tonkin accounted for 98.2% of land allocation.[35] In contrast, cultivable land in Cambodia was still plentiful and the farmers were under no pressure to use every bit of it (Fig. 10–7). Although the small landholders in Tonkin were quite skilled at cultivation, the tiny size of their plots limited their ability to make ends meet. Thus, poverty was deep-rooted and widespread.

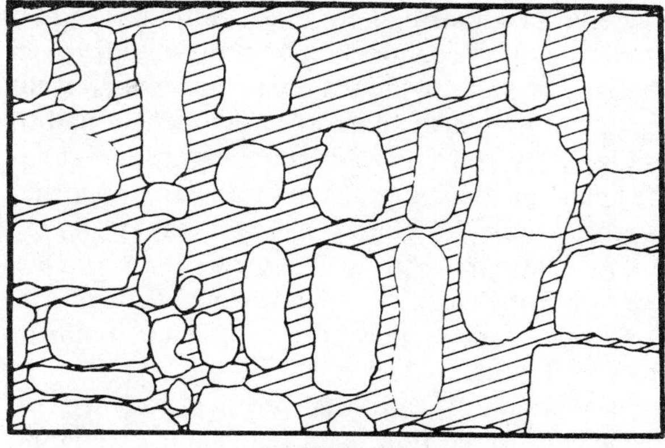

CAMBODIA

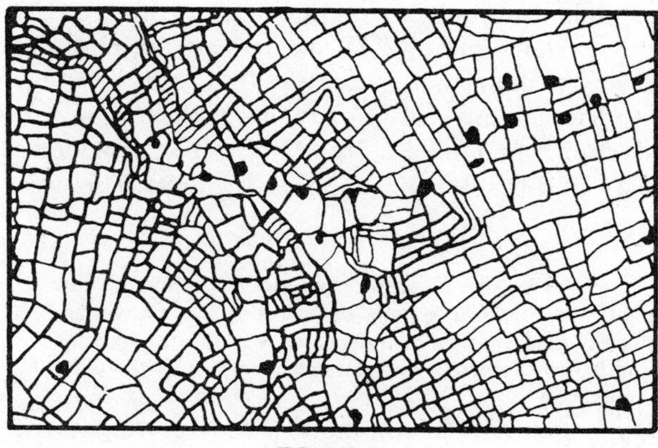

TONKIN

Source: L' Utilisation du Sol en Indochine Francaise, P. Gourou.

Figure 10-7. Parcels of Cultivated Land in Tonkin and Cambodia Before WW II (the areas indicated in the two diagrams are the same in size).

Because of large-scale poverty and antagonism against foreign rule, the communist-led rebellion against the French was centered in Tonkin. The Communists also organized an extensive resistance movement against the Japanese occupation of Indochina in World War II. Because of French success in preventing the establishment of a strong local bourgeoisie by not allowing any sizeable industrialization or higher education, there was no strong middle class in Vietnam and therefore no middle class political party available to lead the nationalistic upsurge. This vacuum was filled by the Communist Party led by Ho Chi Minh who succeeded in establishing a strong peasant-based government in Hanoi in 1946. Although Ho was soon driven out of Hanoi by the French, his provisional government still ruled much of North Vietnam and the Red River delta. When the French were finally forced out of Indochina in 1954, the Communists organized a government of their own in North Vietnam. This opened a new era of *one-party rule*, socialization of the means of production and new interpretations to old social values.

Communization of Tonkin

Since 1954 the Government of North Vietnam, which designated itself as the Democratic Republic of Vietnam, has developed a basic political system of Communist Party rule. In this system, the party and its top hierarchical unit, the Politburo, have the most power in designing government policies. The state was organized on the basis of the renunciation of private property and state control of the means of production, exchange and communication. The party members advocated the nonexistence of gods and spirits in which the Tonkin people had so deeply believed. They also tried to inculcate in the poeple of North Vietnam a sense of sacrificing for a national cause which included: (1) the reunification of North and South Vietnams, (2) help in the "liberation" struggles of neighboring Laos and Cambodia, and (3) the building of an economic base in the country even at the cost of an individual's own comfort and well-being. In other words, narrow individualism had to be replaced by collective thinking. Because of state-owned mass media and efficient means of indoctrination, the people of North Vietnam had probably begun to believe quite strongly in their system and the objectives of the party. This has enabled this state to be one of the most powerful and viable political centers in Southeast Asia.

Such a viability had been further accented by strategic land connections with the People's Republic of China. Since China became a communist country in 1949, the Vietnamese Communists have taken from that country not only ideological thought but also material supplies. The strength of the relationship was so great that one of the first tasks after the North Vietnamese victory of 1954 was the building of the Hanoi-Nam Quam railroad link which provided a regular land-based connection with China. This was completed in 1955.[36]

> The Hanoi-Nam Quam railroad not only links up with the Chinese railroad system, but also provides an overland route to the Soviet Union and Eastern Europe, thus connecting North Vietnam with the other countries of the Communist bloc.[37]

The communist brotherhood was so strong in the case of North Vietnam, even in the face of Sino-Soviet differences, that all communist countries (particularly the U.S.S.R. and the People's Republic of China) continually made up the food deficit in the Red River delta.[38] For several decades this area has been an endemic center of food scarcity. Much of the shortage before 1954 was met by imports from the Mekong delta. To make food matters worse, the population of the Red River delta was growing as much as 3.5% annually.

As compared with the period before World War II, gross rice production had almost doubled in the 1960s, however, the increase had been negated by an even greater increase in population. Hardworking Tonkin farmers not only fertilize their fields by widespread use of dried night-soils, but also irrigate their lands so that more than one crop can be grown from the same plot. Rice production per acre in the Red River delta is very high—over 1,500 pounds per acre. Also the winter rainfall helps grow a second crop. The work-land ratio in the delta in the 1960s, was very close, 1:1.2, which indicated that agriculture is highly labor intensive.

> It takes forty times as many man-hours to grow a pound of rice in North Vietnam as it does in Japan. The imperative need of course is rationalization of the agricultural sector—mechanization, greater use of (chemical) fertilizer, new varieties of seeds, etc.[39]

The increase in rice production after 1954 is credited to collectivization of North Vietnamese farming, in which land, cattle, and other means of production now belong to the community and each individual farmer's earning depended on his hours of work. In the 1960, as many as 95% of the country's families belonged to the 5,000 communes or collective farms.[40] Soviet experience with collectivization has shown that after the initial production increase, the pace slows down in a collective system. The Red River delta had probably already reached such a slow-down stage. Collectivization of rice crops poses some additional problems. Wet rice cultivation needs a great deal of individual care from the nursery stage through the harvesting.[41] Since the farmers feel the collectives belong to everybody, it is doubtful if such care could be generated efficiently. However, a different type of rice cultivation similar to that in California can be done efficiently on a capital intensive basis.

Although mechanization of agriculture would appear to be one of the primary tasks of North Vietnam, it was impossible to achieve under present conditions because it would mean unemployment or underemployment for a large number of agricultural laborers. Also, any spectacular future growth of the industrial sector did not seem probable despite the great emphasis given to industrial development. As much as 80% of North Vietnam's total labor force of 10 million was engaged in food production in early 1970s.[42]

The Red River delta has, no doubt, the greatest potentiality in terms of industrial development in Indochina for five reasons: (1) the availability of ample mineral resources in the nearby A.C.N. Mountains, (2) the climatic diversity which enables the area to produce a wide variety of agricultural raw materials, such as cotton and sugarcane, (3) a stable, well-secured government which visualizes the prosperity of the country mainly through industrialization, (4) easy access to the sea by means of well-established ports like Haiphong, and (5) the recent development of efficient road and railroad communication throughout the delta. France had recognized such potentialities and started to develop cement, textile, and other light industries; however, since 1954, chemical and heavy industries have been particularly emphasized. There has been "backyard" production of several thousand tons of cast iron. In addition, a modern steel plant has been opened in Thai Nguyen and several thermo-phosphate and nitrogenous fertilizer plants have been installed. Other industries of the Red River delta include electric power, mechanical construction, petroleum refining, building materials including cement, cotton textile weaving, food processing (including rice husking mills), paper, rubber, glass, and other light industries.[43]

Tonkin: The Most Viable Core Area in Indochina. Despite Tonkin's difficulty in feeding her people and the heavy bombing of her installations and cities by American planes between 1965 and 1973, she has been able to sustain herself with a stable government, mobilize her people for the war of "liberation," and acculturate her people with new socialist values. When a situation combines with a glorious cultural history, it gives rise to a volatile community which can be used either for territorial/ideological expansion or for internal prosperity. During 1954–75, Tonkin emphasized the cause of extension by helping to organize *liberation* struggles of the Pathet Lao, the Viet Cong (or the Provisional Government of South Vietnam), and the Khmer Rouge. While extension into Laos and Cambodia might not have any colonial type of design, extensionist activities in South Vietnam was definitely for the reunification of Vietnam. The fact remains that due to the strength of the Tonkin core, communist occupation succeeded in all parts of the Indochinese land area.

In 1973, as a result of protracted negotiations in Paris, a ceasefire was agreed upon among all warring parties in Vietnam. The United States' bombing stopped and their troops withdrew from active fighting in Indochina. It seemed for a time that a real peace had come, but after only a year, fierce fighting broke out between the communist-led Provisional Government and Saigon's US-backed Thieu Government. The result was a victory to the Communists in April of 1975 and a final reunification of the North and South Vietnam in 1976. Thus, after a lapse of over a century, the Viets are again one country.

Hanoi became the capital of the new united Vietnam in 1976. From this capital the government leaders commanded an army of over one million: the fourth largest standing army in the world. In 1980, the country's military budget was 28% of the national income and 47% of the total state expenditure; an enormous waste for a country which was trying to take-off to fast industrialization.[44]

One of the expected results of the North-South unification was the overcoming of the chronic food shortages of Tonkin with the Mekong delta surplus. This did not materialize because of the force employed in the collectivization of farms in the South and the reluctance of the farmers there to produce a surplus. The result has been that until the mid-eighties almost 2 million tons of grain was imported annually. Thus the country's scarce resources had to be diverted from any industrialization process in order to feed the people. Though the Tonkin region is the best endowed in Indochina for industrial development, nothing much can succeed there until the Mekong delta improves its rice production and the country's defense budget is drastically slashed to divert limited resources for Tonkin's development.

Footnote References

[1]E.H.G. Dobby, *Southeast Asia* (London: University Press, 1966), p. 315.

[2]Shannon McCune, "The Diversity of Indochina's Physical Geography," *Far Eastern Quarterly*, Vol. 6 (August, 1947), p. 337.

[3]Norton Ginsburg, editor, *The Pattern of Asia* (New Jersey: Prentice-Hall, Inc., 1958), p. 416.

[4]Donald Fryer, *Emerging Southeast Asia* (New York: McGraw-Hill Book Company, 1970), p. 398.

[5]Ginsburg, p. 420.

[6]C.S. Ramage, *Monsoon Meteorology* (New York: Academic Press, 1971), 38.

[7]Dobby, p. 42.

[8]Dobby, p. 309.

[9]They undertake wet-rice cultivation in the valleys where annual deposits of alluvium from the highlands make the land fertile.

[10]*Area Handbook for Vietnam* (Washington, D.C.: U.S. Government Printing Office, 1962), p. 58.

[11]Fryer, p. 426.

[12]*Ibid.*

[13]Frank N. Trager, *Why Vietnam* (New York: Frederick A. Praeger, Inc., 1966), p. 16.

[14]Joseph Buttinger, *Vietnam: A Political History* (New York: Frederick A. Praeger, Inc., 1968), p. 26.

[15]*Ibid.*, p. 25.

[16]*Ibid.*

[17]Charles A. Fisher, *Southeast Asia* (London: Methuen & Co., 1964), p. 531.

[18]For more information see Ashok K. Dutt, "Level of Planning in the Netherlands, with Particular Reference to Regional Planning," *Annals of the Association of American Geographers,* Vol. 58, No. 4 (December, 1968), pp. 670–685; Ashok K. Dutt and Robert B. Monier, "Zuyder Zee Project," *Journal of Geography*, Vol. 67, No. 6 (September, 1968), pp. 374–377; Johan Von Veen, *Dredge Drain Reclaim* (The Hague: Martinus Nijhoff, 1962); Ashok K. Dutt and Frank J. Costa, *Public Planning in the Netherlands* (Oxford: Clarendon Press, 1984).

[19]Fisher, p. 89.

[20]Trager, p. 18.

[21]Paul K. Benedict, "Languages and Literatures of Indochina," *Far Eastern Quarterly*, Vol. 6 (August, 1947), p. 387.

[22]Trager, p. 18.

[23]Buttinger, p. 18.

[24]Hanoi, which means "capital of the East" in Vietnamese, was recaptured by the Chinese in the early 7th century A.D. and thereafter, for over 800 years, witnessed only occasional destruction by Chinese armies, local Tonkinese aspirants for the throne and Chams from Champa.

[25]Buttinger, p. 41.

[26]*Ibid.*

[27]*Area Handbook for Vietnam*, p. 37.

[28]Joseph Buttinger, *Vietnam: A Dragon Embattled*, Vol. I (New York: Frederick A. Praeger, Inc., 1967), p. 102.

[29]*Ibid.*, p. 177.

[30]*Ibid.*

[31]Fisher, p. 546.

[32]*Ibid.*

[33]*Ibid.*, p. 545.

[34]*Ibid.*, p. 546.

[35]Buttinger, 1967, p. 521.

[36]Theodore Shabad, "Economic Developments in North Vietnam," *Pacific Affairs*, Vol. 31 (1958), p. 49.

[37]*Ibid.*

[38]Fifteen percent of the food eaten by the North Vietnamese must be imported.

[39]Douglas Pike, "North Vietnam in 1971," *Asian Survey*, Vol. XII, No. 1 (January, 1972), p. 21.

[40]*Ibid.*, p. 18.

[41]Hoang Van Chi, "Collectivisation and Rice Production," in *North Vietnam Today*, P.J. Honey, editor, (New York: Frederick A. Praeger, Inc. 1962).

[42]Pike, p. 21.

[43]P.H.M. Jones, "The Industry of North Vietnam," *Far Eastern Economic Review*, Vol. 29 (1960), pp. 653–654.

[44]Douglas Pike, "Vietnam in 1980: The Gathering Storm?", *Asian Survey*, Vol. XXI, No. 1 (1981) p. 87.

Chapter 11

Indochina: Evolution of the Core Areas of Champa, the Mekong Delta, Angkor, and the Upper Mekong Valley

Ashok K. Dutt

COASTAL PLAINS AND CHAMPA

A narrow coastal plain about 500 miles long connects the Red river delta with the Mekong Delta. This plain once gave rise to the powerful kingdom of Champa. West of this strip, the Annamite Cordillera rises abruptly; however, at many points, particularly in the south, the Cordillera breaks the continuity of the coastal plain by extending across it to drop sharply to the shores of the South China Sea. Thus, access via the coastal plain from the south was never as easy as it was from the north. This discontinuous coastal strip is generally only a few miles wide although it approaches 40 miles width in the north.

The coastal plain evolved in recent geologic times with the accumulation of alluvium carried by short streams which originated in the Cordillera. A number of small deltas, such as the one at Hue, occur along the plain. Like the Tonkin plains, the coastal strip shows some variation in relief with *levees* along streams, sand dunes along the coast, and patches of old-alluvium.[1]

During the mid-eighth century the Champa capital at Panduranga[2] was established (Fig. 11-1). The coastal plain north of Mui Dinh to the Tonkin Delta is fertile and humid enough to grow rice. In this area the land is capable of producing two or three rice crops per year becasce of additional winter rainfall related to moisture bearing northeast trade winds. However, despite high potential agricultural productivity, the coastal strip north of Hue never became a political core area; as a result of location along a frontier zone with Tonkin, from time to time this land changed hands between Champa and Tonkin. Instability and political insecurity were the consequences.

Although typhoons may inflict maximum damage to this region, several embayments, such as Cam Ranh Bay (Vinh Cam Ranh) and Da Nang Bay provide excellent natural shelter and anchorage, even for modern deep-draft ships. No wonder that within historic times this coast harbored one of the strongest sea powers of Southeast Asia: the naval fleet of the Chams.

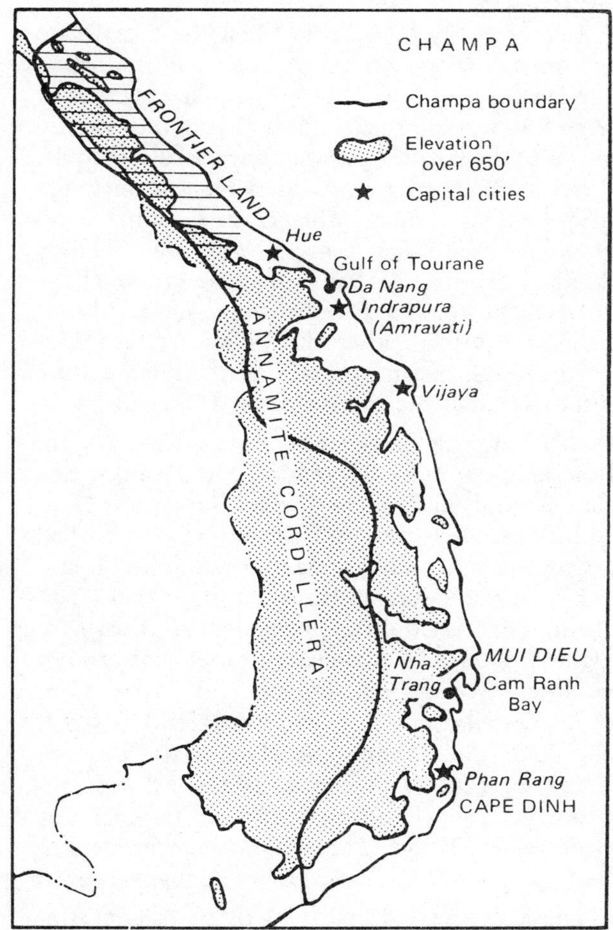

Figure 11-1. Champa: Boundary of Kingdom and Capitals.

The Origin of Cham Power

Chams, Malayo-Polynesian peoples who landed on the eastern coast of Vietnam well before the Christian era, formed the nucleus of a great power known, in Chinese, as Lin-i and Chan-Ch'eng and in Indian Sanskrit, as Champa. Champa in Sanskrit refers to a type of fragrant Indian flower. *"Cham* is the oldest of the 'naturalized' languages of Indochina and might well be looked upon as a 'native son' in terms of squatters' right."[3] Ironically, only a few hundred people now speak this language. Champa, once a flourishing empire with a distinct heritage, culture, and language, has been almost entirely assimilated by Viets who marched south from the Tonkin delta. Let us examine what geographical and other forces caused the rise and decline of Champa.

It was probably in A.D. 192 that the first Cham kingdom was founded with its capital in the region around what is now Hue.[4] The Chams wanted "Lebensraum" and their logical direction of expansion was to the north. They were successful in acquiring part of the northern provinces from Chinese occupied Tonkin. Indian influence in Champa dates back to the midfourth century when the Champa king Bhadravarman (a Sanskrit name) adopted the cult of Siva worship for his state. Quang Nam, known as Amravati after the Indian Pallava Kindgom's capital, became the center of Indian culture and the capital of the empire in the fifth century.

Indianization in Champa was exclusively Hindu. All the later capitals—Indrapura, Panduranga, and Vijya —were given Sanskrit names. Hardly any Buddhist influence occurred until the ninth century when the Cham king, Indravarman II, adopted India-based Mahayana Buddhism. Since the Chams had evidently established direct sea connections with India, the process of Indianization developed directly from India, not through Funan, Angkor, or Lopburi. These sea connections were apparently a result of the China-India trade route which passed through Champa. Perhaps further proof of these direct connections is suggested by the experience of *Gangaraja,*[5] the fifth century Cham king who went to India to bathe in the scared Ganges (Ganga) river.

Champa represented a particularly traditional Hindu way of life. Along with Siva, other Hindu gods, such as Brahma, were worshipped. Widows did not remarry. Queens joined the funeral pyre of their deceased husbands and were known as *Suties*. (*Suti*, widow self-immolation, was in vogue in India until the early nineteenth century.) The Chams also regarded cows as sacred. They practiced Yoga and studied Sanskrit.[6] As in India, the Chams sounded conches and drums as warning signals. The Hindu custom of cremation was also practiced in Champa, and the unburnt remaining bones of the dead were thrown into a river or ocean.[7] Cham generals were termed *Senapati* (chief of army), as were Indian generals, and the Commander-in-chief as *Mahasenapati.*[8]

In many ways, the Indianization of Champa was similar to that of its neighbor Funan and later of Angkor. In all three areas the kings suffixed the Sanskrit royal title of *Varman* to their names. They accepted the cult of Devaraja (god king). Funan, and Angkor, as well as Champa, hired *Brahmins* for their courts to perform rituals and pronounce omens for the kingdom. Considerable energy was spent to erect temples, but Angkor surpassed all limits in this connection. Everywhere, Indian influence was generated by peaceful means.

Despite such similarities, Angkor and Champa differed in the geographic orientation of their empires. The former, because of its primary base on an interior plain, was a land power; however, the coastal geographic situation of Champa influenced it to look to the sea as the basis of its power.

The limited area of the narrow coastal strip of Champa definitely placed limits for the provision of a strong agricultural base required by a great power. Possibilities for expansion were limited. The Annamite Cordillera was a real barrier to westward land acquisiton. Also, to the west were the powerful Khmers who had previously expelled a small number of Chams from Chenla. The only broad and level land connection Champa had was with Tonkin to the north, but Tonkin was a powerful neighbor. The Chams naturally turned to the sea in the east and, nevertheless, to the mountains in the west, the Cordillera for resource exploitation. Although the mountains were agriculturally unproductive and could not support any sizeable number of people, the mountain forests became the Cham source of camphor, sandalwood, ebony, lead and tin which were used primarily for export. Marco Polo, who passed by Champa in 1278, left the following account:

> There are very great number of elephants[9] in this kingdom, and they have lignaloes[10] (fragrant wood) in great abundance. They have also extensive forest of wood called Bonu's (ebony) which is jet-black, and of which chessman and pen-cases are made.[11]

The chams eventually developed a strong naval force which for over 1,300 years protected their existence as an independent and powerful empire. At times the Chams had a fleet of more than 100 turreted vessels. Their navy commanders were usually royal princes. They even functioned as semipirates at sea. Many ships at that time did not venture to travel on the open seas, preferring to take a safer coastal route. Champa's naval extortionists forced coastal plying ships to pay a tariff of 20% of their cargo value. By means of direct sea piracy, Chams also captured slaves who were either employed in their own country or traded to other kingdoms. The greater portion of Cham maritime income was probably gained from such semipiracy.[12] Beginning about A.D. 431, the Cham fleet began pillaging Tonkin coasts for either simple material gains or political reasons. With such naval expeditions, the Tonkin capital was sacked by the Chams several times in history. In 803, the Cham King Harivarman made sea attacks on Chinese provinces north of Hoan-son. The Cham navy also sacked Angkor in 1177.

Champa fleets were aided by certain prevailing winds. Sailing boats of Champa took advantage of southwesterly winds between October and February for their southern travels. With such climatic advantages, meagreness of land-based resources and a long coastline, the Cham kings and peoples had little alternative but to look to the sea for their prosperity.

Decline and Eclipse of Champa

Because Champa was unable to expand via land, she was eventually squeezed to death after the Viets to the north secured their independence in A.D. 939 and began to move outward. In 982, the Viets attacked and subsequently occupied the northern frontiers along Champa's coast. For almost 500 years, there were land and sea struggles between Champa and the Viets. During this period, the pillage and destruction of each other's capital was a routine affair.

The Viets had an enormous advantage over the Chams because their extensive fertile delta (Tonkin) was not only capable of feeding a large population, but also a great source of resources. Moreover, by applying innovative farming techniques, the Viets were able to produce a much greater agricultural surplus whereas the Chams were extremely limited in internal resources. Partly because of agricultural limitations, Champa degenerated into an inferior power and eventually succumbed to the successful southern march of the Viets.

Because Champa realized that the real threat to its existence was to come from the north, it decided to relocate her capital to an area farther south. The first attempt at relocation took place in the fifth century when the capital was shifted from the Hue region to Amravati also known as Indrapura (Quang Nam). However, this shift was also intended to put the capital in the heart of the country. Later, in the middle of the eighth century, the capital was moved farther south to Panduranga (Phan Rang), only to be brought back to Indrapura in 875. Nevertheless, in 988, the capital was moved south again, this time to Vijya (Binh-Dinh Province), the last Cham capital. This final movement of the capital from Indrapura was a great blow to the Chams because Indrapura was not only within the heart of the country, but also close to the holy city of My-Son with its protective god Bhadrashvara. As a result of the removal of its capital from the vicinity of My-Son, "Champa was like a body deprived of its essential organs."[13]

Realizing their survival was in danger, the Chams turned to China for help; however, China did not provide the support necessary to avert the Viet threat from Tonkin. Since its western neighbor, Angkor, was already an enemy of Champa, her leaders turned to the Moslem countries of Malacca and Java for protection. Cham rulers adopted Islam as their religion probably during their final struggle with the Viets in 1470–71.[14] Vietnamese occupation of Champa was decisive in 1471, for the Viets advanced and occupied lands as far as Mui Dieu. The eclipse of Champa accounted for a mass migration of Moslem Chams to Java and Malaysia. The two-thirds of the Chams who remainded continued to be influenced by Hindu traditions.[15]

The Viets in the Coastal Strip

After the demise of the main Champa kingdom, the entire coastal strip became a frontier land for the Viets who, in the sixteenth century, embarked on a conquest of the remaining small Cham kingdoms south of Mui Dieu. Thus the Viets with their political system influenced by China, with their intensive agricultural practices, and with their own version of Buddhism affected the Hinduized coastal strip. Today, a few Hindu traditions are noticeable along this coast. Buddhism replaced Hinduism; Chinese and Vietnamese languages replaced Sanskrit and Cham; and the Buddha image replaced Siva and Brahma in the temples. Sanskritized names such as Panduranga became Vietnamized to Phan Rang. The Tonkin-type mandarin system was introduced in the political sphere.

The southward expansion of Viets created two problems: the divison of the country into two parts, and the shift of the national capital south from Hanoi to Hue. In 1560 the royal Nguyen king, originally of Hanoi, gained control of the coastal strip and began to operate from the newly established capital of Hue as an independent sovereign free of Hanoi. Such division was the natural culmination of the weakening of the central power still at Hanoi. After an extended war (1620–70), the Nguyen family regime obtained final control of the coastal strip. Thus, two Vietnams, North and South, came into existence. The Wall of Donghoi, almost at the 17th parallel, was built north of Hue to separate the two areas physically. Hue remained the southern capital. The Nguyen kings of Hue marched further south seizing the Mekong delta from Khmer Cambodia, thus renewing their resource base. In 1802, Nguyens conquered the Tonkin delta and extended their territory from the Mekong delta to the Red river delta, the land known thereafter as Vietnam. Hue remained the capital but was now given greater status as an Imperial Capital. From a geographic standpoint, the intermediate location of Hue between Tonkin in the North and the Mekong delta in the South made it a logical choice for a national capital.

Annam Under the French

As stated in the foregoing chapter, the Imperial Kingdom of Hue succumbed to French pressure . After the French conquest of the eastern coast of Vietnam in 1884, the king of Hue became known as the king of Annam. The French named the central portion of Vietnam the Protectorate of Annam. Any internal authority the king has was completely taken away by the time Dumer became the French Governor General. Thus, the Hue core not only lost its national leadership, but fell under foreign rule. The king of Annam, with minimized grandeur and practically no power, continued to exist until the French left Indochina.

The French were not particularly interested in the coastal strip since it was not potentially rich in surplus food or in raw materials. Although the coastal plains were extremely fertile as far south as Binh Dinh and two or more crops (mainly rice) were cultivated because of summer and winter rainfall, the area was so heavily populated that no surplus was available for export. In addition, the French had no interest in the supplementary occupation of fishing in which the coastal people were extremely specialized.

The only important development in this area effectuated by the French was the construction of longitudinal railroads and highways along the entire coastal strip. The French desire to connect Saigon with Hanoi accounted largely for the north-south transport routes. However, such a link definitely made the entire coast accessible by all means of transport—rail, road and sea.

The Divided Coastal Strip After 1954

When North and South Vietnam were divided along the 17th parallel in 1954, the coastal strip was also split—the northern part falling under North Vietnam and the southern part under South Vietnam. Thus, two different political and economic systems were imposed on a group of people having the same cultural heritage and living in the same natural area. Taking into consideration the strength developed in the Hanoi core (backed by Peking and Moscow) and the Saigon core (backed by Washington), the importance of the coastal strip remained in the shadows and it had little possibility of developeng into a vaiable core in the near future. Viet Cong capital, Dong Ha, lay in this strip between 1973-75.

MEKONG DELTA AND FUNAN

The Mekong delta, which lies mainly in the southern segment of Vietnam, is of recent geological origin. Sedimentary accumulations from five distributaries of the Mekong river and from three small, but independent, rivers—the Song Vam Co, the Song Sai Gon (Saigon), and the Song Dong Nai—created the delta. Since the delta was built by deposition of new alluvium, the soils are extremely fertile and can be cultivated up to its seaward extremity. The other main distributaries of the Mekong, the Song Hau Giang (Bassac), bifurcates at Phnom Penh and flows south of the Mekong. Between the Mekong and the Song Hau Giang lies Mesopotamia which, like other parts of the delta, is highly susceptible to flooding. Flooding on the delta occurs twice a year, once in July-August due to local rains and waters from melting of snow at the head water region, which swell the Mekong river, and again in November when the Tonle Sap resumes its normal flow back to the Mekong.

Most of the delta has an average elevation of only ten feet above sea level. The only bits of higher elevations are linear ridges of levees and former shore dunes located along both banks of existing or former channels. Because these slightly elevated areas escape inundation, they are coveted sites for human settlements.

Although the 2,800-mile long Mekong is one of the largest rivers in the world, it has only limited use for navigation due to several rapids that occur at various levels along its course. The last rapid is located at Kompong Cham, only 70 miles north of Phnom Penh. Mudbanks and sandbars also prevent deep draft ships from entering delta streams. Only the Song Sai Gon allows modern ships with up to 19 foot drafts to enter Saigon.

Since no area in the delta has less than 45 inches of rainfall a year, rice may be grown everywhere. Warm year-round temperatures are an additional advantage for rice cultivation.

Rise and Fall of the Funan Core

Funan, as it is called by the Chinese, developed its powerful core area with a capital on the Mekong delta at Vyadhapura (present-day Banam). Vyadhapura served as the capital during most of the Funan period. As early as the third century, Fan-tan, king of Funan, extended his empire westward to the Malay peninsula. Funan's relatively high stage of civilization made it powerful. The nation had a productive agricultural base made possible by the cultivation of the delta's watery terrain. Another aspect of civilization was its adoption of certain valuable Indian cultural traits. Funan, thus, grew into a viable organized community in the delta, which in addition maintained a strong contingent of maritime vessels that were responsible for most of its expansion.

Perhaps, Indochina would have developed into a respectable civilization even if it had been left to itself. The introduction of Chinese and Indian cultures which were more advanced than those of native Tonkin or Funan gave the region an initial impetus which resulted in a stepped-up development of the region. The Funan society and political system were highly influenced by Indian 'conquests'. Unlike the Chinese conquest in Tonkin, the Indian conquest was nonviolent and spiritual. Rene Grousset described the Indian influence as one of the greatest contributions to mankind.[16]

Indians came to Funan and the Mekong Delta for trade to collect more spices such as cardamom, pepper, and cloves, and to acquire precious items such as rare stones, rhinoceros horn, and ivory. These items were meant primarily to be exported to the Middle East and Europe, a sea trade already established by India in the first few centuries A.D. Indian traders who depended on the southwest monsoon to move their sailing ships from southern Indian coasts to Indochina, sailed back to India in winter with the help of northeasterly winds. During these several month long waiting periods, large Indian colonies were periodically established in the Mekong delta. Some colonists began to raise food crops according to their cultural traditions; some married local girls and princesses; all worshipped their own gods, Siva, Vishnu, or Buddha; and built their own temples. Such cultural-spiritual colonies of India were established in foreign lands in a sporadic and unplanned fashion. However, within the limits of such disorganization, there lay an embryo of a systematic society which eventually fertilized into mass acculturation and the Indianization of Funan. Although it is difficult to trace the exact beginnings of such Indianization, accounts of Chinese ambassadors showed that the Indian way of life was firmly established by the third century A.D.

The location of the Mekong delta, halfway between India and China, provided many advantages for setting up Indian trading outposts. Delta streams and banks made excellent landing places, mostly free from typhoons. There was already established an organized community of Funan people who recognized the importance of international trade. The forest and mountains of Cambodia offered rich resources which were readily sought by Indians. Finally, Funan had fertile and extensive cultivatable land. Thus, "everything conspired to make it the junction for all the trade of Southeast Asia."[17]

Although Indian influence had an early impact, greater influence occurred when Indian princes and Brahmins began to ascend the royal throne, chiefly by marrying native princesses. About A.D. 357, an Indian, possibly of Scythian origin and descendant of the Indian king Kaniska, ruled Funan and introduced the worship of the sun-god *Surya*. The most important of Indian rulers of Funan was Kaudinya-Jayavarman who ruled between 478 and 514 and, according to Chinese accounts, completely Indianized the customs of Funan.

> He probably (1) systematized and extended the worship of Indian deities (doubtless introduced by earlier Kaundinya), especially the state worship of the Sivalinga; (2) introduced and put into force the Laws of Manu; (3) introduced a central Indian alphabet; and (4) honorific title of Varman, which was suffixed to another name having a religious or political significance to form the name of a king or other person of exalted rank.[18]

Aside from the introduction of the central Indian alphabet, used even today in Kampuchea and Laos, Sanskirt became the literary and ritual language. The Laws of Manu, *Manu Smrti*, originated in India and date back to the second or first century B.C. These laws gave Funan an integrated philosophy of life and systematized the social and political organization of the time. The idea of the divine origin of kings came from the Laws of Manu, where it was said that the king is formed of essential particles derived from different gods.[19] Such belief made the king almighty and a living representative of the gods on earth. The king was also supposed to look after the well-being of his subjects by organizing his administration into several departments (limbs).[20] Also, Indian mathematics and astronomy, the glories of which had attained great heights in India during the Gupta Empire (A.D. 320–535) were introduced in Funan making possible the formulation of an accurate calendar which helped both in planting rice crops according to the rhythm of monsoons and in regulating the oceanic voyages which depended so much on seasonal monsoon winds.

Colonizers from southern India who had had experience with irrigation and land reclamation in Tamilnadu extended their knowledge in Funan. Spiderweb canals were dug; all were interconnected and originated from the Hau Giang river. These canals met the sea in the south, southeast, and west by following the natural slope of the land. Remnants of this canal system can still be recognized from air photos. Like the present-day multipurpose river valley projects, Funan's canal network served several purposes. Salt from the sea was prevented from being deposited on the delta plain, allowing the opening of large tracts of fertile alluvial land for intensive cultivation. Fresh water from Hau Giang was obtained to irrigate fields during the dry season. Ships of relatively deep draft were able to sail to inland towns.[21]

International trade became the backbone of Funan's prosperity and spread from China to Rome. The principal military strength of Funan was its navy. The Funan core, formed in the Mekong delta swamps, looked to water both as a resource and as a means of expansion. Its cities, built on artificial or natural levees, were surrounded by a series of earthen embankments and moats. Because canals extended into the cities, the loading and unloading of items of national and international trade was easy. Thus, water became the lifehood of the common people, who eventually mastered naval and seafaring techniques.

The eclipse and decline of Funan was the result of its land vulnerability. Chenla, a former vassal of Funan and located inland to the north, grew in strenth due to continued new migration from China and Indian acculturation through Funan. Chenla, continentally oriented and with a strong land army, annexed Funan shortly before the middle of the sixth century and turned it into a vassal. At the beginning of the seventh century, Funan was completely absorbed by Chenla (Fig. 11–2). After that, the core area of Funan was obliterated, and no other place on the Mekong delta developed into a core until the fifteenth century, when disintergrating Khmer kings of Angkor moved their capital near Phnom Penh. Thereafter for the following four centuries the Khmer kings based on the Phnom Penh core were busy maintaining their own independent status.

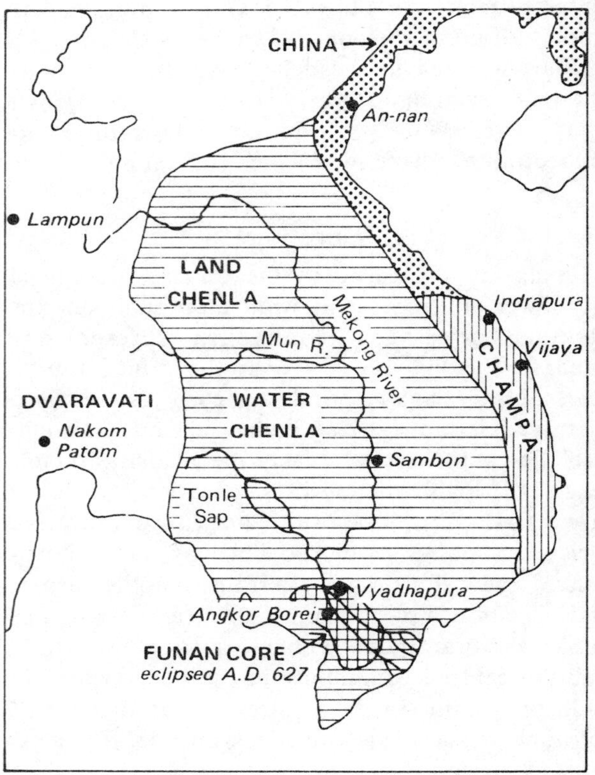

Figure 11-2. Political Boundaries in the Mid-Eight Century A.D. with the Funan Core Area That Eclipsed in A.D. 627.

Mekong Delta on the Eve of French Occupation

The Mekong delta turned into a frontier land for the Vietnamese who advanced into the area from the north. Before the French conquest of the Mekong delta in 1862–63, the Cambodian royal kings ruled a shrinking territory from the capital of Ondong. The Vietnamese and Siamese had already usurped the eastern and western parts respectively of the old Khmer kingdom. At one time during the nineteenth century, Cambodia had become a vassal of Siam and Vietnam and paid tribute to both. In addition, the Siamese vassal of Champassak began to expand at the expense of the Khmer kindgom's northern lands. Such shrinkage of the Cambodian kingdom was the result of its own political weakness and land vulnerability from the north, west, and east. The eastern part of the delta became vulnerable because of the Vietnamese migration in the seventeenth century (Fig.10–3). Prior to that time, the eastern Mekong delta was mostly unexploited virgin land forming an ideal noman's land frontier between the Chams and Khmers.

With the Vietnamese advance into the Mekong delta, there occurred a direct cultural confrontation between the Sinicized Viet and the Indian Khmer cultures. Both cultures had established strong value systems. Viets believed in a Chinese-based Confucian Buddhism which had been assimilated with local animism, whereas Cambodian Khmers were Theravada Buddhists. Khmer and Viet language bases were unrelated. Furthermore, the Viets were organized into communes at the village level and elected a council of men to look after the well-being of the community, to pay communal taxes to the king, and to solve local problems. The Khmers, on the other hand, were more individualistically oriented. A well organized mandarin administrative system[22] existed in the Viet society in which the mandarin administrators were selected from those who were successful in passing a test. In the Khmer system, the administrators were appointed by the king, or his appointees, and were often chosen on a basis of heredity. In this system the king commanded as much respect as a god for the people virturally depended on him. However, in the Viet system, the king relied more on an efficient organization based on communes for the kingdom despite the assumption that the emperor was the son of heaven. When these two cultures confronted each other, the politically more powerful Viets, with their core in Hue, not only pushed the Khmers from most of the delta, but also assimilated the remaining ones into their own culture, with several Khmer traits becoming part of the Viet culture. There still exist some Cambodians in the Vietnamese part of the Mekong delta who adhere to their own ancient traditions.

French in the Mekong Delta

French occupation of the Mekong Delta was legalized by the treaties of 1862 and 1863 when Cochin China and Cambodia were brought under French control. Saigon, already grown into a trading center, was chosen to be the French headquarters for Indochina. Although the capital was shifted to Hanoi in 1902, Saigon not only continued to act as a southern capital with the Governor General spending part of his time there, it provided several capital functions. Saigon was a French creation, with a deep French architectural imprint in its buildings and general atmosphere. Saigon is located on the natural levee of the Sai Gon river which provides a sizeable land area free of inundation for settlement. In addition, the riverine location enabled Saigon to become a seaport, suiting French trade and military strategies.

Immediately after the conquest of Cochin China in 1862, the French turned to subjugate the Cambodian kingdom in the northwestern part of the Mekong delta for two reasons. Possession of Cambodia was necessary if the Mekong was to be used for access to China. In addition, Cambodia's instability could make it easily available to Siam working in collaboration with the British.[23] Eventually, Norodam, the king of Cambodia who ruled between 1860 and 1904, was forced to sign a treaty in 1863 accepting French protection.

The French attitude toward Cochin China, particularly its deltaic part, and Cambodia differed. To the French, Cochin China was the first experimental colony in Southeast Asia whose resources were intended to produce surplus rice and other necessary raw materials and whose administration was molded after the French model. Cambodia, on the other hand, was paid little attention because in the game of colonial economic development it was not of much significance to France. Until 1904, when King Norodam died, direct French rule was only halfheartedly implemented in Cambodia.

French Policy in Cochin China. In Cochin China, the virgin plains of the Mekong delta to the west and south of the Bassac river, not inhabited by the advancing Viets, had received French attention for agricultural expansion since 1870. To produce agricultural surpluses for export these lands were reclaimed by constructing a series of major canals to drain excess water and to provide an infrastructure of navigable waterways. These canals later became the main arteries for transportation of rice from the delta to the mills in Cholan-Saigon which cleaned and polished rice for export and for consumption within the urban area. Within seventy years (1870–1940) the rice cultivation in Cochin China increased more than four times.[24] It actually increased from 0.28 million metric tons of cleaned rice to 1.45 million metric tons.[25] France, essentially a bread consuming country, could not rely on the humid semiequatorial climate of the Mekong delta to produce wheat. Therefore, metropolitan France tried to adjust itself to import and consume the export surplus of one of her colonies or "limbs." However, despite attempts to popularize rice in France—"the effects of which are still evident in the national cuisine"—only half of the delta's rice export had been imported to the mother country.[26] Natural facts of geography (the delta's rice exportable capacity) thus overruled the demands of the man-made "assimilation" policy of the French.

The new lands, opened for cultivation after reclamation in the nineteenth century, were not given to tenant farmers in the Mekong delta as they had been when the British opened up the Irrawaddy delta in Burma. Historically, whenever the Viets reclaimed any land they always distributed it to needy peasants.

However, under the French rule only the large and rich landowners—the French and collaborating Vietnamese—were recipients of new lands on the Mekong delta. The landowners never cultivated the land themselves; instead, they leased parcels of the land to farmers who paid half their produce as rent. Such tenants could be dispossessed at any time at the will of the landowner who lived in Saigon with the comforts of modern amenity. Thus was created a special class of people, *absentee landlords*, a new rural parasite. Individual landlords each held from 1,250 to 2,500 acreas of land as compared with 2 to 12 acres typical of pre-French settlement northeast of Bassac river.[27] Because of the high rent demanded of the farmers, the payment of which was beyond their capacity, they soon were in debt to the rich who also claimed abnormally high interest rates. Eventually, many farmers became semiserfs due to their inability to repay their debts. All the reclaimed land could not be brought under actual cultivation with the new land-tenure system because high rents were not attractive to farmers and landowners themselves were unable to plow such large areage with their primitive tools. Violette, a French authority, commented on this aspect in 1912:

> As a result of great drainage work, land has become fertile but remained unoccupied. Instead of attracting small farmers, we have given vast territories to individuals who doubtless has been of service to us, but who were only our creatures and did not deserve such rich presents, nor did they deserve to have the principle (of settling peasants on available land) overturned in their favor.[28]

However, despite all these difficulties, the rural areas of the Mekong delta continued to be populated. In the South Vietnamese part of the delta, the rural density reached 450 persons per square mile, less than half that of the Red river delta.

France made no effort to increase the potential of the land. Adding new rice fields to old ones was an easier way of making a profit than introducing new crops and better growing methods. The French knew that a surplus of rice for export would always be available to Chinese middlemen and French exporters through the landlords who had the greater share of the harvest.[29] The Mekong delta continued to be cultivated largely in rice without any effort made to have a diversity of crops. At that time the French were merely interested in rice exports.

The principal industries allowed in this part of Indochina were rice milling and cane sugar refining. Before being exported, the paddy had to be separated from its outer kernel (husk), cleaned, and polished to give it a white appearance. Unhusked paddy, weighing about twice that of cleaned rice, would cost more when shipped to France. Thus, the development of local rice mills was to aid French economic interest, and Cholan became the chief rice milling center under Chinese business ownership. Similarly, sugarcane refineries had to be developed in the Mekong delta rather than in France because sugarcane cannot withstand long periods of time in either strorage or transport. Sugarcane loses about 10 times its weight from the raw stage to that of the finished sugar granules. Thus, refineries must locate close to the raw material.

The French required new administrative systems to cater to their colonial needs. One of the first administrative modifications concerned the powers and duties of mandarins. They were replaced from their positions governing cantons and administrative levels above cantons, by French personnel. Although the commune system was retained, its self-sufficient basis and authority were minimized. The French mistakenly saw similar features (such as the position of a "mayor") in the communes to those of their municipal communes in France. Under the directions of the new French administration, "mayors" were appointed in the Vietnamese communes erroneously from a group of lesser notables[30] who did not command as much respect as the decision making, or great notables of the commune council. Because of the increasing interference in the activities of the communes from the French headquarters in Saigon, they started to become less significant in rural life. Thus, the very roots of the Vietnamese rural society, which was traditionally based on communes, were shaken.

Cochin China was the principal money making area for the *colons* who controlled the Colonial Council for Cochin China. This Council was the legislative body for the region and commanded supreme authority until the establishment of the Superior Council of Indochina in 1897. Even afterwards, the Colonial Council continued to be effective in molding French policy for Cochin China. Vietnamese participation in higher level policymaking was negligible. Only the 2,000 local French citizens were allowed to vote for electors to the Colonial Council. The upper level of the old royal administrative system was, thus, completely replaced by a mock democracy which mainly served the interests of the *colons*.

French Policy in the Mekong delta area of Cambodia. Cambodia was allowed to retain some powers of its royal throne until 1904; Cambodians had continued to adhere to the image of a godking. Any replacement would have caused considerable resentment. However, after 1904 the king was virtually stripped of all powers and was replaced by a French resident. He was still called a king and was allowed to stay in his traditional palace. With the help of supporting French administrators and under the direction of the Governor General and the Superior Council, the resident ruled the country from the capital at Phnom Penh. At the beginning of the twentieth century, the French began to initiate many reforms, such as the abolition of slavery.

The French felt that the Cambodian part of the Mekong delta, as well as the other parts of the country, were not as economically attractive as Cochin China. This greatly limited French interest in Cambodia. Lack of concern was so strong that the proposed railway link between Phnom Penh and Saigon never materialized. The only major railway link completed by the French, in 1932, was from Phnom Penh to Poipit along the Saimese border, and that was only to guarantee a year-round rice supply for export from the Tonle Sap Basin. Because Cambodia and its deltaic parts were sparsely populated, there was also a possibility of agricultural expansion. The Cambodian region of the delta had reached a density of only 52 people per square mile. With the stimulus of rice export, several possibilities were further explored to increase rice acreage. Acreage did increase from one-half million acreas at the beginning of the twentieth century to 1.5 million in 1930. Compared with French efforts in canal construction in Cochin China, irrigation construction in Cambodia was minimal. However, port facilities and rice husking mill were constructed in Phnom Penh. Such aids, along with having a small local population to feed, made Cambodia the third largest rice exporter in the world by the end of the 1930s.

Dual Independent Foci of the Mekong Delta After 1954 Independence

With the French acting from two different points—Saigon and Phnom Penh—a logical basis was laid for the delta to develop two different foci: Phnom Penh, which became the capital of Cambodia in 1866, and Saigon, which became the capital of the Republic of Vietnam (or South Vietnam) in 1954. Both are primate cities; Phnom Penh had a population of 393,995 according to the 1962 census and the Saigon metropolitan area (including Saigon's twin-city of Cholan) had over 2,400,000 people in 1965.[31] Not only were both cities political centers with legislative and executive headquarters, but they were also the principal economic and cultural foci of their respective territories. Despite the historical rivalry between the Khmers and the Viets, after their independence in 1954, both nations lived in comparative peace, perhaps the result of their preoccupation with fighting local communism. Rivalry erupted since 1978 culminating into Vietnamese army marching into Kampuchea and installing a puppet government.

Politically, Phnom Penh had a relatively stable government between 1954 and 1969 under the leadership of the Chief of State, Prince Sihanouk, who organized state elections for the first time in Cambodian history. However, after the *coup d'etat* staged in 1969 by one of the generals, Cambodia came under military rule with only a hint of democracy. On the other hand, leadership of the Saigon government changed hands several times during the first decade of independence until General Thieu became President. After that, questionably democratic elections were held. However, the stability of the government was retained mainly due to strong local military backing and subtle American support. The Thieu Government fell in 1975, clearing the way for a communist takeover of Saigon. By that time, Cambodia was also Communist.

Saigon Core: Vietnamese Part of the Mekong Delta. Because the Vietnamese part of the Mekong delta is primarily agricultural, the land problem continued to be the most decisive factor affecting politics in the area. The Viet Minh (later the Viet Cong) was readily supported by the native peasantry as a result of French abuses in the land tenure system before 1954. The Viet Minh controlled a large part of the deltaic countryside, distributing land to tillers and landless. In order to neutralize Viet Cong effort and to decolonize the tenure system, the newly constituted Saigon government issued some reforms in 1956: (1) rent on cultivated land was not to exceed 25% of the current gross yield, (2) tenure was to be secured for a period of 3 to 5 years under terms of a written contract, (3) lands left abandoned for 3 years were subject to redistribution, (4) no one landowner was to be permitted to own more than 294 acres of land, and (5) excess land was to be purchased by the government for distribution to farmers in plots of two to twelve acres.[32]

However, land hungry farmers saw these reforms as only a halfhearted solution to the problem. Although, by 1960, over one million acres were distributed to over 124,000 farmers, these reforms could hardly create confidence among the farmers.[33] Nonetheless, these reforms weakened the power of the landlords.[34] However, when the Saigon government forces reoccupied Viet Cong controlled villages, they replaced the farmers (who had worked the soil and received new title of ownership from the Viet Cong) with the same wealthy landowner who had legally owned the land since the time of the French. As a result, the villages were divided into two factions—the wealthy, who supported the Saigon government and the poor, who supported the Viet Cong. Government forces ruled the villages by day and the Viet Cong ruled by night, both having opposing military forces and tax collections.

In order to deal with this problem, the Saigon government began a rural resettlement scheme, the Agroville Program, in the early sixties. Confirmed and potential Viet Cong families were put under strict surveillance in a particular settlement area, while loyal families were grouped in another place and guarded from Viet Cong attacks. Such a divisive scheme was unworkable because (1) it made necessary a clustering of houses that was unacceptable to these deltaic people who had been living in a more widely dispersed arrangements, and (2) it removed the farmers from their rice paddies where they were needed to take individual care of their crops.[35]

In 1970, as a part of the American "pacification program" a new land policy was introduced to regain the countryside from the Viet Cong control—the Land to the Tiller Program. This scheme guaranteed legal title and ownership of land actually tilled by the farmer to a *maximum* of 7.5 acres (usually less) for each adult member of the family. The landlords, i.e., the legal owners, were compensated financially for the loss of their land by the Saigon government, mainly through American aid. This program further limited the landlords to own a maximum of approximately 50 acres of land provided they made use of it. This policy was carried out. As of 1973, in the delta, most of the land, some 1.3 million acres, had been distributed to the farmers. "Before 1957 some 2,000 families owned about half the rice land in the Delta; today, at least half of the Delta's population are claimed to be individual owners."[36] Americans have been heartened by the response to such a program from the deltaic farmers in spite of the fact that the landlords owned much greater individual acreage of land than that of the farmer.[37]

Nevertheless, the war-ridden countryside and the disruption to farming caused by the Civil War resulted in declining rice production in the delta. Even land reforms could bring no tangible results. Thus, the delta which normally has had a rice surplus (it exported about 300,000 tons in 1963) was importing almost 150 thousand tons of rice every year and had a continual annual deficit since 1965. The overall exports of South Vietnam, however, outweighed the imports by 60 to 1.[38] With the ceasefire of 1973 and the establishement of peace, it was thought possible that the delta would once again produce surplus rice for export. In addition, the possibility of the presence of oil off the deltaic coasts, for which concession contracts were already drawn,[39] might suddenly change the fate of the area.

The Saigon government, which had been engaged in Civil War since 1954, was having some respite due to the 1973 ceasefire. But the land of South Vietnam still remained divided into two segments—one ruled by the Saigon government and the other by the Viet Cong. Sporadic fighting continued between the forces of Saigon and the Viet Cong. During the 19 years of war, South Vietnam became totally dependent on United States aid, which amounted to $396 million in 1971 and $385 million in 1972. Additional United States grants have made up the trade deficit; in 1972, South Vietnam's imports were worth $700 million whereas the exports were only $12 million.[40] The American military not only directly employed 200,000 Vietnamese at the height of American involvement, but also spent considerable money in Vietnamese shops, bars, and transportation systems. Now that only 5,900 official Americans were in South Vietnam in January, 1974, the labor market was faced with unemployed men with the same limited skills as before as well as a lessened retail service sector. Thus, the Saigon government was facing the shock of de-Americanization of its country's economy and existed on its own. The pace of its development depended on the amount and use of foreign aid, which came mostly from the United States.

The *U.S. News & World Report* (January 14, 1974) stated:

> The relationship among the three great powers [U.S.A., U.S.S.R., and China] may dictate the course of war and peace in both South and North Vietnam. But peace would require all three to cut off arms and other aid to both Saigon and Hanoi— and that's not in the cards for now.

In the cards was hidden the inevitable fate of South Vietnam: reunification with the North. When the Viet Cong's Provisional Government, backed heavily by Hanoi, mustered enough strength to register a knock-out victory over the Thieu Government in 1975, the former had completed its strategy of confrontations at and military occupation of the Annamite Cordillera region first, and then to the populated plains; on the plains, they marched from the North to the South, along the coast repeating the centuries old direction of the "March to the South." Saigon was only cordoned off by the Communists; no real war was fought in the city. It was surrendered to the Provisional Government on April 30, 1975, which turned the city into their capital until the 1976 reunification and renamed it Ho Chi Minh City.

Politically, Ho Chi Minh City, in 1976, was relegated to a secondary position as it ceased to be the capital governing a nation for the first time in almost a century. Nonetheless, it remained the most populous city in the nation.

The city and other parts of the Mekong delta region, in the early 1980s, were experiencing the teething problems of socialism as private enterprise and land ownership were discouraged. Wholesale and retail businesses were in disarray in a city with many unemployed people who formerly worked for the national government. A great many businessmen, former civil servants and elites were taken away from the city to concentration camp-like "re-education centers" for brain-washing; some never came back.

The Vietnamese Premier, Pam Van Dong, emphasized, in 1976, that "Ho Chi Minh City will have a very important role in many respects, and will broaden its foreign relations with countries in southeast Asia and the rest of the world."[41] Consequently, the Ho Chi Minh City Import-Export Company was set up, so that 70% of the foreign exchange earned could be used in the city. This resulted in the import of spare parts and raw materials for some 100 industrial enterprises run by the city by early 1981.[42] In spite of these and other efforts for rejuvenation, Ho Chi Minh City remained subdued and much less vibrant than the Saigon of the early 1970s.

The food supply in the city remained rationed in the early 1980s along with shortages of other consumer's goods, such as soap, sugar, coffee, etc.

> "In Ho Chi Minh City, the distribution of rice remains fixed at 3 kilos per month, the rest consisting of wheat or noodles. In Hanoi, a Politburo statement last month [April 1980] disclosed that the collection of rice in the Mekong Delta had reached only a disappointing 40% of the target. Evidently the delta farmers sold it [rice] on the free market in Ho Chi Minh City in order to buy consumer goods rather than delivering their rice to the government."[43]

Phnom Penh Core. The deltaic core surrounding Phnom Penh is primarily devoted to rice production. In this deltaic region, the levees are especially fertile and have the capacity to produce a wide variety of crops. Levees surrounding Phnom Penh are utilized for commerical vegetable gardening to supply the needs of the city. However, beyond the levees where floods spread new alluvium every year, rice is the principal crop. The marshlands, paticularly between the Bassac and Mekong rivers and extending into Vietnam, are used primarily for growing floating rice.[44] As in Vietnam, agriculture in Kampuchea is the primary economic resource. Rice, was its chief exportable surplus. Export was possible because the country was underpopulated and its rice acreage had more than doubled between 1930 and 1960. However, a drastic reduction occurred in the rice production during the 1970–75 civil war and was reflected in the fact that from a peak 3.5 million metric tons in 1969–70, the rice output dropped to 1.1 million in 1972–73. The communist guerrilla (Khmer Rouge) activities beginning in 1969 had virtually deprived the Phnom Penh core of its extensive rice-based hinterland, forcing Phnom Penh to import rice. Thus, the economic and political influence of the Phnom Penh core had been drastically reduced in terms of area which it controlled. The dichotomy was eased after the Khmer Rouge occupation of Phnom Penh, along with all of Cambodia in April of 1975.

The Khmer Rouge, led by Maoist Premier Pol Pot, decided to turn Kampuchea into a hermit republic. Everyone was forced to work in the fields to improve agriculture. Thousands of Phnom Penh city dwellers were driven out into the villages; its population reduced to 200,000 from 2,000,000 by 1976. Formal schooling was abandoned; school-age children were supposed to learn while working. Religion was virtually abolished while pagodas were converted into storage and military places. Except for one hospital in Phnom Penh, all others in the country ceased to operate as the officials believed in self-reliant herbal medicine.[46]

The Khmer Rouge implemented their dogmatic policies ruthlessly. Any opposition or even 'suspicion' of opposition was enough for the extermination of people. Over 90% of 500 doctors of the country were killed; the remaining 10% survived because they distinguished themselves as field workers. Schools were not only turned into ammunition depots, but one of them in Phnom Penh was converted into a prison and Nazi-like interrogation center, where hundreds of Pol Pot opponents were tortured and killed.[47]

All of these ruthless efforts were aimed at achieving selfsufficiency in agricultural products, especially rice; exchanging the surplus rice for necessary imports and generating a simple living formula. The effort pumped a large percentage of workers into agriculture and succeeded temporarily-as dikes were built, canals were dug and reservoirs were constructed all over the country. About one million acres of farmland were irrigated. One-tenth of the cultivated land produced two rice crops a year. By 1977, the country produced almost all the rice it needed to feed itself.

The hermit state's pro-Chinese alignment and unpopularity among its own people induced pro-Soviet

Vietnam to intervene and invade Kampuchea in 1979. The Khmer Rouge were driven out of Phnom Penh and pro-Vietnamese Heng Samrin was installed to rule Kampuchea. The Khmer Rouge operated as guerrillas from the villages in the western part of the country and declared a parallel insurgent government. With the Vietnamese occupation and Khmer Rouge guerrilla activities, agricultural operation in the countryside virtually ceased. It was learned from a U.S. satellite survey in September, 1979, that only 5% of Kampuchea's cultivable land was planted in rice.[48] This brought about an unprecedented famine in 1979–80, widespread malnutrition and disease; only one birth for every ten deaths and thousands of emaciated Kampuchians pouring into Thailand in search of food.[49] Conditions did improve in the early 1980s, but a rice shortage persisted as of 1983 while the pro-Vietnamese, puppet regime controlled only a part of a country still deep in the shock of hunger, shortages, insecurity and instability.

TONLE SAP BASIN, MEKONG LOWLANDS AND ANGKOR

The Tonle Sap Basin and the Mekong Lowlands (Fig. 11-3) are flanked by low-lying hills—the sandstone Dangrek Range in the north, the granitic Cardamom Range in the southwest, and the Elephant Range in the south. The Annamite Cordillera lies to the east. Within this vast area of lowlands, there are only a few isolated islands of higher lands over 1,000 feet, and all these are in the central area. Tonle Sap, which literally means Great Lake, is a unique physiographic area which needs some explanation. Formerly it existed as an arm of the sea, but as a result of gradual silting of the Mekong delta it turned into an inland lake, probably during historic times. This lake is connected to the Mekong by a 40-mile channel known as the Tonle Sap river.[50] The unique mechanism of monsoon backflow to Tonle Sap from the Mekong river has been explained in Chapter 2 (pp. 39–40).

Precursor to Core Area Formation (A.D. 535–802)

The Khmers established a powerful core area based on the Angkor area. They descended essentially from Mongoloid stock and migrated from the north eventually to inhabit the Tonle Sap and Mekong lowland region after ousting the indigenous stock of people. In the early years of the Christian era, the limited number of local Chams were readily overpowered by Khmers. The Khmers assimilated some of the indigenous peoples while the remaining ones were driven to the coasts or to the highlands of the Cordillera in the east. Having obtained control, the Khmers established a kingdom known as Chenla that became a vassal of Funan; however, in A.D. 627 Chenla overpowered Funan. Thus the "March to the Sea" was completed by the Khmers much before the Viets began it from Tonkin. With accessibility via rivers and within an area which had a productive agricultural base, the first capital of Chenla was established at the junction of the Se Mun and Mekong rivers.[51] Isanavarman, one of the subsequent Chenla kings, moved the capital farther south to a place north of Tonle Sap, site of modern-day Samba Prei Kuk; because the surrounding region had greater agricultural potential. This capital he named Isanapura after himself (*pura* in Sanskrit means city). From the new capital, Isanavarman succeeded in extending his empire north to Yunnan in China and west to the Chao Phraya valley. The region around Isanapura later became the great Angkor area of the Khmer kingdoms dating back to the early ninth century. At the beginning of the eighth century, Chenla had been divided into two parts which the Chinese named Land and Sea Chenla according to their locations (Fig. 11-2). *Land Chenla*, in the north, was oriented toward the mainland, whereas *Water Chenla*, in the south, not only had access to the sea but also was susceptible to Mekong inundation. Paradoxically, the great Khmer Empire, whose people had no aptitude to become seafarers, was embryonically embedded in maritime Chenla.

Until the annexation of Funan, the Khmers were a group of homogeneous people with no interest in the sea. Accustomed to farming on relatively dry lands, they never had to face the problem of draining monsoon waters as did the deltaic Funanese people; instead, the Khmer problem was to hold or store water for a second crop in the dry season. In Chenla the water storage problem was solved by enclosing a large area of land served by a canal which originated at an elevation higher than the enclosed area and carried water from a perennial stream. Such an enclosed area with its "captive water" was used for multiple cropping. These agricultural areas, associated with Chenla towns of that time, were used to provide food for urban dwellers.[52] Although the Khmers conquered Funan, they were not interested in the water-control technique which had been developed on the delta; as a result, agriculture in the Mekong delta during the Chenla period was neglected. Instead, people of *Water Chenla* turned to the drier areas north of Tonle Sap to develop their agriculture because that area had a greater potential for im-

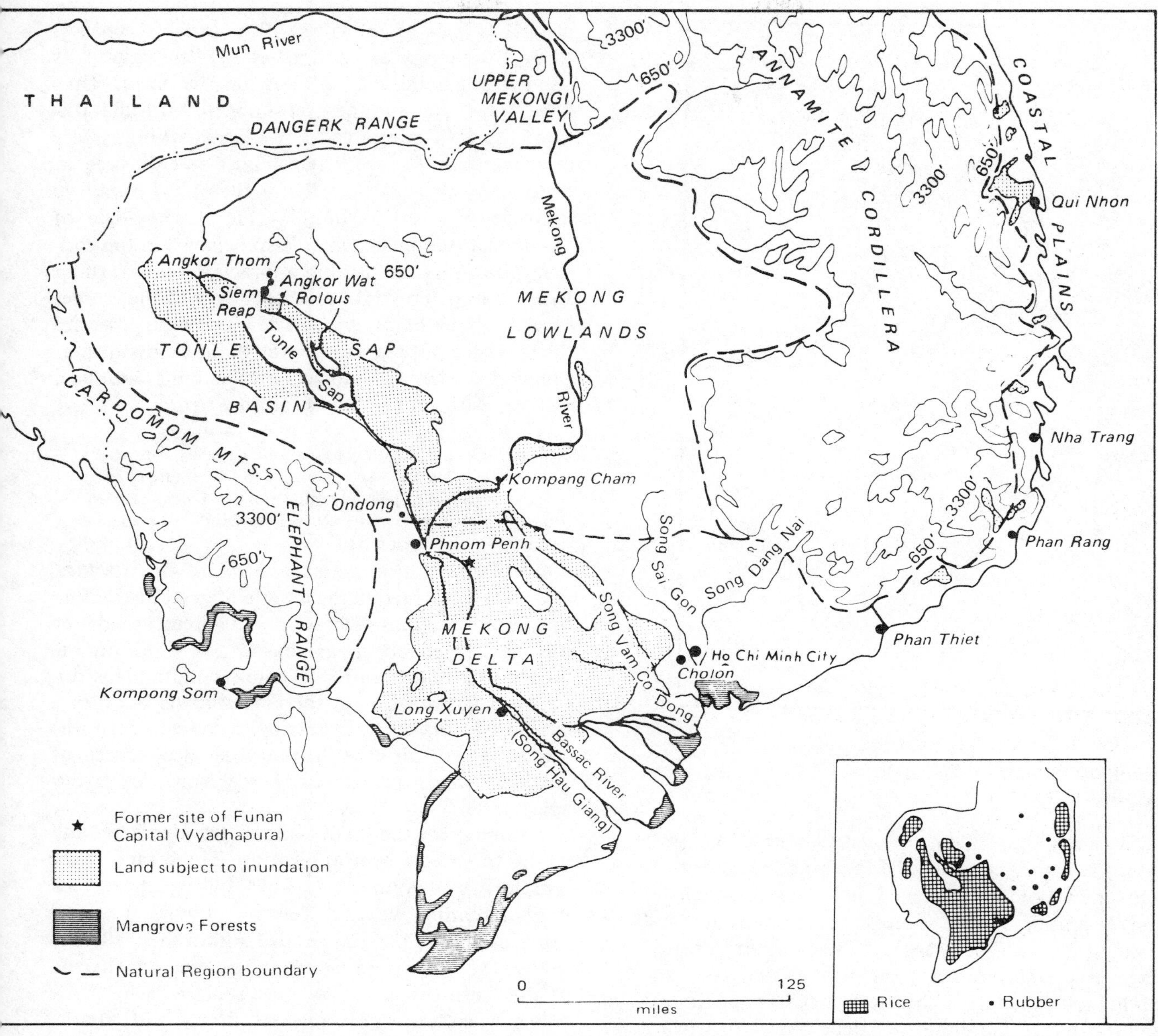

Figure 11-3. Mekong Delta and Tonle Sap Region: A General Map.

plementation of their "water captive" technique.

The Khmers of Chenla, as had their Funanese predecessors, continued to be influenced by Indian Hindu traditions. Sanskrit was the literary language; Sanskrit sacred books were entrenched in the Khmer culture as were rituals performed by the Brahmins, temples representing the idol-gods, worship of Siva *linga*[53] and *Nandi*, the riding bull of Lord Siva which inhabited the central shrine of the temples. Since every Hindu is supposedly descended from a hermit, the Khmer kings were designated by the local Brahmin priests to be descendents of the great Indian hermit *Kambu Svayambhuva*.[54] Thus, they were "sons of Kambu" or "Kambuja,"[55] which later became "Chambodge" to the French and "Cambodia" to the English.

Growth and Maturity of the Angkor Core Area (802–1220)

Despite their seaward location, the Khmers, true to their continental traditions, never were able to become a maritime power. The great Khmer kings in later times extended their territories by marching their armies by land. On the sea, they were vulnerable. At the end of the eighth century, a powerful maritime kingdom developed in Srivijya,

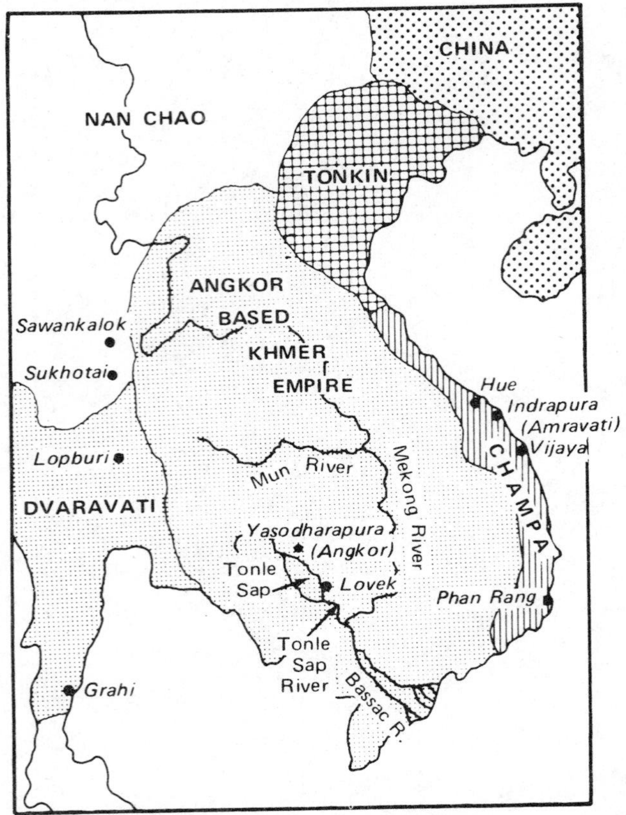

Source: C.A. Fisher

Figure 11-4. Angkor Based Khmer Empire: Eleventh Century.

modern day Palembang in Sumatra, whose Maharaja (king) ravaged the coast of Indochina, beheaded the Khmer king of Water Chenla, and "set up a minister to rule until a suitable successor could be found and trained."[56] Subsequently, the Khmer prince, Jayavarman II, returned from Java as a vassal of the Maharaja and started to rule Water Chenla. In 802 Jayavarman II attained sufficient power to declare Khmer independence through a ritual performed by a Hindu Brahmin who was especially brought from India to proclaim Jayavarman II as *Chakravartin*, the sovereign of the world.[57] Such was the inauguration of the Angkor period, the great Khmer Empire which endured until 1432.

The real glories of the Khmer Empire, however, lasted only until 1215 (Fig. 11–4). Between 802–1215, the twelve kings[58] who ruled the country all used the suffix of *Varman*. The Khmer kingship gave rise to one of the most powerful and long lasting therocratic states in the world and determined not only the dynastic lineage but also the political, social, economic, and agricultural features of the land.

God-king concept. In accordance with the god-king (Indra) concept of the Hindus in India which originates back to about 1500 B.C. in the sacred *Rig Veda*, Brahmin priests designated the Khmer kings as the living embodiment of god on the earth. Thus "the first victim and the first supporter of Indianization was the monarch."[59] Whereas kings were designated as *Devaraja* (god-king) and devotee of Lord Siva; Suryavarman II was the only *Vishnuraja* (devotee of Lord Vishnu).[60] Due to the logic of Mahayana Buddhism which also believed in the god-king concept, and Brahmin practice, Jayavarman VII, the most powerful and legendary of the Khmer kings, became *Buddharaja*. The kings were powerful rulers whose popular image was that of a divine personality to whom all subjects must submit and obey. M. Paul Mus, in his notable words, wrote:

> The royal religion, firmly based both magically and socially on the worship and exploitation of the land, turned every king into a god by placing behind him like a halo the splendor of a celestial divinity of which he was the embodiment and visible representative.[61]

Every king desired to attain *Mokha*[62] or *Nirvana*[63] and to be enshrined in the temple of gods built either by himself or by his successors. No longer would it be necessary to be reborn, as he would be free from the miseries of reincarnation. Temple-building was not only a demonstration of the king's power but also a passport to heaven. Thus, temples came to form the central core of the city; the morphological aspects of Angkor's urban growth emanated from this divine epicenter.[64]

Commencing the ninth century, temples were built as the focus of a central location. The center of the temple was surrounded by walls and had four axial roads radiating outward. The royal family and some other privileged persons resided within the walls. Initially, the walls were wooden; however, by the end of the tenth century, they were replaced with stone which was less vulnerable to decay and attack. Angkor Thom was one of the first temples with stone walls. (The word Angkor has its origin in the Sanskrit *Nagara* which means city.) Beyond the wall lived the common people, unprotected from outside invasion. Still farther away a square or retangular canal-road system, made up mainly of roads on canal embankments, developed. The center of such systems was the temple city.

The Angkor City Complex. At times succeeding kings created their own temple-cities which were a few miles removed from the previous center. Thus, during the Angkor period, the city center shifted from one location to another according to the whims of the kings, an outgrowth of the peculiar *divine dynamism* belief. The final form of the city, chiefly of the northern plains of Tonle Sap surrounding

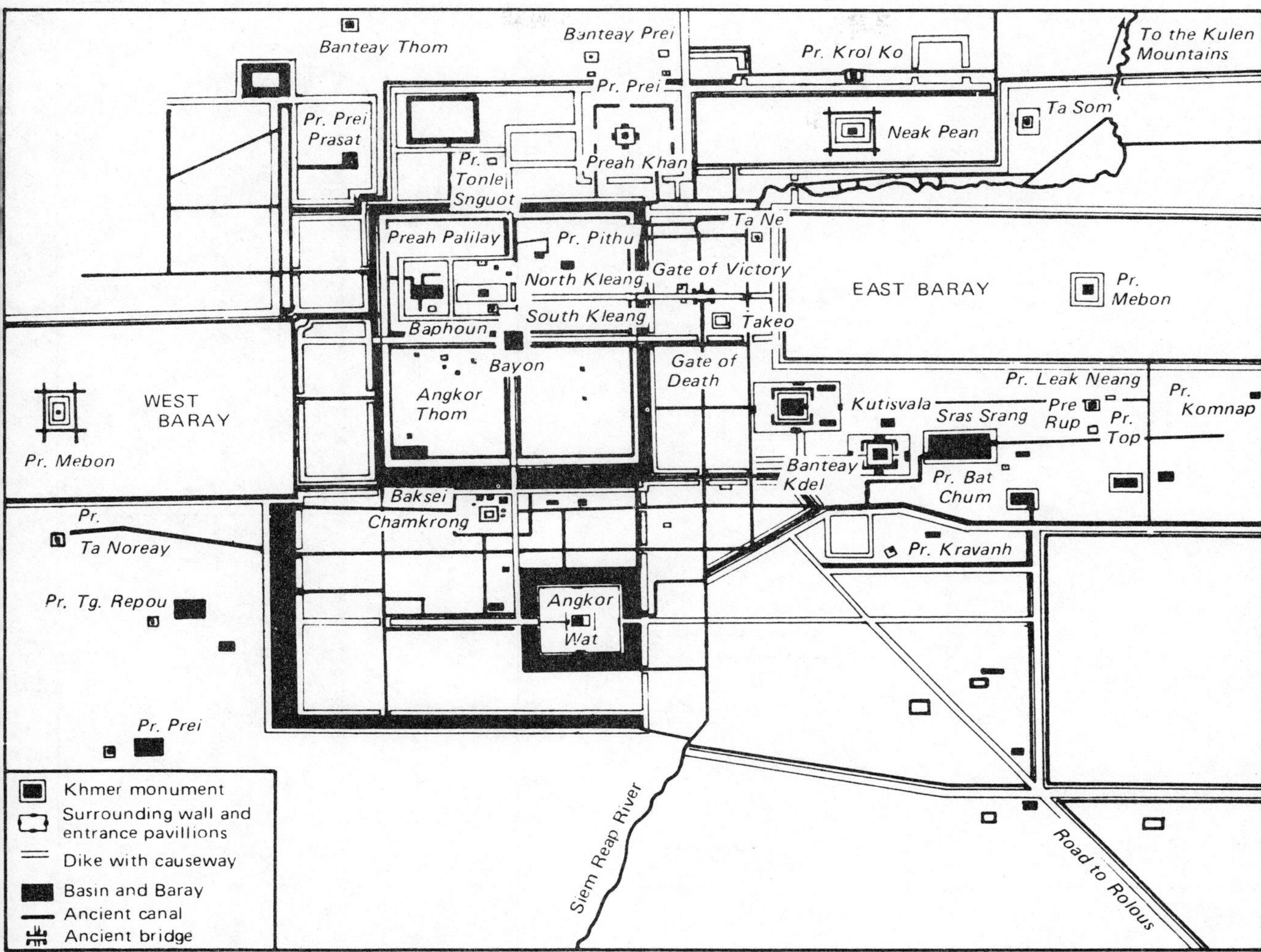

Source: After Groslier 1957 and 1962.

Figure 11-5. Angkor Urban Complex at Its Height.

Angkor Thom, can be seen in Figure 11–5. This type of city provided a successful functional combination of agriculture and administration through the medium of religion.

During the thirteenth century, an estimated one million persons were thought to live in the Angkor city region. However, the city was not truly congested; for the population was distributed within an area of 50 to 100 square miles. The royal palace, which was built of wood in order not to surpass the grandeur of the more permanent temple built of sandstone, laterites, and bricks, was the focal point of the city center. Around the royal palace were clustered the residences of the king's court; the nobles, high officials, foreign ambassadors, and rich businessmen. Booths of craftsmen and guilds of masons also found a place within the city while priests had their quarters in the vicinity of the temples.

City services such as refuse collection or sewerage were not available as they existed in the Indus Valley's older urban civilizations of Mohenjodaro and Harappa. Instead people dug ditches in their backyards for sanitary disposal. Baths, so important to Hindu life, were taken in small ponds dug for one or several families. The communal bathing places were a few large reservoirs or water bodies which were located mainly outside the city walls and occassionally frequented by groups of people. However, these were different from the ancient Roman bathhouses both in organization and design.

City Planning. A landmark in city planning was instituted by Suryavarman I (1002–47), a Tamil-Malaya prince who had a blood relationshiip with Khmer kings and who was the first Mahayana Buddhist king of Angkor (Fig. 11–6). He added a new concept to civic center planning for the capital

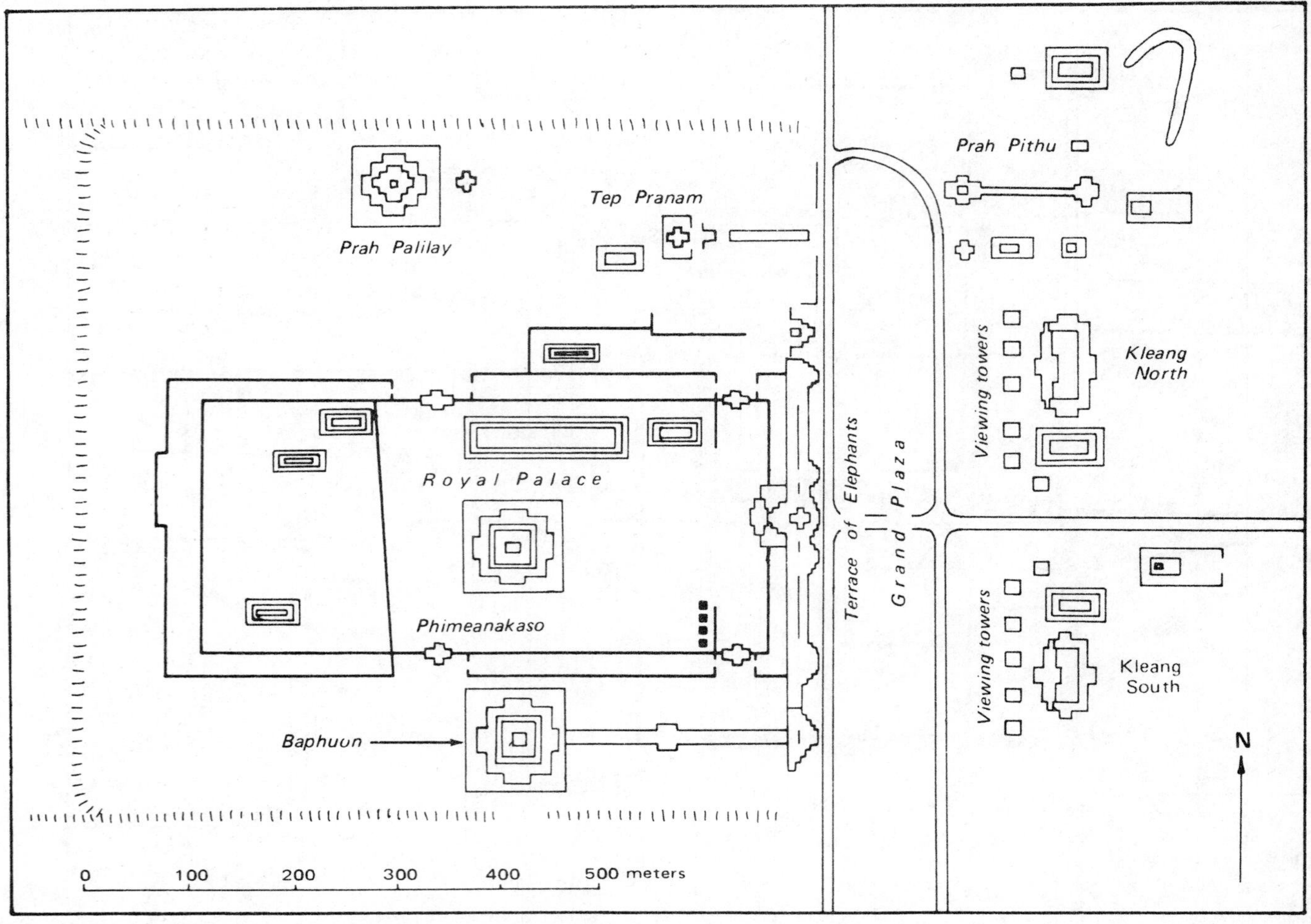

Source: After *Angkor,* G.H. Parmentier (Saigon: Albert Portal, 1950).

Figure 11-6. Angkor Thom Civic Center (Eleventh Century).

(Angkor Thom) by building an administrative complex, the Royal Enclosure, which consisted of the official palace in the front and the household domestic quarters in the rear. The Grand Plaza, a spacious and dignified square, was developed in front of the Royal Enclosure. To the north and south were the Kleangs, residences for foreign missions and provincial viceroys who visited the capital. The twelve viewing towers facing the Grand Plaza were "vantage points from which official personages could watch the processions, sports, wild boar fights, and other ceremonies which were held in the Grand Plaza."[65] Suryavarman further beautified the city with pools, basins, and other ornamental water bodies meant both for commercial fishing and public bathing.[66]

The vertical and horizontal layout of the cities in Angkor reflected the cosmic beliefs of the Hindus. Their gods live in Mount Meru, and this was symbolized by the spires of the temples. The temples were enclosed by four sided walls which represented the surrounding world of mortals (men). The moat or canal around the city reflected the Hindu concept that the known world had an end which bounded a Sea of Milk, the Ocean of Creation. Such cosmological harmony represented in Angkor cities was thought to bless the people of the Khmer empire with prosperity.

With the building of splendid temples, walls, statues, and royal palaces, the period from the ninth through thirteenth centuries brought extensive urban growth to Angkor. The official religion required a considerable expenditure of finances as summarized in the following statement which relates to the year 1191 during the reign of Jayavarman VII:

> there were... more than 20,000 images in gold, silver, bronze, and stone spread all over the kingdom. The service of their cult required 306,372 survitors, living in 13,500 villages and consuming 38,000 tons of rice annually.[67]

Agricultural Revolution. The introduction of a new agricultural production technique in the beginning of the ninth century not only met the subsistence needs of the Khmers, but also provided an adequate surplus for nonagricultural purposes such as empire and city building. An artificial lake, approximately 3 miles by one-half mile, was created by erecting earthen dykes to hold water from Stung Roluos, one of the two major rivers in the area.[68] The lake was named Indratakata after the Hindu god Indra. Irrigation canals leading from the lake followed the sloping terrain, distributing water to the adjacent paddyfields by gravity means. Thus the productivity of the land was increased as extensive areas of land could be used to produce an additional crop during the dry season. This new "artifical lake" technique, which had its origins in southern India where it had been long practiced, was even more beneficial than the ancient "captive water" method used in Chenla because it opened up a much greater area of land for increased agriculture.

The "artificial lake" technique was so effective that later Khmer kings tapped new sources of water. Siemreap river was diverted to create Western Baray, the largest reservior—about 5 miles long and 1 mile wide. The Khmers mastered the art of canal building to such an extent that modern precision instruments can find little error in the straightness of these canals which were miles long.

With the availability of water, a large area of the plain around Angkor was open for intensive cultivation. Now three or four crops could be harvested during the twelve month cycle. Aside from the main crop of rice, the peasants also grew vegetables, sugarcane, and fruits. They used ploughs pulled by water buffalo to cultivate the soil and sickles to harvest the crops. Soil nutrients were renewed by the annual floods which were deployed and distributed by means of the irrigation canals. Subsistence agriculture was replaced with farms, producing surplus crops. In addition to soil cultivation, the farmers fished and kept various livestock; pigs, sheep, goats, cattle, horses, geese, and chickens.[69]

Extension of Khmer Rule. As a result of surplus in agriculture and with the peoples obedience, the Khmer kings succeeded in building an almost invincible army. In the ninth century, all of *Land Chenla* was controlled by the Khmer Empire, and by the eleventh century the Angkor kings ruled a territory from the Chinese borders to the Gulf of Siam and to the Bay of Bengal in the west. Champa was also converted into a province of the Khmer kingdom for a short period between 1203 and 1220.[70] Angkor's geographical location was significant in accounting for land acquisitions. Massive land based expeditions could be made to the north and west via unhindered plains thus expanding the empire in those directions, but the existence of the physical barrier of the Annamite Cordillera to the east prevented the Khmers from dominating Champa for more than a brief period of time. Only once in its heyday was the Khmer imperial capital ransacked, and that was due to its almost always inherent vulnerability by sea. In 1177 the Cham navy followed the water route along the coast, up the Mekong river and to Tonle Sap surprising Angkor rulers. Not only were the Khmers defeated, but their capital was also pillaged, looted, and burned by the invaders.

Fall and Disappearance of Angkor Core (1220–1432)

After the death of Jayavarman VII in 1219, the Khmer kingdom at Angkor continued for a little more than two centuries, but the very backbone of their previous glorious existence had been broken. According to the accounts of the Chinese traveller Chou Ta-Kuan, the apparent riches of Angkor were still flowing in 1296; however, political, spiritual, and economic weaknesses were deeply ingrained in the system. The conditions may be compared to termites destroying the basic structure of a building whose outward appearance remains undisturbed. The culmination of Angkor's image-destruction occurred in 1353 when Thais overran Angkor from their capital of Ayutthaya. The next Thai attack in 1383 prompted the Khmer construction of a strong earth rampart around their capital city. Even this protection did not help. The year 1431 marked the end of the Khmer empire for then the Thai king Paramaraja II not only captured the city of Angkor but also burned what remained of it.[71] Subsequently the Khmers left the Tonle Sap Basin and Angkor region for good and returned to the Mekong delta region which they had left over eight centuries before. Thereafter, the area around modern Phnom Penh became the new Khmer core area.

Wearied Farmers. For several centuries preceding the demise of the Angkor's glories, Khmer monarchs had maintained their stature as god-kings. Such heavenly-earthly grandeur provided great spiritual command over their subjects and enabled them to collect agricultural surpluses and to use slave labor.

The degree of surplus collection and the use of slave labor to erect temples and buildings reached their peak in the twelfth and the beginning of the thirteenth centuries and culminated during the reign of Jayavarman VII. In the short period of one and one-half centuries, gigantic ceremonial and religious structures were completed such as Baphuon (1060), Angkor Wat (first half of the twelfth century), Ta

Prohm (1186), and Prah Khan (1191). During the reign of Jayavarman VII, the government health service alone consumed 11,192 tons of rice annually, grown by 81,640 people living in 838 villages.[72] The enormous staff required for the maintenance of a temple is evident from the example of Ta Prohm temple: 18 high priest, 2,740 officials, 2,202 servers, and 625 dancing girls.[73] However, Khmers were wearied of giving up their surpluses year after year and contributing hard, sometimes torturous, slave labor to erect buildings and temples which they were never permitted to enter upon completion. The appetite of their god-kings appeared insatiable. Khmers had reached their vortex of exploitation and were seeking and striving for a change which culminated with their conversion to Theravada Buddhism.

Loss of City's Surplus Base. With the god-king image shattered, the rulers succeeding Jayavarman VII could hardly mobilize their people for any new impressive construction. The highly centralized power of the kings also weakened, resulting in slackening of both administrative and ecclesiastical bureaucracy. The irrigation system organized by the weakened central machinery, also began to crumble; with reservoirs filled with silt and canals clogged, farmers were deprived of life-giving irrigation water. Due to the absence of annual siltation via floodwaters, the soil became infertile and was changed into latsol (or laterites) by the effects of the humid tropical climate. Thus multiple cropping ceased, and crop production dropped two-thirds.[74] Naturally, the capacity of the Angkor region to sustain a large population decreased signaling an expodus of people from this area. The city, thus, lost its unlimited rural base of support.

Depopulation Due to Malaria. Decline and depopulation of the Angkor region was furthered by undesirable health conditions. Uncared-for, stagnant canals and reservoirs turned into breeding grounds for the Anopheles mosquito, the carrier of malaria. Because no remedy against the deadly disease existed, thousands fell victim to malaria which caused slow death or crippled many. When Khmers migrated to the Mekong delta region, they were rid of this deadly malaria, for Anopheles mosquitos cannot breed in the nonstagnant free-flowing waters of the delta streams.

Advent of Theravada Buddhism. While political, social-economic, and physical changes were taking place, religion was also being modified. The god-king idea derived from Hinduism and Mahayana Buddhism lost its meaning for the common people, even though the kings still clung to Hindu Sivaites. Simultaneously, another branch of the Buddhist religion infiltrated the Khmer land from Ceylon (Sri Lanka) through Siam (Thailand). This was the Theravada Buddhism, which supported the doctrine of resignation and professed individual salvation but did not pay homage to the ideas of serving a god-king. Even a peasant could afford this religion because, unlike the elaborate Hindu rituals, it was administered by priests who pledged to live in poverty. Thus, Theravada Buddhism became immensely popular among the change-seeking Khmer people. As a result, the language of Hindu Brahmins (Sanskrit) began to disappear—the last Sanskrit inscription in Angkor was dated 1327.[75] As with the Latin in the Western World, Sanskrit continues to be used in present-day India as a ritual language for marriage, death, and formal worship; however, it is completely extinct in Cambodia. The people of Angkor replaced Sanskrit with Pali, another India-based language used by the Theravada Buddhists. Pali inscriptions began to appear in Angkor around 1309,[76] a date marking the twilight period of Hinduism in Cambodia.

Army Weakness Leading to Land-Vulnerability. At the end of the thirteenth century, northern and western peripheral territories of the Khmer empire took advantage of Angkor's weakness and began to declare their independence. The same physical factor which contributed to the westward expansion of the Khmer empire was now reversed. The Chao Phraya valley core base Thais had no physical barrier in preventing their access to Angkor. When they acquired sufficient strength, their former subjugators were struck down. Thus, after 1432 Angkor disappeared as a core area.

No other activity of significance took place in the Angkor area until the 1970s, when the Khmer Rouge guerrillas used the area for their operations. The western part of the Tonle Sap basin bordering Thailand was the operation ground of the Pol Pot communist guerrillas in the early 1980s, while the remaining areas of Kampuchea were controlled by the puppet Heng Samrin government based in Phnom Penh. For five years (1979–84), the opposing communist groups, the pro-Chinese Pol Pot guerrillas and the pro-Soviet Heng Samarin government, had been fighting each other ruthlessly, practicing a form of genocide, and creating famine and utter instability in Kampuchea. Such a protracted and savage civil war between two native communist groups is unprecedented in the history of world communism. As of 1984, Samrin's government controlled the major part of the country supported by the Vietnamese. Pol Pot's insurgent bases were potent and were located near the borders of neighboring Thailand, where the insurgents often took refuge whenever strongly pursued by Samrin's army. The exiled Prince Sihanouk and several other non-communist governments supports this insurgency in order to curb Vietnamese expansionism.

UPPER MEKONG VALLEY AND LAOS

The narrow Mekong valley, with its long sinuous alluvial plain, traditionally has been the home of sedentary wet-rice cultivators. This valley developed as a political core of Indochina in the fourteenth century when (a) Angkor began to decay, (b) the Tonkin Viets were engaged in eliminating their centuries-old Cham enemies, and (c) the Siamese kingdom of Sukhotai submitted to Ayutthaya.

The Laos, who are racially akin to the Siamese Thais, constitute most of the population of the valley. Laos, considered "barbarian" by the Chinese, migrated in several stages from Nan Chao, which was conquered by the Mongols under Kublai Khan in the thirteenth century. After the demise of Nan Chao, Thai and Lao migration southward increased, resulting in added Lao strength in the Upper Mekong valley. However, these Laotian migrants had to submit to Angkor sovereignty until the fourteenth century because they were too weak to stand against the Khmers.

Growth of Laotian Core Areas

Fa Ngoun, founder of the Laotian empire Lan Xang, established his capital with the blessing of Angkor in 1353 on the present site of Luang Prabang. Shortly thereafter, Fa Ngoun not only declared independence, but also conquered much of the northern Khmer territory and brought the Siamese kingdom to submission. The kingdoms of Siam and Angkor, lying to the south of Luang Prabang, were easily accessible by land. The numerous rapids in the Mekong river made it virtually impossible for the Luang Prabang based Lan Xang kingdom to extend further south. In any case, the kingdom of Lan Xang had been expanded to cover all of present-day Laos and the northern and eastern parts of Thailand.

By the fifteenth century, the neighboring countries, realizing the extent of Laotian expansion and fearing its emerging power, began to subdue Laos. The Cambodians were too weak to wage war against Laos, but the Burmese, Siamese, and Vietnamese did all that they could to subjugate Laos.

Neighboring Kingdoms Eye on Laos

Vietnamese interest in Laos was limited because any expansion on the other side of the Annamite Cordillera was not only strategically unstable, but also was full of geographical problems. The Vietnamese seized the Laotian capital of Luang Prabang but once, in 1479. Both the Burmese and Siamese competed with each other to subjugate Luang Prabang and Vientiane, the new Laotian capital, in the beginning of the sixteenth century. Burmese attack and rule of Luang Prabang and Vientiane was effective temporarily only during the sixteenth century. For the Burmans, however, the hilly, rugged land between the Irrawaddy and Mekong valleys was, nonetheless, an obstacle to land-based invasions of Laos. In the seventeenth century, when Siam became stronger than Burma, she found it rather easy to attack, govern, and dictate terms to the Laotian kings of Luang Prabang and Vientiane. The Siamese core in the Chao Phraya Valley was more potential resource-wise than the Upper Mekong valley cores at Luang Prabang and Vientiane because the Mekong valley provided only a narrow strip of fertile land. The plains to the west of the Mekong consist of old alluvium which has a tendency to form into infertile laterites. Beginning in 1767, Siam, with a superior resource-based core area, turned the Upper Mekong core areas into vassals.

The vulnerability of Upper Mekong valley core areas was increased when Laos was divided into two kingdoms and later into three. Luang Prabang and Vientiane were formally separated in 1707, while the third Laotian kingdom of Champassak was established in the south in 1713. Each of these kingdoms fought each other and sought Siamese and Burmese aid in their struggles for domination.

Superimposition of Culture in the Mekong Valley

Animistic Base. Despite their residence in China, the Laos had not adopted Buddhism before coming to the Mekong valley. Instead, they believed in a form of animism, the worship of *phi* (spirit). Phi is omnipresent; bad spirits bring misfortune while good spirits must be invited and worshipped. True phi believers bury their dead in unmarked graves since they believe that the "sooner the evidence of grave disappears, the more auspicious it is for the deceased and the family."[77] The longer the signs of a grave remain, it is more likely that the dead man can join the evil *phi pheta.*[78]

Buddhist Influences. Eventually superimposed on such beliefs were two forms of Buddhism-Mayahana Buddhism during Jayavarman VII's reign in the twelfth and thirteenth centuries, and Theravada Buddhism from Angkor, Siam, and Burma beginning in the mid-thirteenth century. Theravada Buddhism influence was more widespread than Mahayana Buddhism because Laotian kings adopted it and made it the state religion. Buddhism remained the state religion in Laos until 1975. No king was enthroned unless he was a Buddhist. Although Buddhists perform cremation, the phi belief of burying the dead is still practiced. In the absence of true Brahminic influence, Mekong valley kings looked to Buddhism as a source to bestow on them the image of god-king. During the sixteenth century, Vientiane became the spiritual center of Theravada Buddhism which was at that time designated as the state religion. Since 1824, the political oath of allegiance to the king had been taken in a specially erected Buddhist Temple of Sisaket. Nearly every sizeable village in Laos has at least one pagoda.[79]

Indian and Hindu Cultures. Along with Buddhism also came a great deal of Brahmin influence. However, it must be made clear that Indian influence in Laos never came directly from India. Indianization was attained with the adoption of religious and cultural traits of her neighbors who had been influenced by Indian culture for centuries. Indian influence was most evident in Laotian religious literature, the main works being the Indian *Jatakas, Ramayana,* and *Panchatantra*. Stories relating to the Vedic god Indra are especially beloved in Laos.[80]

In Laos, even the profane literature is imbued with religious overtones suggestive of Buddhist and Brahminic inspiration. Folklore, prose and verse romances, epics, apologues are all influenced by Indian traditions.[81] Because the Laos who migrated from South China had no written script, there is little phi evidence in their literature. Indeed, Lao writings are composed primarily of Indian forms and contents. The names of Lao kings reveal Indian influence. Visun (1501–1520), Dhamnikaraja (1596–1622) and Chandrakumara (1825–1868)[82] are names of Indian origin. Unlike the custom in Angkor and Champa, the suffix of *Varman* was not added to the end of a name. Indian influence in Laos, on the whole, was not very strong because of the deep-rooted, preexisting animistic beliefs.

The French in the Upper Mekong

As in Cambodia, French interest in Laos and the Upper Mekong valley was aroused by Siamese efforts to bring Laos under control. With a successful naval blockade of Bangkok in 1893, the French ended Siamese claim to Laos which thereupon became a French protectorate. A treaty signed with Siam in 1904 gave the French more control over the Laotian territories that Siam had gained in 1885. The Laotian king, who had his headquarters and palace in Luang Prabang, was stripped of all powers. Instead the French resident ruled Laos from his station at Vientiane. Laos became a part of the Indochina colony, and as with the other four parts, was governed by the French Governor General in Hanoi and Saigon, and his Superior Council.

The Upper Mekong Valley did not provide any economic attraction to the French. It was left in virtual isolation; no significant effort was put forth to make it accessible to the rest of the world. No important changes were brought about in Laos.

> On the whole, French rule rested lightly on Laos. The French accepted the advice and used the services of the local elite, especially the chiefs of the tribal groups. Patterns of local rule were not greatly changed and local custom and tradition went unmolested, insofar as they were not incompatible with the larger French objectives.[83]

Nevertheless, the French abolished slavery and tightened the reigns of administration, particularly regarding the control of all fiscal matters. The Upper Mekong valley remained in its backward state with subsistence agriculture of wet-rice cultivation. Although the area was capable of producing a small amount of surplus rice for export, it was almost devoid of any modern industry.

Independence of Laos and Shrinkage of Influence from the Upper Mekong Core

Laos, an independent nation again by 1953, was by then already divided into two; the Luang Prabang-Vientiane-based royal core, and *Pathet Lao*, the communist occupied parts in the Annamite Cordillera and Northern Mountains. Western powers, particularly the United States, took care of the royal core by providing all kinds of aid to sustain it, while North Vietnam and China helped *Pathet Lao*. Although the royal core held the Upper Mekong valley which accounted for about two-thirds of the total Laotian population of about two million, the *Pathet Lao* occupied two thirds of the area of Laos.

With a long-drawn war in Laos, and an extraordinary military spending, the Upper Mekong had become not only a rice deficit area, but also one of the world's largest recipients of aid per capita. Most of this aid was used for nondevelopmental purposes. The economy persisted in the same primitive subsistence status that it was for centuries. The cease-fire with *Pathet Lao* forces in 1973, which also had resulted into the formation of a coalition government, did not last very long. Soon after the first military victories achieved by the communist forces in South Vietnam and Cambodia in 1975, there was a peaceful takeover of the Laotian Government by the Pathet Lao forces in November of 1975, abolishing the centuries old monarchy, naming the country the "People's Republic of Laos," and thus, completing the formation of Communist governments in all of Indochina.

Unlike Kampuchea, the Laotian communists were able to unite; Kaysone Phomvihane and the former Prince, Souphanouvong became premier and president, repectively, of the new republic in 1976. Continuity of the old communist leadership was maintained. The leaders turned pro-Vietnamese and pro-Soviet and thus, did not have to face the danger of Vietnamese invasion. The former prime minister of Laos, Prince Souvanna Phouma, was named an "Advisor" to the government, but spent most of his time playing cards and died of natural causes in 1984.

Dual control of Laos from Vientiane and Luang Prabang ceased in 1976. The capital, Vientiane, became the only national center of the country, while Luang Prabang, the former royal capital, lost its national reputation and became a regional central place. The royal palace at Luang Prabang is now a museum.

In the early 1980s, Laos was not experiencing any significant food shortages, but its economy remained stagnant.

> "Despite abundant resources in the form of timber, minerals, unused but cultivable land, and vast hydroelectric power, the economy remains extrammelled by a shortage of skilled labor and management personnel, limited financial resources, and the inability to attract much foreign aid because of Vientiane's involvement in Vietnam's Kampuchea adventure. Above all, there remains uncertainity over the future course of economic planning."[84]

Footnote References

[1]Shannon McCune, "The Diversity of Indo-Chinese Physical Geography," *Far Eastern Quarterly*, Vol. 6 (August, 1947), p. 338.

[2]Present-day Phan Rang.

[3]Paul K. Benedict, "Languages and Literatures of Indo-China," *Far Eastern Quarterly*, Vol. 6 (August, 1947), p. 380.

[4]G. Coedes, *The Making of Southeast Asia* (Berkely: The University of California Press, 1967), p. 63.

[5]*Ibid.*, p. 66. Taking a bath in the sacred Ganges River is considered to be holy by the Hindus.

[6]John F. Cady, *Southeast Asia: Its Historical Development* (New York: McGraw-Hill Book Company, 1964), pp. 107–108.

[7]Coedes, pp. 65–66.

[8]R.C. Mazumdar, *Ancient Indian Colonizers in the Far East: Vol. 1 Champa* (Lahore: The Punjab Sanskrit Book Depot, 1927), pp. 79–80.

[9]Marco Polo's account further elaborates that, at that time, Champa sent a tribute of 20 elephants every year to the King of China.

[10]Refers to sandalwood.

[11]Harry Y. Benda, *The World of Southeast Asia* (New York: Harper & Row Publishers, 1967), pp. 11–12.

[12]Cady, p. 107.

[13]Coedes, p. 123.

[14]Cady, p. 168.

[15]G. Maspiro, *The Kingdom of Champa: A Translation of Chapter 1 of the Royaurne du Champa* (New Haven: Yale University Press, 1949), p. 18.

[16]*Area Handbook of Vietnam*, D.A. Pamphlet No. 550–40 (U.S. Government Printing Press, 1962), p. 36.

[17]Bernard Groslier, *The Art of Indochina* (New York: Crown Publishers, 1962), pp. 53–54.

[18]L.P. Briggs, "A Sketch of Cambodian History," *The Far Eastern Quarterly*, Vol. 6 (August, 1947), p. 346.

[19]Wm. Theodore de Bary, (editor), *Sources of Indian Tradition*, Vol. 1 (New York: Columbia University Press, 1967), pp. 236–243.

[20]*Kautilya's Arthasastra* dating back to the 3rd century B.C. defines seven such limbs: the kings, the ministers, the country, the forts, the treasury, the army, and the allies, *Ibid.*, p. 244.

[21]Groslier, p. 56.

[22]Osborne calls this a pyramidal bureaucracy. In this system those mandarins who had gained the doctoral degree in the state organized competitive examinations entered the civil service at the higher level. Mandarinal civil service in the capital of Hue was esteemed over the service in the provinces. Milton E. Osborn, *The French Presence in Cochinchina and Cambodia* (Ithaca: Cornell University Press, 1969), p. 17.

[23]*Ibid.*, p. 176.

[24]C.A. Fisher, *South-East Asia* (London: Metheun, 1966), pp. 539-540.

[25]*Ibid.*

[26]*Ibid.*, p. 539.

[27]*Ibid.*, p. 540.

[28]Joseph Buttinger, *Vietnam: A Dragon Embattled*, Vol. 1 (Frederick A. Praeger, Inc., 1967), p. 39.

[29]*Ibid.*, pp. 38-39.

[30]Osborne, p. 19.

[31]Doxiadis Associates Consultant, *Saigon Metropolitian Area Urban Development Program and Plan 1* (Athens, Greece: 1965). p. 1

[32]*Area Handbook of Vietnam*, pp. 358-359.

[33]*Ibid.*, p. 359.

[34]James B. Hendry, "Land Tenure in South Vietnam," *Economic Development and Cultural Change*, Vol. 9 (1960), p. 40.

[35]Joseph J. Zasloff, "Rural Resettlement in South Vietnam: The Agraville Program," *Pacific Affairs*, Vol. 35 (1962-1963), p. 338.

[36]Benjamin Cherry, "Vietnam Diggin In," *Far Eastern Economic Review* (June 24, 1972), p. 22

[37]*Ibid.*

[38]*Far Eastern Economic Review* (May 13, 1972), p. 33.

[39]*Ibid.*, p. 37.

[40]*Ibid.*, p. 33.

[41]*Asia 1976 Yearbook,* Hongkong: Far Eastern Economic Review p. 320.

[42]Nayan Chanda, "A Last Minute Rescue," *Far Eastern Economic Review* (Feb. 27, 1981), p. 29.

[43]Francois Nivolou, "Correcting Past Mistakes," *Far Eastern Economic Review* (May 16, 1980), p. 62.

[44]*U.S. Army Area Handbook for Cambodia* (Prepared by Foreign Areas Studies Division of the American University, 1963), p. 266.

[45]Nayan Chanda, "The Cambodian Nightmare", *Far Eastern Economic Review* (September 20, 1974), p. 42.

[46]*Asia 1980 Yearbook* (Hongkong: Far Eastern Economic Review Ltd.), p. 207-8.

[47]*Asia 1978 Yearbook* (Hongkong: Far Eastern Economic Review Ltd.), p. 158.

[48]*Op. cit.*, footnote 46.

[49]*Ibid.*

[50]*Op cit.*, footnote 44.

[51]This location falls in Thailand a few miles north of the Cambodian border.

[52]Croslier, p. 70.

[53]Phallic symbol, one of the forms of Siva, worshipped symbolically.

[54]*Svayambhuva* in Sanskrit means self-creating.

[55]Briggs, p. 348.

[56]Lawrence Palmer Briggs, A Pilgrimage to Angkor (Oakland: The Homes Book Company, 1943), p. 72.

[57]Briggs (1947), pp. 349-350.

[58]Chronology of kings who ruled Angkor from A.D. 802 thru 1215: Jayavarman (802-854), Jayavarman III (854-877), Indravarman (877-889), Yasovarman (889-910), Yasovarman's sons-until 944, Rayendra Varman (944-968), Jayavarman V (968-1001), Suryavarman I (1002-1049), Udayditydvarman (1049-1064), Suryavarman II (1113-1152), and Jayavarman VII (1181-1215).

[59]Bernard Groslier and Jacques Arthaud, *The Arts and Civilization of Angkor* (New York: Frederick A. Praeger, Inc., 1957), p. 26.

[60]One of the Hindu gods, who has four names holding a disc, the conchshell, the ball, and the club. According to Brahman trinity, he is the Protector.

[61]Groslier and Arthand, p. 27.

[62]*Mokha* is a Hindu way of salvation, in which one is freed from the pains one has to encounter after being reborn. *Mokha* also means going to heaven directly after death.

[63]*Nirvana* is a Buddhist conception of salvation.

[64]Don Clifford Mills, "Angkor: A Theocratic System of Urban Development," *Ekistics*, Vol. 33, No. 195 (February, 1972), pp. 132-134.

[65]Malcolm MacDonald, *Angkor* (London: Jonathan Cape, 1958), pp. 97-98.

[66]*Ibid.*, p. 98.

[67]George Coedes, *Angkor-An Introduction* (Hong Kong: Oxford University Press, 1963), pp. 105-106.

[68]Groslier, *The Art of Indo-China*, p. 95.

[69]MacDonald, p. 67.

[70]The Cham-Khmer rivalry has already been described in the beginning of this chapter.

[71]Groslier, *The Art of Indo-China*, p. 190.

[72]Coedes (1963), p. 104.

[73]Bernard Groslier, *Angkor Art and Civilization* (Thames and Hudson, 1966), p. 162.

[74]Groslier, *The Art of Indo-China*, p. 189.

[75]*Ibid.*

[76]*Ibid.*

[77]Frank M. LeBar and Adrienne Suddard (editors), *Laos: Its People, Its Society, Its Culture* (New Haven: Hraf Press, 1963), p. 56.

[78]*Ibid.*

[79]*Ibid.*, p. 49.

[80]*Ibid.*, p. 92.

[81]*Ibid.*

[82]G. Coedes, *The Making of Southeast Asia*, pp. 176–177.

[83]LeBar and Suddard, p. 17.

[84]Stanley S. Baddington, "Laos in 1981: Small Pawn on a Larger Board," *Asian Survey*, Vol. XXII, No. 1 (January, 1982), pp. 96–97.

Chapter 12

Thailand: A Geographical Analysis

Ashok K. Dutt

Thailand is the only country in Southeast Asia with a 2,000-year-long history of monarchy, in which the monarchy is still in place today. Though the power of the king has been severely reduced since the revolution in 1932, the king retains his symbolic position. The Kingdom of Thailand, as it is called, was influenced by Indian Hindu and Mahayana Buddhist religions until the seventh century A.D., and later by the Sri Lankan based Theravada Buddhism. Thailand is surrounded by four neighbors; Burma, Laos, Kampuchea (Cambodia) and Malaysia. It is with the first three that the Thais had deeply established cultural and political relationships along with a shared religion. As Malaysia is reached only through a forested isthmus, communication with it had been poor. Culturally, Malaysian Moslems developed different traditions in contrast to Theravada Buddhists of Thailand.

Thailand was controlled by the native Mon Kingdom of Subarnabhumi during the early Christian era. Its capital was then at U Thong. The Mons were subjugated by the Funan Kingdom, centered in the Mekong delta, during the third century A.D. and turned into a vassal state. By the middle of the sixth century, when Funan started to show signs of weakness, a new Mon Kingdom, Dvaravati, developed in the Chao Phraya valley, which lasted from 550 to 1253 A.D. Its capital was Nakom Patom (Fig. 12-1a). By the eleventh century, when the Angkor-based Kampuchean Kingdom expanded westward, the Dvaravati became its vassal like its predecessor Subarnabhumi. The Funan and Angkor sovereigns operating from Kampuchea did not encounter any obstruction in conquering Thailand because no significant physical barrier existed between them. However, starting in the eleventh century, new immigrants from China poured into Thailand in great numbers. These immigrants, known as Thais, were attracted to the Chao Phraya valley because it had a productive wet-rice agricultural base. The two new Thai Kingdoms established were the Sukhotai and Chiang Mai. The Chiang Mai capital was located at the northern end of the Chao Phraya basin. The Sukhotai Kingdom, which lasted from 1236 to 1419, was quite powerful and had no difficulty in conquering Dvaravati in 1238. Sukhotai and Chiang Mai regained the Thai sovereignty by overpowering the Khmers and overrunning their capital, Angkor, in 1353. While different regional kingdoms were rising and falling in different parts of the Chao Phraya basin, there was one that was most powerful, the Kingdom of Ayutthaya (1350–1767). The capital, also called Ayutthaya, was named after the capital of the Indian epic *Ramayana*. Ayutthaya had subdued Sukhotai and the other minor kingdoms of Thailand and had turned Angkor and Laotian kings into vassals. Further, Thai expansion into Laos, also, had no physical obstruction because the headquarters of the Laotian kingdoms centered at Vientiane, Luang Prabang, and Champssak were in the Mekong valley, connected with Thailand by plains and relatively accessible plateaus. As a matter of fact, Laos remained a vassal of Thailand intermittently until the French occupation in 1893.

The Burmans had their core areas in the Irrawaddy-Sittang valley and Tenasserim coast, thus were buffered from the Thai core areas in the Chao Phraya basin by relatively inaccessible mountain ranges and jungles. Hence, neither the Thais nor the Burmans were ever able to subjugate each other for a long time. Even when Burma mustered enough strength in 1758 and 1767 to successfully conquer Ayutthaya, difficulties were encountered in sustaining the occupation and hence it did not last for more than a few years.

After the Burman destruction of the Thai capital of Ayutthaya in 1767, the capital was shifted

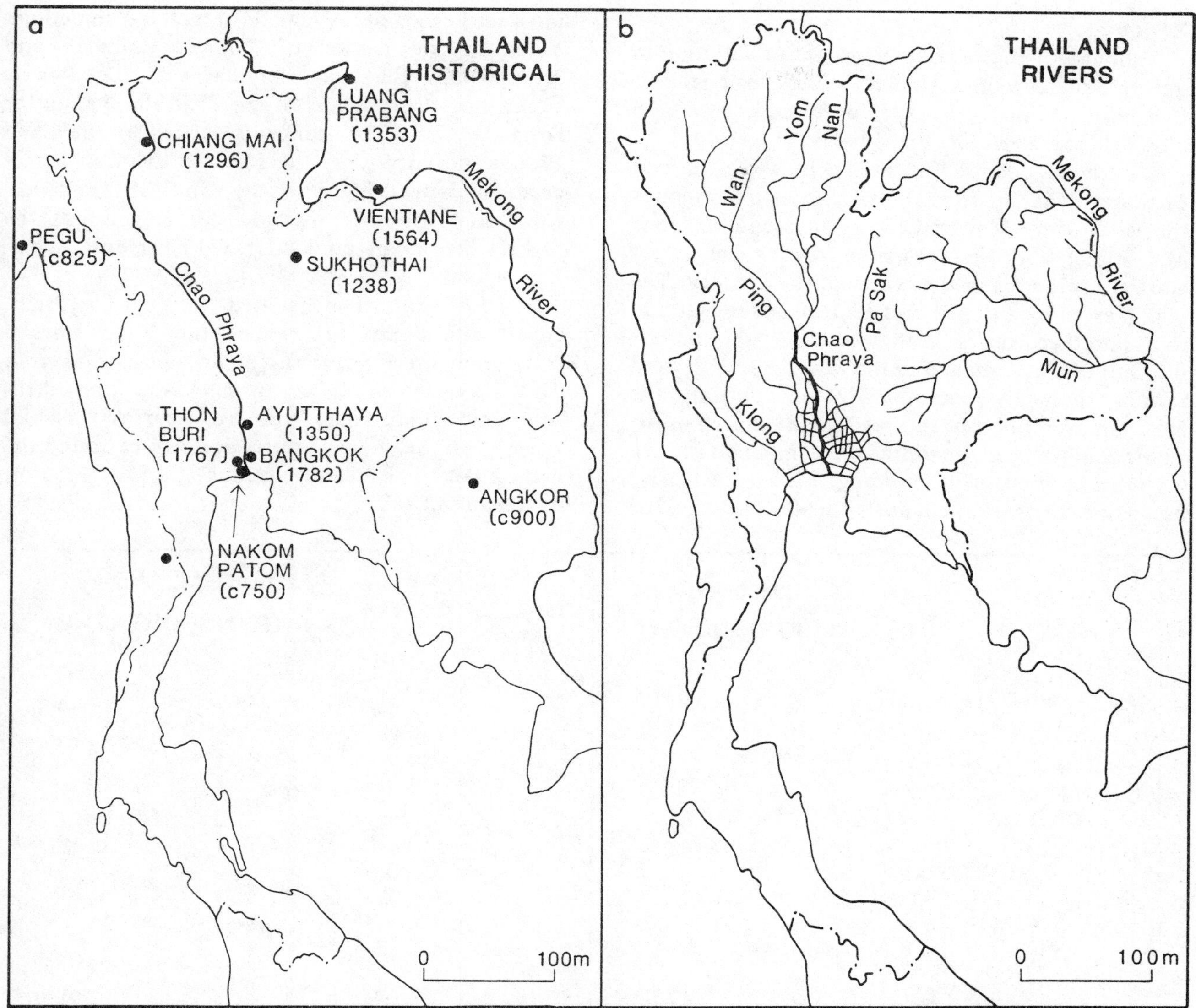

Figure 12-1 a. Capitals and Core Areas of Thailand and Adjacent Countries. b. The River Systems of Thailand. Intricate Network of Canals at the Lower Chao Phraya Valley.

southwards to the right bank of the Chao Phraya, first at Thonburi, then to Bangkok in 1782, on the opposite side of the river. Starting in the late nineteenth century, the Thai Kingdom began to modernize with the establishment of railroads, telegraph services, scientific education and the abolition of slavery.

Thailand is the only country in Southeast Asia which was not occupied by any western colonial power. As a matter of fact, its location between the British colony of Burma to the west and Malay to the south and the French colony of Indochina to the east, gave it a buffer status whereby both the European super powers made a tacit agreement not to occupy Thailand. Thailand, thus, remained a buffer state with sovereign status throughout the colonial era.

PHYSICAL FEATURES

Thailand has an area of some 198,250 sq. miles (514,000 sq. km.)[1] made up of river plains, plateaus and forested mountains. Specifically Thailand is located between latitudes of 5° 30''N and 20°N (not quite 1,000 miles or 1600 km. long). Longitudinally it is about half this distance and lies between 97° 30''E and 105° 30''E.[2] The country can be said to be at the center of mainland Southeast Asia. Due to its position the country experiences a tropical climate. Its coastline extends for some 1,200 miles around the Gulf of Thailand (or Siam) with a 120 mile stretch of coast along the Indian Ocean.

Regions

Although there is a certain amount of variation in the literature as to how Thailand can be regionalized, five basic regions can be said to exist based on physical characteristics (Fig. 12–2a).

The Central Plains. This area is truly the heart of Thailand. It is the great central depression which is the valley of the Menam Chao Phraya and the lesser Mai Klong and Bank Pakong rivers. This great alluvial lowland is in the center of the country. The region extends to the Khorat Plateau in the east and to the northern region in the north.[3] To the south is the Gulf of Thailand and to the west lies the Western region. Physically, economically and politically the most important part of this region[4] and indeed of the whole country, is in the south where the Chao Phraya becomes braided. This braiding, plus an extensive network of irrigation channels, makes this area the most fertile part of the region. In fact, it is sometimes called the "rice basket" of Thailand. Politically and economically this area dominates as Bangkok is situated on the left bank of the Chao Phraya not far from the Gulf. The sediments carried by the Chao Phraya are deposited to form a delta which is gradually advancing into the Gulf of Thailand.[5] Compared to other regions, this region has the highest density of population (311 persons per sq. km. in 1982).

North. The North is that area of the country drained by the upper reaches of the Chao Phraya tributaries (the Ping, Wang, Yom and Nan Rivers). This is a region of 60,000 sq. miles with long north-south mountain ridges and deep, narrow, alluvial valleys.[6] In the west of this region can be found the highest land in Thailand, peaking at 8,514' (2595 m) at Inthanon Peak.

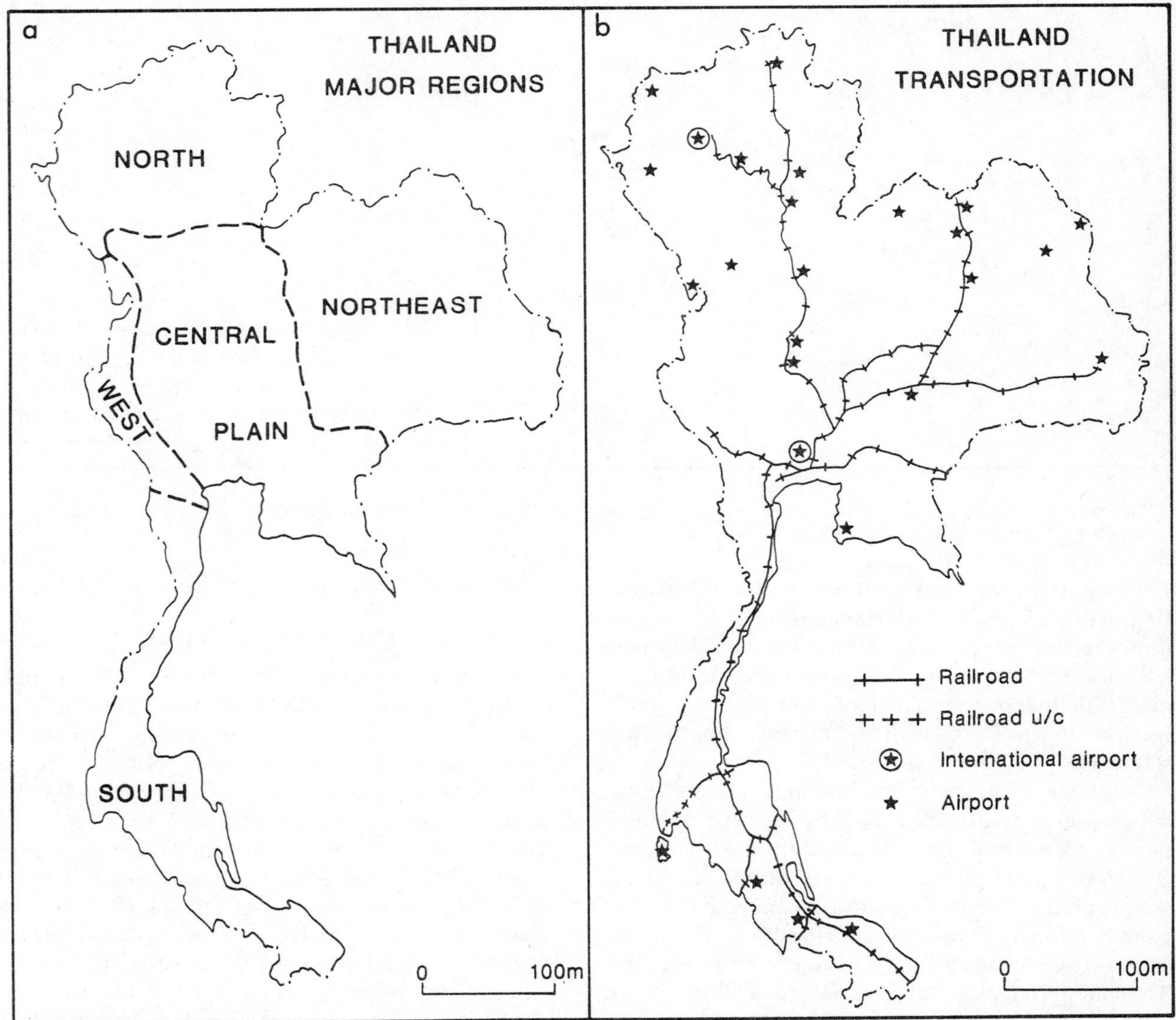

Figure 12-2 a. Five Major Regions of Thailand. b. Transportation Network in Thailand indicating Bangkok's Nodal Location.

The basins of the rivers have largely been cleared of their natural forest cover and rice cultivation based on irrigation can be found.[7] The slopes of this region which receive higher rainfall are still forested and a valuable source of different types of wood. The most valuable of the woods (as far as exports are concerned) is teak and this can be found particularly in the Yom and Wang River areas. This region, however, has a low density of population (60 persons per sq. km. in 1982), about 33% of the national average.

The mountains to the west of this area continue southwards to an area drained by the Khwae Yai and Khwae Noi Rivers. These mountains become the spine of the Malay Peninsula.

Northeast. This region is an elevated and tilted plain which is roughly circular; being about 250 miles (400 km) in diameter. The mean elevation is about 600' (185 m) and the whole area dips to the southeast. Also known as the Khorat Plateau it extends from the limits of the Chao Phraya valley to the Mekong River valley. This area covers a third of the land area of the country and, incidentally, also has a third of the country's population.[8] Communication both within and to other areas is restricted somewhat because the region is isolated from the Chao Phraya valley.[9] Most of the region is drained by the Mae Nam Mun and the Lam Nan Chi which flow into the Mekong. Soils are generally thin and poor and in some areas a "salt cap" develops during the dry season. Due to the indifferent nature of the soils agriculture is limited and greater emphasis is placed on the raising of livestock. Poverty, coupled with its nearness to communist Indochina, makes this region one of the most politically volatile and a future trouble spot for massive guerrilla activities. Though this region has a density of population (105 persons per sq. km. in 1982), that is only about two-thirds of the national average, it is very much hard pressed to support itself.

West. Along the western borders of the country this region is drained by the Khwae Yai and Khwae Noi and is very mountaneous. It receives very heavy rainfall in the monsoon season. The valleys, though, are in a rain shadow and actually receive less rainfall than the Central Plains. This region has the lowest population density (58 persons per sq. km. in 1982) among all regions and the standard of living is also low here due to its isolation from the Chao Phraya core area.[10]

South. The southern region of Thailand extends down the Kra Isthmus to the border with Malaysia. Some 500 miles (800 km) long, this region consists of a ridge of granite hills rising to a maximum height of 6,800' (2,070 m). There is a coastal plain that is narrow and discontinuous on the west but wider on the east, which is densely settled by people dependent on wet-rice cultivation. The overall density of population (86 persons per sq. km. in 1982) for the region, however, is only half that of the nation. Only on the east are there exploitable soils and adequate harbor facilities.[11] Deposits of tin and other minerals occur in this region which also produces the bulk of Thailand's rubber.

Climate

Most of Thailand lies in the tropical wet-dry monsoon belt;[12] the winter months being the dry period (October to May). In both the southeast of the country and in the peninsula, there exist tropical rain forest areas in which there are no seasonal differences in rainfall. Similarly, temperature and rainfall variations throughout the country tend to be split into two types of areas. The peninsula (South region) and southeast have uniformly high temperatures and no month has an average temperature below 64°F (18°C). The rest of the country though, experiences two major temperature seasons; short winter and long summer.

The summer can be sub-divided into hot and wet months. The hot months last from mid-February to mid-April in the central lowlands and to mid-May in the North and Northeast. Temperatures up to 100°F (38°C) are not uncommon at this time of the year. The wet monsoon, which arrives in May, also brings with it a decrease in temperature, especially in the North and Northeast and lasts through October. The winter season (November through February) is pronounced in the North and Northeast, but near Bangkok lasts only a few days.

Rainfall in the southeast and peninsular (South) areas averages between 90''–100'' (2300–2500 mm). However, most of the Central Plain, the North and Northeast receive only 40–45'' (1000mm–1100mm), 90% of which comes during the wet season. The central Chao Phraya valley receives less rainfall than the North and Northeast as it lies in the rain shadow of the Burmese highlands to the west.

Throughout Thailand, except the Central Plains, where relief and soils permit, there is, during the wet season, enough rainfall for rice agriculture. The extensive irrigation system of the Central Plains guarantees effective wet-rice farming. In parts of the Northeast some marginal areas receive less than 1000 mm (39.4") of rain and drought occasionally threatens the crop.[13]

Soils

Thailand possesses a fairly wide variety of soils which tend to correspond to the different regions of the country. For instance, the Central Plains region, particularly the Bangkok delta area, has heavy dark clays suitable for rice growing. One aspect of this soils' suitability for rice growing is that it is fairly impervious and so is good for holding the water in the rice paddies. The Chao Phraya floods, which affect this area, deposit fine sandy and silty soils on the rice paddies. The presence of this soil also permits the growth of mangos and other fruits as well as jute, vegetables, and sugarcane.

The southeastern coastal plain has deep red soils which are ideal for growing rubber, sugarcane, fruit, and even rice where there is enough water. The North has a dark clay soil with considerable alluvial deposits along river valleys. It is in such valleys that rice is grown. Generally the soils support an open forest vegetation which is partly deciduous in drier areas. The soils of the Northeast are fine sandy loams which do not retain water easily and therefore the nutrients in the soil are leached away. Some areas even have saline soils. It is principally because of the poor soils in this area that farmers raise livestock rather than grow crops.

The peninsula soils in the South are a mixture of poor sandy loams and clay loam soils. Rubber trees actually thrive here and rice is also grown in the valleys.[14]

Rivers

Rivers are extremely important to the economy of Thailand to the extent that they deserve special mention here. Until fairly recently rivers were in fact virtually the only means of communications. Another important aspect of the rivers is that they facilitate rice growing in the country. As Blanchard points out, no part of the rice lands of the Central Plain receives the minimum annual rainfall necessary for the growth of rice, yet annual flooding by rivers and irrigation make up this shortfall.[15]

The major river in Thailand is the Chao Phraya, formed by the joining of four rivers from the northern region (Ping, Wang, Yom and Nan). A fifth river adds its water in the central valley. Further south the river then splits into three distributaries which reunite before flowing into the Gulf of Thailand. This central river system has created a 300 mile stretch of fertile, alluvial soil which has become the most important agricultural region in the country (Fig. 12-1b).

The Mekong river in the east forms much of the border with Laos. Other rivers of note are the Chi and the Mun which flow from the Khorat plateau into the Mekong. Also the Mae Klong, which originates in the Tenasserim mountains west of the Chao Phraya delta, flows into the Gulf of Thailand. Lastly, the Bang Pakong flows from the southeastern coastal highlands into the Gulf.

RESOURCES

The mineral resources of Thailand are both extensive and varied[16] although amounts of commercially exploitable minerals are few. Of the most notable minerals, two, tin ore (cassiterite) and wolfran (tungsten) are the most important. Also of importance are scheelite, antimony, coal, copper, gold, iron, lead, manganese, molybdenum, and precious gems (rubies and sapphires). The output of minerals and ore in metric tons in 1978 (most recent figures available) are shown in Table 12-1.

Thailand is troubled by a serious lack of good quality coal. This is hindering industrial development and it also means that charcoal and firewood are used for most domestic cooking. This is leading to a fast depletion of the country's forest resources. A considerable proportion of the mineral wealth is found in the peninsula (South). Already there is concern over the fading tin ore deposits of the country. On the brighter side though there is the possibility that this mineral could be found under the sea in the Gulf. Offshore oil drilling explorations in the Gulf have produced satisfactory results as commercial quantities of natural gas from the Union gasfields have been marketed in the country from the last quarter of 1981. The 200 million cu. ft. per day production replaced about 14% of the country's oil consumption in 1982.[17]

Table 12-1

Mineral and Ore Production in Thailand, 1978

Mineral/Ore	Tons
Iron	88,122
Manganese	72,211
Tin	46,526
Lead	39,121
Antimony	6,759
Wolfram	5,815
Lignite (coal)	638,942
Gypsum	280,905

Source: *Statesman's Yearbook*, 119th edition, 1982, edited by John Paxton (New York: St. Martins Press, 1982), p. 1178.

The importance of minerals to the Thai economy must *not* be overstressed. For instance, less than one quarter of one percent of the labor force is in mining and yet, in spite of increased tin production, mining accounts for less than 2% of total national output.

Power Generation

In 1974, Thailand had an installed electricity generation capacity of 2.4m KW and, in early 1977, only 20% of the population had access to electricity.[18] Two native fuel sources, lignite (coal) and water for hydro-electric power are used for power generation. Only two power plants actually use coal, one near Mae Moh in Lampang Province in the North and the other near Karbi in the South. Even though Thailand has limited supplies of coal, 55% of all electricity generated in 1977 was from steam. This was possible because 81% of the fuel used was imported.

Also in 1977, hydro-electric power supplied 29% of the total amount of electricity generated in the country. Indeed, hydro-electricity is the main, proven potential supplier available for domestic energy. Offshore gas also has future potential.

Existing hydro-electric power sources include the Phuniphon (Yanhee) Dam on the Ping River (140,000 KW installed capacity) and the Ubonratana (Nam Phong) Dam in the Northeast (25,000 KW).[19] Overall, it is the Northeast region that is most power deficient and will remain so until either coal or gas are discovered underground or until agreement is reached between the countries controlling the Mekong river. If there is agreement and cooperation then the hydro-power potential of the river can be exploited to the benefit of all three countries: Thailand, Laos and Kampuchea. An indication of the imbalanced economic growth in Thailand can be seen by the fact that three quarters of the electricity produced is consumed in the Bangkok metropolitan area alone.

Forestry

Forestry is very important to Thailand as a source of export earnings, a supply of firewood and charcoal, and also as an internal supply of building materials. Sixty percent of the land surface of the country is forested but productivity is at a fairly low level. However, forest products, particularly teak, have been an important export earner for more than three quarters of a century.[20]

Figure 12-3. Employment of Trained Asian Elephants in Teak and Other Hardwood Forests of Northern Thailand. Known for an Unusual Sense of Balance, Great Strength and Intelligence, the Elephant responds to Commands by its Mahout. Frequently Two Elephants are required to lift, carry and stack Logs. An Adult Elephant's Work-life is About 20 Years, beginning at 20 Years of Age (Caption and photo by Mildred M. Walmsley.)

Table 12-2
Output of Wood and Wood Products, 1978

Product	Volume ('000 Cubic Meters)
Teak	112
Yang	476
Other	2,019
Firewood	855
Charcoal	284

Sources: *Statesman's Yearbook*, 119th edition, 1982-83, edited by John Paxton (New York: St. Martins Press, 1982), p. 1178.

Most of the other woods produced are used domestically and so are not available for export.

Generally speaking there are three main types of wood producing areas.[21] The North has a mixed deciduous forest with teak intermingled with others. The Northeast provides a supply of other types of hardwoods while all other regions have tropical evergreen forests.

The importance of teak in the forest industry can be seen by the fact that in the early 1970s teak accounted for only 10% of the total volume of timber output but about half of the export volume of 100,000 cubic meters.[22] Some of the teak is transported by specially trained elephants (Fig. 12-3).

Also of importance is the production of Yang wood found in the Southeast and on the eastern side of the peninsula. Overcutting of the forest stock has been of concern in recent years as forest losses are shown to be depleting the capital stock. To offset this the Thai government has started a replanting program but the funds allocated seem to be insufficient.

POPULATION

The Thai population increased significantly after World War II because, as in most other developing nations during this period, the death rate declined very sharply while the birth rate remained high. In this post-war period (1947–82), the nation experienced an almost 300% net growth of population, while during the same three-and-a-half decade period prior to 1947 it grew only a little over 200% (Table 12-3).

Central Plain's High Density

Historically, the population of Thailand had been concentrated in the cultivated areas where rice is produced. The Central Plains, particularly in the southern part around Bangkok, has always had the greatest density of population (Fig. 12-4b). The Chao Phraya valley in the Central Plains region had, in 1960, 200 persons per square mile, but in terms of persons per square mile of cultivated land it was about four times this figure. The lowest densities occur in the mountaneous North and West Regions.[23]

One of the main reasons for the high population density in the Chao Phraya valley is the irrigation on which the people of this area had depended for centuries. Irrigation is used because this area does not receive adequate rainfall for a guaranteed rice crop. The perennially flowing Chao Phraya increases in volume during the rainy season and floods its banks and the adjacent rice paddies providing the needed water for rich rice cultivation. Moreover, canal irrigation is widely practiced in this valley. The Thai government

Table 12-3
Thailand Population Growth

Census Year	Total Population	Annual Rate of Increase in %
1911	8,266,408	
		1.4
1919	9,207,355	
		2.5
1929	11,506,207	
		3.2
1937	14,464,105	
		2.0
1947	17,442,689	
		3.9
1960	26,257,916	
		3.1
1970	34,397,374	
		3.5
1982	48,846,927	

Source: Compiled by the author.

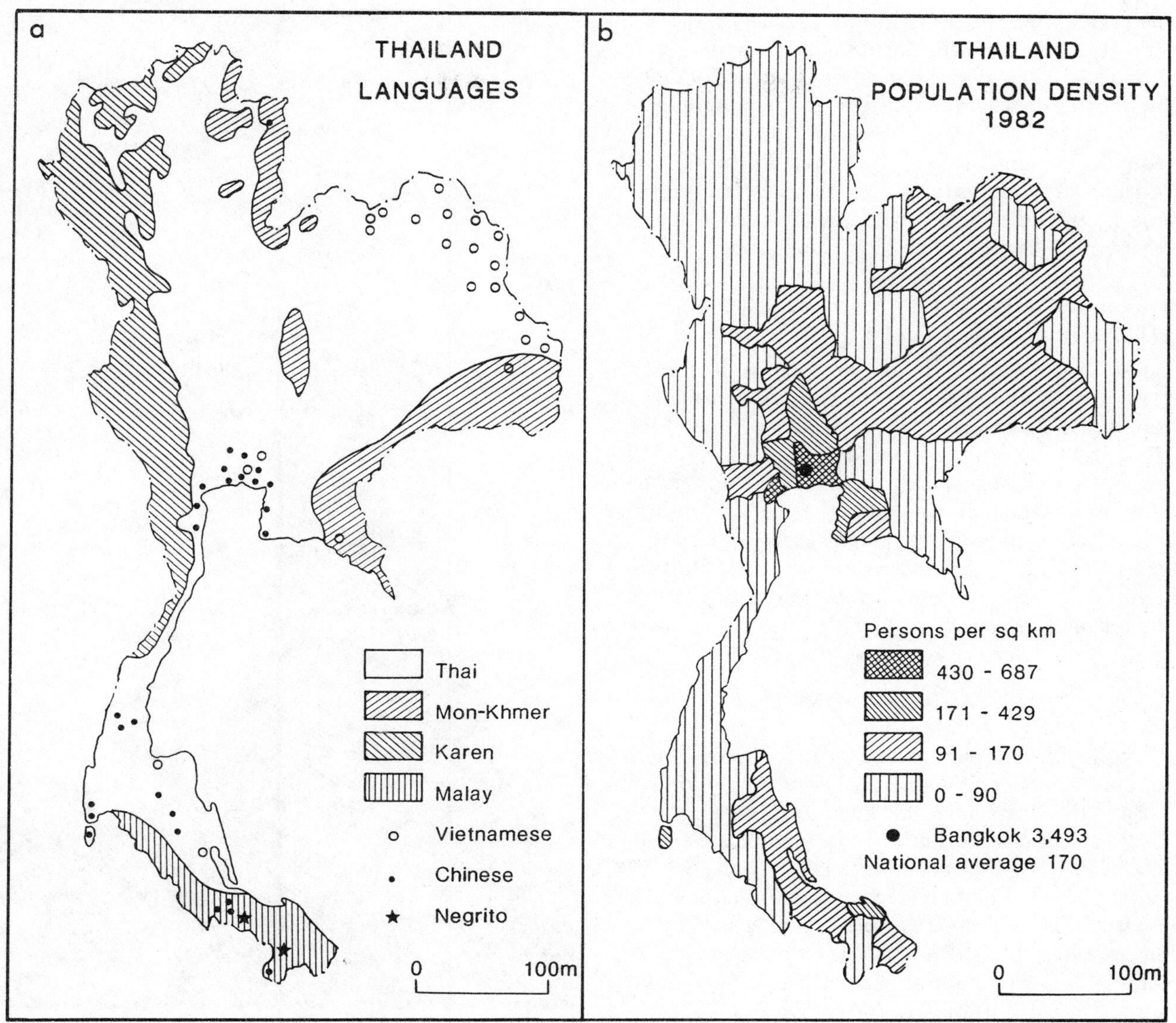

Figure 12-4 a. Ethnolinguistic Pattern of Thailand (Source: Bunge, p. 68). b. Density of Population in Thailand, based on unpublished census data (1982) obtained by the author.

completed the South Pasak Canal Project in 1922 in order to control the spread of natural flood water, needed to avert the problem of overflooding. This was followed by an International Bank and World Bank supported endeavour, the Chainat Project, completed in the mid-1960s. This project included the construction of a dam on the Chao Phraya about 100 miles north of Bangkok, and a system of canals to improve water control on 1.4 million acres.[24] It is no wonder that starting in 1966–77 this valley became the main focus of the high yielding variety of rice (HYV) production because this area already had a system of water control, a *sine qua non* for maximizing yields of HYV. Another reason the Chao Phraya remained the main attraction for the high density of population is the existence of Thailand's political cores in an area in, or very near, the valley, for almost 2,000 years. Such core areas always attract large numbers of people.

Predominance of the Thai Language

The Thai language is spoken by over four-fifths of the people. These people are found all over the country except in the marginal areas (Fig. 12-4a). Though there are eight different Thai dialects, communication among them is not difficult. Those speaking Chinese, about 15% of the country's total population, are immigrants from China and are intermingled with the Thais in the Central Plains. The third most numerically strong linguistic group are the Malays settled adjacent to the borders with Malaysia in the South, where pockets of the Negrito linguistic groups are also found. Semang can also be found in the relatively unaccessible mountains. In the eastern margins the Mon-Khmer are to be found, while to the west there are Tibeto-Burman linguistic groups.

Theravada Buddhism: The Religion of the Country

At least nine out of ten people believe in Theravada Buddhism. It is the state religion in the sense that the King has to be a Buddhist, Buddhist theology is taught in all state-supported schools, except in the four Moslem provinces in the South, and the *wats*, Buddhist monestery-cum-worship places, are supported by the state. The Thonburi Theravada Buddhist temple is also a typical representation of Thai temple architecture (Fig. 12-5).

Figure 12-5. Thonburi Buddhist Temple is a Masterpiece of Thai Architecture (Photo by A.K. Dutt).

AGRICULTURE

Agriculture dominates the Thai economy in terms of employment and makes the largest single contribution to the Gross Domestic Product (GDP) and to export earnings. It is estimated that agriculture employs about 75% of the total active labor force. In 1980, agriculture and livestock accounted for 22.6% of the GDP.[25] The economic growth recorded by Thailand in the 1960s and 1970s was due to the steady expansion of the agricultural sector. The availability of large areas of virgin land for cultivation is seen as a major contribution to this success. Between 1950 and 1980, agricultural holdings nearly doubled in area from 22 million hectares. During this period, Thailand's agricultural base supplied sufficient food for the growing population, and the level of nutrition of the populace, in general, compared favorably to other South and Southeast Asian countries.[26] Starting from the late 1970s, the availability of virgin land for agricultural expansion has declined sharply and thus the only way improvement in production can be achieved is through higher productivity.

The average size of an agricultural landholding was 5.6 hectares in the late 1970s, though sizes did vary due to physical features and the historical evolution of the different regions of Thailand.[27]

In the late 1970s, estimates of overall land use suitability revealed that 50% of the land was considered cultivable. Of this cultivable land, 19% was suitable for paddy, 28% for upland crops and a further 11% for both. The agricultural contribution to the GDP had declined steadily from 1970 to 1980. In sectoral terms, the drop in the growth rate of agriculture is attributable not only to low soil fertility and ineffective governemnt policies,[28] but also to relative increase in the growth rate of other sectors.

On the whole, however, Thailand has proved to be very successful agriculturally. Its chief product, rice has accounted for about 25% of the world's total rice export per annum during the 1970s and early 1980s. Bowring summed up the success:

> It is the only regular, large-scale food exporter in Asia... The existing diversity of Thai agriculture should enable its share of world food trade to grow rapidly...

Most important, Thailand is a highly competitive producer of many food crops, its farmers can, without subsidy, produce sugar cheaper than Filipinos, rubber cheaper than Malaysians, pigs and chickens than the Danes and rice cheaper than anyone.[29]

Crops

The variation in climatic and soil conditions in Thailand permits a wide range of crops to be grown. However, until the late 1950s, the major emphasis in agriculture was on the production of rice and secondarily of rubber. Then these two commodities accounted for over half the value of all commodity exports. Other crops that were grown were usually supplementary to the two mentioned here and were basically for domestic use. Such crops included fruits, sugarcane, beans, potatoes and yams, cassava, maize, cotton, and various oilseeds. A change in the market in the 1960s and 1970s due to increased world demand, (and hence, higher prices) and developing domestic industry spurred independent farmers to grow more of the secondary crops listed above. Hence, in 1980, the major Thai export crops included traditional rice and rubber but also maize, cassava, sugarcane, mung beans, tobacco, jute, keraf, and sorghum.[30]

Rice. It is the country's largest crop and is grown on about three quarters of all farms. About half the production of over 15 million tons was grown in the Central Plains and the major valleys of the North; another two-fifths was produced in the Northeast, and about 6% in the South, which was a rice deficient area.[31] The harvested area of rice was 8.7 and 9.1 million hectares in 1979 and 1980 respectively . This was about two-fifths larger than two decades earlier. Although rice production has been increasing, the volume of rice exports vary from year to year because of variations in the international rice market and the amount of the local harvest. The poor harvest in 1977 reduced exports of rice in 1978 to 1.6 million tons, in 1979 the level rose to 2.8 million tons and 2.65 million tons in 1980. Further, a record level of 3.1 million tons was achieved in 1981.[32]

It is generally believed that the low productivity of rice in the past is attributable to government policies aimed at keeping the consumer price of rice low. The rice premium, an export tap, was the main governmental policy. That, and occasional quantitative export controls were criticized by opponents on the grounds that they reduced profitability and hence discouraged any significant increase in productivity.[33] To help rectify this situation, in 1981, the Ministry of Commerce reduced the level of domestic reserves, simplified export procedures and lowered the export premium. This action had the desired result of increasing rice exports. Export prices for rice increased 12% from 1980 to 1981 and the value of rice rose by 32.9%. The rice sector's percentage share of export value rose from 13.5% in 1980 to 17.2% in 1981.[34]

Rubber. In 1918, there was only one significant rubber plantation in Thailand, yet, since the late 1920s, rubber has been a major crop and a significant export. Until challenged by maize, cassava and sugar in the 1970s, it was Thailand's second most important export earner.[35] Production is mainly in the South, on small holdings often with old, low yielding trees. Climatically the South is the most suited region in the country for rubber production because of year round rainfall averaging over 80'' and warm temperatures.

Thailand had about 1.6 million hectares in rubber in the mid-1970s.[36] The production in 1978 was estimated to be about 467,000 tons (the 1956 figure was 135,600 tons). Problems of the quality of product due to the small scale of operations was in part ameliorated in the 1970s by replanting and reorganization. This was also against a background of rising costs of oil-based synthetic rubber which made natural rubber more competitive in the world market. Since 1971, Thailand has increased rubber production at an annual rate of 5.95%, a rate faster than other producers with the result that in 1979, the country became the third largest producer in the world. In 1980, rubber represented 9.6% of export earnings. Despite an increase in the volume of exports of 3.5%, falling prices have reduced the value of exports by 13.8%. As a result, rubber's share of export earnings fell to 7.1% in 1981.[37]

Maize. It is believed to have been introduced into Thailand in the sixteenth century but it was not until after World War II that it was exported. Maize became an established cash crop in the 1950s and 1960s becoming the third most important agricultural export (after rice and rubber) from 1959 to 1975, when it was overtaken by cassava. Maize is grown throughout Thailand but the northern parts of the Central Plain are the best growing areas. Double cropping is possible for commercial growers.[38]

Domestic demand for this product is quite small and is mainly traded as cattle fodder for Japanese livestock. It is also exported to Singapore, Malaysia, Hong Kong and Taiwan. It was particularly falling Japanese demand and prices for maize which forced a change to the growing of cassava. Thus it was that in 1977 and 1978 exports of maize fell. However, since 1979, both production and exports have increased due to stable prices. Further, new trading agreements with Hong Kong have helped guarantee an export market. In 1978, 2.8 million metric tonnes were produced but this figure had increased to 3.7 million metric tonnes by 1981. This bumper crop in 1981, resulted in a record export of 2.6 million metric tonnes. Hence the fall in prices and the fall in the level of exports that occurred in early 1981, were overcome. As in the case of rubber, a relaxation in the regulations governing the export of maize and a reduction in export taxes have stimulated exports.[39]

Problems of Agriculture

Soils, except in the Central Plains, are generally of low fertility, largely the result of leaching by heavy rainfall.[40] Thailand, on the other hand, has an abundance of agricultural land in relation to its population. Hence, the average farm size of 5.6 hectares in the late 1970s is substantially larger than is usual in Southeast Asia. Large landholdings, by Southeast Asian standards, is also possible because of institutional arrangements which permit a peasant to acquire land simply by clearing it and planting a crop. Thailand alone in Southeast Asia has kept a policy of free land.[41] Nonetheless, the country's productive virgin land has almost all been brought under cultivation and therefore, more and more villagers are apt to become landless, already a major problem.

In the 1970s, the number of landless farmers was thought to be between 500,000 to 700,000. To aid this situation, in 1974 the Agricultural Land Rent Control Act was passed. Basically this act allowed for rental contracts of six years in length but which were renewable indefinitely. Again, in 1975, another law in the form of the Agricultural Land Reform Act made possible the allocation of up to 8 hectares of farmland to landless and tenant farmers. Such land could then be paid for on a long-term installment basis.[42]

Thai agriculture is also facing the problems of transition towards large-scale commercialization. Cecil Werner, a Canadian marketing expert, conducted a survey of local rice trade in Thailand in 1982 and concluded that about US $1000 million was lost annually because of marketing inefficiency, rodent infestation, wasteful processing, overhandling and milling obsoleteness.[43]

MANUFACTURING

The 1978 census data revealed that of an economically active population aged eleven years or more totalling almost 21.9 million, only 1.48 million or some 6.75% were engaged in manufacturing. Even this figure is inflated as it included some 70,000 unpaid family workers and many thousands who work seasonally in rice and sugar milling.

According to an estimate made for the International Bank in 1957, there were approximately 16,000 industrial establishments in Thailand (excluding government factories) but only a little over 300 of these employed over 50 workers. Some 146,000 manufacturing workers in 1960 were engaged in their own production of goods. It is estimated that most of these, together with unpaid family workers, were all probably in cottage industries.

As is common in many third world countries, the industrial sector is dominated by the processing of primary products in small-scale plants. Heavy industry in Thailand is of little significance; the major industries being textiles and processed agricultural products. The textile industry of the country was stimulated in 1981 by the devaluation of the baht allowing Thai textiles to improve their competitiveness on the world market. In 1981, the value of textile exports rose 22.1% over the previous year. Many of the textile factories import silk and cotton yarn from Japan, revealing the inability to completely rely on domestic supply. The stagnation of domestic cotton production and the increased cost of imported yarn is raising production costs, and hence, placing an increased strain on the industry.[44]

Manufacturing employed 6.75% of the work force and contributed 18% to the GDP in 1978; its rate of growth during 1970–78 being ll.5%. Manufacturing's contribution to the GDP in 1980 was estimated to be 20.8%. Although labor force statistics are unreliable and not always collected on the same basis, an overall increase in industrial employment is clearly visible.

Government policy has been directed at stimulating investment, particularly from abroad, through the establishment of the Board of Investment and from private investors through the establishment of the Industrial Finance Corporation in 1959.[45] Even though the Thai government has been interested in private enterprise, the public sector (Ratwisahakit') is quite large and is well established. It consists of 108 enterprises with a total capital of 9 billion baht. State activity is in the areas of agriculture, manufacturing, transportation and energy, including major public utilities. Further, the government is directly responsible for 10% of manufacturing output.[46]

TRANSPORTATION AND COMMUNICATION

Thailand's transportation system is a combination of inland waterways, railroads and roads. Like the old proverb "All roads lead to Rome", all transport arteries converge on Bangkok (Fig. 12-2b). Thailand's strategic position in Southeast Asia, make it a major center of transportation.[47]

Inland Waterways

The system of canals and navigable rivers (principally the Chao Phraya) provides a transportation network of 2483 miles (3999 km). Further, part of this network is navigable all year. Despite the increased use of roads and railroads, water transportation still carries a fair amount of traffic. For instance, in 1976 inland waterways carried 17% of the total freight. Another use of the waterways is that they provide a market place in the form of shop boats which ply the canals (or Klongs) of Bangkok. Passenger boats also travel the canals and often also carry household supplies or fruit and vegetables.[48] The advent of the dry season reduces the distance of navigable waterways to about 1100 km. In the late 1970s, some 7,000 privately owned wooden barges were operational.[49]

Railroads

The railroads of Thailand date back to 1896 when King Ayutthaya inaugurated the first section from Bangkok to Ayutthaya. At this time railroads were not only seen as offering economic opportunity, but also extending administrative control to outlying areas.[50] The railroad did bring considerable economic development as it allowed the expansion of rice growing on the Khorat Plateau and lignite mining in the North.

All railroads in Thailand were nationalized in 1951 and put under control of the State Railway of Thailand (SRT). With help from the World Bank in 1979, Thai railroads were able to replace old steam locomotives with new diesel units. Most of the SRT's 3800 km of meter gauge track is single track except for a two-way 90 km stretch between Bangkok and Ayutthaya. Five main lines radiate out from Bangkok; the 741 km Northern line to Chiang Mai; the Eastern line to Avaryprathet which then joins with the Kampuchian system leading to Phnom Penh; the Northeast line to Nong Khai at the border with Laos near Vientiane; the 150 km line west to Nam Tak; lastly the 990 km southern line joining the Malaysian system. The railroads are the most important means of long-distance travel in Thailand.

Despite increased competition in transport from the road network the railroad is still very important for the transportation of bulk commodities such as petroleum products, cement, and rice.[51]

Roads

Road development in Thailand increased considerably after World War II with help from the USA in the form of aid in the 1950s and 1960s and later also with help from the World Bank. In 1980, there were 13,000 km (8125 miles) of paved, national highways, 22,000 km (13,750 miles) were provincial roads and about 50,000 km (31,250 miles) were tertiary. This gives a total road network of 85,000 km (53,125 miles).[52] One of the important new roads is the Friendship Highway, built with US aid, linking Bangkok with Nong Khai.[53]

Ports and Shipping

Bangkok is Thailand's only major seaport and it is situated 30 km from the mouth of the Chao Phraya. Some 98% of imports and 65% of exports are handled by Bangkok. Despite its importance, Bangkok can only handle ships of 10,000–12,000 tons with a draught of no more than 28 feet. Some 3,300 vessels docked at Bangkok in 1977 and the port handled 18.7 million tons of cargo. Other ports in Thailand of significance are Si Racha and Sattahip (a deepwater supplement to Bangkok) southeast of Bangkok and Songkhla and Phuket in the South. A further 30 smaller ports can be found in the Gulf of Thailand and the Andaman Sea.[54] In 1980, three Thai steamship companies owned 20 vessels between them with a gross tonnage of 151,000.

BANGKOK

Bangkok is situated on the left bank of the Chao Phraya. It not only lies in the center of Thailand, but also is the hub of the country in every sense of the word (Fig. 12–6). Thai peasants and provincial towns look to Bangkok for capital-based political leadership. Further, Bangkok's "residents set standards of behavior, outlook, dress and physical comforts which are imitated in varying degree by," other Thailanders.[55] Bangkok's estimated 5 million (1982) population is about 50 times more than the second largest town in the country. The increasing dominance of the Bangkok Metropolis on the urban structure of Thailand can be assessed from the fact that in 1980 it had 70% of the country's urban population compared to only 42% in 1947.[56] The enormous development gap between Bangkok and other towns makes it most attractive to migrants. As a result of this, the metropolis is growing at an annual rate of 6%, double the national growth rate. Michael points out that despite a critical employment situation, Bangkok may be called the most important growth center of the country.[57] The Greater Bangkok Area, which has only 12% of the country's population, produces about half of the Gross National Product.[58]

Bangkok's main business district lies in China Town and is characterized by bazaar-type shopping with a very high population density in the center. In the periphery of the city the density is considerably lower. The demand for housing is so intense that almost one-quarter of the city's population live in slums, 37% of which are on government grounds and 63% on private land.[59] In contrast, the rich appear to be getting richer with an increasing number of mansions being built on the relatively higher grounds outside the city core, leaving the low lying, flood-prone, unsanitary areas to slum dwellers. In 1972, Bangkok had 43 cars per 1000 inhabitants compared to only 5 per 1000 for Thailand as a whole. It was projected that this number of cars will grow to 50–70 per 1000 in Bangkok in 1990, when the population is expected to reach the 8 million mark.[60] All of these problems necessitated the preparation of a Greater Bangkok Plan (Fig. 12–7).

Soon after the preparation of a plan for the metropolis by an American consultant, the Thai Ministry of the Interior revised the Greater Bangkok Plan in the early seventies to accommodate the increasing number of people. The plan delineated its existing urban area and earmarked areas for redevelopment. Extensive future development areas, both public and private, were planned around the existing urban area. Road traffic arteries were designed to improve transportation.[61] In the mid-1970s, German transport experts, who have suggested further modification to the Bangkok Plan, proposed that the future urbanized areas be further extended, several major and minor sub-centers be created and additional traffic channels be designated.[62] All these grandiose plans need money and legal support for their implementation. The fact is though, that funds are not forthcoming at a pace the planners would like.

THAILAND IN THE EIGHTIES

Thailand faces complex political, economic and demographic problems in the 1980s. Its political problems lie in internal communist insurgency and its situation adjacent to two communist countries: Laos and Kampuchea. In 1979–81, there was a tremendous downswing in communist guerrilla activities, almost 70% lower during the two-year period. The main reason for such a decline was that Soviet-supported Vietnam communists stopped supplying arms and other support to the Thai Communist Party, which traditionally has been allied to the Chinese brand of communism.[63] Fewer guerrilla activities mean a lesser involvement of the government in internal defense spending, leading, in turn, to a greater potential for development expenditure. If the Vietnam-China difference continues and the Thai Communist Party remains inclined to the latter, the law and order situation in Thailand seems to be brighter for the 1980s. This would be in spite of its common borders with Laos and Kampuchea, whose ruling communist parties are aligned with Vietnam.

Thailand is not only a food-sufficient country, but a significant exporter of agricultural commodities. As this country is already using most of its cultivable agricultural land, the only way it can continue to expand its agricultural exports is by increasing productivity, increasing the application of the green revolution technique, expanding irrigation, diversifying crops and improving marketing, processing and storage facilities. Both the Thai government and the farmers are aware of the above facts. If all goes well, by the 1990s the country may be able to lay the foundations for a new industrial nation because only a successful Thai agriculture can be the basis for a strong manufacturing sector. The expansion of natural gas output, started only in 1981, will further guarantee Thailand's transition to industrialization.

Although Thailand's population is generally homogeneous, its fast growth, if it remains unchecked, will cause overall declining development

Figure 12-6. View of Bangkok and the Chao Phraya River (Photo supplied by Royal Thai Embassy, Washington, D.C.).

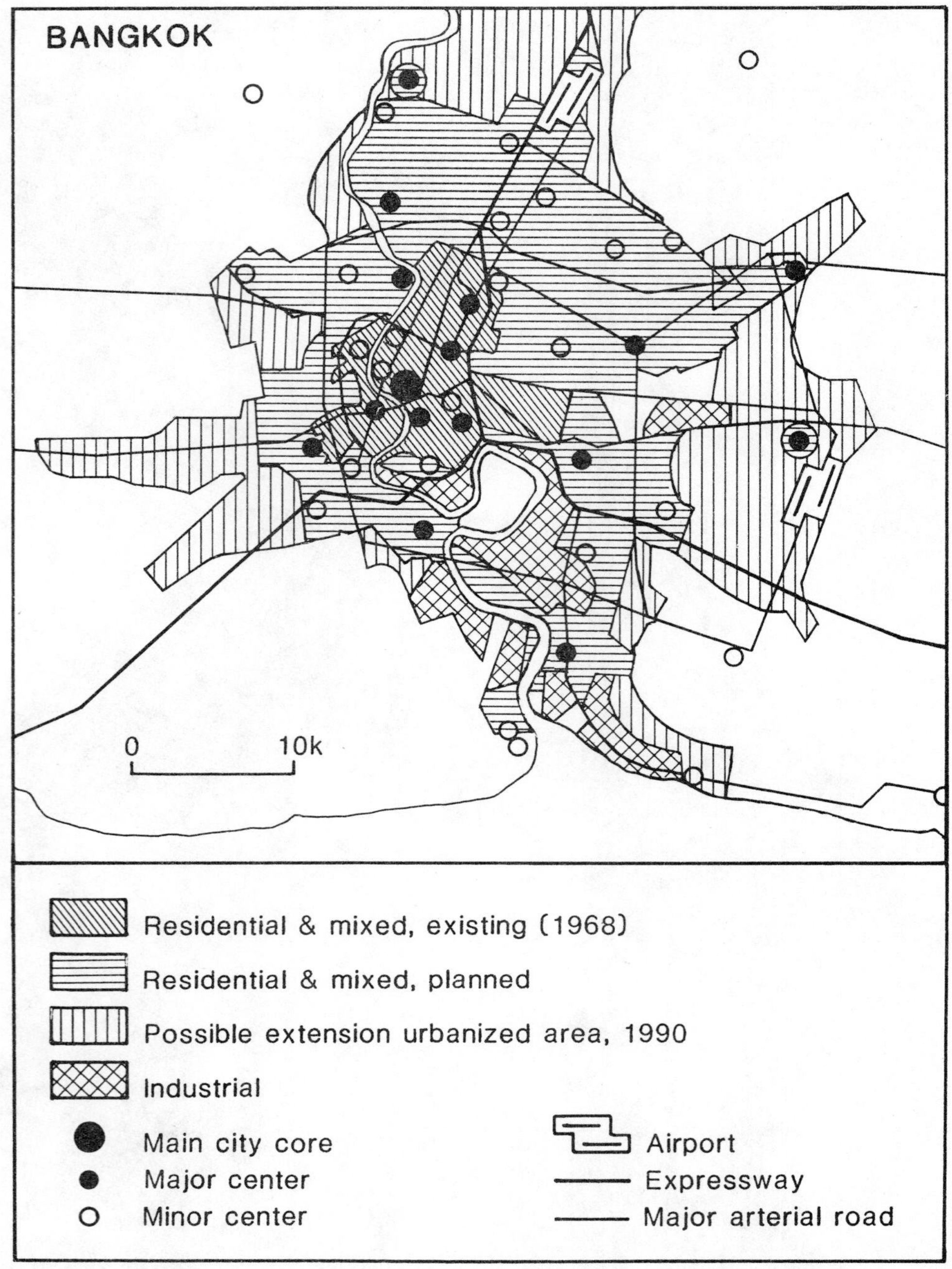

Figure 12-7. Revised and Updated Plan for the Bangkok Metropolitan Area Prepared by the Thai Ministry of Interior, 1973
(**Source:** Michael, p. 7).

for the country. Limited resources which would otherwise be used for further productivity, will have to be diverted to meet the basic needs of the growing population. Family planning which has had limited success until the early 1980s needs to be greatly expanded in the immediate future in order to be able to invest the fruits of development for further development.

In the early 1980s Thailand was in a transitional stage and was trying to emerge as a New Industrial Nation. This can only happen if the pace of development, set since the 1960s, continues through the 1980s.

Footnote References

[1]*The Statesmans Year-Book*, 1982–83, 119th edition, edited by John Paxton (New York: St. Martins Press, 1982), p. 1175.
[2]Wendell Blanchard, *Thailand its people its society its culture* (New Haven: Hraf Press 1958), p. 39.
[3]*Ibid.*, p. 42.
[4]Donald W. Fryer, *Emerging Southeast Asia* (New York: John Wiley and Sons, 1979), p. 143.
[5]*Ibid.*, p. 143.
[6]Blanchard, p. 39.
[7]Fryer, p. 143.
[8]*Ibid.*, p. 147.
[9]Blanchard, p. 40.
[10]Fryer, pp. 144–45.
[11]Blanchard, p. 42.
[12]L.L. Ungur, "Thailand," *Focus, Vol. XXI, No. 3 (November, 1970), p. 5.*
[13]*Ibid.*
[14]Adapted from Wendell Blanchard, p. 46.
[15]*Ibid.*, p. 44.
[16]*The Statesmans Year-Book, pp. 1177#78.*
[17]*Asia Yearbook 1982*, Far Eastern Economic Review, p. 256.
[18]*The Statesmans Year-Book, p. 1177.*
[19]Ungur, p. 6.
[20]Fryer, p. 167.
[21]*Statesmans Year-Book, p. 1178.*
[22]Fryer, p. 169.
[23]*Area Handbook, Thailand* (Washington, D.C.: U.S. Government, 1966), p. 45.
[24]*Ibid.*, pp. 394–95.
[25]*The Far East and Australia 1982-83* - A Survey and Directory of Asia and the Pacific (London: Europe Publications Ltd., 1982), p. 1131.
[26]Bunge Frederica M. (ed.), *Thailand: A Country Study* (U.S. Department of Army, Washington, D.C.: Government Printing Office, 1981), p. 127.
[27]*Ibid.*, pp. 128–29.
[28]*The Far East and Australia 1982-83*, p. 1130.
[29]Philip Bowring, "Asean's darkhorse," *Far Eastern Economic Review* (October 22, 1982), p. 88.
[30]Bunge, pp. 135–36.
[31]*Ibid.*, p. 136.
[32]*The Far East and Australia 1982-83*, p. 1131.
[33]Bunge, p. 136.
[34]*The Far East and Australia 1982-83*, p. 1131.
[35]*Ibid.*, p. 1132.
[36]Bunge, p. 137.
[37]*The Far East and Australia 1982-83*, pp. 1132–33.
[38]Bunge, p. 137.
[39]*The Far East and Australia 1982-83*, p. 1132.
[40]Bunge, p. 129.
[41]Fryer, p. 150.
[42]Bunge, pp. 134–35.
[43]Paisal Sricharatchanya, "Ano-support Scheme," *Far Eastern Economic Review* (March 5, 1982), p. 50.
[44]*The Far East and Australia 1982-83*, p. 1134.
[45]*Ibid.*, p. 1134.
[46]George Thomas Kurain, Encyclopedia of the Third World (New York: Facts on File Inc., 1982), p. 1743.
[47]Bunge, p. 153.
[48]Kurain, pp. 1744–45.
[49]Bunge, p. 153.
[50]*Ibid.*, pp. 153–55.
[51]*Ibid.*, p. 155.
[52]*Ibid.*, pp. 155–56.
[53]Kurain, p. 1745.
[54]Taken from Bunge, pp. 157–58.
[55]*Area Handbook for Thailand*, p. 100.

[56]"Land for Housing Bangkok's Poor", *Asian Institute of Technology Review*, Vol. 21, No. 2 (April 1982), p. 7.

[57]Richard Michael, "Bangkok, Jakarta, and Singapore: A Comparative Analysis of Plans and Problems", *Ekistics*, 266 (January 1978), p. 4.

[58]*Ibid.*

[59]*Asian Institute of Technology Review*, p. 7.

[60]Michael, p. 6.

[61]*Greater Bangkok Plan 2513*, Map No. 15 (Ministry of Interior, Government of Thailand), Undated.

[62]Michael, p. 7.

[63]Larry A. Niksch, "Thailand in 1981: The Prem Government Feels the Heat," *Asian Survey*, Vol. XXII, No. 2 (February 1982), pp. 194–95.

Chapter 13

The Philippines: Emerging Fragmented Nation

Alden Cutshall

The Philippines is a fragmented country of extreme contrasts situated on the rim of Asia. For a quarter of a century, this nation of islands has been attempting to transform a traditional, agricultural, colonial, and family-oriented type of economy into an industrial, national, and market-oriented system. In some respects, significant progress has been made; in others, changes have barely begun. The country has been described as a transition zone between East and West in the Pacific. At best, this is a half truth; because geographically and culturally, the country is truly within the Southeast Asian realm, although on the periphery of that vast area of land and water. But the Philippines is unique among Oriental countries to the extent that is has been affected by western culture. In terms of religion, education, government, recreation, and living standards, Philippine values appear to be those of the West. These values, however, have been superimposed upon a number of older, indigenous values that are truly Asian. Such values include a commitment to the conscious past, a fatalistic attitude toward life, a predisposition to authoritarianism, shame rather than guilt as a reaction to failure, and an emphasis on status rather than function, among others. Hence, outside Manila and a few other cities, the Philippines is only superficially Westernized.

The Philippines is an insular arc, largely of volcanic origin, consisting of more than seven thousand islands, eight hundred of them inhabited (Fig. 13-1). Somewhat like ancient Greece, both the intervening seas and the rugged interior uplands have contributed to physical fragmentation and cultural isolation. Problems of transportation, economic development, and political unity are not unrelated to physical geography. Sixty-five percent of the land is characterized by folding, faulting or recent volcanic activity. With 115,600 square miles, the country is about the size of Arizona, or about twice as large as Illinois. Luzon, the largest island, is about the size of Ohio; Mindanao, about equal to Indiana. But the Philippines extends over 16° of latitude, approximately the distance from Minneapolis to New Orleans, or from Stockholm to Rome.

The tropical position and archipelagic character of the country assure warm, uniform temperatures and generally adequate precipitation, yet northern stations do experience a higher annual range of temperature than most of Southeast Asia, 7° higher at Laoag. Temperatures above 100°F. are extremely rare and occur only at interior, lowland stations as in the Cagayan Valley of northeast Luzon. Sea level temperatures below 70°F. are uncommon and below 60°F. unknown; but temperatures in the sixties do occur at Baguio (elevation, 4860 feet) and some other upland stations.

Although precipitation totals generally appear adequate at all reporting stations, there are marked variations on amount and distribution in different parts of the country. Most of Mindanao, the Sulu archipelago, Palawan, and parts of a few other islands have a representative tropical rain forest regime. Southeastern Luzon, Samar, and parts of some of the other central islands have precipitation throughout the year, receiving adequate moisture during the months of the southwest (summer) monsoon, and even heavier rainfall during the period of the northeast (winter) monsoon (accentuated by northeast trades). Western Luzon has a long, dry season corresponding to the period of the northeast monsoon.

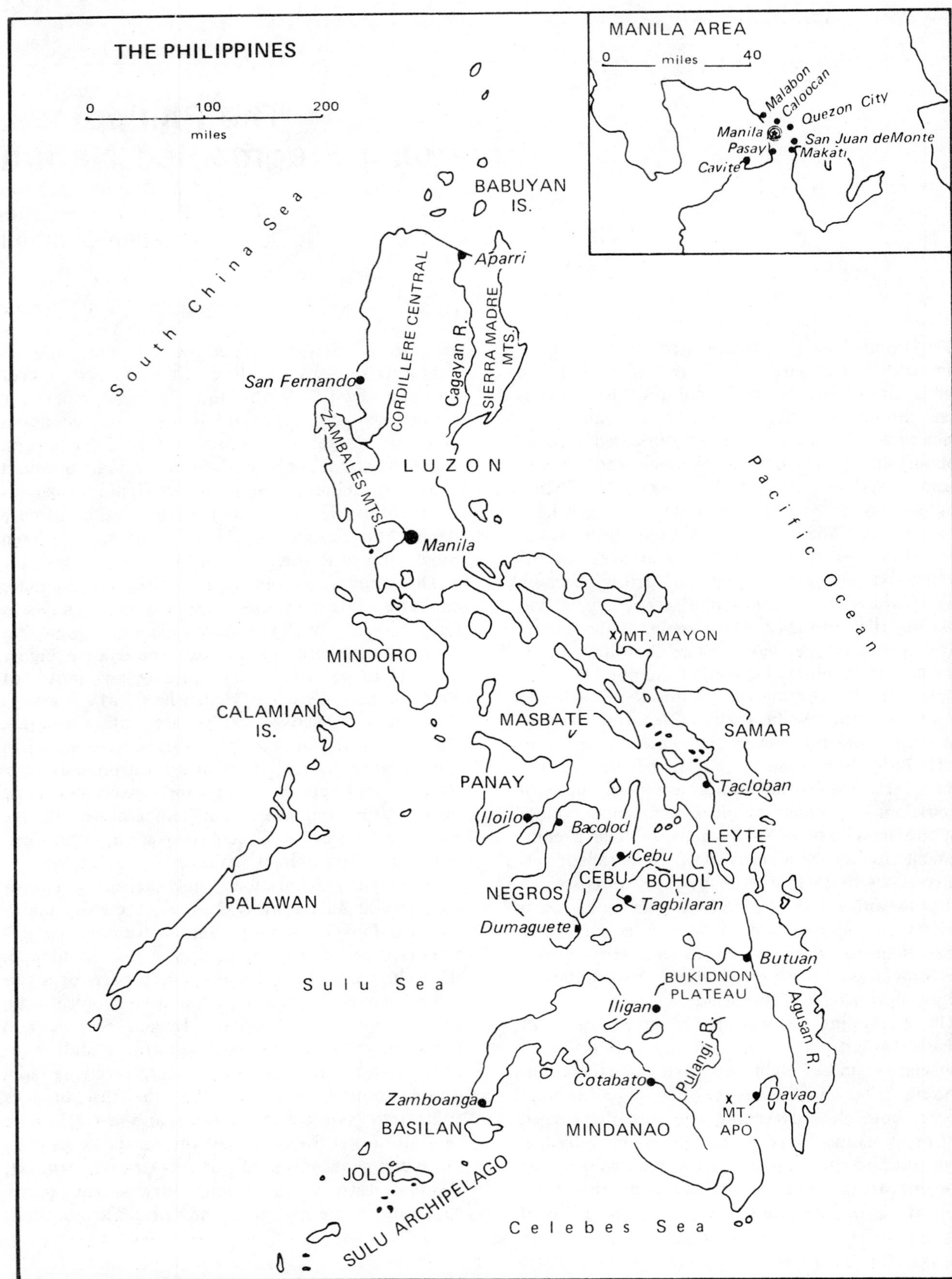

Figure 13-1. Philippines.

The driest areas, generally, are the Ilocos Coast of northwest Luzon, most of Cebu and southeastern Negros, and some of the interior lowlands of Mindanao.

HISTORICAL FACTORS

The first known inhabitants of the islands, some twenty-five thousand years ago, were a pygmy-like people, the ancestors of today's few remaining Negritos, a short black people with negroid traits who live in the remote parts of Luzon and a few other islands. About eleven thousand years ago, a wave of seafaring people arrived from eastern China and possibly from Taiwan as well, with another similar influx about four thousand years ago. They were of Mongoloid stock with Caucasian strains. They had stone tools for growing grain—probably rice—and some knowledge of rudimentary agriculture.

The largest and most significant migrations into the islands occurred in several waves beginning about 300 B.C. They were the ancestors of the present Malays or lowland Filipinos. They are brown-skinned individuals, of medium height, with slender bodies, flat noses, straight black hair, and brown eyes. They had a knowledge of weaving and pottery making and brought Iron Age tools. They organized themselves into many separate communities, *barangays*, named after the crude boats in which they arrived. This was primarily an association of a kinship group at the village level and in a coastal location convenient for trade with Chinese, Hindu and Arab seafaring merchants with whom they may have had previous contacts. A union or crude confederation of barangays oftentimes developed, but seldom endured. Hence, when the Spanish gained control of the area after Magellan's visit in 1521, there was no effective political organization, no centralized governmental structure, no elite culture, no military subjugation; in fact, no group that ruled over a large territory or over thousands of people.

The Colonial Period

Spanish Philippines. Magellan's landing and subsequent Spanish expeditions left no permanent imprint until Miguel Lopez de Legaspi was appointed governor and established a settlement on Cebu in 1565. Four years later, his forces were moved to Panay and in 1671 to Manila. Thus, the then bamboo-barricaded village on the swampy alluvial fill at the mouth of the small Pasig River became the administrative center for the entire archipelago. By 1700, Spanish authority had been extended over most of the coastal and lowland areas north of Mindanao and possibly Palawan.

The Spanish interest was primarily economic, and, secondly, religious. There was little attempt to train Filipinos for self-government or to advance them politically. Within the Spanish central government in Manila, Filipinos held no responsible positions. Economically, most Filipinos remained subsistence farmers and fishermen. However, there was the encouragement and emergence of commercial crops such as sugarcane, tobacco, coconuts, and abaca (Manila hemp); and there was an introduction of the then more advanced techniques of irrigation. Associated with these newer concepts of agriculture and agricultural systems, came the emergence of the Spanish concept of private property, rather than the communal ownership that characterized the barangay.

In most cases, friars marched with soldiers at the time of conquest; and conversion to Catholicism was usually peaceful and generally successful. The only exceptions were those areas that never came under effective Spanish jurisdiction; namely the Moro stronghold of Mindanao and the mountain areas of northern Luzon. The union of church and state was both effective and realistic; the governor-general was also the civil head of the church.

The American Colony. If Spanish contributions to the Philippines were primarily economic and religious, America's contributions were most pronounced in the fields of government, education, health, and sanitation.

From the beginning, the United States' policy stressed a progressively increasing amount of self-government. In support of the initially stated intent of protection, development of a democratic form of government and ultimate independence, autonomous powers were delegated to Filipinos as qualified leaders demonstrated their ability to handle domestic affairs—first at the local level, then on provincial matters, and gradually at the "colonial-nation" level. Unfortunately, the 10-year Philippine Commonwealth, beginning in 1934, never provided a realistic and effective last step to independence. As a result of the great physical destruction of property, loss of political leaders and other factors during World War II, the Philippines were less qualified to assume the role of an independent nation-state when independence finally came in 1946 than at the beginning of the Commonwealth period.

TABLE 13-1

Philippines: Population and Average Growth Rate

Year	Population	Average Rate of Growth
1903	7,635,426	—
1918	10,314,310	1.90
1939	16,000,303	2.22
1948	19,234,182	1.91
1960	27,455,799	3.18
1970	36,684,486	3.10
1980 (est.)	47,914,017	3.00

National Organization

The Philippine Republic is organized as a political democracy with a liberal constitution patterned after the constitution of the United States. There is no legally privileged class; but in practice, the government was dominated initially by a group of wealthy landowners, and with few exceptions, has continued to be in the hands of the wealthy segment of the society.

It is a fact of reality that the Philippines has had a democratic form of government for 27 years (1945–72), but it never enjoyed a democracy as a democracy is known in Anglo-America. It was a paper democracy but not a practicing democracy. Over the years, justice and security became myths. Tax evasion and smuggling made headlines at home and abroad. Violence and corruption became rampant. Private armies were maintained by rural warlords. Hotel doormen wore side arms. And, the civil service payroll was padded with political appointees. The result of these conditions, and many other inequities, brought the Philippines to the edge of chaos and possible political calamity and permitted (if not required) President Ferdinand Marcos to impose martial law in late September, 1972. Most Filipinos accepted the change calmly and philosophically. It appeared to be a way to end political paralysis and high level corruption. Whether the deep social inequalities can and will be remedied is a matter of conjecture. An effective democracy must be a practicing democracy. The Philippines has never had a practicing democracy. From late 1972 until 1984 it was an agitated and excited nation; and the future was still unclear.

POPULATION, URBAN GROWTH, AND CULTURE

The population of the Philippines has more than doubled since independence, and was estimated at almost 48 million in 1980, the 16th largest country in the world in terms of population. With a rate of population growth of more than three percent per year, it is expected that the population will grow by another seventy to seventy-five million in the three remaining decades of the twentieth century. The population problem, then, is not one of present numbers or density or distribution, but of growth.

Generally, the most densely populated areas are the Ilocos Coast, the Central Plain-Manila area, and the central Visayas, especially Cebu along with eastern Panay and parts of Negros. These are the most intensively cultivated areas and the most "urbanized" segments of the country. Outside the mountainous interiors, the least densely populated areas are Palawan, western Mindanao, northeast Luzon, and parts of southern and interior Mindanao.

Urban Growth Patterns

The core area of the Philippines centers on Metropolitan Manila (population 4.3 million). It includes the Central Plain of Luzon which extends from Lingayan Gulf to Manila Bay and the Laguna-Batangas area southeast of Manila. This region includes the heart of the Tagalog area, the capital and financial center, the transportation hub of the country, and most Philippine manufacturing.

The Philippines is changing from a rural to an urban nation. From 1950 to 1960, urban growth proceeded at nearly twice the rate of total population growth. According to the 1960 census, the population living in cities was 4 million, or 15% of the total population. By 1970, there were more than 4 million people in metropolitan Manila alone. Estimates place the national urban population at 34.1% of the total in 1970[1]. In 1980, there were 8 cities with a population of more than 200,000.

The rapid city growth results in part from the high natural increase that characterizes the country and in part from rural to urban migration. One reason for the massive movement from countryside to the city is rural poverty, stemming from rigid systems of land ownership and rural economic stagnation that impede farm families to acquire land, to enlarge small holdings, and to improve their social and economic positions. Another prime factor is the concentration of economic activity, especially the new factories, in or near the larger centers, particularly the Manila region. Also, urban workers' wages and salaries exceed the income of farm workers. A third significant factor reflects the fact that most of the universities are located in the cities and the better health services (hospitals, clinics, doctors, dentists) are likewise concentrated in the larger cities. One other stimulus to migration is the relatively inexpensive transistor radio, which brings urban information (and urban propaganda) to all parts of the country.

Once in the city, however, the typical migrant may find a life quite different from that which he envisioned, for he probably finds himself competing for work among others like himself. Despite the number of newly created industries in the 1950s and 1960s in the cities, jobs are still too few to supply work for all the people seeking employment. As a result, unemployment rates are higher in the urban than in the rural sectors of the Philippine society. Some return to their former rural homes, but most urban migrants remain in the hope of improving their economic and social status, oftentimes living in overcrowded ghettos and "shanty towns."

Ethnic and Linguistic Composition

The Filipino population is predominately of the Malay physical type with cultural differences producing recognizable ethnic categories. Despite the identification of more than fifty ethnic-linguistic groups, 90% of the population fits into a relatively homogenous lowland, Christian, ethnic category. These are the Hispanicized people who have been Christianized and, to varying degrees, Westernized as a result of more than three and half centuries of Spanish and American rule. Within this category are groups, each with its own language, a sense of group identification, and a recognizable geographical distribution. Minority groups not fitting into this broad category reside mainly in the mountains of Luzon and interior Mindanao.

Among these minority groups are remnants of Negritos in the mountains of Luzon, Negros, Palawan, and a few of the other larger islands. The Kalingas, Ifugaos, Bontocs, and other in the mountains of northern Luzon are collectively called Igorots, a Tagalog word meaning mountaineer. There is a variety of minor groups in Mindanao and Palawan, including the Dumagats who are similar to the Papuans of New Guinea and the Tasaday, a small tribe with a Stone Age culture who were discovered only in June, 1971. In contrast, there are some rather sophisticated groups among the minority peoples of Mindanao.

The most important alien ethnic group is the Chinese. For at least one thousand years, Chinese traders and then Chinese migrants have played an active role in banking, have financed much of the surface transportation within the country, and have entered in to retail trade, even in some of the remote areas. Many Filipinos, including prominent figures in the nation are of partial Chinese ancestry. Those who have not intermarried with Filipinos have retained much of their Chinese culture, and they constitute a conspicuous ethnic minority. Philippine Chinese are, for the most part, urban residents; the Chinese farmer and Chinese market-garden-type-farming so conspicuous elsewhere in Southeast Asia is not a feature of the Philippine landscape.

The Western segment of the population consists of some 5,000 Americans, 1,500 Spaniards, and smaller numbers of several other nationalities.

Eight major dialects are spoken. The chief of these are: Cebuano (Bisaya, Visayan) spoken by more than 24% of the population; Tagalog, used in the area around Manila and the dialect upon which the National Language (Pilipino) is based, almost 24% Ilocano, used primarily in northwest Luzon, 11%; and Panay-Hiligayon, 10%. The other four are Bicol (Bikolese) used on southeast Luzon, 7%; Waray-Waray (Samar-Leyte), 5% Pangasinan, used around the southern margin and inland from Lingayan Gulf, 2.5%; and Pampangan, on the Central Plain between the

Tagalog area and the Pangasanan group, 3.2%.

Internal migrations have blurred linguistic boundaries, mostly in the larger cities and in frontier areas. Manila lies within the Tagalog area, but it has larger number of Ilocanos, Bicols, and Cebuanos than Vigan, Legaspi and Cebu City respectively. A somewhat similar situation exists in parts of the Cotobato lowland of Mindanao. Ilocanos settled in the area before World War II; Pampangans and Tagalogs were resettled there during Magsaysay's amnesty program for former Huks in the 1950s; and more recently, Cebuanos have migrated into the area to take advantage of agricultural opportunities. There are also indigenous Moros living in the Cotobato Valley. Hence, a rural area of interior Mindanao and urban metropolitan Manila exemplify regions of a multiple native-language situation.

Religious Factors

The Philippines is predominately Roman Catholic. The Philippine Independent Church (Aglipayan), a local version of Catholicism, is the religion of about five and one-half percent of the population; and almost 3% of the people are Protestants. Almost 5% are Moslems (Moros), Islam having been introduced into Mindanao and the Sulus from the Malay Peninsula in the fourteenth century. The remainder of the inhabitants are members of the Iglesia ni Kristo, or one of several other indigenous cults, or practice one of the diverse beliefs based upon supernatural beings, usually spirits of deceased ancestors, but sometimes with no human affiliations. Most of the non-Christian and non-Islamic people live in the remote areas of the larger islands.

Religion and social life exercise a reciprocal influence with each affecting the other. Filipino culture has been formed, in large part, by religious influence; and the churches play a major role in education and social service. Oftentimes, churchmen have made direct pronouncements on social and political issues.

Language Base

The Philippines is commonly referred to as the third largest English speaking country, next only to the United States and the United Kingdom. Although spoken by only about 40% of the population, it is taught in all schools at all levels and is the required medium of instruction above the primary grades. It is the language of the leading newspapers and magazines and most of the radio and TV stations. It is the language of government, trade, and commerce. Pilipino, which is basically Tagalog, is the national language, is compulsory in all schools at all levels, and is spoken by probably one-half of the population.

Spanish is the third official language; but prob ably no more than half a million people, largely among the social elite, speak or understand it as a second language.

ECONOMIC DEVELOPMENT

Economic growth is proceeding at a respectable rate and generally has spread broadly across the country. But, the rate of growth has not been uniform or consistant in either time or place. As a result, it has been characterized as erratic, or as a lurching economy. Agriculture is dominant and is the listed employment of 57% of the workers. Industry employs 15% of the labor force and accounts for 19% of the GNP. By Western values, Filipinos are poor people. Nonetheless, the 1979 per capita income of $620 was surpassed among the Southeast Asian countries only by Singapore, Malaysia, and Brunei. Unfortunately, half the nation's wealth is in the hands of only 5% of the population. This imbalance of wealth has become a major source of irritation and was one of the factors leading to the violent student-worker demonstrations in 1970.

Agricultural Resources

Agriculture is characterized by subsistence cropping, primarily rice, but replaced by corn or sweet potatoes in certain areas; secondly by export crops such as sugar, coconut products, abaca and pineapples; and in selected areas, by commercial crops for the domestic market (tobacco, rubber, coffee, tropical fruits, onions or garlic, and both tropical and mid-latitude vegetables).

The Philippines is primarily agricultural but less so than most other Southeast Asian countries and does not feed itself. There was a food deficit in late Spanish times, during the American colonial period; and despite concerned efforts at correction, it remains true today. This reflects both the rapidly increasing population and dietary habits. There is now a small rice surplus in some years, a result of the diffusion of the high yielding varieties developed at the International Rice Research Institute, and adequate amounts of most other necessary staples. But the increased demand for wheat products, beef and dairy products, and processed middle latitude fruits and vegetables is not, and generally cannot, be met by domestic agriculture.

In volume, agricultural production more than doubled between 1949 and 1960 then continued to increase at a slower pace during the 1960s. But improvement has been slow. Although Philippine farmers are not as labor intensive as most other Asian countries, they are not as capital intensive as those of western countries. Draft power is inadequate. Farm equipment ranges from the simple digging stick and the Oriental hoe to power machinery. Fertilization, crop rotation, and conservation are not practiced by the representation small farmer; but the recent widespread introduction of the high-yielding IRRI rice varieties, which require more fertilizer, is forcing some change for the better. Although prohibited by law, shifting cultivation continues and is rather widespread in the rugged interiors of the larger islands and some other remote areas.

Rice. About three-fourths of the population depends upon rice for food, and some eight and one-half million acres are planted with rice each year. With 5.7 million tons produced in 1975, it is grown in every province; but the principal producing regions are the major lowlands: the Central Plain of Luzon, the Bicol Region, eastern Panay, parts of the Cagayan Valley, and a few areas in Mindanao. (Sugar is more important than rice on the plain of western Negros.) The famous Ifugao rice terraces of northern Luzon contribute only a very small percentage of the national total and are atypical rather than representative of Philippine rice culture. Two crops of rice are possible in the Bicol and other eastern areas that receive year-round precipitation and is becoming progressively more widespread in the area southeast of Manila and on parts of the Central Plain as more efficient irrigation techniques are developed and utilized. Central Luzon is the chief surplus rice area, but metropolitan Manila easily absorbs this surplus.

Maize. Almost 25% of the Filipinos live chiefly on corn (maize). Cropping practices vary widely, with from one to four crops per year, depending on local conditions. Corn has a greater climatic tolerance than rice and is suited to a wider variety of topographic and soil conditions. Hence, corn is normally relegated to lands that are unsuitable for rice production and is of commercial significance on the coraline limestone areas of the eastern Visayas, in the hilly areas of northern and eastern Mindanao that were settled primarily by Cebuanos, and on the sandy alluvial soils of the middle Cagayan Valley. The surplus from Mindanao and northeast Luzon is shipped primarily to food deficit Cebu and secondly to Manila for consumption by the metropolitan Cebuanos. Davao is now the leading corn producing province.

The cultivation of other food crops such as roots, tubers, legumes, and tropical vegetables appears relatively less important in the Philippines than in Indonesia. There has been a considerable increase in the acreage of both coffee and tropical fruits in the last couple of decades.

Commerical crops. Coconuts, sugarcane, abaca, tobacco, and pineapples occupy almost 20% of the cultivated land and produce some two-thirds of the export earnings. Coconut products and sugar are the large earners of foreign exchange, yet the country is not really an efficient producer of either. Nonetheless, the Philippines is the world's foremost producer of coconut products, with about 40% of the world total and with some four million people dependent on the coconut industry to some extent for their economic livelihood. Coconut production is widespread south and southeast from central Luzon. Sugar production from 21 *centrals* is now more than two million tons annually (two and one-third million in the 1970—71 crop year) and the country ranks sixth as a producer of sugar from cane. Production is concentrated principally on Negros, secondly in central Luzon, and with lesser amounts from Panay, northern Cebu and western Leyte. For a variety of reasons, both internal and external, abaca production has been on the decline for several decades and is now no more than two-thirds of the prewar total. Nonetheless, it is still the third ranking export and the Philippines supply some 90% of this premier hard fiber. Principal producing areas are southeastern Luzon, Samar and Leyte, and parts of eastern Mindanao, all areas of abundant year-round rainfall. Commercial tobacco production is important in only two areas. The middle Cagayan Valley has long been the center for cigar tobaccos. The southern Ilocos Coast and the north portion of Luzon's Central Plain have become of equal, if not greater, importance for Virginia-type cigarette tobacco, first introduced in 1950. Philippine tobacco is produced for the domestic industry, as none of either type is exported in any quantity. Two large leased areas in Mindanao are devoted to pineapple growing, each supporting a modern cannery, and with almost all the production exported.

Mineral Wealth

Mining employs only 0.3% of the estimated national work force of about eleven million persons, but produces some two percent of the national product. The country has no proven petroleum or natural gas resources and only very meager coal deposits. In prewar years, gold mining was important but has decreased to a relatively unimportant position. Chromium, primarily in the Zambales mountain area, has been important since the 1930s; and the Philippines has ranked among the world's leading producers. Copper production has increased from that of a single shaft mine in the Baguio mining district in the 1930s to production from several open-pit deposits of low grade ore in Cebu, Samar, southwestern Negros, and Zambales. With an annual production of about 200,000 metric tons (metal content), the country may be the leading copper producer in Asia. The mining of iron ore is potentially an important activity, but its prosperity for the present must depend upon the strength of the Japanese market. The paucity of mineral fuels has stimulated a modest development of hydroelectricity, of which the most widely known, but not the largest, is at the Maria Cristina Falls in northern Mindanao.

Fish and Forest Products

A wide variety of fish are found in Philippine waters, and there is a catch of some 720,000 metric tons per year. More than half this amount comes from some form of subsistence fishing, about one-third from commercial fish ponds. Although the volume of production has tripled in the last 25 years, the fishing industry is unable to supply the nation with adequate seafood products to meet the growing demand. An expansion of the present 350,000 acres of commercial fish ponds may be the appropriate solution.

Tropical forests, most of which are secondary growth, cover about one-half of the country. Logs, lumber, plywood, and other forest products collectively rank second to coconut products among Philippine exports. The foremost buyer of logs is Japan; most of the lumber is shipped to the United States where it is marketed under the general name of "Philippine Mahogany." Bamboo and rattan, principal secondary forest products, primarily are marketed locally.

Industrial Development

Historically, Philippine manufacturing consisted primarily of cottage or handicraft industries, or of plants that processed agricultural, mineral, or forest products, primarily for export, and oftentimes financed by foreign capital. Illustrative of this latter group were the large saw mills, centrifugal sugar mills, desiccated coconut plants, and the larger cigar factories.

Since independence, there has been a national impetus to develop manufacturing. The processing plants, as compared with their prewar predecessors, have increased production by the use of new machinery or other improved techniques and procedures, by expanding the line of products manufactured, by more efficient use of by-products, or as a result of better labor relations.

Beginning in 1950, too, there was a recognition that Philippine economy was grossly overbalanc ed in favor of agriculture. By a series of import controls and other means, the government encouraged the establishment of new industries, manufacturing primarily for the domestic market. As a result, Philippine manufacturing now includes petroleum refineries, cement plants, fertilizer factories, textile mills, flour mills, and plants making miscellaneous steel products, aluminum foil and sheets, flashlight batteries, rubber tires, plastics, shoes, drugs, and a variety of food products.

The Manila area has been, and remains, the industrial center of the country. However, much of the new industry is outside crowded Manila. It is along the Pasig River in Quezon City or Pasay, in the Marikina Valley of Rizal, or in the nearby provinces of Cavite, Batangas, Bulacan, or even Bataan. The only sizeable industrial complex, apart from metropolitan Manila, is Iligan, Mindanao, where Maria Cristina power is the major localizing factor.

Potentially, the Philippines is in a reasonably strong position with respect to industrial development, in many ways in a stronger position than most of its Southeast Asian neighbors. However, it has not kept pace with Thailand, Malaysia, and Singapore in the past few years and may not do so in the years immediately ahead.

THE SPATIAL PATTERN OF THE TOURIST INDUSTRY

Like many other Southeast Asian countries, the Philippines has attempted to emphasize tourist attractions and thereby attract the foreigner and his money into the Philippine economic sphere. In general, despite the quality of the physical and cultural attractions, this attempt has been unsuccessful. However, some factors merit consideration. The Philippinies has been a high cost country; but with the *peso* allowed to seek its own level on the money market in 1970, this negative factor has become less true. Outside of Manila, tourist accommodations generally have been inadequate; however, there are now excellent hotels in Bocolod, Baguio, Cebu, Davao, Iloilo, Legaspi, Zamboanga, and many other regional centers. Although domestic airlines provide good service, distances are great and fares are expensive. Land and water transportation is cheap but slow, oftentimes uncomfortable and usually overcrowded. The fears of the foreigner with respect to law and order may be real but tend to be overemphasized and overexaggerated. One takes precautions that are appropriate to time and place whenever, and wherever he travels, in the Philippines or in his home community.

However, there are other considerations. It is possible to travel throughout the Philippines with English as the language of intercommunication. The relic walled city, many old and picturesque Spanish cathedrals, several universities and other landmarks are in or near Manila. Historic Corregidor is easily accessible by hydrofoil, as well as by cheaper and slower craft. Beautiful Tagaytay Ridge, Lake Taal and Taal Volcano are only an hour's drive over paved roads from Manila. Baguio, the mountain resort community, is accessible by air, bus, or train. Zamboanga and the colorful sea gypsies are readily accessible by air, as is Cebu city and Mactan Island (famous as landings of Magellan).

Basically, only the Banaue rice terraces are difficult to visit; and only the Morolands of interior Mindanao and the Sulu Archipelago can be considered unsafe for foreigners.

POLITICAL PERSPECTIVES

The government, which operated under the constitution of 1935 as amended until October 1972, was republican in form, was democratic in principle, and in some ways dictatorial in practice.

There is much similarity between the Philippines constitution and the constitution of the United States, logically so because in 1935, approval of the United States congress was as necessary as was a favorable vote in the then Philippine National Assembly and the subsequent approval of the Philippine people. Later revisions diluted some similarities; but the basic pattern remains unchanged.

In the Philippines, the President was a powerful person, partly because he was expected to be the national leader in a variety of ways—not all of them related to political leadership. But the Philippine presidency was a more powerful office in relation to other branches of the government than is the American presidency. "Item veto authority" over money matters and tariff bills was one illustration of this greater power vested in one man, or more specifically, in a single office. Moreover, the political power of the president was greater, relatively, because there was a higher percentage of appointive offices in the Philippine government than in American governmental organization. In no sense was the Philippine Congress inactive, or simply a rubber stamp of approval; but the president is the power that runs the country. The frequent pilgrimages of public officials, both legislative and appointive, to Malacanang (the Philippine White House) to plead for the "release" of funds which have been authorized by Congress is a distinctive feature of Philippine politics.

Domestic politics certainly are vocal and can be violent, as evidenced by "election-eve murders" and lesser acts of violence and coercion. Although only a small group of people really participate meaningfully in political decision making, most people vote. Amost 80% of the qualified voters normally participate in national and local elections. (This is a marked contrast to the 60-65% turnout in recent United States national elections.)

Law and Order

Law enforcement traditionally has been a problem in some areas. The Spanish never established effective control over either the Moro centers of Mindanao or some of the mountain peoples of northern Luzon. These areas were among the last to be brought under jurisdiction by the Americans and remained under military governors until rather late in the American colonial period. Recent murders of non-Moslems in Mindanao's "Moroland" attest to the fact that some of the past conditions are still current. The present Philippine government has some of the same problems as their Spanish and American predecessors. Highway robbery and night-time banditry in Cavite, southeast of Manila, has occurred sporadically throughout modern Philippine history, where the general rule has been, and still is, "Strangers should get off the roads by nightfall."

Huks. The only organized resistance to the Philippine government was the Hukbalahaps, commonly called "the Huks," which was initially the peoples anti-Japanese army. The nature of Huk activities has already been described in Chapter 1. The widespread uprisings in the late 1960s under a quite different name and with a different leadership was said to have been a resurgence of the dissident activities of the 1950s.

In summary, however, the Philippines are not as unsafe as the media seems to indicate. A major Rand Corporation study in 1969–70 using the quantitive tools of modern behavioral science offers these conclusions, among others: (1) Crime is not a nationwide problem; violence and fear of violence are concentrated in a few areas. (2) The HMB (the modern version of the Huks) is not a serious threat to the government. The organization is more an application of terror and coercion than a real attempt (or demand) for social and economic reform.[2] Such conclusions are generally true in the 1980s.

The Role of the Military

The Philippine armed forces is charged with security, both internal and international. The then 50,000 man armed forces was the major factor in the defeat of the communist-led Huks in the early 1950s. And President Marcos used the military to control student rebellions in 1970 and for guard duty and various other tasks in 1972. The President put the entire country under martial law on September 21, 1972 in the name of taking action against "Widespread lawlessness and anarchy—criminal conspiracy to take over the government by force and violence."[3] Thus, the country has continued as a military dictatorship, with some slight modification since that date. Political developments after 1972 have been dealt with in the Introduction Chapter.

EDUCATIONAL SYSTEM

The educational system of the Philippines is the most extensively developed in Southeast Asia, if not in all of Asia. Education is the second largest item in the national budget, about 20% of the total in recent years. It is the only organized institution outside the family with a physical plant and paid personnel in most barrios (districts). There is a working relationship between the barrio people and their school. The local teacher is a person to be respected. Filipino people everywhere place a great importance on education. A diploma is considered a means of social, economic, and political betterment. The literacy rate of those persons ten years old and over is more than 80%, probably the highest in Southeast Asia except Singapore. (However, this figure is somewhat misleading, as anyone who has completed third grade is considered literate for statistical purposes.)

The educational system is highly centralized with administrative control in Manila where an appointed Secretary of Education is one of the posts in the President's Cabinet. At subcabinet rank is a Director of Public Schools and a Director of Private Schools, for the educational system consists of two coordinate branches from elementary through college. And in the Philippines, the private educational system is vitally important, particularly at the secondary, normal, collegiate and university level. Most of the 34 universities (1970) are private universities.

The system of public education is based upon the American principles of free and universal education and of separation of church and state. The philosophy is sound and the overall organization is good. However, there are shortcomings and some marked difference between Philippine education and its American model. Four years of elementary work and only two or three years in the intermediate grades place the student in the secondary system at an earlier age than his American counterpart and into college when he is still quite immature in some ways. With few exceptions, the physical plant is inadequate and classes are overcrowded. Classroom equipment is insufficient, especially in the science areas. Library holdings are meager and oftentimes obsolete. Some teachers are poorly trained, most of them are overworked, probably all of them are underpaid. In brief, despite the percentage of the national budget used for education, there is inadequate financial support to take care of the number of pupils and students that require educational training at the various levels of instruction.

The predicted increase in formal education, superimposed on population growth, may well cause school enrollments (now more than ten million) to more than double within another decade. When and if this becomes a reality, the financial requirements for new classrooms, teachers salaries, and equipment can be expected to accelerate to the point that the national budget for education will be equal to the total current national governmental budget. This is truly a sobering thought.

THE DECADE OF 1972–1982

A Constitutional Convention, called in 1971, was charged with changing the government from a presidential to a parliamentary form of organization. In October, 1972, the Constitutional Convention voted to permit Marcos to assume the position of premier while continuing as president until a regular parliament could be elected. In essense, Marcos ruled by decree. In October, 1976, a referendum amended the constitution so that the Interim National Assembly was replaced by an Interim Batasang Pambansa (IBP). In January, 1981, although martial law had only partially reduced the opposition of rebellious groups, particularly the Moros on Mindanao, Marcos lifted martial law in most provinces and transferred legislative powers to the IBP. Marcos then relinquished the premiership to his Secretary of Finance. In June, 1981 an election, largely boycotted by the opposition, returned Marcos to the presidency for a new six-year term.

For most people, life remains largely unchanged. Nearly three-quarters of the population still live in rural areas. The increased rice yields have barely kept pace with population growth in some years, in most years not at all. Inflation has increased drastically, as it has elsewhere in the world. The personal situation has become worse for the small farm-owner, the tenant farmer, the bus driver, the small owner-operator and others on a marginal income and with a limited lifestyle.

The general economy is largely unaltered. Most of the coconut products are now exported as coconut oil, rather than as copra, and the country now supplies 70% of the world's coconut oil exports. In value of exports, sugar usually has continued as a close rival of coconut products, although the United States has ceased to be the sole market for Philippine sugar. The two copper smelting plants have continued to operate and a giant nickel processing plant was completed. Several small geo-thermal projects and a nuclear energy plant are completed or well underway. The nation has approached self-sufficiency in fishery projects. The export of logs rather than processed wood products continues to predominate. Manufacturing is still on the increase, but concentrations in a few geographical areas adds to urban problems, especially in Metro-Manila. Cottage industries are declining, but over half the labor force employed in industry is still employed in shops with five or less employees. Japan supplies almost one-third of the direct foreign investments, the other two-thirds are shared by the United States and Europe. A very small middle class has evolved and the number of truly wealthy families has declined. Some of the more wealthy and many of the more qualified professionals have emigrated to the Unted States, Canada or Europe; the brain drain continues.

The most visible area of change over the past decade has been in the areas of transportation and construction. The "Marcos Regime" has given the country more roads, bridges and public buildings than any single previous administration. Airport facilities have been improved with several new terminals in Mindanao and the rebuilding of fire-damaged Manila International Airport. There has been a realistic attempt to complete the larger and more visible segments of the Pan-Philippine Highway, including the San Juanico Bridge (1973) between Leyte and Samar and the improved ferry service both between the Bicol Peninsula and Samar and between Leyte and Mindanao. The construction of new federal buildings has continued and has been extended to the provincial level in many cases. The number of new hotels has increased, to give greater impetus to the expanded tourist industry. And, new office and office-related buildings in downtown Manila has created a new skyline along the Pasig River.[4]

Footnote References

[1]Estimates for urban population vary, apparently dependent upon the definition of "urban"; i.e., people living in the truly urban segments of chartered cities, or all residents of chartered cities, or residents of chartered cities and other large "towns." This estimate is based on W.A. Withington's chapter 6 of this book, Table 6-1, p. 73.

[2]Harry A. Averch, John E. Kochler and Frank H. Denton, *The Matrix of Policy in the Philippines* (Princeton: 1971), p. 151.

[3]*Americana Annual 1973* (Americana Corporation, 1973), p. 535.

[4]For more recent information see the following books: David A. Rosenberg, (editor), *Marcos and Martial Law in the Philippines* (Ithaca, NY: Cornell University Press, 1979); Harord C. Conklin, *Ethnographic Atlas of Itugoa: A Study of Environment, Culture and Society in Northern Luzon* (New Haven, Conn.: Yale University Press, 1980); T.J.S. George, *Revolt in Mindanao: The Rise of Islam in Philippine Politics* (Kuala Lumpur: Oxford University Press, 1980); Andrew B. Gonzalez, The Philippine Experience Thus Far (Quezon City: Aleneo de Manila University Press, 1980).

Chapter 14

Malaysia: Multiethnicity and New Settlement Schemes

Miriam Lo

Malaysia, a former British colony, is a multiethnic nation. In terms of political geography, its shape may be characterized as fragmented.

From the nineteenth century to the formation of the Federation of Malaysia in 1963, the word "Malaysia" or Malaya included the Malay archipelago that occupies the present day insular Southeast Asia. This "Malaysia" had some definite things in common. All the main languages indigenous to the area were related to Malay; Malay was the *lingua franca* of trade and communications. The majority of the people shared similar forms of social organization, laws, and ways of life. The peoples were physically similar as well, and most of them, for at least four hundred years, had shared a common religion: Islam.

The Federation of Malaysia, established in 1963, comprised the eleven states of the Malayan peninsula, two states in the island of Borneo (Sarawak and Sabah), and the insular city-state of Singapore. It had then a total population of over 10 million and an area of about 130,000 square miles. In 1965, Singapore seceded from the Federation and is now an independent nation.

MULTIETHNIC CHARACTERISTICS

Today, a Malaysian is a citizen of the Federation; he may be ethnically a Malay, a Chinese, an Indian, an Indonesian, a European, or a member of some other ethnic group. A Malay, on the other hand, is constitutionally defined as a person belonging to the Malay ethnic group, which constitutes slightly over half of the Malaysian population. A Malay is distinguished by the use of the Malay language and generally by practice of the Islam faith.

The Malaysian ethnic groups are legally classified and their positions are constitutionally defined and protected accordingly.[1] The Malays, together with the Dayaks of Sarawak, the Kadazans of Sabah and all other smaller indigenous groups of Sarawak and Sabah form the *bumiputra* (sons of the soil). The aborigines of the Malayan peninsula are *orang asli* (original people). The Chinese and the Indians constitute another category. Figures in Table 1 show the population of the Federation by ethnic origin in 1957 (for Malaya), 1960 (for Sarawak and Sabah) and 1970 and 1980 for Malaysia. The majority of the ancestors of today's Malay Malaysians were migrants from continental Southeast Asia and they arrived at the Malayan peninsula around 1500 B.C. There are also Malay Malaysians whose ancestors migrated from Indonesian islands—especially Sumatra and Java—most of whom arrived at the peninsula in the early twentieth century. Today, the majority of Malay Malaysians reside in the peninsula. The ancestors of Chinese Malaysians were from southern China; especially the province of Kwangtung. Most of them reside in urban centers of the Federation, as it is reflected by figures in Tables 2 and 3. Indian Malaysians migrated from southern India and today they reside principally in the peninsula. Indian contacts with the peninsula can be traced as far back as several centuries before the Christian Era, while Chinese contacts first began in the 1400's. Large-scale Indian and Chinese immigration took place, however, only in the eighteenth and nineteenth centuries under the British colonial rule. In Malaysia, throughout the past few centuries, the Chinese have maintained the highest economic position among the various ethnic groups, a feature common in Southeast Asia.[2] As observed, by Milne,[3] the ethnic composition of Malaysia is, more than anything else,

TABLE 14.1
Malaysia: Population By Ethnic Groups

Year	1957 (for Malays) 1960 (for Sarawak & Sabah)		1970		1980
Territory	Population Number	% of Total in Territory	Population Number	% of Total in Territory	Population Number
Peninsular Malaysia					
Malays	3,125,474	49.78	4,685,838	53.13	n.a.
Chinese	2,333,756	37.17	3,122,350	35.40	n.a.
Indians	735,038	11.71	932,629	10.57	n.a.
Total	6,278,758	98.66	8,819,928	99.10	11,138,227
Sarawak					
Indigenous*	377,952	50.76	489,454	50.08	n.a.
Chinese	229,154	30.79	294,020	30.08	n.a.
Malays	129,300	17.38	182,709	18.69	n.a.
Total**	744,529	98.93	977,438	98.85	1,294,753
Sabah					
Indigenous***	306,498	67.45	418,713	63.93	n.a.
Chinese	104,542	23.01	139,509	21.30	n.a.
Malays	1,645	0.36	18,365	2.80	n.a.
Total	454,421	90.82	654,943	88.03	n.a.
Malaysia			10,452,309	95.33	13,435,588

Sources: *1970 Population and Housing Census of Malaysia, Community Groups* (Kuala Lumpur: Government Printer, 1971), pp. 45-46. *Initial Counts of 1980 Population and Housing Census* (Kuala Lumpur: Government Printer, 1981).

*Include Sea Dayaks, Land Dayaks, Melanaus, and other Indigenous Populations of the State.

**The percentage total does not equal 100 due to the lack of availability of precise statistics.

***Include Kadazens, Muruts, Bajaus, and other Indigenous Populations of the State.

n.a. ⁼ not available

the key to the understanding of the country. It dictates the pattern of the economy, has helped to shape its constitution, and has influenced its democratic process and party system. In a letter to the editor, K. George, while rebuking "Bumiputra" separatism, advocates a concern for racial unity in the following words:

> "Bumiputra" claims that the Malays are culturally and racially much closer to the Malayan aborigines than the Chinese and the Indians. If it were so, I fail to understand why the aborigines are called "orang asli" and not "bumiputra." It is sheer ignorance for Bumiputra to state that the Chinese and Indians came to exploit the natural resources of Malaya. History says they came originally to work in mines and plantations as indentured labour. Malaysia's economic progress is undoubtedly attributable to the sacrifice and hard work of those indentured labourers who were treated more like semislaves than human beings by their colonial masters. The word "bumiputra" means son of the soil. But in the Malaysian contest, it is a misnomer and negates the national goal of racial unity.[4]

MULTIETHNICITY, ECONOMIC DEVELOPMENT AND SETTLEMENT GEOGRAPHY

The multiethnicity of Malaysian society is distinguished in the economic and political realms of life of her people. This produces a problem for the governmental efforts on planning for regional economic development. The series of Five-Year Development Plans, as well as the national policy for settlement and agricultural development, demonstrate the amount of attention and intensity of effort called for to cope with the problem of multiethnicity over time.

Efforts on Economic Development

A discussion of the Development Plans of Malaysia has already been made in Chapter 7. The Plans identify major problems concerning the country's economic development. They also set goals designed to overcome these problems. The 1961-65 and 1966-70 plans laid out the

TABLE 14-2
Malaya: Population By Ethnic Groups of Ten Connurbation Areas,* 1970

Connurbations / Ethnic Groups	Malays	Chinese	Indians	Total
1. Kuala Lumpur Municipality	184,419 (27.2%)	394,517 (58.1%)	118,067 (17.4%)	697,003 (100.0%)
2. City of Georgetown	51,077 (15.7%)	231,198 (71.0%)	43,415 (13.3%)	325,690 (100.0%)
3: Ipoh Muncipality	41,851 (16.4%)	177,125 (69.4%)	36,299 (14.2%)	255,275 (100.0%)
4. Johor Bahru Town Council	72,504 (51.4%)	55,832 (39.6%)	12,771 (9.1%)	141,107 (100.0%)
5. Melaka Municipality	17,921 (18.5%)	72,179 (74.5%)	6,812 (7.0%)	96,912 (100.0%)
6. Seremban Town Council	18,866 (20.9%)	54,718 (60.7%)	16,529 (18.3%)	90,113 (100.0%)
7. Alor Star Town Council	35,580 (42.1%)	40,580 (48.0%)	8,335 (9.9%)	84,495 (100.0%)
8. Kota Baharu Town Council	51,744 (74.6%)	16,147 (23.3%)	1,482 (2.1%)	69,373 (100.0%)
9. Kuala Trengganu Town Council	49,244 (83.8%)	8,636 (14.7%)	914 (1.6%)	58,794 (100.0%)
10. Kuantan Town Council	17,667 (41.0%)	21,539 (50.0%)	3,855 (9.0%)	43,061 (100.0%)

Source: *1970 Population and Housing Census of Malaysia, Community Groups* (Kuala Lumpur: Government Printers, 1971), p. 287.
*These areas are defined as the totality of the gazetted (officially incorporated) areas of the towns being studied and the built-up areas lying outside their boundaries.

TABLE 14-3
Sabah and Sarawak: Population by Ethnic Groups of Major Towns and Townships, 1970

Towns/Townships / Ethnic Groups	Indigenous	Chinese	Malays	Total
Sabah				
1. Kota Kinabalu Town	10,794 (28.7%)	24,591 (65.5%)	2,143 (5.7%)	37,558 (100.0%)
2. Sandakan	7,412 (20.4%)	27,337 (75.4%)	1,531 (4.2%)	36,280 (100.0%)
3. Tawau Town	2,703 (16.2%)	12,695 (76.2%)	1,255 (7.5%)	16,653 (100.0%)
4. Labuan Town	1,586 (24.5%)	2,788 (43.1%)	2,098 (32.4%)	6,472 (100.0%)
Sarawak				
1. Kuching	3,094 (5.0%)	43,909 (71.6%)	14,342 (23.4%)	61,345 (100.0%)
2. Sibu	2,745 (5.7%)	38,161 (79.0%)	7,385 (15.3%)	48,291 (100.0%)
3. Miri	4,025 (12.1%)	20,059 (60.1%)	9,311 (27.9%)	33,395 (100.0%)

Source: *1970 Populations and Housing Census of Malaysia, Community Groups* (Kuala Lumpur: Government Printers, 1971), pp. 279-281.

specific economic and social problems facing the economy at those periods.

The 1961–65 Plan recognized three major problems: the high birth rate; the economically depressed conditions in rural areas; and the need for economic diversification.[5] The birth rate was then three to three and one-half percent per year. At the same time the rural areas were overcrowded with living conditions physically inadequate and little being done to assist the small farmer to acquire his own land. The single major export item—rubber—kept the entire economy dependent upon the fluctuation of the world market rubber price which was, in turn, influenced by the synthetic rubber industry in other countries.

Several major socioeconomic problems were also recognized in the 1966–70 Plan.[6] The birth rate remained high and the economy was still dependent upon the export of rubber, though the export of tin had increased significantly enough to be considered a major export item. The problem in rural areas was now seen as one of disparity of income distribution between rural and urban dwellers. The additional problem recognized in the 1966–70 Plan was lack of human-resource development which resulted in a lack of skills needed for economic and technological development. Surveys carried out in the late 1950's and early 1960's[7] indicated the rural family income as ranging from M$60 to M$120 per month. This was far short of the target of M$400 per month that is set by the government as the minimum family income. Natural rubber accounted for over two-thirds of the country's total exports in the 1940's. Although this has been reduced, mainly through increasing production of other agricultural crops and the export of tin, rubber remained the dominant item in the export sector. The 1970 figures indicated that the export of rubber constituted 30.6% of Malaysia's export by value.[8]

Both Plans (1961–65 and 1966–70) identified similar problems for the country.[9] They were:

1. rapid population growth rate;
2. excessive dependence on two export items—rubber and tin; and
3. economic imbalance between the rural and urban population.

The Plans also offer a similar procedure for rectifying the problems. Basically, their proposal is to increase the economy's total output through agricultural and industrial diversification.

Malaysia has been confronted with the problems as envisaged by the planners for a very long period, and the period of planning had not seen them significantly alleviated. Malaysia still has one of the fastest population growth rates in Asia. The economy has actually grown more dependent on the sales of rubber and tin since World War II. The growth of the export sector has continuously created the imbalance of growth between export and the rest of the economy and this trend did not slow down in the last decade. In other words, the problems are persistent and remain so despite conscious attempts to check them. Essentially, the difficulties do not lie in the Plans themselves. It is not a question of whether the Plans are good or bad as instruments of growth and development. The failure lies rather in the internal economic, social and political conditions, which are now more clearly distinguished in the country and are reflected by the 1971–75 Plan.

The 1971–75 Plan puts forth a "two-pronged" New Economic Policy for development:

1. to reduce and eventually eradicate poverty by raising income levels and increasing employment opportunities for all Malaysians, irrespective of race; and
2. to accelerate the process of restructuring the Malaysian society to correct economic imbalance, so as to reduce and eventually eliminate the identification of race with economic functions.

The Plan maintains that the two prongs of the new economic policy are not mutually exclusive but are in many ways, interdependent and mutually reinforcing. It also maintains that the strategy for restructuring the economy is founded on the "philosophy of active participation, not on disruptive-redistribution."[11] In a later section, however, the Plan states that its fundamental objective is "greater participation by Malays and other indigenous people (that is, the aborigines) in manufacturing and commercial activities." The government has set a target so that, within the next twenty years, at least thirty percent of the total commercial and industrial activities in all categories and scales of operation should have participation by "Malays and other indigenous people" in terms of ownership and management. The objective of the government is to create a Malay middle class to counterbalance that of the existing Chinese and Indians, to set up a catching-up race of competition, as it were, with the Chinese and Indians so that Malays are represented within the present wealthy section of the Malaysian population, which is perceived by the government to be principally Chinese.

When the 1971-75 Plan was presented to Parliament in the middle of 1971, local newspapers were flooded with reports and comments about the Plan and the attitudes of the government regarding the ethnic groups of the country. The government encourages the Malays to participate in the economic activities of the country. It calls on them to adopt "new attitudes," to "follow the example of the Chinese," to "cultivate the virtue of hard work that the Chinese have." It was acknowledged by some members of Parliament that the Malays are "one hundred years behind the Chinese" in business acumen, that the Malays are hardworking only in the kampongs, but are not so in the towns, and that "to better their lot, the Malays have to go into business and the Chinese should help them."[12]

The government has assumed that the economic inconsistencies of Malaysia are caused by the ethnic differences within the population. As a result, it is trying to solve an economic problem by deliberately favoring one ethnic group—the Malays—over the rest of the Malaysian population. The rationale for instituting such policies on the part of the government are the following:

1. With respect to planning for economic development, the goals of the government may be summarized in terms of raising the total gross national product and diversifying the economy.
2. To achieve these goals, however, the community problems of the society reflected in economic imbalances, have first to be solved.
3. The identification of economic roles with ethnic groups has to be removed.
4. To the government, the only solution lies in the 1971-75 Plan, which is engaged in removing the economic, social, and psychological problems of the Malays.

Rural Settlements

Ownership of land being granted to specific groups of people in a country occurs in many parts of the world. Malaysia has land, known generally as reserve land, which is normally only granted to the Malays and to other indigenous peoples. The distribution of such land in the Malayan peninsula is shown in Fig. 14—1. Another system of land distribution in Malaysia is by relocation of people to specific areas containing planned villages. There are two kinds of planned villages: the New Villages and the Land

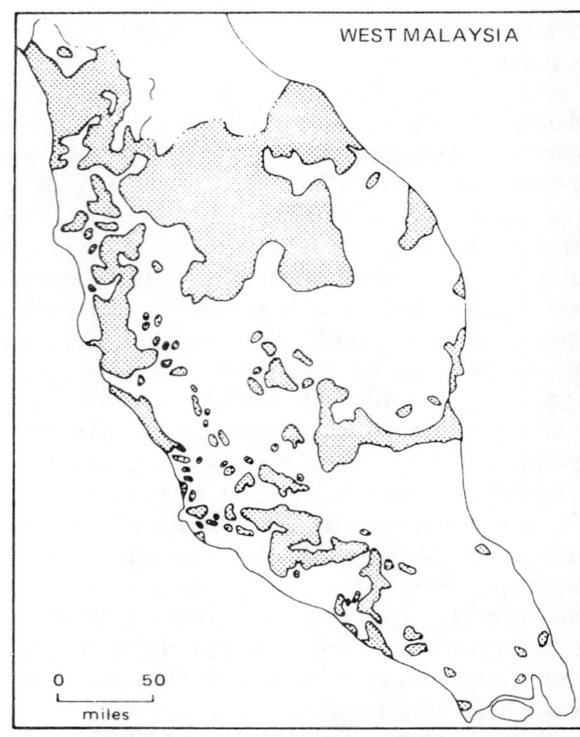

Source: 1958 Report of Land Administration Commission.

Development Settlement Schemes. There are, in Malaya, over five hundred New Villages. The number of such villages in Sabah and Sarawak is unknown. There are over one hundred Land Development Settlement Schemes in Malaya, over ten in Sabah, and about ten in Sarawak.

New Villages. A New Village in Malaya means a resettlement village built under the auspices of the government. Theoreticallly, it is a village for any community whose original homes are situated in territories that are deemed by the government to be unsafe for settlement because they are close to areas infested by communist terrorists. In practice, by far the majority of the New Village settlers are Chinese, though some Indian and Malay settlers can be found as well. Most of the New Village settlers were originally squatters. The squatters, during the depression of the 1930s and the period of the Second World War and the Japanese Occupation (1942-1945), left the towns and cities and occupied the edges of estates, other rural communities, abandoned tin mines or anywhere at all. Much of the land which they came to occupy legally belonged to others. Even where they occupied state land which was opened to settlement, many squatters did not obtain title to the plots where they have come to live. Only a small percentage of them ever sought title, and they were given Temporary Occupation licenses.

The Chinese squatters were principally market-gardners. Their role as food producers was generally accepted as significant and a valuable asset to the country; especially in times of depression. At the outburst of communist insurgency in 1948, a "state of emergency" was declared in the country. It was at this time that the plan for resettlement of the Chinese squatters and market-gardners received the most urgent attention of the government. The squatters had been the major suppliers of food and other items of necessity, including money and information, to the communist-insurgents. The government argues that if the main source of food of the insurgents was cut off, they would be put to a disadvantage in their struggle against the government. By 1950, the resettlement plan began to take shape. The distribution pattern of New Villages in Malaya is shown in Fig. 14–2.

According to Nyce, whenever possible, each family was given one-sixth of an acre of land to build their house and to set up their vegetable gardens.[13] The house was usually very small since most of the land of the plot was given over to growing vegetables. The whole New Village was enclosed by barbed wire. In the beginning, each New Village was laid out immediately along a main road, with the road dividing the village in half. The entrances to both ends of the village were heavily guarded and all through traffic was compelled to stop for police checks. Outside of the barbed wire, land was alotted for agriculture. The plan of a typical New Village is shown in Fig. 14–3. By the end of 1953, 40,000 acres of land had been set aside for resettlement and agriculture, and close to M$2 million had been spent. Suitable land for farming could not always be found immediately outside the village, but where possible, farming plots were located within a two-mile radius of the village. A subsistence allowance was generally given, but primarily to those families who had been moved more than two miles from their old homes and could not continue to work there. For those whose old fields were within the two-mile radius of the New Village, financial assistance was given for a period of two weeks. Curfews were imposed in the New Villages and settlers were not allowed adequate time to go to their fields to work and come back to the villages. Most of the settlers had no means of transport; the best that a villager could obtain was a bicycle. What was most conspicuous was that the settlers

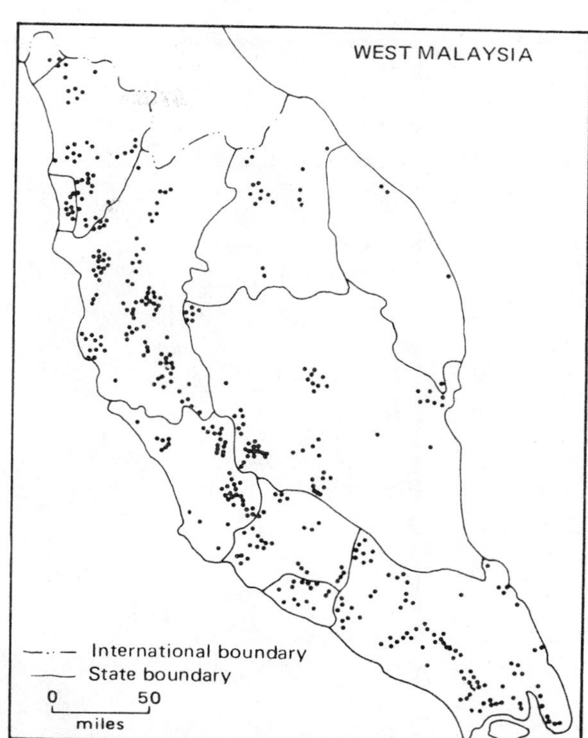

Figure 14-2. Distribution of New Villages.

Source: K.S. Sandhu, *Journal of Tropical Geography*, vol. 18, Aug. 1964.

were not allowed to go back to their old fields and those crops were, therefore, unattended and sometimes, the harvest went unreaped.

The bulk of New Villages were established in the 1950–1960 period. Some settlements were extremely crowded, with lots 20' x 30' in size. Some of the land on which the settlements were set up did not belong to the government at the time of settling. The government did not itself settle all the squatters. Whenever possible, it attempted to assign responsibility for a New Village to a private organization, preferably one which was already involved in the lives of the squatters to be relocated. The organizations most commonly involved were rubber and tin companies, the major nonagricultural employers of the squatters. As far as possible, the government maintained ethnic segregation in the resettled communities.

In September, 1971, the government began to collect land-title fees and land taxes in New Villages. Owing to the poor conditions of living that prevailed in the New Villages, the settlers did not have the incentive to apply for land titles even though the government had been issuing Permanent Occupation titles (titles that are effective for a period of thirty-three years) since 1968. Only one-third of all settlers have applied since then. The government had notified the settlers

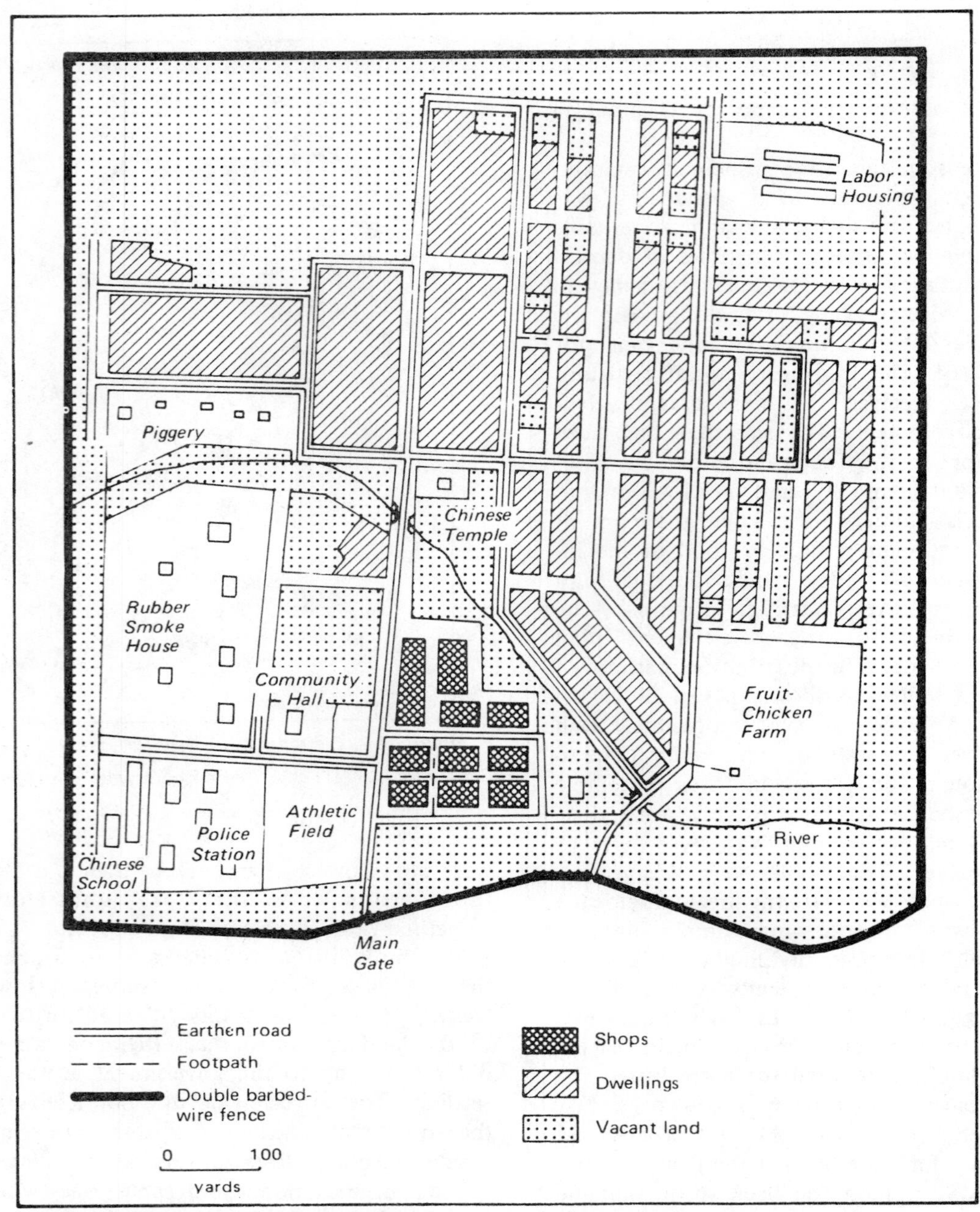

Source: K.S. Sandhu, *Journal of Tropical Geography*, vol. 18, Aug. 1964.

that by the end of 1971, should they fail to apply for the permanent land titles and pay the fees and land taxes, their Temporary Occupation licenses would not be renewed and their houses would be torn down. At present, some New Villages are still encircled by barbed wire and controlled by curfew regulations. Some settlers do not yet possess citizenship. The definition of a New Village has not been made clear by the government so that, under the present policy of the government on economic development, no money is allocated for their improvement. They are loosely put in the category of "traditional towns," and they do not belong to the jurisdiction of rural development authorities but they are not taken care of by any city municipality.

As is reported by local newspapers, the majority of the settlers who are employed are rubber-tappers and tin-mining laborers. Throughout the years, they have been unable to pay the land taxes, and many of them are in debt to their local councils. The present fees required to obtain permanent titles and the annual land taxes as set by the government are higher than the expectations of the settlers. The last time period in which application for permanent land titles could be made was the four-month period from September to December of 1971. For example, in the district of Ipoh in Perak, where there are eighteen New Villages, there was a significant change of fees and taxes since August, 1971. For every lot measuring 90' x 45', the highest land value fixed before August was M$700; after August, it became M$6075. The title fee before August was M$105; after August, it became M$912. And the annual land tax changed from M$21 to M$183. For the least valued lot, the price changed from M$30 to M$151 and the annual land tax changed from M$30 to M$121. How the government conceived this set of price changes is quite beyond the knowledge of the people in the country. Even the most high-class housing estates in Ipoh do not have to pay an annual land tax of M$2.50 for every 1,000 square feet.

Land Development Settlement Schemes. In Malaya, the Federal Land Development Authority (F.L.D.A.) was established under the Land Development Ordinance of 1956. The F.L.D.A. was first conceived by the government as a major way to create a prosperous Malay peasantry and help offset, as much as possible, the ethnically identified economic imbalance that was in existence between the Malays and the non-Malays. The aim of the F.L.D.A. was to create an environment wherein a Malay settlement family would earn an income of approximately M$400 per month from agriculture alone. The F.L.D.A. programs form the most significant programs of the government for rural land and agricultural development. Its efforts are aided by various other agencies such as the State Economic Development Corporations and the Federal Rehabilitation and Consolidation Authority.

As originally conceived, each F.L.D.A. program would involve four hundred families (approximately 1,200–3,600 people) with per family holdings of above ten acres in area. The general criteria for choosing settlers are:

1. preferably Malays;
2. preferably the near or totally landless—but people having more than six acres of land are eligible;
3. preferably people with larger families—seven to ten and over;
4. preferably people in the 35 and 45 year age-groups;
5. preferably with agricultural background, but people of all walks of life are eligible; and
6. preferably physically fit people.

The distribution of F.L.D.A. programs in Malaya is shown in Fig. 14–4. Each settlement is provided with specific facilities. A typical settlement is shown in Fig. 14-5. There is a village center located as close to the geographic center of the settlement as possible so that distances from the village center to the cultivated lot are kept to a minimum. The settlement, therefore, has a compact, near circular or hexagonal shape. Areas with gentle gradients are chosen for roads and relatively flat areas for the village center and school sites. The area should have suitable soil for such agricultural purposes as rubber and oil palms, as well as sufficient availability of water. An excess of water which could cause flooding is to be avoided. There should be reasonable access to a main road but the village should not be too close to it. Each residential lot is limited in size: a quarter-acre lot with a house 20' x 20'. Open spaces are provided at the rate of six to seven acres per one hundred population. There are also reserved lands within each settlement for future development; mainly for industry.

The program is planned to follow four steps: (1) the jungle is felled; (2) the land is cleared; (3) crops planted; and (4) houses constructed. This is all done by contract work financed by the F.L.D.A. All the material needed for building and planting, and the machinery and tools are considered as part of the cost of a program and are chargeable to the loan funds and are recoverable by the government. The settlers then come in and begin to "develop their land." The basic foodstuffs required by the settlers are obtained on credit from the government's cooperatives. Living allowances are given for the first two years, at the rate of M$60–75 per family per month. A 400-family settlement has a resident manager, two assistant-managers, thirteen field assistants, a chief clerk, a junior clerk, and a storekeeper.

Some studies have been done on the F.L.D.A. programs to assess their benefits and costs to the economy, as well as to the settlers. Singh finds that the settlements he investigated provided an opportunity for the settlers to become relatively prosperous peasants with incomes substantially higher than they had before joining the programs.[14] He also finds that without considering the secondary effects, the programs can be advantageous to the settlers. However, these programs are very heavily subsidized by the government. His findings, which are based on benefit-cost analysis, do not show that the land development programs examined are better than other

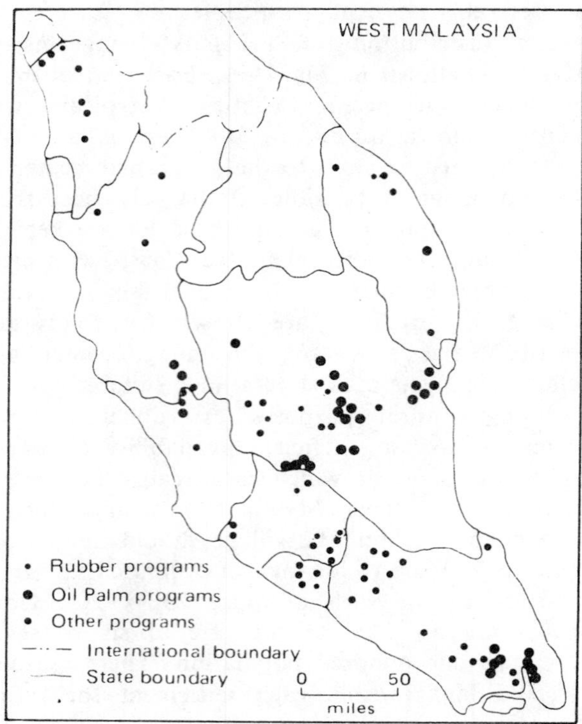

Source: R. Wikkramatileke, *Pacific Viewpoint*, May 1972.

CONCLUSION

Multiethnicity is still regarded as the country's chief obstacle to development in the 1980s. Given such a perception on the part of the government, development efforts continue to foster the eradication of Malay poverty and the enlargement of control margin in Malay investment and management in business (industrial, manufacturing as well as agriculture) and banking. Nowhere is the issue of common poverty, that is, poverty as a feature prevailing among all ethnic groups in both rural and urban areas, addressed to by the planning authorities. So long as the perception of the problem of poverty and underdevelopment continues along the ethnic line, the Malaysian society will perpetuate her communal problems that have existed since the time of British colonization. The continued emphasis of the federal government on the eradication of Malay poverty has alienated the rest of the native population of the country. The native people of Sabah and Sarawak have begun to show their discontent. Under the circumstances of tight central govern-

forms of investment that the government can be involved with. His analyses do not indicate that the total land development program should be expanded at the cost of other development programs.

The analysis of a few programs by the F.L.D.A. itself, show that although the settlers can indeed become prosperous peasants by working on their land in the villages, their major source of income, at the time of the analysis, comes from off-farm work: rubber-tapping and maintenance work in other private estates.

Without a systematic analysis of the attitudes of the settlers, it is not possible to assess the effect the F.L.D.A. programs have on the settlers in the context of success or failure of the F.L.D.A. to attempt to foster a spirit of self-help among the Malays. It will not be possible to assess the long-term results of the F.L.D.A. programs until the attitudes of the next generation begin to appear. The paternalistic attitude of the government toward the Malays may, instead of developing this spirit of self-help, be creating and perpetuating a pattern of reliance upon governmental programs as the solution to all their problems.

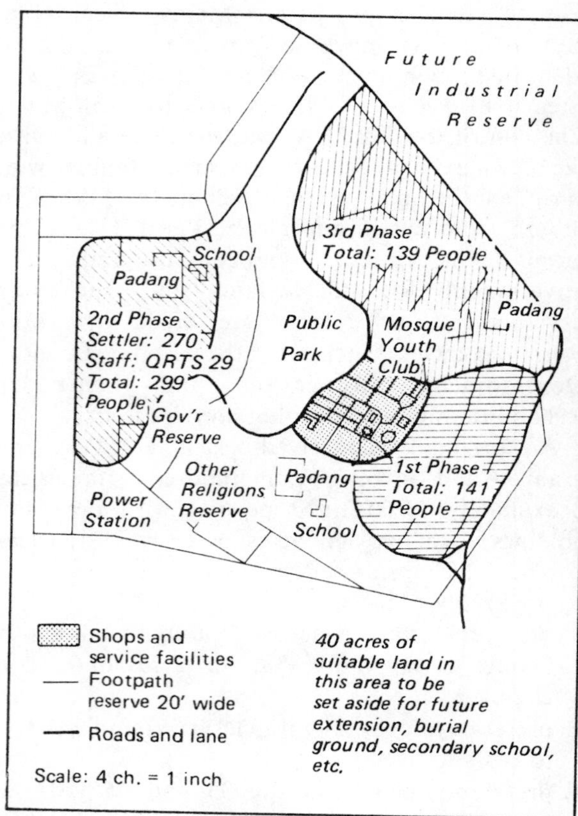

Source: F.L.D.A. *Annual Report,* 1962.

ment control on economic planning, investment, police and military as well as the continued victory of the ruling government party, little change to the present situation can be expected.

Footnote References

[1]See Article 153 of *Malaysia, Federal Constitution. Incorporating All Amendments up to 1st June, 1970* (Kuala Lumpur: 1970).

[2]For accounts of historical incidents leading to the present economic differences of Malaysians, see J.M. Gullick, *Malaya* (London: Earnest Benn Ltd., 1963). There are, in addition, many other excellent works on the subject.

[3]R.S. Milne, "National Ideology and Nation-Building in Malaysia," *Asian Survey* (July, 1970). See also G. Means, *Malaysian Politics* (London: University of London Press, 1970) and MacDoughall, *Shared Burdens, A Study of Communal Discrimination* (unpublished Ph.D. dissertation, Harvard University, 1968).

[4]K. George, in Kuala Lumpur, printed in *Far Eastern Economic Review* (July 1, 1972), p. 7.

[5]*Malaya, Second Five-Year Plan (1961-1965)* (Kuala Lumpur: Government Press, 1960), p. 15.

[6]*Malaysia, First Malaysia Plan (1966-1970)* (Kuala Lumpur: Government Press, 1965), p. 1.

[7]See, for example, T.H. Silcock and H.C. Fisk, *Political Economy of Independent Malaya* (London: Angus and Robertson Ltd., 1963).

[8]*Malaysia, Second Malaysia Plan (1971-1973)* (Kuala Lumpur: Government Press, 1971), pp. 54–55.

[9]The similar nature of the goals of both plans may also be recognized from the following details about the plans. The 1961–1965 plan has five goals: (a) to provide facilities and opportunities for rural economic and social development; (b) to raise the per capita output of the economy; (c) to provide agricultural and industrial diversification; (d) to create jobs for the rapidly increasing working-age population; and (e) to improve and expand social services; particularly education and health care. From *Malaya, Second Five-Year Plan (1961-1965)* (Kuala Lumpur: Government Press, 1960), p. 15.

To reinforce these goals, the 1966–1970 plan has the following aims: (a) to promote the integration of all races; (b) to provide steady increases in levels of income and consumption; (c) to raise the productivity of the rural people and to generate employment opportunities for them; (d) to provide agricultural and industrial diversification; (e) to educate and train the young to participate in the process of economic and social development; (f) to initiate family planning to reduce the high birth rate; (g) to reduce the number of landless by opening up new lands; (h) to provide social-overhead capital; and (i) to make further progress with health care and other social welfare development. From Malaysia, First Malaysia Plan (1966-1970) (Kuala Lumpur: Government Press, 1965), p. 1.

[10]*Malaysia, Second Malaysia Plan (1971-1975)* (Kuala Lumpur: Government Press, 1971), p. 1.

[11]*Ibid.*, p. 158.

[12]See reports in *Nanyang Siang Pau*, November 1971 issues.

[13]R. Nyce, *The New Villages of Malaya, A Community Study* (unpublished Ph.D. dissertation, Hartford Seminary Foundation, 1963).

[14]S. Singh, *Economic Aspects of Three New Land Development Schemes* (unpublished Ph.D. dissertation, Australian National University, 1965).

Chapter 15

Southeast Asia's Most Progressive Country: Singapore

Ashok K. Dutt
David Liversedge

Singapore, Southeast Asia's most prosperous country—second only to Japan, in Monsoon Asia, has undoubtedly attained a very high level of development, one unmatched by any other equatorial country in the world. Singapore's progress negates further the outdated theories of environmental determinism, such as that of Huntington, that the hot, tropical, and equatorial regions of the world are not suited for modern development. The name Singapore originated from the Sanskrit word singhapura (*singha* means lion and *pura* means city) because, in the thirteenth century, an Indian prince of Palembang, saw some lionlike animals roaming around the island.

PHYSICAL FEATURES

The Republic of Singapore lies to the south of the Malaysian Peninsula; East Malaysia lies to the east, and Indonesia to the south. More specifically, it lies between latitudes 1°09'N and 1°29'N, and longitudes 103°38'E and 104°06'E. It is, thus, a true equatorial country.

Singapore is made up of a main island plus a group of 50 or so smaller islets. The total land area of the state is some 247.12 sq. miles (617.8 km^2), the main island having an area of 228.64 sq. miles (571.6 km^2). The main island is roughly diamond shaped and is 25.1 miles (41.84 km) long and 13.5 miles (22.53 km) wide. It has a coastline of 116.22 miles (193.7 km) (Fig. 15-1).

The three quarter mile wide Jahore Strait separates the island of Singapore from West Malaysia to the north. A causeway across the Strait (1161.6 yds. or 1056 m in length) provides a vital road and rail link to West Malaysia. The causeway also carries a water pipe which supplements the islands own inadequate water supply. When the Japanese invaded Singapore in 1941, they surprised the British by coming by land through Thailand and Malay instead of by sea and used the short span of the strait for entering the island.

The island is generally low lying; the highest point being at only 581' or about 174 m (Bukit Timah). In this higher central region there can be found the island's three water reservoirs (Seletar, Peirce, and MacRitchie). Also this area has the only remnant of the forest covering of the island and is made of dense, mixed evergreen trees.

Physically, Singapore is an outlier of rocks and structures running through the Malay Peninsula and can easily be divided into three distinct regions:

1) The central area is a hilly granite outcrop that forms the highest point of this generally low lying island. Bukit Timah, the highest peak, is situated in this area.

2) To the west of this region lies an area of Triasic quartzites and shale that dip to the southwest and form low degraded scarps. These scarps have been heavily eroded into hills aligned in a northwest—southeast direction. The steepest ridge in the area is behind Pasir ("sand") Panjang.

3) To the east of the central granite zone is an area of weathered detritus averaging 100 ft. (30 m) in height. Weathered red and yellow lateritic soils and a thick iron pan cap all soils.

Ship contact with Singapore is possible via the deepwater channel of Keppel harbor (on the southern part of the island) which is sheltered from the south by the hilly islands of Blakang Mati and Brani. Elsewhere, along this part of the coast, there is silting up in progress and dangerous coral reefs and sandbanks lie offshore. At the eastern end of the Jahore Strait is a deep scoured channel, which permits large vessels to approach the naval dockyards at the northern 'corner' of the island. The western end of the Strait is inaccessible to the through movement of

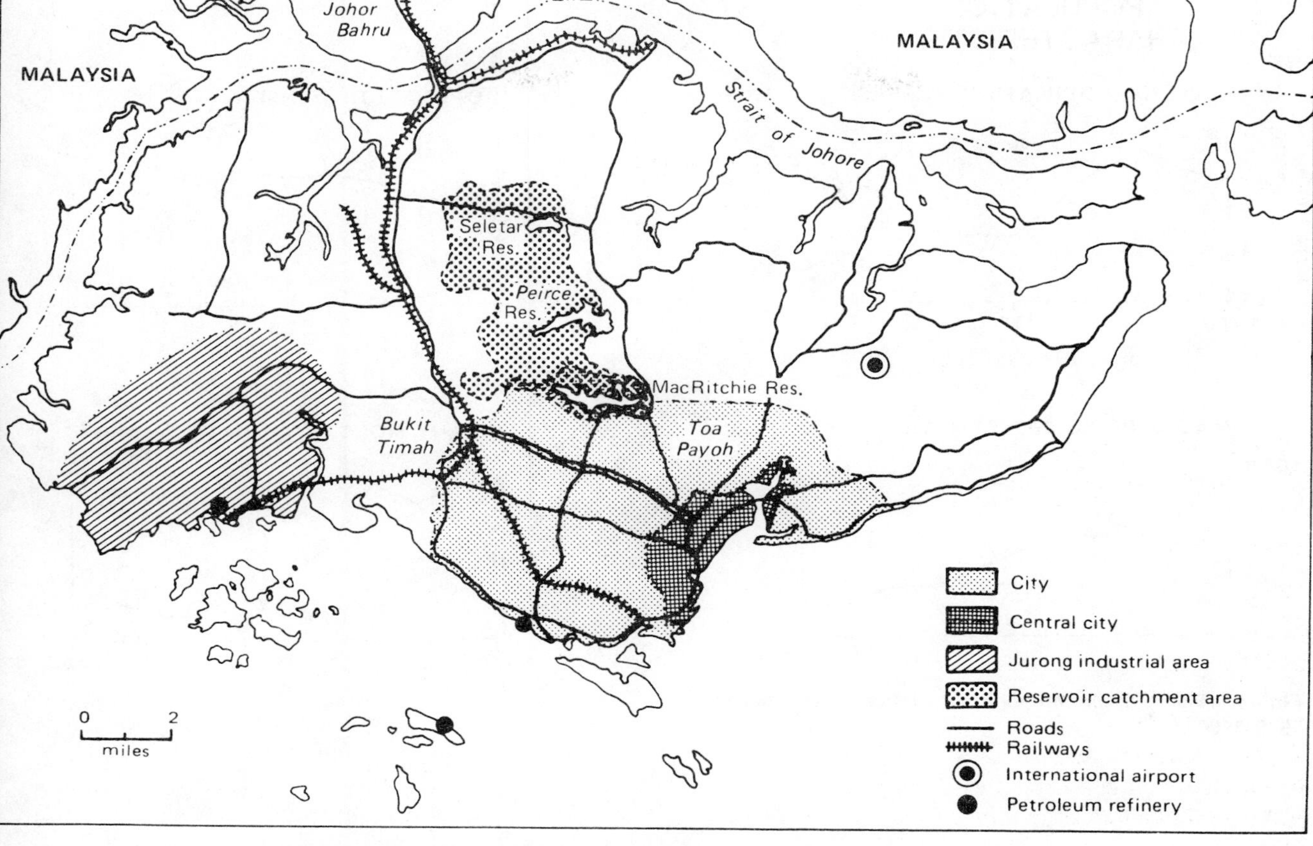

Figure 15-1. Singapore: A General Map.

vessels due to the construction of the causeway which has also hastened silting in the area.

Climate

Climatologically the island of Singapore can be said to be equational. It has an average daily maximum temperature of 87°F (30.5°C) and an average night time minimum of 75°F (23.8°C). It is also quite humid with a relative humidity greater than 90% at night but in afternoons it drops to about 65-70%.[3]

The island receives about 96" (24000mm) of rain per year and although it rains all year the heaviest rainfall period is between November and January. This is the time of the northeast monsoon and there can be as much as 2" (50mm) of rain in a day.[4] Thunderstorms are prevalent in the inter-monsoon months of April–May and October–November. Early morning thunderstorms (*sumatras*) also occur 3–4 times a month from April to November.

DEMOGRAPHIC CHARACTERISTICS

The most recent comprehensive census of the population was undertaken in 1980, the eleventh decennial census taken in Singapore. This revealed a total population of 2,413,945, and this was an increase of 1.2% over the previous year. This increase raised the population density from 3,858 persons/km^2 in 1979 to 3,907 persons/km^2 in 1980 (Fig. 15–2). In actual numbers there were 1,231,760 males and 1,182,185 females giving a relatively even sex ratio of 1,042 males per 1,000 females.

The breakdown of the population into groups of ethnic origin reveals that 76.9% of the population are Chinese Singaporeans while Malay Singaporeans form the next largest group of 14.6%. The other significant ethnic group is the Indian population which comprises 6.4% of the total. All other groups total 2.1% of the population. The growth of the population by ethnic group is shown in Figure 15–3. Here the proportional sizes of the various ethnic groups can be seen quite clearly indicating the fact that although Singapore is multi-ethnic the vast majority of people are Chinese Singaporeans. As Singapore was largely peopled after British occupation, the latter encouraged the Chinese to migrate in large numbers as traders and coolies while the Indians, mainly Tamilians, came with some education to man the education and merchantile system. Many

POPULATION CHARACTERISTICS

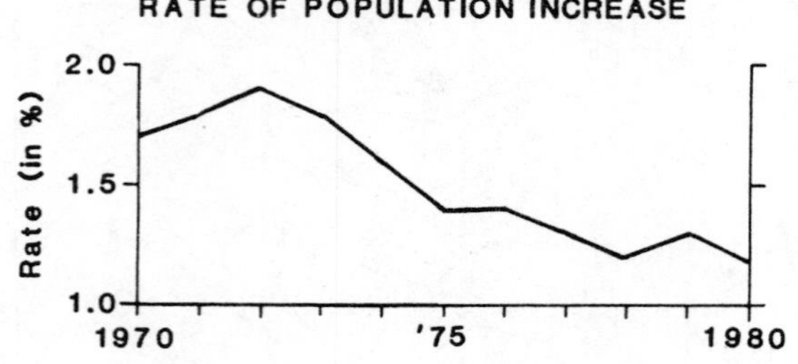

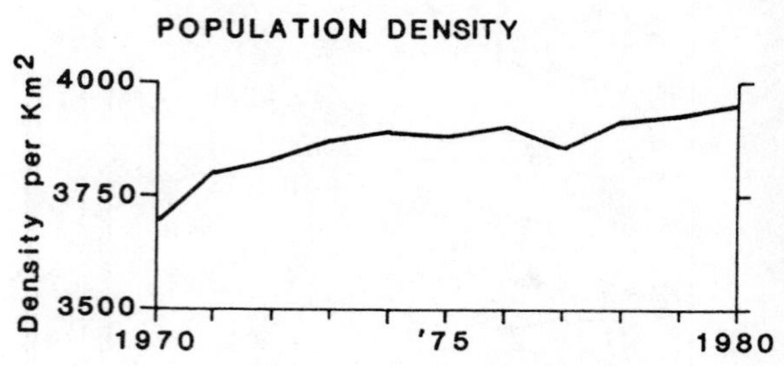

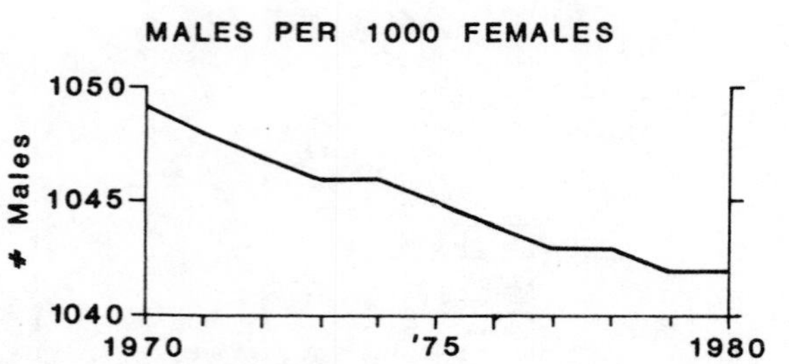

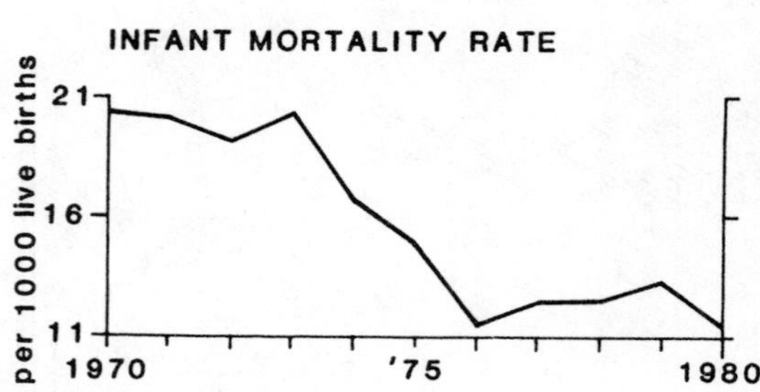

Figure 15-2. Population Characteristics and Change, 1970-1980.

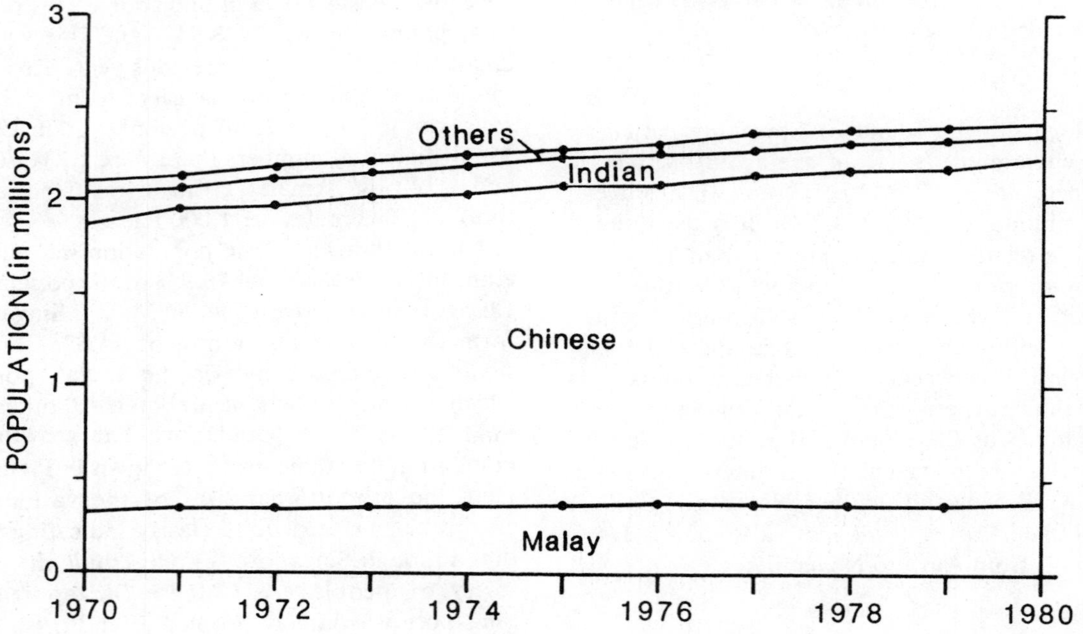

Figure 15-3. Growth of Singapore Population by Ethnic Groups (Source: Ministry of Culture, Sinapore).

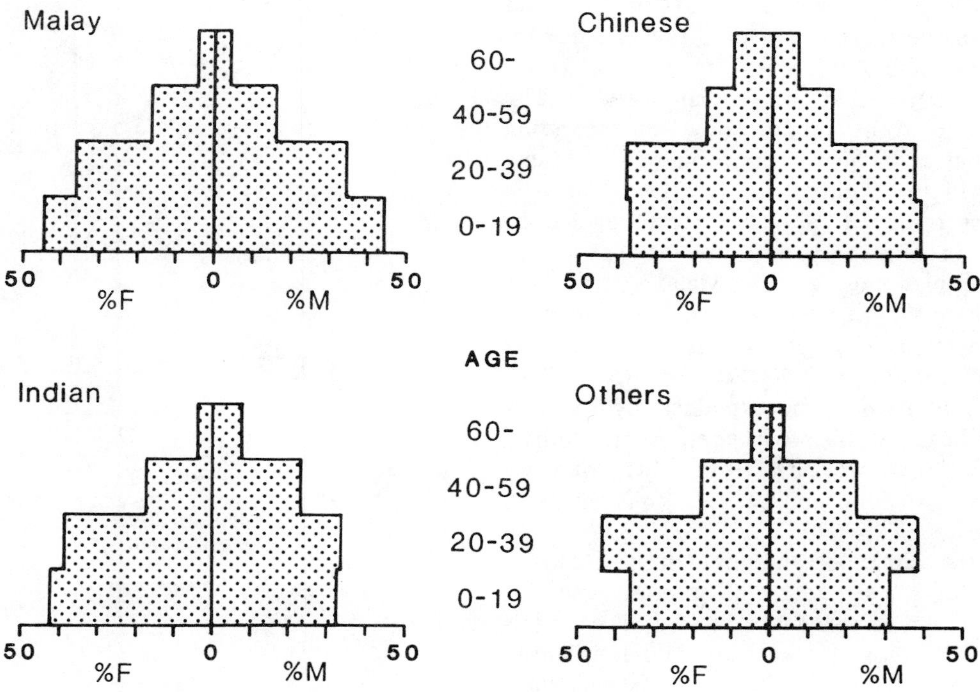

Figure 15-4. Age-Sex Pyramids for the ethnic/racial classes of Singapore (Source: Ministry of Culture, Singapore).

Tamailians also turned to business.

Over the inter-censal period of 1970–1980 the population aged on average from 24.7 to 27.9 years. During 1970–1980, the percentage of the population less than 15 years declined from 38.8 to 27.1. This also shows the effectiveness of family planning acceptance in the country. However, there has been a set-back in the family planning policy. The higher income, educated mothers have had a lesser number of babies than the poor uneducated ones. To counter the effects of such 'inferior breeding' a unique elitist policy was operating in early 1984. This program encouraged 'better genetic breeding' by giving an incentive to higher income educated mothers to have more children, who will receive preferred admission in the highly competitive better schools.

Further, the proportion between 15 and 59 years rose from 55.5% to 65.7%. Also, the proportion in the age group over 60 increased from 5.7 to 7.2%. The increase in older people's percentage is indicative of higher life expectancy. What is also significant about these changes is that the dependency ratio declined from 80.2% to 52.1% in the same 10 year period; showing an increasing work force.

This decline in the birth rate and hence in the dependency ratio is also due to the efforts of the Family Planning and Population Board. The Board has set a net reproduction goal of less than one percent till the year 2000 and projects that the population of Singapore will stabilize at 3.5 million by 2030. Indeed, since 1953 the growth rate of the Singapore population has declined from an annual rate of 5.7 to 1.2%. This has been achieved by legal and cheap abortions and sterilizations. Financial incentives to have a small family are also used, for instance, income tax relief is claimable on only the first three children and not the first 5, as in previous years; paid maternity leave is only available for a woman's first two children; and delivery and ante-natal charges in hospitals increase with each additional child. Family planning, however, is not equally effective in all ethnic groups of Singapore.

Figure 15–4 shows the age-sex pyramids for the four ethnic/racial groups of population (Malay, Chinese, Indian, and other). The age structures of these four groups effect some of the important characteristics of the Singapore population as a whole. Chinese Singaporeans, by far the largest section of the population, have a fairly stable age structure, with a lesser percentage of children compared to the Malays. This explains that family planning is widely practiced among ethnic Chinese. The Chinese in Singapore have continuously dominated business and politics and have been in the mainstream of life ever since independence. Family planning is also effective among the population of Indian origin. The Malays, on the other hand, show an expanding pyramid, that is, a high proportion of the Malay population in the younger age groups. This is a reflection or result of the fairly recent arrival of Malaysians in Singapore and the lack of extensive family planning among Malays, who are largely Moslems. The "other" category shows a small proportion of younger people and the largest age group is the 20–39 year group. This structure could perhaps be explained by the fact that a significant number of people in the 'other' category are 'guest workers' from other countries and so they have few families, i.e., children, with them.

Overall the Singaporean population shows a high degree of social and racial harmony and this can be put down to two main factors. The first is the state of the Singaporean economy. It is growing, and extremely quickly by Western standards. When an economy is booming everybody in society benefits and so no one group of the population is suffering or being victimized for the country's ills. This is so often found to be the case in societies where the economy in not so sound and often a scapegoat is found for the country's troubles.

The second major factor has been the continuous dominance of the Chinese section of the population. This has led to the development of a stable society as control has always been in the hands of Chinese Singaporeans. Even during the time of British colonial rule the Chinese majority made local administration not only easier but more importantly helped assure a smooth transition to self-governing independence.

Other factors which are also worthy of note are the composition of the government and the State's attitude to housing. All governments of Singapore have always had representatives from the major population groups and hence as a result no one group has felt the threat of racial/ethnic dominance by another group. Lastly, the role of the state in the provision of housing, with its belief in equality of opportunity and guaranteed accessibility to such housing ensures that no one racial group is excluded from the housing market. Such equality of opportunity ensures that racial/ethnic tensions do not develop in this area.

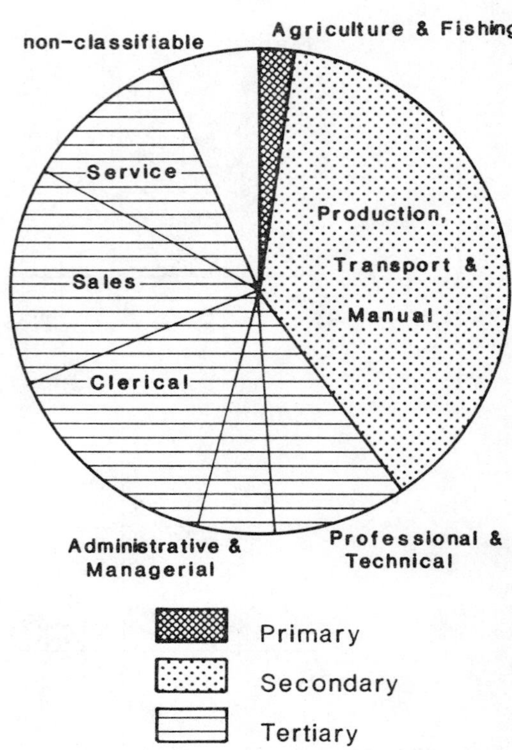

Figure 15-5. Singapore Occupational Structure (Source: Ministry of Culture, Singapore).

Occupational Structure

The occupational structure of the working population of Singapore in 1980 has been shown in Fig. 15-5. Those people employed in the primary sector, principally agriculture and fishery, only account for 1.75 percent of the total working population. Compared to the 1970 figure this represents a very slight increase.

Those people, in secondary (industrial) activities, that is, those classed as production and manual, account for 38.86 percent of the total. This figure represents a small decrease in proportion compared to 1970. This change reflects the changing structure of industry as brought about by an active government policy. As will be discussed later, the Singapore government is actively encouraging industry to modernize and automate by increasing wages. A higher wage bill is, of course, a significant spur to industry to increase productivity per worker by mechanization. If such a policy is maintained then it can be expected that the proportion of people engaged in the secondary sector to decline but without a decline in either the volume or value of manufactures.

The tertiary (service) sector in Singapore currently accounts for about 54% of total employment. Overall, the proportion to total employment has remained quite stable in relation to the 1970 figure, however, this is not the complete picture. Within this group the sales sector has increased the largest and is followed by proportionate increase in those classified as administrative and managerial. There has been also a decrease in the proportion classified as service, professional and technical, and clerical, during the decade of the 1970s. The decline in these areas could well be due to increased business efficiency and again, reflecting the desire to cut down or at least minimize wage costs. It must be stressed though that porportions are being used here and not whole numbers. So even if proportions have decreased the actual numbers may have increased.

ECONOMY

Singapore has a progressive economy. In 1981 alone the manufacturing sector grew by 12 percent in real terms and new investment commitments totaled $1.4 billion. Further, as the world drifted into depression the Singapore economy, as measured by GDP growth, rose 10 percent in 1981 and had a fairly low inflation rate of 6.7 percent. The main growth has taken place in manufacturing, trade, tourism and transport.

The relatively healthy state of the Singaporean economy is due to many factors. Not least of these factors is the role of the government in the stimulation of the economy. In recent years government expenditure has been kept to a minimum for maintaining the present level of government services and has, thereby, maximized the proportion of finite government resources available for development expenditure designed to, "stimulate the economy and accelerate economic recovery."[5] Indeed, in the 1981–82 budget, recurrent government expenditure was, for the first time, less than development expenditure.

A detailed analysis of economic policies and plans of the 1960s and 1970s has been given in Chapter 7. The government devised an economic strategy in the early eighties to stimulate industrial and manpower development; to improve infrastructure and communications both within and to Singapore; and to make the country a center for international finance and tourism. To put it another way, Singapore wishes to transform itself into an industrial center and make itself a base for regional and international services. In economic terms, the country is aiming for an annual growth rate in GDP of between 8–10 percent in the 1980s and with this there will be a restructuring of industry.[6] The government wishes to increase the manufacturing component in the GDP to 31 percent of the total and for manufactures to account for 60% of all exports by 1990.[7] To this end one of the recent budgets (1981–82) has been expansionary in nature, that is, with a deficit. Further, the development expenditure component of government spending is mostly in fixed capital formation and it now accounts for roughly 50 percent of overall capital formation.

It was back in the 1960s that Singapore wanted to shed its entrepot image and change it to one of a manufacturing center. To this end, in the early 1970s, Singapore allowed subsidiaries of foreign firms to establish freely in the country.[8] The aim of this policy was two fold; to create jobs in Singapore and to diversify the economy to make the country less vulnerable to the fluctuations in the world economy.

This policy has been largely sucessful in recent years as can be seen by the recent growth in GDP. After the oil crisis in 1973, the rate of GDP growth fell to 7 percent and 4 percent in 1974 and 1975, respectively.[9] Since 1976, however, the rate of GDP increase has risen annually; for instance, in 1970 it was 8.6 percent, in 1975 it was 9.3 percent, and in 1980 it was 10.2 percent.[10]

Given this type of growth and the concentration in industrial development it is hoped that Singapore will be a fully industrialized nation by the 1990s. Singapore attributes its success in diversifying both its domestic economy and its external markets.

Although all the current indicators of economic well-being are good for Singapore a targeted or projected level of development could be affected by two important factors. The Singaporean economy is really dependent upon the health of its trading partners; its principal export markets and countries most responsible for its foreign investment. Singapore's main trading partners are the USA, Japan and the European Economic Community.[11] Investment from these countries, it is believed, is being stifled somewhat by a strong Singapore dollar and the increasing labor costs in the country.

Further, Singapore will face future competition in the market from newly industrializing countries both for investment and for exports. In addition to these factors, there is the fear of protectionism. Protectionism not only threatens markets for existing domestic manufacturers and for entrepot trade, but also promises to cancel out some of the benefits of foreign direct investment in Singapore. For instance, it would be of little use setting up factories in Singapore if it cannot export those products back to the investing nation.

Despite these possible problems that could be faced by Singapore, the government is not hesitating in its push to industrialize. Indeed, over the years the government has subtly changed its policy in this regard so as to maximize the benefit to Singapore. For instance, in the late 1960s and for most of the 1970s, Singapore encouraged any type of industry as it was mainly concerned to reduce unemployment. In more recent years, though the government has been more selective about the type of industry it wishes to encourage. In the early 1980s, it wanted high technology, high investment industries to build a strong economy. The types of industry encouraged include: computers, integrated circuits, industrial electronics, automated machine tools, and medical equipment.[12] In fact, it can be said that Singapore wanted to reconstruct its economy so as to improve the productivity of the existing work force (although Singapore had few unemployed it did not wish to encourage further guest workers from other countries in the 1980s)[13]. It was hoped to increase productivity by automating existing industries where possible and to encourage the relocation of those industries which could not increase it.

The advantages to Singapore of such an industrial policy are many-fold.[14] Up-market products, such as electronics and computers, will alter the country's competitive sphere with regard to other nations having a cheap labor supply (e.g., China, Taiwan) and it will so relocate its comparative advantage.

Further, the kinds of new products will, it is hoped, be far less vulnerable to protectionist pressures which are usually aimed at the traditional manufactures of the industrializing countries, like textiles, clothing, and furniture. By concentrating on invisible components like aircraft electronic components and quality precision parts that can be supplied to larger foreign manufacturers, Singapore hopes to avoid trade barriers and to enhance its attractions to other high technology industry.

Singapore in the early 1980s was faced with the inescapable necessity to conserve labor as recent figures showed the labor force was growing at a decreasing rate. In fact, limitations of the labor force is the principal spur to efforts for Singapore to move onto knowledge and capital intensive industries where output and value added are higher and where labor costs as a percentage of total production can be reduced.[15]

This economic/industrial policy of moving to the production of up-market goods started in 1979 under the direction of the National Wages Council (an organization with members of the government, employers, and the Trade Union Council). Prior to this date, it had been the policy of the Wages Council to moderate wage rises to keep production costs down for industry. This maintains Singapore's competiveness in the world market and maintains an inflow of investment into the country.[16] With a change in policy, it was decided to increase wages so as to increase production costs, which in turn was a spur to industry for augmenting per worker productivity. This was to be done by mechanization and automation. These wage increases were also implemented to compensate for the admittedly excessive wages restrictions in years 1974–78.

The scale of wage increases is really quite large, especially for the low wage earners. For instance, in 1979 and 1980 wages were increased for low income groups by 20% and 19%, respectively. Wage hikes of this magnitude have the detrimental effect of causing "wage pull" inflation. To offset this effect though part of wage hike is drawn off by increased contributions to the Central Provident Fund. This is a compulsory savings account for all employers and employees. Employees' contributions remained at 20.5% of one's income and the net effect is that a low wage earner effectively received a pay rise of only 8–12%.[17]

Singapore's economic success of recent years has been the result of the interplay of several key factors. As outlined above, an active and progressive government attitude to industrialization has been possibly the most important factor. Less tangible factors though are also of importance. The development of a work ethic and a desire for personal wealth backed up by a progressive capitalistic system are examples of such intangible factors.

From a geographic point of view, Singapore's economic success is also due to the crossroads position at the tip of the Malay Peninsula. It dominates the Strait of Malacca that leads from the Indian Ocean to the South China Sea; a very important trading route both to and from Southeast Asia. Due to the fortunate geographic position of Singapore, it managed to become the fourth largest port in the world in the 1970s.

The Port

The economic development of Singapore is closely linked to the amount of trade the port handles. This was particularly so in the nineteenth century. For instance, in 1842 the economy of Singapore suffered with the development of Hong Kong and later with the French occupation of Indochina. However, the opening of the Suez Canal in 1869 and the development of steamships encouraged the growth of both the port facilities in Singapore and of the local economy. This period of trade development led to the construction of three miles of wharves at Tanjong Pagar and finally in 1921 to a naval base. Further, the economic growth of the Malay States after they became British protectorates enlarged the transit trade handled by Singapore. In addition, the demand of the industrial west for tin and rubber made Singapore one of the greatest ports in the world.

The port of Singapore, being and integral node of the former "British Life Line" and also the only deep draft harbor of the area, performed a very important entrepot function. The British Life Line was the oceanic route that joined the East and West from London to China through Gibraltar, Malta, Suez, Aden, Colombo, Singapore, and Hong Kong. The colonial conquest by Britain was so well designed that it ruled all those strategic locations in the Line before World War II. However, with the eventual growth of nationalism and each Southeast Asian nation seeking its own port outlet, Singapore began to lose this entrepot base created during the colonial era.

Despite regional competition, Singapore has the fourth largest port trade in the world and the figures are impressive. Over 300 shipping lines use Singapore's six specialized gateways. The port facilities are:

(1) The Container Terminal with an area of 132.5 acres (53 ha) has eight berths of varying sizes. One berth has roll-on/roll-off facilities. The main marshalling yard can accommodate some 28,000 TEU's and there is a 17.5 acre (7 ha) yard for the storage of 3,000 empty containers.

(2) Keppel Wharves—a conventional wharf with a total length of 2.88 miles (4.8 km) it can handle 26 ocean-going and 5 coastal vessels simultaneously.

(3) Pasio Panjang Wharves is a combination port terminal and warehousing center and it is the largest warehousing complex in Southeast Asia.

(4) Tebok Buyer Wharves—over 1100 yds. (1000 m) of wharves.

(5) Sembawang Wharves is the main gateway for handling low value, high volume, homogeneous cargos and is also a container terminal for a major container line.

(6) Turorg Port—has a total of 10 berths for bulk cargo handling.

The port of Singapore authority operates 1,337,280 yd^2 (1,114,400 m^2) of storage space within the Free Trade Zone and some 416,400 yd^2 (347,000 m^2) outside it. Another 232,800 yd^2 (194,000 m^2) of warehousing space has recently been completed.

HOUSING

A distinctive factor of Singapore is in the field of state planning, particularly, with reference to public housing. The government of Singapore through the operation of the Housing Development Board (HDB) has housed some 1.64 million people, that is, some 68% of the total population of the country in 1981. It is the very magnitude of the level of direct government intervention in the housing market (i.e., the actual construction of homes) that not only distinguishes Singapore from other Southeast Asian countries but positively makes it unique.

The HDB, set up in 1960, has successfully implemented four five year plans. The fifth plan for the years 1981–1985, aims to add 100,000 housing units to the housing stock of the country. By 1985 almost 75% of the entire population of Singapore will be housed in HDB apartments.

Previous HDB plans have all met with success and are a credit to the government of Singapore for it has effectively solved the housing problem in the country. The first plan of 1960–65 was mainly concerned with the quantity of housing it built because it had to rehouse slum dwellers. In all 50,000 housing units were built of which 15,822 were only one room emergency dwellings. Once the immediate crisis of the slum dwellers had passed the second plan (1966–70) emphasized instead the call for home ownership of the dwellings. In all, some 60,000 dwellings were constructed.

The third plan spanned the period from 1971 to 1975 and instead of cutting back at this time during the oil crisis and world recession the government tried to fight the economic recession by accelerating the rate and number of dwellings constructed. Indeed, the plan target of 100,000 dwellings was exceeded by a further 13,000. Continuing this expansion in housing construction the fourth plan aimed to build 125,000 to 150,000 housing units. In actuality some 130,396 were constructed.

The Housing Development Board, responsible for all public housing construction, operates under the auspices of the Ministry for National Development. Specifically, it is responsible for the whole range of functions associated with public housing. It builds new towns and housing estates, provides loans for purchases, provides community facilities such as parks, open space

Figure 15-6. New and older colonial buildings blend with each other in the central parts of Singapore. (Photograph, A. K. Dutt).

and so on, manages the new towns and estates, and even acquires land for public housing. Further, it also clears land for redevelopment and resettles any displaced persons.

Being a government body the HDB is financed by loans from the government. Indeed, for the financial year 1980–81 S$1,133 million was loaned by the government to the HDB. This amounted to almost one-third of total government development expenditures of S$3,617 million. The loans supplied by the government, via the HDB, for the construction of public housing for sale is repayable over 10 years with a low interest rate of 6%. Similar loans for the construction of housing to be rented are repayable over 60 years with an interest rate of only 7¾%.

Figure 15-7. Central City Area with Ground-Floor Shopping and Upper Floors used for Residences. (Photo by A. K. Dutt).

Public housing was first sold to people who wish to be owner-occupiers back in 1964 and the idea was actively encouraged in the second HDB plan of 1966–70. People who wished to purchase under the Home Ownership Scheme must put 20% of the selling price down as an initial down payment. Most people do this mainly by providing from funds everyone makes to the Central Provident Fund (a nationally run savings bank). The outstanding debt is usually paid for over the following 20 years at a very reasonable interest rate of 6¼%.

The active state intervention in the provision of housing and the institutionalization of factors that enables people to not only rent government built apartments but buy them as well, is indeed unique. Not only is a considerable proportion of the governments budget devoted to housing construction but the provision of subsidized rents and the very attractive rates of interest for potential buyers makes Singapore one of the world's success stories as far as housing provision is concerned.

THE CITY

The city of Singapore so dominates the main island of the Republic of Singapore that to many, they are one and the same thing. There are, however, certain distinctive features about the city. It is the capital of the Republic and a free port which is situated at the mouth of the Singapore River.

The city itself was created by Royal Charter in 1951 and was administered as a municipality by a mayor-council from 1957–59 when the colony became self-governing. Since 1963 the administration of both the city and the surrounding rural areas has been by the central government.

The built-up area is concentrated in the south part of the main island and now covers some 50 sq. miles (128 km^2) or some 24% of the land. The main concentrations of buildings are found to the north and east of the port area and span both the Singapore and Rochor Rivers.

The site of the original settlement, on the left bank of the Singapore River, is now the heart of the city. This area has a "Chinatown" and is the principal commercial, governmental, and public buildings sectors. It is particularly in this area that skyscraper hotels and office buildings blend with British colonial architecture, Chinese shophouses, and thatched roof dwellings (Fig. 15-6 and 15-7). Many main street front buildings have shops on the ground floor and residences on the 2nd and 3rd floors. Lying beyond these areas are extensive suburban areas composed of a mixture of semi-detached houses, bungalows, flats and thatch-roofed rural style dwellings. The active role of the Singapore government in the provision of public housing has meant that more and more apartment buildings and complexes are emerging on the suburban landscape. The government has also prepared a long-range land use plan for the city (Fig. 15-8).

Singapore does have limited squatter settlements and it is these areas that often have the thatched roofs and even roofs made of corrugated iron.

The dominance of the city on the island of Singapore is partly reflected in the amount of people it contains. The city area is 38.9 square miles (97.4 km^2) or about 16% of the total land area of the state. However, approximately 60% of the entire population of the Singapore Republic live in the city.

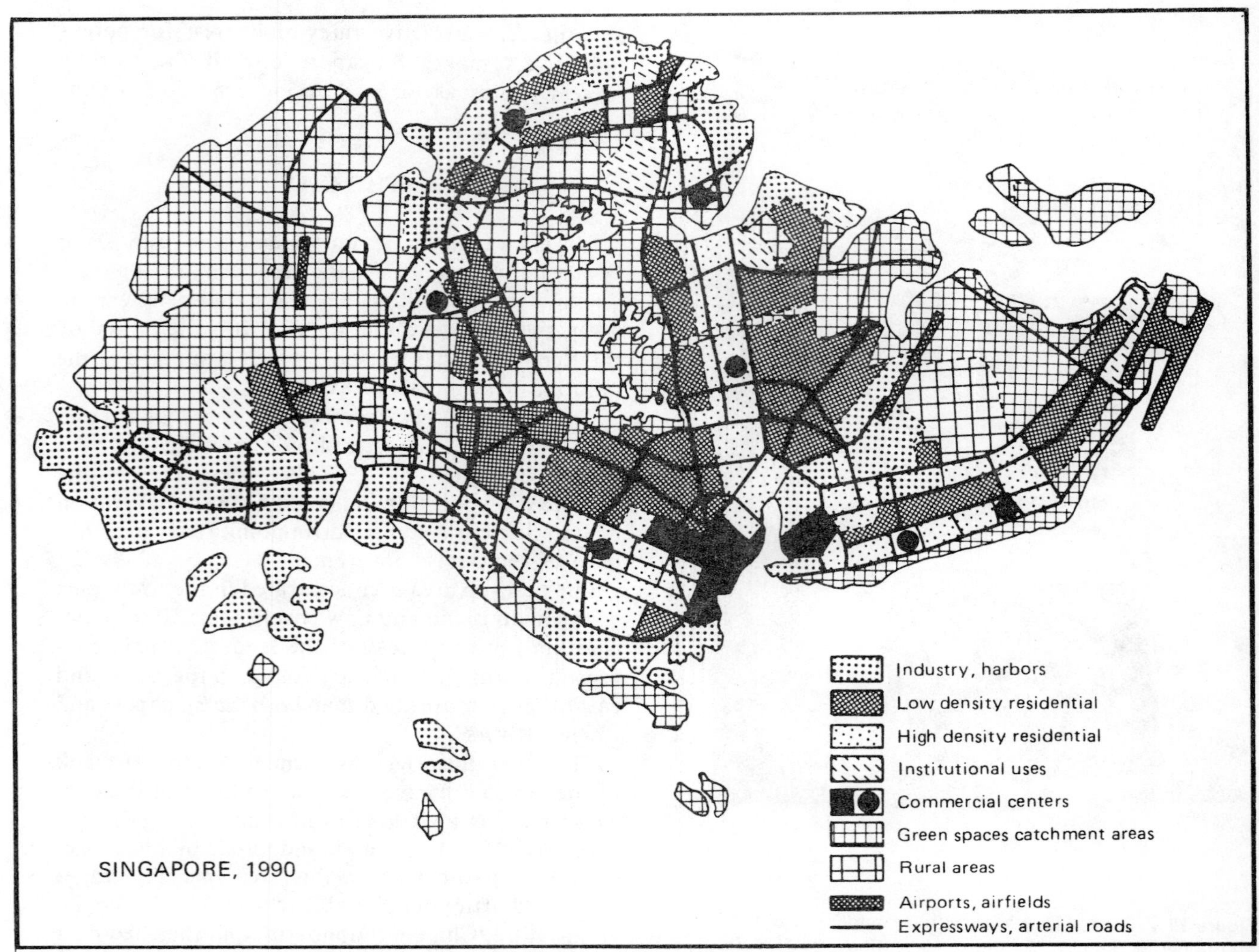

CONCLUSION

Singapore is Southeast Asia's most progressive country. No other country in the realm has reached its level of economic progress. Despite its multi-racial, multi-ethnic and multi-lingual characteristics, it has a disciplined democracy and its effective bureaucratic apparatus continually encourages development. Certain minimum levels of economic well-being are enjoyed by everyone in the country and the 'fruits of its recent development' are reasonably shared by all.

Footnote References

[1]Ellsworth Huntington, *Principals of Human Geography* (New York: John Wiley and Sons, Inc., 1940), 5th edition, p. 339 and various other parts of the book.

[2]*Singapore—Facts and Pictures 1981* (Singapore: Information Division Ministry of Culture), p. 1.

[3]*Ibid.*, p. 4.

[4]*Singapore '81*, (Singapore: Information Division, Ministry of Culture), p. 167.

[5]*Far Eastern Economic Review* Vol. 95, No. 10 (March 1977).

[6]Chee-Meow Seah, "Singapore in 1980: Institutionalization System Manintenance", *Asian Survey*, Vol. XXI, No. 2 (February 1981).

[7]*Ibid.*
[8]*Far Eastern Economic Review*, Vol. 101, No. 32 (August 1978).
[9]*Far eastern Economic Review*, Vol. 97, No. 32 (August 1977).
[10]*Far Eastern Economic Review*, Vol. 113, No. 32 (July 1981).
[11]*Ibid.*
[12]*Ibid.*
[13]Chee-Meow Seah, "Singapore 1979: The Dialects of Survival", *Asian Survey*, Vol. XX, No. 2 (February 1980).
[14]*Far Eastern Economic Review*, Vol. 113, No. 32 (July 1981).
[15]*Ibid.*
[16]*Far Eastern Economic Review*, Vol. 97, No. 32 (August 1977).
[17]*Far Eastern Economic Review*, Vol. 113, No. 32 (July 1981).
[18]*Singapore '81*, (Singapore: Information Division, Ministry of Culture, 1981).
[19]*Ibid.*, pp. 78–81.

Chapter 16

Brunei: A Country with Surplus Balance of Payments

Ashok K. Dutt

Brunei is one of the smallest countries in Southeast Asia, but the richest in terms of per capita income. It is situated on the north coast of the island of Borneo (Kalimantan) and is bordered by the Malaysian state of Sarawak. On the north Brunei is bordered by the South China Sea. The state is in fact two separate but unequal areas of land. The capital, Bandar Seri Begawan, is situated in the larger western part of the two enclaves of Sarawak.

Physiographically, the country is mainly hilly and has elevations over 3000' in the southeast. The coastal area is more lowlying but this strip of land is quite narrow. Soils in the hilly areas are quite poor being red laterites while the coastal areas have more fertile alluvial and peat soils deposited by the country's rivers. Four rivers drain the country (the Belait, Tutong, Brunei and Temburong) all of which flow in a northerly direction (Fig. 16-1).[1]

Brunei feels the effects of equatorial monsoons and the rainfall varies from 100 inches on the coast to 200 inches on the more hilly inland areas. Most of the rain comes from the northeast trade winds in the period from November to March. Temperatures do not vary as much as precipitation as the average range is from 76° to 86°F (24° to 30°C).

Vegetation in the country is that which is typically associated with an equatorial monsoon climate and that is equatorial rainforest; some 75% of the land area is covered by such growth.[2]

PEOPLE

Permanent settlers in the country are found in the river valleys although most of the population lives near the oil fields at Seria and Kuala Balai or in the capital of Bandar Seri Begawan. The capital has all the features of a modern bustling city although it also has an older section (Kampong Ayer) where 10,000 Brunei Malays live in small houses on stilts near the river.

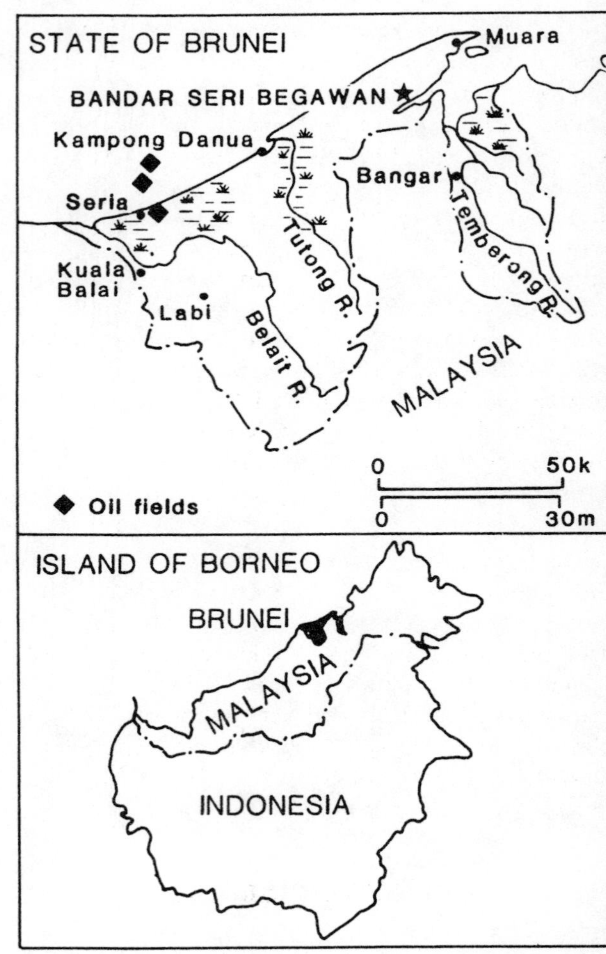

Figure 16-1. Location of Brunei with a General Map of the State.

According to the 1981 census the population of Brunei was 193,000 of which at least 22,000 were immigrant workers. About 80% of the people are Malay or other indigenous peoples while the remaining 20% are mostly Chinese.[3] Since Brunei's total independence from Great Britain in January of 1984 all the Chinese changed from being British-protected persons to being the responsibility of the Brunei government. As the Brunei government will not let the Chinese become Bruneians they are technically stateless.[4] Religiously two-thirds of the people are Moslem, a small number of the indigenous people are Christian, while the Chinese are usually Buddhist, Taoist or Confusionist.

POLITICAL SETUP

Brunei is essentially a monarchist state in which the present Sultan, Sir Muda Hassanal Balkiah Muizzadin Waddaulah, has absolute power. Legitimate elections were once held in the country back in 1962. Those elections were the result of the British policy to withdraw from areas east of Suez but leaving democratic institutions behind. Thus, Britain pressured the then Sultan to hold the elections. In the election Sheik Azahari, an opposition party leader, led his followers to victory in 35 of the 36 legislature seats. Azahari was pro-Indonesia and he was fearful that the Sultan would lead Brunei into federation with Malaysia, hence, he declared a rebellion. The rebellion was put down with the help of a British Gurkha battalion dispatched to the country.[5]

The Sultan has made no moves to join with Malaysia as then the country's great wealth, derived almost entirely from oil and gas, would be dispersed throughout Malaysia and not benefit Brunei to the extent it is now doing. Thus, the country was the only former British dependency inhabited by a Malay people that did not join the Federation of Malaysia in 1963.[6]

ECONOMIC VIABILITY

Economically, Brunei is a very secure nation. In 1982 per capita GDP was equivalent to $25,600, the highest for any nation in East Asia. The country's great wealth is derived almost entirely from the extraction of oil and gas (Fig. 16-2). Together these comprise 85% of GDP and generate 99% of all export revenues.[7] This financial security which derives from oil and gas is expected to last for at least 30 years as there are an estimated 1.8 billion barrels of oil and several billion cubic feet of gas which are unexploited reserves.[8] The oil and gas are now being drawn on comes from the inland field at Seria and from the offshore fields that stretch from the capital to Seria.

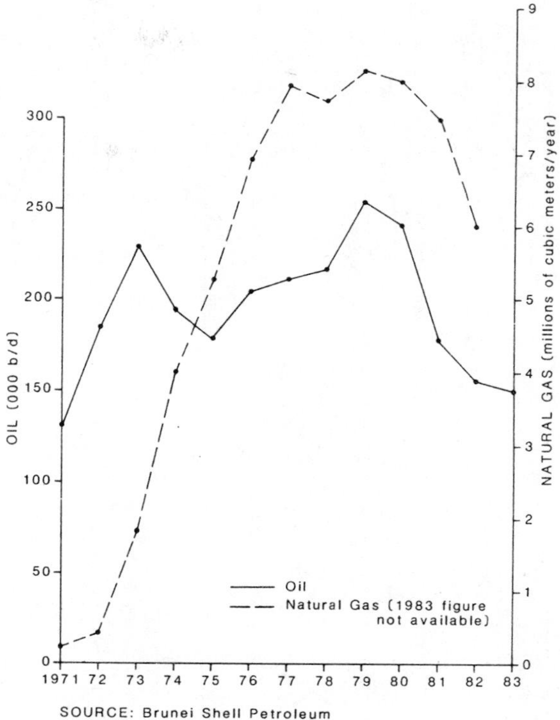

Figure 16-2. Oil and Natural Gas Production of Brunei (1971–83).

Oil production in Brunei comes completely from the Brunei Shell Petroleum (BSP) Company and as such it is not surprising that BSP is the largest contributor to state revenues. Total oil and gas revenues for 1982 alone were estimated at $3.77 billion. Overall Brunei runs a very large trade and government budget surplus. The balance of trade in 1982 was $3,800 million in surplus and the government surplus was $2,500 million. As oil and gas create so much income for the government there is no need for a personal income tax to generate money. Further, there are no import quotas and import duties are low, and company tax is at a most reasonable 30%.

The healthy economy and a secure high income for the government has enabled it to greatly increase its spending. Thus the budget for 1983 was 22% greater than 1982 with outlays totaling B$2,200. The remainder of government income is

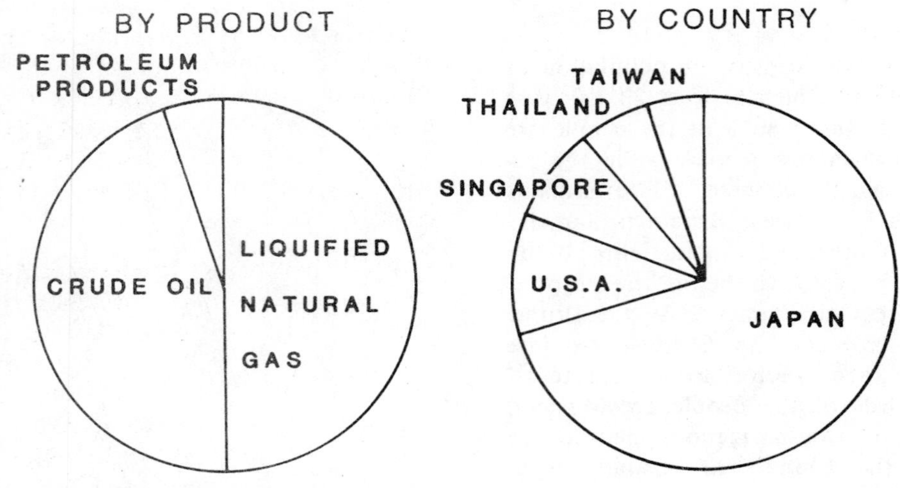

Figure 16-3. Exports of Brunei (1983).

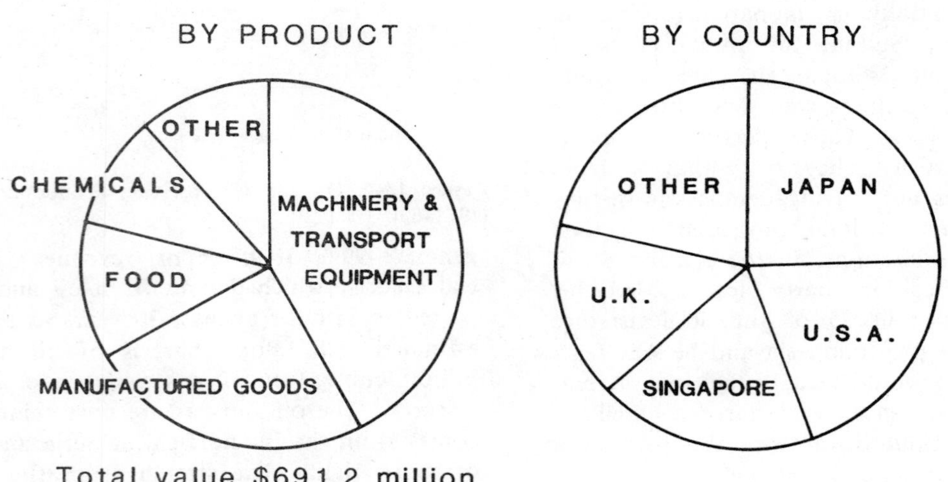

Figure 16-4. Imports of Brunei (1983).

invested abroad and foreign reserves in 1982 were estimated at $9,900 million.[9]

Brunei's trade with other nations involves the export of hydrocarbon products (62% of which is crude oil, 31% is natural gas and 6% other petroleum products)[10] and the importation of such goods as machinery, transport equipment, manufactured goods, and food (Figs. 16-3, 16-4). It is noticeable that the trading patterns of Brunei are not too dissimilar from OPEC countries. That is the country is exporting a valuable raw material at a very good price and is being able because of this, to buy capital goods. Such purchases help to develop the country's infrastructure and diversify its industrial base so as not to be so dependent on oil and gas in the future. Approximately 24% of all imports into Brunei come from Japan with a further 20% from the United States, 19% from Singapore and 15% from the United Kingdom (Fig. 16-4). Exports from the country are dominated by the trade with Japan, some 71% of the total, due mainly to the purchasing by Japan of natural gas. Other significant destination countries of Brunei's exports are the United States (10%), Singapore (8%), Thailand (6%), and Taiwan (5%) (Fig. 16-3).[11]

Total employment in Brunei numbers about 70,000 of which only 50,000 are native Bruneians. Half of the work force either work for the government or in public service provision while a further quarter work for Brunei Shell Petroleum.[12] This shows, once again, the doninance of the mineral extraction industries in the Brunei economy.

Agricultural production in the country while not as important financially as oil and gas is, nevertheless, significant. There are some 27,000 acres of land in rubber cultivation, about 3,000 acres of which are of the high yield variety. Rice production, although significant at more than 10,000 tons per year, is not sufficient to meet domestic needs. Other agricultural crops include sago, coconuts and pepper[13] and other typical tropical products such as cassava, banana, and pineapple.[14] Livestock in the country number 15,000 for buffalo and pigs, but there is also 4,000 head of cattle and well over a million chickens.[15] The timber industry of the nation is not yet developed but with about 70% of the land forested serviceable timber must be exploitable.[16]

There are only 916 miles of roads in Brunei (451 miles bituminous surfaced). The main road in the country (84 miles) runs the length of the country from the capital, Bandar Seri Begawan, to Kuala Balai and Seria. There are approximately 60,000 vehicles on the road and as the country has less than 200,000 people the vehicle/population ratio (1:3) is quite good when compared to the rest of Southeast Asia. Three of the country's four rivers are navigable (the Brunei, Belait and Tutong) and the government has encouraged the development of a new port at Maura. There is an international airport near the capital served by three foreign airlines these are in addition to the Royal Brunei Airways which, of course, also serves the capital.[17]

Brunei has strong defense forces and a high expenditure on armaments and other military equipment. In fact, almost a third of the government budget in 1983 was devoted to the Royal Brunei Malay Regiment. To further ensure the country's defense in 1984 Brunei became the sixth member of ASEAN.

Overall Brunei appears to be a stable and prosperous country which has gone a long way to share the benefits of its wealth. Although there is still great disparity between the very rich and the poor the general levels of welfare are good compared to other Southeast Asian countries. The Sultan's firm control over the country means that free elections appear to be a thing of the distant future. However, with the country's great wealth the people apppear to be contented.

Footnote References

[1]*Encyclopaedia Britannica* Macropaedia (Chicago: Encyclopaedia Britannica Inc., 1980), vol. 3, p. 342-2.

[2]*Ibid.*

[3]*Quarterly Economic Review, Malaysia, Singapore, Brunei*, Annual Supplement (London: Economist Intelligence Unit Ltd., 1983), p. 27.

[4]*The Times*, London, Oct. 3, 1983, p. 7.

[5]Joseph Judge, "Brunei Borneo's Abode of Peace," *National Geographic*, vol. 145, no. 2 (Feb. 1974), p. 216.

[6]*The Stateman's Yearbook 1982-83*, 119th ed. edited by John Paxton (New York: St. Martins Press), p. 242.

[7]*Quarterly Economic Review*, Annual Supplement (1983), p. 27.

[8]*Ibid.*, p. 28.

[9]*Ibid.*, p. 31.

[10]*Encyclopaedia Britannica Book of the Year 1983* (Chicago: Encyclopaedia Britannica Inc., 1983).

[11]*Quarterly Economic Review*, Annual Supplement (1983), p. 32.

[12]op. cit., p. 27.

[13]*Quarterly Economic Review, Malaysia, Singapore, Brunei*, Annual Supplement (1979), p. 34.

[14]*Encyclopaedia Britannica Book of the Year 1983.*

[15]*Ibid.*

[16]*The Stateman's Yearbook 1982-83*, p. 242.

[17]*Ibid.*

Chapter 17

Perspectives on Southeast Asia

Ashok K. Dutt

Southeast Asia is a land of diversity, yet it has evolved an identity for itself based on its centuries old civilization. Since the 1940's, when the area was first recognized as a realm in the modern world, Southeast Asia has been identified by distinctive characteristics. Several events and special features of international significance have taken place in the realm strengthening its regional personality. Such events and features can be classified in political, economic, and cultural settings.

POLITICAL SETTING

Politically, the realm today represents three different systems: democratic, military dictatorship, and communist. Two countries (Malaysia and Singapore) have maintained a democratic form of government since independence. Malaysia, before becoming independent, attracted worldwide attention for its extensive, communist-led guerilla activities in the 1950's. The British, however, succeeded in completely obilterating the ethnic Chinese guerillas in Malaysia by, a) starving them in the jungles and rubber plantations, b)separating them from ethnic Malay rice cultivators, c) not letting them establish any direct sea or land connection with any communist country, and d) encouraging the growth of liberal, middle class, Malay political groups to evolve into a majority force.

The British success offered a ray of hope to the western countries that communist guerilla activities could be suppressed in other Southeast Asian countries, particularly in Burma and Indochina. The western world believed that China considered the realm to be a "frontier", and to international communism it became an arena in which to topple the non-communist regimes. After three decades of much publicized conflict, which ended in the mid-1970's, the Indochinese countries (Vietnam, Kampuchea, and Laos) fell to communism. Burma, however, has not succumbed to communism due to its a) non-aligned status, b) guerillas lacking decisive power to strike a knockout blow to the Rangoon government, and c) turning inward by separating itself from the rest of the world.

During the long period of political unrest in Southeast Asia, following World War II, four countries, Burma, Thailand, the Philippines and Indonesia, turned to military dictatorships and away from freely elected democratic governments. In two cases the transition was accomplished by the government leaders who had been democratically elected. Two democratically elected Presidents, Sukarno of Indonesia and Marcos of the Philippines, using their popularity and their peoples' faith in them, advanced their countries into military dictatorships and thus perpetuated their role as rulers. In Burma, once the military was in power, it never returned the country to true civilian rule, except for a two-year period (1960–62). In Thailand, however, the military often sits on the sidelines and takes power whenever it feels that the elected or the appointed civilian government does not come up to their expectations. Thus, these four southeast Asian countries followed the pattern of most developing countries which also have become dictatorial after democratic beginnings.

The communist governmental system of Indonchina evolved (1954–75) mainly because of 1) their direct connection with China which supplied food, training and a regular supply base to the rebel military; 2) massive arms and other military logistics supply by the Soviet Union; 3) the lack of a strong middle class and associated values; 4) a lack of domestic liberal political groups; and 5) the existence of a strong anti-imperialist tradition led by communists. As the governments of Vietnam, Kampuchea, and Laos have adopted the communist system, the intensity of one-party political control accentuates along with a thorough brainwashing campaign in favor of communism and thus, the continuity of the system is perpetuated. The problem will surface in the realm when Vietnam settles its conflict in Kampuchea and, starts actively supporting the guerillas in Thailand and Burma. Things may also turn worse if China changes its current policy in the area. This policy, established in the late 1970s, is of putting great emphasis on its own internal development. As such China, at present, refrains from making large commitments to keep insurgent or guerilla activities in both Southeast Asian and other countries. If China changes this policy and resumes its active support to the guerillas and joins with Vietnam it might be able to topple the non-communist governments of Thailand and Burma. Both Thailand and Burma have direct land connections with more than one communist country and such a situation assures the local guerillas a consistent flow of supplies from outside sources if Vietnam and China wish to do so. Thailand and Burma are the frontiers between communist and non-communist nations of Southeast Asia in the early 1980's and their fall to communism, if it occurs at all in the future, will mean the shifting of frontiers in Southeast Asia and directly with South Asia. All these possibilities depend on several questions. Will Vietnam divert its scarce resources from much needed internal development to advance the guerilla cause in Southeast Asia? If the answer is yes, how soon? How long will it take for Thailand and Burma to establish firm and progressive economic bases, so that poverty, the main breeder of communism, can be reduced to a "reasonable" level? Will internal dissention among communist nations, especially between China and Russia, be resolved in order for them to put up an united front for the expansion of communism in Southeast Asia?

ECONOMIC SETTING

The economies of Southeast Asian countries, like those of all other countries of the world, reflect the political systems they possess. Vietnam, Kampuchea, and Laos have systems where the state already owns, or is in the process of obtaining, ownership and management of all the means of production, exchange, and transportation. Private ownership of land and industry is considered capitalistic and, hence, such ownership must be eliminated. They belong to communist block countries and look to the Soviet Union for technology, aid, trade and leadership.

The other countries of Southeast Asia, except Burma, are essentially capitalistic with some legacies of feudalism. Land, industry, business, and many transport systems are, by and large, owned by private businesses and individuals. Private enterprise and free economy principles operate there. They look to the western countries for aid, development, trade and leadership.

Burma has an atypical economic status because the state owns the major industries, transport network, and banks; organizes foreign trade either fully or partly; but the country is not ruled by communists. Its rulers may be described as national socialists with a strong slant to Buddhism. Private ownership of land, however, still prevails. Thus, Burma combines socialist and capitalist principles in running its economy.

No economic system thrives in isolation today. It influences and is influenced by others; often benefiting them both at the same time. The communist systems of Southeast Asia react to the changes in the economic strategies of the Soviet Union. Similarly, the capitalistic systems of neighboring Southeast Asian countries, as well as other nations of the world, have influenced these communist states to introduce "private incentives" and the idea of "individual profit", mainly to augment their productivity.

The Southeast Asian countries with free enterprise economies similarly have been tremendously influenced by the state intervention policies initiated by India and west European countries. Thailand, Malaysia, Singapore, Indonesia, and the Philippines do not allow a totally "free' enterprise to prevail in their economies. They set policies directing the course of the economy; state investments are used to accelerate economic growth; welfare benefits are given to the needy. All of these steps are possibly the most practical inputs, partly borrowed from the socialist systems or ideology and partly generated by the need for economic advancement and to maintain political stability.

The Southeast Asian economic systems are, thus, moving within their own sphere while their aspects are being influenced by others and, at the same time, are influencing others. The progress of each country's system depends on how well endowed the country is in resources and how skillfully they are organized.

CULTURAL SETTING

Culture is essentially reflected in the psychological make-up of people, influenced by religion, language, customs, heritage, environment, material well-being, and a stable political system. When, for a long time, a region experiences a totality of these generated forces, a regional culture evolves in relative isolation. In Southeast Asia, unlike the United States, there exists several micro-regional cultures because these regions have stayed in relative isolation during long periods of history. A single culture is sometimes politically divided between two countries in Southeast Asia; the Vietnam-Kampuchea border is an example in the case where Viet ethinc groups are found well within Kampuchea. At the same time a country may give rise to various cultures; the Javanese Moslem culture is different from the Balinese Hindu tradition; the North and Central Philippine's Catholic culture contrasts with its southern Moslem society. Thus, Southeast Asia is a realm of varied cultures, and where clashes of culture frequently occur.

A clash of cultures has been taking place in Southeast Asia since the beginning of historic times. It is not only that the different cultures within the realm have clashed with each other, but cultures have invaded from abroad. Apart from Indian, Chinese, Islamic and Western cultures which have invaded from without, modernization and communization processes of contemporary times clash with the traditional cultures in the area. The modernization process is represented in Southeast Asia by western secular ideas and scientific explanations associated with technologically advanced means of production. The urban elites in all Southeast Asian countries represent the elements of modernization and their ideas are in constant opposition to the traditional cultures of the rural areas.

Similarly, the communization process represents not only the elements of modernization, but adds Marxist ideology to it, which aims at changing the economic base, creating disbelief in religion, and eventually creating a classless, crime-free, avarice-free, homogeneous society, where each person will work according to his ability and will be remunerated according to his needs. The communist regimes of Vietnam, Kampuchea, and Laos are experiencing a cultural pressure that emanates from the communization process and is trying to generate a new "psyche" in an age-old cultural system. In practice, however, this process means one-sided brainwashing in the schools, at work and by the media to convert each nation more towards a single communist culture, rather than developing respect for deep-rooted regional cultures.

Whatever may be the culture of the regions, with the ever-growing contacts, interchange, and migration, all cultures of Southeast Asia will not only foster mutual exchange, but will develop the same exchange with the cultures from outside the realm. Further dilution of cultures will take place in the future.

THE SOUTHEAST ASIAN REALM IN COMPARISON TO OTHER REALMS OF ASIA

Southeast Asia stands out as distinctly different from other realms in Asia because it has a) a proliferation of individual country units with no single dominating nation, b) two politically different systems—communist and capitalistic, in different parts of the realm, c) a tropical humid land mass with relatively insignificant dry land, d) archipelagos forming the major physical element and e) a situation between two great historic cultures of China and India, which have remained regularly connected with each other over the last 2000 years using the realm as a midway halt. The South Asian and Siberian realms lack all the above elements, whereas East Asia has only one similarity with the Southeast Asia, i.e., existence of two politically different systems. Similarly the Middle East like Southeast Asia has a proliferation of individual country units without a single country dominating the realm. Southeast Asia possesses enough physical, economic and cultural oneness to be called a realm with unique characteristics of its own yet it is, at the same time, a realm full of contrasts.

INDEX